RESEARCH DESIGN EXPLAINED

RESEARCH DESIGN EXPLAINED Second Edition

MARK MITCHELL
Clarion University

JANINA JOLLEY
Clarion University

Harcourt Brace Jovanovich College Publishers
Fort Worth   Philadelphia   San Diego   New York   Orlando
Austin   San Antonio   Toronto   Montreal   London   Sydney   Tokyo

Publisher/Ted Buchholz
Acquisitions Editor/Tina Oldham
Senior Production Manager/Annette Dudley Wiggins
Cover Designer/Brian K. Salisbury
Cover/The Image Bank, Douglas Kirkland
Editorial, Design, and Production Service/Michael Bass & Associates

Library of Congress Cataloging-in-Publication Data

Mitchell, Mark L.
    Research design explained / Mark Mitchell, Janina Jolley. — 2nd ed.
    p.   cm.
  Includes bibliographical references and index.
  ISBN 0-03-055972-3
    1. Psychology—Research—Methodology. 2. Psychology,
Experimental—Research—Methodology. I. Jolley, Janina M.
II. Title
BF76.5.M57   1992
150'.72—dc20

                                         91-39985
                                           CIP

Address for Editorial Correspondence: Harcourt Brace Jovanovich, Publishers, 301 Commerce Street, Suite 3700, Forth Worth, TX 76102

Address for Orders: Harcourt Brace Jovanovich, Publishers, 6277 Sea Harbor Drive, Orlando, FL 32887

Printed in the United States of America
2 3 4 5 016 9 8 7 6 5 4 3 2 1

DEDICATION
TO OUR PARENTS

Preface

This book uses the same strategies that professors use when they teach research methods. Specifically, it

- *Focuses on goals*. Professors do not simply give students isolated facts and concepts. Instead, they give students information in the context of making a design decision, reading an article, generating a research idea, or in evaluating the value of the scientific approach. That is, rather than merely presenting facts, design professors teach students the strategies, tactics, and knowledge needed to achieve course goals. This goal-orientated approach decreases the number of times students ask "Why do I have to know this?"; invites students to think along with the professor (rather than merely memorize terms); helps students connect concepts; and increases students' chances of achieving course goals. In this text, we focus on the goals of showing students why psychology is a science, how to be critical consumers of research, how to propose a research project, what to consider when making a design decision, and how to conduct a study.

  Our emphasis on the how and why of research is reflected throughout the book and is even evident in the table of contents. For example, the book has chapters on why psychology is a science (chapter 1), generating research hypotheses (chapter 2), critically reading research (chapter 9), and on writing research proposals and reports (chapter 13).

- *Helps students avoid common or serious errors*. Teachers know what mistakes students are tempted to make and warn students about those errors. To know what errors students might make, we relied not only on the errors our students had made, but also errors we saw when attending undergraduate research conferences and when reviewing articles for professional journals. In addition, we looked at surveys about what errors reviewers tend to find in articles they reject (e.g., Fiske & Fogg, 1990).

- *Explains concepts*. Teachers realize students learn by examples and analogies. They also know that to explain something, one has to remember what it is like not to know (Wurman, 1990). Furthermore, they realize that once one knows something very well, it is difficult to remember what it is like not to know (Wurman, 1990). To help us remember, we had students, English professors, and a journalist read and review our text. We are indebted to these reviewers for letting us know when another example was needed or when a step in an explanation was glossed over. These reviewers have allowed us to write a book that talks to—but not down to—students.

- *Demonstrates that the course is "relevant."* Professors realize that some students come into the class with the view that the design class is an arbitrary hurdle. We take three steps to show students that the course is relevant. First, we emphasize that without the scientific approach, there is no psychology. Second, we show how understanding research design can help students get jobs or go on to graduate school. Third, we show how thinking like a researcher can help students think smarter about real-life problems.

- *Addresses student fears.* Some students come into the class with "design phobia." This interferes with their ability to understand and apply concepts. We take several steps to reduce irrational fears about research design. We avoid unnecessary terms and complex computations. We use examples and analogies to explain concepts. We adopt an unpretentious, conversational style. That is, rather than acting like research is something only scientists can think about and do, we invite the reader to think about, evaluate, and propose research. Put another way, rather than making research design seem foreign, mysterious, and abstract, we demonstrate that scientific thinking is often a refinement of the way students already think.

CHANGES FROM THE FIRST EDITION

In many respects, first editions are like pilot studies. They may be charting new areas, they may be well thought out, their basic logic may be appealing, but they still benefit from further refinement. In the pilot study, the refinements may come from subjects' feedback. In the case of this text, the refinements have primarily come from professors' comments. Because one of the things we most admire about science is its self-correcting aspects, we have tried to incorporate these comments into this second edition. The result is a book that is much better than the first edition.

The primary changes in the second edition are

- more tables and graphs to summarize and reemphasize major points, as well as to help students see connections between concepts, similarities between designs, and tradeoffs involved in making different design decisions
- more emphasis on what science is and how it progresses
- more examples from current research
- revised Instructor's Manual and Test Bank

Beyond these changes and updating, more specific changes are as follows:

Chapter 1—Introduction
- more emphasis on showing the value of the scientific approach
- more emphasis on showing why psychology is a science

- more reasons for studying research design
- clearer explanation of the different types of validity

Chapter 2—Generating Research Ideas

- more emphasis on the value of reading research
- added tips on how to do a literature review
- more instruction on how to convert an idea into a hypothesis
- more information about how to use theory
- even more ways of generating research ideas

Chapter 3—Measuring and Manipulating Variables

- reorganized for clearer organization
- streamlined and shortened
- extensively rewritten

Chapter 4—Internal Validity

- more figures added
- organization tightened

Chapter 5—The Simple Experiment

- more tables to help students understand statistical significance and tradeoffs involved in making design decisions

Chapter 6—The Multiple-Group Experiment

- better explanation of confounding

Chapter 7—Factorial Designs

- clearer definition of interactions
- better graphs of interactions
- better explanation of ordinal interactions
- expanded coverage of three-way interactions
- more tables

Chapter 8—Within Subjects Designs

- reorganized to focus on within subjects designs and when to use them

Chapter 9—Critically Reading Research

- much more information on how to critically read articles
- more information about types of journals
- more emphasis on building on existing research

Chapter 10—Beyond Lab Experiments

- deleted unnecessary terms
- better job at explicitly making the connections between experimental and quasi-experimental research

Chapter 11—Descriptive Research

- expanded coverage of the logic of correlation coefficients
- clearer connections drawn to chapter 3

Chapter 12—Survey Research

- rewritten to be easier to understand
- more practical advice
- clearer connections drawn to chapter 3

Chapter 13—Planning and Conducting Research

- boxes showing strategies for writing the article and examples of how actual research-ers use these strategies

Appendix A—Ethics

- rather than simply reporting the ethical principles, we explain the general idea behind the ethical guidelines, explain the guidelines, outline a general strategy for deciding whether a study is ethical, and provide some practical advice that should help students propose and conduct ethical research

Appendix B—Conducting a Literature Search

- even more advice on how to conduct a literature review

Appendix F

- sample paper drawn from a published experiment

ACKNOWLEDGMENTS

Writing *Research Design Explained* was a monumental task that required commitment, love, effort, and a high tolerance for frustration. If it had not been for the support of our friends, family, publisher, and students, we could not have met this challenge.

Robert Tremblay, a Boston journalist, has our undying gratitude for the many hours he spent critiquing the first draft of our book. We also give special thanks to Christina Oldham, Susan Pierce, and the rest of the folks at Holt for sharing and nurturing our vision.

In addition to thanking Bob and Holt, we would like to thank three groups of dedicated reviewers whose valuable comments have made this edition of the book superior to the previous edition. First, we would like to thank the competent and conscientious professors who made useful comments and shared their insights with us: Tracy L. Brown, University of North Carolina—Wilmington; Walter Chromiak, Dickinson College; James J. Ryan, University of Wisconsin—La Crosse; Raymond Ditrichs, Northern Illinois University; James R. Council, North Dakota State University; James H. Beaird, Western Oregon State College; Joel Lundack, Peru State College; Mary Ann Foley, Skidmore College; Charles A. Levin, Baldwin-Wallace College; John Nicoud, Marian College of Fond du Lac; and Robert Hoff, Mercyhurst College. Second, we would like to thank our student reviewers for this edition: Susanne Bingham, Chris Fenn, and Shari Custer. Third, we would like to thank the English professors who critiqued our book: William Blazek, Patrick McLaughlin, and John Young. In addition to improving the writing style of the book, they also provided a valuable perspective—that of the naive, but intelligent, reader.

Finally, we offer our gratitude to Agatha and Max for allowing us the time to complete this project.

ABOUT THE AUTHORS

After graduating summa cum laude from Washington and Lee University, Mark L. Mitchell received his M.A. and Ph.D. in psychology at The Ohio State University. He is currently an Associate Professor at Clarion University.

Janina M. Jolley graduated with "Great Distinction" from California State University at Dominguez Hills and earned her M.A. and Ph.D. in psychology from The Ohio State University. She is currently a consulting editor of *The Journal of Genetic Psychology* and *Genetic Psychology Monographs*. Her previous book was *How to write psychology papers: A student's survival guide for psychology and related fields*, which she wrote with J. D. Murray and Pete Keller. She is currently a Professor of Psychology at Clarion University.

Drs. Mitchell and Jolley are married to research, teaching, and each other—not necessarily in that order.

CONTENTS

RESEARCH DESIGN EXPLAINED

1 Introduction

"The whole of science is nothing more than the refinement of everyday thinking."

—Albert Einstein

"Psychology . . . has risked everything on being a science."

—Edna Heidbreder
Seven Psychologies

OVERVIEW

In this chapter you will learn why psychologists embrace scientific research. You will learn what obstacles they face in applying classical scientific techniques to the study of behavior. Most importantly you will learn how understanding research can benefit you.

WHY PSYCHOLOGY USES THE SCIENTIFIC APPROACH

Since the first cave dweller, humans have asked themselves: "Why are people the way they are?" Everyone seems to have an opinion about what causes someone to break the law, be a hero, flunk a class, or run for president.

A little over 100 years ago, a few individuals used a novel approach to answer these questions—the scientific approach. As a result, psychology, the science of behavior, was born. What is it about the scientific approach that psychologists find so attractive?

CHARACTERISTICS OF SCIENCE

Psychologists find the scientific approach attractive because it has proven to be a useful tool for anyone trying to solve a mystery. For example, forensic detectives have used the scientific approach to solve crimes. Biologists have used the scientific approach to track down the genes responsible for a variety of inherited disorders. Similarly, behavioral scientists, such as psychologists, use the scientific approach to unravel the mysteries of the human mind. Science is able to help all of these detectives get accurate answers to their questions because it

1. seeks general rules
2. collects objective evidence
3. makes verifiable statements
4. adopts a skeptical attitude
5. is open-minded

6. is creative
7. is explicit
8. is public
9. is productive

General Rules

Just as police detectives assume crimes have motives, scientists assume events happen for reasons. Scientists are optimistic they can find general patterns, regularities, or rules that will allow us to better understand our world. Their hope is that by finding the underlying reasons for events, they will find order, predictability, simplicity, and coherence in what often seems a chaotic, random universe. Thus, contrary to what happens in some science classes, the goal of science is not to make things seem bewilderingly complex. Instead, science's goal is to make things easier and simpler to understand by finding the common threads that connect diverse experiences.

Objective Evidence

Scientists hope they can find the common, connecting threads *by looking at concrete, physical evidence.* That is, they want to avoid the speculations and biased perceptions that have caused people to see an orderly, predictable world. For example, some believe their lives are controlled by the stars and the world is very predictable as long as one has a good astrologer. In contrast to the speculations and biased perceptions that have led some to "discover the truth" of astrology, the scientific laws of gravity and magnetism were discovered through careful observation and experimentation.

Verifiable

We are not saying that scientists don't speculate—they do. Like other detectives, scientists are encouraged to go out on a limb, make specific predictions, and then track down leads to find out whether their speculations were correct. As long as scientists make specific, verifiable, before-the-fact predictions, they are not concerned about having their ideas proven wrong. After all, a major goal of science is to identify false beliefs. However, scientists are concerned if a statement cannot be tested. Untestable statements are not scientific because they cannot be adjusted, refined, or corrected by evidence. The two main kinds of untestable statements that scientists avoid making are vague statements and after-the-fact statements.

Vague statements are as useless as they are unverifiable. Consequently, a police detective who tells us that the murderer lives in this universe will neither be proven wrong nor promoted. Vague statements are often the province of pseudo-sciences, such as palmistry and astrology (see figure 1.1). For example, one of the authors' horoscopes read: "Take care today not to get involved with someone who is wrong for you and you for him or her. Trouble could result." This horoscope tells us nothing. It does not say trouble will result or even that trouble will probably result. It only says that trouble is, like anything else, a possibility. Furthermore, it does not give us a clue as to what "wrong for you" means. Finally, "trouble" could mean almost anything. Because the horoscope does not

Vague and unfalsifiable statements fool the naive; profit the quack; and disturb the scientist.
Reprinted with special permission of King Features Syndicate.

FIGURE 1.1 Verifiable Statements

tell us anything, it cannot be proven wrong. But because it does not tell us anything, it is also useless.

Like vague statements, after-the-fact statements do not involve making testable predictions and are therefore virtually impossible to prove wrong. Indeed, the horoscope just quoted could be construed as making after-the-fact statements. If, after becoming involved with someone, "trouble" resulted, then that person was wrong for us. If no trouble resulted, the astrologer would say that the person was right for us.

After the fact, almost anyone can generate a plausible explanation for why the stock market went down, why a team lost the championship, or why a company succeeded. Although these explanations may seem reasonable, they may be incorrect. To dramatize the fact that plausible-sounding explanations may be wrong, people were asked to explain various "facts" such as why Russia has been involved in more armed conflicts than the U.S., why forming extremely bizarre images of an object helps you remember more than forming other images, why the elderly are lonelier than teenagers, and why property values go down when group homes for the mentally handicapped move into a neighborhood. The responders were able to generate logical, persuasive reasons as to why these "facts" were true—*even though all of these "facts" are false* (Greenwald & Johnson, 1989; Myers, 1990; Slovic & Fischoff, 1977; Stanovich, 1990; Teigen, 1986).

Skeptical

Despite being willing to make speculative predictions, scientists are very skeptical. Like other detectives, scientists want evidence to support even the most "obvious" of statements. For example, Galileo tested the "obvious fact" that heavier objects fall faster and found it to be false. Thus, like the police detective, scientists' approaches range from "show me" to "let me see" to "let's take a look" to "can you verify that?" In short, detectives and scientists do not accept things merely because an authority says it is true, because another person is sure that it is true, or because everyone says it is true. Instead they demand evidence.

However, even once they have evidence, they continue to be skeptical. They do this by asking themselves: "What other explanations are there for these facts?" Consequently, scientists are experts at considering other explanations for events. For example, malaria means "bad air" ("mal" means bad as in malpractice, "aria" means air) because people thought malaria was caused by breathing the bad-smelling air around swamps. People pointed out that malaria cases were more common around swamps and swamps contained foul-smelling marsh gas. Scientists countered that foul-smelling marsh gas is not the only thing that happens around swamps. For example, insects, such as mosquitoes, breed in swamps. As we now know, it is the bite of mosquitoes, not the smell of marsh gas, that transmits malaria.

Like other detectives, scientists realize that sometimes an event may merely be the result of a coincidence. A suspect may be near the victim's house on the night of the murder for perfectly innocent reasons, a patient may suddenly get better without treatment or even after getting a quack treatment, a volcano may erupt exactly twenty years after an atomic bomb went off, or we can have one warm summer for reasons having nothing to do with the "greenhouse effect."

Open-minded

Despite being such critical skeptics, scientists are extremely open-minded. Just as they are reluctant to accept an idea because everyone believes in it or because some powerful person claims the idea is true, they are reluctant to rule out an idea simply because nobody believes in it. That is, just as a good police detective initially considers everyone a suspect, scientists are willing to entertain all possibilities. Consequently, scientists will not automatically dismiss something as nonsense, not even ideas that seem to run counter to existing knowledge, such as telepathy. The willingness to test "odd" ideas has led scientists to important discoveries, such as finding that certain jungle herbs have medicinal properties.

Creative

To test such ideas, scientists have to be clever and creative. Unraveling the mysteries of the universe and solving riddles that have never been solved are not tasks for the unimaginative. Dreams, brain-storming, and clever analogies have helped scientists ask questions in such a way that nature would answer.

Explicit

Once scientists make predictions or do studies, they make their knowledge explicit. They spell out the logic behind their research or theory by publishing it in books and journals. One advantage of explicitness is it makes contradictions painfully clear. Because explicitness makes contradictions obvious, police detectives take copious notes looking for contradictions in witnesses' stories. As you can see by looking at box 1.1, common sense would not be taken seriously for long if it were made explicit because its contradictions would be too apparent.

BOX 1.1   The Inconsistency of Common Sense

Partly because common sense is not written out, many people fail to notice its inconsistencies. As you can see below, when we make common sense explicit, we find that, unlike scientific theory, common sense is full of inconsistencies.

Absence makes the heart fonder,
BUT:
Absence makes the heart wander.

Like attracts like,
BUT:
Opposites attract.

Haste makes waste,
BUT:
A stitch in time saves nine.

Too many cooks spoil the broth,
BUT:
Two heads are better than one.

To know you is to love you
BUT:
Familiarity breeds contempt.

Public

Although explicitness alerts scientists to contradictions, the most important aspect of publishing ideas and research is it allows science to be public. By being public, flaws and biases can be spotted and corrected. Rival investigators can repeat studies and challenge conclusions.

Without such openness science does not work, as the case of cold fusion illustrates. In 1989, two physical scientists called a press conference to announce they had invented a way of creating nuclear fusion, a potential source of safe electric power, without heating atoms to enormous temperatures. (Before their announcement, all known ways of producing nuclear fusion used more energy to heat atoms than the fusion reaction produced. Thus, nobody could seriously consider using nuclear fusion to commercially produce electricity.) However, they did not submit their research to peer-reviewed journals and they failed to give details of their procedures.

All these actions worked against science's self-corrective and *unbiased* nature. By not sharing their work, they removed the checks and balances that make science the reliable source of evidence it is. People were expected to accept the findings only on the basis of the investigators' press conference. Fortunately, skeptical scientists refuse to accept statements, whether from astrologers or physical scientists, without evidence untainted by personal bias.

Thus far we have skeptically assumed cold fusion did not really happen. But what if it did? The researchers' lack of openness would still be tragic because science only flourishes in the open. The reason science is so powerful is that people can build on one another's work. Each individual scientist does not have to reinvent the wheel. By cooperating, they can discover more than any single individual could by working alone. Indeed, by combining their efforts, ideas and facts multiply to such an extent that the knowledge in some fields doubles every five to ten years.

Productive

The power of science to make discoveries and progress is obvious. The technology created by science has vaulted us a long way from the dark ages or even the pre-VCR, pre-personal computer, pre-microwave early 1970s.

The progress science has made is remarkable considering that it is a relatively new way of finding out about the world. During the 1400s, people were punished for studying human anatomy and even for trying to get evidence on such basic matters as the number of teeth a horse has. As recently as the early 1800s, the scientific approach was not applied to medicine or psychology. Until that time, people were limited to relying on tradition, common sense, intuition, and logic for medical and psychological knowledge. Once science gained greater acceptance, people used the scientific approach to test and refine many common sense, traditional, and intuitive notions, as well as test the assumptions on which logical inferences were based. As a result of supplementing and complementing other ways of knowing, science helped knowledge in the Western world progress at an explosive rate.

IS PSYCHOLOGY A SCIENCE?: A LOOK AT ITS CHARACTERISTICS

Although most people agree that science has allowed physics, chemistry, and biology to progress at an enormous rate, some wonder whether the scientific approach can have the same benefits for psychology. They wonder whether psychology can, like the physical sciences, be evidence-oriented, make falsifiable statements, be skeptical yet open-minded, critical but creative, explicit, public, and productive in the pursuit of individual facts as well as simple, general rules that explain human behavior.

General Rules

Perhaps the most serious question about psychology as a science is: Can it find relatively general rules that can predict, control, and explain human behavior? Skeptics argue that whereas finding rules to explain the behavior of molecules is possible, finding rules to explain the behavior patterns of people is not. Psychologists respond by saying that even though people are not simple nor all alike, human beings do have certain things in common. Furthermore, they argue that most behavior has reasons. Finally, they argue that if human behavior is not governed by rules, then psychologists will not find any rules. However, the fact is that psychologists have found a wide variety of rules that underlie human behavior (see table 1.1). For example, psychologists have discovered laws of

TABLE 1.1   Examples of General Rules That Apply to Human Behavior

"All or none" law of neural firing.

Laws of operant conditioning.

Laws of classical conditioning.

Psychophysical laws.

Gestalt laws of grouping.

Short-term memory holds between 5 and 9 chunks.

Meaningful information is easier to recall.

First and last bits of information presented are most likely to be recalled.

Credible communicators are more persuasive.

Reaction to stressors follows the general adaptation principle: alarm, followed by resistance, and finally, exhaustion.

Orthogenetic Principle: development progresses from global responding to differential responding to responding in which different components are integrated into a hierarchical organization. For example, in learning anything, people progress from over-generalizing concepts (be it the term "dada" or "experiment") to discriminating when a concept applies to finally developing an organized way of understanding the relationships between the concepts.

Beyond a certain point, arousal fails to increase performance (follows from the Yerkes-Dodson Law).

If a stimulus produces a certain reaction, the body will counter with an opposite reaction, thus accounting for negative after-images and drug withdrawal symptoms.

Avoidance gradients are steeper than approach gradients (when an action [getting married, donating time to a charitable organization] is in the distant future, the positive aspects are more salient relative to the negative aspects than they will be as the time to do the action approaches. Consequently, a person who is ecstatic about being engaged to be married in a year may get "cold feet" in the weeks or days before the wedding.)

---

operant and classical conditioning, laws of memory (Banaji & Crowder, 1989), and even laws of emotion (Frijda, 1988). (If you doubt that emotions follow rules, then ask yourself why movie directors can control the audience's emotions.)

Psychology's situation is similar to medicine's. Until recently, people believed everyone needed their own special treatment. One person's flu was caused by totally different circumstances than another's. "Each patient regarded his own suffering as unique, and demanding unique remedies" (Burke, 1985). Consequently, one person's treatment was totally different from another's. Partly because what cured one person was supposed to be totally irrelevant for curing anyone else, knowledge about cures was not shared. As a result, medicine did not progress and many people died unnecessarily. It was only after physicians started to look for general causes of disease that cures were found.

Nevertheless, *general* rules do not always work. A treatment that cures one person may not cure another. For example, one person may be cured by penicillin whereas another may be allergic to it. This is not to say that reactions to a drug follow no rules. It is simply that how an individual will respond to a drug is affected by many rules. Predicting a person's reaction to a drug would require knowing at least the following: the individual's weight, family history of reactions to drugs, when they last ate, condition of their vital organs, other drugs they are taking, and level of dehydration.

Like human physiology, human behavior is governed by many factors. Because there are so many rules that may come into play in a given situation, predicting what a given individual will do in that situation would be difficult even if you knew all the rules. Thus, psychologists agree with cynics that predicting and explaining an individual's behavior is difficult. However, psychologists disagree with the cynic's assumption that there are no rules underlying behavior. Instead, psychologists know there are rules that are useful in predicting the behavior of many of the people much of the time—although we are not as bold as Sherlock Holmes who said, "You can never foretell what any man will do, but you can say with precision what an average number will be up to. Individuals may vary, but percentages remain constant."

All sciences, not just psychology and medicine, produce general rules that apply to the average case yet do not hold for every individual case. For instance, take the case of statistics. On the basis of statistics, we can predict that if you flip many coins, numerous times, you will average about 50 percent heads. However, we have trouble applying this general rule to a single coin flip. It is not that the outcome of a coin flip does not follow rules; it follows very simple rules: The outcome depends on what side was up when the coin was flipped and how many times the coin turned over. Nevertheless, since we do not know how many times the coin will turn over, we cannot predict the outcome of a single coin toss. Similarly, most would agree that weather is determined by specific events. However, since there are so many events and since we do not have data on all events, we cannot predict weather with perfect accuracy. Likewise, if a physicist knew how fast a car was going, the condition of the tires, the road temperature, the condition of the road, and a few other variables, the physicist should be able to predict precisely how far a given car will skid on a certain road on a certain night. After all, the car's skid should conform to physical laws. However, because physicists do not have measures of all of those variables, they have trouble predicting such real life events. In short, just because a given behavior in a given situation cannot be predicted, we should not conclude that the behavior does not follow rules. That behavior might be perfectly predictable—if we knew the rules and could measure the relevant variables.

Objective Evidence

A second question raised about psychology's ability to be a science is: Can psychology collect objective evidence about human behavior? Whereas physical sciences study the physical world, psychologists often study the invisible, mental world of thoughts and feelings. There are two answers to this question. First, as with all sciences, there are some questions psychology cannot answer. Physics and biology do not pretend to find evidence for or against the existence of God; psychology does not attempt to prove or refute the idea that people have souls. To get answers to these questions, we must go outside science and use other ways of knowing. Second, physical sciences have studied things they could not see. Genetics was well advanced before anyone had seen a gene; physicists and chemists were discussing electrons long before electrons were seen; and nobody has yet seen gravity, time, or magnetism. Unobservable events can be inferred from observable events: Gravity can be inferred from observing objects fall, and psychological variables like love can be assessed by observable indicators such as how long a person gazes into their partner's eyes, pupil dilation at sight of partner, physiological arousal at sight of partner, and passing up the opportunity to date attractive others. Partly as a result of relying on objective observations, psychological research is highly reliable. That is, when psychologists repeat another's study, they are very likely to get the same pattern of results. In fact, psychological research is just as reliable as physics research (Hedges, 1987).

Verifiable

A third question about psychology is: Can it make verifiable statements? If it cannot, then it would share the weaknesses of palmistry and astrology. Fortunately, most individual research studies make verifiable predictions. Indeed, psychology journals are full of articles in which predictions made by investigators were disconfirmed. For example, to his surprise, Charles Kiesler (Kiesler, 1982; Kiesler & Sibulkin, 1987) found that many mentally ill individuals are hurt, rather than helped, by being put in mental institutions.

Skeptical

A fourth question about psychology is: Are psychologists as skeptical as other scientists? After all, it would seem difficult for psychologists to be constantly skeptical when many ideas are so intuitively appealing. It would be sad, but understandable, if psychologists did not test ideas that were so logical that they "sounded right" or if psychologists failed to test ideas that "ring true" because they seem to be verified by personal experience. Fortunately, however, psychologists seem quite willing to test even the most "obviously true" of ideas. For example, Greenberger and Steinberg (1986) did a series of studies testing the "obviously true" idea that teenagers who work do better in school and better understand the value of hard work. They found, contrary to conventional wisdom, that teenagers who work do more poorly in school and are more cynical about the value of hard work than non-working teens. Similarly, Shedler and Block (1990) tested the "obviously true" idea that drug use is the cause of psychological problems. Their evidence suggested conventional wisdom was wrong—heavy drug use was a symptom rather than a cause of psychological problems. Likewise, Laurie Chassin and her colleagues (Chassin et al., 1990) found, contrary to the "obviously correct" view that the peer group always pressures the adolescent to smoke, that the adolescent often approaches the group and asks to smoke.

In addition to being skeptical about conventional wisdom, psychologists are also skeptical about the evidence they collect. That is, they question what the evidence means. As we shall see, they question whether

1. the measures tap the mental states they claim to tap
2. the evidence proves that one factor causes something else to happen

3. the results of a study would occur if the study were repeated in a different place with a different type of subject.

They may question the degree to which measures, such as love scales, truly capture the psychological concepts the measures purport to assess. They are not easily convinced that a "love scale" measures love or that an "intelligence test" measures intelligence. They would need evidence documenting that these tests really measured what the tests claimed to measure.

Psychologists are also very skeptical about drawing cause-effect conclusions. If they find that better students have personal computers, they do not leap to the conclusion that computers cause academic success. They realize the computer-owning students may be doing better because they went to better preschools, got better nutrition, or got more parental encouragement, etc. Furthermore, they may have gotten a computer because they were doing well in school. Until these other explanations are eliminated, psychologists would not assume that computers caused academic success.

Finally, many psychologists are skeptical about the extent to which results from a study can be generalized. They do not assume that a study done in a particular setting can be generalized to other kinds of subjects in a different setting. For instance, they would not automatically assume that a study originally done with gifted six-year-olds at a day-care facility would obtain the same results if it were repeated with adult subjects studied at a work place.

Open-minded

Paralleling the concern that psychologists do not test "obvious facts," is the concern that psychologists are not open to ideas that run counter to common sense. However, contrary to these concerns, psychologists have tested all sorts of ideas, such as the idea that subliminal, backward messages (back-masking) on records can force teens to suicide and Satanism (Custer, 1985); the idea that people can learn in their sleep; and the idea that ESP can be reliably used to send messages (Swets & Bjork, 1990). Although psychologists found no evidence for any of those ideas, psychology's willingness to try to test virtually anything has led to tentative acceptance of some novel ideas such as the effectiveness of acupuncture; the idea that meditating causes people to live longer (Alexander et al., 1989); and the idea that beliefs people hold to be unquestionably true, such as "you should brush your teeth three times a day" are very easy to change (McGuire, 1985).

Creative

Whereas psychologists' open-mindedness has been questioned, few have questioned psychologists' creativity. Coming up with testable research ideas requires creativity. Coming up with a way of objectively measuring a psychological state, finding a way to get subjects to become emotionally and psychologically engaged in a laboratory task, or figuring out how to do a study in the real world, all require a certain degree of ingenuity. Some psychologists have combined the best techniques of "Candid Camera" and "Totally Hidden Video." Others, much like the first inventors of the wind tunnel, have created ingenious models of real world situations. Still others have come up with beautifully direct predictions and remarkably simple and elegant ways of conclusively testing those predictions.

Explicit and Public

Psychologists have also been very good at making their ideas explicit and public, as shown by the hundreds of journals in which they publish their work. Indeed, psychologists may enjoy more candor and cooperation than scientists in other fields because psychologists usually gain little by keeping results secret. For example, if you wanted to be the first to patent a new technology, it would pay to keep secrets from competitors. In such a race, if you were first, you might make millions; if you were second, you would make nothing. Whereas such "races for dollars" are common in chemistry, they are rare in psychology because psychologists produce few patents or inventions.

Productive

Perhaps because of this candor psychologists have made tremendous progress in the last 100 years. To see the effect of research on the teaching and practice of psychology, compare introductory textbooks published in 1910, 1930, 1950, 1970, and 1990. Even a cursory examination of these texts will dramatize two facts. First, research has radically changed knowledge in every field of psychology. Second, the rate of research discovery is rapidly accelerating—especially in the fields of counseling, developmental, personality, cognitive, physiological, social, and applied psychology.

Because research has contributed to every area of psychology, even former opponents of research now praise research. For example, Abraham Maslow (1970), the founder of the "Third Force"—an approach that initially rebelled against scientific psychology and doubted whether scientific psychology was relevant to human concerns—later wrote: "Clearly, the next step for this psychology . . . is research, research, research." (p. 1).

Today, because psychologists still have many unanswered questions and relatively few pat answers, scientific research is as relevant as ever. To take just a few examples, researchers have identified ways of getting people to behave in ways that will stop the spread of the AIDS virus (O'Keeffe, Nesselhof-Kendall, & Baum, 1990), ways of increasing volunteerism (Snyder & Omoto, 1990), ways of encouraging energy conservation (Aronson, 1990), and ways of understanding and helping married couples get along (Holmes & Boon, 1990). No wonder people outside psychology, professionals in areas such as education, communication, marketing, economics, and medicine, now adopt our methods. (See table 1.2 for a summary of the similarities between physical scientists and psychologists.)

THE IMPORTANCE OF SCIENCE TO PSYCHOLOGY: CONCLUSIONS

Not only is the scientific method responsible for the tremendous progress in psychology, but it is also what makes psychology unique (Stanovich, 1990). The reason every

Table 1.2 Similarities Between Physical Scientists and Psychologists

APPROACH	EXAMPLES	
	PHYSICAL SCIENTIST	**PSYCHOLOGIST**
Seeks general rules	Laws of gravity	Laws of operant and classical conditioning; laws of memory (meaningless information is hard to remember, memorizing similar information such as Spanish and Italian leads to memory errors); laws of motivation (up to a point, motivation can help performance, but after that point motivation will hurt performance)
Collects objective evidence	Measures heat given off by a reaction, weights product of reaction	Records subjects' behavior: number of words written down on memory test, ratings made in judgment task, personality test responses, reaction times, etc.
Makes verifiable statements	Makes specific predictions that are sometimes found to be wrong and thus revised (heavy objects fall faster)	Makes specific testable predictions that are sometimes found to be wrong (rewarding someone for doing a task will always increase their enjoyment of that task)
Skeptical	Demands evidence for statements; considers alternative explanations for evidence (UFO sighting may be due to airplane, smog, mass hysteria, etc., rather than the presence of a space ship)	Demands evidence for almost any statement; challenges common sense and traditional notions; does not take evidence (subjects' statements or ratings) at face value; considers alternative explanations for evidence (group given memory pill may do better than another on memory task because they had naturally better memories, because they were tested later in the day, or because they believed the pill would work)
Open-minded	Entertains possibility that UFO's and cold fusion may exist.	Willing to entertain virtually any hypothesis, from acupuncture being effective to ESP being effective to meditation prolonging life
Creative	Cleverly asks questions in such a way as to pry answers out of nature	Needs cleverness to measure psychological concepts, generate hypotheses, and devise studies that rule out alternative explanations for findings
Explicit	Theories and predictions are spelled out and published	Theories and predictions are spelled out and published
Public	Research is presented at conferences, and published in journals	Research is presented at conferences and published in journals
Productive	In some scientific fields, knowledge doubles every 5 to 10 years	Psychological knowledge is increasing at a dramatic rate

definition of psychology starts out "the science of . . ." is that whereas other fields—from astrology to philosophy—study individuals, only psychology studies individuals scientifically (Stanovich, 1990). Without the scientific method, psychology might simply be a branch of astrology.

The success of psychology as a science depends, in part, on discovering the rules that guide human behavior. Like all sciences, psychology has had to contend with people who argued that its subject matter followed no rules. That is, since the beginning of recorded history, there have been people who have argued that finding rules or laws that govern nature is impossible. For centuries, most people believed the stars followed no pattern. Not that long ago, it was believed diseases follow no patterns. Even today, some people believe human behavior follows no discernible pattern. Yet, each of these assumptions has been disproven. The stars, the planets, diseases, and humans behave for reasons that we can understand. Admittedly, the rules determining human behavior may be complex and numerous—and it may be that some behaviors do not follow rules. However, to this point, searching for rules of behavior has been fruitful.

Despite the success of scientific psychology, we should point out that the scientific approach has its limitations. If scientists become corrupt, overly arrogant, or stop being skeptical, science's ability to be objective would suffer. Furthermore, science, even at its best, is only one way of obtaining information. Some important philosophical and religious questions (such as "does the fetus have a soul?") cannot be answered by science.

Yet, despite not being able to answer some questions, a strength of science is its flexibility. Science can work in concert with a variety of other ways of knowing. It can verify knowledge passed down by tradition or from an authoritative expert. It can test knowledge obtained by intuition or common sense. By anchoring speculation in reality, psychology can create, refine, or verify common sense and eliminate superstitions (Kohn, 1988; Stanovich, 1990). For example, consider the following findings from research.

1. Punishment is not very effective in changing behavior.
2. Having teens work does not instill the "work ethic."
3. Drug use often is a symptom, rather than a cause, of psychological problems.
4. We may like a task because we do it, rather than doing it because we like it.
5. Misery loves miserable company.
6. Absence makes the heart fonder only for couples who are already very much in love.
7. If you tell somebody what happened, they will tend to think they could have predicted the event, that "they knew it all along."

All of these findings are refinements of the traditional, old-fashioned, common sense of a few years ago. All of these findings are, or will soon become, part of the common sense of the 1990s.

In short, science is a powerful tool that can be used to solve some human problems. If we have such a tool, why shouldn't we use it, especially when it does not rule out the use of other tools?

QUESTIONS ABOUT APPLYING TECHNIQUES FROM OLDER SCIENCES TO PSYCHOLOGY

Thus far, we have talked about the value of using an important tool: the scientific method. Specifically, we have emphasized that psychology, like other sciences, should collect objective evidence, make verifiable statements, be explicit, and be public.

We are not saying, however, that psychology should use the same equipment and techniques as other sciences. Obviously, what you study affects how you study it. Thus, the biologist, the astronomer, and the chemist all use different equipment and techniques. Clearly, live subjects (rats, pigeons, humans, etc.) cannot be studied the same way molecules are studied.

To appreciate how sensitive research psychologists are to the unique challenges and responsibilities involved in studying the behavior of living things, let us see how a research psychologist would react if someone ignored those challenges and responsibilities. For instance, suppose that a novice investigator tried to model his psychological research after the following chemistry experiment:

> A chemist has two test tubes. Both test tubes contain a group of hydrogen and oxygen molecules. She leaves the first test tube alone. She heats the second over a flame. She observes that water forms only in the second test tube. Because there was only one difference between the two test tubes (the flame), she concludes that the flame caused the group of molecules in the second test tube to behave differently than the molecules in the first tube. She then concludes that heat always causes hydrogen and oxygen to combine.

Instead of filling two test tubes with hydrogen and oxygen, the novice investigator fills two rooms with both men and women. He treats both groups identically, except that he makes the second group's room ten degrees warmer than the first group's room. He then compares the behavior of the two groups and observes more "aggression" in the second room. Consequently, he concludes that "feeling warmer" makes people more "aggressive."

Because of the vast differences between humans and molecules, an experienced research psychologist would have four sets of very serious questions about the novice investigator's study. The first three deal with the validity of the novice investigator's conclusions: (1) Did the treatment manipulation really *cause* the differences in *behavior?*; (2) Did the investigator really measure and manipulate the variables he thought he did? (Did the manipulation make subjects feel warmer and did the subjects' behavior really reflect aggression?); and (3) Would the results *generalize* to other settings and subjects? The fourth, and final, set of concerns is the most serious: Was it ethical to perform the study?

INTERNAL VALIDITY QUESTIONS: DID THE TREATMENT CAUSE A CHANGE IN BEHAVIOR?

The first set of questions deals with the study's *internal validity:* the degree to which the study demonstrates that the treatment *caused* a change in behavior. If the study clearly establishes that putting the subjects into different rooms *caused* the warm-room group to behave differently from the normal-room group, the study has internal validity. If something other than being in different rooms is causing the groups to differ, then the study does not have internal validity.

For the chemist, establishing internal validity is fairly simple. If the flame condition yields water and the no-flame condition does not, the flame manipulation must be responsible. The chemist does not have to worry that the oxygen molecules in one tube were more likely to combine with hydrogen than were the molecules in the other tube. Since all oxygen molecules are basically alike, she knows she would have gotten the same results if he had applied the flame to the second tube rather than to the first. Similarly, since oxygen molecules in the well-controlled laboratory tend to stay the same, the chemist does not have to worry about treating both tubes identically. For example, she could do the no-flame part of the study in the morning and do the flame part of the study at night. She can be confident that her results will not be affected by time of day because laboratory oxygen in the morning behaves just like laboratory oxygen at any other time.

In psychological research, on the other hand, it is not easy to determine whether a *treatment* is the *cause* of an *effect*. In this study, for example, the warm-room group may have naturally been more aggressive than the normal-room group. Since we do not know that the groups were the same at the start of the study, finding a difference between the groups at the end of the study is not conclusive that the room manipulation caused the groups to differ. Furthermore, even if the groups were initially equivalent, they may not be equivalent at the time of testing. For example, suppose the novice happens to test the normal-room group in the morning and the warm-room group in the evening. In this case, many events completely unrelated to the room manipulation might cause the warm-room subjects to behave differently from the normal-room subjects. For example, during the afternoon or early evening, the warm-room group may have had a few drinks or learned of some act of terrorism. Although these events have nothing to do with the room manipulation, they might affect the subjects' behavior.

To reiterate, if we cannot be sure that the *manipulation* is *the one and only* systematic difference between our subjects, we cannot determine that the manipulation is the cause of an effect (see figure 1.2). That is, if we cannot be sure that the groups were the same except that they were placed in different rooms, we cannot conclude that being in the different rooms caused the difference in their behavior.

CONSTRUCT VALIDITY QUESTIONS: WHAT DOES SUBJECTS' BEHAVIOR REALLY MEAN? WHAT DOES THE TREATMENT REALLY MANIPULATE?

In the example, the novice carelessly assumed that the room manipulation *caused* the subjects to behave differently. However, that was not the only questionable assumption he made. Unfortunately, he also presumed the manipulation made warm-room subjects "feel warm" and he had accurately measured "aggression."

The professional researcher would point out the novice did not see subjects "feel warm" or "be aggressive." The novice manipulated the physical environment by raising

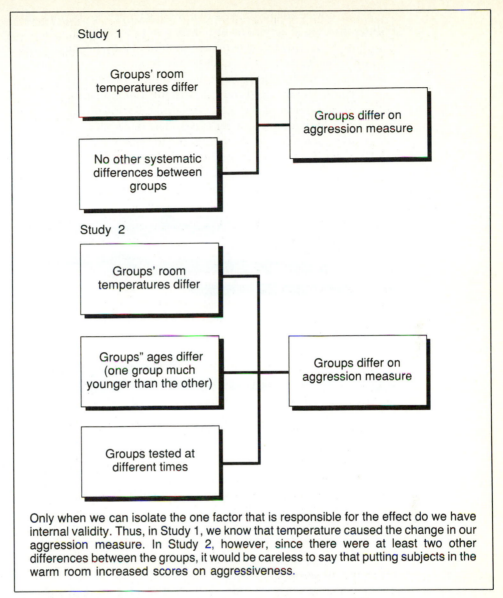

Study 1

Groups' room temperatures differ

No other systematic differences between groups

Groups differ on aggression measure

Study 2

Groups' room temperatures differ

Groups" ages differ (one group much younger than the other)

Groups tested at different times

Groups differ on aggression measure

Only when we can isolate the one factor that is responsible for the effect do we have internal validity. Thus, in Study 1, we know that temperature caused the change in our aggression measure. In Study 2, however, since there were at least two other differences between the groups, it would be careless to say that putting subjects in the warm room increased scores on aggressiveness.

FIGURE 1.2: The Challenge of Establishing Internal Validity

the thermostat and observed behaviors, but the novice did not directly manipulate or directly observe subjects' psychological states. Yet, the novice is talking about psychological states. He is labelling his room manipulation as a manipulation of "feeling warm" and he is labelling subjects' behavior as "aggressive." How can he justify using those arbitrary labels?

The novice might respond that most scientists go beyond talking about the procedures they use. That is, scientists' conclusions do not deal with the actual actions they performed, but with the underlying variables that they manipulated. For example, the chemist's conclusions would not deal with the effects of "a lit bunsen burner," but rather would deal with the effects of the underlying variable—heat.

The researcher would point out that the leap from assuming that the bunsen burner manipulates the heat of the molecules in the test tube is relatively safe and short. It is unlikely the burner has any other effects. The molecules do not notice the flame's color, are not irked or terrified by its intensity, do not care if it discolors the test tube, and do not smell it. Manipulating the temperature of molecules is clearly simpler than manipulating how people feel. Furthermore, the chemist makes virtually no inference when it comes to observing the results of the reaction: Water is easy to observe and measure. In contrast, it is difficult to accurately measure "aggression."

In short, the research psychologist realizes that measuring and manipulating people's thoughts, feelings, and behaviors is much more difficult than measuring and manipulating the behavior of molecules. If you are not careful, going from objective, observable, physical concepts to inferring invisible, subjective, psychological concepts may involve jumping to conclusions. For instance, some people are quick to infer that a person who works slowly is unintelligent. Others are quick to infer that such a person is lazy. However, the individual may be cautious, new to the task, or ill. Because the possibility of error is so great, psychologists are extremely cautious about inferring private mental states from publicly observable behavior. Therefore, the research psychologist would question the temperature study's **construct validity:** the degree to which the study measures and manipulates the **underlying concepts** the researcher claims. The research psychologist would have four major reasons to doubt that the novice's aggression study had adequate construct validity.

First, turning up the thermostat is not necessarily a "pure" manipulation of room temperature, much less of "feeling warm." For example, turning up the thermostat in the "warm" room might also decrease the room's air quality (if the heater's filters were dirty) or make the room noisier (if the heater's belts or fans were noisy). Thus, the room manipulation might be a temperature manipulation, a noise manipulation, **and** an air quality manipulation.

Second, even if the researcher has a pure manipulation of heat, the researcher does not necessarily have a pure manipulation of "feeling warm." That is, unlike molecules, subjects may interpret the research situation or manipulation differently from how the researcher intended. Consequently, the subjects may not **feel warm** in the "warm" room. For example, they may take off jackets and sweaters to cool off or they may find the room's temperature "comfortable." But even if the novice investigator did make the warm-room subjects feel warm, he may also have made them frustrated about being unable to open the windows to cool off the room or he may have made subjects angry with him for being so inconsiderate as to put them in such an uncomfortable room. Thus, in addition to being a manipulation of temperature, the treatment may have had other side effects, such as being a manipulation of frustration or anger.

Third, unlike molecules, people know they are in a research project and may act accordingly. In the novice's study, warm-room subjects may realize that they have been deliberately placed in an abnormally warm room and then given a questionnaire that asks them how aggressive they feel. If they like the investigator, they may *act* aggressive for the researcher's benefit. The investigator may misinterpret or mislabel this acting as genuine aggression.

Fourth, unlike the amount of water produced by a chemical reaction, psychological concepts such as aggression are abstract, invisible, and therefore impossible to measure directly. We can only indirectly assess inner reality from clues we find in outer reality. Guessing what is on the inside from the outside, like guessing what is inside a package, is a gamble. Because there is no direct pipeline to the mind, subjects' behaviors and reactions may not be correctly labelled. For example, the novice investigator may have misinterpreted "kidding around" and attention-getting behaviors as aggression. The novice may have misinterpreted physiological changes (sweating, flushed face) as signs of anger rather than merely the body's automatic reaction to being warm.

In conclusion, our novice wants internal and construct validity (see figure 1.3). With only internal validity, he would be limited to concluding that "turning up the thermostat *causes* a difference in how people fill in circles on a multiple-choice answer sheet." With only construct validity, he would be limited to concluding that "members of the group who felt warm were more aggressive, but the aggression could be due to many factors unrelated to feeling warm, such as the possibility that people in the group who felt warm were naturally more aggressive than those in the other group."

EXTERNAL VALIDITY QUESTIONS: CAN THE RESULTS BE GENERALIZED TO OTHER SETTINGS, SUBJECTS, AND TIMES?

Even if the novice actually manipulated "feeling warm" and measured aggression (construct validity) and established that results in this particular study were due to the treatment (internal validity), the experienced researcher would still question the study's *external validity:* the degree to which the results could be *generalized* to different subjects, settings, or times (see figure 1.4 and table 1.3). There are at least two reasons to question the aggression study's external validity.

First, since people differ, a result that occurs with one group of people might not occur with a different group of people. The novice investigator might have obtained different results had he studied all female groups instead of mixed-sex groups, if he had studied Soviet sixth-graders instead of midwestern college students, if he had studied people used to working in very warm conditions, or if he had studied less aggressive individuals.

Second, since people's behavior may change depending on the situation, the results might not hold in another setting. For instance, suppose the novice investigator used a very sterile laboratory setting to eliminate the effects of non-treatment factors. By isolating the treatment factor, the novice may have succeeded in establishing internal validity. However, results obtained under such controlled situations may not generalize to more

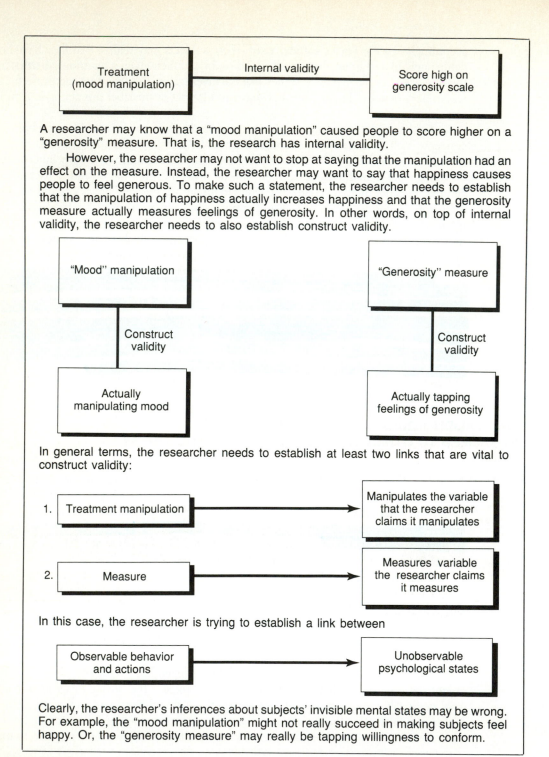

A researcher may know that a "mood manipulation" caused people to score higher on a "generosity" measure. That is, the research has internal validity.

However, the researcher may not want to stop at saying that the manipulation had an effect on the measure. Instead, the researcher may want to say that happiness causes people to feel generous. To make such a statement, the researcher needs to establish that the manipulation of happiness actually increases happiness and that the generosity measure actually measures feelings of generosity. In other words, on top of internal validity, the researcher needs to also establish construct validity.

In general terms, the researcher needs to establish at least two links that are vital to construct validity:

In this case, the researcher is trying to establish a link between

Clearly, the researcher's inferences about subjects' invisible mental states may be wrong. For example, the "mood manipulation" might not really succeed in making subjects feel happy. Or, the "generosity measure" may really be tapping willingness to conform.

FIGURE 1.3: The Challenge of Establishing Construct Validity

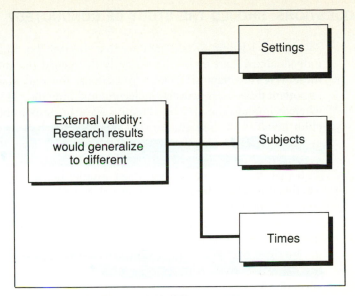

FIGURE 1.4: External Validity

complex situations, such as the work place or the home where other factors, such as frustration and pressure, come into play.

In short, even if temperature increased aggression in this particular lab with this particular group of subjects at this particular time, the experienced researcher would not automatically assume that temperature would have the same effect in future studies conducted with different subjects in different settings. To maximize external validity, the experienced researcher might repeat the study using different types of subjects and different situations.

Table 1.3	Common Threats to the Three Kinds of Validity	
TYPE OF VALIDITY	**DEFINITION**	**MAJOR SOURCES OF PROBLEMS**
Construct validity	Manipulating and measuring psychological states researcher claims to be measuring	Faulty measures, resulting in mislabelling or misinterpreting behavior
Internal validity	Determining cause-effect relationship between manipulation and behavior *in* a given study	Allowing factors other than the manipulation to vary (treatment and no-treatment groups differ before study begins)
External validity	Producing results that can be generalized *outside* the study to other situations and subjects	Artificial situations, unusual subject population

The novice's failure to take into account the fact that humans are more complex and individualized than molecules seriously threatened the validity of his study. Although those were important differences to overlook, the student also overlooked the two most important differences between molecules and humans: (1) Molecules do not have rights, whereas humans do; and (2) Chemists have no responsibility for the welfare of molecules involved in their studies, but psychologists have a responsibility for the welfare of their subjects. Therefore, in the researcher's mind, the most important question about the study is whether it should have been done. This question is so important that no professional researcher would do a study without first determining whether the study should be conducted as well as considering how ethical concerns could be addressed.

In deciding whether the subjects' rights had been protected and whether the novice investigator had lived up to his responsibilities, the experienced researcher would consult the *Ethical Principles in the Conduct of Research with Human Participants,* published by the American Psychological Association (1990). (These principles are summarized in appendix A.)

The principles state that participants have the right to know what will happen in the study, the right to refuse to be in the study, and the right to anonymity. According to these principles, the novice should have told participants the study would involve sitting in a warm room with a group of people. Knowing what the study was about, participants should have freely volunteered to be in the study. Once in the study, they should have been told they could quit the study at any point and do so without being penalized. Furthermore, the novice should have taken extensive precautions to ensure that no one other than the investigator found out how each subject behaved during the study.

The ethical principles not only discuss subjects' rights, but also discuss investigators' responsibilities (see table 1.4). According to the APA's ethical principles, the investigator is responsible for behaving in an ethical manner and, under some circumstances, may be responsible for ensuring that others also behave ethically. For example, if the novice had others working on the aggression study, those people would be responsible for their own conduct, but the novice would also be responsible for their conduct. In other words, if the people working with or for the investigator behaved unethically, the novice could not avoid responsibility by saying that he personally did not misbehave or that he did not know what the others were doing.

Furthermore, the investigator should try to anticipate all possible risks to subjects and protect subjects from these risks. In this study he should have taken steps to prevent subjects from suffering due to heat (heart attack, heat stroke) or aggression (hurt nose, hurt feelings, hurt relationships).

Yet taking preventative measures is not enough. The investigator should also try to find out if anyone has been harmed. The investigator cannot merely assume that no one has been harmed. Instead, he should have actively looked for evidence of harm. He should have probed subjects to find out if anything unpleasant had happened to them. Of course, if he detected harm, he should have tried to undo that harm.

Table 1.4   Selected Ethical Principles

1. Subjects should volunteer to be in the study.
2. Subjects should have a general idea of what will happen to them if they choose to be in the study. In addition, they should be well informed about anything that they might perceive as unpleasant. That is, they should know about anything that might cause them to decide not to participate.
3. Subjects should know that they can quit the study at any point.
4. Subjects have the right to anonymity.
5. Investigators should keep subjects' responses confidential.
6. Investigators should make sure all subordinates behave ethically.
7. Investigators should try to anticipate all possible risks to subjects and take steps to prevent these potential problems from occurring.
8. Investigators should probe subjects for signs of harm and take steps to undo any harm detected.
9. Investigators should explain the purpose of the study and answer any questions subjects may have.

Finally, after subjects finished participating, the investigator should explain the study to them. Educating subjects about the study is the least an investigator can do to compensate subjects for their participation. Furthermore, telling subjects about the study may help subjects by assuring them that their reactions are not unusual. For example, subjects might think they were anti-social or highly aggressive unless they were told the study was designed to make them act and feel that way.

Unfortunately, the professional researcher cannot determine the novice's study was ethical simply by observing that the investigator followed a few simple rules. Instead, as the first sentence of the *Principles* states, "The decision to undertake research rests upon a considered judgment by the individual psychologist about how to **best contribute to psychological science and human welfare**" (italicizing added).

The first sentence of the *Principles* has two important implications. First, it implies that even if none of the principles were compromised, the study would still be unethical if the study were unlikely to contribute to psychological science and human welfare. Second, it implies that the investigator could compromise some of these principles and still be ethical if the expected benefits of the study would compensate for those compromises. Consequently, an important step in determining whether the study was ethical is determining the likelihood that the study would lead to human betterment.

The experienced researcher would determine whether the study might lead to human betterment by evaluating the importance of the research question and by determining how well the study could answer that question by evaluating the proposed study's internal, external, and construct validity. Unfortunately, determining the value of the research question is highly subjective. One person may find the idea very interesting, another may find it extremely dull. In the aggression study, the novice may believe that determining the relationship between temperature and aggression is extremely valuable and might lead to ways of preventing riots. Others, however, may disagree. A novice investigator should always consult and defer to a higher authority's opinion. *Never conduct a study without approval from your professor!*

To further complicate the problem of assessing the potential value of a piece of research, no one knows what the investigator will discover. A study that looks promising may discover nothing. On the other hand, many scientific studies designed to answer one question have ended up answering a very important but unrelated question (Burke, 1985; Coile & Miller, 1984). Because it is so hard to judge the value of a research question, the experienced researcher would probably acknowledge that the novice's research question has some merit.

The only way the experienced researcher would consider the research question totally worthless was if he discovered that the research question had already been answered. For example, suppose there was an abundance of research on aggression and temperature, including several studies identical to our novice's study. Suppose further that the novice would not have done his study if he had known about this published research. In other words, the only reason the novice performed the study was because he failed to do a proper literature review. Under these circumstances, the experienced researcher would consider the novice's study unethical. No investigator has the right to put subjects at any risk, no matter how small, if the study has no chance of contributing to human betterment.

As you can see, outside of showing that previous research has already answered the question, judging the quality of a research question is difficult. Therefore, to estimate the potential value of the novice's study, the professional research psychologist would put less emphasis on his subjective impression of the importance of the research question and put more emphasis on the more objective judgment of how well the study would answer the research question. That is, he would ask whether the study would provide valid data. Of course, he would not consider the study worthless if it failed to have high levels of all forms of validity (see table 1.5). Few studies even attempt to have all three validities. However, in this particular study, he would demand a reasonable level of internal validity.

After carefully considering the potential value of the novice's study, the professional research psychologist would again consider the potential risks to subjects. If the benefits outweighed the risks (the ends justified the means), he would believe that conducting the study was ethical.

To reiterate, the psychological researcher's most important concerns about the aggression study are ethical concerns. Indeed, since ethical concerns include concerns about validity and since the goal of research is human betterment, one could argue that ethical concerns are the competent researcher's only concerns.

But what if the study had used animals instead of human subjects? In that case, some might think the psychologist would not have been concerned about ethics. Nothing could be further from the truth. Psychologists have always been concerned about the ethics of animal research, and, in recent years, animal rights have received more attention from the APA than human rights. If the aggression study had used animals as subjects, the experienced researcher would have consulted APA's *Ethical Principles for the Care and Use of Animals* (1989), summarized in appendix A.

Table 1.5   Valid Conclusions Can be Made Without Having All Forms of Validity

CONSTRUCT VALIDITY	INTERNAL VALIDITY	EXTERNAL VALIDITY	CONCLUSIONS
Yes	Yes	Yes	Increasing temperature caused increased aggression and this finding would generalize to other settings and subjects.
Yes	Yes	No	Increasing temperature caused increased aggression. However, this finding probably does *not generalize* to many other situations or subjects.
Yes	No	Not applicable	The warm-room group was more aggressive, but the investigator failed to establish that the groups were equally aggressive before the study started. Therefore, we cannot say that temperature *caused* aggressiveness.
No	Yes	Yes	Putting subjects in the warm room caused them to behave differently than putting subjects in the normal room. However, we cannot say the warm room caused *aggressiveness,* possibly because we have a *poor measure* of aggression.

ISSUES RESEARCHERS FACE: CONCLUSIONS

Professional research psychologists must be aware of the responsibilities and challenges of studying human and animal behavior. In other chapters we will discuss the wide range of methods psychologists use to meet these challenges and responsibilities. Investigators may use a single subject or thousands of subjects, human subjects or animal subjects, laboratory studies or field studies, experiments or surveys, depending on ethical considerations, the type of validity the researcher is after, and the research problem.

WHY SHOULD YOU KNOW ABOUT RESEARCH?

Thus far, we have explained why professional psychologists are interested in scientific research. Psychologists see research as a useful tool to obtain answers to their questions. But why should you know about this tool?

TO UNDERSTAND PSYCHOLOGY

The classic answer is that you cannot really understand psychology, the *science* of behavior, unless you understand its methods. Without understanding psychology's scientific aspects, you may know some psychological facts and theories, but you will not understand the basis for those facts and theories. Thus, to major in psychology without knowing about research would be like buying a car without looking at the engine or a house without inspecting the foundation. Furthermore, as a young science, psychology does not have as much technology as some other sciences have. Consequently, in some complex, applied situations, the most useful thing psychology can offer is not a pre-packaged answer to the problem based on established facts, but rather its method of getting answers to problems (Levy-Leboyer, 1988).

TO CONVINCE OTHERS THAT PSYCHOLOGY IS A LEGITIMATE SCIENTIFIC FIELD

Although you are keenly aware of the fact that psychology is a science, not everyone accepts this fact. Many psychology majors report that their peers majoring in physical sciences look down on them as being less than "real scientists." Even non-science majors express doubts about psychology's scientific merit and are consequently less likely to trust its findings.

To illustrate the value of being able to convince people that a field is indeed a science, contrast the credibility of physics with that of psychology. Because physics is considered "real science," people will accept any statement a physics major makes about the physical world. The physicist has little fear of being contradicted, even when making statements that run counter to everyone's perceptions, such as: the earth, rather than standing still, is spinning at thousands of miles per hour; heavy objects fall at the same rate as light-weight objects; a solid steel wall has billions of holes in it; or the sun does not set, it stays still while the earth revolves. Psychologists, on the other hand, know that virtually any statement they make will be contested if it does not perfectly coincide with people's perceptions (Stanovich, 1990). Specifically, people's reactions to counterintuitive findings often follow this pattern: "Who says? . . . Psychology? That's not a science, that's their opinion. I don't agree with that at all. They're wrong." From people's reactions, one might suppose psychologists get together at conventions to decide what fable about human behavior they are going to fabricate this year.

If you are going to defend the validity of the psychological statements you make, you need to be able to explain to people why psychology is a science. Otherwise, your credibility, as well as that of your field, will suffer.

SO YOU CAN READ RESEARCH

Not only will knowing about research help you to motivate others to take advantage of psychological knowledge, but it also will help you become more able to take advantage of such knowledge. Specifically, knowing about research will allow you to tap the most recent psychological discoveries about whatever problem interests you. For instance, you may want to know something about the latest treatment for depression, the causes of shyness, factors that lead to better relationships, or new tips for improving work-place morale. If you need the most up-to-date information, if you want to draw your own conclusions, or if you want to look at everything that is known about a particular problem, you need to read research. You cannot rely on reading *about* research in textbooks, magazines, or newspapers. Textbooks will only give you sketchy summaries of the few out-of-date studies selected by the textbooks' authors. Magazine and newspaper articles, on the other hand, may talk about up-to-date research, but these reports may not correctly represent what really happened. A knowledge of research terminology and logic will allow you to bypass second-hand accounts of research. Instead, you will be able to read original research for yourself and come to your own conclusions.

SO YOU CAN EVALUATE RESEARCH

If you understand research, you will not only be able to get recent, first-hand information, but you will also be in a position to critically evaluate that information. You may also be able to critically evaluate many second-hand reports of research in magazines and newspapers.[1] Thus, you will be able to take full advantage of the knowledge that psychologists are giving away, knowledge that is available to you for free in libraries, in newspapers, and on television. Your critical abilities will also enable you to judge how much weight you should place on a particular research finding—a very useful skill, especially when you encounter two conflicting research findings.

TO PROTECT YOURSELF FROM QUACKS

Perhaps more important than encountering conflicting research findings is the problem of identifying quacks. The lack of restrictions on free speech protects quacks, just as the lack of the Food and Drug Administration protected "snake oil" salespeople in the old days. Back then, patent medicine vendors could sell the public anything, even pills that contained tapeworm segments. Today, "experts" are free to go on talk shows and push "psychological tapeworms." Common "psychological tapeworms" include unproven and sometimes dangerous tips on how to lose weight, quit smoking, discipline children, and solve relationship problems. Unfortunately, without some training in research, it is hard to distinguish which free information is useful and which is worthless or even dangerous.

TO BE A BETTER THINKER

Not only can understanding the scientific approach improve your access to psychological knowledge, but it can also improve your thinking. As you will discover, science is an

---

[1]Assuming, of course, that the articles provide you with enough information about the study's methodology, If they do not, you will have to go to the original scientific publication.

elaboration of everyday thinking. The skills you learn in this course—problem-solving skills, decision-making skills, how to look for objective information, and being able to judge and interpret information—are transferable to real life. Consequently, the same scientific thinking skills you will learn in this book are also taught in books that purport to raise your practical intelligence (e.g., Lewis & Greene, 1982). Furthermore, those same skills are measured by some tests of "practical intelligence" (Frederikson, 1986) and are necessary for understanding certain real life situations (Lehman, Lempert, & Nisbett, 1988). Finally, Lehman, Lempert, and Nisbett's (1988) research suggests that learning about research methodology in psychology transfers to understanding real life applications of methodological principles better than does learning about other sciences, such as chemistry or medicine (see figure 1.5).

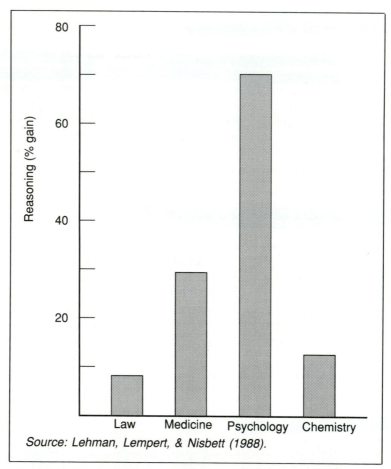

Source: Lehman, Lempert, & Nisbett (1988).

FIGURE 1.5: Changes in Reasoning Ability Scores as a Function of Program of Study

Another reason students take a psychological research methods course is that it is a relatively easy way to learn about how science works. Intelligent people are supposed to be able to profit from experience, and in today's world, many of our experiences are shaped by scientific and technological changes. Unfortunately, despite the scientific progress we have made and despite the fact that the results of science surround us, many people do not know how science works.

Many argue that this scientific illiteracy threatens our democracy—and they have a point. How can we make intelligent decisions about the so-called "greenhouse effect," if we cannot properly interpret the data about global warming? We would like to rely on experts, but "experts" contradict each other on many important issues. Therefore, if we are going to make an informed decision about global warming, acid rain, whether drugs are the cause or a symptom of societal problems, the extent of the drug problem, the extent and nature of the homelessness problem, the extent of the AIDS problem, the effectiveness of a highly expensive heart operation, the effects of pornography, the inhibiting effects of capital punishment, the effects of sex education classes, or the psychological effects of a woman having an abortion, we need to know how to interpret scientific research.

Regrettably, it appears that many people are not scientifically literate. Most high school students (and some high-ranking politicians) believe in astrology. Furthermore, many astrology skeptics can easily be convinced to believe in it (Glick et al., 1989). In addition to astrology, other scientifically invalid procedures such as handwriting analysis, foot reflexology, and scientology also enjoy surprising popularity.

Against this backdrop, there is an amazing emphasis of hype over objective facts. Politicians, for example, often say, "We don't need to do research on the problem, we know what we need to do" or "I don't care what the research says, I feel . . ." Similarly, contrary to the scientific belief in research and openness, products that include "secret ingredients" or "mysterious secrets of Europe" are more appealing to many consumers than ones that were carefully tested in the open and proved to be effective.

With flagrant disregard for internal validity, people often make careless cause-effect statements. Leaders take credit for random or cyclical changes in the economy. Advertisers try to convince us that models are attractive because they use their products. Even people who are not trying to sell us products use very weak evidence. For example, *Sports Illustrated*, hyping the problem of youngsters wanting high-priced tennis shoes, presented the following evidence "proving" that teens are being killed for shoes: a young man was found dead, and his money, cocaine, and shoes had been stolen. Couldn't it be that he was killed for the money, the drugs, or some other reason? Does it have to be the shoes alone?

With blatant disregard for internal, external, and construct validity, talk show hosts periodically parade a few people who claim "success" as a result of some dieting or parenting technique. Similarly, advertisers still successfully hawk products using testimonials from a few satisfied users and political leaders "prove" what our country needs by telling us stories about one or two individuals rather than boring us with facts.

Unfortunately, research shows that, to the naive, these nonscientific and often misleading techniques are extremely persuasive (Nisbett & Ross, 1980).

TO INCREASE YOUR MARKETABILITY

Besides making you a better citizen and consumer, knowing about research makes you a more employable individual. In today's information age, you probably will **not** be hired for what technical information you know because such information is quickly obsolete and will soon be available at the punch of a keystroke from a computer database. Instead, you probably will be hired for your ability to evaluate and create information. That is, as you will see in appendix D, you will be hired for your analytical abilities rather than your knowledge of facts. For example, even marketing majors are told that, at least for their first few years, their scientific skills, not their marketing intuition, is what will pave the way to future career success (Edwards, 1990). These same analytical skills will, of course, also be helpful if you plan to go to graduate school in business, law, medicine, or psychology.

SO YOU CAN DO YOUR OWN RESEARCH

To get into graduate school or enhance your marketability, you may do your own research. Or, you may do research as part of your job or graduate school experience. It seems that everyone is doing research these days. Movie moguls do research to decide whether the music, length, ending, and so forth are effective. As a result of such research, the ending for the movie *Fatal Attraction* was re-shot (at a cost of $1.3 million). Some of our former students have been surprised that they ended up doing research to get government grants or get more staff for their social service agencies.

Beyond the employment angle, you may find that doing research is its own reward. Some students like research because it allows them to "do psychology" rather than read about it. Others enjoy the teamwork aspect of working with professors or other students. Still others enjoy the excitement of trying to get answers to questions about human behavior. Once you start an investigation into one of the many uncharted areas of the human psyche, we think you will understand what Carl Rogers (1985) meant when he said, "We need to sharpen our vision of what is possible . . . to that most fascinating of all enterprises: the unearthing, the discovery, the pursuit of significant new knowledge" (p. 1).

CONCLUDING REMARKS

In conclusion, no matter what you do in the future, a knowledge of scientific research will be useful (see table 1.6). The skills you learn will allow you to attack problems systematically, criticize data, and become a scientifically literate citizen or consumer—almost necessities in our science-dominated world.

Furthermore, you will need to read and evaluate the merit of specific psychological

Table 1.6 Nine Reasons to Understand Psychological Research Methods

1. To better understand psychology
2. To convince others that psychology is a legitimate scientific field
3. To keep up with recent discoveries by reading research
4. To evaluate research claims
5. To protect yourself from quacks and frauds
6. To be a better thinker
7. To be scientifically literate and thus a better educated citizen and consumer
8. To improve your marketability
9. To do your own research

research findings. If you become a counseling psychologist, you will want to use the best, most up-to-date treatments with your clients. Partly for this reason, licensing exams for counseling psychologists include questions testing knowledge of research methods. If you become a manager, you will want to know the most effective management techniques. If you become a parent, you will want to evaluate the relative effectiveness of different child-rearing strategies. To get accurate answers in any of these areas, you will need to understand research. Unless you understand the research process, you will be limited by insufficient, out-of-date, or inaccurate information.

The reason *you* need to know about psychological research is, unlike other fields, psychological knowledge is not useful if only the experts have it. If only a few experts know how to design computer chips or drugs that stop illnesses, we can all benefit. The experts can apply the knowledge for us and businesses can make a profit mass-producing and marketing the technology. We do not have to understand or apply the technology, all we need to do is buy it. Furthermore, our ignorance should not hurt us because the government will usually protect us from defective products, such as computers that do not work or drugs that harm rather than help. Psychological technology, on the other hand, is not available in stores. If we are to benefit from psychological research, we usually have to find the research and apply the technology ourselves. Consequently, even seventeen years after psychologists have discovered proven ways of reducing prejudice and easing racial tensions, people are unaware of and fail to use these techniques (Aronson, 1990). Because advice is protected by laws that govern free speech, the government cannot protect you from bad advice. You are the only one who can protect yourself.

Of course, if you plan to pursue a career in psychology, the need to keep up with psychological research is even more important. Psychological knowledge is growing at such a rapid rate that much of what you know now will be obsolete in ten years (it's even worse in engineering where knowledge becomes obsolete in less than five years). Thus, a person graduating at age twenty-three could be hopelessly out-of-date by age thirty-three.

Last, but not least, knowing about research will give you the tools you need to find answers to your questions. By reading this book, you will learn how to generate research ideas, manipulate and measure variables, collect objective data, ensure validity, choose the right design for your particular research question, treat subjects ethically, interpret your results, and communicate your findings. We hope you will use this knowledge to join the most fascinating quest of our time—exploring the human mind.

SUMMARY

1. Science seeks objective evidence and simple, general rules. Science is also skeptical, verifiable, creative, open-minded, explicit, public, and productive.
2. Psychology is a science.
3. Scientific research is a logical, proven, and ethical way of obtaining important information about human behavior.
4. Researchers want to conduct ethical research. Part of being ethical is ensuring that the research has some degree of validity.
5. If a study has internal validity, it establishes that a particular, observable, physical stimulus or manipulation *causes* a certain, observable response.
6. A study's external validity is the degree to which its findings can be generalized to other people, places, and times. Often, people question whether a result can be generalized to real world situations.
7. When investigators are studying the psychological states they claim to be studying, their reseach has construct validity.
8. Threats to construct validity include
   a. poor measures of variables—for example, if researchers measure "sense of humor" by how funny subjects rate sexist cartoons, they may be measuring sexism rather than sense of humor;
   b. treatments that do not succeed in doing what they claim to do—for example, if researchers tried to make subjects happy by having a mime play tricks on people, the "happiness" manipulation might really be an "irritation" manipulation; and
   c. subjects figuring out how the researchers want them to behave and then acting that way.
9. Subjects in research studies have many rights, including the right to decide whether they want to be in the study, the right to privacy, and the right to learn what the study's purpose is.
10. No study should be done without doing a literature search first, and no student should conduct a study without the approval of a professor.
11. Skills learned in research design are transferable to real life.

KEY TERMS

construct validity   external validity
internal validity

1. Abraham Maslow and other humanistic psychologists have argued that psychologists have studied rats and neurotic individuals, but have not studied extremely well-adjusted people. This is a criticism about the _____ validity of research.

2. The professor of a Psychology of Women class notes that a study used only male subjects. The professor is probably attacking the _____ validity of that research.

3. The professor of a Psychology of Women class notes that a study claiming women were more conforming than men could be interpreted as showing that women are more cooperative than men. The professor is probably attacking the _____ validity of that research.

4. A survey finds that diet Coke–drinkers are less irritable than diet Pepsi–drinkers. The investigator concludes that consuming diet Pepsi causes enhanced irritability. This conclusion lacks _____ validity.

5. Some subjects drink two cans of caffeinated Coke; others drink two cans of decaffeinated Coke. The caffeinated Coke–group reports being more refreshed. The investigator concludes that consuming caffeine causes enhanced alertness. This conclusion lacks _____ validity. What changes would you make in the study?

6. Don and Julie are engaged to be married this summer. However, upon taking a "couple compatibility" test in a popular magazine, they find they are not compatible. Before breaking off their engagement, Don and Julie should determine the _____ validity of the test.

7. An investigator wants to determine if being put in a happy mood makes people more likely to help others. To put people in a good mood, the investigator allows them to "find" twenty dollars. However, rather than feeling happy, subjects feel guilty. This study lacks _____ validity.

8. A medical school does a study and asks for volunteers for a drug study that involves medical and psychiatric testing. The researchers conclude that the drug calms people down. Given the subjects used in this study, the _____ validity of the research could be questioned.

9. Near the end of the last lecture before the exam, a professor asks the class whether they have any questions. Because there are none, the professor concludes that the students know and understand everything. The professor's measure of "knowing and understanding everything" may lack _____ validity.

10. Identify the type of validity (internal, external, or construct) being questioned in each of the following statements.

CRITICISM	VALIDITY BEING QUESTIONED
Two groups differ, not because of treatment, but by chance.	
Subjects studied are not typical of average people.	
Measure used is not very good.	
Subjects only included gifted ten-year-olds.	
Groups were not the same before treatment was introduced.	
Subjects' reports of their feelings may be inaccurate.	
Only males were used.	
Subjects may have guessed hypothesis and played along.	
Measure does not capture construct.	
Subjects may have changed even without treatment, so researcher should not conclude that treatment caused change.	
Results would not hold in a real life situation.	
Task was boring and meaningless, so subjects were not psychologically involved in the study.	
Manipulation may not have produced intended effect on subjects' psychological states.	
Measure is biased.	

11. Public officials often cite studies linking drugs and crime and then conclude that drugs cause crime. However, if drug use is not the cause of crime, but rather a symptom of some other problem, such as alienation that does cause crime, the studies cited by those officials may lack _____ validity.

12. "A rose by any other name would smell as sweet." Perhaps. But if a scale that measured conservatism were re-labelled "close-mindedness scale," there would be _____ validity problems with studies using this "close-mindedness" scale.

13. *Teen* magazine put a survey form in a recent issue. Of those who reply, 40 percent claim to have used drugs. As a result, the magazine concludes that 40 percent of teens have used drugs. Even assuming the respondents are honest, the study may lack _____ validity.

14. A police officer puts a drunk in a blue room. The prisoner acts in a way that the officer describes as "violent." Then, the officer moves the prisoner to a pink room. This prisoner then acts in a way that the officer describes as "less violent."
    a. A scientist doubts that the pink room changed the prisoner's behavior. Instead, he thinks the change in the prisoner's behavior in the pink room might just be a coincidence. The prisoner may have changed his behavior for reasons that have

nothing to do with the pink room at all (the prisoner has calmed down by the time he enters the pink room). Since the scientist is doubting that the pink room caused the effect, he is questioning the study's _____ validity.

b. A second scientist believes that even if the pink room changed this prisoner's behavior—that is, the study had _____ validity—there would be serious doubts as to whether the pink room would change the behavior of sober prisoners. The second scientist is questioning the degree to which the results would generalize. Thus, this scientist is questioning the study's _____ validity.

c. A third scientist agrees that the prisoner's behavior changed, but does not agree that the behavior became "less violent." Instead, the scientist thought the prisoner was simply less active in the pink room. Since the scientist is disputing the way the behavior was labelled, the scientist is attacking the study's _____ _____ validity. Specifically, the scientist is attacking the _____ validity of the study's measure of aggression.

15. Can you have external and construct validity without internal validity? (Hint: Think about surveys.)

16. If biologists and chemists do research that has external validity in extremely artificial settings, can psychologists do the same? Why or why not? (Hints: Could interesting stimulus materials help? Do people react in a "psychologically real" way in such artificial settings as video-game rooms and movie theaters? Are there basic processes that are relatively unaffected by the psychological reality of the setting?)

17. Why don't chemists do more research in natural settings like bakeries and biologists do more research in the woods? What implications does this have for psychological research?

18. Is it ethical to treat a patient with a method that has not been scientifically tested? Why or why not?

19. What APA ethical principles are violated by television shows such as "Candid Camera," "Totally Hidden Video," and "America's Funniest Home Videos?"

20. Do you think individual researchers are capable of making responsible judgments about whether their research is ethical? Or, should committees make these decisions? If so, who should serve on these committees?

21. The APA ethical principles are general guidelines that give recommendations as to what researchers should do. Do you support the idea of general guidelines or do you think there should be hard and fast rules that all researchers must obey? If you support the idea of establishing some absolute laws about what researchers should and should not do, what would your laws be? If you do not think absolute rules should be enacted, why not?

22. Two of the most ethically questionable studies in the history of psychology are Milgram's obedience study (where subjects were told to deliver dangerous shocks to an accomplice of the experimenter) and Zimbardo's prison study (where well-

adjusted students pretended to be either prisoners or guards). In both of these studies, there would have been no ethical problems if subjects had behaved the way common sense told us they would. No one would have obeyed the order to shock subjects and none of the "guards" would have mistreated the prisoners.

  a. Argue that the inability to know how subjects will react to a research project means that research should not be done.
  b. Then, argue the opposite side of the coin: Because we cannot yet predict human behavior, certain kinds of research should be performed so we can find out the answers to these important questions.

23. From the brief description in exercise 22, what ethical principles, if any, were violated in Milgram's shock experiment?

24. From the brief description in exercise 22, what ethical principles, if any, were violated in Zimbardo's prison study?

2

Generating the Research Hypothesis: Tapping Intuition, Theory, and Existing Research

"Questions show the mind's range, and answers its subtlety."

—Joseph Joubert

"If you do not ask specific questions, I cannot be responsible for your misinterpretation of the answer."

—Solitaire
"Live and Let Die"

OVERVIEW

Scientists do research to get answers to questions. Therefore, to do research, we should start with a question worth answering and we *must* start with an answerable question. This question is usually stated as a ***hypothesis***: an idea or prediction capable of being disproven.

In this chapter, you will learn how to extract fascinating research ideas from three sources: intuition, theory, and existing research. Then, you will learn how to convert these interesting ideas into testable hypotheses. By the end of this chapter you should be well on your way to being able to conduct creative, exciting, and fruitful research.

USING INTUITION TO GENERATE RESEARCH IDEAS

Intuition is a time-tested way of generating research ideas. If it were not for intuition, physics might be without Einstein's theory of relativity, chemistry without an understanding of the carbon molecule, medicine without penicillin, and psychology without the principles of classical conditioning.

WHAT IS INTUITION?

Although science has certainly benefitted from the intuitions of such geniuses as Einstein, Curie, Kekule, and Pavlov, intuition is not a magical quality that only a gifted few possess. All members of a society share the same intuition in the form of common sense. Common sense, like an informal theory, gives us general rules from which we can deduce specific hypotheses. These hypotheses help us understand the world and predict what will happen next. For instance, suppose we know that Jim and Joan are two very different people. What would happen if we put them together? Common sense tells us that opposites attract. On that basis, we would predict that Jim and Joan will be attracted to each other. Our conclusion is an example of **deduction**: applying a general rule to a specific situation. (A problem with common sense, however, is that it also tells us that "likes attract likes." Therefore, we could also deduce that Jim and Joan will not like each other.)

In addition to common sense rules, we create our own unique "uncommon sense" rules by finding patterns in our personal experiences. These uncommon sense rules are often formed by **induction**: creating a general rule by seeing similarities among several specific situations. For example, after seeing people fight repeatedly in bars, you may induce that alcohol leads to aggression.

GENERAL APPROACHES TO USING YOUR INTUITION

You will find that your intuition is a valuable source of potential research ideas—*if you concentrate exclusively on generating ideas about real-life behavior.* When you begin thinking of ideas, do not worry about whether your idea is a testable idea. Just generate as many ideas as you can. Once you have completed this first step, you can move on to the second step—deciding which ideas are testable.

Unfortunately, rather than generating ideas about real-life behavior (step 1) and then narrowing down these ideas (step 2), a common tendency is to combine these steps into a single step—thinking about what can be done in a lab. Although this shortcut is tempting, using it will prevent you from fully capitalizing on your intuition. If you constantly remind yourself of the following five facts, you will be able to resist that temptation (see table 2.1).

First, you are probably more interested in real-life behavior than "what could be done in the lab." Therefore, you are more likely to think longer about real-life behavior than laboratory behavior. Since creative ideas are largely the result of persevering (Pronko, 1969), you will be more likely to have creative ideas about real-life behavior than laboratory behavior.

Second, trying to come up with an idea about behavior is less restrictive than coming up with an idea that can be tested in a laboratory. Research suggests that the more broadly defined the problem is, the more creative the solutions will be (Adams, 1974). Thinking of ideas that can be tested in a laboratory is extremely restrictive, especially because research does not have to be done in a lab.

Third, while you do not have a lifetime of experience in a lab, you do have a lifetime of experience in real life. As Wolfgang Kohler showed back in 1917, you are

---

TABLE 2.1   Five Reasons to Generate Ideas about Real-world Behavior Rather than Asking Yourself "What Can I Test in a Lab?"

1. You will persevere longer in developing ideas about real-life situations.
2. You are not prematurely restricting what you can think about.
3. Because you have more experience in thinking about real-life behavior, you are better at it.
4. You will be more likely to follow an important rule of creative thinking: Producing ideas should be kept separate from criticizing them.
5. Not all research is done in the laboratory.

---

much more likely to be creative in an area in which you have a background than one in which you do not.

Fourth, not all research is done in the lab. Although most psychological research is done in the lab, important research is also done in non-lab settings.

Fifth, if you try to generate an idea that can be tested in a laboratory, you will tend to do two things simultaneously: generate the idea and evaluate how testable it is. Many psychologists believe that the key to creativity is to keep production of ideas and criticism of ideas separate. Indeed, the number one rule in brainstorming is that no ideas are criticized until the idea-generation stage is completed (see figure 2.1).

Because of these five principles, many students prefer the two-step ([1] generate ideas, then [2] narrow down) model over trying to directly generate an idea that can be tested. They find by using the two-step approach they have a relatively easy time coming up with ideas, and they end up with hypotheses that really interest them.

Although most students have an easy time coming up with ideas, they often have trouble generating their first idea. We suspect they have trouble getting started because they are afraid of having a bad idea. Excessive self-criticism is a common barrier to creative thinking (Adams, 1974). Remember the first idea does not have to lead to the Nobel Prize. Also realize that your idea does not have to be absolutely original. Indeed, the strength of science is that scientists build on one another's ideas.

Finally, do not automatically reject your idea because you feel it is "too simple." Simple ideas are not necessarily bad. One goal of science is to come up with simple principles to explain phenomena. After all, the principles of gravity, reinforcement, and modeling are as powerful as they are simple. Even if an idea turns out to be "too simple," the idea may prove a good "jumping off point" for a better idea. That is, by combining it with another simple idea or considering an additional factor, you may end up with an extremely promising idea.

In short, in the early stages of generating ideas, you should emphasize quantity over quality. Once you have a large pool of ideas, you and your professor can start judging the ideas to determine which can be developed into hypotheses.

TWELVE WAYS TO TAP YOUR INTUITION

To help you get the first idea and to get in the habit of generating ideas without judging them (see table 2.2), we have developed twelve techniques to help you get the first idea. We think you will find these "ice-breakers" both fun and useful.

Think of Some "Old Sayings"

Although "old sayings" are stated as fact, they are often assumptions that can be tested. For example, Stanley Schachter (1959) tested the saying "misery loves company." Wohlford (1970) tested the saying "like father, like son" in terms of smoking. Bob Zajonc (1968) found the saying "familiarity breeds contempt" to be false in many situations. Ellen Bersheid and her colleagues (1971) found that "birds of a feather" did flock together. Don Byrne (1971) found that opposites don't attract. Latane, Williams, and Harkins (1979) found evidence for the idea that "too many cooks spoil the broth."

FIGURE 2.1 Some Students Shoot Down Ideas Before They Have a Chance to Develop

TABLE 2.2 Questions that Should Not Be Asked When Trying to Generate Research Ideas

1. Is my idea perfect?
2. Is my idea completely original?
3. Is my idea too simple?

If a saying you were planning to test was previously mentioned, do not automatically abandon plans to test that saying. Sayings are usually broad enough that all aspects of the saying cannot be completely tested in a single study. For example, researchers still do not have definitive answers on the extent to which many of a son's behaviors (other than smoking) are modeled after his father's. Similarly, even though in 1971 Byrne found evidence that opposites (in terms of attitudes) do not attract, it was not until seven years later that researchers found that opposites—in the form of "psychologically masculine" males and "psychologically feminine" females—do not attract in short-term blind dates (Ickes & Barnes, 1978). And it was twelve years later that researchers discovered that "psychologically masculine"males and "psychologically feminine" females do not attract in long-term marriage relationships (Antill, 1983). However, if you want to test completely untested sayings, there are many to choose from. Perhaps you could test hypotheses generated from common sense such as "the more, the merrier," "brevity is the soul of wit," or some other saying you find in a fortune cookie, in a package of Salada tea (Dillon, 1990), in a book of quotations, on a bumper sticker, or on a T-shirt.

Rather than trying to prove or disprove old sayings, you might try to refine them. For example, you might ask yourself: "Under what circumstances is the saying accurate?" Or, you might try to reconcile the inconsistencies of common sense. For example, when does "like attract like" and when do "opposites attract?" Under what circumstances are "two heads better than one" and under what circumstances is it better to do it yourself? One undergraduate student and her adviser used this technique to get an article published in one of the most prestigious journals in psychology. Specifically, they did a survey to find out under what situations women said "no" when they meant "yes" (Muehlenhard & Hollabaugh, 1988). (More examples of "intuitive" research can be found in table 2.3.)

Analyze Songs

Interestingly, Muehlenhard and Hollabaugh could have found their idea in Dan Fogelberg's song "You Say No When You Mean Yes." A few psychologists readily admit they are willing to take advantage of the many research ideas suggested by songs. For instance, Pennebaker et al. (1979) investigated the hypothesis proposed by the country song "The Girls Get Prettier at Closing Time" (he discovered that women appeared more attractive to men as closing time approached). Perhaps you can convert some of your favorite songs into research ideas. Some songs only offer questions (e.g., "Why Do Fools Fall In Love?") whereas others make predictions. For instance, a prediction and a question come from Miami Sound Machine's "Nothin' New" lyrics "How come love is never new for long?" So, listen to music if you want an easy way to get research ideas.

Read

Books by psychological theorists and thinkers, such as William James' *The Principles of Psychology* (1890), are full of stimulating ideas about why we act the way we do. But you do not have to limit yourself to books written by psychologists. Most classic literature provides or stimulates explanations for why people act in certain ways. For example,

TABLE 2.3 Examples of "Intuitive" Research

Anderson, C. A. (1987). Temperature and aggression: Effects on quarterly, yearly, and city rates of violent and nonviolent crime. *Journal of Personality and Social Psychology, 52,* 1161–1173.

Archer, D., Iritani, B., Kimes, D. D., & Barrios, M. (1983). Face-ism: Five studies of sex differences in facial prominence. *Journal of Personality and Social Psychology, 45,* 725–735.

Baron, R. A. (1987). Effects of negative ions on interpersonal attraction: Evidence for intensification. *Journal of Personality and Social Psychology, 52,* 547–553.

Carli, L. L. (1989). Gender differences in interaction style and influence. *Journal of Personality and Social Psychology, 56,* 565–576.

Coleman, M., & Ganong, L. H. (1985). Love and sex role stereotypes: Do macho men and feminine women make better lovers? *Journal of Personality and Social Psychology, 49,* 170–176.

DePaulo, B. M., Dull, W. R., Greenberg, J. M., & Swaim, G. W. (1989). Are shy people reluctant to ask for help? *Journal of Personality and Social Psychology, 56,* 834–844.

Gonzalez, M. H., Pederson, J. H., Manning, D. J., & Wetter, D. W. (1990). Pardon my gaffe: Effects of sex, status, and consequence severity on accounts. *Journal of Personality and Social Psychology, 58,* 610–621.

Isen, A. M., Daubman, K. A., & Nowicki, G. P. (1987). Positive affect facilitates creative problem solving. *Journal of Personality and Social Psychology, 52,* 1122–1131.

Krosnick, J. A., & Alwin, D. F. (1989). Aging and susceptibility to attitude change. *Journal of Personality and Social Psychology, 57,* 416–425.

Levenson, M. R. (1990). Risk taking and personality. *Journal of Personality and Social Psychology, 58,* 1073–1080.

Mori, D., Chaiken, S., & Pliner, P. (1987). "Eating lightly" and the self-presentation of femininity. *Journal of Personality and Social Psychology, 52,* 693–702.

Myerscough R., & Taylor, S. (1985). The effects of marijuana on human physical aggression. *Journal of Personality and Social Psychology, 49,* 1541–1546.

Nevo, O. (1985). Does one ever really laugh at one's own expense? The case of Jews and Arabs in Israel. *Journal of Personality and Social Psychology, 49,* 799–807.

Padilla, E. R., & O'Grady, K. E. (1987). Sexuality among Mexican Americans: A case of sexual stereotyping. *Journal of Personality and Social Psychology, 52,* 5–10.

Pliner, P., Chaiken, S., & Flett, G. L. (1990). Gender differences in concern with body weight and physical appearance over the life span. *Personality and Social Psychology Bulletin, 16,* 263–273.

Siegel, J. M. (1990). Stressful life events and use of physician services among the elderly: The moderating role of pet ownership. *Journal of Personality and Social Psychology, 58,* 1981–1081.

Smith, R. E., Smoll, F. L., & Ptacek, J. T. (1990). Conjunctive moderator variables in vulnerability and resiliency research: Life stress, social support, and coping skills, and adolescent sport injuries. *Journal of Personality and Social Psychology, 58,* 360–370.

Snodgrass, S. E. (1985). Women's intuition: The effect of subordinate role on interpersonal sensitivity. *Journal of Personality and Social Psychology, 49,* 146–155.

Thorne, A. (1987). The press of personality: A study of conversations between introverts and extraverts. *Journal of Personality and Social Psychology, 53,* 718–726.

Wegner, D. M., Schneider, D. J., Carter, S. R., & White, T. L. (1987). Paradoxical effects of thought suppression. *Journal of Personality and Social Psychology, 53,* 5–13.

Wyer, R. S., & Budesheim, T. L. (1987). Person memory and judgments: The impact of information that one is told to disregard. *Journal of Personality and Social Psychology, 53,* 14–29.

many of Shakespeare's works suggest unconscious influences on behavior (e.g., Lady Macbeth washing her hands in her sleep in an attempt to remove the king's death from her conscience). Writers of syndicated columns also are good at generating plausible-sounding, if totally unsupported, statements. For example, one columnist wrote that morality was being undercut by lotteries because people begin to believe wealth is not the result of hard work, but of luck. Although it is plausible that learning about a person winning millions in a lottery may reduce your belief in the value of hard work, this idea is untested.

Even the lowest forms of literature can provide research ideas. For instance, some tabloids (such as the *National Enquirer*) present intriguing ideas stated as documented fact. Some of these ideas can be tested and may, occasionally, be correct. For example, in one issue, a tabloid asserted that deliberately smiling would improve your mood. This idea has some support (Laird, 1984; Strack, Martin, & Stepper, 1988). If nothing else, reading a tabloid should stimulate ideas about why people read that stuff!

Argue

Find a person who disagrees with you about everything and then argue with her about the effects of various activities. Many of these arguments can be converted into research projects. For example, suppose your acquaintance feels that jogging increases creativity whereas you do not. Or, suppose you feel that fast-talkers are more persuasive, but your acquaintance vehemently disagrees. If neither of you can use logic to win these arguments, you have an ideal situation for generating research ideas. If you cannot prove your acquaintance wrong, then it is time to get evidence to show that you are right: It's research time. So, seek out those ornery friends and crusty acquaintances, or play the role of devil's advocate. If you cannot find any disagreeable sorts, look at the editorial page of *USA Today*. On that page, two sides of an issue and different points of view expressed by "person in the street" quotes are presented. (See also figure 2.2.)

Look Through a Dictionary

Start at any page in a dictionary and begin looking for a personality trait (e.g., aggressive, creative, persistent). Once you find a trait, convert it into a trait-noun by finding the noun form of it. Thus, aggressive would become aggression, creative would become creativity, persistent would become persistence, and so on. The first trait-noun you find could be what you will try to measure. Then, think about factors that might influence this trait-noun. If you cannot think of anything, go back to the dictionary again. Flip through the pages, looking at a couple of words on each page. Ask yourself if these words could have anything to do with your first trait-noun. If the answer is "yes," you may have a research idea.

An example will give you a clearer picture of how this method works. Suppose you pick up a dictionary, open it near the middle, and start looking for traits. Assume the first trait you find is the word "nervous." Your dictionary dutifully informs you that "nervous" is an adjective and that "nervousness" is the noun form. You now know what you want to measure. Next, you must find a factor that would affect nervousness. On a lark, you start

FIGURE 2.2 Talking to "Different" People will Alert You That Your Commonsense Ideas Aren't Shared by Those Who Have Different Perspectives.

looking for words that start with "ba" that might affect nervousness. Baboon, baccarat (a gambling game), backbiting, the backfiring of a car, bacteria, badge, badmouthing, bagpipes (especially off-key), balloons (popping), bang (as from a gun), barbarity, barometer (do changes in air pressure make people nervous?), barracuda, basil (does the smell of the herb make people less nervous?), bat, battle, bawl, and bazooka, all have some appeal. Using two or more words in combination may provide you with additional ideas. For example, are *ba*chelors more nervous than others, especially around *ba*bbling *ba*bies?

You will probably eliminate some of these variables (e.g., barracuda, battle, and bazooka) because you would not want to expose your subjects to these stimuli. However, you will still have many factors you could study. Some of these variables are easy to manipulate, such as the scent of basil, the presentation of loud noises, and so on. The other variables can also be manipulated, if you use a little imagination. For example, while you may not be able to present an actual baby, you could play a tape of a baby crying.

Ask Five Key Questions

Begin by thinking about any phenomenon that interests you. The phenomenon could be something well established such as keeping a diary, getting a good job, getting ill, wearing a watch, complaining, calling a request line, putting a bumper sticker on a car, forgetting, having nightmares, drinking, watching talk shows, being greedy, being popular, being ignored, etc. Or, the phenomenon could be a relatively recent one, for example, wearing personal stereos, playing video games, leaving messages on answering machines, fearing computers, placing personal ads, calling "900" numbers, etc.

Once you have picked a phenomenon, adapt Rudyard Kipling's wisdom: "I keep six honest serving-men (They taught me all I knew); Their names are what and why and when and how and where and who." Specifically, ask five basic questions: who, what, when, why, and what are the short- and long-term consequences? Thus, if the phenomenon you were interested in was wearing personal stereos, you might ask the following questions:

1. **Who** wears personal stereos (or how do heavy users differ from light users)? To answer this question, you might consider
   a. demographic variables, such as age and gender
   b. personality traits, such as anxiousness, extraversion, openness to experience (daring, nonconforming, broad interests), agreeableness, conscientiousness, impulsiveness, reflective, self-esteem, status conscious, achievement-oriented, relaxed or tense, self-sufficient or dependent, suspicious or trusting, serious or happy-go-lucky, or shrewd or forthright
   c. abilities such as verbal, spatial, musical, or social intelligence and creativity
   d. attitudes wearers may hold
   e. other possessions they may have
   f. other habits or behaviors
2. **What** do they do?
   a. what do they listen to? (music without lyrics, songs that express intense emotions, songs that are not popular with their friends, songs that are repetitive)
   b. what do they attend to when listening? (lyrics, beat, own thoughts)
   c. at what volume?
3. **When?**
   a. how often?
   b. in what situations? (when bored, when exercising, when studying)
4. **Why?** (to relax, wake up, to avoid others)
5. **What** are the **effects?** (are they perceived as less friendly? does it distract them from unwanted thoughts? does it make them less creative? more creative? less reflective? more reflective? On what tasks does it help? hurt?)

To take another example, you might look at recent graduates from your school who got a "good" first job. How did they differ from graduates who had less successful job searches? Were there personality differences? What behaviors did they exhibit that less successful graduates did not? When did they initiate these behaviors? What prompted them to exhibit those behaviors? What were the consequences of getting these good jobs (increased self-esteem; being stressed out; increased liking for their college)?

Watch Television Commercials

Ask yourself what makes a certain commercial effective or ineffective. For example, suppose you think the television commercial for "Scrumptious Candy" is ineffective because it is too serious, whereas you think the ad for "Jerby's Candy" is effective because it is funny. You now have a research idea: Humor increases the effectiveness of a persuasive message.

Be Negative

Rather than being frustrated about what is wrong with the world, try to find out why things are wrong. For example, rather than being upset by how irrational people can be, some psychologists (Kahneman, Slovic, & Tversky, 1982; Nisbett & Ross, 1980) have done research to find out why people make illogical decisions. So, the next time you think things are not the way they are supposed to be (road signs being in the wrong place, traffic being a mess, obnoxious commercials being aired, professors using poor instructional techniques, etc.), realize that you have at least one kind of research question: Why does the behavior occur?

Attack a Practical Problem

Practical problems often are good sources of hypotheses because they are easy to visualize and because different people have different "solutions" to almost any given problem. For example, consider the problem of spouse abusers. Some people think spouse abusers should be arrested. Others believe abusers should be kicked out of the home. Still others feel spouse abusers should be left alone. In Minneapolis, a study was conducted to determine which of these "solutions" was most effective. On the basis of random assignment, police either arrested the abuser or left the abuser alone. Several months later, social workers went back to the home to check on the family. They found that abusers who had been arrested were less likely to engage in further violence against their spouses (Sherman & Berk, 1984).

Of course, just because the hypothesis comes from a practical situation does not mean that research needs to be conducted in the field. For example, laboratory studies on jury decision making, eyewitness testimony, violence, productivity, and human error have been inspired by practical problems.

To illustrate that practical problems may stimulate researchers to do laboratory studies that allow them to model the key aspects of a real-life situation, suppose you were concerned about the effect of television violence on aggression. Specifically, suppose you were concerned about television shows that include scenes in which hundreds of shots are fired without a serious injury occurring. You feel this kind of violence could lead to more viewer aggression than equally violent shows where people got hurt. You do not have to take over a major television network to test this hypothesis. Instead, you could make several tapes—one that had no violence, one that had violence with people getting killed, and one that had the same violence but people were not killed. Next, you could randomly assign subjects to watch one of three films (no violence film, violence-without-consequences film, or violence-with-consequences film) and then measure aggression. You could conduct the entire study without leaving the comfort of the lab.

Think About Statistics Reported by the Popular Press

Each day you are bombarded with statistics that no one bothers to explain (see table 2.4). For example, you might read that 61 percent of people surveyed believe television news is more objective than newspaper news. Or, you may hear that the home-court advantage is very important in basketball. If you can come up with a possible explanation for a given fact, then you may be able to do a research project to test this explanation. If you need provocative statistics in a hurry, pick up *Harper's* magazine and look up "Harper's Index." "Harper's Index" contains facts such as 5 percent of the people making under $15,000 a year say they have achieved the American dream, whereas 6 percent of those earning more than $50,000 say they have; only 4 percent of U.S. citizens claim they would not change anything about their appearance; and 72,504 people have died from AIDS since 1981, whereas 14,000,000 people have died of measles.

Create a New Situation

Rather than trying to answer the question "Why does _____ happen?", you could ask the question "What would happen if . . .?". Just as a chemist can produce new molecules by creating conditions that never happen in real life, you may be able to produce novel effects by exposing people or animals to new, never-before-experienced environments. There are numerous novel experiences you could expose people or animals to—from novel scents to special diets to films of self-actualized models.

Examine Your "Mental Block"

If you are still stuck for an idea, ask yourself what factors are decreasing your creativity. You could then do research to investigate these factors.

TABLE 2.4 Left-handers and Right-handers

In sports	lefties have 20% more accidents
At work	25% more accidents
At home	49% more accidents
Using tools	54% more accidents
Driving an auto	85% more accidents

Reprinted with the permission of Dr. Stanley Coren and World Features Syndicated, based upon data from Coren (1989).

THE ART OF CREATING INTUITIVE HYPOTHESES: A SUMMARY

You can generate research ideas if you are persistent and concentrate on trying to figure out why people or animals act the way they do. To focus on this task, you can use two basic approaches.

First, you can take advantage of existing common sense. You can find common sense ideas by reading literature, listening to songs, or thinking about old sayings, Second, you could stimulate your intuition by thinking about how to solve a practical problem; trying to find out why certain mistakes are made; creating what you would consider the ideal situation for a certain event to occur; explaining the reason for a statistic; questioning assumptions made in books, magazines, and newspapers that you read; asking basic questions about a phenomenon; talking to people whose intuitions differ from yours; reconciling apparent contradictions; glancing through a dictionary; analyzing ads; and even by reflecting on why you are having problems coming up with an idea (see table 2.5).

TABLE 2.5 Twelve Ways to Tap Your Intuition

1. Test or refine an "old saying."
2. Test assumptions or predictions made in songs.
3. Test assumptions about human nature that are stated in classic or popular literature.
4. Transform the opposing views of an argument into a research idea.
5. Look through a dictionary for interesting research variables.
6. Ask five key questions about an interesting phenomenon:
    1. Who does the behavior? How do people who are high and low on the behavior differ?
    2. What precisely is the behavior? For example, what do people complain about?
    3. When is the behavior most likely? At what time of day? What events precede the behavior?
    4. Why do people engage in the behavior?
    5. What are the long- and short-term effects of the behavior?
7. Analyze television commercials.
8. Figure out why bad or irrational actions occur.
9. Attack a practical problem (ecology, illiteracy, prejudice, apathy, alcoholism, violence).
10. Try to explain survey and research findings reported in the media.
    Look at *USA Today, Harper's* magazine, or *Sports Illustrated.*
11. Create a new—and perhaps ideal—situation.
12. Investigate factors that decrease your creativity.

GETTING IDEAS FROM THEORY

Thus far we have concentrated on generating ideas from informal observations and from common sense. Yet, following hunches is not the only, or even the most preferred, method of generating ideas. Many psychologists prefer ideas derived from theory.

WHAT IS A THEORY?

To understand why many psychologists prefer to derive research ideas from theory, you need to understand what a theory is. Unfortunately, theory is hard to define and may be confused with related terms (see table 2.6). It can be defined as a set of assumptions about causes of a phenomenon (Cozby, 1990). However, because theories usually have received some research support, you might prefer the definition "a partially verified statement of a scientific relationship that cannot be directly observed" (Martin, 1985). According to this definition, we can have theories of motivation, learning, and gravity, even though we cannot directly observe any of these concepts. Even this definition, however, can be debated. It does not emphasize the idea that theories, unlike hypotheses, are usually an organized *set* of propositions. Therefore, you might prefer the definition "a system of

---

TABLE 2.6   Hypotheses, Models, Theories, and Laws

Even psychologists do not always properly distinguish between hypotheses, models, theories, and laws. However, there are differences.

Hypothesis:

A specific prediction that can be tested.

Theory:

More complex than a hypothesis because a theory is a ***set of related propositions*** that attempt to specify the relationship between a set of variables and some behavior. Usually, a theory summarizes a body of empirical evidence. Theories may be used to derive hypotheses, explain laws, or build models.

Model:

A model is a theory or set of theories applied to a specific area (job satisfaction) or situation. Often, the goal is to describe the exact mathematical relationships among variables in a certain situation. The cost of this precision is that models are generally narrower in scope than theories and may also tend to be less parsimonious.

Law:

Definition #1: A relationship between variables that has been so strongly supported by many studies that it is almost universally believed to be basically correct. That is, laws can be ***verified hypotheses.*** These laws are often expressed mathematically. Scientists may develop theories to explain why this relationship occurs. For example, scientists have theorized about why Weber's Laws hold in many situations.

Definition #2: A theory that has been substantially verified. Behaviorists may argue that their theories of behavior are really laws that have been verified.

generalizations that specify lawful relationships between specific behaviors and their causes" (McBurney, 1983). However, this definition would seem to do a better job of describing laws than theories.

Although no definition is perfect, we think that, for researchers, the most relevant definition of **theory** is: an integrated set of principles that explains facts and from which a large number of *new* observations can be deduced. This definition highlights two important facts about good theories. First, they use a *few* principles to explain and summarize a large number of facts. Second, they stimulate *new* discoveries. Thus, researchers used "germ theory" to discover the bacteria responsible for certain diseases, "gene theory" to discover DNA, Newton's theory of gravity to discover Neptune, Einstein's theory of relativity to develop nuclear weapons, and social learning theory to discover ways of reducing aggression and shyness. In short, theory, like common sense, is a good source of research ideas. But why do many psychologists prefer theory to common sense?

ADVANTAGES OF USING THEORY TO GENERATE IDEAS

First, theories tend to be more internally consistent than common sense. That is, a theory usually does not contradict itself. Common sense, on the other hand, often contradicts itself ("absence makes the heart grow fonder," "absence makes the heart wander"). Researchers find it easier to make clear, consistent predictions from a consistent theory rather than from inconsistent common sense.

Second, theories tend to be more consistent with existing facts than common sense. Often, theories are constructed by systematically collecting data and carefully analyzing the data for patterns. But even when facts do not play a dominant role in giving birth to a theory, facts will usually shape the theory's development. Generally, if a deduction from a theory is incorrect, the theory should be changed or abandoned. Unlike common sense, theories do not ignore facts. Consequently, a hypothesis based on an established theory is a more educated guess and should have a greater chance of turning out than one based on common sense or superstition.

Third, theories are not restricted to making common sense or intuitively obvious predictions. Theories can make predictions that are counter-intuitive. For example, social learning theory predicts punishment will not be an effective way of changing behavior. In fact, some theories not only make new predictions, but incite controversy by suggesting new ways of viewing the world. For instance, Darwin's theory on evolution had us look at apes as relatives, Einstein's theory of relativity had us look at matter and energy as being the same thing, Freud's theory had us look at ourselves as being motivated by forces we were not aware of, and Watson's theory had us look at ourselves as a set of reflexes.

Fourth, theories summarize and organize a great deal of information. Just as the plot of a movie may connect thousands of otherwise unrelated images, theories connect individual facts and give them meaning. That is, theories try to explain facts. The ability of theories to connect facts means that, unlike some intuitive research, theory-based research will not produce isolated bits of trivia. Instead, the findings will fit into a framework that connects many other studies. In other words, the facts revealed by theory-based research are not merely of interest for their own sake, but also for how they relate to the theory's explanation of how the world works. For example, the fact that around age seven children stop believing in Santa Claus is relatively trivial in its own right. However, when put in the context of Piaget's theory, which states around age seven children are able to think logically about concrete events (and thus realize Santa Claus cannot be everywhere at once and cannot carry that many toys), the finding has deeper significance.

Fifth, in addition to giving individual facts a meaningful context, theories focus research. Because many researchers try to test theories, findings from theory-based research are not only relevant to the theory's explanation of events, but also to the findings of other researchers. Because progress in science comes from researchers building on each other's work, the importance of a theory's ability to coordinate individual scientists' efforts should not be underestimated.

Sixth, theories are often broad in scope. Because theories can be applied to a wide range of situations, researchers can generate a wide variety of studies from a single theory. For example, social learning theory can be applied to prisons, businesses, advertising, politics, schizophrenics, smokers, librarians, mad dogs, and Englishmen. Similarly, Freud's theory of the unconscious can be applied to virtually any situation.

Seventh, theories try to explain the facts with only a few core ideas. That is, they tend to be **parsimonious**: explaining a broad range of phenomena with a few principles. The value of parsimony is evident when you consider that a major function of science is to simplify our world. The parsimonious theory provides a few simple rules that summarize hundreds of observations. These "rules of thumb" make existing knowledge easier to understand, remember, and use. Therefore, scientists prefer theories with a few far-reaching principles to theories that require a different principle to explain each new phenomenon. Thus, it should be no surprise that two theories that have enjoyed great popularity—evolutionary theory and social learning theory—possess only a few broad-ranging principles. (For a summary of this section, see table 2.7. See table 2.8 for examples of theory-related research.)

TABLE 2.7 Contrasting Theory and Common Sense

THEORY	COMMON SENSE
Internally consistent	Makes contradictory statements
Consistent with existing facts	Not overly concerned with being consistent with existing knowledge
May make novel, counter-intuitive predictions	Makes intuitively obvious, common-sense predictions
Summarizes and organizes information	Common sense summarizes, but not as extensively or accurately as theories; furthermore, some studies derived from "intuition" yield results that cannot be integrated with existing knowledge
Focuses research on a particular set of problems	Rarely focuses research on a problem
Broad in scope	Broad in scope
Parsimonious	Parsimonious, often to the point of grossly oversimplifying reality

TABLE 2.8 Resources Relevant to Theory-related Research

Bandura, A. (1969). *Principles of behavior modification.* New York: Holt, Rinehart, & Winston.

Bandura, A. (1973). *Aggression: A social learning analysis.* Englewood Cliffs, NJ: Prentice-Hall.

Bandura, A. (1982). Self-efficacy mechanism in human agency. *American Psychologist, 37,* 122–147.

Bandura, A. (1989). Human agency in social cognitive theory. *American Psychologist, 44,* 1175–1184.

Bierman, D., & Winter, O. (1989). Learning during sleep: An indirect test of the erasure-theory of dreaming. *Perceptual and Motor Skills, 69,* 139–144.

Bless, H., Bohner, G., Schwarz, N., & Strack, F. (1990). Mood and persuasion: A cognitive response analysis. *Personality and Social Psychology Bulletin, 16,* 331–345.

Buss, D. M. (1984). Evolutionary biology and personality psychology: Toward a conception of human nature and individual differences. *American Psychologist, 39,* 1135–1147.

Buss, D. M. (1985). Human mate selection. *American Scientist, 73,* 47–51.

Cirillo, R. A., George, P. J., Horel, J. A., & Martin-Elkins, C. (1989). An experimental test of the theory that visual information is stored in the inferotemporal cortex. *Behavioural Brain Research, 34,* 43–53.

Crane, L. L., & Hicks, R. A. (1989). Preference for the color red and activation: A test of Thayer's theory. *Psychological Reports, 64,* 947–950.

Dykman, B. M., & Abramson, L. Y. (1990). Contributions of basic research to the cognitive theories of depression. *Personality and Social Psychology Bulletin, 16,* 42–57.

Engs, R., & Hanson, D. J. (1989). Reactance theory: A test with collegiate drinking. *Psychological Reports, 64,* 1083–1086.

Festinger, L. (1957). *A theory of cognitive dissonance.* Stanford, CA: Stanford University Press.

Goldman, M., Pulcher, D., & Mendez, T. (1983). Appeals for help, prosocial behavior, and psychological reactance. *The Journal of Psychology, 113,* 265–269.

Goodson, J. R., McGee, G. W., & Cashman, J. F. (1989). Situational leadership theory: A test of leadership prescriptions. *Group and Organization Studies, 14,* 446–461.

Harrington, D. M., Block, J. H., & Block, J. (1987). Testing aspects of Carl Rogers' theory of creative environments: Child-rearing antecedents of creative potential in young adolescents. *Journal of Personality and Social Psychology, 52,* 851–856.

Hauenstein, N. M., & Lord, R. G. (1989). The effects of final-offer arbitration on the performance of major league baseball players: A test of equity theory. *Human Performance, 2,* 147–165.

Keller, R. T. (1989). A test of the path-goal theory of leadership with need for clarity as a moderator in research and development organizations. *Journal of Applied Psychology, 74,* 208–212.

Kuhlman, T. L. (1985). A study of salience and motivational theories of humor. *Journal of Personality and Social Psychology, 49,* 281–286.

Mellers, B., & Hartka, E. (1988). Test of a subtractive theory of "fair" allocations. *Journal of Personality and Social Psychology, 56,* 691–697.

(continued)

TABLE 2.8 Continued

Meyers, R. A. (1989). Persuasive arguments theory: A test of assumptions. *Human Communication Research, 15,* 357–381.

Mikulincer, M. (1989). Cognitive interference and learned helplessness: The effects of off-task cognitions of performance following unsolvable problems. *Journal of Personality and Social Psychology, 57,* 129–135.

Mullen, B., Copper, C., & Driskell, J. E. (1990). Jaywalking as a function of model behavior. *Personality and Social Psychology Bulletin, 16,* 320–330.

Myers, H. M., & Siegel, P. S. (1985). The motivation to breastfeed: A fit to the opponent-process theory? *Journal of Personality and Social Psychology, 49,* 188–194.

Rusbult, C. E. (1980). Commitment and satisfaction in romantic associations: A test of the investment model. *Journal of Experimental Social Psychology, 16,* 172–186.

Schifter, D. E., & Ajzen, I. (1985). Intention, perceived control, and weight loss: An application of the theory of planned behavior. *Journal of Personality and Social Psychology, 49,* 843–851.

Seligman, E. P. (1975). *Helplessness: On depression, development, and death.* San Francisco: Freeman.

Simpson, J. A. (1987). The dissolution of romantic relationships: Factors involved in relationship stability and emotional distress. *Journal of Personality and Social Psychology, 53,* 683–692.

Skinner, B. F. (1963). Behaviorism at fifty. *Science, 140,* 951–958.

Skinner, B. F. (1966). What is the experimental analysis of behavior? *Journal of Experimental Analysis of Behavior, 9,* 213–218.

Solomon, R. L. (1980). The opponent-process theory of acquired motivation. *American Psychologist, 35,* 691–712.

Williams, B. A., & Royalty, P. (1989). A test of the melioration theory of matching. *Journal of Experimental Psychology: Animal Behavior Processes, 15,* 99–113.

Wickelgren, W. A. (1973). The long and the short of memory. *Psychological Bulletin, 80,* 425–438.

DETERMINING WHETHER A THEORY IS TESTABLE

Despite their similarities, all theories are not equally useful. Some theories are more testable—and thus more useful—than others. Therefore, when choosing a theory, make sure it is testable. To be testable, a theory must

1. make predictions rather than rely entirely on after-the-fact explanations;
2. predict one outcome rather than several contradictory outcomes;
3. make a specific, rather than an extremely vague prediction; and
4. make a prediction that can be verified through objective observation.

Prediction Rather than Postdiction

To make testable predictions, the theory must tell you what will happen in the future. Yet, not all theories make predictions about the future. Instead, some, such as

McDougall's (1908) instinct theory, only explain what happened after the fact. For example, *after* a person picked apples from an orchard, McDougall might say "the person picked apples because the instinct to pick apples from an orchard was activated." However, McDougall's theory could not make before-the-fact predictions because his theory did not tell us when to expect instincts to be aroused or how to tell whether someone would inherit a high level of an instinct.

Prediction Rather than Predictions

To be testable, a theory must be capable of making one and only one prediction about what would happen in a certain situation. To illustrate the problem of making more than one prediction, consider Freudian theory. According to Freudian theory, receiving a severe beating from one's father would result in any of the following outcomes:

1. no apparent effect (we try not to think about it: repression or suppression),
2. deep anger and resentment at people similar to our father (displacement),
3. great love for our father (reaction formation), or
4. hate for ourself (internalization).

Given all these predictions, it is hard to imagine an outcome that would not agree with one of these predictions. The theory would probably be more testable if it made one prediction.

Precision in Prediction

Almost as useless as making many predictions about what would happen in a certain situation is making one extremely vague prediction. Some theories purport to make predictions about the future, but these predictions are so vague that they are untestable. An extremely vague prediction may remind us of a fortune cookie that read: "You will make a decision soon."

Precision is the reason we often like to see quantitative statements in theories. For instance, the statement "People taking the drug A will remember twice as much as those not taking A" is more precise than the statement "People taking A will remember more than those not taking A."

Operationalism

Even if a theory makes specific, unambiguous predictions about the future, these predictions must be publicly observable for the theory to be testable. That is, for the relevant variables, we must be able to provide **operational definitions**: publicly observable set of procedures (operations) to manipulate or measure a variable.

To illustrate the importance of operational definitions, consider the statement "If you have lived a good life, you will go to heaven." Although this is a prediction about future events, it cannot be scientifically tested because we cannot find any *publicly observable*, physical evidence that would help us determine whether a person has gone to heaven. Because religion makes such metaphysical (beyond the physical world) statements, science and religion usually do not mix. Analogously, a few scientists have argued that science and psychoanalysis do not mix because one cannot observe the unconscious.

We should caution, however, that not all variables in a theory must be *directly* observable. Many theories discuss **hypothetical constructs:** entities that we cannot, with our present technology, observe directly. Gravity, electrons, love, learning, and memory are all hypothetical constructs because they are invisible. Although hypothetical constructs cannot be seen, we may be able to infer their presence from their traces or impact. With enough indirect, physical evidence, scientists can make a very convincing case for the existence of an invisible entity (a hypothetical construct). Thus, although no one has ever seen an electron, physicists swear they exist.

In psychology, the challenge has not been to see inside the atom, but to see inside the head. Like electrons, mental states cannot be directly observed. For example, we cannot directly observe learning. However, we can see its effect on performance. That is, we can operationally define learning as an increase in performance. Thus, if we see someone improve their performance after practicing a task, we would conclude that learning has occurred. Similarly, we can provide operational definitions for such intangible, hypothetical constructs as hunger, thirst, mood, or love.

PREPARING TO TAKE ADVANTAGE OF A HELPFUL THEORY

You now know how to judge whether a theory can help you generate research ideas. But where do you find theories?

Finding a Theory

From our earlier discussion, you might expect to find theories in the form of a list of hypotheses, as in box 2.1. Unfortunately, psychological theories, especially ones that are broad in scope, are not always presented so elegantly. Instead, psychological theories may ramble on for hundreds, even thousands of pages. For example, Gall's theory of phrenology (determining personality from bumps on the head) occupies seven volumes. Even with more widely accepted theories, hypotheses and core assumptions are often hidden among tons of verbiage.

Faced with the problem of clumsily stated theory, the theory-oriented researcher has two basic options. The first option is to read summaries of the theory from texts or journal articles. Reading a textbook summary should at least acquaint you with some of the theory's propositions. The problem with this approach is the textbook summary may oversimplify the theory. The researcher who relies exclusively on textbook summaries may be accused of ignoring key propositions of the theory or of using a "straw" theory (an exaggerated, oversimplified caricature of the theory). Therefore, in addition to reading textbook summaries, you might want to see how other researchers have summarized the theory. To find these summaries, consult journal articles that describe studies based on the theory (e.g., Elation and Depression: A Test of Opponent Process Theory). Usually, the beginning of these articles includes a brief description of the theory that the study tests.

BOX 2.1 Theory of Social Comparison Processes (Leon Festinger 1954)

Hypothesis 1—There exists, in the human organism, a drive to evaluate his opinions and his abilities.

Hypothesis 2—To the extent that objective, non-social means are not available, people evaluate their opinions and abilities by comparison respectively with the opinions and abilities of others.

Hypothesis 3—The tendency to compare oneself with some other specific person decreases as the differences between his opinion or ability and one's own increases.

Hypothesis 4—There is a unidirectional drive upward in the case of abilities which is largely absent in opinions.

Hypothesis 5—There are non-social restraints which make it difficult or even impossible to change one's ability. These non-social restraints are largely absent from opinions.

Hypothesis 6—The cessation of comparison with others is accompanied by hostility or derogation to the extent that continued comparison with those persons implies unpleasant consequences.

Hypothesis 7—Any factors which increase the importance of some particular group as a comparison group for some particular opinion or ability will increase the pressure toward uniformity concerning that ability or opinion within that group.

Hypothesis 8—If persons who are very divergent from one's own opinion or ability are perceived as different from oneself on *attributes consistent with the divergence*, the tendency to narrow the range of comparability becomes stronger.

Hypothesis 9—When there is a range of opinion or ability in a group, the relative strength of the three manifestations of pressures toward uniformity will be different for those who are closer to the mode of the group than those who are distant from the mode. Specifically, those close to the mode of the group will have stronger tendencies to narrow the range of comparison and much weaker tendencies to change their own positions compared to those who are distant from the mode of the group.

The second option is to read the theory and generate a complete list of its propositions yourself. Often, authors of recently developed theories describe their theories in *American Psychologist* or *Psychological Bulletin*. If you are interested in a more established theory, you should be able to find a textbook that includes a reference to the original statement of the theory. With established theories, you will also want to consult *Psychological Abstracts* (see appendix B), to find books and review articles devoted to the theory. These sources will help keep you up-to-date about changes in the theory.

Which of these options should you use? Perhaps the most prudent strategy is to select a theory based on textbook descriptions of the theory. Then, if the original theory is extremely lengthy, rely on review articles or textbooks to obtain the main principles of the theory. If the original statement of the theory is brief (e.g., Kelley's attribution theory, Festinger's social comparison theory, equity theory, Latane's social impact theory, Seligman's learned helplessness theory, Solomon's opponent processes theory, Aronson's gain-loss theory of attraction, dual theory of memory, reactance theory) or if the theory explicitly states its propositions like many learning theories (e.g., Guthrie's contiguity theory, Hull's drive reduction theory, Anderson's associative network theory), read the original source.

Ways of Deducing Hypotheses from Theory

Once you understand the theory, your task is to apply your powers of deduction. You have these powers or you would not have passed high school geometry and you would not be able to write an essay. In fact, much of your everyday thinking involves deductive logic. For example, you may say, "The important thing about a college education is to learn how to think. This assignment doesn't help me learn how to think. Therefore, this assignment is not important to my college education." If your premises were sound, your statement would be an example of sound, deductive logic.

In deducing hypotheses from theory, you will use the same deductive logic illustrated above. That is, you will apply a general rule to a specific instance. The only difference is the general rule comes from a theory instead of from the top of your head. To reassure yourself that you can apply deductive reasoning to propositions that were made up by someone else, try this deductive reasoning test:

1. All people treated like b turn out c.
2. Person A is being treated like b.

3. Person A will turn out _____.

1. All behavior can be changed by controlling its consequences.
2. Bob's behavior is bad.

3. Bob's bad behavior can be changed by _____.

1. Unconscious thoughts affect one's task performance.
2. Presenting a stimulus such as "Mommy and I are one" on a screen so quickly that the subject is not consciously aware of it (subliminal presentation) will produce the unconscious thought "Mommy and I are one."

3. Flashing "Mommy and I are one" subliminally will _____.

As this "test" illustrates, if you know the premises and set them up correctly, deductive logic can be as simple as 1-2-3. Thus, because you know common sense's premises, you probably had no problem deducing research ideas from common sense. Consequently, once you know a theory's premises, your problem is not *how* to think deductively, but *what* to think about. To help focus your deductive reasoning, we have listed ten ways to use a theory.

Apply It to Solve a Practical Problem

Contrary to common stereotypes about theories, theories can be applied to practical situations. As Kurt Lewin said, "there is nothing so practical as a good theory." For example, social learning theory has been used to cure shyness, promote energy conservation, address speech problems, reduce violence, and improve studying behavior.

To take a closer look at how theory can help you determine what factors to manipulate to improve a practical situation, consider cognitive dissonance theory (Festinger, 1957). According to cognitive dissonance theory, if a person holds two thoughts that the individual considers inconsistent, the person will experience dissonance (see table 2.9). Since dissonance is unpleasant, the individual will try to reduce it, much as the individual would try to reduce hunger, thirst, or anxiety (Aronson, 1990).

Michael Pallak and his colleagues (1980) used dissonance theory to tackle the problem of energy conservation. After being told they would get their names in the paper if they conserved energy, people cut back on their energy use. Then, dissonance was induced by telling them their names would not be printed. This created dissonance between two inconsistent ideas: (1) I do things for a reason, and (2) I went without air conditioning for no reason. Subjects resolved the dissonance by cutting energy use even more! That is, they decided (1) I do things for a reason, and (2) I went without air conditioning because I believe in energy conservation.

To take yet another example, attribution theory tries to explain how people interpret behavior. For instance, if you do poorly on a test, you could attribute your performance to yourself or to the test. If you attribute your performance to yourself, you could attribute it to a permanent aspect of yourself ("I'm not bright when it comes to school work") or to a temporary condition ("I was sick" or "It was a crazy week"). Timothy Wilson and Patricia Linville (1985) found they could improve performance of freshmen by making freshmen understand that getting low grades during their first year was a normal and temporary result of adjusting to college.

Finally, consider the hypothesis that having pets will cause the elderly to be more mentally alert and healthy. Such a hypothesis could come from intuition, but it could also come from learned helplessness theory, which states that a lack of control over outcomes may cause depression. Having a pet, or even a plant, may give one more of a

---

TABLE 2.9   Basic Propositions of Cognitive Dissonance Theory

1. If a person has two thoughts that the person considers inconsistent, the individual will experience dissonance.
2. Dissonance is an unpleasant state, like anxiety or hunger.
3. A person will try to reduce dissonance.
4. Changing one of the thoughts to make it consistent with the other is one way of reducing dissonance.

---

sense of control and thus make one less vulnerable to helplessness (Langer & Rodin, 1976).

Use Theory to Understand a Real-Life Situation

Many researchers take advantage of the fact that a major purpose of theories is to explain what happens in the world. For example, researchers wanted to understand why fraternities engage in hazing (Aronson & Mills, 1959; Gerard & Mathewson, 1966). They wondered if cognitive dissonance theory could explain hazing. Consequently, they tried to induce dissonance in some subjects by having them suffer electric shocks as a requirement for being accepted into a "boring" group, whereas other subjects were able to join the group without an "initiation." The researchers found the subjects receiving shocks resolved the dissonance caused by the opposing thoughts "I am a logical person" and "I went through unpleasantness to join a boring group" by deciding that the boring group was a pretty good group after all.

Apply It to a Different Subfield of Psychology

Often, theories generated in some subfields of psychology take years to affect other subfields of psychology. For example, years passed between the inception of Skinner's theory and its application to therapy, and between the inception of Piaget's theory and its application to educational psychology. Consequently, when asking yourself "how could this theory be applied?", do not forget to think about applied areas of psychology such as educational psychology, counseling psychology, legal psychology, health psychology, industrial psychology, and sports psychology. Thus, if you were trying to apply cognitive dissonance theory, you might start by asking yourself how dissonance could occur in

1. therapy (patients who pay the most may be happiest with the treatment)
2. a school (students doing work for no extra credit may decide they like school work)
3. a courtroom (a prosecuting attorney might not be able to accept evidence that proves the defendant innocent)
4. a hospital (a cancer patient may smoke more after the doctor tells him that his type of cancer is related to smoking because he cannot accept responsibility for his condition)
5. the workplace (a worker's loyalty may increase if he hears that he would have made more money if he had taken the other job he was offered)

Even if the theory originates in one applied area of psychology, try to apply it to another. For example, you might apply a theory of job satisfaction—e.g., Hackman and Oldham's (1980) theory of job satisfaction or Locke and Latham's (1990) theory of motivation and satisfaction—to school or marital satisfaction.

Applying theories to different subfields of psychology prevents the subfields of psychology from becoming independent collections of undigested information (Rotter, 1990) and can make the theories broader and more powerful. Cognitive dissonance theory was originally limited to situations in which people were subtly pressured to engage in a behavior contrary to their beliefs, such as telling someone a boring task was interesting or advocating the merits of a religion other than their own (Festinger & Carlsmith, 1959). Then it was expanded to consider other situations in which people might face conflicting thoughts. Specifically, researchers (Brock & Balloun, 1967; Frey, 1986; Knox & Inkster, 1968) found dissonance theory applied to consumer behavior ("I bought this brand when the other brand is cheaper and seems just as good"), gambling behavior (people are most sure of their bet right after they put down their money), and political behavior (we ignore information that runs counter to our beliefs, such as political editorials that argue against our position).

Similarly, theories of psychophysics were originally used only to understand how we make judgments about physical objects, such as determining the weight of a ball. Eventually, researchers applied the theory to social judgments (Helson, 1964; Parducci, 1984). For example, researchers found, as is the case in judging weights, the context (what you have to compare the stimulus with) affects your judgments of how attractive a person is (Wedell, et al. 1987), how hostile you judge someone to be (Herr, 1986), and even how satisfied you are with your life (Strack, Schwarz & Gschneidinger, 1985). In one interesting study, Parducci found that clinical psychologists were more likely to judge a patient as having a serious problem if the psychologist's previous clients had mild symptoms than if the previous clients' problems were moderate or severe (Wedell, Parducci, & Lane, 1990).

Apply Theory to Fields Related to Psychology

After considering how the theory might apply to psychology's subfields, think about how the theory might apply to fields related to psychology. After all, much of the research in education, nursing, medicine, marketing, political science, criminology, management, personnel relations, advertising, and consumer behavior involves applying basic psychological theories to different situations. For example, researchers have looked at how principles of operant conditioning, such as using rewards and lottery-type games, can be used to increase school attendance, increase patient's compliance with doctor's orders, reduce criminal behavior, improve employee morale, and get consumers to buy more.

Look for Moderator Variables

Theories are general rules that, ideally, hold most of the time under specific conditions. Therefore, ask yourself, "under what situations or conditions does the theory not apply?" Because researchers asked this question about cognitive dissonance theory, we now know that people do not experience dissonance every time they do a behavior that goes against their attitudes. Instead, certain conditions must be met. Specifically, if performing a counter-attitudinal behavior is going to change subjects' attitudes (Aronson, 1989; Brehm & Cohen, 1962; Festinger & Carlsmith, 1959), subjects must (1) believe they engaged in the behavior of their own free will; (2) not receive a large reward for the behavior; and (3) view the attitude as important to their self-concept.

Thus, if a smoker is forced at gunpoint to say smoking is bad, or given $10,000 for saying smoking is bad, or does not view smoking as important to his self-concept, the smoker will tolerate the inconsistency between thought and behavior and not feel dissonance. Can you think of other factors or situations that might cause people to accept, rather than rationalize, inconsistencies between their thoughts and actions?

When looking for limiting or boundary conditions for a theory, ask yourself whether the theory might be too parsimonious. For example, Ajzen and Madden (1986) found that the theory of reasoned action could be more accurate if it included more principles (see figure 2.3). The original theory (Fishbein & Ajzen, 1975) postulated that behavior depended on intentions. Intentions, in turn, depended on two factors: your attitude toward the behavior and your beliefs about how your reference group would view the behavior. By adding another factor, the person's sense of perceived control over the outcome, Ajzen and Madden (1986) found they could better predict behavior. Similarly, operant conditioning theory's rule that a behavior reinforced under a partial reinforcement schedule is more resistant to extinction is too simple. A behavior reinforced under a partial reinforcement schedule is more resistant to extinction *only* when the person believes the reward is controlled by external forces such as chance, fate, or the ex-

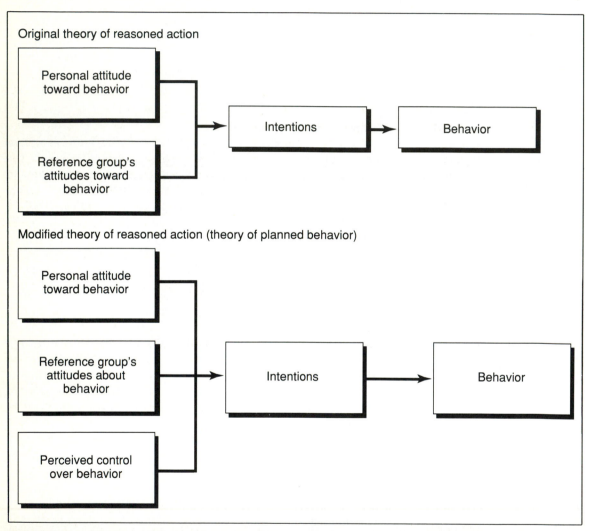

FIGURE 2.3 Making a Theory More Accurate by Making it Less Parsimonious: The Case of the Theory of Reasoned Action

perimenter's whim. Partially reinforced behaviors are *not* more resistant to extinction when the subject believes that getting reinforcement depends on skill (Rotter, 1990).

When trying to think of what kinds of people or what kinds of situations may cause a theory not to hold, do not forget to consult other theories. To illustrate, consider attribution theory, which postulates that people, like naive scientists, logically combine information to determine the causes of social behavior. According to attribution theory, what would happen if an impartial witness says a defendant murdered someone whereas the defendant's sister says he did not? According to attribution theory, jurors would discount the sister's testimony, realizing that she might be lying to help her brother. Under what conditions might attribution theory be wrong? That is, when would people be unable to realize that the sister's testimony should carry very little weight?

Obviously, to ignore the testimony of a loyal sister, a juror must remember that the person who said the defendant was guilty had no connection with the defendant whereas the person who said the defendant was innocent was his sister. If the juror fails to realize these relationships or misremembers them, the juror may be unable to discount the sister's testimony. Drawing on associative network theories of memory (Anderson & Bower, 1973; Collins & Loftus, 1975), Devine and Ostrom (1985) decided that unless the information was properly organized in memory, people would be unable to accurately synthesize the information in the way postulated by attribution theory. Consistent with associative network theories, Devine and Ostrom found that only when information was presented in a way that subjects could easily form impressions of each witness, did subjects properly discount the testimony of the defendants' relatives.

To find another factor that might limit people's ability to make rational, logical attributions, Allen, Walker, Schroeder, and Johnson (1987) used another theory—Piaget's theory of cognitive development. Piaget's theory suggests that only those people who have attained the highest level of cognitive development, formal operational thought, could make the abstract, complex, and logical judgments that attribution theory assumes everyone makes. Allen et al.'s finding were consistent with Piaget's theory.

Apply the Theory to a Different Subject Population

Trying to identify a theory's boundaries may suggest that a theory is not applicable to all populations. For example, Carol Gilligan (1982) argues that theories, such as Kohlberg's theory of moral development and Erikson's theory of personality development, are based on research with males and do not hold for females.

If there is a valid reason for expecting that a theory will not hold with a certain subject group, the theory should be tested on that group. Occasionally, such tests may simultaneously refine *and* broaden the theory. For example, Skinner's theory of operant conditioning was initially developed based on research on lower animals. Although research applying the theory to humans has found situations where the "laws" of behavior do not always apply (Rotter, 1990), such research has also found the theory does apply to much human behavior.

Take It to the Limit

In addition to determining to whom the theory applies, you can determine to what degree it applies. For example, if a theory predicts that increasing rewards will lead to greater liking of the task, you might see whether extremely large rewards lead to greater liking (by comparing first-graders who either receive a nickel for five minutes' work with those who receive ten dollars for the same amount of work).

Testing whether a theory holds in the extremes can injure or bolster a theory. Fechner's theory of psychophysics was weakened by the fact that the theory did not hold well for extremely powerful or extremely weak stimuli (Stevens, 1957). On the other hand, the modified theory of reasoned action has been bolstered by its ability to predict extreme situations such as whether someone opts for an abortion.

Improve Its Accuracy

Instead of seeing whether the theory holds in extreme cases, you may choose to increase its precision. For instance, you may want to more accurately map the relationship between the theory's key variables. Is the relationship a straight line (what slope?) or a curve? This mapping will require accurate measurement of both variables (e.g., amount of dissonance and attitude change, the amount of difference between two people's opinions and their tendency to compare themselves with each other) and may seem rather dull. However, the more precise a rule is, the more useful it is. Wouldn't you prefer specific directions (e.g., "Go straight for a mile and a half, then turn right.") to general directions (e.g., "Turn to the right up the road a piece.")?

Historically, progress in chemistry and physics has been marked by coming up with more precise mathematical equations to explain relationships among variables. For example, rather than saying that objects fall or that gases expand when heated, physical scientists have formulated laws that specify the rate at which objects fall and the extent to which gases expand. Similarly, psychologists have become famous by carefully mapping relationships among variables. For example, in the 1800s, Fechner's psychophysics mapped the relationship between physical stimulation and sensation (Fechner, 1860), providing the impetus for the development of psychology as a science (Schultz & Schultz, 1990). Fechner's general finding—that the more intense the stimulus, the more intensely we feel it—was not that exciting. The exciting thing was that Fechner was able to precisely specify the relationship between stimulation and sensation.

More recently, Latane's (1981) theory of social impact is popular not for what it says, but for how precisely it says it. The theory's thesis—the more people in the group, the more influence the group can have—is not unique. What makes the theory unique is it tells us, with more accuracy than any previous theory, how much more influence the group will gain by adding members.

Increasing the precision of a theory is of enormous value. Being specific is often the only thing that distinguishes scientific predictions from common sense predictions. Furthermore, accurate and precise theories are necessary if we are to accurately make the precise predictions that would be useful in a practical, real-life situation. Because improving the precision and accuracy of a theory is so important, it may be worthwhile to assess the relationship between key variables in a theory.

Go for the Jugular

Another tactic is to design a study that tests the accuracy of the theory's core assumptions. Often, attacking the heart of the theory involves determining whether the physiological or cognitive events that are—according to the theory—the underlying causes of behavior. For instance, cognitive dissonance theory assumes that when people have two beliefs that they see as contradictory, they experience an unpleasant, anxiety-provoking state called dissonance. To reduce dissonance, people will reconcile the inconsistency. In other words, dissonance theorists assume that dissonance mediates attitude change.

To test this assumption, you might try to induce and maintain dissonance in subjects and determine whether they do find dissonance an unpleasant, anxiety-provoking state. If subjects felt *decreased* arousal, it would seem that you had disproved a core assumption of the theory.

In addition to trying to measure the mediating state, you may try to manipulate it. For example, suppose that a certain manipulation tends to cause attitude change, presumably because it creates a cognitive and physiological state of dissonance that people then reduce. You might expose subjects to that manipulation, but do something so subjects would be less likely to experience the physiological arousal of the dissonance state. For example, you might give them a tranquilizing drug that would reduce arousal. If reducing the physiological state of dissonance is what mediates attitude change, subjects who experienced less arousal (tranquilizer condition) should experience less attitude change than the subjects who simply went through the conventional dissonance manipulation.

By either measuring or manipulating mediating variables, you should be able to test most theories' core assumptions. The first step, however, is to find a core assumption to test. Looking at table 2.3, do you see any core assumptions of social comparison theory that you might be able to test?

Pit Two Theories against Each Other
Rather than trying to torpedo a theory, some researchers think the best hypotheses are those in which two theories make opposite predictions. Ideally, these studies, often called "critical studies," try to settle the question of which theory's view of the world is more correct (see box 2.2). One of the first critical studies was simple but persuasive. Subjects looked at two lights. Almost as soon as one went on, the other went off. According to structuralism, the person should see one light going on, another going off. However, according to Gestalt theory, subjects should see the illusion of a light going back and forth. Gestalt theory was supported.

More recently, cognitive dissonance has challenged behaviorism and psychoanalysis. According to behaviorism, people should like things for which they are rewarded (Aronson, 1990). If you reward people for saying something, they should become attached to the statement and believe it. The larger the reward, the more they should believe it. However, Festinger and Carlsmith (1959) showed that people believe lies for which they get small rewards, but not lies for which they get big rewards.

In taking on psychoanalysis, dissonance researchers tested the psychoanalytic position that if you express hostility towards a person, you'll release pent up anger and consequently feel better about the person. Dissonance theory, on the other hand, predicts that if people hurt someone with whom they are angry, they will justify their aggression by

BOX 2.2 Tolman's Critical Experiments

As you have read, critical studies have sometimes led to enormous changes in psychology. The Gestalt psychologist's critical study involving the illusion of moving light not only weakened structuralism, but launched Gestalt psychology. Similarly, critical experiments that supported dissonance theory over behaviorism were partly responsible for psychology's cognitive revolution—during which psychologists pursued the study of thoughts with renewed vigor.

The "king" of critical experiments was E. C. Tolman. Tolman's reputation as one of the most influential people in the history of psychology comes mostly from a series of critical experiments he and his students conducted. The experiments supported his theory over the prevailing theory of the time: radical behaviorism. In one experiment, he challenged the behaviorists' position that no learning occurs without reinforcement. This assertion was in conflict with Tolman's cognitive theory, which stated that organisms naturally form cognitive maps of their environment (Tolman, 1932). To support his view, Tolman had groups of rats run a maze. The group that was always rewarded showed steady progress. The rats that were not rewarded did not seem to progress. However, one day the unrewarded rats were rewarded. The next day, they ran the maze just as fast as the rats who had always been rewarded, suggesting that the unrewarded rats had learned, but until they had been rewarded, they did not have any motivation to show what they had learned (Tolman & Honzik, 1930).

In another experiment that supported Tolman's cognitive view over the behaviorist position, he showed rats did develop cognitive expectations and these expectations affected their behavior. He started out by giving one group of rats one pellet for running a maze, whereas the other group got ten. After several trials, he changed the rewards so that all rats got five pellets. The group that was accustomed to getting one pellet greatly improved their performance (an elation effect), whereas the group that was accustomed to getting ten pellets ran the maze much more slowly (depressed effect). The results directly contradicted the behaviorist position that amount of reward, not expectation, affects performance.

In yet another critical experiment, he tested another discrepancy between his cognitive theory and behaviorism. Behaviorism, at that time, claimed organisms learn individual motor movements. Tolman, on the other hand, believed organisms create a mental map of the world. To test this idea, Tolman had rats learn to run a simple maze. All they had to learn was to turn right. Then, he put them on the opposite side of the maze. If they had only learned motor movements, they would turn right. If they had made a mental map of the area, they would turn left. Tolman's rats turned left.

denigrating the person and will, therefore, feel more hostility. Experiments support the dissonance prediction (Aronson, 1990).

If you can devise a situation where two theories make different predictions, you have probably designed a study your professor will want to hear about. However, even if you perform a critical study, do not expect the "loser" of your study to be replaced. The loser has only lost a battle, not a war. There is usually enough vagueness in any theory for its arch-supporters to minimize the extent of the damage. They may argue that your experiment was a near-miss (their theory didn't really say that, you put words in its mouth, or it mumbled something and you misunderstood it). If that is not possible, they may concede that their theory applies to a more limited set of situations than they thought or they may modify the theory to account for the results (Greenwald et al., 1986). Because scientists usually respond to a damaging set of findings by modifying an established theory rather than "throwing the baby out with the bath water," Darwin's theory of evolution, Adam Smith's theory of capitalism, and Festinger's theory of cognitive dissonance survive today, but not in their original form. That is, by adapting to new data, theories evolve.

GENERATING RESEARCH IDEAS FROM THEORY: A SUMMARY

As you have seen, theory is a very useful tool for developing research ideas and tying those ideas to existing knowledge (see table 2.10). Without research based on theory, psychology would chaotically move in every direction with little purpose, like an amoeba or a government bureaucracy. Indeed, theory-based research is responsible for much of psychology's progress since 1890, when psychology was described by William James (p. 468) as:

"a string of raw facts; . . . but not a single law in the sense in which physics shows us laws, not a single proposition from which any consequence can causally be deduced. . . . This is no science. . . ."

TABLE 2.10 Ten Ways to Use Theory to Obtain Research Ideas

1. Apply it to solve a practical problem.
2. Use it to understand a real-life situation.
3. Apply it to a different subfield of psychology.
4. Apply it to fields related to psychology.
5. Look for moderator variables.
6. Apply it to a different subject population.
7. Take it "to the limit."
8. Improve its accuracy.
9. "Go for the jugular."
10. Pit two theories against each other.

TABLE 2.11   Pros and Cons of Theory-based Research

PROS	CONS
Theory focuses research on specific issues and problems	Theory may divert attention away from other important issues and problems
Theory provides a way of interpreting and explaining facts, a way of looking at the world	Theory may provide a wrong way of looking at the world and may prevent us from finding more accurate ways of viewing phenomena

Yet, not everyone believes that theory-based research is always best (Greenwald et al., 1986; Kuhn, 1970; Skinner, 1956). (See table 2.11 for pros and cons of theory-based research.) Thomas Kuhn (1970) argues that theories can serve as blinders, causing us to ignore problems that do not fit nicely into existing theory. Skinner (1956) also argues that sticking to a theory's narrow path may cause us to ignore interesting side streets. Specifically, Skinner's advice to investigators was "when you find something of interest, study it."

In addition to making us fail to seek new facts, theories may also cause us to fail to see old facts in new ways. Thus, we may fail to make the kind of discoveries Darwin, Freud, and Skinner made—the ones that result from seeing what everyone else has seen, but thinking what no one else has thought. As physicists learned when Newton's theory was largely overturned by Einstein, looking at things exclusively through a theory's perspective is especially dangerous when the theory has not been extensively tested. In other words, some experts (Greenwald et al., 1986; Kuhn, 1970; Skinner, 1956) would agree with Sherlock Holmes' statement about the danger of premature theorizing: "One begins to twist facts to fit theories rather than theories to fit facts."

Fortunately, as Aronson (1989) points out, science is like a big circus tent. Under the tent, there is room for the programmatic research derived from theory. There is also room for researchers who have hunches or who drop everything to follow an interesting lead, as Pavlov did when he saw his dogs salivate at the sight of the experimenter and Skinner did when he saw pigeons in his operant conditioning chamber hopping around on one leg.

Not only is there room for both hunch-based and theory-based research, but hunches and theory can often be combined. For example, suppose you had a hunch that consuming alcohol might make people more helpful under certain conditions. To determine what "under certain conditions" are, you might refer to theories on the effects of alcohol and theories on helping behavior. As a result, you might conclude that alcohol consumption might increase helpfulness if the helping situation entailed a great deal of risk. If your results supported your hypothesis, your results would not only add to knowledge about the relationship between drinking and helpfulness, but would also support Latane's theory of bystander apathy that people tend to weigh the risks of helping before they act (by the way, a study supporting the hypothesis that alcohol can increase helping in risky situations has already been published [Steele & Southwick, 1985]).

GENERATING IDEAS FROM PREVIOUS RESEARCH

The research circus tent not only has a ring for researchers using intuition and a ring for researchers using theory, but also a third ring for research based on previous studies (see table 2.12). Although one survey suggests that fewer than one in seven professional research efforts originate from reading research (Garvey & Griffith, 1971), for a beginning researcher, basing an idea on previous research has at least three major advantages. First, research based on previous studies, like theory-based research, allows you to build on other scientists' work. Consequently, your research will probably not produce an isolated, trivial fact. Second, a hypothesis based on previous research is indeed an educated guess and has a reasonable chance of panning out. Third, doing research based on other people's work is easier. Other people have done the groundbreaking research, built the foundation, and discovered what tools to use; all you have to do is finish the basement or paint a few rooms.

SPECIFIC STRATEGIES

To take advantage of other people's work, you have to be able to find their work and, once you find it, you have to have a strategy of how to build on it. Therefore, in the next sections, we will give you some tips for developing ideas from previous research and then we will show you how to find research relevant to your needs.

Find Gaping Omissions

As you review the literature, you may find that some obvious aspect of the problem has not been studied. For example, Montepare and Zebrowitz-McArthur (1988) found that many studies looked at how we form impressions of people based on their facial expressions, but that no studies looked at the first thing we see—the person walking toward us. Consequently, they studied how we form impressions of people based on their gait.

TABLE 2.12 Relative Advantages of Three Primary Ways of Generating Research Hypotheses

ADVANTAGES	COMMON SENSE	THEORY	LITERATURE SEARCHES
Rationale for predictions	Yes	Yes	Yes
Make hypothesis a more *educated* guess	No	Yes	Yes
Connect findings to other people's work so research does not merely contribute trivial facts	No	Yes	Yes
May provide different perspective on problem	No	Yes	Yes
May provide suggestions for how to manipulate or measure variables	?	Yes	Yes

Repeat Studies

Science relies on skepticism. If a finding does not seem believable to you and it has not been replicated, you should repeat the study (see table 2.13). You may also want to repeat studies that yield conflicting findings. For example, in texts or in lectures, you may be presented with a study that claims to show one thing and another study that seems to show the opposite. In that case, you may want to repeat both studies.

Do a Study Suggested by the Journal Article's Author(s)

In *Psychological Science, American Psychologist, Psychological Bulletin,* and the *Annual Review of Psychology,* you will find articles that introduce or review a subfield of psychology such as commitment, health psychology, or instructional psychology. Those articles will not only say what has been done, but suggest research studies that should be done.

Review articles are not the only ones to suggest research studies. At the end of many research articles, the researchers suggest additional studies that should be done. For example, they may point out that the research should be repeated using a different sample of subjects or should be done in a different setting.

Repeat the Study with a Different Group of Subjects

Even if the researchers do not suggest it, you may believe the findings would not hold for another subject group. For example, most of the research on mid-life crises (Gould, 1978; Levinson, 1978) only studied middle-class males. Would the results be different if middle-class women were studied?

Look for Situational Factors That May Moderate the Effect

Just as results of a study may not generalize to different groups of people, the results may not generalize to different situations. There are usually several situational factors that could strengthen or weaken the relationship between two variables. If you are blocking on moderating variables, just ask yourself "When might the opposite occur?" For example, you might read of research saying alcohol makes people sad and "cry in their beer." Clearly, you can think of opposite situations, instances when alcohol seems to make people happier. Similarly, you may read about situations where eyewitness testimony was inaccurate, but you can think of times when it was accurate. What is different about the two situations?

Look for Factors That Were Not Controlled

As you learned in chapter 1, establishing that one factor caused an effect is very difficult, partly because it is hard to control other factors. For example, Gladue and Delaney (1990) argued that a study (Pennebaker et al., 1979) finding that "girls get prettier at closing time" at bars left unanswered the question of whether time or alcohol consumption was responsible for increased perceptions of attractiveness. Are there other factors, besides alcohol consumption, that the researchers should have controlled or considered?

TABLE 2.13   Examples of Published Research Involving Replications

Alterman, A. I., Searles, J. S., & Hall, J. G. (1989). Failure to find differences in drinking behavior as a function of familial risk for alcoholism: A replication. *Journal of Abnormal Psychology, 98,* 50–53.

Braud, W. G. (1989). A possible proximity effect on human grip strength: An attempted replication. *Perceptual and Motor Skills, 68,* 157–158.

Breederveld, H. (1989). The Michels experiments: An attempted replication. *Journal of the Society for Psychical Research, 55,* 360–363. (*Note:* They were unable to replicate a study that appeared to provide evidence for ESP.)

Bryan, T., Pearl, R., & Fallon, P. (1989). Conformity to peer pressure by students with learning disabilities: A replication. *Journal of Learning Disabilities, 22,* 458–459.

Burgard, P., Cheyne, W. M., & Jahoda, G. (1989). Children's representations of economic inequality: A replication. *British Journal of Development Psychology, 7,* 275–287.

De Jonghe, J. F., & Baneke, J. J. (1989). The Zung self-rating depression scale: A replication study on reliability, validity, and prediction. *Psychological Reports, 64,* 833–834.

Gleeson, S., Lattal, K. A., & Williams, K. S. (1989). Superstitious conditioning: A replication and extension of Neuringer (1970). *Psychological Record, 39,* 563–571.

Harris, M. J. (1989). Personality moderators of interpersonal expectancy effects: Replication of Harris and Roenthal (1986). *Journal of Research in Personality, 23,* 381–397.

Houghton, S. (1989). Improving social behaviour and academic performance of a secondary school pupil through self-recording: A replication of Merrett and Blundell. *Educational Psychology, 9,* 239–245.

Latham, G. P., & Frayne, C. A. (1989). Self-management training for increasing job attendance: A follow-up and a replication. *Journal of Applied Psychology, 74,* 411–416.

Levinson, E. M. (1989). Job satisfaction among school psychologists: A replication study. *Psychological Reports, 65,* 579–584.

Lindsay, R. C., Wells, G. L., & O'Connor, F. J. (1989). Mock-juror belief of accurate and inaccurate eye-witnesses: A replication and extension. *Law and Human Behavior, 13,* 333–339.

Nilson, I., & Ekehammar, B. (1989). Social attitudes and beliefs in heredity: A replication and extension. *Personality and Individual Differences, 10,* 363–365.

Norman, T. R., Judd, F. K., Burrows, G. D., & McIntyre, I. M. (1989). Platelet serotonin uptake in panic disorder patients: A replication study. *Psychiatry Research, 30,* 63–68.

Okaichi, H., Oshima, Y., & Jarrard, L. E. (1989). Scopalamine impairs both working and reference memory in rats: A replication and extension. *Biochemistry and Behavior, 34,* 599–602.

Sher, K. J., Frost, R. O., Kushyner, M., & Crews, T. M. (1989). Memory deficits in compulsive checkers: Replication and extension in a clinical sample. *Behavior Research and Therapy, 27,* 65–69.

Stith, M. T., & Goldsmith, R. E. (1989). Race, sex, and fashion innovativeness: A replication. *Psychology and Marketing, 6,* 249–262.

Thyer, B. A., Himle, J., & Miller-Gogoleski, M. A. (1989). The relationship of parental death to panic disorder: A community-based replication. *Phobia Practice and Research Journal, 2,* 29–36.

Trute, B., Tefft, B., & Segall, A. (1989). Social rejection of the mentally ill: A replication study of public attitude. *Social Psychiatry and Psychiatric Epidemiology, 24,* 69–76.

Tryon, W. W., & Cicero, S. D. (1989). Classical conditioning of meaning: A replication and higher order extension. *Journal of Behavior Therapy and Experimental Psychiatry, 20,* 137–142.

Reduce the Effects of Expectancies

Suppose you are reading a study and you say to yourself, "If I were a subject, I would know how the experimenter wanted me to behave." In that case, the study should be repeated with a change to reduce the effects of expectancies. One way to reduce the effects of expectancies is the so-called **double-blind technique:** neither the subjects nor the researcher knows what treatment the subjects are getting. This double-blind technique is often used in drug studies to make sure the patient's improvement is due to the drug itself rather than to the patient's or physician's expectations that the drug will work.

Please note that the double-blind technique is not limited to drug studies. If you can administer two or more treatments that would seem very similar to the subjects, you can probably use the double-blind technique. For example, Greenwald et al. (1990) used a double-blind technique to look at the effects of listening to tapes with subliminal messages. Subjects got either subliminal messages designed to improve their memory or messages designed to improve their self-esteem. They found out it did not matter what messages subjects actually got—it only mattered what they thought they got. That is, if subjects thought they got messages designed to improve their memory, they did better on memory tasks, If, on the other hand, they thought they were hearing messages designed to increase their self-esteem, their self-esteem appeared to improve.

Use More Realistic Amounts of the Treatment Factor

Some studies use unrealistically extreme levels of the treatment factor to get an effect. Early studies on the effects of cigarette smoke, for example, gave rats the human equivalent of more than 400 cigarettes a day. The next logical step is to determine if life-sized variations in the treatment will have an effect.

Uncover the Functional Relationship

Even if the study used realistic amounts of the variables, you may still want to test additional amounts of the factor to get a better idea of the relationship between the variables. For example, a study finding that exercise increases alertness may use only two amounts of exercise (none and one hour per day). As a practical matter, we would like to know how much exercise produces what level of alertness. Can we get away with exercising for five minutes or do we need a full hour to get the effect? To find out, you may want to repeat the study using different levels of the predictor variable. Sometimes, looking for functional relationships can lead to discovering laws. For example, by examining the relationship between motivation and performance, researchers discovered the **Yerkes-Dodson Law,** which states, in part, that motivation will improve performance except at very high levels of motivation, at which point increases in motivation will decrease performance.

Use More Realistic Stimulus Materials

Memory research progressed from having subjects memorize nonsense syllables to having them recall life-like re-enactments of car accidents (Loftus, 1980). Similarly, research in impression formation has evolved from having subjects read lists of traits about a target person to watching videotapes of the target person. Therefore, you may be able to repeat a study using more complex or realistic stimulus materials.

See If Another Factor Would Have the Same Effect

Occasionally, researchers will argue that a general psychological or physiological process accounts for the effect of their treatment. If they are right, then any factor that can affect that process should have a similar effect. For example, Steele and Joseph (1990) hypothesized that limited ability to attend to and process stimuli is responsible for many of alcohol's effects. If limited attention and processing capacity do mediate the effects of alcohol, then other factors that limit the ability to attend to and process stimuli may mimic alcohol's effects. Thus, exposing subjects to a powerful distracting stimulus or having subjects exercise to the point of exhaustion may be manipulations that mimic some of alcohol's effects (since these manipulations should limit the ability to process stimuli).

Bridge Fields and Try to Find a Practical Implication of the Research

Advances in sciences often occur when information from one field is transferred to another. This cross-fertilization can produce remarkable progress (Burke, 1978). As we already mentioned, extending research done on animals to human subjects has produced important results. In this era of increased specialization, it is easy for findings in one area of psychology to stay in that field. However, most research, especially in basic fields of psychology, can and should be extended to many different areas. Short-term memory capacity has implications not only for memory, but for educational psychology, industrial psychology, social psychology, health psychology, and personality psychology. For example, people with limited short-term memories may be slower readers, consider fewer options when making business decisions, be more likely to stereotype others, less likely to follow a physician's instructions, and be more impulsive.

Look at the Studies from a Different Level of Analysis

One perspective probably cannot completely explain a phenomenon. Therefore, if the studies are looking at cognitive effects of a treatment, you might look at physiological, behavioral, or social effects. If research looked only at the effects of inheritance, look for the effects of environment. If the research looked exclusively at personality variables, look for situational variables, and vice-versa. For example, when psychologists initially tried to understand why people's behaviors sometimes did not match their attitudes, psychologists looked primarily at situational factors. More recently, however, Snyder (Snyder, 1974; Snyder & Gangestad, 1986) has proposed a measure of individual differences to partially account for why behaviors sometimes do not match attitudes. Similarly, whereas some experts felt tobacco addiction was only psychological, research has found it to be, in part, physiological (Schachter, 1971). Conversely, whereas the effects of alcohol were assumed to be physiological, Steele and Joseph (1990) have shown that much of alcohol's effect depends on the environmental situation.

Look for Patterns in Conflicting Studies

When you find studies that produce conflicting results, look for subtle differences in how the studies were conducted. What do the studies that find one pattern of results have in common? What do the studies that find a different pattern have in common? Answering these questions is a creative and potentially productive task. For example, many studies found a "social facilitation" effect—that the presence of others improved performance. However, many other studies found a "social inhibition" effect, such that the presence of others decreased performance. Bob Zajonc (Zajonc, 1965; Zajonc & Sales, 1966) looked at all the studies and found how the two sets of studies differed: studies finding social facilitation involved tasks that were easy for subjects to do whereas studies finding social inhibition involved tasks that were hard for subjects to do. Zajonc then designed several studies to test his hypothesis that task difficulty determines whether social inhibition gets social facilitation was correct. More recently, Steele and Joseph (1988, 1990) found studies that showed strong effects for alcohol differed from studies that showed weak effects for alcohol. Specifically, studies showing strong effects introduced some sort of conflict (If I gamble this large amount, I could win a lot, but I could also lose a lot; If I hurt this person, they may hurt me back) whereas studies showing weak effects introduced very little conflict (gambling very small amounts, being able to shock a person without getting shocked back). They then conducted a series of studies that systematically varied level of conflict and found that their explanation held.

Look for a Factor's Immediate Relationship to Other Variables

Even if there is no contradiction in the literature, it can still pay to look for patterns. For example, Steele and Joseph (1988) knew from the literature that alcohol caused people to gamble more, aggress more, and engage in risky sex more often. They decided to see if alcohol affected other behaviors that involved some kind of risk, such as helping other people.

Similarly, there has been an avalanche of research on the correlates of attachment style. Initially, researchers looked at how one's attachment to parents corresponded to security in romantic love relationships (Hazan & Shaver, 1987). Then researchers looked at the relationship between attachment style and feelings about death (Mikulincer, Florian, & Tolmacz, 1990). Finally, researchers looked at the relationship between attachment style and orientation toward work (Hazan & Shaver, 1990). Soon we will probably see studies examining how attachment to parents is connected to how people relate to their possessions. Such avalanches seem to occur with any new personality measure that gains prominence, as subject's scores on that measure are correlated with their scores on popular personality measures.

Although rarely reaching avalanche proportions, researchers may extend findings of a study to a different behavior, using the original study as a model of how to do the study. For example, Festinger, Schachter, and Back (1950) found that group norms affected certain key attitudes and that deviation from these attitudes caused rejection. Crandall (1988) replicated this study, only he looked at binge-eating in sororities. He found that binge-eating followed the same pattern as the original attitude study: women who purged the "right" amount were most popular.

Look at Long-Term Effects

You may read studies that examined the short-term effects of pushing preschoolers to learn or the short-term effects of divorce on children, but what about the long-term effects? Similarly, many memory, attitude change, and physiological studies look only at short-term effects.

Look for "Down the Road" Effects

In addition to asking whether an effect lasts, you should ask "and what else would happen?" Taking a finding one step further can lead you to a chain of questions. For example, suppose you read that arousal reduces short-term memory capacity. Since short-term memory is used in making judgments, arousal should affect judgments. Furthermore, since behavior is based on judgments, arousal may affect behavior.

To take a more detailed example, suppose you read research showing that physically attractive people are more highly rated than others. You might ask how these high ratings will, in turn, affect how attractive people will be treated; how being treated, in turn, will affect how attractive people will view themselves; and how they view themselves and the way they are treated will affect how they treat others. The wonderful thing about studying human behavior is that a change in one factor can have a very large ripple effect (see figure 2.4).

Repeat the Study Using a Different Measure of the Same Construct

As you learned in chapter 1, it is difficult to properly measure a psychological state of mind. Any single measure of a construct may be flawed. Therefore, a study that finds a relationship between two operational definitions of a construct is not conclusive. However, if we again find the same relationship using different operational definitions, we can be more confident that a relationship really exists between the two constructs. For example, suppose a memory researcher finds that rehearsal strategy affects organization, as measured by the order in which subjects recall information. To be more confident that rehearsal strategy affects organization, the study might be repeated using a reaction time measure of organization (e.g., how much seeing a concept on the immediately preceding trial speeds up response to a related concept on the next trial).

Ironically, it may be especially valuable to use a different measuring procedure if virtually all studies are using the same measuring technique. For example, researchers once used the pecking rate of pigeons as a measure of *motivation.* However, it turned out pecking rate was not a voluntary behavior. Instead, pigeons peck almost reflexively when they are aroused, regardless of whether it is food or shock that *arouses* them. Consequently, even if you shock pigeons for pecking, their pecking will increase.

Keep in mind that what is a consequence at one moment may be a cause the next. This may help you in generating research ideas from reading research. For example, suppose you read that increasing arousal decreases short term memory. You realize that changes in short term memory could affect judgments, which, in turn, could affect behavior. That is,

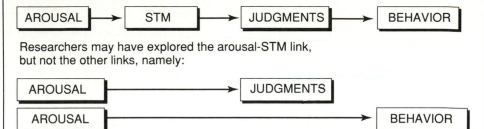

Researchers may have explored the arousal-STM link, but not the other links, namely:

AROUSAL	⟶	JUDGMENTS
AROUSAL	⟶	BEHAVIOR

Similarly, Walter Mischel told children if they could wait, and resist the reward that was immediately present, they could get a better reward. In his original studies (Mischel, 1973, 1981), he looked at factors that allowed children to delay immediate gratification. Later, he and his associates (Mischel, Shoda, & Peake, 1988) looked to see if ability to delay gratification could predict other consequences. Mischel and his colleagues found that ability to delay gratification (wait for a reward) predicted many other events. Children who were able to wait for a reward when they were four or five were more academically and socially competent, verbally fluent, rational, planful, and able to deal with stress and frustration. That is:

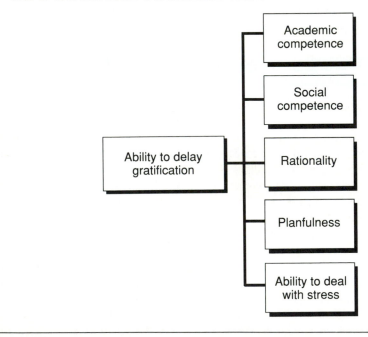

FIGURE 2.4 Looking for "Down the Road Effects"

Repeat the Study with a More Sensitive Way of Detecting the Effect

Just as you may repeat a study that found an effect, you may repeat a study that failed to find an effect. Your hope is that just as higher power microscopes and telescopes and more sensitive scales and clocks have helped other sciences discover new phenomena, more sensitive measuring techniques may help psychologists discover new relationships and phenomena. For example, if you ask people to write down anything they can remember from tapes that were played while they slept, it appears that no sleep learning whatsoever occurs. However, to determine if any learning takes place, experts (Swets & Bjork, 1990) have suggested using several more sensitive ways of measuring learning. One method involves replaying the tape, while subjects are awake, at such a low volume that subjects would ordinarily be unable to understand the tape. Can subjects who have heard the tape in their sleep understand more of what is being said than subjects who have never before heard the tape? Another method involves seeing if subjects who hear the tape in their sleep and then hear a lecture on the material do better than those who only hear the lecture.

Take Advantage of "Component" Measures

Scientific progress often results from developing more differentiated measures. You may read a study finding that certain situations or characteristics cause individuals to do poorly on a memory task. To get a more detailed, up-close view, you may decide to repeat the study using measures of memory that will allow you to isolate where memory is breaking down. Is the memory problem due to poor encoding, lack of rehearsal, slow search speed, failure to organize the material, or failure to take advantage of retrieval cues? Similarly, measures of different kinds of love may allow you to go beyond saying that a factor increases love, to finding out what type of love is increased by this factor.

To emphasize that component measures introduce new questions, consider research suggesting attitudes are composed of three different measurable dimensions: emotional, behavioral, and cognitive (Breckler, 1984). This finding raised many new questions. For starters, all the old questions that had been asked about attitudes had to be asked again for each of the three components. For example, although we knew about persuasive techniques that changed attitudes, we now had an opportunity to find out which component(s) were changed by each technique (Edwards, 1990; Millar & Millar, 1990). Similarly, although research suggested that men were just as difficult to persuade as women, new questions arose, such as "Is it easier to change emotional attitudes of men than women?" and "Is it easier to change cognitive attitudes of women than men?" Furthermore, there were questions about the relationship between the components, such as "Do changes in the emotional component bring about greater changes in the behavioral component than changing the cognitive component?" In short, when a component measure is introduced, all the old questions are asked again, except, instead of looking at a generic, global measure, psychologists try to answer them for each component, as well as trying to understand the relationship between the components (see figure 2.5).

Take Advantage of Measures of Entirely New Concepts

A new measuring instrument or measurement strategy may open up a new psychological frontier, thereby allowing any willing psychologist to be a pioneer. Many psychologists have stampeded into the new frontiers opened up by such newer and better mousetraps as the Skinner Box, the Memory Drum, the electroencephalogram (EEG), the Prisoner's Dilemma Game, the Bem Androgeny Scale, the Minnesota Multiphasic Personality Inventory (MMPI), the Buss Aggression Machine, measures of the order in which words are recalled, and various reaction time measures of recognition memory.

Valid measures of previously unmeasured concepts or behaviors make it relatively easy to do something that no one has done before. For instance, medical research institutes spend thousands of dollars to gain access to the newest measure. Such access allows these institutes to be the first to see how the measure is affected by such well-known variables as caffeine, diet, alcohol, and exercise. In addition, they can be among the first to discover how the measure correlates with other measures of psychological and physical fitness, as well as how it correlates with variables such as sex and age. Fortunately, new psychological measures are usually less expensive and more easily accessible than medical instruments. In fact, many of our newest measures are paper-and-pencil devices (e.g., psychological tests, interview forms, attitude scales). These paper-and-pencil measures can often be copied from journal articles or obtained from the article's author.

Unfortunately, not all psychological devices are so easily and cheaply obtained. Indeed, some of these measuring instruments have price tags that may be beyond your department's budget. To avoid the expense problem (and become famous to boot), invent a way of measuring a heretofore uninvestigated variable (see figure 2.6). Suggestions on developing measures will be discussed in the next chapter.

DOING A LITERATURE SEARCH

Clearly, doing a literature search can help you obtain research ideas (see table 2.4). But what if you already have many research ideas? Even then, you should still do a literature search. Without a literature search, you may unnecessarily and unintentionally repeat a study that has already been done. Without a literature search, you may invent crude measures when refined measures already exist. Without a literature search, you will be ignorant of how other people have approached and thought about similar problems. Therefore, to avoid reinventing the wheel, all good researchers conduct a thorough literature search before conducting their study (see table 2.16).

How can you conduct a literature search? Generally, the easiest way to start is to find a citation of an interesting finding in a textbook. You might begin with some of the newest general psychology texts and then move to new editions of more specialized texts. For example, if you are interested in cognition, you might look at general psychology texts and then examine cognition texts. Look up the studies that appear promising in the text's

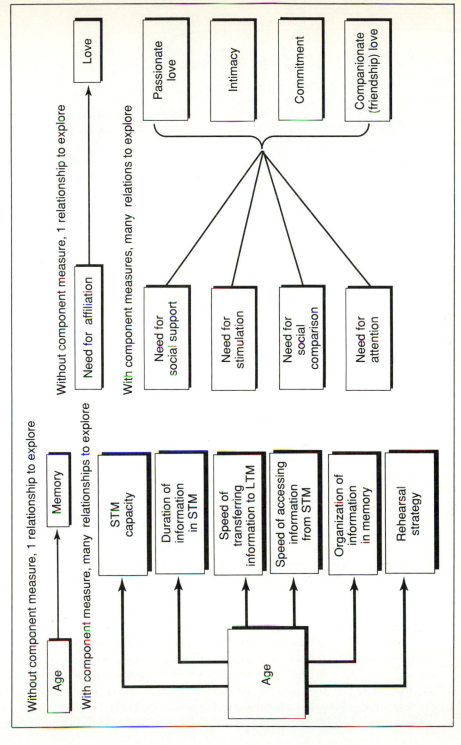

FIGURE 2.5 Two Examples of How Component Measures Generate New Relationships to Explore

FIGURE 2.6 New Measures Sometimes Produce Immense Amounts of Research

bibliography. Go to the library, read that study, and look up any interesting articles listed at the end of that article.

Once those leads are exhausted, you might consult more specialized recent books on your topic. These books may be listed in your library's card catalog or in its on-line computer catalog. In the event you cannot find recent texts in your field and your librarian does not have ads for publishers of books on current topics in psychology (American Psychological Association, Lawrence Erlbaum and Associates, and Sage Publications), consult *Books In Print* and order relevant books through interlibrary loan.

TABLE 2.14   Twenty-one Ways to Get Ideas by Searching the Literature

1. Find gaping omissions.
2. Repeat studies.
3. Do a study suggested by the journal article's authors.
4. Repeat the study with a different group of subjects.
5. Look for situational factors that may moderate the effect.
6. Look for factors that were not controlled.
7. Reduce the effects of expectancies.
8. Use more realistic amounts of the treatment factor.
9. Uncover the functional relationship.
10. Use more realistic stimulus materials.
11. See if another factor would have the same effect.
12. Bridge fields and try to find a practical implication of the research.
13. Look at the studies from a different level of analysis.
14. Look for patterns in conflicting studies.
15. Look for a factor's immediate relationship to other variables.
16. Look at long-term effects.
17. Look for "down the road" effects.
18. Repeat the study using a different measure of the same construct.
19. Repeat the study with a more sensitive way of detecting the effect.
20. Take advantage of "component" measures.
21. Take advantage of measures of entirely new concepts.

TABLE 2.15   Idea Generation Techniques Applicable to Common Sense, Theory, and Literature Searches

1. See if results would generalize to different subjects or settings.
2. Look for moderating variables that would either strengthen, weaken, or reverse the relationship between the variables. Asking "When does the opposite occur?" may help you think of moderators.
3. See if the effect could be applied to a practical problem.
4. See if you can more precisely state the relationship between the variables.
5. Reconcile contradictions between conflicting studies, theories, or common-sense expressions.
6. Examine variables that may mediate the hypothesized or observed relationship—that is, even if psychologists have documented a relationship between two behaviors or know that putting a person or animal in a certain situation causes a certain response, they may have very little evidence about the cognitive or physiological states that mediate the relationship. Consequently, you might either seek evidence that the physiological or cognitive changes they hypothesize are occurring or you may try to see if, by interfering with or intensifying the hypothesized mediating process, you can interfere with or intensify the relationship.

TABLE 2.16 Reasons to Do a Literature Review

1. To get a research idea.
2. To find operational definitions of your measures.
3. To determine whether your study has already been conducted.
4. To find a rationale for your prediction.
5. To see how your research idea might contribute to existing knowledge.

Also, see if your topic is described in any recent editions of *Annual Review of Psychology*. If you still cannot find any books, the American Psychological Association produces *PsychBooks* which reference and summarize recent books and chapters on psychological topics.

Once you have consulted these books, looked up articles they reference, and then looked up the articles that those books reference, you have a good start on your literature review. There is only one problem. You may be two or three years behind the times.

To become more current, you should look up your topic in subject indexes of recent volumes of *Psychological Abstracts*. The subject index tells where in the *Psychological Abstracts* you can find a short summary of articles related to your topic. For example, if you are looking at the index for volume 80 under reaction time and find 176 listed, you would go to volume 80 of the *Psychological Abstracts* and find the abstract numbered 176. If the abstract seems relevant, you would then go to the original source which is referenced in the abstract. You also should use the author index to see if the author of a study you have already found has recently published additional work in the field.

Another tactic is to find recent research that cites the studies you have identified as important. Articles that cite your key articles are probably relevant to your research project. But how do you find articles that cite your key studies? Fortunately, you do not have to go through the reference sections of the more than 70,000 articles published each year to determine which articles have cited a certain article. Other people have done that work for you and have published it as the *Social Sciences Citation Index* (see appendix B). For example, suppose you wanted to base your research on an article Bandura published in 1991. Naturally, you would want to find out if anyone else had followed up on that work. Therefore, you would look up Bandura in the most recent volumes of the *Citation Index* and search until you found the 1991 article. There, you would find a listing of recent articles that cited Bandura's 1991 article. You would then look up those articles.

In addition to looking up references, you might be able to save some time by doing a computerized search of the literature using sources such as "Psych Lit," "Psych Info," and "ERIC" (see appendix B). Finally, you might get the most recent articles by scanning the last several months of *Psychological Bulletin, Current Contents, Psych Scans,* and other journals that have published articles relevant to your proposed research (see table 2.17).

TABLE 2.17   How to Do a Literature Search

1. Consult general sources, e.g., introductory psychology texts or specialized texts.
2. Consult professional texts. You may be able to find good sources by (1) looking in *Books in Print,* (2) looking at *PsychBooks,* (3) seeing if library has *Annual Review of Psychology,* and (4) consulting card catalog.
3. Track down articles referenced in those books.
4. Read those articles and their reference sections. Track down research that they reference.
5. To see if the authors have done more recent research, look them up in the author index of *Psychological Abstracts.*
6. Look up topic in subject index of *Psychological Abstracts.*
7. See what recent articles have referenced your key articles by consulting the *Social Science Citation Index.*
8. Scan recent issues of journals where you have found previous articles related to your topic or that are general in scope (for example, *Psychological Bulletin, American Psychologist, Psychological Science, Psych Scans, Current Contents*).
9. Consider doing a computerized search of the literature.

CONVERTING AN IDEA INTO A RESEARCH HYPOTHESIS

If you apply our tips, you should have some research ideas, but you may not have a research hypothesis. Converting an idea into a workable research hypothesis is often a challenging task. However, you do need to state your idea in the form of a hypothesis. Therefore, the rest of this chapter is devoted to helping you generate a workable research hypothesis.

MAKE IT TESTABLE

When converting an idea to a hypothesis, you want to be sure that your hypothesis is testable. In general, a testable hypothesis has the same basic characteristics as a testable theory or of a verifiable bet. As with any bet, you must be able to define your terms. For example, if you bet "Gene will be in a bad mood today," you need some publicly observable way of ascertaining what a bad mood is. Similarly, if you hypothesize a relationship between two variables, you must be able to obtain operational definitions of your key variables. For example, if you plan to measure the effects of physical attractiveness on how much a person is liked, you must be able to objectively measure liking, and you must be able to define attractiveness according to publicly observable criteria.

Also, as with any bet, your prediction should be specific so that it is clear what patterns of results would indicate that your hypothesis "won" and what results would indicate that your hypothesis "lost." You do not want to do a study and then have to debate whether the results supported or refuted your hypothesis. Usually, the easiest way to avoid such disputes is to make your hypothesis as specific as possible. Therefore, when stating your hypothesis, specify not only a relationship between two or more variables, but also the *direction* of that relationship. Thus, rather than saying aggression will vary with temperature, it would be better to say increases in aggression will correspond to increases in temperature. Ideally, you would be even more specific. For example, you might predict that increasing the temperature from 80 to 90 degrees Fahrenheit will increase aggression more than increasing the temperature from 70 to 80 degrees. To check that your prediction is precise enough, ask yourself, "What kind of result would disconfirm my prediction?" and "What kind of result would confirm my prediction?" Then, either graph or describe your predicted results as well as results that would disconfirm your prediction.

By being precise, you can avoid making predictions that are so vague that no pattern of results will disprove them. Unlike some fortune tellers and unscrupulous gamblers, you want to be fair by giving yourself the opportunity to be proved wrong. Of course, you also want to give yourself the opportunity to be proved right. Consequently, you not only have to beware of making bets you cannot lose, but also bets you cannot win. In particular, you must be wary of one kind of bet you can never win—the **null hypothesis:** A prediction that there is no relationship between your variables. No pattern of results can support the null hypothesis. To illustrate, suppose you hypothesize no relationship between attraction and liking. Even if you find no relationship, you cannot say there isn't a relationship. You can only say you did not find the relationship. Failing to find something, whether it be your keys, a murder weapon, a planet, or a relationship is hardly proof that the thing does not exist.

BE SURE TO HAVE A RATIONALE

In addition to spelling out your prediction, you should spell out the rationale for your hypothesis. If you cannot think of a good reason why your hypothesis should prove correct, your hypothesis is probably a "bad bet." For example, if you hypothesized, without giving any rationale, that people would be more creative after drinking seven glasses of water—it is doubtful that your prediction would pan out. Instead, it would appear that you were simply going on a hopeless fishing expedition with little chance of catching anything. Therefore, always write out the reasons for making your prediction. Your rationale can come from theory, common sense, or the fact that related research has found similar findings.

DEMONSTRATE ITS RELEVANCE

In addition to having a reasonable chance of turning out, you should explain how your research fits in with existing theory and research or how it solves a practical problem. Scientists frown on doing research to find isolated bits of trivia. For example, without any other rationale, doing a study to show that alcohol decreases ping-pong performance is meaningless, except possibly to people who bet on ping-pong in bars.

If your hypothesis is testable, reasonable, and relevant, then you should still ask two additional questions. First, can *you* test it? Sometimes, you may not have the skills or the resources to test it. For example, testing some hypotheses in physiological psychology may require equipment or surgical skills that you do not possess. Second, should your hypothesis be tested? That is, can the hypothesis be tested in an ethical manner?

Get Approval from Your Professor

You have a serious obligation to make sure your study is ethical. Clearly, you do not have the right to physically or psychologically harm another. Reading chapter 13 and appendix A can help you decide whether your study can be done in an ethical manner. However, because conducting ethical research is so important, do not make the decision to conduct research without consulting others. Specifically, *never conduct a study without your professor's approval!* (See table 2.18.)

In their present form, some of your ideas may be impractical or unethical. However, with a little ingenuity, many of your ideas can be converted into workable research hypotheses. Basically, many practical and ethical obstacles can be overcome by making the key variables more abstract, constructing a smaller scale model of the situation, using animals as subjects, toning down the strength of the manipulation, not using manipulations, or finding ways to operationalize the crucial variables.

TABLE 2.18   Quesions to Ask about a Potential Hypothesis

1. Can it be proved wrong?
   a. Can you obtain operational definitions of the variables?
   b. Is the prediction specific?
2. Can it be proved right?
   a. Are you predicting you will find an effect or a difference?
   b. Beware the null hypothesis.
3. Are there logical reasons for expecting the prediction to be correct?
   a. Is it predicted by theory?
   b. Is it consistent with past research findings?
   c. Does it follow from logic or common sense?
4. Would the results of the test of your prediction be relevant to
   a. previous research?
   b. existing theory?
   c. a practical problem?
5. Is it practical and ethical to test your prediction?
   a. Do you have physical and financial resources to conduct tests of your idea?
   b. Would testing the hypothesis not cause physical or psychological harm to subjects (see appendix A)?
   c. Do you have approval from your professor?

Ways of Making Your Ideas More Ethical and Practical

To understand how these principles can turn even the most impractical and unethical idea into a viable research hypothesis, consider the following hypothesis: Receiving severe beatings causes one to be a murderer. How could we convert this idea into a workable research hypothesis? (See table 2.19.)

Make Variables More General

One possibility is to make your key variables more abstract. That is, you might view murder as a more specific instance of **aggression.** Similarly, you might view beating as a specific instance of either aggression, pain, or punishment. Thus, you now have three research hypotheses that have been studied in controlled settings: "aggression leads to more aggression," "pain causes aggression," and "punishment causes aggression."

Use Smaller Scale Models of the Situation

Of course, you are not going to have human subjects hitting each other to measure aggression. Instead, you may give subjects an opportunity to destroy something that supposedly belongs to the other person, an opportunity to write a negative evaluation, an opportunity to press a button which supposedly (but doesn't really) deliver a shock to the other person.

Smaller scale models of the situation have not only ethical, but practical advantages. For example, if you are interested in the effects of temperature on aggression, you cannot manipulate the temperature outside. However, you can manipulate the temperature in a room. Similarly, you cannot manipulate the size of a crowd at a college football game to see the effect of crowd size on performance. However, you can manipulate audience size at a dart contest that you sponsor. By using a dart contest, your audience-size hypothesis is not only testable, but also practical. For instance, if audience size has an effect, you could probably find it by varying the size of the audience from zero (when you are hiding behind a one-way mirror) to three (yourself and two friends).

Once you have a small scale model of a phenomenon, you can test all kinds of ideas that previously seemed impossible to test. For example, can you imagine using the dart contest situation to test the effects of audience involvement or size of reward on performance?

Because smaller scale models of situations are so valuable, researchers often do a literature review to find out if someone else has already made a smaller scale model of the

---

TABLE 2.19 Ways of Making a Test of a Research Idea More Practical and Ethical

1. Make variables more general.
2. Use smaller scale models of the situation.
3. Use less extreme manipulations.
4. Do not manipulate variables.
5. Carefully screen potential subjects.

---

phenomenon. That is, just as an airplane designer may use a wind tunnel to test new airplane designs, researchers may use someone else's scale model of a situation to see if their ideas fly.

Carefully Screen Potential Subjects

In some research, you might decrease the ethical problems by choosing subjects who would be unlikely to be harmed by the manipulation. Therefore, if you were to do a frustration-aggression study, you might only use subjects who

1. were, according to a recently administered personality profile, well adjusted;
2. were physically healthy;
3. volunteered after knowing about the degree of discomfort they would experience;
4. were fully aware they could withdraw from the study at any time without any penalty; and
5. will be fully debriefed about the study immediately after they finish participating in the study.

Alternatively, you might use animal subjects rather than human subjects to minimize harm. Using animal subjects has the added advantages of allowing you to control aspects of their environment. For example, if you wanted to manipulate punishment in childhood, you could make sure that some rats received punishment from early infancy to adulthood. Such a manipulation would not only be unethical, but impossible with human subjects.

Use "Moderate" Manipulations

In addition to restricting what subjects can be in the study, you may also want to restrict what levels of the manipulation you use. For example, if you were to use frustration to see its effects on aggression, you would want to use only very low levels of frustration.

Do Not Manipulate Variables

Finally, you may decide not to manipulate the variables at all. To understand the basic advantages and disadvantages of this approach, let's return to the original hypothesis: Receiving severe beatings causes one to be a murderer. You might pursue this idea by interviewing murderers and non-murderers to see whether murderers were more likely to have been beaten as children. Of course, even if you found that murderers were more likely than non-murderers to have been beaten, your results would not necessarily mean that the beatings caused the murders. Beatings may have no impact on murders. Instead, murderers may only say they were beaten as children to get sympathy. Or, murderers may have been beaten more than non-murderers because, even as children, murderers were more aggressive and more disobedient than non-murderers. Or, perhaps children who are beaten tend to come from poorer families and poorer families tend to live in environments that encourage murder. People who live in these environments may be more likely to murder, regardless of whether or not they were beaten. Although interviewing would not allow you to discover whether beatings *cause* children to become murderers, it might allow you to address a related research hypothesis: "Are murderers more likely to have been beaten by their parents than non-murderers?".

CONCLUDING REMARKS

In this chapter, you have learned how to generate research ideas from intuition, theory, and previous research. You now have hypotheses about how two or more variables are related. However, before you can test these ideas, you must find a way to obtain or generate operational definitions of your variables. To help you with this task, we wrote chapter 3.

SUMMARY

1. The purpose of scientific research is to test ideas.
2. Research ideas may come from existing research, from intuition, or from theory.
3. To generate research hypotheses, first come up with an idea about behavior. Then, determine if you can convert this idea into a testable hypothesis.
4. Science allows us to test our own intuitions as well as benefit from the intuitions of others.
5. Creative ideas are the product of persistence.
6. Analyzing literature, songs, tabloids, commercials, practical problems, honest differences of opinion, old sayings, and even your own difficulty in generating ideas are productive ways of developing research ideas.
7. Like intuition, theories are good sources of ideas. Unlike intuition, theories are formally stated and internally consistent.
8. Hypothetical constructs are abstract variables that cannot be directly observed (love, learning, thirst, etc.). Researchers can deal with abstract constructs by devising **operational definitions**: concrete ways (recipes, if you will) of manipulating or measuring abstract constructs.
9. Testable theories make specific predictions and have variables that can be operationalized.
10. You can generate hypotheses from a theory by testing the theory's core assumptions, seeing how well it holds in extreme cases, checking its precision, applying the theory to novel or practical situations, or comparing two theories that make opposing predictions.
11. Scientists like theories that are broad in scope, parsimonious, and provocative.
12. Theories evolve and change as a result of adapting to new findings.
13. Never do a study without first doing a literature review.
14. Never do a study without first getting your professor's permission.
15. The null hypothesis is that there is no relationship between two variables. While it can be disproven it cannot be proven.
16. A research hypothesis must be testable and must be testable in an ethical manner.

17. Even the most impractical and unethical of ideas may be converted into a practical and ethical hypothesis if you create models of the phenomenon rather than studying the phenomenon itself, make critical variables more abstract, carefully screen your subjects and tone down or eliminate your manipulation.

KEY TERMS

"critical" studies
deduction
double-blind technique
hypothesis

hypothetical construct
induction
null hypothesis
operational definition

parsimonious
straw theory
theory

EXERCISES

1. What are the characteristics of a good hypothesis? How are the characteristics of a good hypothesis similar to the characteristics of a good theory?
2. How are the qualities of a good theory similar to the qualities of a good answer to an essay test?
3. Is theory or intuition more valuable in generating useful research? Support your conclusions by listing the strengths and weaknesses of each.
4. Why do scientists like theories?
5. Why should you always do a literature review before conducting a study?
6. What similarities are there between getting ideas from theory, research, and common sense?
7. What is the difference between deduction and induction?
8. In terms of the null hypothesis, what is wrong with the following research conclusions?
   a. There is no difference in outcome among the different psychological therapies.
   b. There is no difference in effectiveness between generic and name brand drugs.
   c. Viewing television violence is not related to aggression.
   d. Nutrasweet has no side effects when used by the normal population.
   e. There are no gender differences in emotional responsiveness.
9. Using the "Twelve Ways to Tap Your Intuition" (table 2.5), generate at least five research ideas. If you get stuck, you may wish to consult table 2.3.
10. a. List at least four ways to use a theory to generate research ideas.
    b. Apply one of those principles to a theory such as Bandura's social learning theory, Skinner's theory of operant conditioning, Solomon's opponent process

theory, learned helplessness theory, Piaget's theory, dual memory theory, cognitive dissonance theory, attribution theory, equity theory, reactance theory, or evolutionary theory. If you are having trouble, you may want to consult one or more of the sources in table 2.8.

11. Generate five hypotheses from published reports of research. Hint: You may find it useful to consult tables 2.14, 2.17, and appendix B.

3

Measuring and Manipulating Variables

Overview

Obtaining Measures

Using a previously developed measure

Inventing measures

General Issues in Validity

Valid measures of behavior versus valid measures of mental states

Reliability

Reducing observer bias: Seeing what we hope or expect to see

Beyond Valid Measurements of Behavior: Construct Validity

Reactivity biases

Convergent validation strategies

Discriminant validation strategies: Showing that you are not measuring the wrong construct

Internal consistency: Are all items measuring the same thing?

Content analysis: Is everything represented?

Summary of construct validity

Selecting the Best Measure for Your Study

Sensitivity: Will the measure be able to detect the differences you need to detect?

Scales of Measurement: Will the measure allow you to make the kinds of comparisons you need to make?

Ethical and practical considerations

Manipulating Variables

Common threats to validity

Evidence used to argue for validity

The value of "powerful" manipulations

Tradeoffs among three common types of manipulations

Manipulating variables: A summary

Concluding Remarks

Summary

Key Terms

Exercises

"Science begins with measurement."

Lord Kelvin

OVERVIEW

In chapter 2, we discussed how to generate research hypotheses. If you took our suggestions to heart, you have several interesting research ideas. But, before you can test any of your ideas about how certain variables are related, you must generate *operational definitions* of those variables. For example, if you were to test the idea "bliss causes ignorance," you must define the vague, general, abstract, and invisible concepts "ignorance" and "bliss" in a clear, specific, concrete, and visible way. That is, you must spell out the exact procedures you would follow to create "bliss" and the exact procedures you would follow to measure "ignorance."

Without operational definitions, scientists could not repeat each other's studies to verify findings. Without knowing the "recipe" you followed to create "bliss," scientists would not be able to repeat your study. Without a concrete, observable way of measuring "ignorance," researchers would not know whether they were seeing the same "ignorance" you saw. Clearly, having publicly observable, systematic ways to measure and manipulate variables is crucial to research.

Because all research involves measuring variables, this chapter will focus on measurement. We will begin by showing you how to find or create measures of the variable(s) you wish to measure. Then, we will show you how to assess—and, if necessary, improve—the degree to which your measure really is an unbiased, objective, reliable, and accurate measure of *behavior.* Next, we will discuss the special challenges involved in measuring invisible mental states such as love, hunger, and motivation. You will see that accurately measuring a mental state involves not only getting an accurate measure of a behavior, but also being sure the observable behavior you measure is an accurate indicator of the invisible mental state you wish to assess. Finally, we will show you how to choose the right measure for your study.

After discussing how to choose operational definitions of variables you want to measure, we will turn our attention to choosing operational definitions of variables you may want to manipulate. You will see that many of the principles of choosing and validating measures also apply to choosing and validating manipulations. That is, many of the same principles and concerns you would have if you were to measure happiness would also apply if you were to try to manipulate happiness.

In short, at this very instant, coming up with objective, publicly observable ways to measure and manipulate variables may seem like pulling a rabbit out of a hat: it is magical, mysterious, impossible, and impressive. Admittedly, there is something impressive about measuring constructs as abstract and as subjective as love, motivation, shyness, religiosity, or attention span. However, by the end of this chapter, you will understand that generating valid operational definitions of variables is more a matter of logic than of magic.

OBTAINING MEASURES

There are two basic ways to obtain a measure. You can use one that someone else developed or you can invent your own. Since inventing and refining a measure is a challenging task, your first step should be to see if any suitable measures exist. As you can see from table 3.1, well-established operational definitions exist for many variables. Furthermore, even if you found that no suitable operational definitions of your variable exist, the time spent looking for measures would not necessarily be wasted. What you learn about existing measures' strengths and weaknesses may help you in developing your own measure.

USING A PREVIOUSLY DEVELOPED MEASURE

To find a previously developed measure, you should conduct a literature review of relevant books, journal articles, and other manuscripts. A good first step in conducting your literature review is to consult an introductory psychology textbook. For example, if you are interested in measuring love, turn to the back of your text and look up "love" in the index. The index will refer you to pages in the texts where love is discussed. You will find, embedded in these discussions, the names of researchers who have published love research. Look up these researchers' names in your textbook's bibliography to find out where they published their articles. Next, go to the library and read their articles. In their articles, the researchers will describe, in great detail, how they operationalized love. The researchers may also explain why they chose to operationalize love the way they did.

After digesting these articles, track down the articles they reference in their bibliographies. Then, to get more recent measures, consult *Psychological Abstracts, Social Sciences Index, Social Science Citation Index, Current Contents,* and computerized searches (see appendix B). After looking at these sources and the sources listed in table 3.2, you will soon read enough to either (1) identify other well-accepted measures of

TABLE 3.1 Selected Operational Definitions of Popular Concepts	
CONCEPT	OPERATIONAL DEFINITION(S)
Memory	Number of Words Recalled
Motivation	Rate of Bar Pressing
Learning	Time it Takes Rat to Get to End of Maze
Personality	Score on Standard Personality Test Such as the MMPI or Cattell's 16 PF
Arousal	Heart Rate, Blood Pressure, Respiration Rate, Galvanic Skin Response
Attitude	Number Circled on a Five-Point Attitude Scale

TABLE 3.2   Common Sources of Measures

Beere, C. A. (1979). *Women and women's issues: A handbook of tests and measures.* San Francisco: Jossey-Bass.

Buros, O. K. (1978). *The eighth mental measurements yearbook.* Lincoln: University of Nebraska, Buros Institute of Mental Measurements.

Chun, K., Cobb, S., & French, J. R. P. (1976). *Measures for psychological assessment.* Ann Arbor: University of Michigan, Institute for Social Research.

Comrey, A. L., Backer, T. E., & Glaser, E. M. (1973). *A sourcebook for mental health measures.* Los Angeles: Human Interaction Research Institute.

Goldman, B. A., & Busch, J. C. (1978). *Directory of unpublished experimental mental measures, Vol. 2.* New York: Human Sciences Press.

Johnson, O. G. (1976). *Tests and measurements in child development,* handbook 2, vols. 1 and 2. San Francisco: Jossey-Bass.

Robinson, J. P., Rusk, J., and Head, K. (1968). *Measures of political attitudes.* Ann Arbor: University of Michigan, Institute for Social Research.

Robinson, J. P., & Shaver, P. R. (1973). *Measures of social psychological attitudes.* Ann Arbor: University of Michigan, Institute for Social Research.

Shaw, M. E., & Wright, J. M. (1967). *Scales for the measurement of attitudes.* New York: McGraw-Hill.

love, (2) learn that their measure is pretty well accepted, or (3) determine there are no well-accepted measures of love.

INVENTING MEASURES

Rather than copying someone else's measure, you could invent your own measure. Inventing your own measure is easiest when you are interested in observable behavior for its own sake. For example, if you were interested in measuring a behavior such as cigarette smoking, then figuring out what behavior you want to measure is fairly straightforward. Your challenge is to measure that behavior accurately and to determine what aspect of the behavior you wish to measure. Do you want to measure the behavior's

1. frequency (total of ten cigarettes smoked)
2. rate (rate of two cigarettes per hour)
3. duration (e.g., smoked for two hours)
4. intensity (how much smoke was inhaled with each puff)
5. accuracy (errors)
6. **latency:** how long it takes for the behavior to emerge (reaction time or time it took before the subject lit up the first cigarette)

Questions about what aspects of behavior to measure have to wait if your ultimate goal is to tap an invisible mental concept such as love or memory. In that case, before deciding on what aspect of behavior to measure, you must first find a behavior that is a sign, a symptom, or an indicator of your concept. The behavior could be

1. a *verbal behavior* (the answer to the question "How much do you love Mary?")
2. a *nonverbal behavior* (how long a subject gazes into Mary's eyes)
3. a *physiological response* (increase in blood pressure when Mary walks into the room)

Once you think of a behavior that taps the construct, you can then determine whether you want to measure the behavior's frequency, rate, duration, intensity, latency, or accuracy. Before you start determining how often, how fast, how long, how hard, how suddenly, or how accurately a behavior is performed, you must first have a behavior that reflects your concept. Fortunately, you can generate verbal, nonverbal, and physiological behaviors that may tap your construct if you take advantage of three important resources: definitions, theories, and intuition.

Definitions

When trying to invent a measure, your first step should be to use a dictionary and an introductory textbook to look up the definition of your concept. Until you know what it is you want to measure, you will have a hard time measuring it.

Not only may reading textbook and dictionary definitions give you a clearer picture of what it is you want to measure, but they also may give you a clearer picture of what you do not want to measure. For example, reading definitions of love might help you realize you want to measure mature love and you want to avoid unintentionally measuring concepts such as liking or infatuation.

Besides helping you define exactly what it is you want to measure, ordinary dictionaries, psychological dictionaries, and glossaries may provide hints about how to measure the concept. For instance, the *Random House Dictionary* (1990) defines love in several ways, including "sexual desire or its gratification" and "a feeling of warm personal attachment." These definitions suggest that frequency of sex or reports of feelings of attachment may be promising operational definitions of love.

Theory

Like dictionaries, theories may suggest ways of measuring its constructs. Thus, if you are interested in measuring a concept, you should look at different theories of that concept. Careful questioning of these theories will give you ideas about what kinds of measures to use. For example, if you read a theory of love, you might determine whether, according to the theory, a person is aware of being in love. If people are unaware of being in love, asking people how much they love someone is useless. If, on the other hand, people are aware of how much love they feel, then asking them direct questions about the extent of their love might be useful. You might also determine whether the theory mentions any physiological or behavioral changes that accompany love. If you ask these questions of several theories, you will have several measures. In fact, as you can see from box 3.1, we asked these questions of just one theory of love and came away with several measures. (For another example, see box 3.2.)

BOX 3.1 An Example of a Lovely Theory that Tells Us How to Measure Various Concepts

Rafael Frank's (1984) theory of love tells us how love can and cannot be measured. According to the theory, you *cannot* accurately measure love by asking a person how much they love someone because people simply do not know the extent of their love.

According to the theory, there are two ways to measure love. One way can be used only if the person loses their loved one. According to the theory, love can be accurately assessed by determining how long it takes for the person's grief to become half as intense. For example, suppose John were jilted by Linda. Furthermore, suppose that the day he was jilted his grief was a "90" on a zero to one hundred scale. The time it takes for John's grief to go to half that ("45") will tell us how much in love he was with Linda. If it takes two days, he was not deeply in love. If it takes six years, he was.

The theory also says that love can be assessed by the following formula:

$$\text{Love} = \text{liking} \times \text{maturity/dependency} \times 20 \text{ (sexual attraction)/age}$$

Because zero times any number is zero, this formula tells us that if liking, maturity, or sexual attraction equals zero, then love equals zero. Thus, if Bruno does not like Broomhilda, he does not love her. Likewise, if Bruno is not at all mature, Bruno cannot love Broomhilda.

The theory tells us not only how to measure love, but also how to measure the other concepts in the formula. For example, the theory states that liking may be measured by simply asking people how much they like someone; by having them rate how much time they want to spend with that person; rating how comfortable they feel with the other person; how similar they perceive the other to be to themselves in terms of values, respect, and admiration; how many topics they can discuss; the number of activities they do together; and how favorably they rate the other person.

According to the theory, maturity can be measured by assessing the degree to which the person is concerned with people or things other than oneself, an internal locus of control, and the ability to delay gratification.

Dependence, according to the theory, can be measured by the degree to which one could sleep alone, one's self-confidence, and one's ability to do things alone, such as approaching a stranger to talk, inviting people over for dinner, or going to a restaurant.

According to the theory, sexual attraction can be easily measured in physiological terms.

Thus, as you can see below, asking questions of the theory gives us ideas about how to—and how not to—measure love.

QUESTION	THEORY'S ANSWER
Can we use a self-rating scale to measure love?	No, because people are not consciously aware of the extent of their love.
Can we use a disguised measure to assess love?	Yes, if a person loses their loved one. Love can be assessed by determining how long it takes for the person's grief to become half as intense.
What other ways can you use to measure love?	By using this formula: Love = liking × maturity/dependency × 20 (sexual attraction)/age

Source: From "A Half-life Theory of Love" by R. Frank, 1984. Paper presented at the 92d Annual Convention of the American Psychological Association. Adapted by permission of the author.

BOX 3.2 Theory Has Implications for Measures

What Is Successful Therapy?

Psychoanalytic Theory: Better memory for early childhood events, fewer errors of speech (Freudian slips), less self-destructive behavior, feeling less anxiety.

Rogers's Self Theory: Less of a difference between what the person thinks he or she is and what the person wants to be. A Q-sort is used to measure difference between the ideal and real self.

Maslow: Being less dependent on others, having a sense of humor, being concerned about other people, being able to laugh at oneself, having very close interpersonal relationships, being happy to be alive, feeling energetic.

Gestalt Psychology (Perls): Being more spontaneous, being more concerned about the present, being less inhibited by others.

Reality Therapy (Glaser): More accepting of society's norms, taking responsibility for your own behavior.

Behavior Therapy: Decreasing the undesired behavior, increasing the incidence of more desirable behavior.

Intuition

The same questions you ask of theory, you can ask of your intuition. Thus, if you were trying to measure love, you might ask yourself how someone in love would talk and act differently from someone who was not in love.

To help yourself articulate the behavioral signs or symptoms of love, think of three people: a person who is very much in love, a person who is slightly in love, and a person who is not at all in love. Then, act as though you are describing the behaviors of these different people to a skeptical stranger—a stranger who wants behavioral evidence that your perceptions of these people are correct. You might start by discussing how the person who is deeply in love is now bumping into things, spending three hours in the bathroom, smiling more, speaking to only one other person, singing songs, not eating, and not sleeping. Next, you might move to describing the person's verbal behavior: claiming to be in love, claiming that it's great to be alive, and using "cute" words when in the presence of their partner. Finally, you might address physiological symptoms of their condition: increased heart rate, higher blood pressure, or nervous stomach.

GENERAL ISSUES IN VALIDITY

After conducting a literature review and consulting definitions, theory, and intuition, you should have several potential measures. But how do you know if any of these measures are **valid**: measuring what you think they are measuring?

VALID MEASURES OF BEHAVIOR VERSUS VALID MEASURES OF MENTAL STATES

How you demonstrate that your measure is valid depends on *what* you intend to measure. If you are trying to measure a concrete, observable behavior like cigarette smoking, then establishing validity is relatively easy. You need only to accurately measure behavior. If, on the other hand, you are trying to measure an invisible, mental construct, establishing validity may be more difficult (see box 3.3). You not only will have to accurately measure behavior but will also be able to accurately infer the construct from the behavior (see figure 3.1).

To illustrate the additional challenges of trying to measure a construct, consider two researchers who are both measuring the number of cigarettes subjects smoke. The first researcher is trying to find ways of getting people to stop smoking and is therefore only interested in cigarette smoking for its own sake. The second researcher is not interested in cigarette smoking for its own sake, but only as a means to an end. Specifically, she is only interested in smoking as an indicator of nervousness. In other words, because she cannot measure the invisible mental state of nervousness directly, she hopes to *infer* nervousness from smoking behavior.

The first researcher can establish validity merely by establishing that he is really

How can we measure someone's unconscious mind, a mind that they themselves do not know? Here are some measures of the unconscious. We will let you judge their validity.

1. Remembering events under hypnosis that you could not recall before
2. Failure to recall important events, even under the influence of sodium pentothal
3. Freudian slips
4. Symbolism of dreams
5. Inability to remember early childhood
6. Having strong feelings toward therapist
7. Having long pauses or quickly changing the subject while associating
8. Unusual response to word association games. For instance, "mother" to the word "sex" or not responding at all to the word "father"
9. Analyzing self-destructive behavior
10. Feeling anxiety for no apparent reason

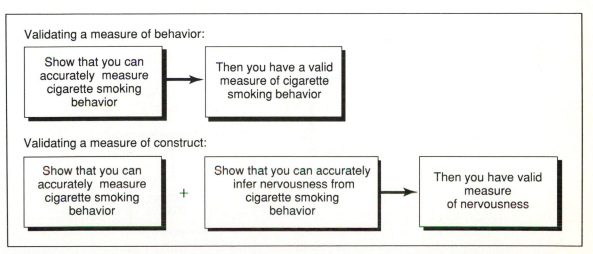

FIGURE 3.1: Validating a Measure of a Construct Usually Involves at Least One More Step Than Validating a Measure of Behavior

measuring smoking behavior. The second researcher, on the other hand, must establish two things: (1) that he has accurately measured smoking behavior, and (2) that he can accurately *infer* nervousness from the number of cigarettes a person smokes.

In short, if you are interested in measuring behavior as a way of getting a clue to the subject's mental state, establishing validity is more complex than if you are simply trying to establish that you are measuring behavior. However, regardless of whether you measure a behavior because you are interested in that behavior or whether you measure it only because you think it will let you tap an abstract mental construct, the first step to establishing validity is the same—you must accurately measure that behavior.

As we mentioned, establishing that you are accurately measuring a behavior is relatively easy. For example, if you are directly observing smoking behavior, there are only two ways that you could go wrong.

First, your measurements would be off in some systematic way if your study was victimized by **observer bias:** observers seeing or recording what they expect or hope subjects are doing rather than what subjects are actually doing. For example, after a smoking treatment was introduced, observers might become less likely to observe or record that a subject was smoking. They might also become much stricter about what they considered "smoking one cigarette." That is, before the treatment was introduced, taking one puff from a cigarette might have been counted as smoking an entire cigarette, but now "only one puff" is not considered smoking. In this case, observer bias would be systematically pushing cigarette smoking scores in a given direction: down. By decreasing the average smoking score, observer bias may lead us to believe that our cigarette-smoking treatment worked, even if it did not.

Second, measurements could be off due to unsystematic, random error (see figure 3.2). That is, rather than push or bias the scores in a consistent direction, random error

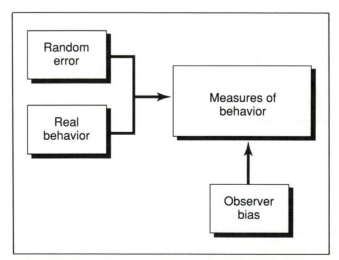

FIGURE 3.2: Measures of Behavior May Reflect More Than Just Behavior

erratically inflates some scores while deflating others. Consequently, unlike observer bias, random error may not change the overall, average score. However, random error does cause individual measurements to be erratic and less accurate than they would otherwise be.

RELIABILITY

If you were to weigh a small amount of gold three times, you would prefer to get the same measurements all three times. That is, you want your measurements to be **reliable**: stable, consistent. If you did not get the same results each time, you would take steps to correct the situation. You might find a more reliable scale, be more careful about reading the scale, or you might move the scale inside, away from the gusts of winds that could be affecting your measurements.

This example demonstrates that you intuitively realize three important principles. First, one reason you may be getting inconsistent, unreliable readings is random error. Second, the more your measure is affected by the fickle winds of chance, the less it can be affected by what you want to measure (the gold). Third, you can—and should—take steps to reduce the effects of random error.

These principles apply not only to measuring gold, but to measuring behavior. If your measurements of behavior are reliable, then you can be confident that your measurements are not unduly influenced by **random error**: chance fluctuations.

Determining If a Measure Has Adequate Reliability

Clearly, you do not want your measurements to be wildly bounced around by the erratic winds of chance. Consequently, when deciding whether to use a measure, you want to know whether it is strongly contaminated by chance.

Perhaps the most obvious way to find out the degree to which a measure produces consistent results is to obtain its **test-retest reliability.** As the name suggests, test-retest reliability requires subjects to be tested and then retested. The test-retest coefficient is based on how well subjects' scores on the first measurement correspond to their scores on the second measurement. Usually, test-retest correlations range between +.30 (poor reliability) to +.98 (excellent reliability). However, it is conceivable to get any number from 0.00 to +1.00.[1] A test-retest coefficient of zero would mean there was absolutely no relationship between scores subjects got the first time and scores they got the second time. A coefficient of +1.00, on the other hand, would mean there was a perfect correspondence between the first and second time of measurement—all those who scored high the first time also scored high the second time.

If you are examining a previously published measure, the test-retest reliability coefficient may have already been calculated for you. The measure's test-retest reliability coefficient may be cited in the original research report, in the test's manual, or in *Mental Measurements Yearbook* (Buros, 1978).

[1]The test-retest reliability coefficient is not a correlation coefficient. Instead, it is the square of the test-retest reliability (Anastasi, 1982).

Improving Reliability by Reducing Random Error

If you find or suspect that a measure has low reliability, what can you do? Clearly, one possibility is to search for or invent another measure. A second possibility is to improve the measure's reliability. The two easiest ways to improve reliability are to make observers more consistent and to make sure the measure is administered in a more consistent way (see figure 3.3).

Determining if Random Observer Error Is a Problem

If a measure appears unreliable, the problem may be due to the human observer. Attention lapses, random perceptual and judgment errors, carelessness in recording observations, and differences among observers on how behaviors are rated, can all contribute to random observer error.

Looking for Potential Sources of Random Observer Error

To determine whether the unreliability is due to random observer error, you might begin by determining the degree to which human judgment is involved. If all the observers do is score a multiple-choice test, you would not be worried about excessive random observer error. If the observers have to count behaviors, you would want to make sure that the researcher had clearly defined what constituted an instance of a behavior. For example, if the researcher defined the behavior so that all the observers had to do was count certain clear-cut behaviors (number of bar presses, number of horn honks, etc.), you would not be overly concerned with random observer error. However, if the observers had to categorize behavior by putting some qualitative label on it (low, medium, high; good, bad; fair, unfair), you would want the investigators to give some indication about the degree to which observers who saw the same behavior rated it similarly.

Getting Evidence of Random Observer Error

Typically, the researchers would have two or more observers *independently* (without talking to one another) rate the same behaviors. The researchers would then compare how different raters judged the same behavior (see figure 3.4). Sometimes, the researchers

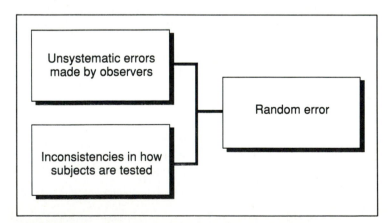

FIGURE 3.3: Primary Sources of Random Error

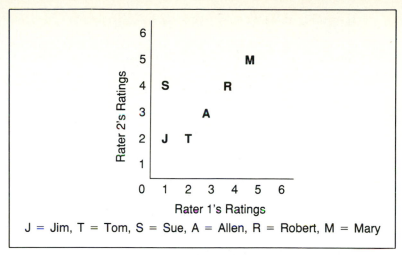

FIGURE 3.4: Graph of How Rater 1's Ratings of Six Subjects Might Relate to How Rater 2 Rated the Same Six Subjects

would simply report **inter-judge agreement**: the percentage of times the raters agree. For example, the researchers might report that the raters agreed 98 percent of the time.

Often, researchers will report another index of the degree to which different raters give similar ratings: **inter-observer reliability**. To obtain inter-observer reliability, researchers calculate a correlation coefficient between the different raters' judgments of the same behavior and then square that correlation.[2]

Like overall reliability coefficients, inter-observer reliability coefficients can range from 0 to +1. An inter-observer reliability coefficient around zero (0.00 to +.20) indicates there is virtually no relationship between the observers' ratings. Knowing how one observer rated a behavior gives you almost no idea about how the other observer rated the same behavior (see figure 3.5).

Because observers usually agree to some extent, and journals usually require a high degree of inter-rater reliability, you will almost never see a published study report an inter-observer reliability coefficient below +.60. Therefore, when reading a study, your question will not be: "Did the observers agree?" but "To what extent did the observers agree?" Generally, you will expect inter-observer reliability coefficients of around .90. (See figure 3.6.)

---

[2]There are two main reasons for squaring the correlation coefficient. First, it allows researchers to directly compare observer reliability with the test-retest reliability (which is also a squared correlation coefficient). Second, squaring the correlation coefficient gives the percentage of variation in scores that is **not** due to random observer error. That is, subtracting these coefficients from 100 percent gives you the percentage of variation that is due to random error. Thus, inter-observer reliability of .80 tells you that 20 percent of the variation in scores is due to random observer error (100 – 80 = 20). Similarly, if you also know that test-retest reliability coefficient is .70, you realize that 30 percent of the total variations in scores are due to random error (100 – 70 = 30). Thus, without doing any sophisticated calculations, you realize that ⅔ (20%/30%) of the measure's unreliability is due to random observer error. Therefore, you would know that if you could substantially reduce random observer error, the measure would be fairly reliable.

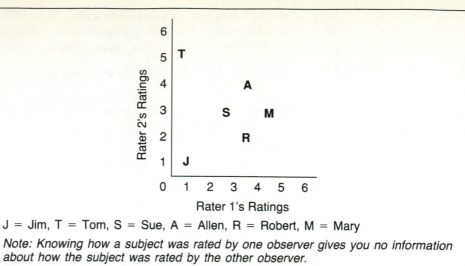

FIGURE 3.5: Graph Indicating a Near Zero Inter-Rater Reliability Coefficient between Rater 1's Ratings of Six Subjects and Rater 2's Ratings of the Same Six Subjects

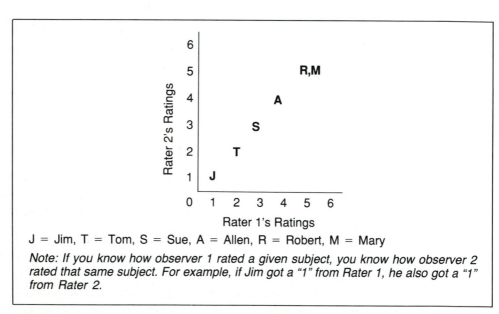

J = Jim, T = Tom, S = Sue, A = Allen, R = Robert, M = Mary

Note: If you know how observer 1 rated a given subject, you know how observer 2 rated that same subject. For example, if Jim got a "1" from Rater 1, he also got a "1" from Rater 2.

FIGURE 3.6: Graph Indicating a High Inter-Rater Reliability Coefficient between Rater 1's Ratings of Six Subjects and Rater 2's Ratings of the Same Six Subjects

Reducing Random Error Due to Observer

If you find low inter-rater agreement or suspect a high degree of random error due to observers, one obvious alternative is to use another measure. Another, almost equally obvious tactic is to reduce random observer errors by simplifying or eliminating the job of the human observer. Specifically, a researcher could

1. use machines rather than humans to observe and record behavior
2. simplify the observer's task by using objective measures such as multiple-choice tests
3. ask observers to count behavior rather than judge its intensity
4. emphasize to observers that they are to record and judge observable behavior rather than invisible psychological states
5. videotape subjects' behavior so observers can recheck their original observations
6. carefully define your categories so that all observations will be interpreted according to a consistent, uniform set of criteria
7. make recording observations as simple and as undemanding to memory as possible by using checklists, tape recorders, or other machines such as counters
8. train raters
9. motivate raters
10. use only those raters who were consistent during training

Reduce Random Error Due to Measurement Situation

Just as random observer error can hurt the reliability of your observations, so too can random variations in the testing environment. Therefore, we should try to keep the testing environment the same from one data gathering session to the next. Random changes in noise levels, room temperature, or how the instructions are given, may result in unwanted changes in subjects' behaviors.

In the abstract, the key to stopping random fluctuations in the measurement situation from causing fluctuations in the subjects' behaviors is simple: administer the measure in the same way every time. Although you may not be able to administer the measure in exactly the same way and under the exact same conditions each time, you should strive to do so. Ideally, you would test all your subjects in the same soundproof, temperature-controlled setting. At the very least, you should write out a detailed description of how you are going to test your subjects and stick to those procedures. For example, you would make sure all subjects got the same instructions by writing and you would make sure all subjects got the same instructions. To further standardize procedures, you might put instructions and measures in a booklet, on a tape, on a videotape, or have a computer administer the measure to the subjects.

Conclusions about Reliability

We have described steps you can take to assess and reduce unreliability. Ideally, we would like to reduce random error because getting inconsistent, unreliable measurements virtually guarantees inaccuracy. Put another way, the more reliable the measure, the greater the opportunity for validity. For example, if a junior high student measures your systolic blood pressure three times and measures it as 100 one day and 200 the next day, you would suspect the student's average measurement was off by *at least* 50 points. If, on the other hand, your systolic blood pressure is measured by a health-care professional as 150 one day and 160 on the next day, the professional's measurements *may* be accurate to five points.

In a way, the relationship between random error and validity in a measure is similar to the relationship between ice and cola in a glass. Where there is ice, there cannot be cola. Where there is random error, there cannot be validity. Thus, if your glass is entirely full of ice, there can be no cola, and if your measure is completely dominated by random error, there is no room for validity. Consequently, if you use a measure that is completely dominated by random error, then your measure will have no validity. For example, if your measure of IQ was based completely on random error (on how close people came to predicting that night's lotto jackpot number), your measure would have no reliability and no validity. In short, reliability puts a ceiling on validity. Consequently, *a valid measure must be reliable.*

However, *a reliable measure is not necessarily valid.* A consistent, reliable measure could be consistently and reliably wrong. For example, a thoroughly incompetent person might always measure your blood pressure as 0.

The reason that reducing random error, by itself, does not guarantee validity is that random error is not the only source of measurement error. Random error is only one reason your measure might not have validity, just as having your glass full of ice is only one reason you might not have cola in your glass. Thus, just as the absence of ice in your glass does not mean the glass is completely full of cola, the absence of random error does not mean the measure is completely valid.

In fact, in small quantities, random error may be the least serious of the many threats to validity. Random error is not as serious as some threats because it is inconsistent: Random error will not systematically or reliably bias your measurements in any given direction. Thus, just as the ice displaces and dilutes—but does not poison—the cola, random error dilutes—but does not poison—validity. Therefore, even a measure with a moderate degree of reliability may have a moderate degree of validity and be relatively free of systematic bias.

In conclusion, reliability puts a ceiling on validity. Therefore, all other things being equal, the most reliable measure will be the most valid measure. However, because all other things are rarely ever equal, you cannot determine the validity of a measure from reliability alone. Indeed, reliability has nothing to do with whether a measure is free from systematic biases. Therefore, when determining the validity of a measure of behavior, look at both reliability and at the extent to which the measure is free from systematic biases. (See table 3.3 and figure 3.7 for guidelines on assessing a measure's reliability.)

REDUCING OBSERVER BIAS: SEEING WHAT WE HOPE OR EXPECT TO SEE

The reason systematic bias is more serious than random error is perhaps most evident when we contrast random observer error to *observer bias:* observers reporting what they hope or expect to see, rather than seeing what is really there. To understand the

TABLE 3.3   Key Points to Remember about Reliability

1. Two major avoidable sources of unreliability are
   a. random fluctuations in the measurement environment
   b. random fluctuations in how observers interpret and code observations
2. Reliability is necessary for validity: valid measures are reliable.
3. Reliability does not guarantee validity: reliable measures are not always valid.
4. Unreliability weakens validity but does not introduce systematic bias into the measure.

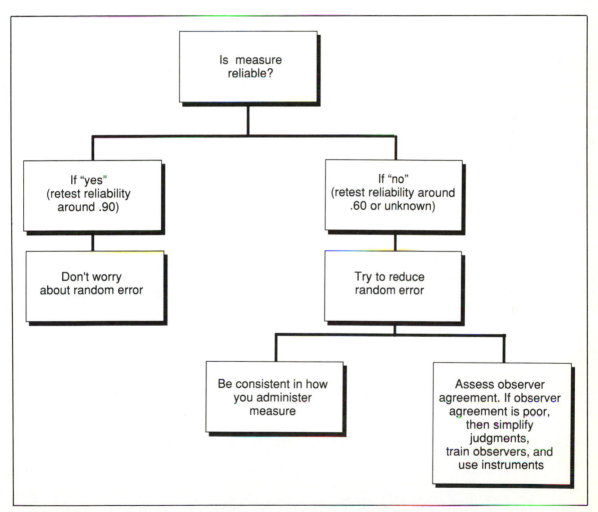

FIGURE 3.7: Primary Steps to Addressing Concerns about Reliability

difference, consider two basketball referees. An inattentive, emotional, and generally incompetent ref is aggravating. However, in the course of a game, his errors will tend to balance out, thus not necessarily giving either team an advantage. Such a ref's calls are marked by a large degree of random observer error. A biased referee who makes "home town calls," on the other hand, may consistently give the home team a several point advantage.

Clearly, observer bias should be minimized. One way to eliminate bias due to human observers seeing what they expect to see is to replace human observers with scientific recording devices.

If you cannot eliminate observer bias by eliminating the human observer's role in measuring behavior, you may be able to reduce observer bias by reducing the observer's role. Rather than having observers interpret open-ended responses, you could limit the observer's role to that of recording answers subjects made to fixed-response items. In short, as you can see from table 3.4, many of the steps you might take to reduce random, unsystematic observer error can be used to reduce systematic observer error.

Yet, even though these tactics should reduce observer bias by making subjects' behaviors less open to interpretation, these tactics may not eliminate observer bias. To see why, suppose you were having observers judge essays to determine whether males or females used more "aggressive" words. Even if you conducted a thorough training program for your raters, the raters might be biased if they knew whether the writer was a male or a female. Therefore, instead of letting your raters know whether an essay was written by a male or female, you should consider making your raters *blind:* unaware of the subject's characteristics and situation.

In essence, the tactics you would use to reduce observer bias are the same tactics a professor would use to avoid favoritism in grading. The professor who is concerned with

---

TABLE 3.4 Techniques That Reduce Both Random Observer Error and Observer Bias

1. Use machines rather than humans to observe and record behavior.
2. Simplify the observer's task by
   a. using objective measures, such as multiple-choice tests.
   b. replacing tasks that ask observers to judge a behavior's intensity with tasks that ask observers to count.
   c. make recording observations as simple and as undemanding to memory as possible by using checklists, tape recorders, counters, or other recording devices.
3. Tell observers that they are to record and judge observable behavior rather than invisible psychological states.
4. Record subjects' behavior so observations can be re-checked.
5. Carefully define your categories so that all observations will be interpreted according to a consistent, uniform set of criteria.
6. Train raters and motivate them to be accurate.
7. Use only those raters who were consistent during training.

---

avoiding favoritism in grading would certainly not determine students' grades solely by sitting down at the end of term and trying to recall the quality of each student's class participation. On the contrary, a professor who was solely concerned with avoiding favoritism would give multiple-choice tests that were computer-scored. If the favoritism-conscious professor were to give an essay exam, the professor would establish clear-cut criteria for scoring the essays, follow those criteria to the letter, and not look at students' names while grading the papers.

BEYOND VALID MEASUREMENTS OF BEHAVIOR: CONSTRUCT VALIDITY

If you are interested in behavior, and only behavior, then all you need is a measure that is both reliable and free from observer bias. Thus, health psychologists interested in cigarette-smoking behavior and blood pressure would only require that their measures be free of observer bias and be reliable measures of overt behavior (e.g., amount of cigarette smoking). That is, they would be content to have valid measures of overt behavior.

However, psychologists are often interested in more than behavior. Specifically, psychologists often measure and interpret behavior so they can infer what is going on in subjects' minds. For example, they might measure cigarette smoking or blood pressure not because they care about smoking or blood pressure, but because these behaviors are indicators of nervousness. When trying to infer a mental state from behavior, showing that you have a valid measure of behavior is only a first step. The second step is to show that you can validly infer the construct from the behavior.

To illustrate why accurately measuring a construct requires that you do more than accurately measure behavior (see figure 3.8), consider the errors that people often make when they infer mental states from behavior. For example, if someone does not speak to us, we may infer they are "stuck up." If someone works slowly, we may infer they are lazy. Obviously, these inferences may be incorrect: the person who does not speak to us may be shy; the slow performer may lack ability or may be extremely cautious. Likewise, when psychologists infer that choosing certain multiple-choice answers means a person is intelligent or that shocking someone after they shocked you indicates aggressiveness, these inferences may be incorrect. In short, even though we may have accurately observed subjects' behavior, we should be very careful about *inferring* psychological states from that behavior.

REACTIVITY BIASES

One reason we may make incorrect inferences from subjects' behavior is **reactivity:** subjects changing their behavior because they are being observed. If we think a behavior reflects a subject's true feelings, but the behavior is really produced to make a good impression on us, we would be misinterpreting the behavior's meaning.

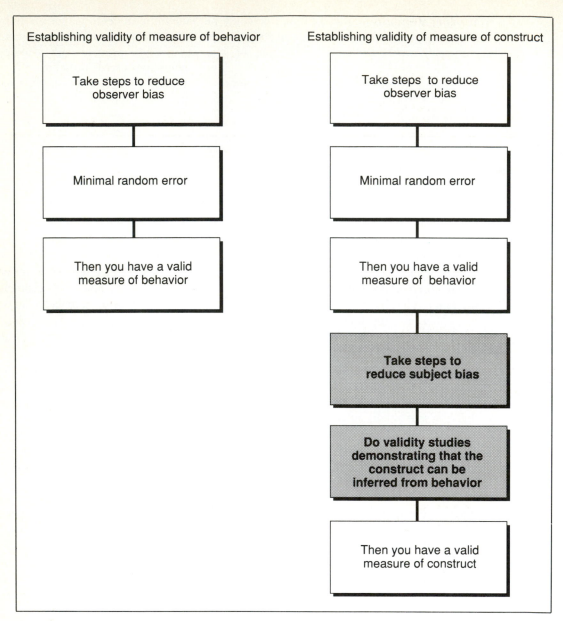

FIGURE 3.8: Establishing the Validity of a Measure of a Construct is More Challenging Than Establishing the Validity of a Measure of a Behavior

Types of Reactivity

One of the earliest documented examples of the problem of subjects reacting to being watched was the case of Clever Hans, the mathematical horse (Pfungst, 1911). Hans would answer mathematical problems by tapping his hoof the correct number of times. For example, if Hans's owner asked Hans what three times three was, Hans would tap his hoof nine times. Hans's secret was that he would watch his owner—his owner would stop looking at Hans's feet when Hans had reached the right answer. Thus, although people interpreted Hans's hoof tapping as evidence that Hans was mentally performing mathematical calculations, hoof tapping only really meant that Hans was watching and reacting to his owner's gaze.

Social Desirability Bias

If animals can produce the "right" answer when they know what you are measuring, so can humans. In fact, for humans, there are two kinds of "right" answers. The first kind is the **socially desirable response:** answers that make the subject look good. Subjects are quite willing to give socially desirable responses. For example, many studies have shown people claim to be much more helpful (Latane & Darley, 1970) and less conforming (Milgram, 1974) than they really are.

Demand Characteristics

The second kind of "right" answer is the one that makes you, the researcher, look good by ensuring that your hypothesis is supported. Martin Orne (1962) believes subjects are very willing to give researchers whatever results the researcher wants. In fact, subjects are so eager to please that they look for clues or hints as to how the researcher wants them to behave. According to Orne, if subjects find these hints, subjects follow the hints as surely as if the researcher had *demanded* that they follow the hint. Hence, Orne calls clues about the nature of the study **demand characteristics.**

To see how demand characteristics might come into play, suppose you have subjects rate how much they love their partner. Next, you give them fake feedback, supposedly from their partner, showing that their partner loves them intensely. Finally, you have subjects rate how much they love their partner a second time. In this study, subjects may realize that they are supposed to rate their love higher the second time. Therefore, if subjects reported they loved their partner more the second time, you would not know whether learning about their partner's devotion increased love or whether subjects merely obeyed the study's demand characteristics.

How did subjects know what you wanted them to do? Your measure made it obvious you were measuring love. Once subjects knew you were measuring love, they were able to guess why you showed them their partners' ratings. You gave them all the clues they needed to figure out what you would consider a "good" response.

Reducing Reactivity Biases

Fortunately, you do not need to give subjects such clear-cut cues about what you are measuring. Specifically, you could make your intentions less obvious by

1. preventing subjects from knowing they were being observed,
2. preventing them from knowing what particular behavior you were observing,

3. preventing them from knowing why you were observing the behavior you were observing, or

4. choosing a response that most subjects could not or would not change.

Measuring Subjects in a "Non-research" Setting

One way to stop subjects from acting the way they think the researcher wants them to act is not to let them know they are being observed. One way to observe subjects without their knowledge is to observe them in a "non-research" setting. For example, you may observe them in some real-world setting (library, restaurant, etc.) or while they are ostensibly in the study's waiting area. Although observing subjects in these settings may reduce demand characteristics, such observations raise ethical questions. We will address these ethical concerns in chapter 8, chapter 12, and appendix A.

Unobtrusive Observation

Even if subjects are observed in a research setting, they can be unobtrusively observed. For example, you might observe subjects' hand-holding behavior through a one-way mirror.

Unobtrusive Measures: Observing Subtle Behaviors or Physical Evidence of Behaviors

Even if subjects know they are being observed, they do not have to know what behaviors you are observing. That is, you could measure behaviors that were so subtle that subjects would not think you would notice, much less record. For example, your measure might be some nonverbal behavior, such as their posture, how close they sat to each other, or how long they gazed into each other's eyes. Or, you might use a computer to unobtrusively record each subject's behavior. Without subjects knowing it, the computer could measure the number of errors subjects made, how fast subjects responded, or even how hard subjects pressed down the keys.

But what if you cannot observe subjects unobtrusively? Then, instead of directly measuring behavior, you might play detective by looking for the physical consequences of behavior. For instance, you might determine how close two people were sitting by measuring how far apart their chairs were; you might determine whether subjects read two pages by seeing whether they broke a seal you had placed between two consecutive pages; you might determine the popularity of a candidate by seeing how many of the leaflets that were handed out in his behalf ended up in the nearest garbage can; you might compare the relative popularity of paintings at a museum by measuring how much the tile had eroded under each painting; or you might assess the degree of communication among professors, staff, and administration by seeing how many classroom clocks kept accurate time (Webb, Campbell, Schwartz, Sechrest, & Grove, 1981).

"Unexpected Measures"

Rather than measuring subtle behaviors, you could use readily observable behaviors that appear so irrelevant to the study that subjects would never expect these behaviors to be measures. For example, you might use measures like how long it takes subjects to ask for help when their computer "unexpectedly" breaks down (Williams & Williams, 1983), whether subjects mail a lost letter (Milgram, 1966), how many peanuts a subject eats

(Schachter, 1971), or whether the subject asks the researcher for a date (Dutton & Aron, 1974). If you wanted to use an "unexpected" measure to assess love, you might see if subjects would be willing to help repair some damage allegedly caused by their partner (picking up hundreds of data cards their partner had knocked over or paying for some equipment their partner had broken).

Disguised Measures

Even if subjects know what behavior you are recording, you may be able to keep them from knowing *why* you are recording it. If they do not know why you are recording it, you may be able to minimize reactivity bias. For example, suppose you were measuring attitudes toward the president using the Hammond-Error Choice Technique. In that case, you would give your subjects a multiple-choice "knowledge" test. Unlike ordinary multiple-choice tests, subjects would have to choose between two or more wrong answers. Thus, if taxes had increased 20 percent during the president's first term, subjects might be given a test question that read:

At the end of the president's first term:
  a. Taxes had increased by 10 percent.
  b. Taxes had increased by 30 percent.

Subjects would know that you were interested in how they responded to this question. However, they would incorrectly assume this was a "knowledge" test. Consequently, they would not realize that by choosing "a," they are indicating they like the president and by choosing "b," they are indicating they dislike the president.

If you were using a disguised measure to assess love, you might take advantage of one fact: If a male subject loves his partner, he will overestimate how similar that partner is to him or her (Gold, Ryckman, & Mosley, 1984). Thus, you could have subjects rate their partners on a variety of characteristics. Subjects would probably think you wanted to know how accurately or how positively they rated their partner. Actually, you would not be looking at either of those things. Instead, you would compare their own self-ratings to their ratings of their partners. The more these ratings corresponded (the more subjects believed they and their partner were similar), the higher the love score.

Overwhelming Subjects with Measures

Another way of confusing subjects about what you are up to is to have them respond to many measures. If subjects respond to several measures, they may be less likely to guess what you are really interested in. For instance, even if you were interested in attitude toward the president, you might give subjects "decoy" questions about foreign affairs, mathematical principles, their mood, in addition to questions about the president. In fact, you could combine the strategy of disguising your measures and overwhelming subjects with measures by embedding your question about the president in the middle of some "Current Events Quiz" or "Belief in Democracy Scale." Analogously, if you were measuring love through the disguised measure of perceived similarity, you could devise a "How Well Do You Know Your Friends?" questionnaire, in which you embed questions that are relevant to your purposes ("What does your boyfriend/girlfriend think about gun control?") among questions that are irrelevant to your purposes ("What does your best same-sex friend think about gun control?" "How old is your boyfriend/girlfriend?").

Important Behaviors and Physiological Responses

Thus far, we have discussed ways to prevent subjects from knowing what you are really trying to measure. We explored several techniques that would either prevent subjects from knowing they were being observed or prevent them from knowing what behavior or construct you really wanted to measure.

But what if subjects know what behavior or construct you are trying to measure? Even then, there are two ways you can stop subjects from merely going along with your hypothesis or trying to seem nobler than they are.

First, you can choose a response that is so important to your subjects they would not be willing to cooperate with you or to lie for the sake of making a good impression. Therefore, if you want to reduce subject biases, do not ask subjects hypothetical questions about how likely it would be that they would vote for the president or donate money to charity. Instead, use more personally involving responses, such as asking them to volunteer to work for the president or actually donate money to charity. When subjects make a response that is personally involving, such as choosing which person to go out on a date with or volunteering to go without food, they will focus on what they need, rather than on what might impress you or on what you might want.

Second, you might choose a measure that subjects cannot voluntarily control such as a physiological response (blushing, sweating, heart rate, brain wave activity). Therefore, if you were measuring love, you might measure the degree to which subjects' pupils dilate when they see their partner (see box 3.4).

CONVERGENT VALIDATION STRATEGIES

Let us assume you have shown you have a valid measure of behavior. Furthermore, let us assume your measure is not affected by reactivity. In other words, you have shown that scores on your measure are

1. *not* unduly influenced by random error,
2. *not* biased by observer bias,
3. *not* biased by demand characteristics, and
4. *not* biased by social desirability.

The next step is to show that your measure *is* measuring the construct you claim it is. One way to convince people your measure is valid is to show that it correlates with other indicators of the same construct, such as

1. other measures of the construct
2. membership in a group composed of individuals known to possess a high level of the construct

BOX 3.4 Ways to Avoid Subject Biases when Measuring Love

TECHNIQUE	EXAMPLE
Measure subjects in non-research settings	Observe hand holding in college cafeteria
Unobtrusive observation	Observe hand holding through one-way mirror in lab
Unobtrusive measures (non-verbal)	Observe time spent gazing into each other's eyes
Unobtrusive measures (physical traces)	Measure how far apart couples' chairs were
"Unexpected measures"	Asking subject to repair damage "caused" by partner
Disguised measures	Asking subjects to rate themselves and their partners and then looking at how similar they think their partner is to themselves
Overwhelming subjects with measures	Asking subjects to rate several acquaintances (including their partner) on a wide number of dimensions
Physiological responses	Pupil dilation or increased blood pressure in presence of partner
Important behavior	Whether subject passes up opportunity to date a very attractive other

3. membership in an experimental group that has been given a treatment that should cause the members to have a high level of the construct

4. behaviors known to correlate with the construct

The process of getting evidence that your measure correlates with other indicators of the construct is called **convergent validation.** The general idea is that your measure and these other indicators correlate because they are all converging on the same thing—your construct.

Perhaps the most obvious step in convergent validation is to show that your measure correlates with other measures of the same construct. Thus, if you were measuring love, you might correlate your measure with another measure of love. Since both measures are supposed to be measuring the same thing, the two measures should correlate with one another.

Another obvious tactic is to find two groups: one known to be high on the characteristic you want to measure and one known to be low on that characteristic. Clearly, you would hope that subjects in the first group would score higher on your measure than subjects in the second group. This tactic is called the **known-groups technique.** Thus, in validating your love scale, you might give your scale to two groups:

one that is known to be in love (dating couples) and one that is known not to be in love (friends). You would hope to find, as Rubin (1970) did when he validated his love scale, that the two groups score differently on your scale.

In addition to looking at whether your measure distinguishes between two existing groups, you could determine whether your measure predicts whether subjects will later belong to different groups. For instance, you might see if your measure could predict which dating couples would get engaged and which would soon split up (Rubin, 1970).

You also could see if your measure distinguishes between two groups exposed to different experimental manipulations. For example, if you had an experimental group that was expecting a shock and a control group that was not, you would expect the experimental group to score higher on a measure of anxiety than the control group.

Finally, you could determine whether your measure correlated with other verbal or nonverbal indicators of the concept. Thus, you could correlate scores on the love scale with a behavior that lovers are supposed to do. For example, Rubin (1970) showed that his love scale correlated with how long the couples looked into each other's eyes.

DISCRIMINANT VALIDATION STRATEGIES: SHOWING THAT YOU ARE NOT MEASURING THE WRONG CONSTRUCT

Even if you show that your measure correlates with other criteria of love, some critics may still believe that you are not measuring love, but some other construct. For example, they might argue that you are not measuring love, but instead are measuring liking, empathy, intelligence, extraversion, or social desirability. Therefore, you might anticipate these attacks by correlating your measure with measures of liking, empathy, intelligence, extraversion, and social desirability. Obviously, you would hope your measure would not correlate with unrelated constructs (intelligence and social desirability) and only modestly with measures of related constructs (liking). If you succeed in showing that your measure does not correlate highly with other constructs, you have established your measure's **discriminant validity.**

INTERNAL CONSISTENCY: ARE ALL ITEMS MEASURING THE SAME THING?

Another way of supporting your belief that you are measuring the one construct you say you are measuring is to show you are measuring *one* construct. Thus, if you were measuring sexual attraction with a fifty-item test, you might assess your measure's validity by looking at its **internal consistency:** the degree to which each item is correlated with the overall test score. You would expect that if all your items were measuring the same unidimensional construct, all of the items should correlate with one another. Therefore, you would expect the measure to have a high degree of internal consistency. When researchers report inter-item correlations, Cronbach's alpha, split-half reliabilities, or Kuder-Richardson reliabilities, they are telling you the extent to which their measure is internally consistent.

But what if you were measuring a construct that was more complex than sexual attraction? For example, suppose you were measuring love and you believed love had two dimensions (sexual attraction and willingness to sacrifice for the other). If love is made up of two separate constructs, then your love measure should be made up of two different subscales. Although the measure **as a whole** might have a low degree of internal consistency, each of the subscales should have a high degree of internal consistency. All the responses to items related to sexual attraction should correlate with one another and all the responses to items related to sacrifice should correlate with one another. In cases where a scale is made up of subscales, each measuring a separate factor, researchers may not only report the internal consistency of each subscale, but may do a factor analysis to provide evidence the test is measuring the number of factors the researcher claims.

CONTENT VALIDITY: IS EVERYTHING REPRESENTED?

Finally, you might try to make a case for your measure's validity by establishing its **content validity**: the extent to which it represents a balanced and adequate sampling of relevant dimensions, knowledge, and skills. For example, if you defined love as "feeling sexual attraction toward a person and a willingness to make sacrifices for that person," then you would make sure your measure had both kinds of items. As we mentioned above, you would probably want to have both a "sexual attraction" and a "sacrifices" subscale.

Usually, content validity is a concern for achievement tests that assess knowledge or skills. For achievement tests, content validity may be extremely important. For example, a test to assess what you have learned about psychology should cover all areas of psychology, not just classical conditioning. Similarly, a test of oral communication skills should not merely test speaking skills, but also listening skills.

SUMMARY OF CONSTRUCT VALIDITY

As you can see, building a strong case for your measure's construct validity is several research projects in itself. Since validating a measure takes so much time and since most researchers are interested in finding out new things about a construct rather than finding new ways to measure it, most researchers do not invent their own measures. Instead, they use measures that others have already validated (see box 3.5 and box 3.6). (In fact, while reading about what it would take to validate your own love scale, you may have been saying to yourself: "Let's use Rubin's scale instead.")

SELECTING THE BEST MEASURE FOR YOUR STUDY

When selecting a measure, you might think that you should always choose the most valid measure. After all, you want to make sure your instrument measures what it is supposed to measure. However, the best measure for your study is not always the most valid one.

For example, imagine you have found four measures that have roughly the same validity. However, the different measures have different sources of invalidity. The first measure's validity is weakened by demand characteristics, the second measure's validity is weakened by social desirability bias, the third measure's validity is weakened by observer bias, and the fourth measure's validity is weakened by unreliability. Which measure should you choose?

Clearly, the answer depends on your particular study. If your hypothesis is one that subjects should not be able to figure out, you might not be concerned about a measure's vulnerability to demand characteristics. Thus, you might choose the first measure. If you are comparing a treatment group and a no-treatment group, both groups should be equally influenced by social desirability. Therefore, you would not be overly concerned about social desirability and might choose the second measure. If you were able to keep observers "blind," you would not be concerned with observer bias. Consequently, you might choose the third measure. Finally, if you are very concerned about avoiding bias, you may choose the fourth measure.

In short, even if validity were your only concern, you would not always choose the most valid measure. However, validity is never your only concern. For example, ethical and practical concerns will always affect your choice of measure. In addition, you should also choose a measure based on whether it will allow you to answer the specific research question.

SENSITIVITY: WILL THE MEASURE BE ABLE TO DETECT THE DIFFERENCES YOU NEED TO DETECT?

To understand how a measure could prevent you from answering your research question, imagine a cell biologist's reaction to being told she could only use a magnifying glass. Obviously, she would be horrified. Without a microscope, the cell biologist could not determine the effect of different treatments or see how cells differed.

Like cell biologists, psychologists often look for rather subtle differences. Consequently, psychologists usually want their measure to be **sensitive:** have the ability to detect differences among subjects on a given variable.

BOX 3.6 Validating Empathy Measures

Convergent validity:

- Child abusers score lower on empathy measures than non-abusers.
- Social workers with graduate training score higher on empathy than clerical employees.
- Prisoners who volunteer to help disadvantaged people score higher on empathy than prisoners who do not help.
- Medical students who score higher on empathy measures have more humanistic reasons for choosing medicine as a career than low scorers.
- Delinquents have lower empathy scores than non-delinquents.
- High scorers are more likely to help people than low scorers.
- Therapists with high scores tend to have better success rates than therapists with lower scores.
- High scorers tend to become more anxious when watching a speaker make a fool of himself.
- Groups with low empathy scores have intense internal feuding.
- High scorers are better able to convey ideas during a charade performance.
- Higher scoring salespersons have better sales records.
- High scorers tend to have greater knowledge of leadership.
- Higher scorers are more extroverted and more self-disclosing than low scorers.
- Higher scorers are less aggressive than low scorers.
- Higher scorers have more affiliative urges than low scorers.
- Higher scorers are more anxious than low scorers.
- Studies have correlated empathy measures with one another.

Discriminant validity: Studies have been done to show that empathy scores are not highly correlated with intelligence.

Content validity: Experts have analyzed measures to see whether they tap two basic aspects of empathy: being able to take another's perspective and vicariously experiencing the emotion that another is feeling.

Adapted from Chlopan, Bruce E., McCain, M. L., Carbonell, J. L., & Hagen, R. L. (1985), Empathy: Review of Available Measures. *Journal of Personality and Social Psychology,* 48; 635–653.

Achieving the Necessary Level of Sensitivity

How can you find or develop a sensitive measure? Much of the process is simply common sense. For example, if subjects can only get one or two scores, the measure will not be sensitive to subtle differences among subjects. But beyond common sense considerations, a sensitive measure will also tend to be valid and reliable.

Look for High Validity

The desire for sensitivity is a major reason why researchers often insist on having the most valid measure available. That is, even though they have several valid measures to choose from, they want the most valid one because it will tend to be the most sensitive.

The reason validity may aid sensitivity is clear. The less the measure is affected by irrelevant factors, the more valid and the more sensitive it will tend to be. For example, if you were weighing people to find out whether a diet had an effect, you would be more likely to find the diet's effect if subjects were weighed unclothed rather than clothed. Both the clothed and unclothed measures would be valid. However, because the "unclothed" measure is not assessing the weight of the clothes, it is more valid and more sensitive to actual weight changes.

For similar reasons, measures that involve fewer inferences tend to be both more valid and more sensitive. That is, scientists would prefer to measure weight on a scale rather than by the depth of the impression a footprint left in the sand. They would rather measure body fat using calipers rather than by estimating it from overall body weight. Consequently, researchers may avoid "clever" measures such as "disguised measures" and "physical traces of behavior" in favor of methods that involve fewer and safer inferences, such as direct observation of behavior (see figure 3.9).

Look for High Reliability

Sensitivity is also a reason psychologists value reliability. In our example of choosing among the four measures, you might have wondered why we did not simply suggest choosing the one whose Achilles' heel was random error. After all, given a choice between random error and bias, it would seem that one should choose random error. However, in some cases, a researcher may decide to use a more reliable, but potentially biased measure over a less reliable and less biased measure. Why? Because to the extent that a measure is varying because of random error, it is not sensitive to variations in subjects' behavior.

Unreliability is to data what static is to television reception. With a little static, you can still enjoy your TV show. However, as the static increases, it becomes increasingly difficult to receive the signal the TV station is sending you. Similarly, with a lot of random error in your measurements, it becomes hard to pick up the signal your data are sending you. If your measures are very unreliable, even a large difference between your groups may be due to random measurement error. Therefore, if you see that your groups score differently on a measure, you do not know if these differences are due to measurement error or whether they represent actual differences. To illustrate this point, suppose you were measuring the time it took two different rats to run a maze. Suppose that rat A and rat B ran the maze four times. Their actual times were:

	TRIAL 1	TRIAL 2	TRIAL 3	TRIAL 4
Rat A	6 seconds	6 seconds	6 seconds	6 seconds
Rat B	5 seconds	5 seconds	5 seconds	5 seconds

If you had obtained these data, you could clearly see rat B was the faster rat. However, suppose your measuring system was unreliable. For example, suppose you were having some problems with the stopwatch or you were not always paying close attention. Then, you might record the rats' times as follows:

	TRIAL 1	TRIAL 2	TRIAL 3	TRIAL 4
Rat A	7 seconds	6 seconds	5 seconds	6 seconds
Rat B	8 seconds	4 seconds	6 seconds	2 seconds

Despite the random error in your measurements, you correctly calculated that rat A averages six seconds to run the maze and rat B averages five seconds to run the maze. Thus, random error does not bias your observations. However, because of the unreliable, erratic nature of your measuring system, it is hard to determine whether rat B is really the faster rat. That is, the unreliability of the measuring system causes static that makes it harder to get a clear picture of the message the data should be sending you.

You have seen that too much random error in your measuring system can prevent you from detecting true differences between subjects. In other words, all other things being equal, the more reliable the measure, the more sensitive it is. Therefore, if you want to have a sensitive measure, you should probably choose a measure that has a pretty high (above .70) test-retest reliability coefficient. At the very least, you should avoid measures with very low reliability coefficients. For example, if a measure's reliability is under .50, then more than half the variation in subjects' scores ($1.00 - .50 = .50$) is due to random error.[3]

Allow Scores to Vary

Thus far, we have discussed cases in which you could increase sensitivity by increasing validity and reliability. However, often a measure is insensitive not because it is invalid, but because—like a scale that will only measure you to the nearest 100 pounds—it fails to differentiate between subjects.

To see how a valid measure might fail to be sensitive, imagine you are trying to detect small changes in how much a man loves a woman. What flaws in your measure could stop you from detecting changes in the man's love?

Avoid Behaviors That Are Resistant to Change

One thing that could prevent you from detecting small changes in love is if you choose to measure a behavior that is very resistant to change. Important behaviors, such as getting married or buying a car, and well-ingrained habits, such as smoking or cursing, are resistant to change and therefore may not change as readily as the man's love changes. For instance, suppose your measure of love was whether the man asked the woman to marry

---

[3]Remember, the test-retest reliability coefficient is not a correlation coefficient. Instead, it is the **square** of the test-retest correlation. As such, it is an index of the percentage of variation in scores that is **not** due to random error.

him. Since the man would only ask the woman to marry him once his love had reached a high level, this measure would be insensitive to many subtle changes. For instance, it would not be able to detect the man's love changing from a near zero level of love to a moderate level.

So, if you are interested in sensitivity, stay away from measures that cannot detect low levels of a construct. Do not use death as a measure of stress, tile erosion in front of a painting as a measure of the painting's popularity, or quitting smoking as a measure of willpower.

Avoid Measures That Produce a Limited Range of Scores

A second reason that a marriage proposal is an insensitive measure is there are only two scores the man could receive (asked or did not ask). You are trying to distinguish between numerous subtly differing degrees of love, but you are only letting your subject respond in two different ways. If a measure is going to discriminate between many different degrees of love, subjects must be able to give many different responses.

Ask How Much Instead of Whether

One obvious way to allow subjects to get a variety of scores on a measure is to add scale points to your measure. Adding scale points to your measure may increase its precision just as adding inch marks to a yardstick makes the yardstick more useful for detecting subtle differences in the length of boards. For instance, if you are measuring generosity, do not just record **whether** someone gave to charity. Instead, record **how often** (frequency) she donated, or **how much** she gave (amount), or **how long** you had to talk to her before she was willing to give (response latency). Similarly, if you are using maze running to measure motivation, do not simply record whether or not the rat ran the maze. Instead, time the rat to determine **how fast** the rat ran the maze.

Scientific equipment can help you add scale points to your measure. For instance, with the proper instruments, you can measure reaction time to the nearest ten thousandth of a second. Or, by using a sound meter to measure how loudly a person is speaking, you can go beyond saying that the person was speaking softly or loudly: you can specify exactly **how many** decibels the person produced.

Add Scale Points to a Rating Scale

You also can add scale points to self-report measures. For example, do not measure love by asking the question: "Are you in love? (1 = yes, 2 = no)." Instead, ask: "**How** in love are you? (1 = not at all 2 = slightly 3 = moderately 4 = extremely)." Similarly, rather than having an observer rate whether a child was aggressive, you could have the observer rate the extent to which the child was aggressive.

Obviously, there comes a point where adding scale points to a measure will not enhance sensitivity. Asking people to report their weight to the nearest 1/10000 of a pound or asking them to report their love to the nearest 1/1000 will probably not boost sensitivity. That is, after a certain point, any apparent gains in precision are wiped out by the fact that responses are unreliable guesses. Besides, such questions may cause subjects to be frustrated or to doubt your competence. Therefore, to boost sensitivity without frustrating your subjects, you should not unnecessarily add scale points beyond a certain point. But what is that point?

According to conventional wisdom, the point at which you should stop adding scale points depends on the kind of question you are asking and the kind of subject you are asking. If you are asking about something your subjects think about a lot and your subjects are intelligent, you might be able to use an eleven-point scale. If you are asking about a feeling they are relatively ignorant of (or apathetic toward) and they are not very intelligent, you may want to use a three-point scale. When in doubt, use a five- or seven-point scale.

Pilot Test Your Measure

However, just because there are many possible scores a subject **could** get on your measure, that does not mean there are many different scores that your subjects **will** get. To determine if scores will vary, pilot test your measure. That is, before conducting a full-blown study, try out your measure on a few subjects. Often, you will find—or would have found—that subjects' behavior on the measure does not vary. For example, one investigator did an experiment to see if reading along with a videotape would help children remember more than if they just saw the videotape. To measure memory, she asked the children several questions about the story. Unfortunately, the questions were so hard that none of the children got any of the questions right. Thus, the results of her study were hard to interpret. Conversely, if the questions had been so easy that all the children got all the questions correct, the effect of the videotape would also have been impossible to assess.

Sensitivity: Conclusions

You have seen that if a measure is to be sensitive to differences between subjects, subjects must vary on the measure. Subjects are most likely to vary on measures that are relatively simple, relatively direct, and that allow subjects to show how much of the trait or behavior they have.

For a measure to be sensitive, it is not enough that subjects get different scores. Subjects should get different scores because they differ in the degree to which they possess the behavior or construct you are trying to measure. In other words, all other things being equal, your measure should be as valid as possible. Consequently, you should minimize the extent to which subjects' scores vary because of random measurement error or factors unrelated to your construct. Thus, if you use simple, anonymous behaviors as measures (such as self-rating scales), you may be more likely to detect differences between subjects than if you observe complex, public behaviors.

As you can imagine, sometimes the goal of sensitivity sometimes conflicts with the goal of validity. For example, you might want to use a complex, public behavior (sacrificing for one's partner) as your measure of love to avoid reactivity biases. However, you might want to use a simple rating scale because it would be more sensitive. Do you choose the complex behavior that might be insensitive? Or, do you use the rating scale, even though it would be invalid if subjects simply give you the ratings they think you want?

In certain situations, some researchers would choose the more sensitive rating scale.

To understand why, realize that a sensitive measure can help you find small differences so you can make discoveries. An insensitive measure, on the other hand, may stop you from finding these differences. Because you fail to find these differences, you will overlook discoveries. Consequently, some scientists would use a sensitive measure that would allow them to find differences and then they would debate what those differences mean (the validity question). They would prefer debating what their difference meant to doing a study that had virtually no chance of finding any differences at all.

In short, even though validity is important, it is not the only factor to consider when selecting a measure. Depending on the circumstances, having the ability to detect subtle differences may also be important. For example, if we wanted to know how much gold weighed, most of us would choose a scale sensitive to a thousandth of a gram over a scale that gave weight to the nearest pound.

SCALES OF MEASUREMENT: WILL THE MEASURE ALLOW YOU TO MAKE THE KINDS OF COMPARISONS YOU NEED TO MAKE?

Insensitive and invalid measures are not the only kinds of measures that can prevent you from answering your research question. You can also be thwarted by measures that do not allow you to make the kinds of comparisons you need to make.

The kinds of comparisons you need to make depend on your research question. For example, consider these four questions:

1. Do the two groups differ on the variable?
2. Does one group have more of the variable than the other?
3. How much more does one group have of the variable than the other group?
4. Does one group have more than three times as much of the variable than the other group?

Obviously, the questions differ in the amount of information needed to answer them. What is less obvious is that some measures could help answer all four questions; some could only address the first three questions; some could only address the first two; and some measures could only be used to address the first question. The fact that not all valid measures of the variable can be used to make all four comparisons seems strange given that all these questions could be answered by using numbers, and all measures can provide numbers. The key to the mystery lies in the fact that not all these numbers are alike. Just as some descriptive phrases are more informative and specific than others ("they love each other twice as much as the other couple" versus "their relationship is different from the other couple's"), some numbers are more descriptive than others.

The Different Scales of Measurement

Rather than saying that some numbers provide more specific information than other numbers, psychologists say that different numbers represent different **scales of measure-**

ment. In the next few sections, we will show you (1) how these numbers differ, (2) why some measures provide more informative numbers than others, and (3) how to determine what kind of number you need.

Nominal Numbers: Different Numbers Representing Different States

The least informative numbers are **nominal** numbers: numbers that front for names. Like names, nominal numbers identify or classify things. That is, things having the same number are alike, things with different numbers are different. Like names, nominal numbers cannot meaningfully be ordered. That is, just as we do not say that Jan is a bigger name than Jim, we do not say that someone possessing the uniform number 36 is better than someone wearing 35. In everyday life we run into nominal numbers constantly— social security numbers, players' uniform numbers, charge card numbers, license plate numbers, and serial code numbers.

In psychological research, the best use of nominal numbers is when the subjects can be clearly classified either as having a certain quality or not. For example, we may characterize people as male/female or as student/faculty. That is, this most basic way of using numbers is perfect when you are not interested in measuring different amounts, but **different types.** For example, someone scoring a "1" might have a platonic love characterized by friendship whereas someone scoring a "3" might have passionate, romantic love.

Sometimes, we use nominal scale measurement because our measurements are primitive and crude. This may happen in the early stages of developing a measure, if we only have a rough idea of what the measure is assessing. For instance, suppose that when subjects see their partners, some subjects produce one pattern of brain waves whereas others produce a different pattern. Labelling the first brain wave pattern "1" and the other pattern "2" is arbitrary. We could have just as easily labelled the first pattern "2" and the other pattern "1." In other words, we have nominal scale measurement because we do not know whether "2" indicates a greater reaction than "1." We only know that "2" is a **different** pattern than "1." Once we find out that one pattern indicates more arousal than another, we can give the more aroused state the higher number. At that point, we have moved beyond nominal scale measurement.

Ordinal Numbers: When Bigger Means More

Often, we want to move beyond nominal scale measurement. Rather than merely saying that subjects getting different numbers differ, we often want to say that subjects receiving higher scores have more of a given quality. In addition to saying that people scoring "3" are similar to each other and different from those scoring "1," we want to make the additional statement that people scoring "3" have more of a given quality than those scoring "1." In other words, we may want to be able to meaningfully **order** scores from lowest to highest—that is, higher scores mean more of the quality. For example, people scoring a "5" feel more love than people scoring "4" who feel more love than people scoring "3," and so on.

If you can assume higher numbers indicate more love than lower numbers, your measure is producing at least **ordinal** scale numbers: numbers that can be meaningfully ordered from lowest to highest. When you assume you have ordinal data, you are making a very simple assumption: the numbers are ordered. Note, however, you are **not** assuming the difference between "2" and "1" is the same as the difference between "3" and "2." You are assuming "2" is bigger than "1" and "3" is bigger than "2," but you have no idea how much bigger "3" is than "2."

To illustrate what ordinal data assume and do not assume, suppose you successfully ranked ten couples in terms of how much they loved each other. Because the numbers can be meaningfully ordered from highest to lowest, this is definitely ordinal data. Yet, because it is ordinal data, the difference between "1" and "2" may be very different from the distance between "9" and "10." For example, there might be little difference between the couple getting rank "1" and the couple getting rank "2," but there might be an enormous difference between the couple getting rank "9" and the couple getting rank "10."

Interval Scale Numbers: Knowing How Much More

However, you may want to go beyond assuming your measure produces ordinal scale numbers. In addition to assuming numbers can be ordered, you might also want to assume the psychological distance between "1" and "2" is the same as the psychological distance between "2" and "3," which is the same as the psychological distance between any two consecutive whole numbers. In technical terminology, you are assuming your numbers are on an **interval scale:** a scale for which equal numerical intervals represent equal psychological intervals.

Unfortunately, the assumption of equal intervals is not easy to defend, no matter what measure you use. As we have seen, ranked data is typically assumed not to be interval.

Furthermore, if you use a measure of nonverbal behavior, you could still fail to meet the assumption of equal intervals. For example, suppose you had couples come into a lab for ten minutes and recorded the total amount of time each couple stared into each other's eyes. Who would argue that the difference in love between a couple who looks for 120 seconds and a couple who looks for 110 seconds is the same as the difference between a couple who looks for a total of 10 seconds and a couple who does not look at all?

Generally, rating scales are assumed to produce interval data. Yet, even if you use a rating scale, the assumption of equal intervals might be hard to justify. For example, suppose you had people rate how they felt about their partner on a −30 (hate intensely) to a +30 (love intensely) scale. Would you be sure that someone who changed from −1 to +1 had changed to the same degree as someone who had changed from +12 to +14?

Ratio Scales: Zeroing in on Perfection

If you are ambitious, it may not be enough for you just to assume that your measure's numbers can be meaningfully ordered from lowest to highest and that equal intervals between numbers represent equal psychological distances. You may want to make one last, additional assumption: that your measure has an absolute zero. That is, you might assume someone scoring a zero on your measure feels absolutely no love. The assumption of having an absolute zero is not automatic even when measuring physical reality. For example, zero degrees Fahrenheit does not mean no temperature. If it did, we could make ratio statements such as saying that fifty degrees is half as warm as 100 degrees. Similarly, if a score of "0" on your love measure represented absolutely no love (and you had equal intervals), then you could say that the couple who scored a "3" on the love measure was three *times* as much in love as the couple scoring a "1." Because measures that have an absolute zero and equal intervals allow you to make ratio statements, these measures produce **ratio scale** numbers.

When measuring psychological characteristics, it is hard to meet the requirements of ratio scale measurement. It is hard to say that a "0" score means a complete absence of a psychological characteristic. Furthermore, it is hard to say that the numbers generated by a measure correspond perfectly to psychological reality. It is tough enough to have some degree of correspondence between scores on a measure and psychological reality, much less to achieve perfection. Indeed, most researchers do not even ask subjects to try to make ratio scale judgments. For example, they often ask subjects to rate on a one to five scale rather than on a zero to four scale. Furthermore, even when subjects rate on a zero to four scale, subjects are rarely asked to think of "2" as having twice as much of the quality as "1," "3" as three times "1," and "4" as twice as much as "2" and four times as much as "1." Of course, even if subjects were asked to make such judgments, there is no guarantee subjects would be able to successfully do so.

Why Our Numbers Do Not Always Measure up

But why don't you get ratio scale numbers from your measures? For example, why isn't time staring into each other's eyes a ratio scale measure? Isn't zero the complete absence of gazing? Isn't three seconds of gazing three times as much as one second? Yes and no. Yes, seconds of gazing is a ratio scale measure if you are interested in knowing about gazing. But you are not measuring gazes for gazing's sake. You are using gazes to measure love. You are not trying to measure physical reality (gazes); you are trying to use physical reality to measure psychological reality (love). As an indirect, imperfect, reflection of love, time of gaze is not a ratio scale measure. You cannot measure love, or any other construct, directly. You can only measure constructs indirectly. It is unlikely you will be able to indirectly measure a concept with the perfect accuracy that ratio scale measurement requires (see box 3.7).

Which Level of Measurement Do You Need?

You have seen that there are four different levels of measurement: nominal scale, ordinal scale, interval scale, and ratio scale. As you go up the scale from nominal to ordinal to interval to ratio scale measurement, the numbers become increasingly informative (for a review, see tables 3.5 and 3.6). Furthermore, as you go up the scale, it becomes harder to find a measure that provides that level of measurement. For example, a measuring system that ranks subjects provides ordinal data, but not interval data. Therefore, if you need interval data to answer your research question, you cannot use a measure that involves ranking subjects from lowest to highest. This is true no matter how valid the ranking system is.

Thus, when choosing a measure for a study, you should ask two questions: (1) What scale of measurement do I need to answer the research question? and (2) Which of the measures that I am considering will give me this level of measurement? The next sections and tables 3.7 and 3.8 will help you answer these questions.

BOX 3.7　Numbers and the Toll Ticket

Exit No.	Toll by Vehicle Class (in dollars)					No. of Miles
	1	2	3	4	5	
1	.25	.35	.60	.35	.50	3.0
2	.40	.45	1.00	.60	.90	10.0
3	.50	.60	1.35	.80	1.25	40.0
4	.80	.90	2.15	1.30	1.95	45.0
5	.90	1.10	2.65	1.55	2.40	49.0
6	1.45	1.65	3.65	2.15	3.30	51.0
7	3.60	4.15	9.95	5.85	9.30	117.0

The humble toll ticket shows us many kinds of numbers in action. For example, the numbers representing vehicle class (1–5) at the top of the ticket (under toll by vehicle class) are nominal numbers. The only reason the toll people used numbers instead of names is that numbers take less room. So, instead of writing car, sixteen-wheeled truck, small truck, etc., they wrote "1," "2," "3," "4," and "5." There is no particular order to these numbers as shown by the fact that a "3" is charged more than any other number.

The exits, when used as an index of distance, represent ordinal data. You know that if you have to get off at exit 4, you will have to go farther than if you get off at exit 5, but—without looking at the miles column—you do not know how much farther. Thus, missing exit 4 is not too bad, the next exit is only four miles away. Missing exit 6, on the other hand, is terrible—the next exit is sixty-six miles further down the road.

Money, as a measure of miles, is also an ordinal measure. That is, while the more money you spend, the farther you go, you cannot predict how much farther you will go merely by looking at how much money you spend. For example, if you are vehicle class number 1, it costs you twenty-five cents to go three miles, ten cents more to go seven additional miles, and only ten more cents gets you thirty additional miles. That is, amount of money spent and number of exits passed are only ordinal measures when trying to indirectly measure another variable (distance). Similarly, some behavioral and physiological measures (eye gazing or blood pressure increases) may only be ordinal measures when used to indirectly assess invisible psychological states (love).

When You Need Ratio Scale Data

Suppose you want to find out whether engaged couples are *twice* as much in love as dating couples that are not engaged. Because you are hypothesizing a 2 to 1 ratio, you need a measure that gives you ratio scale numbers. As table 3.8 indicates, there are very few measures you can use if you need ratio scale numbers.

TABLE 3.5 Assumptions Made by Different Scales of Measurement

Nominal
Different scores represent different types of behavior or different levels of the constructs ("3" is a different kind of love than "1" or a different level of love, but you cannot say that "3" indicates more love than "1").

Ordinal
Different scores indicate different amounts *and* higher scores represent greater amounts of what is being measured ("3" is more love than "1").

Interval
Higher scores represent more of the construct *and* equal distances between numbers represent equal psychological differences ("3" is more love than "1" to the same extent that "5" is more love than "3").

Ratio
Higher scores represent more of the construct *and* equal distances between numbers represent equal psychological differences **and** a zero means a complete absence of the construct. The numerical ratio between the higher and the lower score represent their relationship ("3" is three times as much love as "1").

TABLE 3.6 Degree of Correspondence between Different Scales of Measurement and Psychological Reality

Psychological reality	0	1	2	3	4	5	6	7	8
Ratio measurement	0	1	2	3	4	5	6	7	8
Interval measurement		0	1	2	3	4	5	6	7
Ordinal measurement		0		1	2		3	4		5

TABLE 3.7 Different Research Questions Require Different Levels of Measurement

RESEARCH QUESTION	MINIMUM SCALE OF MEASUREMENT REQUIRED
Are members of group A more likely to be ＿＿ *types* than members of group B?	Nominal
Is group A *more* ＿＿ than group B?	Ordinal
Is the difference between group 1 and group 2 *as much as* the difference between group 3 and group 4?	Interval
Did group A change *as much* as group B?	Interval
Is group A ＿＿ *times* more ＿＿ than group B?	Ratio

TABLE 3.8 Measuring Instruments and the Kind of Data They Produce

SCALE OF MEASUREMENT	MEASURING TACTICS ASSUMED TO PRODUCE THOSE KINDS OF NUMBERS
Ratio	Magnitude estimation
Interval	Rating scales (Magnitude estimation)
Ordinal	Nonverbal measures Physiological measures Rankings (Rating scales) (Magnitude estimation)
Nominal	Any valid measure (all of the above)

Fortunately, you only need ratio scale level of measurement if you are trying to make ratio statements like John is twice as attractive as Mike or Sue's joke is one-third as funny as Amy's, married women are twice as happy as widows or Mary is four times smarter than Bob.

When You Need at Least Interval Scale Data

Because you probably will not be comparing groups to find out whether one group is twice as much in love as another group, you rarely will need to assume your measure has ratio properties. However, you may have to assume your measure does have interval properties. For example, suppose you are trying to estimate the effects of therapy on relationships. Before relationship counseling is offered on your campus, you measure the degree to which couples are in love. Next, you observe who goes to counseling and who does not. Finally, at the end of the term, you measure the couples' love again. Suppose you got the following pattern of results:

	BEGINNING OF TERM	END OF TERM
Did not go to counseling	3.0	4.0
Went to counseling	5.0	7.0

Note: The higher the score, the more in love. Scores could range from 1 to 9.

Did the couples who went to counseling change more than those who did not? Do not say yes too soon! If you say yes, you are **assuming** that the psychological distance between "3" and "4" is less than the distance between "5" and "7." However, it could be that the psychological distance between "3" and "4" is more than the psychological distance between "5" and "7." Thus, to answer the question of which group changed more, you must assume your data conform to an interval scale. Therefore, to answer this research question, you would have to use a measure that has interval properties, such as a self-rating scale.

When Ordinal Data Is Sufficient

Suppose you do not care how much more in love one group is than the other. Rather, all you want to know is which group is most in love. For example, suppose you want to be able to order these three groups in terms of amount of love:

Did not go to counseling at all	3.0
Went to counseling for one week	5.0
Went to counseling for eight weeks	7.0

Note: The higher the score, the more in love.
Scores could range from 1 to 9.

From these numbers, you may conclude that subjects who went to counseling for eight weeks were most in love, those who went for one week were less in love, and those who did not go to counseling were least in love. You can make these conclusions if you assume you have data that are at least **ordinal**: higher numbers mean higher degrees of love.

Thus, if you only had ordinal data, you would have no idea about how much happier the eight-week group was from the one-week group. It could be that one week of counseling did an enormous amount of good and the additional seven weeks made a very small difference. Or, it could be just the opposite: one week of counseling did very little good, but an additional seven weeks made a big difference.

If you simply want to know which group is higher on a variable and which group is lower, then all you need are ordinal data. If all you need are ordinal data, you are in luck. As you can see from table 3.8, most measures are assumed to produce data that are at least ordinal.

When You Only Need Nominal Data

It is conceivable that you are not interested in discovering which group is more in love. Instead, you might have the less ambitious goal of merely trying to find out whether or not the groups experience different levels or types of love. If that is the case, nominal data are all you need. Because you only need to make the least demanding and safest assumption about your numbers (that different numbers represent different things), any valid measure you choose will measure up.

Conclusions about Scales of Measurement

Your research question may dictate your choice of measures. If you need to make ratio statements, then you need a measure that produces ratio level data. If you need to make "how much more" statements, you need to use a measure that provides either ratio or interval data. If you need to make "more than" statements, you must use a measure that provides either ratio, interval, or ordinal data.

Consequently, you may find the type of data you need will dictate the measure you choose. That is, you may find the only measure that will give you the type of data you want is not as sensitive or as free from biases as another measure. Two examples may clarify this point.

Example #1: Measuring a physiological response or a nonverbal behavior will give you a less reactive measure of love than a rating scale measure. However, you want to know if a treatment is more effective for couples having relationship problems than it is for couples that are very much in love. Your research question requires interval scale data. Consequently, if the rating scale is the only measure that gives you interval scale data, you will have to use it, even if the other measures are more valid.

Example #2: Suppose you are studying retention of a list of material. You may like a multiple-choice measure of memory because it is so sensitive. That is, if subjects have any memory for the material, they should be able to recognize it and correctly respond to a multiple-choice question about it. However, you want to find out how many times more effective one memory technique is than another. With the multiple-choice test, you cannot say that someone who got 30 percent right knows twice as much as someone who got 15 percent right. However, with a recall test, like an essay or fill-in-the-blank test, you can say that a person who recalled thirty facts recalled twice as much as someone who recalled fifteen. Therefore, to answer your research question, you would have to use a recall rather than a multiple-choice test—even if the multiple-choice test was more sensitive.

ETHICAL AND PRACTICAL CONSIDERATIONS

As important as validity, sensitivity, and scales of measurement are, you should *always* be concerned about ethics when choosing a measure. You may decide against using disguised, unobtrusive, or unexpected measures because you feel subjects should be fully informed about the study before they agree to participate. Similarly, you may reject unobtrusive or field observation because you feel those tactics threaten subjects' privacy.

Although you should always be concerned about ethical issues, you often have to be concerned about practical issues. You may have to reject a measure because it is simply too time-consuming or expensive to use. Or, you might choose a measure primarily because it has high **face validity**: the extent to which it looks, on the face of it, to be valid. Although there is nothing scientific about face validity, face validity may be important to the consumer (or the sponsor) of your research. For example, how loud a person yells and how many widgets a person produces may be equally valid measures of motivation. But, if you were going to get a manager to take your research seriously, which measure would you use?

MANIPULATING VARIABLES

In all research, you will measure variables. In experimental research, you will also manipulate variables. To select a manipulation, you go through many of the same steps as when you select a measure. You could find both measures and manipulations by doing a literature review. To invent your own manipulation, you consult the same sources you would use to invent your own measure: intuition, theory, and definitions.

COMMON THREATS TO VALIDITY

When evaluating manipulations, you have the same concerns as you do when you measure variables: random error, researcher bias, demand characteristics, providing evidence for validity, and detecting differences (see table 3.9).

Random Error

Just as you want to minimize random error when measuring variables, you want to minimize random error when manipulating variables. Therefore, just as you standardized the administration of your measure, you want to standardize the administration of your treatment. You want to administer the treatment the same way every time.

Researcher Bias

If you were worried about researchers being biased in their observations, you will also be worried about **experimenter bias**: researchers being biased when they administer the treatment. For example, researchers may be more attentive and friendlier to the subjects they expect or want to do better on the task. As is the case with observer bias, the key is to use scientific equipment to administer the manipulations, to use paper-and-pencil instructions, to standardize procedures, or to make the researcher blind to what condition the subject is in.

Subject Biases

Just as you were concerned that your measure might tip subjects off to how they should behave, you should also be concerned that your manipulation might tip subjects off as to how they should behave. One of the most frequently cited examples of how a treatment could lead to demand characteristics was a series of studies done in the 1920s at the Hawthorne electric plant. The investigators, Roethlisberger and Dickson, were looking at the effects of lighting on productivity. At first, everything seemed to go as expected: increasing illumination increased productivity. However, when they reduced illumination, productivity continued to increase. The researchers concluded that the treatment group was reacting to the special attention, rather than to the treatment itself. This effect became known as the **Hawthorne effect** (Roethlisberger & Dickson, 1939).

TABLE 3.9 Similarities Between Measuring and Manipulating Variables

MEASURE	MANIPULATION
Reduce random error by standardizing administration of measure.	Reduce random error by standardizing administration of manipulation.
Reduce observer bias by training, standardization, instruments, and making researcher "blind" about the subject's condition.	Reduce experimenter bias by training, standardization, instruments, and making researcher "blind" about the subject's condition.
Concern that subjects will figure out what the measure is measuring and then act in such a way as to make a good impression or give the researcher the "right" results. Sometimes problem dealt with by not letting subjects know what the measure is or what the hypothesis is.	Concern that subjects will figure out what the manipulation is designed to do and then act in such a way as to make a good impression or give the researcher the "right" results. Sometimes problem dealt with by not letting subjects know what the manipulation is or what the hypothesis is.
Want sensitive measure to pick up differences between subjects.	Want powerful manipulation to create differences between subjects.
Show that operational definition of measure is consistent with theory's definition of manipulation.	Show that operational definition of manipulation is consistent with theory's definition of manipulation.
Convergent validity shown by correlating with other measures of construct.	Convergent validity sometimes demonstrated by showing that manipulation has same effect that other manipulations of the construct have and that it has an effect on a simple, direct measure of the construct (the manipulation check).
Discriminant validity demonstrated by showing measure does not correlate strongly with measures of related constructs.	Discriminant validity demonstrated by showing that manipulation has little effect on measures of unrelated constructs.

Although many experts now believe that Roethlisberger and Dickson's results were not due to the Hawthorne effect, no one disputes that subjects may act differently just because they think they are getting a treatment. Therefore, researchers use a wide variety of techniques to avoid the Hawthorne effect. Some of these techniques are similar to the techniques used to make a measure less vulnerable to subject biases. That is, just as researchers measure subjects in non-research settings or use unexpected measures, researchers may manipulate the treatment in a non-research setting or use unexpected manipulations (for example, a remark the subject "accidentally" overhears).

A more common way of offsetting subject biases is to give the "no-treatment" group a placebo: a treatment that is known to have no effect. For example, in drug studies, some subjects may get a caffeine pill (the treatment), whereas others get a sugar pill (the placebo). If both groups improve equally, the researchers can conclude the improvement was due to subjects expecting to get better. If, however, the treatment group improves more than the placebo group, we know the results were not due to subject expectancies.

EVIDENCE USED TO ARGUE FOR VALIDITY

As with measures, you would like to provide evidence that your treatment is doing what you claim it is. The difference is that making a case for the validity of a treatment is less involved than making a case for the validity of a measure. The two most common ways of establishing validity are to (1) argue that your treatment is consistent with a theory's definition of the construct and to (2) use a **manipulation check**: a question or set of questions designed to determine whether subjects perceived the manipulation in the way the researcher intended.

Consistency with Theory

For example, suppose you were manipulating cognitive dissonance: a state of arousal caused when subjects are aware of having two inconsistent beliefs. You would want to argue that your manipulation meets three general criteria that dissonance theory says must be met for dissonance to be induced.

1. Subjects must believe they are voluntarily performing an action that is inconsistent with their attitudes (a smoker writing an essay about why people shouldn't smoke).
2. Subjects should believe the action is public and will have consequences (before writing the essay, they must know others will read their essay and know they wrote it).
3. Subjects must not feel they did the behavior for any reward (you did not pay them for doing the behavior).

To make the case that the manipulation is consistent with dissonance theory, you might argue that (1) you told subjects their cooperation was voluntary and they could refuse, (2) you told them their essay would be signed and children who were thinking about smoking would read it, and (3) you did not pay subjects for writing an anti-smoking essay.

Manipulation Checks

Your procedures would seem to induce the mental state of dissonance. However, that is assuming subjects perceived the manipulation as you intended. To check on that assumption, you might use a manipulation check. For example, you might ask subjects if they felt aroused, if they felt their attitudes and behavior were inconsistent, if they felt they were coerced, if they felt their behavior was public, or whether they foresaw the consequences of their behavior. Many researchers believe you should always use a manipulation check when doing research on human subjects.

But, what if giving people the manipulation check tips subjects off to the study? In that case, manipulation check advocates would say to use the manipulation check, but only with practice subjects or only after subjects had responded to your measure.

But, what if it is obvious you are manipulating whatever you think you are manipulating (physical attractiveness, concrete versus abstract words, etc.)? Even then, manipulation check advocates would urge you to go ahead with a manipulation check for two important reasons. First, a manipulation check could establish the discriminant validity of your treatment. For example, wouldn't it be nice if you could show that your attractiveness manipulation increased perceptions of attractiveness, but did not change perceptions of age or quality of clothes? Second, because you are doing research to test assumptions rather than make assumptions, you should be willing to check your assumption that you know what you are manipulating.

THE VALUE OF "POWERFUL" MANIPULATIONS

As with measures, you are concerned with more than just validity. Just as you are concerned with whether your measure is sensitive enough to pick up differences, you are concerned about whether your manipulation will be strong enough to create sizeable differences. The way to have a strong manipulation is to give one group a large amount of the treatment while giving the other no treatment. However, it may be unethical, impractical, or invalid to use such a strong manipulation. In short, as with choosing a measure, choosing a manipulation usually involves making tradeoffs.

TRADEOFFS AMONG THREE COMMON TYPES OF MANIPULATIONS

Choosing a manipulation usually involves making tradeoffs, because, as with measures, there is no such thing as the perfect manipulation. Different manipulations have different strengths and weaknesses (see table 3.10). The following discussion will briefly highlight the strengths and weaknesses of three common kinds of manipulations: instructional, environmental, and stooge.

TABLE 3.10 Tradeoffs Between Three Different Kinds of Manipulations

INSTRUCTIONAL	ENVIRONMENTAL	STOOGES
East to do	Not as easy to do	Not easy to do
Easily standardized, reduces (1) random error and (2) potential for experimenter biases	Not easily standardized, may lead to concerns about (1) random error and (2) potential for experimenter biases	Not easily standardized, may lead to concerns about (1) random error and (2) potential for experimenter biases
May not involve subjects and thus not be powerful	Could be powerful if subjects attend to it	Could be a very powerful manipulation producing big effects in subjects' behavior
Vulnerable to reactivity biases	Less vulnerable to reactivity biases	Not very vulnerable to reactivity biases

Instructional Manipulations

Perhaps the most common treatment manipulation is the **instructional manipulation:** manipulating the variable by giving written or oral instructions. The advantage of an instructional manipulation is you can standardize your manipulation easily. All you have to do is give each subject the same mimeographed instructions or play each subject the same tape. This standardization reduces random error and also reduces experimenter bias.

However, just because you can consistently *present* instructions to subjects, do not assume your instructions will be *perceived* the same way every time. Subjects may ignore, forget, or misinterpret instructions. To reduce random error due to subjects interpreting your instructions differently, be sure to repeat and paraphrase your most important instructions. Many researchers advise you to hit subjects over the head with your manipulation. Thus, if you were manipulating anonymity, you would tell "anonymous" subjects that their responses would be anonymous *and* confidental *and* private *and* that no one would know. Furthermore, you would also tell them not to write their name on the paper. In the public condition, you would do just the opposite. You would tell "public" subjects that everyone would see their paper, that you were going to make Xerox copies of their paper, and you would make a big deal of their signing their names to the paper.

If subjects do not understand or do not pay attention to the manipulation, the instructional manipulation will have little effect on your subjects. However, by making the instructions clear, this problem can be overcome. Unfortunately, subjects may understand your manipulation too well. That is, subjects may figure out what you are trying to manipulate and can play along. Fortunately, placebo treatments, counter-intuitive hypotheses, and unobtrusive measures can reduce the threat of subject biases.

Environmental Manipulations

If you are concerned that subjects will "play along" with an instructional manipulation, you may use an **environmental manipulation:** changing the subject's environment. Some environmental manipulations take the form of "accidents." For instance, smoke may fill a room, the subject may be induced to break something, or the subject may overhear some remark.

When considering an environmental manipulation, ask two questions. First, will subjects notice the manipulation? Even when manipulations have involved rather dramatic changes in subjects' environments (smoke filling a room), a sizeable proportion of subjects report not noticing the manipulation (Latane & Darley, 1970).

Second, can you present the manipulation the same way every time? Fortunately, many environmental manipulations can be presented in a consistent, standardized way. All animal research, for example, involves environmental manipulations that can be consistently presented (food deprivation). Likewise, research in perception, sensory processing, cognition, and verbal learning usually involves environmental manipulations (presenting illusions or other stimuli). These manipulations vary from the routine—presentation of visual stimuli by computer, tachistiscope, memory drum, or automated slide projector—to the exotic. For example, Neisser (1984) has done studies where the manipulation consists of silently moving the walls of the subject's cubicle.

Manipulations Involving Stooges

A special kind of environmental manipulation employs **stooges:** confederates who pretend to be subjects, but are actually the researcher's assistants. By using stooges, social psychologists and others get subjects to respond openly, thus avoiding the demand characteristics that accompany instructional manipulations. The problem is that it is very hard to standardize the performance of a stooge. At best, inconsistent performances by stooges create unnecessary random error. At worst, stooges may bias the results. Some researchers try to get the advantages of stooges without any of the disadvantages by having subjects listen to tapes of actors rather than relying on stooges to give the exact same performance time after time. For example, both Aronson and Carlsmith (1968) and Latane and Darley (1968) had subjects believe they were listening to people talking over an intercom when subjects were actually only listening to a tape-recording.

As you can see, choosing manipulations usually means making tradeoffs. To choose the right manipulation for your study, you must determine what your study needs most. Is experimenter bias your biggest concern? Then, you might use an instructional manipulation. Are you most concerned with demand characteristics? Then, you might use an environmental manipulation.

MANIPULATING VARIABLES: A SUMMARY

In conclusion, when manipulating variables, you have many of the same concerns you have when measuring variables. However, when manipulating variables, you have one set of concerns that you do not have when measuring variables: How many levels of the treatment should you have and how different should your levels be? We will deal with the important decision of choosing treatment levels in chapters 5 and 6.

CONCLUDING REMARKS

In chapter 2, you developed a research idea: a prediction about how two or more variables were related. In this chapter, you learned how to operationalize these variables. Now that you have the raw materials to build a research design, you can take advantage of the rest of this book.

SUMMARY

1. You may be able to use a measure or manipulation that someone has already published. Therefore, look for references in your textbook's bibliography, visit the library, and consider a computerized literature search.

2. Consulting a dictionary may help you to be more precise about what it is you want to measure.

3. Both theory and intuition may suggest ways of measuring abstract concepts.

4. Sensitivity, reliability, and validity are highly valued in a measure.

5. Sensitivity is a measure's ability to detect small differences.

6. Validity refers to whether you are measuring what you claim you are measuring.

7. A reliable measure is relatively free from random error.

8. Two major sources of unreliability are human error in making or recording observations, and random variations in how the measure is administered.

9. An unreliable measure cannot be valid, but a reliable measure may be invalid.

10. An unreliable measure cannot be sensitive, but a reliable measure may be insensitive.

11. By asking "how much" rather than "whether," by knowing what you want to measure, by avoiding unnecessary inferences, and by using common sense, you can increase the sensitivity of your measure.

12. A valid measure must have some degree of reliability and be relatively free of observer bias and subject biases.

13. Two common subject biases are social desirability (trying to make a good impression) and obeying demand characteristics.

14. By not letting subjects know what you are measuring, you may be able to reduce subject biases.

15. Establishing discriminant validity, convergent validity, and internal consistency are all ways of validating a measure.

16. Different kinds of measures produce different kinds of numbers.

17. Nominal numbers only let you say that subjects differ.

18. Ordinal numbers only let you say which subjects have more of a quality than others.

19. Interval and ratio numbers let you say how much more of a quality one subject has than another.

20. Ratio scales let you say how many times more _____ (e.g., intelligent) one subject is than another.

21. Since no measure is perfect, choosing a measure involves making tradeoffs.

22. Depending on the research question, a measure's sensitivity and its level of measurement may be almost as important as validity.

23. Choosing a manipulation involves many of the same steps as choosing a measure.

24. Placebo treatments can reduce subject bias.

25. "Blind" procedures and standardization can reduce experimenter bias.

26. You can use manipulation checks to make a case for your manipulation's validity.

blind
construct validity
content validity
converging operations
convergent validity
correlation coefficient
demand characteristics
discriminant validity
hypothetical construct

internal consistency
interval data
inter-observer reliability
known-groups technique
latency
nominal scale data
observer bias
operational definition
ordinal data

placebo treatment
random error
ratio scale data
reliability
response latency
sensitivity
social desirability
subject biases (reactivity)
test-retest reliability

EXERCISES

1. Define a concept you would like to measure (memory, love, arousal, etc.).

2. Locate two published measures of that concept (see appendix B). What search strategy did you use to find these measures?

3. For that concept, develop or find a self-report measure, a physiological measure, and a nonverbal behavior measure.

4. Take one of your measures and discuss how you could improve its sensitivity.

5. If you had one year to try to validate your measure, how would you go about it? (Hint: Refer to the different kinds of validities discussed in this chapter.)

6. What kind of data (nominal, ordinal, interval, or ratio) do you think your measure would produce? Why?

7. Why is reliability important?

8. What could you do to improve your measure's reliability?

9. How vulnerable is your measure to subject and observer biases? Why? Can you change your measure to make it more resistant to these threats?

10. Becky wants to know how much students drink.
    a. What level of measurement could Becky get? Why?
    b. Becky asks subjects: How much do you drink: (a) 0–1 drinks, (b) 1–3 drinks, (c) 3–4 drinks, (d) more than 4 drinks. What scale of measurement does she have?
    c. Becky ranks subjects according to how much they drink. What scale of measurement does she have?
    d. Becky assigns subjects a "1" if they are a wine drinker and a "2" if they are a beer drinker. What scale of measurement is this?
    e. Becky asks subjects: How much do you drink: (a) 0–1 drinks, (b) 1–3 drinks, (c) 3–4 drinks, (d) more than 4, (e) don't know. If she codes the data as follows: a = 1, b = 2, c = 3, d = 4, e = 5, what scale of measurement does she have? Why?

11. What factor would you like to manipulate? Define this factor as specifically as you can.

12. Find one example of this factor being manipulated in a published study. (See appendix B.)

13. How would you manipulate that factor? Why?

14. How could you perform a manipulation check on the factor you want to manipulate? Would it be useful to perform a manipulation check? Why or why not?

15. Compare the relative advantages and disadvantages of using an instructional manipulation versus an environmental manipulation.

16. Assume that facial tension is a measure of thinking.
    a. How would you measure facial tension?
    b. What scale of measurement is it on? How would you know?
    c. How would you validate that measure?

17. If an investigator wants to know whether one drug awareness program is more effective than another, what scale of measurement does the investigator need? What if the investigator wants to show that one program is better for informing the relatively ignorant than it is for informing the fairly well informed?

18. Researchers have used a certain measure to find rather subtle differences between groups. What can you infer about the measure's reliability?

19. A researcher wants to measure "aggressive tendencies." The researcher is considering two choices: a paper-and-pencil test of aggressive impulses or observation of actual aggression.
    a. What problems might there be with observing subjects' aggressive behavior?
    b. In evaluating the test, what should the researcher beware of? What information about the test would suggest that the test is a good instrument?

4 INTERNAL VALIDITY

"All things are possible until they are proved impossible"

—Pearl S. Buck

OVERVIEW

As you may recall from chapter 1, for a study to have internal validity, it must clearly demonstrate that a specific factor causes an effect. Thus, if you establish that turning on blue lights in a room causes higher scores on a happiness questionnaire, your study has internal validity.

The logic of establishing internal validity is simple. First, you determine that changes in a treatment (blue lighting) are *followed* by changes on a variable (increased happiness). Then, you determine that the treatment (blue lighting) is the *only* factor responsible for the effect (increased happiness). That is, you show that the results could not be due to anything other than the lighting. Or, as a psychologist would say, you rule out **extraneous factors:** factors other than the treatment.

The most direct way to rule out the possibility that your results are due to the effects of extraneous factors is to eliminate all extraneous factors from your study. If there are no extraneous factors in your study, extraneous factors obviously cannot be responsible for your results. In the abstract, there are two ways you can get rid of extraneous factors:

1. Get two identical groups, treat them identically, except you only give one of the groups the treatment, and then compare the treatment group to the no-treatment group.
2. Get some subjects, measure them, make sure nothing in their lives changes except that they get the treatment, and then measure them again.

In actual practice, however, neither of these methods succeed in eliminating extraneous variables. As a result, these approaches—contrary to what a naive person might believe—*cannot* prove a treatment caused an effect.

In this chapter, you will learn why these two approaches fail to establish internal validity. Specifically, you will learn about Campbell and Stanley's (1966) eight general threats to internal validity:

1. selection
2. selection by maturation interactions
3. regression
4. maturation
5. history
6. testing
7. instrumentation
8. mortality

In addition, you will know enough about these threats to (1) be cautious about accepting a claim that one factor causes a certain effect, (2) identify flaws in research that erroneously claims to prove that a certain factor has an effect, (3) avoid using a design that is vulnerable to these threats, and (4) take steps to prevent these threats from affecting the results of your research.

WHY WE CANNOT GET TWO IDENTICAL GROUPS: SELECTION

To begin our exploration of Campbell and Stanley's (1966) eight threats to validity, let us examine the first approach to ruling out extraneous variables: getting two identical groups. Specifically, suppose you get two groups of subjects and treat them identically, except only one of the groups gets the treatment (blue lighting). Then, you give both groups the happiness scale and note they have different levels of happiness.

What do you conclude? If the groups were identical before you introduced the treatment, you would correctly conclude the treatment caused the groups to differ. However, if the groups were not identical before you introduced the treatment, the effect (see figure 4.1) could be due to **selection**: choosing groups that were different from one another before the study began.

SELF-ASSIGNMENT TO GROUPS AS A SOURCE OF SELECTION ERROR

How can you avoid the selection error? That is, how can you get two identical groups? Obviously, one key to avoiding selection error is to prevent subjects from choosing what condition they want to be in (self-selection). If your subjects choose their own conditions, then you know the groups will differ on at least one dimension: one group chose the treatment, the other chose to avoid the treatment. Furthermore, the groups probably differ in ways you do not know about. As a result, if you let subjects choose what condition they will be in, you will probably end up comparing apples and oranges.

Sometimes the effects of self-selection are obvious. For example, suppose you compare two groups—one group volunteers to stay after work to attend a seminar on "Helping Your Company," the other does not. If you find the seminar group is more loyal to the company than the no-seminar group, you cannot conclude the effect is due to the seminar. The groups obviously differed in loyalty before the study began.

Sometimes the effects of self-selection are not as obvious. For instance, what if you let subjects choose whether they get blue lighting or no lighting? If you find the blue lighting group is happier than the no-lighting group, you cannot conclude the effect was due to the blue lighting. People who prefer blue lighting may be happier than people who prefer no lighting. You really do not know how subjects who choose one condition differ from those who choose another condition. But you do know that they differ. And these differences may cause the groups to differ at the end of the study.

FIGURE 4.1 An Anti-health Care Demonstration Organized by Citizens Who Don't Understand Selection.

RESEARCHER ASSIGNMENT TO GROUPS: AN OBVIOUS SOURCE OF SELECTION BIAS

Obviously, letting subjects assign themselves to a group creates unequal groups. However, if you assign subjects to groups, you might unintentionally bias your study. For example, you might put all the smiling subjects in the blue light condition and all the frowning subjects in the no-treatment condition.

ARBITRARY ASSIGNMENT TO GROUPS AS A SOURCE OF SELECTION BIAS

To avoid the bias of "picking your own team," you might assign subjects to groups on the basis of some arbitrary rule. For example, why not assign students on the right-hand side of the room to the no-treatment group and assign students on the left side of the room to the treatment group? The answer is simple: Because the groups are obviously **not** equal.

At the very least, the groups differ in that one group prefers the right side, while the other group prefers the left side. They probably differ in many other ways. For example, if the left side of the room is near the windows and the right side is near the door, we can list at least four reasons why left-siders might be happier and/or more energetic than right-siders.

1. People sitting on the left side of the room may be more energetic because they walked the width of the room to find a seat.
2. People sitting on the left side of the room may be early-arrivers (students who came in late would tend to sit on the right side so they would not disrupt class by crossing the width of the room).
3. People sitting on the left side may be more interested in the outdoors since they chose to have access to the window.
4. People sitting on the left side may have chosen those seats to get a better view of the professor's performance (if the professor shows the typical right-hander's tendency of turning to the right, which would be the students' left).

You can probably come up with many other differences between "left-siders" and "right-siders" in a particular class. But the point is that the groups definitely differ in at least one respect (choice of side of room) and they almost certainly differ in numerous other respects.

What is true for the arbitrary rule of assigning subjects to groups on the basis of where they sit is true for any other arbitrary rule (see figure 4.2). Thus, researchers who assign subjects on the basis of an arbitrary rule (the first subjects to arrive are assigned to the treatment group, people whose last names begin with a letter between A and L are assigned to the treatment group, etc.) make their research vulnerable to selection bias.

The reason arbitrarily assigning subjects to groups does not work is because you are assigning subjects to groups based on their differences. You are insuring that they are different on some variable (preference for side of the room, etc.).

MATCHING: A VALIANT BUT UNSUCCESSFUL STRATEGY FOR GETTING IDENTICAL GROUPS

If you can assign subjects in a way that guarantees they are different, why not assign subjects in a way that guarantees they are identical? In other words, why not use **matching**: choosing your groups so that they have identical characteristics.

The Impossibility of Perfectly Matching Individual Subjects: Identical Subjects Do Not Exist

In the abstract, matching seems like an easy, foolproof way of making sure your two groups are equal. In practice, however, matching is neither easy nor foolproof. Imagine the difficulty of finding two people who match on every characteristic and then assigning one to the no-treatment condition and the other to the treatment condition. It would be impossible. Even identical twins would not be exactly alike—they have different health histories and different experiences.

4.2(a) The rule of choosing "every other person" to get the treatment is not random. The problem with this rule is most obvious when applied to situations where people are encouraged to line up "boy/girl."

FIGURE 4.2 Problems with Arbitrary Assignment to Group

The Difficulty of Matching Groups on Every Variable: There Are Too Many Variables

Obviously, you cannot create the situation where each member of the treatment group has an identical clone in the no-treatment group. Try as you might, there would always be some variable you had not matched on—and that variable might be important. Thus, even if you created two groups that had the same average age, same average intelligence, same average income, same average height, same average weight, there would still be thousands of variables on which the groups might differ. For example, the groups might differ in how they felt on the day of the experiment, how they were getting along with their parents, how many books they had read, or their overall health.

4.2(b) The arbitrary rule of assigning the front of the class to one treatment and the back of the class to no-treatment does not work. Ask any teacher! The two groups are definitely different.

FIGURE 4.2 Continued.

4.2(c) An attention study goes awry. Assigning by row. The students on the window-side of the room are sitting there because they want to look out the window. The students on the other side of the room may be sitting there to avoid distractions.

FIGURE 4.2 Continued.

Two Difficulties with Matching Groups on Every Relevant Variable

Clearly, you cannot match your no-treatment and treatment groups on every single characteristic. However, making groups identical in every respect may be unnecessary. You only need them to be identical in respect to the variable you want to measure (happiness). Therefore, all you need to do is match your groups on characteristics that will influence their performance on your measure (the happiness scale).

Unfortunately, there are two problems with this "solution." First, matching only on those factors that influence the outcome variable may be impossible because there may be thousands of factors that influence that variable (happiness). Second, you probably do not know every single characteristic that influences the outcome variable (happiness). If you knew everything about happiness, you probably would not be doing a study to find out about happiness.

PROBLEMS WITH MATCHING ON PRETEST SCORES

Instead of matching subjects on every characteristic that affects your outcome variable, why not match subjects on the outcome variable itself? In your case, why not match subjects on their happiness scores? That is, before you assign subjects to groups, test people on the happiness scale (what psychologists call a **pretest**). Next, match your groups so that the treatment group and no-treatment group have the same average pretest score. Finally, at the end of the study, test the subjects again, giving subjects what psychologists call a **posttest**. If you find a difference between your groups on the posttest, then you should be positive the treatment worked, right? *Wrong!*

Even if the treatment had no effect whatsoever, there are two possible reasons why two groups that scored the same at pretest could differ on the posttest: selection by maturation interactions and regression effects.

Selection by Maturation Interactions: Subjects Growing in Different Ways

The first reason is the **selection by maturation interaction**: the groups started out the same on the pretest, but afterward developed at different rates or in different directions. That is, subjects that start out the same on a dimension may grow apart because they differ in other respects.

To visualize the strong impact that selection by maturation interaction can have, imagine you found a group of fourth grade boys and girls. You put all the boys in one group. Then, you had them lift weights. You saw that the average weight they could lift was forty pounds. You then picked a group of fourth grade girls who could also lift forty pounds. Thus, your groups are equivalent on the pretest. Then, you introduced the treatment: strength pills. You gave the boys strength pills for eight years. When both groups were in the twelfth grade, you measured their strength. You found the males were much stronger than the females. This effect might be due to the strength pills. However, the effect may also be due to the males naturally developing strength at a faster rate than the females. That is, the effect may be due to failing to match on a variable (gender) that influences muscular maturation.

You have seen that groups may grow apart because of different rates of physical maturation. Groups may also grow apart because of different rates of social, emotional, or intellectual maturation. To illustrate this point, let us examine a situation where the two groups are probably changing in different ways on virtually every aspect of development.

For example, suppose a researcher matched—on the basis of job performance—a group of nineteen-year-old employees with a group of sixty-three-year-old employees. The researcher then enrolled the nineteen-year-olds into a training program. When the researcher compared the groups two years later, the researcher found the nineteen-year-olds were better than the sixty-three-year-olds. Why?

The difference may have been due to training. However, the difference also may have been due to the fact that nineteen-year-olds' productivity should increase even without training because they are just learning their jobs. The sixty-three-year-olds' performance, on the other hand, might naturally decrease as this group anticipates retirement. Therefore, the apparent treatment effect may really be a selection by maturation interaction.

You may be saying to yourself that you would never make the mistake of matching nineteen-year-olds and sixty-three-year-olds on pretest scores. If so, we are glad. You intuitively know you cannot make groups equivalent by merely matching on pretest scores. We would caution you, however, to realize that age is not the only—or even the most important—variable that might affect maturation.[1] Many factors, such as intelligence, motivation, and health, might affect maturation. Thus, if you are going to match on pretest scores, you must also match on all of the variables that might affect maturation. Otherwise, you run the risk of a selection by maturation interaction.

In reiteration, matching on pretest scores is incomplete. Pretest scores are a good predictor of posttest scores, but not a perfect predictor. Many factors affect how a subject does on the posttest. If the groups are not matched on these other relevant variables, two groups that started out the same on the pretest may naturally grow apart.

If you were somehow able to match on pretest scores and all other relevant variables, you would be able to rule out selection by maturation. However, even then, your matched groups may not be equal.

The Regression Effect

How could your groups not be equal if you measured them and made sure they were equal? The problem is that you cannot measure them to make sure they are equal. In other words, measuring them as equal does not mean they are equal. Even though you tend to assume that measurement is perfect, it is not. For example, if a police officer stops you for speeding, the officer might say, "You were going seventy-five." Or, the officer

---

[1]Note, contrary to ageist stereotypes, we might find the older workers improved more than the younger workers. That is, older workers are much more productive and involved than they are often given credit for. Indeed, this ageism is probably why our poor researcher was forced to do such a flawed study. The researcher was able to get management to invest in training for younger workers but not for the older workers. That is, the researcher used the older workers as a comparison group because management gave him no choice—not because he wanted to.

might say, "I clocked you at seventy-five." The officer's two statements are very different. You may have been going forty and the radar mistimed you (radars have clocked trees at over one hundred miles per hour) or you may have been going ninety-five. In any event, you probably were not going at *exactly* the speed the officer recorded. Even in this age of advanced technology, something as simple as measuring someone's height is not immune to measurement error. In fact, one of the authors regularly fluctuates between 5'5" and 5'8", depending on who measures her. Needless to say, if measurements of variables as easy to measure as height are contaminated with random error, measurements of psychological variables—variables that are not as easy to measure as height—are probably also victimized by random measurement error.

You can capitalize on measurement error to make two groups that are very different *appear* to be very similar and later *appear* to become very different. For example, suppose you were offered one thousand dollars to find and take pictures of a white sheep and a black sheep that are the same color. Then, you were asked to take another picture that would make the two sheep differ in terms of color. What would you do?

To get a photo of a black sheep that looks like a white sheep, you would take hundreds of pictures of white sheep and hundreds of pictures of black sheep. Eventually, due to some random measurement error (overexposure, underexposure, mistimed flash, error in developing film, etc.), you would get at least one photo of a white sheep that looks black, or a black sheep that looks white, or a black sheep and a white sheep that both look gray. You got the results you wanted by selectively taking advantage of measurements that were heavily contaminated by random measurement error.

After you have a photo of a white sheep and a black sheep that appear to be the same color, it is easy to make the sheep "become" different colors. You would simply rephotograph the two sheep. The second time you photograph the two sheep, the white one would probably look white and black one would probably look black. The photographic illusion you created was temporary because extreme amounts of random measurement error rarely strike the same measurements twice in a row. In other words, to create the illusion of change, you took advantage of regression to the mean: the tendency for scores that are extremely unusual to revert back to more normal levels on the retest.

Regression toward the mean occurs because unusual scores tend to be unusually affected by chance. As a result, when subjects receiving unusual scores are retested, their scores tend to be affected by chance to a more normal (and lesser) degree the second time around.

In the example above, you intentionally took advantage of the erratic nature of random measurement error. That is, you "matched" two groups on a factor in which they differed. Then, when they scored differently on the posttest, it *looked* like the groups had changed. Unfortunately, a reseacher might *unintentionally* rely on measurement error to match two groups on a factor in which they differ. For instance, suppose a researcher working at an institution for the mentally retarded wants to see whether a specially developed training program can increase intelligence. The researcher wants to have two groups that are identical in intelligence, give one group the training program, and see whether the training program group does better on a second intelligence test than the no-training group. However, the researcher also wants both groups to have near normal intelligence. Unfortunately, after testing all the patients, the researcher only finds eight patients who score between eighty-five and ninety-five on the IQ test.

The researcher decides that eight subjects are only enough for the treatment group. Therefore, he still needs to find a no-treatment group, preferably one that has the same IQ as his treatment group. As he drives by your school, he has an idea: use some of your school's students as subjects. After clearing it with your school and taking precautions so that no one will be harmed by his procedures, he begins work. He sets up an office at your school and offers $25.00 to anyone who will take an IQ test.

After testing many people, he finds eight college students who score around ninety on the IQ test. He makes this group his no-treatment group. At the end of the study, he administers IQ tests to both the treatment and no-treatment groups. When he looks at his results, he is horrified. He finds the eight college students scored much higher on the second IQ test (the posttest) than the institutionalized people. On closer examination, he finds the college students' IQ scores increased dramatically from the pretest to posttest while institutionalized patients' IQ scores dropped from pretest to posttest.

What happened? Did the true intelligence of the college students increase even though the researcher did nothing? Did the training program shrink the true intelligence of the institutionalized patients?

What happened was the investigator selected scores that were likely to be heavily contaminated with measurement error. To understand how this occurred, think about what would cause your classmates to score ninety on an IQ test. They certainly would not score ninety because that was their true level of intelligence. Instead, they must have scored so low because of some factors having nothing to do with intelligence. Perhaps pulling an all-nighter, being hung-over, or suffering from the flu would cause such a poor performance. If they did score ninety on an IQ test because they were very ill, would it be likely they would score ninety the second time? No, chances are they would not be as ill the second time they took the test. As a result, their second score should be higher because it would probably be a closer reflection of their true intelligence.

Likewise, the investigator chose those retarded patients' scores that were most likely to be loaded with measurement error. Consider how a retarded person could score ninety on the IQ test. What could account for a person scoring so far above their true score? Probably some form of luck would be involved. That is, just as you might have found yourself getting lucky on a multiple-choice test for which you were unprepared, a retarded person might get lucky the first time the test was administered. That is, if you test eight thousand retarded people, eight might score fairly high due to chance. But would these same eight be as lucky the next time? It is a good bet they would not. Instead, their second score should be a more accurate reflection of their true score. Consequently, they would get lower scores than they did the first time.

Conclusions about Matching on Pretest Scores

In conclusion, there are two reasons why matching on pretest scores does not totally eliminate extraneous variables. First, because *scores* are flawed indicators of actual *characteristics,* matching does not eliminate the extraneous variable of measurement error. Because of measurement error, it is possible to get two groups that match on pretest scores but that are actually very different. That is, random error may create the mirage that two dissimilar groups are similar. As convincing as this mirage may be, it is only temporary. Often, the mirage will vanish on the posttest, as chance exerts less of an influence on scores so that the extremely deviant scores revert back to more typical levels (regression to the mean). If the mirage disappears during the posttest, two groups that *appeared* to be similar on the pretest may reveal their true differences during the posttest. Although the change in scores is only due to changes in measurement error, you can understand how people could mistakenly interpret these changes as a treatment effect.

Second, matching on pretest scores is incomplete. It is incomplete because the pretest performance is not a perfect indicator of posttest performance. Subjects change from pretest to posttest and many factors determine how subjects will change from pretest to posttest. Therefore, to predict a subject's posttest score, you need to match not only on the pretest score, but on every other variable that might affect how a subject will change. If you do not, you may have two groups that started out the same, but naturally grew apart—no thanks to the treatment. In other words, you may have what appears to be a treatment effect, but is really a selection by maturation effect. (For a summary, see table 4.1.)

PROBLEMS WITH THE PRETEST-POSTTEST DESIGN

No matter how much we match, we cannot form two identical groups of subjects. The only way we could get two identical groups of subjects would be to have the same subjects in both groups. That is, each subject could be in both the no-treatment group and in the

TABLE 4.1 Why the Selection Problem Is so Difficult to Eliminate

1. Self-assignment causes selection bias.
2. Researcher assignment can cause a selection bias.
3. Arbitrary assignment to group causes selection problems by making the groups differ in at least one respect.
4. We cannot match subjects on every single variable.
5. We cannot even match subjects on all relevant variables. Therefore, "matched" groups may differ from each other in terms of "unmatched" variables. These "unmatched" variables may cause the groups to behave differently at the posttest.
6. We have to worry about the effects of "unmatched" variables even when we match on pretest scores. As cases of selection by maturation interactions demonstrate, just because subjects scored the same at pretest, it does not mean they would score the same at posttest.
7. Even if there were no selection by maturation interactions, matching on pretest scores is imperfect because scores may be heavily influenced by random error. The groups may only *appear* to be similar because one or both groups' pretest scores are heavily influenced by random error.

treatment group. For instance, we might use a **pretest-posttest design,** where we give each subject the pretest, administer the treatment, and then give the posttest. If we make sure that the subjects in the treatment group are the same subjects that were in the no-treatment group, we have eliminated the threat of selection.

THREE REASONS SUBJECTS MAY CHANGE BETWEEN PRETEST AND POSTTEST

Our solution seems perfect if we assume the treatment is the only reason a subject's posttest score would be different from his pretest score. Unfortunately, there are two major reasons why this assumption is wrong. First, even without the treatment, subjects may change over time. For example, a subject's mood may change by the minute. Second, how subjects are measured, how well subjects are measured, and how many subjects are measured may change over time. Therefore, even if subjects do not really change between pretest and posttest, their scores may change because of changes in measurement.

Maturation

A subject may change between the time of the pretest and the time of the posttest as a result of becoming more mature. For example, suppose you instituted a weight-lifting program for high school sophomores. You find later, as seniors, they can lift forty pounds more than they could as sophomores. Your problem is you do not know whether the weight training or natural development is responsible for the change. Similarly, if you give a baby ten years of memory training, you will find the child's memory has improved. However, this difference may be due not to the training, but to **maturation:** changes due to natural development (see figure 4.3)

History

A subject may change between pretest and posttest because the subject's environment has changed between pretest and posttest. These environmental changes are called **history.** To understand the effects of history, suppose two social psychologists have a treatment they think will change how Americans feel about space exploration. However, between pretest and posttest, a spacecraft explodes. Or, suppose an investigator was examining the effects of diet on maze-running speed. However, between pretest and posttest, the heat went off in the rat room and the rats nearly froze to death. Obviously, events that happen in a subject's life (history) between the pretest and the posttest can have a powerful effect on a subject's posttest score. (For an example, see figure 4.4.)

Testing

One event that always occurs between the start of the pretest and the start of the posttest is the pretest itself. If the pretest changes subjects, you have a **testing effect.** For example, if your instructor gave you the same test twice, you would score better the second time around. However, your improvement might not be due to better studying habits, but

FIGURE 4.3 A Happy Case of Maturation

rather to remembering some of the questions (see figure 4.5). People who have taken many intelligence tests (e.g., children of clinical psychologists) may score very high on IQ tests, regardless of their true intelligence.

The testing effect is not limited to knowledge tests; it can occur with virtually any measure. To illustrate, let us choose a pretest that has nothing to do with knowledge. For instance, suppose we were to ask people their opinions about Greenland entering the world bank. Would we get another answer the second time we asked this question? Yes, because the very action of asking for their opinion may cause them to think about the issue more and to develop or change their opinion. In short, by measuring something, you may change it.

HOW MEASUREMENT CHANGES MAY CAUSE SCORES TO CHANGE BETWEEN PRETEST AND POSTTEST

Obviously, subjects' scores may change over time because subjects have changed. What is less obvious is that subjects' scores may change over time even if subjects have not changed. Instead, subjects' scores may change because of changes in how subjects are measured. Specifically, scores may change because of instrumentation, regression, and mortality.

A notable case of history.

FIGURE 4.4 The Therapist Thinks the Last Therapy Session Made Rudolph the Red-Nosed Reindeer Feel Better About His Nose. However, Glancing at the Calendar Suggests Another Reason—Greater Peer Acceptance Because Rudolph Guided the Sleigh Last Night.

Instrumentation

An obvious reason for a subject's score changing from pretest to posttest is that the measuring instrument used for the posttest is different from the one used during the pretest. If the difference between pretest and posttest scores is due to changes in the measuring instrument, you have an **instrumentation** effect.

Sometimes, changes in the measuring instrument are unintentional. For example, suppose you are measuring aggression using the most changeable measuring instrument possible: the human rater. As the study progresses, raters may broaden their definition of aggression. Consequently, raters may give subjects higher posttest scores on aggression, even though the subjects' behavior has not changed. Unfortunately, there are many ways raters could change between pretesting and posttesting. Raters could become more conscientious, less conscientious, more lenient, less lenient, etc. Any of these changes could cause an instrumentation effect.

Often, changes in the instrument occur because the researcher is trying to make the

An eye-doctor becomes aware of the testing bias.

Figure 4.5 To Dr. Stern's Consternation, Zebo Remembers (with the Help of Some Crib Sheets) the Eye Exam Chart.

posttest better than the pretest. Thus, the researcher may get rid of typographical errors, bad questions, or make the scales neater. Unfortunately, these changes, no matter how minor they may seem, no matter how logical they may be, are changes. And these changes may cause instrumentation effects.

We are not saying that you should not administer the best measure possible. Of course you should. But you should refine the measure *before* beginning the study.

Regression Revisited

Even if the measuring instrument is the same for both the pretest and posttest, the amount of chance measurement error may not be. In other words, with a pretest-posttest design, you still have to deal with regression toward the mean. To show that you do not get away from regression toward the mean by using the pretest-posttest design, think back to the researcher who was investigating the effects of a training program on intelligence. Suppose that he had decided not to compare the eight highest-scoring patients with a group of college students. Instead, after having the eight highest-scoring patients complete the training program, he administered a second IQ test as his posttest. What would he observe?

As before, he would have observed the patients' IQ scores dropped from pretest to posttest. This drop is not due to the training program robbing patients of intelligence. Rather, the posttest scores more accurately reflect the patients' true intelligence. The posttest scores are lower than the pretest scores because only the pretest scores were inflated with random measurement error.

The pretest scores were destined to be inflated with measurement error because the investigator selected only those subjects whose scores were extreme. Extreme scores tend to have extreme amounts of measurement error. To understand why, remember that a subject's score is a function of two things: the subject's true characteristics and measurement error. Thus, an extreme score may be extreme because measurement error is making the score extreme. To take a concrete example, let us consider how a student might get a perfect score on a quiz. There are three basic possibilities for the perfect score:

1. the student is a perfect student,
2. the student is a very good student and had some good luck, or
3. the student is an average or below average student but was incredibly lucky.

As you can see, if you study a group of people who got perfect scores on the last exam, you are probably studying a group of people whose scores were inflated by measurement error. If subjects were measured again, random error would probably be less generous. (After all, random error could not have been more generous. There is only one place for perfect scores to go—down.) Therefore, if you were to give them a treatment (memory training) and then look at their scores on the next exam, you would be disappointed. The group that averaged 100 percent on the first test might average "only" 96 percent on the second test.

In the case we just described, regression's presence is relatively obvious because it is taking advantage of a rather obvious source of measurement error—error in test scores. But regression may take advantage of less obvious sources of random measurement error.

The subtlest form of measurement error seems more like an error in sampling than an error of measurement. For example, suppose you are trying to make inferences about a subject's typical behavior from a sample of that subject's behavior. If the behavior you observe is not typical of the subject's behavior, you have measurement error. Even if you measured the behavior you observed perfectly, you have measurement error because you have not measured the subject's *typical* behavior perfectly. This measurement error can, of course, lead to regression toward the mean.

To illustrate how a sample of behavior may not be typical of normal behavior, let us look at a coin's behavior. Suppose you find a coin that comes up heads six times in a row. Although you have accurately recorded the coin came up heads six times in a row, you might be making a measurement error if you concluded the coin was biased toward heads. In fact, if you were to flip the coin ten more times, you probably would not get ten more heads. Instead, you would probably get something close to five heads and five tails.

Coins are not the only ones to exhibit erratic behavior. Virtually every behavior is inconsistent and therefore prone to atypical streaks. For example, suppose you watch someone shoot baskets. You accurately observe he made twelve out of twelve shots. Based on these observations, you may conclude he is a great shooter. However, you may be wrong. Perhaps if you had observed his shooting on a different day, you would have seen him make only two out of twelve shots.

To illustrate how this subtle form of measurement error can lead to regression toward the mean, suppose a person who has been happy virtually all of his life feels depressed. This depression is so unlike him that he seeks therapy. Before starting the therapy, the psychologist gives him a personality test. The test verifies that he is depressed. After a couple of sessions, he is feeling better. In fact, according to the personality test, he is no longer depressed. Who could blame the psychologist for feeling proud?

But has the psychologist changed the client's personality? No, the patient is just behaving in a way consistent with his normal personality. The previous measurements were contaminated by events that had nothing to do with his personality. Perhaps his depressed manner reflected a string of bad fortune: getting food poisoning, his cat running away, and being audited by the IRS. As this string of bad luck ended and his luck returned to normal, his mood returned to normal.

Regression toward the mean is such an excellent impersonator of a treatment effect that regression fools most of the people most of the time. Many people swear that something really helped them when they had "hit bottom." Thus, the baseball player who recovers from a terrible slump believes hypnosis was the cure; the owner whose business was at an all time low believes a new manager turned the business around; and a man at an all time emotional low feels that his new girlfriend turned him around. What these people fail to take into account is that things are simply reverting back to the norm (regressing to the mean). When listening to stories about how people bounced back due to some miracle treatment, remember comedian Woody Allen's line: "I always get well, even without the leeches."

Mortality

The last, and perhaps most obvious, reason you could find differences between pretest and posttest scores would be if you were measuring fewer subjects at posttest than you were at pretest. In other words, your study may fall victim to **mortality**: subjects dropping out of the study before it is completed.

To illustrate how much of an impact mortality can have, imagine you are studying the effect of diet on memory in older adults. You pretest your subjects, give them your new diet, and test them again. You find the average posttest score is higher than the average pretest score. However, if the pretest average is based on one hundred subjects and the posttest average is based on seventy subjects, your results may well be due to mortality. Specifically, the reason posttest scores are higher than pretest scores may be that the people who scored very poorly on the pretest are no longer alive at the time of the posttest.

Of course, you do not have to have subjects die to suffer mortality. In fact, mortality usually results from subjects deciding to quit the study, subjects moving away, or from subjects failing to follow directions.

CONCLUSIONS

We tried to create a situation where we manipulated the treatment while keeping everything else constant. However, nothing we tried worked.

When we tried to compare a treatment group versus a no-treatment group, we had to worry that our groups were not identical before the study started. Even when we matched our groups, we realized the groups might not be identical because (1) we could not match on every single characteristic and (2) we had to match based on imperfect measures of subject's true characteristics.

Because we could not get equivalent groups at the start of the study, we did not even bother to dwell on the problems of keeping them equivalent. That is, we did not discuss the mortality problem that would result if, for example, more subjects dropped out of the treatment group than out of the no-treatment group.

Because of the problems with comparing a treatment group against a no-treatment group (see table 4.2), we tried to measure the same group before and after giving them the treatment. Although this before-after tactic got rid of some threats to validity, it created others. As table 4.3 shows, subjects may change from pretest to posttest for a variety of reasons having nothing to do with the treatment. Subjects may change as a result of (1) natural development (maturation), (2) other things in their lives changing (history), or (3) learning from the pretest (testing).

Furthermore, subjects may *appear* to change from pretest to posttest as a result of (1) the posttest measure being different from the pretest measure (instrumentation), (2) their

Maturation: Could the before-after (pretest-posttest) differences have been due to natural changes resulting from subjects becoming older?

History: Could other events in the subjects' lives have caused the pretest-posttest differences?

Testing: Could subjects score differently on the posttest as a result of the practice and experience they got on the pretest?

Instrumentation: Were subjects measured with the same instrument, in the same way, the second time?

Regression: Were subjects selected for their extreme pretest scores? Subjects who get extreme scores have a tendency to get less extreme scores the second time around.

Mortality: Did everyone who took the pretest take the posttest? Or, were the pretest group and the posttest group really two different groups?

---

pretest scores being unduly influenced by chance (setting up regression to the mean), or (3) subjects dropping out of the study so that the posttest group is not the same as the pretest group (mortality).

RULING OUT EXTRANEOUS VARIABLES

Why could we not eliminate extraneous variables? Was it because we used improper designs? No, we did not fail to establish internal validity because we used flawed designs. As you will see in later chapters, matching subjects and testing subjects before and after treatment are useful research techniques.

We failed because our strategy of trying to keep everything constant was flawed. Keeping everything the same is impossible. Imagine, in our ever-changing world, trying to make sure that only one thing in a subject's life changed!

Accounting for Extraneous Variables

Fortunately, you do not have to eliminate extraneous variables to rule out their effects. Instead of eliminating extraneous variables, you can rule out their **effects.** That is, you could try to track down a treatment's effect the way a detective tracks down a murderer. The detective is confronted with more than one suspect for a murder, just as you are confronted with more than one suspect for an effect. The detective cannot make the suspects disappear, just as you cannot eliminate extraneous factors. However, like the detective, you can use logic to rule out the role of some suspects and implicate others.

Of course, before you can begin to account for the actions of every suspicious extraneous variable, you have to know "who" each of these variables are. At first glance, identifying all the thousands of variables that might account for the relationship between the treatment and the effect seems as impossible as eliminating all those variables.

Identifying Extraneous Variables

Fortunately, identifying the extraneous variables is not as difficult as it first appears because every one of these thousands of factors fall into eight categories: Campbell and Stanley's (1966) eight threats to validity. Thus, you really have only eight suspects (see table 4.4). If you can show that selection, history, maturation, testing, regression, mortality, instrumentation, and selection by maturation were not responsible for the effect, then you can conclude the treatment was responsible.

THE RELATIONSHIP BETWEEN INTERNAL AND EXTERNAL VALIDITY

If you rule out these threats, you have established **internal validity.** That is, you have demonstrated that a factor causes an effect in a particular study. But you have not demonstrated that you can generalize your results outside your particular study. Internal validity alone does not guarantee an investigator doing the same study, but with different subjects (depressed patients instead of college students) or using a different setting (a library instead of a lab), would obtain the same results. If you want to *generalize* your results, you need **external validity.**

If internal validity does not guarantee external validity, why bother with establishing internal validity? The obvious answer is you may not care about external validity. Some

---

TABLE 4.4 Campbell and Stanley's (1966) Eight Threats to Internal Validity

History: Variables other than the treatment that have changed in the subjects' environments.

Testing: Changes resulting from the practice and experience subjects got on the pretest.

Instrumentation: The way subjects were measured changed from pretest to posttest.

Regression effects: If subjects are chosen because their scores were extreme, these extreme scores may be loaded with extreme amounts of random measurement error. On retesting, subjects are bound to get more normal scores as random measurement error abates to more normal levels.

Mortality: Differences between conditions are due to subjects dropping out of the study.

Maturation: Apparent treatment effects are really due to natural growth or development.

Selection: Treatment and no-treatment groups were different before the treatment was administered.

Selection by maturation interaction: Treatment and no-treatment groups were predisposed to grow apart.

---

researchers do not care about generalizing their results; they may want only to show that a certain treatment causes a certain effect in a certain setting. For example, researchers may want to show that with their patients, in their hospital, giving the patients an exercise program reduces patients' alcohol consumption. The researchers may not care whether the treatment would work with other kinds of patients at other hospitals (external validity). They only care that they have a method that works for them.

However, few people are so single-minded that they are totally unconcerned with external validity. If you are concerned with external validity, why should you bother with internal validity? After all, in one sense, it seems that things you would do to improve your study's internal validity would reduce its external validity. For example, to reduce the problem of selection bias, you might use twins as your subjects. Although using identical twins (or clones) as subjects would increase internal validity by reducing differences between your treatment and no-treatment groups, it might hurt the generalizability of your study. Your results might apply only to identical twins. Similarly, you might reduce the threat of history by testing your subjects in a lab situation where they are isolated from non-treatment factors. This artificial situation may increase internal validity because the treatment was the only thing to change during the study. However, you would have to wonder whether the treatment would have the same effects outside this artificial situation. Would the results generalize to real life, where the factors you isolated your subjects from come into play?

As you have seen, internal validity and external validity are *sometimes* in conflict (see table 4.5). The same procedures that increase internal validity may decrease external validity. Fortunately, however, internal validity and external validity are not incompatible. As you will read in future chapters, you can have studies that have both internal and external validity. In fact, internal validity is often a prerequisite for external validity. Before you can establish that a factor causes an effect in every situation, you must show that the factor causes an effect in at least one situation (your study).

Thus, the first step to establishing external validity is often establishing internal

TABLE 4.5 Classic Conflicts between the Goals of Internal and External Validity

TACTIC USED TO HELP ESTABLISH INTERNAL VALIDITY	TACTIC'S IMPACT ON EXTERNAL VALIDITY
Use subjects that are very similar to each other to reduce the effects of selection. For example, only study identical twins or only study a specific strain of rats.	Studying a limited group raises questions about the degree to which the results can be generalized to different subject populations. Do the results hold for people who are not twins? Animals that are not rats?
Study subjects in a highly controlled environment, such as a lab, to reduce the effects of extraneous factors, such as history.	Studying subjects in an isolated, controlled, laboratory setting raises questions about the extent to which the results might generalize to more complex, real-life settings.

validity. In the next chapter, you will learn the easiest and most automatic way to take this step: the simple experiment.

SUMMARY

1. If you observe an effect in a study that has internal validity, you know what caused that effect.
2. Campbell and Stanley (1966) described eight major threats to internal validity: selection, selection by maturation, regression, maturation, history, testing, mortality, and instrumentation.
3. When you compare a treatment group to a no-treatment group, beware of the selection bias: the groups being different before you administer the treatment.
4. To reduce selection bias, subjects should never get to choose what amount of treatment they get. In addition, subject's characteristics, attitudes, or behaviors should have nothing to do with what group (treatment or no-treatment) they are put in.
5. It is impossible to match two groups of subjects so that they are identical in every respect. Subjects simply differ in too many ways.
6. Even matching subjects on pretest scores is not perfect because of the problems of selection by maturation and regression.
7. Selection by maturation effects occur when your two groups mature at different rates or in different directions.
8. The fact that extreme scores tend to be a little less extreme the second time around is called regression toward the mean. Regression toward the mean can cause two groups that appear to be matched on a pretest to score differently on the posttest.
9. In the pretest-posttest design, you measure a group, administer the treatment, and measure the group again.
10. Using the pretest-posttest method is not as perfect as it first appears. It is vulnerable to testing, history, regression, maturation, mortality, and instrumentation biases.
11. Regression can occur in the pretest-posttest design because the person may have gotten the treatment when he most needed it. There was no place to go but up.
12. Maturation refers to biological changes that occur to people merely as a result of time. In some cases, becoming more mature—not the treatment—accounts for pretest to posttest differences.
13. Events having nothing to do with the treatment that occur in a subject's life between pretest and posttest (history) can cause changes in a subject's posttest score.
14. Testing bias refers to the fact that taking a pretest may affect performance on a posttest.
15. The instrumentation bias occurs when the pretest is different from the posttest.

16. External validity is the degree to which the results from a study can be generalized.

17. Internal and external validity are not necessarily incompatible.

KEY TERMS

external validity
extraneous factors
history
instrumentation
internal validity

matching
maturation
mortality
pretest-posttest design
regression

selection
selection by maturation
  interaction
testing

EXERCISES

1. What questions would you have of a researcher who said the no-treatment and treatment groups were identical before the start of the study?

2. In all of the following cases, the researcher wants to make cause-effect statements. What threats to internal validity is the researcher apparently overlooking?

    a. Employees are interviewed on job satisfaction. Bosses undergo a three-week training program. When employees are reinterviewed a second time, dissatisfaction seems to be even higher. Therefore, the researcher concludes the training program caused further employee dissatisfaction.

    b. After completing a voluntary workshop on improving the company's image, workers are surveyed. Workers who attended the workshop are now more committed than those in the "no-treatment" group who did not attend the workshop. Researcher's conclusion: the workshop made workers more committed.

    c. After a six-month training program, employee productivity improves. Conclusion: the training program caused increased productivity.

    d. Morale is at an all time low. As a result, the company hires a "humor consultant." One month later, workers are surveyed and morale has improved. Conclusion: the consultant improved morale.

3. A hypnotist claims hypnosis can cause increases in strength. To "prove" this claim, the hypnotist has subjects see how many times they can squeeze a hand-grip in two minutes. Then, she hypnotizes them and has them practice for two weeks. At the end of two weeks, they can squeeze the hand-grips together many more times than they could at the beginning. Other than hypnosis, what could have caused this effect?

4. How could a quack psychologist or doctor take advantage of regression to the mean to make it appear that certain phony treatments actually work?

5. How could a subject's score on an ability test change even though the person's actual ability had not?

6. A memory researcher administers a memory test to a group of residents at a nursing home. He finds a group of grade school students that score the same as the older patients on the memory pretest. He then administers an experimental memory drug to the older patients. One year later, he gives both groups a posttest.
   a. If the researcher finds the older patients now have a worse memory than the grade school students, what can the researcher conclude? Why?
   b. If the researcher finds the older patients now have a better memory than the grade school students, what can the researcher conclude? Why?

7. What is the difference between history and maturation?

8. A psychologist's daughter scores much higher on an IQ test than you expect. The score seems extremely inconsistent with the child's grades and your general impressions of the child. What is one possible explanation for the unusually high score?

9. A researcher reports that a certain argument strategy has an effect, but only on those subjects who hold extreme attitudes. Why might the researcher be mistaken about the effects of the persuasive strategy?

10. What is the difference between internal and external validity? Can you have internal validity without external validity? Can you have external validity without internal validity?

5 The Simple Experiment

OVERVIEW

In this chapter, you will learn the easiest way to establish that a treatment causes an effect: the **simple experiment.** You will start by learning what a simple experiment is and how it works its magic. Next, you will see why knowing how the simple experiment works will help you make intelligent decisions about how to conduct your experiment. Then, you will examine the tough decisions involved in planning a simple experiment: making tradeoffs among ethics, construct validity, external validity, and internal validity. Finally, you will learn how to analyze the results of a simple experiment.

CAUSALITY: THE SIMPLE EXPERIMENT'S PURPOSE

The purpose of the simple experiment is to determine whether a treatment causes an effect. That is, the simple experiment's purpose is not to describe what happens, but rather to explain *why* things happen.

THE LOGIC OF CAUSALITY

To determine that a treatment causes an effect, you must create a situation where you show that (1) the treatment comes before the effect, (2) the effect occurs **after** the treatment is introduced, and (3) nothing but the treatment is responsible for the effect.

For example, if you were doing a chemistry experiment, you could show heat caused a reaction by keeping everything except the heat constant, systematically varying the heat, and then observing a change in the behavior of the molecules **after** you increased the heat. Similarly, if you were doing a psychological experiment, the ideal setup for demonstrating causality would be to find two identical groups of subjects, treat them identically except only one group gets the treatment, test them under identical conditions, and then compare the behavior of the two groups.

THE VARIABILITY PROBLEM

Clearly, you cannot create this ideal situation. You cannot find two identical groups of subjects. Furthermore, you cannot test all your subjects under absolutely identical conditions. Because you give your treatment and no-treatment groups different instructions or manipulations, you usually have to test them separately—either in different rooms or at different times. But even if you could test them at the same time, in the same room, the two groups of subjects would still be sitting in different chairs.

What are the implications of the facts that groups cannot be identical and different groups cannot be tested under identical conditions? It means that if you see a difference between your treatment and no-treatment groups, you have to accept the *possibility* this difference may be due to nontreatment factors.

If You Cannot Eliminate Variability, Account for It

Because you cannot completely eliminate the possibility the difference between your groups is due to nontreatment factors, you will have to settle for the next best thing: determining how unlikely this possibility is (see table 5.1). If you could show that it is very unlikely nontreatment variables are responsible for the group differences, then you could be confident the difference between groups is due, at least in part, to the treatment. You might be wrong occasionally but you would be playing the percentages.

How can you set up a situation that allows you to determine the odds against the difference between groups being due to nontreatment factors? Use **independent random assignment:** randomly determining, for each individual subject, whether that subject gets

TABLE 5.1 Random Assignment versus Keeping Variables Constant

ACCOUNTING FOR EXTRANEOUS VARIABLES BY RANDOM ASSIGNMENT	ELIMINATING EXTRANEOUS VARIABLES BY KEEPING THEM CONSTANT
Ideally, the treatment is the only *systematic* difference between groups. Random changes in testing conditions do not destroy study.	Ideally, the treatment is the only difference between conditions. Treatment and no-treatment subjects would be identical, testing conditions would be identical, time of testing would be identical, etc. The only difference would be the treatment.
Can be used in virtually any setting because extraneous variables do not need to be held constant. Extraneous variables (differences between subjects, changes in temperature, etc.) are allowed to vary—as long as they vary randomly.	Usually requires a lab or highly controlled environment that permits control of extraneous variables.
Difference between groups could be due to treatment *or* random error.	Difference between groups must be due to the treatment—everything else stayed the same.
Need to use inferential statistics to estimate and then account for the effects of random sampling error. Difference between groups could be due to treatment or to random variables.	No need to use inferential statistics. If there is a difference between conditions, it must be due to treatment—nothing else changed.
Failure to correctly account for effects of random variables will result in incorrectly assessing the treatment's effect (Type 1 or Type 2 errors).	Failure to keep all nontreatment variables constant may result in incorrectly assessing the treatment's effect. If treatment is not the only thing that varies, difference between groups may not be due to treatment.

the treatment. For example, you might flip a coin for each subject. If the coin comes up heads, the subject gets the treatment; if the coin comes up tails, the subject does not get the treatment.[1]

The Advantages of Turning Variability into Random Variability

What are the benefits of independent random assignment? First, by assigning subjects on the basis of a coin flip (or a random numbers table, see box 5.1), you guarantee that treatment subjects and no-treatment subjects would *systematically* differ in only one way: the treatment.

Second, you guarantee that the only other differences between groups are due to chance. Put another way, the groups are random samples of the same population: the total number of subjects who were in your study. Therefore, there are only two reasons why they might differ from one another: random sampling error and treatment. This is good news because you can use the science of random sampling error—the science of inferential statistics—to determine the probability the difference between your groups is due to chance. If, at the end of your study, the groups differ by more than would be expected by chance alone, then you can conclude the difference is due to the one factor that varied systematically: the treatment. Since the science of chance is not an exact science, you cannot be absolutely positive the treatment had an effect. But you can be sure beyond a reasonable doubt.

If, on the other hand, the difference is not more than would be expected by chance, you cannot rule out the possibility the difference between your groups is due to chance. Although the difference between your groups may be due to treatment, the difference also could be due to nontreatment variables. When the difference between your groups is less than could reasonably be expected by chance, your results are inconclusive. (The advantages and disadvantages of using random assignment are summarized in table 5.2.)

BOX 5.1   Randomly Assigning Subjects to Two Groups

There are many ways to randomly assign subjects to groups. Your professor may prefer another method. However, following these steps guarantees random assignment and an equal number of subjects in each group.

Step 1: On the top of a sheet of paper, make two columns. Title the first "Control Group." Title the second "Experimental Group." Under each group name, draw a line for each subject you will need. Thus, if you were planning to use eight subjects (four in each group), you would draw four lines under each group name.

---

[1]As you will see in box 5.1, psychologists usually do not use pure independent random assignment. They typically use independent random assignment with the restriction that an equal number of subjects is in each group.

CONTROL GROUP   EXPERIMENTAL GROUP

_____   _____

_____   _____

_____   _____

_____   _____

Step 2: Turn to a random numbers table, like the one tabled below. Roll a die to determine which column in the table you will use.

Random Numbers Table

LINE	COLUMN					
	1	2	3	4	5	6
1	10480	15011	01536	02011	81647	69179
2	22368	46573	25595	85393	30995	89198
3	24130	48360	22527	97265	76393	64809
4	42167	93093	06243	61680	07856	16376
5	37570	39975	81837	76656	06121	91782
6	77921	06907	11008	42751	27756	53498
7	99562	72905	56420	69994	98872	31016
8	96301	91977	05463	07972	18876	20922

Step 3: Assign the first number in the column to the first space under Control Group, the second number to the second space, etc. When you have filled all the spaces for the control group, place the next number under the first space under Experimental Group and continue until you have filled all the spaces. Thus, if you rolled a "5," you would start in the fifth column and your sheet of paper would look like this:

CONTROL GROUP   EXPERIMENTAL GROUP

81674   06121

30995   27756

76393   98872

07856   18876

Step 4: At the end of each control group score, write down a "C." At the end of each experimental group score, write down an "E." In this example, our sheet would now look like this:

CONTROL GROUP   EXPERIMENTAL GROUP

81674C   06121E

30995C   27756E

76393C   98872E

07856C   18876E

Step 5: Rank these numbers from lowest to highest. Then, on a second piece of paper, put the lowest number on the top line, the second lowest number on the next line, and so on. In this example, your page would look like this:

06121E
07856C
18876E
27756E
30995C
76393C
81647C
98872E

Step 6: Number the top line, subject 1, the second line, subject 2, etc. The first subject who shows up will be in the condition specified on the top line, the second subject who shows up will be in the condition specified by the second line, and so forth. In this example, the first subject will be in the experimental group, the second in the control group, the third and fourth in the experimental group, the fifth, sixth, and seventh in the control group, and the eighth in the experimental group. Thus, our sheet of paper would look like this:

Subject 1 = 06121E
Subject 2 = 07856C
Subject 3 = 18876E
Subject 4 = 27756E
Subject 5 = 30995C
Subject 6 = 76393C
Subject 7 = 81647C
Subject 8 = 98872E

Step 7: To avoid confusion, recopy your list, but make two changes. First, delete the random numbers. Second, write out "experimental" and "control". In this example, your recopied list would look like this:

Subject 1 = Experimental
Subject 2 = Control
Subject 3 = Experimental
Subject 4 = Experimental
Subject 5 = Control
Subject 6 = Control
Subject 7 = Control
Subject 8 = Experimental

TABLE 5.2 Advantages and Disadvantages of Random Assignment

ADVANTAGES	DISADVANTAGES
The treatment is the only variable that will vary systematically.	Nontreatment variables will vary randomly.
Because random assignment does not rely on holding variables constant, experiments can be done outside the lab, in less controlled, more natural settings.	Because random assignment does not hold variables constant, differences between groups may not be due to treatment. Instead, group differences may be due to random variables.
Statistics can be used to estimate the effects of random variables.	Statistics may underestimate or overestimate the effects of random variables, resulting in incorrectly determining the effects of treatment.
If you can randomly assign subjects to a group, you can determine the effects of a given manipulation.	You often cannot randomly assign subjects to a group. Assigning subjects to a group may be unethical (if the treatment is stressful), impractical, and impossible—you cannot assign subjects to variables to which they are already assigned (personal characteristics such as age, gender, race, or personality).

BASIC TERMINOLOGY

Now that you understand the logic of random assignment, let us look at the simplest application of independent random assignment: the simple experiment. In the simple experiment, subjects are independently and randomly assigned to one of two groups, usually to either a treatment group or to a no-treatment group.

EXPERIMENTAL HYPOTHESIS

The simple experiment starts with an **experimental hypothesis**: a prediction that the treatment will *cause* an effect. In other words, the treatment and no-treatment groups will differ because of the treatment's effect. For example, you might hypothesize that getting three hours of full-spectrum lighting causes an increase in mood. Specifically, you might predict that the group getting three hours of full-spectrum light will be happier than the group not getting full-spectrum light.

NULL HYPOTHESIS

The experimental hypothesis is pitted against the **null hypothesis**: the hypothesis that there is *no* evidence the treatment has an effect; any difference between the treatment and no-treatment groups is due to chance. Thus, the null hypothesis would be: Getting three hours of full-spectrum lighting has no demonstrated effect on happiness.

If your experimental results show the difference between groups is probably not due to chance, you can reject the null hypothesis. By rejecting the null hypothesis, you embrace the experimental hypothesis.

But what happens if you fail to demonstrate the treatment has an effect? Can you say there is no effect for full-spectrum lighting? No, you only can say you did not demonstrate full-spectrum lighting causes a change in happiness. In other words, you are back to where you were before you began the study: you do not know whether full-spectrum lighting causes a change in happiness.[2]

We cannot overemphasize the point that *the failure to find a treatment effect does not mean the treatment has no effect.* If you had looked more carefully, you might have observed an effect (just as companies who conveniently failed to find a difference in quality between their brand and another brand may have found a difference had they looked more carefully). Put another way, the null hypothesis is a "maybe" hypothesis, stating the difference between conditions may be due to chance. Note that saying a difference *may* be due to chance is not the same as saying a difference *is* not due to chance.

ADMINISTERING THE INDEPENDENT VARIABLE

Once you have your hypotheses, your next step is to administer (assign) the treatment to some subjects and withhold it from others. In the experiment we have been discussing, you need to vary the amount of full-spectrum light people get. Furthermore, the amount of full-spectrum light a person gets should be independent of the individual's personal characteristics, as well as independent of both the subject's and researcher's preferences. Specifically, the amount of full-spectrum light subjects receive should be determined by independent random assignment. Because full-spectrum light *varies* between the treatment group and the no-treatment (comparison) group, because full-spectrum light varies *independently* of each subject's characteristics, and because the amount of full-spectrum lighting a subject gets is determined by *independent* random assignment, full-spectrum lighting is the *independent variable.*

In simple experiments, the independent variable will always vary between two amounts or *levels.* In this example, subjects are assigned to one of the following two levels of the independent variable: (1) getting three hours of full-spectrum lighting and (2) getting no full-spectrum lighting.

[2]Those of you who are intimately familiar with confidence intervals may realize that null results do not necessarily put the researcher completely back at square one. Admittedly, we do not know whether the effect is greater than zero, but the data do allow us to estimate a range in which the effect may fall. That is, before the study, we may have no idea of the potential size of the effect. We might think the effect would be anywhere between -100 units and $+100$ units or we might simply guess the effect was between $+30$ and $+40$ units. However, based on the data collected in the study, we could estimate, with 95 percent confidence, the effect is between a certain range. For example, we might find, at the 95 percent level of confidence, the effect is somewhere between -1 units and $+3$ units.

EXPERIMENTAL AND CONTROL GROUPS

The subjects who are randomly assigned to get the higher level of the treatment (three hours of full-spectrum light) are called the experimental group. The subjects who are randomly assigned to get a lower level of the treatment (in this case, no treatment) are called the control group.

Please note that the control group and the experimental group should be roughly equivalent at the start of the experiment—the only systematic difference between them occurs during the experiment when they receive different levels of the independent variable. Therefore, if the groups differ at the end of the experiment, the difference may be due to being assigned to different levels of the independent variable. In other words, the control group is a comparison group—by comparing the control group with the experimental group, we can determine whether the treatment had an effect.

As the terms experimental *group* and control *group* imply, you should have several subjects in each of your conditions. The more subjects, the more random assignment will thoroughly stir up and spread out nontreatment factors, making your two groups more similar before the study begins. If you are doing an experiment on a strength pill and only have two subjects—a 6′4″, 280-pound offensive tackle and a 5′1″, 88-pound weakling recovering from a long illness—randomization will not have the opportunity to make your groups equivalent. Thus, just as you would want to flip a coin more than two times if you were trying to get approximately 50 percent heads and 50 percent tails, you would use more than two subjects if you wanted to make your two groups equivalent before the study began.

The Value of Independence

Although we have noted the experimental and control groups are groups in the sense that there are several subjects in each "group," that is the only sense in which these "groups" are groups. To conduct an experiment, you do not find two groups of subjects and then randomly assign one group to be the experimental group and the other to be the control group. To see why not, suppose you were doing a study involving 10,000 janitors at a Los Angeles company and 10,000 managers at a New York company. You have 20,000 people in your experiment—one of the largest experiments in history. Then, you flip a coin and, on the basis of that single coin flip, assign the L.A. janitors to no treatment and the New York managers to treatment. Even though you have 10,000 subjects in each group, your treatment and no-treatment groups differ in a systematic way before the study begins. Your random assignment is no more successful in making your groups similar than it was when you had only two subjects. To get random assignment to equalize your groups, you need to assign each subject **independently**: individually, without regard to how previous subjects were assigned.

Even after you have assigned subjects to a condition, you do not want your control subjects to form a "group" nor do you want the experimental subjects to become a "group." To prevent your groups from becoming "groups," you do not test the control subjects in one group session and the experimental subjects in a separate group session. There are several reasons why you should not have one testing session for the control group and a second session for the experimental group. First, subjects may interact and influence other members of the group. That is, instead of giving their own individual, independent responses, subjects might respond as a conforming mob. As a concrete example of the perils of letting subjects interact, imagine you are doing an extrasensory perception (ESP) experiment. In the experimental group, all fifty subjects correctly guessed the coin would turn up heads. In the control group, all fifty subjects incorrectly guessed the coin would turn up tails. If each subject had made his or her decision independently, the results would certainly defy chance. However, if all the experimental group members talked to one another and made a group decision, they were not acting as fifty individual subjects, but as one. In that case, the results would not be so impressive—because all fifty experimental subjects acted as one, the odds of them correctly guessing the coin flip were the same as the odds of one person correctly guessing a coin flip: fifty to fifty.

Although the above example shows what can happen if subjects are tested in groups and allowed to interact freely, interaction can disturb independence even when group discussion is prohibited. Subjects may influence one another through inadvertent outcries (laughs, exclamations like "Oh no!") or through subtle nonverbal cues. In our happiness experiment, one sobbing subject might cause the entire experimental group to be unhappy. Consequently, we might conclude falsely that the unhappiness must be due to the treatment. If, on the other hand, we test subjects individually, the unhappy subject's behavior does not affect anyone else's responses. (For similar reasons, a public opinion poll would ask each person individually rather than asking a group of people for their opinion.)

The second reason for not testing the experimental group as a group and the control group as a group is that such testing causes the inevitable, random differences between testing sessions to become systematic effects. For example, suppose when the experimental group was tested, there was a distraction in the hall, but there was no such distraction while the control group was tested. Like the treatment, this distraction was presented to all the experimental group subjects, but to none of the control group subjects. As a result, if the distraction did have an effect, its effect might be mistaken for a treatment effect. However, if subjects were tested individually, it is very unlikely that only the experimental subjects would be exposed to distractions. Instead, distractions would have a chance to even out so that both groups would be affected by these factors to a similar extent.

But what if you are sure you will not have distractions? Even then, the sessions will differ in ways unrelated to the treatment. If you manage to test the subjects at the same time, you will have to use different experimenters and different experimental rooms. If you manage to use the same experimenter and room, you will have to test the groups at different times. So, if you find a significant difference between your two groups, is the effect due to differences on the treatment variable or due to differences in the two treatment sessions (an experimenter effect, a time of day effect, etc.)? To avoid these problems in interpreting your results, make sure the treatment is the only factor that systematically varies. In other words, test subjects individually or in small groups so that random differences among treatment conditions can even out.

The Value of Assignment

Independence is vital because the essence of the simple experiment is to begin with two groups of subjects that are essentially equivalent before the experiment begins. In other words, the groups differ only in that the experimental group is **assigned** to receive a higher level of the independent variable and the control group is **assigned** to receive a lower level of the independent variable.

If you cannot start with two equivalent groups or you cannot randomly **assign** subjects to groups, then you cannot do a simple experiment. Thus, if you want to compare a group of males with a group of females, a low-IQ group with a high-IQ group, a tall group with a short group, or a shy group with an out-going group, you cannot do a simple experiment. You cannot do a simple experiment to compare these groups because the groups would be different before the study began. Furthermore, you cannot do a simple experiment because you cannot randomly assign subjects to these kinds of groups. For example, it makes no sense to assign a male to be in the "female" group, or a 7'2" person to be in the "short person" group. Because we cannot randomly assign subjects to have certain personal characteristics, simple experiments cannot be used to study the effects of personal characteristics such as sex, race, personality, and intelligence.

Admittedly, we can randomly sample from groups having certain personal characteristics, but that is not the same as randomly assigning subjects to have those characteristics. To emphasize the importance of the distinction between random sampling from groups and randomly assigning to groups, let us go back to our lighting experiment. We could, perhaps, take a random sample of subjects who were not exposing themselves to full-spectrum light and compare them to a group of subjects who were not exposing themselves to full-spectrum light. However, determining whether differences between the groups were due to lighting would be difficult because the groups differed in many ways before the study started. For example, if the full-spectrum lighting group were more depressed, the lighting might be a symptom—rather than a cause—of their depression. That is, they are using the lights to cure their depression, just as a person uses penicillin to stop an infection. If the full-spectrum lighting group is less depressed, it may be because they are richer and can afford such convenience items as full-spectrum lights. If, on the other hand, you start with one group of subjects and then randomly assign half to full-spectrum lighting and half to no lighting, interpreting differences between the groups would be much simpler: the groups were probably equivalent before the treatment was introduced, large group differences are probably due to the treatment.

COLLECTING THE DEPENDENT VARIABLE

Of course, before you determine whether the groups differ in happiness, you must measure their happiness. You know each person's happiness will **vary depending** on the individual's personality and you hope their happiness will also **depend** on lighting (the independent variable). Therefore, happiness is your **dependent variable.** Since the dependent variable is what the subject does that you measure, the dependent variable is often called the **dependent measure.** (For brief definitions of the terms we have discussed, see table 5.3.)

TABLE 5.3 The Simple Experiment: Key Terms

Experimental hypothesis: A prediction the treatment will *cause* an effect.

Null hypothesis: The hypothesis that there is *no* treatment effect. This hypothesis can be disproved, but cannot be proved.

Independent variable: The treatment variable. The variable manipulated by the experimenter.

Dependent variable: The subject's behavior that is measured because the experimenter hopes it will be affected by the independent variable.

Experimental group: The subjects who are randomly assigned to get the treatment.

Control group: The subjects who are randomly assigned to get no treatment.

THE STATISTICAL SIGNIFICANCE DECISION

After measuring the dependent variable, you will want to compare the experimental group's happiness scores to the control group's. One way to make this comparison is to subtract the average of the happiness scores for the control (comparison) group from the average of the experimental group's happiness scores.

Statistically Significant Results

Unfortunately, knowing how much the groups differ does not tell you how much of an effect the treatment had. After all, the entire difference between groups may be due to random error. To determine the probability that the difference between groups is not due exclusively to chance extraneous variables, you need to use statistics: the science of chance.

If, by using statistics, you find the difference between your groups is greater than could be expected if only chance were at work, then your results are **statistically significant** (see table 5.4). The term means that you are sure, beyond a reasonable doubt, the results were not a fluke.

What is a reasonable doubt? Usually researchers want to be at least 95 percent sure the treatment is responsible for the difference. In other words, they want less than a 5 percent chance the results are due solely to random error. Therefore, if you found a statistically significant effect in your lighting experiment, you would conclude the

TABLE 5.4 Verdicts from Tests of Significance

SIGNIFICANT	NOT SIGNIFICANT
Results probably not due to chance	Results may be due to chance
Able to conclude that treatment has effect	Unable to conclude that treatment has effect

TABLE 5.5 Limits of Statistical Significance

Statistically significant differences are
1. *Probably* not due to chance
2. Not necessarily large
3. Not necessarily important

independent variable caused a change in subjects' scores on the dependent variable. You would be relatively confident that if you repeated the study, you would get the same pattern of results.

Realize that statistically significant results are only significant in a statistical sense. Statistical significance does not mean the results are significant in the sense of being large. Even a very small difference may be statistically reliable. For example, if you flipped a coin five thousand times and it came up heads 52 percent of the time, this small deviation from 50% would be statistically significant.

Nor does statistical significance mean the results are significant in the sense of being important (see table 5.5). If you have a meaningless hypothesis, you may have results that are statistically significant, but meaningless.

Null Results

You now know how to interpret statistically significant results. But what if your results are not statistically significant? That is, what if you cannot reject the hypothesis that the difference between your groups is due to chance? Then, you have failed to reject the null hypothesis. Therefore, your results would be described as "not significant," or "null results."

The terms "null results" and "not significant" accurately describe the *inconclusiveness* of these findings. With null results, you do not know whether the treatment has an effect you *failed* to find or whether the treatment really has no effect.

The situation is analogous to a "not guilty" verdict: Is the defendant innocent or did the prosecutor present a poor case? Often, defendants get off, not because of overwhelming proof of their innocence, but because of lack of conclusive proof of their guilt.

Despite the fact that null results neither confirm nor deny that the treatment had an effect, people commonly abuse null results. Sometimes, people abuse null results by arguing that null results secretly confirm their suspicions. For example, they may say, "The difference between my groups shows the treatment had an effect, even though the difference is not significant." Reread this statement because you are sure to hear it again—it is the most commonly stated contradiction in psychology (see table 5.6). People making this statement are really saying, "The difference is due to the treatment, even though I've found no evidence the difference isn't simply due to chance."

Some people make the opposite mistake, believing that null results disconfirm their suspicions. That is, some people falsely conclude that null results definitely establish the treatment had no effect. This is a mistake because it overlooks the difficulty of finding and proving that a treatment has an effect.

TABLE 5.6 Common Errors in Interpreting or Discussing Null Results

STATEMENT	FLAW
"The results were not significant. Therefore, the independent variable had no effect."	Failing to prove beyond a reasonable doubt that a treatment had an effect is not the same as proving the treatment had no effect. An experiment using more subjects, more powerful manipulations of the independent variable, and more sensitive measures may have found an effect. In short, saying "not that I know of" is not the same as proving "there isn't any."
"The treatment had an effect, even though the results are not significant."	"Not significant" means you failed to find an effect. You cannot say, "I didn't find an effect for the treatment, but I really did."

People should realize that not finding something is not the same as proving the thing does not exist. After all, people often fail to find things that clearly exist: they fail to find books that are in the library, items that are in the grocery store, and keys that are on the table in front of them. Even in highly systematic investigations, failing to find something does not mean the thing does not exist. For example, in 70 percent of all fingerprint investigations, investigators do not find a single identifiable print at the murder scene—not even the victim's. Thus, the failure to find the suspect's fingerprints at the scene is hardly proof the suspect is innocent. For essentially the same reasons, the failure to find an effect is not proof there is no effect.

SUMMARY OF THE "IDEAL" SIMPLE EXPERIMENT

Thus far, we have said that the simple experiment gives you an *easy* way to determine whether a factor causes an effect. If you can randomly assign subjects to either a treatment or no-treatment group (and you often cannot for ethical or practical reasons), all you have to do is find out whether your results are statistically significant. If they are, then your treatment had an effect. No method allows you to account for the effects of nontreatment variables with as little effort as random assignment.

ERRORS IN DETERMINING WHETHER RESULTS ARE STATISTICALLY SIGNIFICANT

Unfortunately, however, there is one drawback to random assignment—it creates chance differences between groups. This drawback is a concern because you may make errors in accounting for chance. Although statistics will allow you to predict chance much of the time, you cannot totally predict chance all of the time.

TYPE 1 ERRORS

If you underestimate the role of chance, you may make a **Type 1 error:** mistaking a chance difference for a treatment effect. Examples of Type 1 errors in nonpsychology settings would include convicting an innocent person (mistaking a series of coincidences as evidence of guilt) or making a "false-positive" medical diagnosis, such as telling someone they were pregnant when they were not or diagnosing someone as having AIDS when they do not.

Preventing Type 1 Errors

What can you do about Type 1 errors? Although you cannot completely eliminate them, you can decide what risk you are willing to take. Usually, experimenters decide they are going to take a five percent risk of making a Type 1 error. They feel that 20 to 1 are great odds. But why take even that risk? Why not take less than a 1 percent risk?

To understand why not, imagine you are betting with someone who is flipping a coin. He always calls heads, you always pick tails. He is winning most of the flips because he is cheating. Let us suppose you will continue betting until you have statistical proof he is cheating. You do not want to make the Type 1 error of attributing his results to cheating when they are really due to luck. At what point would you stop betting? If you wanted to be absolutely, 100 percent sure, you would never stop betting because any kind of lucky streak is possible. If you wanted to be 99.9 percent sure, you would bet for quite a while. But, if you only wanted to be 90 percent sure, you would not have to bet very long.

TYPE 2 ERRORS

The point of this example is that in trying to be very, very sure an effect is due to treatment and not to chance, you may make a **Type 2 error:** overlooking a genuine treatment effect because you think it might be due to chance. Examples of Type 2 errors in nonpsychological situations would include letting a criminal go free (mistakenly attributing the evidence as a set of coincidences because the jury wanted to be sure beyond *any* doubt) or making a "false-negative" medical diagnosis, such as failing to detect someone was pregnant or failing to find they had AIDS.

As you can see, you may have to make tradeoffs between the risk of a Type 1 error you will take and the risk of a Type 2 error you will take (see table 5.7). You want to be careful not to say that two groups differed because of the treatment when they really differed only by chance (just as you would not want to be so reckless as to accuse someone of cheating merely because 6 of 10 coin flips came up heads). On the other hand, you do not want to be so cautious that you fail to detect real treatment differences. In other words, you want your study to have **power:** the ability to find differences or, put another way, the ability to avoid making Type 2 errors.[3]

---

[3]More precisely, power = 1 – probability of making a Type 2 error. Thus, as the probability of making a Type 2 error decreases, power goes up. Power can range from 0 (no chance of finding a significant result) to 1.00 (guaranteed of finding the difference significant).

TABLE 5.7   Possible Outcomes of a Statistical Significance Decision

STATISTICAL SIGNIFICANCE DECISION	REAL STATE OF AFFAIRS	
	TREATMENT HAS AN EFFECT	TREATMENT DOES NOT HAVE AN EFFECT
Significant—reject null hypothesis	Correct decision	Type 1 error
Not significant—do not reject null hypothesis	Type 2 error	Correct decision

Preventing Type 2 Errors by Increasing Power

Unfortunately, many undergraduate research projects are so powerless they are doomed from the start. The students carrying out these powerless experiments would not consider looking for a cell's nucleus with anything other than a clean, high-powered microscope. Yet, like someone using a dirty, dusty, cracked magnifying glass to look for changes in the structure of a cell's nucleus, they are using an under-powered experiment that will be unable to find what they are looking for. In other words, even if their treatment has an effect, statistical tests on their data will not find that effect to be statistically significant.

One reason they fail to design powerful experiments is they simply do not think about power—a "sin" of which many professional researchers are also guilty (Cohen, 1990). Another reason is students are tempted to think "power is a statistical concept and has nothing to do with design of experiments. There is nothing I can do about statistics." Admittedly, power is a statistical concept. However, statistical concepts should influence the design of research. Indeed, by taking power into account, you can design a study with adequate power—without increasing your chances of making a Type 1 error.

To increase your study's power, *you have to reduce the likelihood that chance differences will hide the treatment effect.* Two ways of doing that are (1) to reduce the effects of random error and (2) to increase the size of the treatment effect (see figure 5.1).

Reducing Random Error

One of the most obvious ways to reduce the effects of random error is to reduce the potential sources of random error. The major sources of random variability are differences among testing situations, unreliable dependent measures, differences among subjects, and sloppy coding of data.

Standardize Procedures and Use Reliable Measures   Since a major source of random variability is variation in the testing situation, you can reduce random error by standardizing your experiment: keeping the testing environment and the experimental procedures as constant as possible. Therefore, to improve power, you might want the noise level, illumination level, temperature, room, and time of day to be the same for each subject. Furthermore, you would want to treat all your experimental group subjects identically and all your control group subjects identically. Finally, you would also like to use a

Jungle of random error

Lost treatment effect

Cut down on random error

Build up Treatment effect

FIGURE 5.1 Two Ways to Avoid Losing Your Treatment Effect in a "Jungle" of Random Error

reliable and sensitive dependent measure. As we discussed in chapter 3, some measures are more affected by random error than others.

The desire for standardization and reliable measures is responsible for some psychologists' love of instruments and the laboratory. Under the lab's carefully regulated conditions, experimenters can create powerful and sensitive experiments.

Other experimenters (as you will see in chapter 10) eschew the laboratory setting for real-world setting. The price they pay for leaving the laboratory is that variables experimenters could control in the lab vary randomly in the field. These variables, free to vary wildly, create a jungle of random error that may hide real effects. Because of the variability in real-world settings, the difficulties of standardizing administration of the independent variable, and the difficulties of using sensitive, reliable measures in the field, even die-hard field experimenters may first look for a significant treatment effect in the lab before venturing out to find the treatment's effect in the field.

Use a Homogeneous Group of Subjects   Between subject differences may hide treatment effects. Even if the treatment effect is large, you may overlook it, mistakenly ascribing the difference between your groups to the fact your subjects are years apart in age and worlds apart in terms of environment and genetic heritage.

To prevent between subject differences from obscuring treatment effects, select subjects who are similar to one another. For instance, select subjects who are the same sex, same age, and have the same IQ. Or, use rats as subjects. With rats, you can select subjects that have grown up in the same environment, have similar genes, and even have the same birthday. By studying homogeneous subjects under standardized situations, rat researchers can detect very subtle treatment effects.

Code Data Carefully   Obviously, sloppy coding of the data can sabotage the most sensitively designed study. Why do we mention this obvious fact? First, many undergraduates are guilty of sloppy coding. Although sloppiness does not necessarily bias the results, it will probably introduce random error that will rob you of power. Therefore, check and recheck the coding of your data. Second, careful coding is a cheap way to increase power. If you increase power by using animal subjects, you may lose the ability to generalize to humans. If you increase power by using a lab experiment, you may lose the ability to generalize to real-world settings. But careful coding costs you nothing except for a little time.

Let Random Error Even Out   Thus far, we have talked about the most obvious way to reduce the effects of random error—reduce the sources of random error. But there is another way. You can reduce the effects of random error by giving random error more chances to balance out. As you know, random error balances out in the long run. In the short run, you might get five heads in six coin flips, but in the long run, you will end up with almost as many tails as heads.

To take advantage of the fact random error balances out in the long run, use more subjects. If you use five subjects in each group, your groups probably will not be very equivalent before the experiment begins. Therefore, even if you found large differences between the groups at the end of the study, you might have to say the difference could very well be due to chance. However, if you use 60 subjects in each group, your groups should be fairly equivalent before the study begins. Consequently, a treatment effect that would be dismissed as due to chance if you used five subjects per group, might be statistically significant if you used 60 subjects per group.

Create Larger Effects

Until now, we have talked about increasing power by making our experiment more sensitive to small differences. Specifically, we have talked about reducing the amount of random error or giving random error a chance to even out so it will not obscure our treatment effect. We have left out the most obvious way to increase our experiment's power: increase the size of the effect. Bigger effects are easier to find.

Your best bet for increasing the size of the effect is to give the control group subjects a very low level of the independent variable while giving the experimental group a very high level of the independent variable. The reasoning is that if the treatment has an effect, the more treatment, the more effect. Consequently, the more the groups differ in terms of the treatment, the more the groups should differ in terms of behavior. Hence, to have adequate power in the lighting experiment, rather than giving the control group one hour of full-spectrum light and the experimental group two hours, you might give the control group no full-spectrum light and the experimental group six hours of blue light.

The strategy of giving your experimental and control groups widely different levels of the treatment can also be applied to more advanced experimental designs. For example, Wilson and Schooler (1991) wanted to determine whether thinking about the advantages and disadvantages of a choice could hurt one's ability to make the right choice. In one experiment, they had participants rate their preferences for jams. Half the subjects rated their preferences after filling out a "filler" questionnaire asking them to list reasons why they chose their major. The other half rated their preferences after filling out a questionnaire asking them to "analyze why you feel the way you do about each jam in order to prepare yourself for your evaluations." As Wilson and Schooler predicted, the participants who thought about why they liked the jam made lower quality ratings than those who did not reflect on their ratings. Specifically, the ratings of the group that merely rated the jams corresponded better to experts' ratings of jam quality than did the ratings of the "reflective" group. Although the fact that one can think too much about a choice is intriguing, we want to emphasize another aspect of Wilson and Schooler's study: the difference between the experimental and control group. Note that the researchers did not encourage the control group to do any reflection whatsoever. They did not have the control group do a moderate amount of reflection and the experimental group do slightly more reflection. If they had, they might not have found the effect.

SUMMARY OF THE EFFECTS OF STATISTICAL CONSIDERATIONS ON DESIGNING THE SIMPLE EXPERIMENT

You have seen that statistical considerations dictate and influence virtually every aspect of the design process (see table 5.8). Because you cannot accept the null hypothesis (you can only reject it or fail to reject it), you cannot do an experiment to prove two treatments have the same effect. Nor can you use the simple experiment to show that a treatment has no effect. The only hypotheses you can hope to support are hypotheses that the groups will differ. Statistical considerations also mandate how you should assign your subjects (independent random assignment) and how you should treat your subjects (taking care to maintain their independence).

Even when statistics are not dictating what you must do, they are suggesting what you should do. To avoid making Type 2 errors, statistics suggest that you

TABLE 5.8 Implications of Statistics for the Simple Experiment

STATISTICAL CONCERN/REQUIREMENT	IMPLICATIONS FOR DESIGNING EXPERIMENT
Observations must be independent	Need to use independent random assignment and not allow one subject to influence another's response
Groups must differ for only two reasons—random differences and the independent variable	Must use random assignment
Cannot accept null hypothesis	Cannot use experiment to prove that independent variable has no effect
Need sufficient power to find effect	1. Standardize procedures 2. Use sensitive, reliable dependent variables 3. Carefully code data 4. Use homogeneous subjects 5. Use many subjects 6. Use extreme levels of the independent variable

1. Standardize your procedures
2. Use sensitive and reliable dependent measures
3. Carefully code your data
4. Use homogeneous subjects
5. Use many subjects
6. Use extreme levels of the independent variable

NONSTATISTICAL CONSIDERATIONS

Yet, statistical considerations are not the only things you should consider when designing a simple experiment. For example, if you only consider statistical power, you may unwittingly harm your subjects as well as your experiment's external and construct validity. Therefore, in addition to statistical issues such as power, you should also consider external validity, construct validity, and ethical issues.

EXTERNAL VALIDITY VERSUS POWER

Many of the things you can do to improve your study's power may hurt your study's external validity. By using a lab experiment to stop unwanted variables from varying, you may have more power to find an effect. However, by preventing unwanted variables from varying you may hurt your ability to generalize your results to real life—where these unwanted variables do vary. By using a homogeneous set of subjects (eighteen-year-olds,

Caucasian males with IQs between 120 and 125), you reduce between subject differences, thereby enhancing your ability to find treatment effects. However, because you used such a restricted sample, you may not be as able to generalize your results to the average American as a researcher who used a more heterogeneous sample (see figure 5.2). Finally, although using extreme levels of the independent variable might help you detect a treatment effect, using extreme levels may prevent you from determining the effect of realistic, naturally occurring levels of the treatment variable.

CONSTRUCT VALIDITY VERSUS POWER

Not only may your efforts to improve power hurt external validity, but they also may hurt your experiment's construct validity. For example, you might use the most reliable dependent measure rather than one that has the most construct validity.

Or, you might compromise the validity of your independent variable manipulation.

FIGURE 5.2 Using a Homogeneous Group of Subjects Increases Power, But May Raise Questions About the Study's External Validity

For instance, to maximize your chances of getting a significant effect for full-spectrum lighting, you would give the experimental group full-spectrum lighting and make the control group an **empty control group**: a group that does not get any kind of treatment. Unfortunately, if you found an effect in this study, you could not say it was due to the effects of the full-spectrum lighting. It could be due to some other incidental effect of the manipulation: the treatment group getting a gift (the lights) from the experimenter; getting more interaction with and attention from the experimenter (as the experimenter checks subjects to make sure they are using the lights); adopting more of a routine than the controls (using the lights every morning from 6 A.M. to 8 A.M.); and having higher expectations of getting better (because they have more of a sense of being helped) than the controls.

To minimize the side effects of the treatment manipulation, you might give your control group a **placebo**: a substance or treatment that has no effect. Thus, rather than using a no-light condition, you might expose the control group to yellow light. Furthermore, you might reduce the chances of experimenters biasing the results if you made experimenters and subjects **blind**: unaware of which kind of treatment the subject was getting. The use of placebos, the use of **single blinds** (where *either* the subject or the experimenter is blind) and the use of **double blinds** (where *both* the subject and the experimenter are blind) all reduce the chances you will obtain a significant effect. However, if you use these procedures and you find a significant effect, you can be relatively confident the treatment itself, not some side effect of the treatment manipulation, is the cause.

The techniques of avoiding the use of an "empty" control group and the use of the double-blind technique were incorporated in Wilson and Schooler's (1991) jam experiment. Wilson and Schooler did not have an empty control group. That is, their control group did not simply sit around doing nothing while the experimental group filled out the questionnaire analyzing reasons for liking a jam. Instead, the control group also completed a questionnaire. The questionnaire was a "filler questionnaire" about their reasons for choosing a major. If Wilson and Schooler had used an empty control group, critics could have argued that it was the act of filling out a questionnaire—not the act of reflection—that caused the treatment group to make less accurate ratings than the controls. For example, critics could have argued that the controls' memory for the jams was fresher because they were not distracted by the task of filling out a questionnaire.

To reduce the effects of experimenter expectations, Wilson and Schooler used two experimenters. The first experimenter supervised the tasting of the jams and the filling out of the questionnaires. This experimenter introduced subjects to experimenter 2 and then left the room. Experimenter 2 was unaware of (blind to) whether subjects had filled out the "reasons" or the "filler" questionnaire. Experimenter 2 gave subjects a questionnaire on which to evaluate the jams and left the room while subjects made their ratings.

ETHICS VERSUS POWER

Ethical considerations may conflict with your desire for power. For example, suppose you want to use extreme levels of the independent variable (food deprivation) to insure large differences in the motivation of your animals. In that case, you need to weigh the benefits of having a powerful manipulation against ethical concerns (see appendix A).

Not only do you have to be concerned about your experimental group, but also your control group. That is, not only might it be unethical to administer a potentially stressful stimulus to a subject, but it might also be unethical to completely withhold a potentially beneficial treatment, such as a possible cure for schizophrenia. Instead, it ethically might be less questionable to give the control group a low or moderate dose of the treatment. (For a summary of power versus other goals, see table 5.9.)

ETHICS VERSUS THE SIMPLE EXPERIMENT

Finally, you must determine whether it is ethical to perform a simple experiment. Although the ethical ramifications of any research must be carefully considered before it is conducted (see chapter 13 and appendix A), some believe experiments should be considered even more carefully than other types of research because experiments involve administering treatments to (doing something to) subjects. If either you or your professor do not feel it is ethical to randomly assign volunteers to different levels of your treatment, do not use a simple experiment.

TABLE 5.9 Conflicts Between Power and Other Goals	
ACTION TO HELP POWER	HOW ACTION MIGHT HURT OTHER GOALS
Use a homogeneous group of subjects to reduce random error due to subjects	May hurt ability to generalize to other groups of subjects
Test under controlled conditions (lab) to reduce effects of extraneous variables	1. May hurt ability to generalize to real-life situations where extraneous variables are present 2. Artificiality **may** hurt construct validity—if setting is so artificial that subjects are constantly aware that what they are doing is not real and just an experiment, they may act to please the experimenter rather than expressing their "true" reaction to the treatment
Use artificially high and low levels of independent variable to get big differences between groups	1. May be unable to generalize to realistic levels of the independent variable 2. May be unethical
Use empty control group to maximize chance of getting difference	Construct validity threatened because significant difference may be due to subjects' expectations rather than to treatment
Using many subjects to reduce the effects of random error	May be too expensive or time-consuming

ANALYZING DATA FROM THE SIMPLE EXPERIMENT

To understand how you are going to analyze your data, remember why you did the simple experiment. You did it to find out whether the treatment would have an effect on your subjects. More specifically, you wanted to know the answer to the hypothetical question: "If I had put all my subjects in the experimental condition, would they have scored differently than if I had put all of them in the control condition?" To answer this question, you need to know the averages of two **populations**:

> Average of population #1: what the average score on the dependent measure would have been if **all** your subjects had been in the control group and
>
> Average of population #2: what the average score on the dependent measure would have been if **all** your subjects had been in the experimental group.

Unfortunately, you cannot directly measure both of these populations. If you put all your subjects in the control condition, then you will not know how they would have scored in the experimental condition. If, on the other hand, you put all your subjects in the experimental condition, you will not know how they would have scored in the control condition.

ESTIMATING WHAT YOU WANT TO KNOW

Since you cannot directly get the population averages you want, you do the next best thing—estimate them. You can estimate them because you created two random samples of your population of subjects: the control group and the experimental group (see figure 5.3). The average score of the *random sample* of your subjects who received the treatment (the experimental group) is an estimate of what the average score would have been if all your subjects received the treatment. The average score of the *random sample* of subjects who received no treatment (the control group) is an estimate of what the average score would have been if all of your subjects had been in the control condition.

Calculating Sample Means

Even though only half your subjects were in the experimental group, you will assume the experimental group is a fair sample of your entire population of subjects. Thus, the experimental group's average score should be a good estimate of what the average score would have been if all your subjects had been in the experimental group. Similarly, you will assume the control group's average score is a good estimate of what the average score would have been if all your subjects had been in the control group. Therefore, the first step in analyzing your data will be to calculate the average score for each group.

Usually, the average you will calculate is the **mean**: the result of adding up all the scores and then dividing by the number of scores. After you have collected the data, add up all the control subjects' scores on the dependent measure, then divide by the number

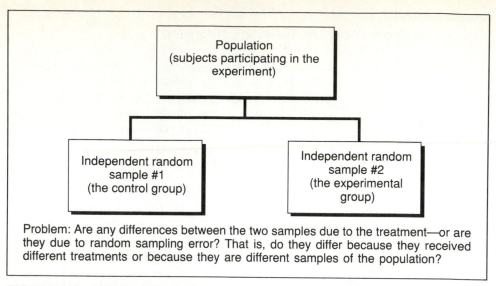

Problem: Are any differences between the two samples due to the treatment—or are they due to random sampling error? That is, do they differ because they received different treatments or because they are different samples of the population?

FIGURE 5.3: The Control Group and the Experimental Group are Two Samples Drawn From the Same Population

of control group subjects to get the control group mean. Next, add up all the scores for the experimental group subjects, divide by the number of experimental group subjects to obtain the experimental group mean.

Comparing Sample Means

Once you have your two sample means, you can compare them. If the treatment had no effect, the control and experimental groups *still* would both be random samples from the same population—the population consisting of every subject who participated in the study—just as they were before the treatment was introduced. As you know, two random samples from the same population will be similar to each other. For example, two random samples of the entire population of New York City should be similar to each other, two random samples from the entire population of students at your school should be similar to each other, and two random samples from the entire group of subjects who participated in your study should be similar to each other. Thus, if the treatment has no effect, the experimental and control groups should be similar to each other.

But, even if the treatment has no effect, the means for the control group and experimental group will rarely be identical. In other words, even if the groups represent the same population, they may still differ. They may differ because of one of the hazards of random sampling from a population: **random sampling error.** You are aware of sampling error from reading about public opinion polls that admit to a certain degree of sampling error or from reading about two polls of the same population that produced slightly different results. Furthermore, if you played around with box 5.1, you also may have realized that which subjects end up in which group varies greatly depending on where on the random numbers table you happen to start—and there are many different places you could start. Obviously, not all of these possible ways of splitting subjects into control and experimental groups are going to produce identical groups. Indeed, you may find random assignment sometimes results in having all males in the experimental group and all females in the control group.

As you have seen, merely as the result of chance, some random samples will be less representative than others. Because of the possibility a sample is affected by random sampling error, your sample means may differ even if your population means do not.

INFERENTIAL STATISTICS: JUDGING THE ACCURACY OF ESTIMATES

Anyone can tell you that two random samples of the same population may differ from one another because of sampling error. You need to know more about sampling error than the mere fact that it exists. You need to know enough to decide whether the difference between your sample means could easily be the result of sampling error.

If you knew that the difference between your sample means was probably **not** due to sampling error, then you could conclude that the population means actually differ. In other words, you could conclude that if all the subjects had been in the experimental group their average score would be different than if they had all been in the control group. In short, you would conclude that the treatment had an effect.

To decide whether the treatment had an effect, you must rely on **sampling statistics** (also called **inferential statistics**): the science of inferring the characteristics of a population from a sample of that population. Just as the science of anatomy allows an archaeologist to infer the characteristics of a dinosaur from a few bones, sampling statistics allow you to make inferences about a population mean from a sample mean.

Estimating the Accuracy of Individual Sample Means

If you knew how accurate each of your individual sample means were, it would help you decide whether the difference between your groups was due to sampling error. For example, suppose you knew the control group mean was within one point of its true population mean. Furthermore, suppose you knew the experimental group mean also was within one point of its population mean. In other words, suppose you knew the estimate for what the mean would be if everybody had been in the control group was not off by more than one point and also the estimate for what the mean would be if everyone had been in the experimental group was not off by more than one point.

If you knew all that and if your control group mean differed from your experimental group mean by ten points, then you would know the two populations differ. That is, you would be confident that if all subjects had been given the treatment they would score differently than if they had all been given no treatment. Based on a 10 point difference between sample means, you were able to conclude that the treatment had an effect. However, if you had not known that the sample means were such accurate reflections of their population means, then you would not have been able to conclude that the treatment had an effect. For example, if each of the sample means could easily be off by

25 points, then the 10 point difference between group means could easily be due to chance.

Consider Population Variability: The Value of the Standard Deviation

But how can you determine how closely your sample means are to the true population means? Obviously, one factor that would affect how well a random sample reflects its population is the amount of variability in the population. If there is no variability in the population (everyone in the population scores a "5"), then all scores in the population will be the same as the mean. Consequently, there would be no sampling error because every random sample will always have a mean of five. For example, because all Roman Catholic cardinals hold very similar positions on the morality of abortion, almost any sample of Roman Catholic cardinals you took would accurately reflect the views of Roman Catholic cardinals on that issue.

If, on the other hand, scores in a population vary considerably (e.g., ranging anywhere from zero to one thousand), then independent random samples from that population can be very inaccurate. Different samples may have very different sample means. Therefore, to know how accurate you can expect each of your samples to be (and thus how likely they might differ from each other due to sampling error alone), it would be nice to have an index of the variability of scores within a population.

The ideal index of variability is the population's **standard deviation**: a measure of the extent to which individual scores deviate from the population mean. Unfortunately, to get that index, you have to know the population mean (for the control condition, the average of the scores if all the subjects had been in the control condition; for the experimental condition, the average of the scores if all the subjects had been in the experimental condition). Obviously, you do not know the population mean for either the control or experimental condition—that is what you are trying to find out!

Although you cannot calculate the population standard deviation, you can estimate it by looking at the variability of scores within your samples. In fact, by following box 5.2, you can estimate what the standard deviation would have been if everyone had been in the control group (by looking at variability within the control group) and what the standard deviation would have been if all your subjects had been in the experimental group (by looking at variability within the experimental group).

One reason the standard deviation is a particularly valuable index of variability is that many populations can be completely described simply by knowing the standard deviation and the mean. You probably already know the mean is valuable for describing many populations. You know that, for many populations, most scores will be near the mean and as many scores will be above the mean as will be below the mean.

What you may not know is, for many populations, you can specify precisely what percentage of scores will be within a certain number of standard deviations of the mean. For instance, you can say 68 percent of the scores will be within one standard deviation of the mean, 95 percent will be within two standard deviations of the mean, and 99 percent of the scores will be within three standard deviations of the mean. If a population's scores are spread out (distributed) in this manner, the population is said to be *normally distributed.*

BOX 5.2   How to Compute a Standard Deviation

Assume we have four scores (108, 104, 104, 104) from a population. We could estimate the population's standard deviation by going through the following steps.

STEP 1 (CALCULATE THE *MEAN*)	STEP 2 (SUBTRACT SCORES FROM MEAN [105] TO GET *DIFFERENCES*)		STEP 3 (SQUARE DIFFERENCES)
108	−105 = +3	×	+3 = +9
104	−105 = −1	×	−1 = +1
104	−105 = −1	×	−1 = +1
104	−105 = −1	×	−1 = +1
Mean = 420/4 = 105			SS = 12

Step 4: Add (sum) the squared differences obtained in step 3 to get sum of squared differences, otherwise known as sum of squares and often abbreviated (SS). Sum of squares (SS) = 12.

Step 5: Get variance by dividing SS (which was 12) by one less than the number of scores (4 − 1 = 3). This yields a variance of 4 (12/3 = 4).

Step 6: Get standard deviation by taking square root of variance. Since the variance is 4, the standard deviation is 2 (because $\sqrt{4} = 2$).

For those preferring formulas, $s = \sqrt{\Sigma(X - \overline{X})^2 / N - 1}$ where $\overline{X}$ is the sample mean, s is the estimate of the population's standard deviation, and N is the number of scores.

As the term "normally distributed" suggests, many populations are normally distributed—from test scores to the heights of American women. Because normally distributed populations are common, plotting the distribution of scores in a population will often produce a **normal curve:** a bell-shaped, symmetrical curve that has its center at the mean (see figure 5.4).

It is convenient to summarize an entire distribution of scores with just two numbers: the mean, which gives you the center of a normal distribution, and the standard deviation, which gives you an index of the width of the distribution. It is comforting to know 68 percent of the scores will be within a standard deviation of the mean, 95 percent of the scores will be within two standard deviations of the mean, and virtually all the scores will be within three standard deviations of the mean.

But the standard deviation has more uses than merely describing a population. You could use the standard deviation to make inferences about the population mean. For example, suppose you do not know the population's mean, but you know that the set

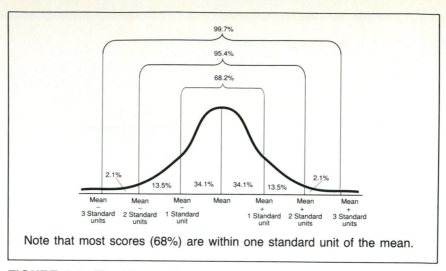

Note that most scores (68%) are within one standard unit of the mean.

FIGURE 5.4: The Normal Curve

of scores is normally distributed and its standard deviation is two. Then, you know that if you randomly selected a single score from that population, there would be a 68 percent chance the population mean would be within two points (one standard deviation) of that score and a 95 percent chance the population mean would be within four points (two standard deviations) of that score.

Consider Sample Size: The Role of the Standard Error
Of course, to estimate your control group's population mean, you would use more than one score. One obvious reason for using a sample mean based on several scores is that the bigger your independent random sample, the better your random sample will tend to be—and the better your sample, the closer its mean should be to the population mean.

Because you use more than one score to calculate the sample mean and because the number of scores you use affects the accuracy of your sample mean, the standard deviation is not an adequate index of your sample mean's accuracy. Any index that assesses the degree to which a sample mean may differ from its population mean must assess the two factors that influence the accuracy of a sample mean: population variability and sample size.

Both of these factors are included in the formula for the **standard error of the estimate of the population mean:** an index of the degree to which random sampling error may cause the sample mean to be an inaccurate estimate of the population mean.

The standard error (of the estimate of the population mean) equals the standard deviation (a measure of population variability) divided by the square root of the number of subjects in the sample (an index of sample size).

Thus, if the standard deviation were forty and you had four people in your sample, the standard error would be twenty: 40 ÷ 2 (the square root of 4) = 20.

Reflecting the fact you have less random sampling error with larger samples, if you had used one hundred subjects, your standard error would have shrunk to four because:

$$40 \div \sqrt{100} = 40 \div 10 = 4.$$

What does the standard error tell you? Clearly, the larger the standard error, the more likely a sample mean will misrepresent the population mean (see table 5.10). But does this random error contaminate all samples equally or does it heavily infest some samples while leaving others untouched? Ideally, you would like to know precisely how random error is distributed across various samples. You want to know what percentage of samples will be substantially biased by random error so you know what chance your sample mean has of being accurate.

Using the Standard Error Fortunately, you can know about how sample means are distributed. As statisticians have shown by drawing numerous independent random samples from normally distributed populations, the distribution of sample means will be normally distributed. Most (68%) of the sample means will be within one standard error of the population mean, 95 percent will be within two standard errors of the population mean, and 99 percent will be within three standard errors of the population mean. Therefore, if your standard error is 1.00, you know there is a 68 percent chance the true population mean is within one point of your sample mean, a 95 percent chance the population mean is within two points of your sample mean, and a 99 percent chance the population mean is within three points of your sample mean.

When you can assume the population is normally distributed, you can estimate how close your sample mean is to the true population mean. You do this by taking advantage of the fact that sample means will follow a very well-defined distribution: the normal distribution. But what if the population is not normally distributed?

Even then, as the **central limit theorem** states: the distribution of sample means will be normally distributed *if your samples are large enough* (thirty or more subjects). To

TABLE 5.10 How Close Is a Sample Mean to the Population Mean?	
FACTORS INCREASING THE CHANCES OF HAVING A SAMPLE MEAN THAT IS CLOSE TO THE ACTUAL POPULATION MEAN	FACTORS INCREASING THE CHANCES OF HAVING A SAMPLE MEAN THAT IS FAR AWAY FROM THE ACTUAL POPULATION MEAN
Sample mean based on population that has a *small standard deviation* (most of the scores center around the population mean, most scores close together)	Sample mean based on a population that has a *large standard deviation* (few of the scores close to the population mean, most scores far apart)
Based on *large sample* (big random samples are good random samples)	Based on *small sample*

understand why the central limit theorem works, realize that if you take numerous large random samples from the same population, your sample means will differ from one another for only one reason—random sampling error. Since random sampling error is normally distributed, your distribution of sampling means will be normally distributed—regardless of the shape of the underlying population. Consequently, if you take a large random sample from any population, you can use the normal curve to estimate how closely your sample mean reflects the population mean.

Estimating Accuracy of Your Estimate of the Difference between Population Means

Because you know sample means are normally distributed, you can determine how likely it is that a sample mean is within a certain distance of the population mean. But in the simple experiment, you are not trying to estimate whether a single sample is an accurate reflection of a certain population. Instead, you are trying to find out whether (1) the two samples come from the same population or (2) the two samples represent two different populations. Your focus is not on the individual sample means, but on the difference between the two means. Thus, rather than knowing how sample means from the same population are distributed, you would like to know how differences between sample means (drawn from the same population) are distributed.

How the Differences between Means Are Distributed:
The Large Sample Case

Fortunately, statisticians know how differences between sample means drawn from the same population are distributed. Statisticians have repeated the following steps thousands of times:

1. take two random samples from the same population,
2. calculate the means of the two samples (group 1 and group 2), and
3. subtract the group 1 mean from the group 2 mean to get the **difference** between group 1 and group 2.

What do they conclude would happen in the long run? That is, what would happen if these steps were repeated an infinite number of times? There are three basic statements we can make about the distribution of the differences between group 1 and group 2.

First, if we took the average of all the differences between groups 1 and 2, the average of all the differences would equal zero. This follows from what you know about estimating a single mean. You know the mean of sample means would, in the long run, be the same as the population mean. Therefore, the mean of all the group 1 means would be the same as the mean of the group 2 means: both would equal the population mean. Consequently, the average difference between them would be zero.

Second, the differences would be normally distributed. You may have already figured this out, especially if you (1) remembered that random sampling error is normally distributed and (2) realized the only way random samples from the same population can differ is because of random sampling error.

Even if you did not remember that random sampling error was normally distributed, you may still have guessed that the distribution of differences was normally distributed. That is, since the statisticians were subtracting scores coming from one normal distribution (the distribution of sample means for a specific population) from scores that come from the same normal distribution (the distribution of sample means from the same population), you might have suspected the distribution they ended up with would have a mean of zero and would be normally distributed.

Third, the standard for the distribution of differences between means is not the standard deviation or the standard error, but the **standard error of difference between means**. The standard error of the difference between means is larger than the standard error of the mean. This fact should not surprise you because the difference between sample means is influenced by the random sampling error that affects the control group mean **and** by the random sampling error that affects the experimental group mean. That is, sample means from the same population could differ because the first sample mean was inaccurate, because the second sample mean was inaccurate, or because both were inaccurate. The formula for the standard error of the difference reflects the fact that this standard error is the result of measuring **two** imperfect estimates. Specifically, the formula is:

$$\sqrt{\frac{s_1^2}{N_1} + \frac{s_2^2}{N_2}}$$

Where s_1 is the estimate of the population standard deviation for group 1 and s_2 is the estimate of the population standard deviation for group 2; N_1 is the number of subjects in group 1 and N_2 is the number of subjects in group 2.

We know that with large enough samples, the distribution of differences between means would be normally distributed. Thus, if the standard error of the difference was 1.0, we would know 68 percent of the time, the true difference would be within 1.0 of the difference we observed; 95 percent of the time, the true difference would be within 2.0 of the difference we observed; and 99 percent of the time, the true difference would be within 3.0 of the difference we observed. Therefore, if we observed a difference of 5.0, we could be very confident the difference between the groups' **populations** was not zero. In other words, we could be confident the groups are samples from different populations: if all the subjects had received the treatment they would have scored differently than if they all had been in the control group. If, however, we observed a difference of 1.0, we realize such a difference might well reflect random sampling error, rather than the groups coming from different populations. Therefore, with a difference of 1.0 and a standard error of 1.0, we could not conclude the treatment had an effect. (For easy reference, see table 5.11.)

How Differences Are Distributed: The Small Sample Case
Although the distribution of differences would be normally distributed if you used large enough samples, your particular experiment probably will not use enough subjects. Therefore, you must rely on a more conservative distribution, especially designed for small samples: the **t-distribution**. Actually, the t-distribution is a family of distributions. The bigger your sample size, the more the t-distribution you use will approximate the normal distribution.

TABLE 5.11   Terms to Keep Straight

Sum of squared differences, more commonly referred to as the **sum of squares:** Calculated in three steps. First, get the *difference* between each score and the mean by taking each score and subtracting it from the mean. Second, *square* each of these differences. Third, add *(sum)* these squared differences. The sum of squares provides some indication of how closely scores stay to the mean. However, because it is calculated by summing differences, the more scores, the larger the sum of squares will tend to be—regardless of the variability of the scores.

Variance: A measure of variability based on the sum of squares. However, unlike the sum of squares, having more scores does not automatically make the variance bigger. Specifically, the variance corrects for having more scores by dividing the sum of squares by the number of scores (in the case of calculating the variance from the population) or by dividing the sum of squares by one less than the number of scores (in the case of estimating the population variance from a sample).

When the population variance is estimated from a sample, this variance is abbreviated s^2. The square root of this variance (s) is the standard deviation.

Standard deviation: A measure of the extent to which individual scores deviate from the population mean. Could be used as an index of the extent to which a randomly selected *score* from a population could be expected to *differ from its population's mean.*

Standard error of the mean: An index of the degree to which the mean of several scores that were randomly selected from a population *(a sample mean)* could be expected to differ *from its population's mean.*

The standard error of the mean can never be bigger than the standard deviation. The standard error will be small when the standard deviation is small and when the sample mean is based on many scores.

Standard error of the difference: An index of the degree to which *two sample means* representing the same population could be expected to *differ from each other.*

The t-distribution you will use depends on how many degrees of freedom (*df*) you have. To calculate your degrees of freedom, simply subtract two from the number of subjects in your experiment. For example, if you had thirty-two subjects, your *df* would be thirty (because 32 − 2 = 30).

Executing the t-test   Now that you understand the basic logic behind the t-test, you are ready to do one (see box 5.3). Start by subtracting the means of your two groups. Then, divide this difference by the standard error of the difference. The number you will get is called a *t-score.* Thus,

$$t = \frac{\text{difference between means}}{\text{standard error of the difference.}}$$

Once you have your t-score and your degrees of freedom, you refer to a t-table to see whether your t-score is significant. Thus, if you used thirty-two subjects, you would look at the t-table in appendix E under the row labelled "30 *df.*" If the number in the table is larger than the absolute value of your t-score, your results are *not* statistically significant at the .05 level. If the number in the table is smaller than the absolute value of your t-score, then your results are statistically significant at the .05 level: there is less than a 5 percent

BOX 5.3 Calculating the Between Subjects t-test for Equal Sized Groups

$$t = \frac{\bar{X}_1 - \bar{X}_2}{\text{standard error of the difference}}$$

Where X_1 is the mean of group 1 and X_2 is the mean of group 2.

And where the standard error of the difference can be calculated in either of the following two ways:

1.
$$\sqrt{\frac{SS \text{ group } 1 + SS \text{ group } 2}{N - 2}} \times (1/N_1 + 1/N_2)$$

Where SS error equals the sum of squares, N_1 equals number of subjects in group 1, N_2 equals number of subjects in group two, and N equals the total number of subjects.

2.
$$\sqrt{\frac{s_1^2}{N_1} + \frac{s_2^2}{N_2}}$$

Where s_1^2 equals the variance for group 1, s_2^2 equals the variance for group 2, N_1 equals number of subjects in group 1 and N_2 equals number of subjects in group 2.

chance the difference between your groups is solely due to chance. Consequently, you can be reasonably sure your treatment had an effect.

Assumptions of the t-test   As with any statistical test, the t-test requires you to make certain assumptions. First, because the t-test compares the two sample means, the t-test requires you to have data that allow you to compute meaningful means. You cannot use ranked data because you cannot meaningfully average ranks. For example, although averaging the ranks of second and third place finishers in a race would result in the same average rank (2.5) as averaging the ranks of the first and fourth place finishers, the average times of the two groups might vary greatly. The average times of the first and fourth place finishers could be much faster or much slower than the average of the times of the second and third place finishers. Nor can you have qualitative data. (Try averaging scores when 1 = nodded head, 2 = gazed intently, and 3 = blinked eyes—what does an average of 1.8 indicate?) In short, to do the t-test you must be able to assume you have either interval scale or ratio scale data.

Second, since the t-test is based on estimating random sampling error, the t-test requires that you independently and randomly assigned each subject to group. If this requirement is violated, the results of the t-test are worthless.

In addition to these two pivotal assumptions, the t-test makes some less vital assumptions. First, the t-test assumes the population from which your sample means was drawn is normally distributed. The reason for this assumption is that if the populations are normally distributed, then the sample means will tend to be normally distributed. This assumption is usually nothing to worry about for two reasons. First, most distributions are normally distributed. Second, as the central limit theorem states, with large enough samples, the distribution of sample means will be normally distributed, no matter what.

The second assumption is that scores in both conditions will have the same variances. This is not a very strict assumption. If you have unequal variances, it will not seriously affect the results of your t-test, as long as one variance is not more than two and one half times larger than the other.

QUESTIONS RAISED BY RESULTS

Obviously, if you violate key assumptions of the t-test, your results raise very serious questions (see table 5.12). Even if you do not violate any of the t-test's assumptions, your results still will raise questions—and this is true whether or not your results are statistically significant.

Questions Raised by Nonsignificant Results

Nonsignificant results raise questions because the null hypothesis cannot be proven. Therefore, null results inspire questions about the experiment's power, questions such as

1. Did you have enough subjects?
2. Were the subjects homogeneous enough?
3. Was the experiment sufficiently standardized?
4. Was the data coded carefully?
5. Was the dependent variable reliable enough?

TABLE 5.12 Effects of Violating Assumptions of the t-test

ASSUMPTION	CONSEQUENCES OF VIOLATING ASSUMPTION
Random assignment	Serious violation, nothing can be done to salvage your study
Observations are independent (random assignment is used and subjects do not influence one another's responses)	Serious violation, probably nothing can be done to save study
Data are interval or ratio scale numbers. (They do not represent ranks [1st, 2nd, 3rd, etc.] and they do represent different amounts of a quality)	Do not use t-test, however, there are other statistical tests you can use (e.g., chi square.)
The population from which your sample means was drawn is normally distributed	If used more than thirty subjects per group, not a serious problem, with small sample size, may decide to use different statistical test
Scores in both conditions have the same variances	Usually not a serious problem, especially if used a large number of subjects

6. Did you choose the wrong levels of the independent variable? In other words, would you have found an effect if you had chosen two different levels?

Questions Raised by Significant Results

If the absolute value of your t-score is greater than the tabled value, your effect is statistically significant. Since you found an effect for your treatment, you do not have to ask any questions about your study's power. But that does not mean your results do not raise any questions. On the contrary, your significant effect raises many questions.

Some of these questions may be the result of making tradeoffs to obtain adequate power. For example, if you used an empty control group or failed to use double-blind procedures, does your significant effect represent a placebo effect rather than an effect for the treatment? Or, if you used an extremely homogeneous group of subjects, do your results apply to other kinds of subjects? Or, if the experiment was very standardized, would the results occur in a less standardized, more naturalistic setting? Or, if you chose two extreme levels of your independent variable, would you have obtained the same pattern of results if you had used more realistic levels of the independent variable?

Some questions raised by significant results are the inevitable results of the limits of the simple experiment—only being able to study two levels of a single variable. Therefore, with any simple experiment, you might ask to what extent do the results apply to levels of the independent variable that were not tested? To what extent could other variables modify the treatment effect?

CONCLUDING REMARKS

Clearly, the results of a simple experiment always raise questions. Although results from any research study raise questions, many of the questions raised by the results of the simple experiment are the direct or indirect result of the fact that the simple experiment is limited to studying only two levels of a single variable. If the logic of the simple experiment could be expanded to designs that would study several levels of several independent variables at the same time, these designs could answer the questions raised by the simple experiment. Fortunately, as you will see in the next two chapters, the logic of the simple experiment can be extended to produce experimental designs that will allow you to answer several research questions with a single experiment.

SUMMARY

1. The experimental hypothesis predicts the treatment will cause an effect.
2. The null hypothesis, on the other hand, states the treatment will not cause an observable effect.

3. With the null hypothesis, you only have two options: you can reject it or you can fail to reject it. You can *never* accept the null hypothesis.

4. The simple experiment is the easiest way to establish that a treatment causes an effect.

5. In the simple experiment, you administer a low level of the independent (treatment) variable to some of your subjects (the control group) and a higher level of the independent variable to the rest of your subjects (the experimental group).

6. Then, near the end of the experimental session, you observe how each subject scores on the dependent variable: a measure of the subject's behavior.

7. To establish causality with a simple experiment, you must use independent random assignment to assign subjects to groups. The best way to do this is to use a random numbers table.

8. Your goal in using independent random assignment is to create two samples that accurately represent your entire population of subjects. You use the mean of the control group as an estimate of what would have happened if all your subjects had been in the control group. You use the experimental group mean as an estimate of what the mean would have been if all your subjects had been in the experimental group.

9. Does the treatment have an effect? In other words, would subjects have scored differently had they all been in the experimental group than if they had all been in the control group? This is the question statistical significance tests ask.

10. If the results are statistically significant, the difference between your groups is greater than would be expected by chance (random sampling error) alone. Therefore, you reject the null hypothesis and conclude your treatment has an effect.

11. There are two kinds of errors you might make when attempting to decide whether a result is statistically significant.

12. Type 1 errors occur when you mistake a chance difference for a treatment effect.

13. Type 2 errors occur when you mistake a genuine difference for a chance difference.

14. Because Type 2 errors can easily occur, nonsignificant results are inconclusive results.

15. To prevent Type 2 errors, reduce random error, use many subjects to balance out the effects of random error, and try to increase the size of your treatment effect.

16. If your experiment minimizes the risk of making Type 2 errors, your experiment has power. Technically, power is 1 – the probability of making a Type 2 error. Less technically, power refers to your ability to find true differences statistically significant.

17. Improving power may hurt your study's external and construct validity.

18. Using placebo treatments, single blinds, and double blinds can improve your study's construct validity.

19. Ethics may temper your search for power and may even rule out your experiment.

20. Many distributions can be approximated by the normal curve.

21. The normal curve is a symmetrical, bell-shaped curve that can be described by two numbers: the mean and a standard term. The center of the normal distribution is the mean. Half the scores will be below the mean and half will be above.

22. The standard deviation is an index of how much variation there is in your sample or population. Usually, 68% of the scores will be within one standard deviation of the mean and 95% will be within two standard deviations of the mean.

23. The standard error is an index of the variability of your sample means. It can be used to give you an idea of how much error has affected your estimate of the population mean. Usually, 68% of the sample means will be within one standard error of the mean and 95% will be within two standard errors of the mean.

24. The standard error of the difference is an index of the degree to which your control and experimental groups may differ due to chance alone. If your independent variable manipulation had no effect, your experimental group and control group means will probably (68% of the time) be within one standard error of the difference of each other and will almost certainly (99% of the time) be within three standard errors of the difference of each other.

25. The degrees of freedom for a two group, between subjects t-test are two fewer than the total number of subjects.

26. The formula for the t-test is: (mean 1 − mean 2)/standard error of the difference.

KEY TERMS

central limit theorem
control group
dependent variable
double blind
empty control group
experimental group
experimental hypothesis
independence
independent random
  assignment

independent variable
inferential statistics
internal validity
mean
null hypothesis
null results
placebo
power
sampling statistics

single blind
standard deviation
standard error of the
  difference
standard error of the
  mean
statistical significance
Type 1 error
Type 2 error

EXERCISES

1. What three criteria must be met to establish that a factor causes an effect? How is the simple experiment able to establish all three criteria?

2. Why isn't it necessary to do an experiment in a lab? What advantages are there to doing an experiment in a lab? What advantages are there to doing an experiment in a real-world setting? What are the disadvantages?

3. A professor has a class of forty students. Half of the students chose to take a test after every chapter (chapter test condition). The chapter tests were taken outside of class. The other half of the students chose to take in-class, "unit tests." Unit tests covered four chapters. The professor finds no statistically significant differences between the groups on their scores on a comprehensive final exam. The professor then concludes that type of testing does not affect performance.
   a. Is this an experiment?
   b. Is the professor's conclusion reasonable? Why or why not?

4. Subjects are randomly assigned to a meditation or no-meditation condition. The meditation group meditates three times a week. The meditation group reports being significantly more relaxed than the no-meditation group.
   a. Why might the results of this experiment be less clear-cut than they appear?
   b. How would you improve this experiment?

5. Can gender differences be studied in a simple experiment? Why or why not?

6. Theresa fails to find a significant difference between her control group and her experimental group. Specifically, her t-test is reported as: $t(10) = 2.11$, not significant.
   a. What would you advise her to conclude?
   b. What would you advise her to do? (Hint: you know her t-test, based on 10 degrees of freedom, was not significant. What does the fact that she has 10 degrees of freedom tell you?)

7. A training program significantly improves worker performance. What should you know before advising a company to invest in such a training program?

8. Jerry's control group is the football team, the experimental group is the baseball team. He assigned the groups to a condition using random assignment. Is there a problem with Jerry's experiment? If so, what is it? Why is it a problem?

9. Leslie tests the experimental group at 10 a.m. and the control group at 11 a.m. Is this appropriate? Why or why not?

10. Students were randomly assigned to two different strategies of studying for an exam. One group used visual imagery, the other group was told to study their normal way.
    a. The visual imagery group scored 88 percent on the test as compared to 76 percent for the control group. This difference was not significant. What can the experimenter conclude?
    b. If the difference had been significant, what would you have concluded? What changes in the study would have made it easier to be sure of your conclusions?
    c. "To be sure they are studying the way they should, why don't you have the imagery people form one study group and have the control group form another study group?" Is this good advice? Why or why not?
    d. "Just get a random sample of students who typically use imagery and compare them to a sample of students who don't use imagery. That will do the same thing as random assignment." Is this good advice? Why or why not?

11. Sarah and Rudy are doing basically the same study. However, Sarah has decided to

put her risk of a Type 1 error at .05, whereas Rudy has put his risk of a Type 1 error at .001. That is, Sarah is willing to take a five in one hundred risk that the results declared significant are due to chance, whereas Rudy is only willing to take a one in one thousand risk of significant results being due to chance.

    a. If Rudy has twenty-two subjects in his study, what t-value would he need to get significant results?

    b. If Sarah has twenty-two subjects in her study, what t-value would she need to get significant results?

    c. Who is more likely to make a Type 2 error? Why?

12. Jody claims that the sample's standard deviation is two and the standard error is four. Why must Jody be wrong?

13. Why do control group scores differ from each other?

14. Complete the following chart:

Action	Implication for Standard Deviation	Implication for Standard Error of the Mean
Using a Homogeneous Group of Subjects		
Using a Highly Reliable Measure		
Standardizing Procedures		
Using a Large Number of Subjects		

15. Why will the standard error of the difference tend to be larger than the standard error of the mean?

16. Your dependent measure is when people arrive for class. This distribution is not normally distributed. It tends to be "J"-shaped. That is, whereas the average arrival time might be a minute before class, some people show up much earlier, but few show up much later. Can you do a t-test on these data? Why or why not?

17. Gerald's dependent measure is the order in which people turned in their exam (1st, 2d, 3rd, etc.). Can Gerald use a t-test on his data? Why or why not? What would you advise Gerald to do in future studies?

18. Are the results of experiment A or experiment B more likely to be significant? Why?

EXPERIMENT A		EXPERIMENT B	
CONTROL GROUP	EXPERIMENTAL GROUP	CONTROL GROUP	EXPERIMENTAL GROUP
3	4	0	0
4	5	4	5
5	6	8	10

19. Are the results of experiment A or experiment B more likely to be significant? Why?

| EXPERIMENT A | | EXPERIMENT B | |
CONTROL GROUP	EXPERIMENTAL GROUP	CONTROL GROUP	EXPERIMENTAL GROUP
3	4	3	4
4	5	4	5
5	6	5	6
		3	4
		4	5
		5	6
		3	4
		4	5
		5	6

20. What would be the t-value for the following data?

| EXPERIMENT C | |
CONTROL GROUP	EXPERIMENTAL GROUP
3	2
4	4
5	6

6

Expanding the Simple Experiment: The Multiple-group Experiment

OVERVIEW

In chapter 5, you learned how to perform a simple experiment. You now know the simple experiment is internally valid and easy to do. However, you are also aware the simple experiment is limited: with it, you can study only two values of a single independent variable.

In this chapter, you will see why you might want to go beyond studying two values of a single variable and how the logic of the simple experiment (random assignment of subjects to groups) can be extended to accommodate your wishes. Specifically, you will learn how and when to use random assignment to study the effects of three or more values of a single independent variable.

THE ADVANTAGES OF USING MORE THAN TWO VALUES OF AN INDEPENDENT VARIABLE

The simple experiment is ideal if an investigator wants to compare two different kinds of treatments. But investigators often want to compare three or more different kinds of treatments. For instance, Roedigger (1980) wanted to compare five kinds of memory strategies (rote rehearsal, imagery, method of loci, the link method, and the peg system). Clearly, he could not compare all five treatments in one simple experiment.

COMPARING MORE THAN TWO KINDS OF TREATMENTS

Therefore, instead of randomly assigning subjects to two different groups, he randomly assigned his subjects to five different groups. To learn how to randomly assign subjects to more than two groups, see box 6.1.

Admittedly, Roedigger could have compared the five treatments by using a series of simple experiments. However, using a single multi-valued experiment has several advantages over using a series of simple experiments. We will only mention the two most obvious.

First, by doing a single five-value experiment, Roedigger greatly reduced the number of experiments he had to perform. To compare all five treatments with one another, Roedigger would have had to do ten simple experiments. Specifically, he would have had to do

1. one experiment to compare rote rehearsal with the imagery,
2. another experiment to compare rote rehearsal with the method of loci,
3. another to compare rote rehearsal with the link method,
4. another to compare rote rehearsal with a peg system,
5. another to compare imagery with the method of loci,

BOX 6.1 Randomly Assigning Subjects to More than Two Groups

Step 1: Across the top of a piece of paper write down your conditions. Under each condition draw a line for each subject you will need.

GROUP 1	GROUP 2	GROUP 3
___	___	___
___	___	___
___	___	___
___	___	___

Step 2: Turn to a random numbers table. Roll a die to determine which column in the table you will use.

Step 3: Assign the first number in the column to the first space under group 1, the second number to the second space, etc. When you have filled the spaces for group 1, put the next number under the first space under group 2. Similarly, when you fill all the spaces under group 2, place the next number in the first space under group 3.

GROUP 1	GROUP 2	GROUP 3
692	996	870
027	469	504
030	061	679
795	923	544

Step 4: Assign the first subject to the condition with the lowest random number, the second subject to the condition with the second lowest number, and so on. In this example, the first two subjects would be assigned to group 1 and the third subject would be assigned to group 2.

6. another to compare imagery with a link method,
7. another to compare imagery with a peg system,
8. another to compare method of loci with a link method,
9. another to compare a method of loci with a peg system, and
10. another to compare a link method with a peg system.

Second, he reduced the number of subjects he had to test. If he had conducted 10 simple experiments, he would have needed 20 groups of subjects. To have any degree of power, he would need at least 15 subjects per group[1] or 300 (15 × 20) subjects. With the five-group experiment, he could have the same power with 75 (15 × 5) subjects.

COMPARING MORE THAN TWO LEVELS (AMOUNTS) OF AN INDEPENDENT VARIABLE TO INCREASE EXTERNAL VALIDITY

In the simple experiment, you want to pick two levels of the independent variable that will allow you to find an effect. Intuitively, you realize the greater the difference between how the two groups are treated, the greater the chances of finding a significant effect. Therefore, when choosing levels of the independent variable, you will usually try to choose levels that differ from each other as much as possible. Thus, if you were investigating the effects of exercise on depression, half of your subjects would exercise very little, whereas the other half of your subjects would exercise a great deal. Your results might be as follows:

Group 1: Low amounts of aerobic exercise = High levels of depression
Group 2: High amounts of aerobic exercise = High levels of depression

Uncovering Relationships

Based on these results, you would be tempted to conclude there is no relationship between aerobic exercise and depression. However, this is a generalization: you have not tested other levels of the independent variable. Out of the many possible amounts of the independent variable you could have chosen, you have only sampled two. In this case, your generalization would be wrong if aerobic exercise had the following effects on depression:

Low amounts of aerobic exercise: Increase depression
Medium amounts of aerobic exercise: Reduce depression
High amounts of aerobic exercise: Increases depression

The "u"-shaped relationship we have postulated between exercise and depression is fairly common. Psychologists often find "u"-shaped and upside down "u"-shaped relationships. Perhaps the most famous case is the Yerkes-Dodson law, which states, in part, that (1) with little motivation, performance is poor; (2) with moderate levels of motivation, performance is good; and (3) with too much motivation, performance is poor.

You can probably think of many examples where (to paraphrase Goldilocks) too little of some factor can be bad, too much can be bad, but a medium amount is just right.

If the relationship between aerobic exercise and depression is "u"-shaped and you pick extreme levels of your independent variable, you will falsely conclude the treatment

---

[1]Many researchers would say that 30—not 15—should be the absolute minimum number of subjects per group. In that case, Roediger would have needed 600 subjects had he done several simple experiments versus 150 with a multiple-group experiment. In many cases, researchers should have at least 60 subjects per group (Cohen, 1990).

has no effect. Therefore, you might be tempted to choose moderate levels of the treatment. However, if the relationship is not "u"-shaped and you use moderate levels, your levels may not be far enough apart to allow you to detect a treatment effect. Thus, as you can see, picking the right levels of your independent variable for a simple experiment is a risky business.

To avoid making hard choices about which two levels to use, avoid simple experiments. Instead of choosing two levels, do experiments that use several levels of the independent variable. Thus, if you had used an experiment that examined three levels of aerobic exercise, you might have obtained the following pattern of results:

Group 1: Low aerobic exercise   = High levels of depression
Group 2: Medium aerobic exercise = Low levels of depression
Group 3: High aerobic exercise   = High levels of depression

Based on these results, you would correctly conclude aerobic exercise affects depression—regardless of whether the relationship between variables was like a straight line or "u"-shaped. In short, using multiple levels of an independent variable allows you to uncover effects that might not have been detected if you had used a simple experiment.

Discovering the Nature of Relationships

You have seen that the researcher using the simple experiment may falsely conclude a factor has no effect. Thus, in the worst case scenario, the results from a simple experiment apply only to the two levels used in the experiment.

But what if the researcher using a simple experiment finds a significant effect? Even in that case, the researcher would have difficulty generalizing the simple experiment's results to unexplored levels of the independent variable. Why? Because to generalize results to unexplored levels of an independent variable, the researcher must not only know a relationship exists, but the researcher must also know the nature of that relationship. That is, the researcher must know the independent and dependent variables' **functional relationship**: the shape of the relationship. Simple experiments do not enable you to uncover the nature of a functional relationship.

To illustrate the weakness of the simple experiment in detecting functional relationships, let's return to our simple experiment investigating the effects of aerobic exercise on depression. Suppose we obtained the following results:

Control group: 0 minutes of exercise per day   1.0 self-rating of depression
Experimental group: 100 minutes of exercise per day   10.0 self-rating of depression

Can you tell what the nature of the functional relationship between aerobic exercise and depression is? Perhaps the functional relationship is linear (like a straight line), as in figure 6.1.

However, the true relationship between exercise and depression might not resemble a straight line. Instead, it might be a nonlinear function, such as one of the curved lines in figure 6.2.

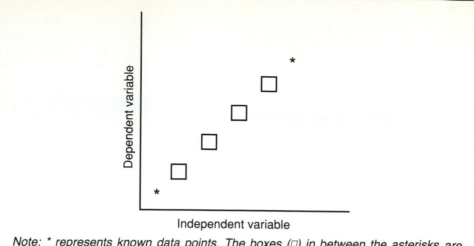

Note: * represents known data points. The boxes (□) in between the asterisks are what would happen at a given level of the independent variable if the relationship between the variables is linear. As you can see in figure 6.2, the relationship does not have to be linear.

FIGURE 6.1: Linear Relationship Between Two Points

Clearly, the simple experiment does not help you discover the functional relationship between two variables. Since you would not know the functional relationship, you could do little more than guess if we asked you about the effects of 70 minutes of aerobic exercise. You might **assume** the relationship is linear and therefore say that exercising 70 minutes a day would be better than no exercise and 70 percent as effective as exercising for 100 minutes a day. But if your assumption of a linear relationship is wrong—and it well could be—your guess would be inaccurate.

To get a line on the functional relationship between variables, you need to know more than two points. Therefore, suppose you expanded the simple experiment into a multi-level experiment by adding a group that gets 50 minutes of exercise a day. Then you would have a much clearer idea of the functional relationship between exercise and depression. As you can see in figure 6.3, using three levels can give you a pretty good idea of the functional relationship among variables. If the relationship is linear, you should be able to draw a straight line through all three points. If the relationship is "u"-shaped, you will detect that too.

Because you can detect the nature of the functional relationship when you use three levels of the independent variable, you can make accurate predictions about unexplored levels of the independent variable. Thus, if the functional relationship between aerobic exercise and depression were linear, you would obtain the following pattern of results:

Group 1:   0 minutes of exercise per day   1.0 self-rating of depression
Group 2:   50 minutes of exercise per day   5.0 self-rating of depression
Group 3:   100 minutes of exercise per day   10.0 self-rating of depression

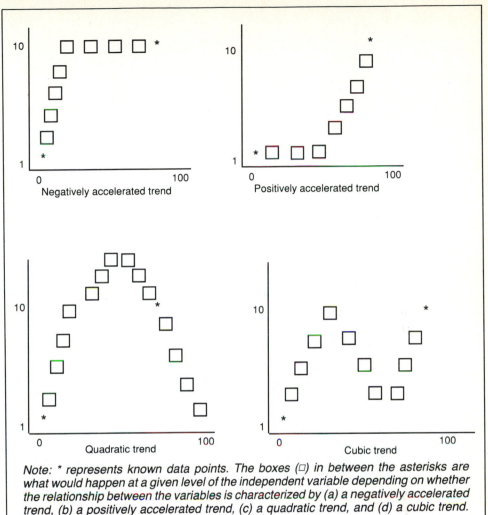

Note: * represents known data points. The boxes (□) in between the asterisks are what would happen at a given level of the independent variable depending on whether the relationship between the variables is characterized by (a) a negatively accelerated trend, (b) a positively accelerated trend, (c) a quadratic trend, and (d) a cubic trend.

FIGURE 6.2: Some Possible Nonlinear Relationships

In this case, you could confidently predict that 70 minutes of exercise would be 70 percent as beneficial for reducing depression as 100 minutes of exercise. If, on the other hand, the relationship was "s"-shaped, you would get the following pattern of results:

Group 1:	0 minutes of exercise per day	1.0 self-rating of depression
Group 2:	50 minutes of exercise per day	10.0 self-rating of depression
Group 3:	100 minutes of exercise per day	10.0 self-rating of depression

In this case, you would predict that a person who exercised 70 minutes would do as well as someone exercising 100 minutes a day.

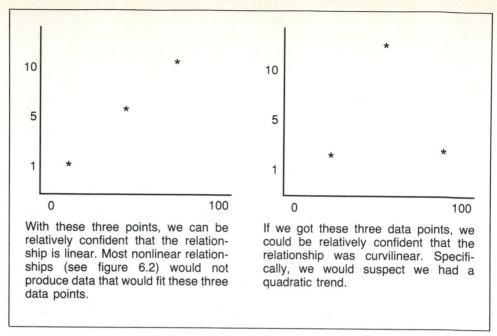

With these three points, we can be relatively confident that the relationship is linear. Most nonlinear relationships (see figure 6.2) would not produce data that would fit these three data points.

If we got these three data points, we could be relatively confident that the relationship was curvilinear. Specifically, we would suspect we had a quadratic trend.

FIGURE 6.3: Having Three Levels of the Independent Variable (Three data points) Aids Greatly in Determining the Shape of the Functional Relationship

The more groups you use, the more accurately you can pin down the shape of the functional relationship. Yet, despite this fact, you do not have to use numerous levels of the independent variable because nature prefers simple patterns. That is, most functional relationships are linear and few are more complex than "u"-shaped functions. As a result, you will rarely need more than four levels of the independent variable to pin down a functional relationship. In fact, you will usually need no more than three carefully chosen levels to identify the functional relationship among variables.

Summary: Multi-level Experiments and External Validity

In summary, knowing the functional relationship between two variables is almost as important as knowing a relationship exists. You want to be able to say more than: "If you exercise 100 minutes a day, you will have less tension than someone who exercises zero minutes a day." Who exercises exactly 100 minutes a day? You want to be able to generalize your results so that you can tell people the effects of exercising 50 minutes, 56 minutes, 75 minutes, and so forth. Yet, you have no intention of testing the effects of every single possible amount of exercise a person might do. Instead, you want to test only a handful of exercise levels. If you chose these levels carefully, you would be able to identify the functional relationship between the variables. Knowing the functional relationship will allow you to make educated predictions about the effects of exercise levels you have not directly tested. Because of this ability to generalize the results to different levels of the treatment variable, multi-level experiments may have a fair degree of external validity.

USING MULTIPLE LEVELS TO IMPROVE CONSTRUCT VALIDITY OF EXPERIMENTS

You have seen that multi-level experiments have more external validity than simple experiments. In this section, you will learn that multi-level experiments also can have more construct validity than simple experiments.

Confounding Variables in the Simple Experiment

Simple experiments are effective in establishing that a treatment manipulation has an effect. Specifically, a statistically significant difference between the control group and the experimental group is probably due to the treatment manipulation rather than to some reason having nothing to do with the treatment, such as the two groups being different before the experiment begins.

However, simple experiments are less effective in identifying what it was about the treatment manipulation that caused the effect. The problem is that most treatment manipulations do not create one—and only one—difference between the experimental and control group. Rather than being pure manipulations of a variable, the independent variable manipulation is often contaminated by **confounding variables**: variables that are unintentionally manipulated along with the treatment.

The following example[2] illustrates the general problem of confounding variables. Imagine being in a classroom that has five light switches. You want to know what the middle light switch does. Assume that in the control condition, all the light switches are off. In the experimental condition, you want to flick the middle switch on. However, because it is dark, you accidentally flick on the middle three switches. The janitor bursts into the room and your experiment is finished. What can you conclude? You can conclude that your manipulation of the light switches had an effect. In other words, your study has internal validity. However, because you manipulated more than just the middle light switch, it would be improper for you to conclude that you knew what the middle light switch did.

Because of confounding variables, it is often hard to know what it is about the treatment that caused the effect. In real life, variables are often confounded. For example, someone may know they got a hangover from drinking too much wine, but not know whether it was the alcohol in the wine, the preservatives in the wine, or something else about the wine that produced the awful sensations. A few years ago, a couple of our students joked that they could easily test the hypothesis that alcohol was responsible. All they needed us to do was donate enough money to buy mass quantities of a pure

[2]We are indebted to an anonymous reviewer for this example and other advice about confounding variables.

manipulation of alcohol—180 proof, totally devoid of impurities. These students clearly understood how confounding variables can contaminate real-life manipulations, thus making it hard to know what about the manipulation caused the effect.

To understand how confounding variables can contaminate a simple experiment, let us take a hard look at our simple experiment on the effects of exercise. You will recall that the experimental group got 100 minutes of exercise class per day, and the control group got nothing. Clearly, the experimental group subjects are being treated very differently than the control group subjects. The groups did not merely differ in terms of the independent variable (exercise), they also differed in terms of several other (confounding) variables: they got more attention and they had more structured social activities than the control group.

Hypothesis Guessing in Simple Experiments

Furthermore, subjects in the experimental group knew they were getting a treatment whereas subjects in the control group knew they were not being treated. If experimental group subjects suspected the exercise program should have an effect, the exercise program may **appear** to have an effect—even if exercise does not really improve mood. In other words, the construct validity of the study might be ruined because the experimental group subjects guessed the hypothesis.

Because of the impurities (confounding variables) of this manipulation, you cannot say the difference between groups is due solely to exercise. Although all manipulations have impurities, this study's most obvious—and avoidable—impurities stem from the fact that the control group is an **empty control group:** a group that does not receive any kind of treatment. Thus, if you could get rid of the empty control group, you would reduce the impact of confounding variables.

How the Multi-level Experiment Can Eliminate the Need for an Empty Control Group

One way to get rid of the empty control group would be to do a multi-level experiment. For example, you might have one group that gets 25 minutes of aerobic exercise, one group that gets 50 minutes of aerobic exercise, one group that gets 75 minutes of aerobic exercise, and a fourth group that gets 100 minutes of aerobic exercise.

Such an experiment has several advantages over a simple experiment that used an empty control group. First, unlike in the simple experiment, hypothesis guessing will be unlikely to produce the illusion of a treatment effect. For example, even if subjects guess that the exercise group is supposed to have improved mood, they all think they are in the exercise group. Thus, they all have the same expectations. Consequently, differences between groups' moods cannot readily be explained by expectations. Second, a number of other confounding variables are controlled. For example, all groups are having relatively equal opportunities to socialize with others. Furthermore, all groups are setting and achieving goals (attending class and finishing the workout). Therefore, confounding is not as serious a problem as when you had an empty control group.

How Multi-level Experiments Can Detect Problems with Empty Control Groups

If you insist on using an empty control group, the multi-level experiment may alert you if there are problems with such a group. To illustrate, imagine you have a four-level experiment where

1. the first group gets no treatment,
2. the second group gets 20 minutes of aerobic exercise,
3. the third group gets 40 minutes, and
4. the fourth group gets 60 minutes.

In this multi-level experiment, the three experimental groups are being treated almost identically. They only differ in terms of how much exercise they get. Consequently, any difference between the experimental groups is probably due to the amount of exercise, rather than to incidental, confounding variables (e.g., socializing with class members, setting goals).

The subjects in the three experimental groups would also have a hard time figuring out the hypothesis and playing along with it. Experimental group subjects should not be able to determine whether they are in the medium- or high-exercise group because (1) 40 minutes could be a high level or a moderate level of exercise and (2) subjects may not even realize there is more than one experimental group. Furthermore, even in the unlikely event that medium-exercise subjects correctly sensed they were in the medium-exercise group, they would have a hard time figuring out how they could cooperate with the experimenter's hypothesis. How would they know how much depression they should report when given a medium level of exercise?

You have seen that subjects in a multi-level experiment would have a hard time figuring out the hypothesis and even a harder time playing along with it. Even if subjects guessed the hypothesis and tried to play along with it, they would only be partially successful. Consequently, you should be able to detect whether the results of a multi-level experiment are solely due to hypothesis guessing. To illustrate, look at table 6.1. The results from one of these experiments are invalid because of hypothesis guessing. Do you think it is experiment A or experiment B? How do you know?

TABLE 6.1   A Comparison between Two Experiments

EXPERIMENT A		EXPERIMENT B	
CONDITION	DEPRESSION	CONDITION	DEPRESSION
No exercise	8.0	No exercise	8.0
Medium exercise	9.5	Medium exercise	11.5
High exercise	11.5	High exercise	11.5

If you think experiment B is the tainted experiment, you are correct! Why did you suspect experiment B? You probably assumed that if exercise has an effect, a high level of exercise will have a greater effect than a medium level of exercise. It is important to recognize this as an assumption—and this assumption could be wrong. However, it is remarkable how often nature conforms to this assumption.

Increasing Validity Through Several Control Groups

You have seen that using a multiple group experiment allows you to do something you cannot do with a simple experiment—have a control group *and* have more than one treatment group. You have seen that using several treatment groups can sometimes allow you to do without a control group or detect a problem with a control group. In addition to allowing you to use multiple treatment groups, multiple-group experiments allow you to do something else you cannot do with a simple experiment—use multiple control groups.

Because you cannot use multiple control groups in a simple experiment, the person using a simple experiment is often forced to choose between control groups. The researcher may have to choose between using a placebo treatment group that gets a pseudo treatment *or* an empty control group that gets no treatment whatsoever. Alternatively, the researcher may have to decide between one kind of placebo group and another kind of placebo group. With a multiple-group experiment, on the other hand, you do not have to choose. You can have as many control groups as you need.

To see how hard it can be to choose between an empty control group and a placebo group, let us go back to the problem of examining the effects of aerobic exercise on depression. If you use an empty control group that has nothing done to them, interpreting your results may be difficult. If the aerobic exercise group does better than this "left alone" group, the results could be due to hypothesis guessing or to any number of confounding variables (e.g., socializing with other students in the class, being put into a structured routine, etc.). If, however, you use a placebo-treatment group (e.g., a meditation group), you would be able to control many of these confounding variables. Still, your problems are not over.

Your problems are not over because you do not know what the effect of your placebo treatment will be. For example, suppose you find the exercise group is more depressed than the meditation group. Would you conclude that exercise increases depression? No, because it might be that although exercise reduces depression, meditation reduces it more. Conversely, if you found the exercise group is less depressed than the meditation group, you could not automatically conclude that exercise decreases depression. It may be that meditation increases depression greatly and exercise increases depression only moderately (see figure 6.4). That is, exercise may simply be the lesser of two evils. To find out whether exercise increases or decreases depression, you need to compare the exercise group to a no-treatment group. Thus, if you were interested in the effects of exercise on depression, you have two options: (1) use a simple experiment and make the hard choice between an empty control group and a placebo group or (2) use a multiple-group experiment so you can include both an empty and a placebo control group.

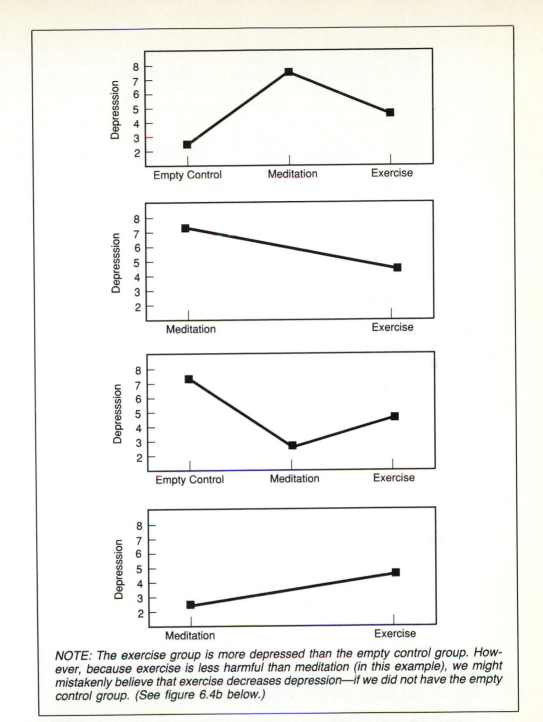

NOTE: The exercise group is more depressed than the empty control group. However, because exercise is less harmful than meditation (in this example), we might mistakenly believe that exercise decreases depression—if we did not have the empty control group. (See figure 6.4b below.)

FIGURE 6.4: How Not Having an Empty Control Group Could Produce Misleading Results

Even if you are sure you do not want to use an empty control group, you may still need more than one control group. Admittedly, if there was only one difference between how the placebo group was treated versus how the experimental group was treated, you might only need one placebo control group. However, you often will not have the perfect control group. Instead, you may have several groups, each of which controls for some extraneous variables, but not for others. If you were to do a simple experiment, you may have to decide which of several placebo groups to use. Choosing one control group—when you realize you need more than one—is frustrating. It would be better to be able to use as many as you needed.

But how often do you really need more than one control group? More often than you might think. In fact, it is so easy to underestimate the need for control groups that even professional psychologists sometimes underestimate the need for control groups. Indeed, many professional researchers get their research articles rejected because the reviewer concluded they failed to include enough good control groups (Fiske & Fogg 1990).

To illustrate how even a good placebo control group may still differ from the experimental group in several ways having nothing to do with the independent variable, consider the meditation control group. The meditation control group has several advantages over the empty control group. For example, if the exercise group was less depressed than a meditation control group, we could be confident this difference was not due to hypothesis guessing, engaging in structured activities, or being distracted from worrisome thoughts for a while. Both groups received a "treatment," both engaged in structured activities, and both were distracted for the same length of time.

However, the groups may differ in that the exercise group did a more social activity, listened to louder and more upbeat music, and interacted with a more energetic and enthusiastic instructor. Therefore, the exercise group may be less depressed for several reasons having nothing to do with exercise: (1) liking their exercise partners, (2) feeling arousal and positive mood as a result of the music, and (3) being exposed to a very upbeat person.

To rule out all these possibilities, you might use several control groups. For example, to control for the "social activity" and the "energetic model" explanations, you might add a group that went to a no-credit, acting class taught by a very enthusiastic professor. To control for the music explanation, you might add a control group that listened to music or perhaps even watched aerobic dance videos. If the exercise group differed significantly from all these control groups, you could say that it was the exercise itself, rather than the variables confounded with the exercise manipulation, that had the effect.

ANALYSIS OF MULTIPLE-GROUP EXPERIMENTS

To this point, you have learned that the multi-level experiment can be used to reduce the effects of hypothesis guessing and other confounding variables. You know you can reduce these threats to construct validity by using multiple experimental groups, multiple control groups, or both. You have also learned that the multiple-group experiment is useful for determining the functional relationship between variables. Thus, there are good reasons to do and to read about multiple-group experiments.

To read or do multiple-group experiments, you must understand the logic behind analyzing the results of such experiments. Obviously, understanding this logic will be useful if you plan to do a multiple-group experiment. But even if you do not plan on doing a multiple-group experiment, understanding the logic and the vocabulary used in analyzing multiple-group experiments is necessary if you are to understand research articles that report analyses from such experiments. Therefore, in the next few sections, you will learn the logic behind analyzing the results of a multiple-group experiment.

AN INTUITIVE OVERVIEW OF THE ANALYSIS OF MULTIPLE-GROUP EXPERIMENTS

As a first step to understanding how multiple-group experiments are analyzed, let us look at data from three experiments that compared the effects of no-treatment, meditation, and aerobic exercise on happiness. All of these experiments had 12 subjects rate their feelings of happiness on a 1 (not at all happy) to 100 (very happy) scale. Here are the results of experiment A:

	NO-TREATMENT	MEDITATION	EXERCISE
	50	51	53
	51	53	53
	52	52	54
	51	52	52
	—	—	—
Group means	51	52	53

Compare these results to the results of experiment B:

	NO-TREATMENT	MEDITATION	EXERCISE
	40	50	58
	42	50	62
	38	48	60
	40	52	60
	—	—	—
Group means	40	50	60

Are you more confident that experiment A or experiment B found a significant effect for the treatment variable? If you say "B," why do you give "B" as your answer? You answer "B" because the group means for experiment B are farther apart than the group means for experiment A. That is, the difference between 40 and 60 is greater than the difference between 51 and 53.

Why does having the means farther apart—what statisticians call greater variability between group means—make you decide experiment B is more likely to be the study that obtained significant results? Intuitively, you realize it is easy for chance to account for small differences among group means, but more difficult for chance to account for large differences. In other words, the more variability there is among group means, the more likely that at least some of that variability is due to treatment.

Now, compare experiment B with experiment C. The results of experiment C are:

	NO-TREATMENT	MEDITATION	EXERCISE
	10	10	100
	80	90	100
	60	60	10
	10	40	30
Group means	40	50	60

Do you think the results from experiment B or experiment C are more likely to indicate a real treatment effect? Both experiments have the same amount of variability between group means. Therefore, you cannot choose one over the other simply because the group means differ more in experiment B than in experiment C. Yet, once again, you will pick experiment B. Why?

You will pick experiment B because you are concerned about one aspect of experiment C: the extreme amount of variability within each group. You realize the only reason the scores within a group vary is because of random variability. (The scores within a group cannot differ due to treatment because they all got the same treatment.) Thus, you see that experiment C is more affected by random variability than experiment B. The large amount of random variability in experiment C (as revealed by the within groups variability) disturbs you because you realize this random variability might be the reason the groups differ from one another. That is, the same random variability that makes scores within a group vary from each other might also make the groups vary from each other.[3] In experiment B, on the other hand, the lack of any within group variability indicates there is virtually no random variability in your data. Therefore, in experiment B, you feel fairly confident random variability is *not* causing the group means to differ from one another. Instead, you believe the means differ from one another because of the treatment.

Intuitively then, you understand the three most important principles behind analyzing the results of a multiple-group experiment:

1. You realize between group variability alone is not an adequate measure of treatment effects. Although treatment effects should cause the groups to differ from one another, random variability will also cause the groups to differ from one another. That is, even if no treatment was administered, the group means would probably differ. In other words, between group variability is not a pure index of variability due to treatment (treatment effects) because it is also affected by random variability.

[3]To get a sense of how random sampling error might cause the group means to differ, randomly sample two scores from the no-treatment group. Compute the mean of this group. If you do this several times, you will get different means. These different means cannot be due to a treatment effect because you are sampling from a group of subjects who are *all* getting no treatment. The reason you are sampling the same group but getting different means is random sampling error. Fortunately, statistics can help us determine how likely it is that the differences among group means are entirely due to random sampling error.

2. You realize within group variability is due solely to random variability.
3. You realize that if you compare between group variability (the effects of random variability + treatment) to within group variability (the effects of random variability), you may be able to determine whether the treatment had an effect.

A CLOSER LOOK AT THE ANALYSIS OF MULTIPLE-GROUP EXPERIMENTS

You now have a general idea of how to analyze data from a multiple-group study. To see how to perform an analysis, look at box 6.2. To more fully understand the logic and vocabulary used in these analyses—a must if you are to understand an author's or a computer's report of such an analysis—read the next few sections.

Assessing Within Group Variability

As you already know, within groups variability does not reflect the effects of treatment. Instead, it reflects the effects of random variability. For example, because all the subjects in the meditation group are getting the same treatment (meditation), any differences among meditation subjects' scores are unrelated to the treatment. Instead of being due to systematic treatment effects, the differences among scores of meditation group subjects are due to such unsystematic, random factors as individual differences, unreliability of the measure, and lack of standardization. Similarly, differences among the scores of subjects in the no-treatment group are not due to treatment, but to irrelevant, random factors. The same is true for the exercise group subjects. Thus, calculating within groups variability will tell us the extent to which individual scores differ from each other by chance. If we know how much individual scores differ from each other by chance, we may be able to figure out the extent to which group means might differ from each other by chance.

To measure within groups variability, we first calculate the variance of the scores

---

BOX 6.2   Analyzing Data From a Multiple-Group Experiment

To analyze data from a multiple-group experiment, most researchers use analysis of variance. To use analysis of variance, as was the case with the t-test,

1. your observations must be independent,
2. your scores should be normally distributed,
3. each of your groups should have approximately the same variance, and
4. you should be able to assume your data are either interval or ratio.

In analysis of variance, you set up the F-ratio: a ratio of the between groups variance to the within groups variance. Or, to use proper terminology, you set up a ratio of means square between (MSB) to mean square within (MSW).

To calculate mean square within groups, you must first calculate the sum of squares for each group. You must subtract each score from its mean, square each of those differences, and then add up all those squared differences. If you had the following three groups, your first calculations would be as follows:

	GROUP 1	GROUP 2	GROUP 3
	5	6	14
	4	5	12
	3	4	10
Group mean:	4	5	12

Sum of squares for group 1:

$$
\begin{aligned}
(5 - 4)^2 + (4 - 4)^2 + (3 - 4)^2 &= \\
1^2 \quad\quad + 0^2 \quad\quad + (-1^2) &= \\
1 \quad\quad + 0 \quad\quad + 1 &= 2
\end{aligned}
$$

Sum of squares for group 2:

$$
\begin{aligned}
(6 - 5)^2 + (5 - 5)^2 + (5 - 6)^2 &= \\
1^2 \quad\quad + 0^2 \quad\quad + (-1)^2 &= \\
1 \quad\quad + 0 \quad\quad + 1 &= 2
\end{aligned}
$$

Sum of squares for group 3:

$$
\begin{aligned}
(14 - 12)^2 + (12 - 12)^2 + (10 - 12)^2 &= \\
2^2 \quad\quad + 0^2 \quad\quad + (-2)^2 &= \\
4 \quad\quad + 0 \quad\quad + 4 &= 8
\end{aligned}
$$

To get the sum of squares within groups, you add all of these sums of squares together ($2 + 2 + 8 = 12$).

To get the mean square within groups, you divide the sum of squares within groups by the within groups' number of degrees of freedom. The number of degrees of freedom in a multiple-group experiment equals the number of subjects minus the number of groups. Because you had nine subjects and three groups, your within groups degrees of freedom are 6 (because $9 - 3 = 6$). So, your mean square within is 2 (because $12/6 = 2$). Note that you would have obtained the same mean square if you had calculated the variance for each of your groups ($1 + 1 + 4$) and averaged those variances ($6/3 = 2$).

To get the mean square between groups, calculate the variance of the group means, as follows:

Calculate mean of group means (4 + 5 + 12)/3 = 21/3 = 7.

Subtract each group mean from the overall mean and square each difference:

4 − 7 = −3; −3 squared = 9
5 − 7 = −2; −2 squared = 4
12 − 7 = 5; 5 squared = 25

Add up all these squared differences (25 + 9 + 4 = 38).

Divide this term by one less than the number of groups. Since you have three groups, divide by two.

So, your variance among groups is 19 (38/2 = 19).

To transform your variance among groups to a mean square between, multiply it by the number of subjects in each group. In this case, you have three subjects per group, so you multiply 19 × 3 and get 57.

Because your F-ratio is just the ratio of mean square between to mean square within, your F-ratio is 57/2 or 28.5.

Thus, at this point, your ANOVA summary table would look like this:

SOURCE OF VARIANCE	SUM OF SQUARES	DEGREES OF FREEDOM	MEAN SQUARE	F-RATIO
Treatment	?	?	57	28.5
Error	12	6	2	

To fill in the rest of the table, you need to know the sum of squares treatment and the degrees of freedom for the treatment. The degrees of freedom for the treatment are one less than the number of groups. Since you have three groups, your *df* treatment is 2. To get the sum of squares treatment, simply multiply the *df* treatment by the mean square treatment (2 × 57 = 114). Thus, your completed ANOVA summary table would look like this:

SOURCE OF VARIANCE	SUM OF SQUARES	DEGREES OF FREEDOM	MEAN SQUARE	F-RATIO
Treatment	114	2	57	28.5
Error	12	6	2	

To determine whether the *F* of 28.5 is significant, you would look in the F-table for the critical value for 2 degrees of freedom in the numerator and 6 degrees of freedom in the denominator. If 28.5 is larger than that value, the results would be statistically significant.

within each group. If we have three groups, then this gives us three measures of within groups variability, or three estimates of random variability. Because we only need one estimate of the variability due to random variability, we average all these within group variances to come up with the best estimate of random variability—the within groups variance. Because the **within groups variance** gives us an index of the degree to which *random error* may cause your group means to differ, within groups variance is also referred to as **error variance**.

Assessing Between Group Variability

Once you have the within groups variance, the next step is to get an index of the degree to which your groups vary from one another. It is at this step where it becomes obvious you cannot use a t-test to analyze data from a multiple-group experiment. When using a t-test, you determine the degree to which the groups differ from one another in a very straightforward manner: you subtract the average score of group 1 from the average score of group 2. Subtraction works well when you want to compare two groups, but does not work well when you have more than two groups. You can only subtract two scores at a time. So, if you have three groups, which two groups do you compare? Group 1 from group 2? Or, group 2 from group 3? Or, group 1 from group 3?

You might answer this question by saying "all of the above." Thus, with three groups, you would do three t-tests: one comparing group 1 against group 2, a second comparing group 1 against group 3, and a third comparing group 2 against group 3. However, that is not cricket.

An analogy will help you understand why you cannot use multiple t-tests. Suppose a stranger comes up to you with a proposition: "Let's bet on coin flips. If I get a head, you give me a dollar. If I don't, I give you a dollar." You accept the proposition. He then proceeds to flip three coins at once and then makes you pay up if even one of the coins comes up heads. Why is this unfair? This is unfair because he misled you: You thought he was only going to flip one coin at a time, so you thought he had only a 50 percent chance of winning. But since he is flipping three coins at a time, his chances of getting at least one head are much better than 50 percent.

When you do multiple t-tests, you are doing basically the same thing as the coin hustler. You start by telling people the odds that a single t-test will be significant due to chance alone. For example, if you use conventional significance levels, you would tell people the odds of getting a statistically significant result for a particular t-test by chance were less than 5 in 100. In other words, you are claiming that your chance of making a Type 1 error is no more than 5 percent.

Then, just as the hustler gave himself more than a 50 percent chance of winning by flipping more than one coin, you give yourself a more than 5 percent chance of getting a statistically significant result by doing more than one t-test. The 5 percent odds you quoted would only hold if you had done a single t-test. If you are using t-tests to compare three groups, you will do three t-tests. If you do three t-tests, the odds of at least one turning out significant is much more than 5 percent.

If you do multiple t-tests, the more groups you use in your experiment, the greater the difference between the significance level you report and the actual odds of at least one result being significant by chance. Just to give you an idea of how great the difference between your stated significance level and the actual odds can be, suppose you had six levels of the independent variable. To compare all six groups with one another, you would need to do 15 t-tests. If you did 15 t-tests and used a .05 significance level, the probability of getting at least one significant effect by chance would be more than 50 percent! That is, your risk of making a type 1 error is more than 10 times greater than what you are claiming it is.

As you have seen, the t-test is not useful for analyzing data from the multiple-group experiment because the t-test measures the degree to which groups differ by using subtraction—and you can only subtract two group averages at a time. To calculate the degree to which more than two group means differ, you need to calculate a variance.

The variance you want to calculate should do more than indicate the extent to which the group means differ. When there is no treatment effect, you want this variance to be equivalent to the within groups variance. Furthermore, when there is a treatment effect, you want this between groups variance to be larger than the within groups variance. In other words, the **between groups variance** should be the sum of two quantities: an estimate of random error plus an estimate of treatment effects. (To calculate the between groups variance, see box 6.2.) By making the between groups variance comparable to the within groups variance, you should be able to estimate treatment effects by comparing between groups variance to within groups variance.

Comparing Variances

Once you have the between groups variance (an estimate of random error plus any treatment effects) and the within groups variance (an estimate of random error), the next step is to compare the two variances. If the between groups variance is bigger than the within groups variance, then some of the between groups variance may be due to a treatment effect. Because you will determine whether the treatment had an effect by comparing *(analyzing)* the between groups variance to the within groups variance, this statistical technique is called *an*alysis *of va*riance (**ANOVA**).

But how do you compare your two variances when doing an ANOVA? You might think you would compare your two variances by subtracting them from one another. That is, you might hope to do something like this:

between groups variance   within groups variance
(random error + possible treatment effects) −   (random error)   = treatment effect

However, in ANOVA you compare your two indices by dividing rather than by subtracting. Specifically, you set up the following ratio:

$$\frac{\text{between groups variance}}{\text{within groups variance}}$$

Let's now take a closer look at this ratio and the terminology used to describe it. In technical terminology, the index of between groups variance is referred to as the **mean square between subjects** (abbreviated *MSB*). Because the groups may differ due to treatment, this index of between groups variance is also referred to as **mean square treatment** (abbreviated *MST*).

The index of within groups variance is called the **mean square within** *(MSW)*. Because within groups variance is also an estimate of the degree to which random error is affecting estimates of the treatment group means, mean square within is also called **mean square error** *(MSE)*.

Finally, the ratio of two variances is called the **F-ratio.** Mathematically, the F-ratio reduces to

$$\frac{MSB}{MSW} \text{ which is the same as } \frac{MST}{MSE}$$

Thus, when reading articles, you may see tables similar to:

SOURCE	MS	F
Treatment	10	2
Error	5	

Conceptually, the F-ratio can be portrayed as follows:

$$F = \frac{\text{random error} + \text{possible treatment effect}}{\text{random error}}$$

By looking at the formula, you can see that the F-ratio will rarely be much less than one. If there is no treatment effect, the formula reduces to random error/random error, and if you divide anything by itself (5/5, 8/8), you will get one. Put another way, if the null hypothesis were true, the between groups variance and the within groups variance should be roughly equivalent because both are measuring the same thing—random error.

You now know that if the null hypothesis were true, the F-ratio would be approximately 1.00. That is,

$$F = \frac{\text{random error}}{\text{random error}} = 1.00^4$$

But what would happen if the treatment had an effect? Again, group 1's scores differ from one another only because of chance. The same is true of group 2's scores differing from one another and group 3's scores differing from one another. In other words, within groups variance is still due only to random error.

But what about the variance among the three group means? Will they vary from each other merely because of chance? No, the groups differ from each other because they received different levels of the treatment. Thus, the variance among group means would be due not only to random error, but also to the treatment causing real differences among

---

[4]If you get an F below 1.00, it indicates you have found no evidence of a treatment effect. Indeed, in the literature, you often will find statements such as "There were no other significant results, all *F*'s less than 1." If you get an *F* substantially below 1.00, you may want to check to be sure you did not make a calculation error. Having said this, we should point out two caveats about this formula. First, the value of *F* that you will tend to get when the null hypothesis is true will not always—or even most of the time—be 1.00. The precise value will vary depending on the degrees of freedom. Second, even under the degrees of freedom in which this formula holds, *F* will often not be exactly 1.00 because random error is variable.

groups. Therefore, the between groups variance would be larger than the within groups variance because, in addition to estimating random error (the only thing within groups variance is doing), the between groups variance is also estimating the treatment effect. Consequently, if the treatment has an effect, you would expect the ratio of between groups variance to be greater than 1.00. To reiterate,

$$F = \frac{\text{between groups variance}}{\text{within groups variance}} \frac{(\text{treatment + random error})}{(\text{random error})} > 1.00 \text{ when the treatment has an effect}$$

Using an F-table

However, not all F's above 1.00 are statistically significant. To determine whether an F-ratio is large enough to indicate a statistical difference between your groups, you need to consult an F-table like the one in appendix E. Just as the t-table told you how big a t-score had to be to reach significance, the F-table tells you how big an F-ratio has to be to reach significance. As was the case with the t-scores, how large a ratio has to be to reach significance depends on the degrees of freedom. The more degrees of freedom the error term has, the smaller the F-ratio has to be to reach significance.

Calculating Degrees of Freedom To use the F-table, you need to know two degrees of freedom: one for the top of the F-ratio (between groups variance, MST) and one for the bottom of the F-ratio (within subjects variance, MSE).

Calculating the degrees of freedom for the top of the F-ratio (between groups variance) is simple. It is just one less than the number of values of the independent variable. So, if you have three values of the independent variable (no-treatment, meditation, and exercise), you have two degrees of freedom. If you had four values of the independent variable (no-treatment, meditation, archery, aerobic exercise), then you would have three degrees of freedom. Thus, in experiments using one independent variable, the degrees of freedom for the between groups variance = number of groups − 1.

Computing the degrees of freedom for the error term in ANOVA is similar to computing the degrees of freedom for the t-test. The formula for the degrees of freedom for the t-test is N − 2. Thus, if there are twenty subjects, the degrees of freedom are 18 (20 − 2 = 18). Another way of looking at the formula is N − G, where G = total number of groups.

As we have indicated, this logic applies to ANOVA as well as to the t-test. Indeed, in a two-group ANOVA with twenty subjects, the *df* for the error term is 18—just as it is for a two-group t-test involving twenty subjects.

Extending this logic to a multiple-group ANOVA is simple. If we have 33 subjects and three groups, the *df* is 30 (because 33 − 3 = 30). If we have 30 subjects and five groups, the *df* is 25 (because 30 − 5 = 25) (see table 6.2).

Once you know the degrees of freedom, you can simply find the column in the F-table that corresponds to those degrees of freedom. If your F-ratio is larger than the value listed in the table, then the results are statistically significant at the .05 level.

The Meaning of Statistical Significance

If your results are statistically significant, what does that mean? As you know, statistical significance means you can reject the null hypothesis. In the multiple-group experiment, the null hypothesis is usually that all the differences among your group means are due to chance. That is, all your groups are essentially the same. Rejecting this hypothesis means, because of treatment effects, all your groups are not the same. In other words, you can conclude that at least two of your groups differ. But which ones? Even in a three-group experiment, there are numerous possibilities: group 1 might differ from group 2 and/or group 2 might differ from group 3 and/or group 1 might differ from group 3. A significant F does not tell you which groups differ. Therefore, once you have performed an F-test to determine that your groups differ, you need to do additional tests to determine which groups differ from one another.

Pinpointing a Significant Effect

You might think that all you would have to do to determine which groups differ is compare group means. However, some group means may differ from another solely as a result of chance. To determine which group differences are due to treatment effects, you need to do additional tests. These additional tests are called **post hoc t-tests.**

Post Hoc t-tests Among Group Means: Which Groups Differ?

At this point, you may be saying that you wanted to do t-tests all along. Before you chastise us, please hear our two-pronged defense.

First, you can only go in and do post hoc tests after you get a significant F-test. That is why post hoc tests are called post hoc ("post hoc" means after the fact). To do post hoc tests without finding a significant F is considered statistical malpractice. Such behavior would be like a physician doing a specific test to find out what strain of hepatitis you had after doing a general test that established that you did **not** have hepatitis. At best, the test will not turn up anything. At worst, the test results will be misleading because the test is being used under the wrong circumstances. Consequently, you may end up being treated for a hepatitis you do not have. Analogously, a good researcher does not ask which groups differ from one another unless the more general, overall analysis of variance test has established that some of the groups do indeed differ.

Second, post hoc tests are not the same as conventional t-tests. Unlike conventional

TABLE 6.2 Calculating Degrees of Freedom

Source of Variance (SV)	Calculation of DF
Treatment (between groups)	Levels of treatment − 1
Within subjects (error variance)	Number of subjects minus levels of treatment

t-tests, post hoc t-tests are designed to correct for the fact you are doing more than two comparisons.

At this point, there is no reason for you to know how to do post hoc tests. You should simply be aware that if you choose to do a multiple-group experiment, you should be prepared to do post hoc analyses. You should also be prepared to encounter post hoc tests if you read a journal article that reports a significant F for a multiple-group experiment. If you read about a Bonferroni t-test (Dunn test), Tukey test, Scheffe' test, Dunnett test, Newman-Keuls test, Duncan, or LSD test, do not panic. The author is merely reporting the results of a test to determine which means differ from one another. (If you want to know more about post hoc tests, see appendix E.)

Post Hoc Trend Analysis: What Is the Shape of the Relationship?

If you are interested in generalizing your results to unexplored levels of the independent variable, you may not be extremely interested in determining **which particular groups** differ from one another. Instead, you may be more interested in determining the **shape** of the relationship between the independent and dependent variables. If so, instead of following up a significant main effect with post hoc tests between group means, follow up the significant effect with post hoc trend analyses.

But why should you do a trend analysis to determine the shape of a relationship between your independent and dependent variables? Can't you see this relationship by simply graphing the group means? Yes and no. Yes, graphing allows you to see the pattern in the data produced by your experiment. No, graphing does not tell you whether the pattern is a reliable one. Just as you needed statistics to tell you whether the difference between two groups was significant (even though you could easily see whether one mean was higher than the other), you need statistics to know whether the pattern you observe in your data (a straight line, a curved line, a combination of a curve and a straight line, etc.) would occur if you repeated the experiment. Specifically, you must do a post hoc trend analysis. If you want to see how to do a post hoc trend analysis, refer to appendix E and box 6.3.

Obviously, to plan an experiment, you do not need to know how to do a trend

---

BOX 6.3   Requirements of a Post Hoc Trend Analysis

1. Your independent variable must have a statistically significant effect.
2. Your independent variable should be quantitative and the levels used in the experiment should vary from one another by some constant proportion.
3. The number of trends you can look for is one less than the number of levels of your independent variable.
4. Your dependent variable must yield interval or ratio scale data.

---

analysis. However, if you want to do a trend analysis on your data, there are three things you should know before you run your first subject. First, to do a post hoc analysis, you must have selected levels of your independent variable that increase proportionally (e.g., 10, 20, 30 mg, or 10, 100, 1000 mg). Second, to do a trend analysis, you must have an interval or ratio scale measure of your dependent variable. Third, the more levels of the independent variable you have, the more trends you can look for. Specifically, the number of trends you can examine is one less than the number of levels you have. If you have three groups, you can test for straight lines (linear component) and for a "u"-shaped curve (quadratic component). With four levels, you can test for straight lines, "u"-shaped curves, and double–"u"-shaped curves (cubic component). Thus, if you are expecting a double–"u"-shaped curve, you must use at least four levels of the independent variable.

CONCLUDING REMARKS

You have seen that you can expand a simple experiment by using more than two values of the independent variable. You have seen that expanding the simple experiment in this way can pay off in two important ways. First, using more control groups allows you more opportunities to rule out the effects of confounding variables. Second, using more treatment groups allows you to more accurately generalize your results to more values of the independent variable.

Yet, as valuable as expanding the simple experiment by adding more levels of the treatment can be, there is an even more powerful way to expand the simple experiment— by adding treatment variables. As you will see in the next chapter, adding variables can not only increase construct and external validity, but open up a whole new arena of research questions.

SUMMARY

1. As compared to the simple experiment, the multiple-group experiment's sensitivity to nonlinear relationships makes it more likely to obtain significant treatment effects and to detect the functional relationship between your independent and dependent variables.
2. Knowing the functional relationship allows more accurate predictions about the effects of unexplored levels of the independent variable.
3. To use the multiple-group experiment to discover the functional relationship, you must carefully select your levels of the independent variable and your dependent variable must be measured on an interval or ratio scale.

4. Multiple-group experiments may have more construct validity than a simple experiment because they can have multiple control groups and/or multiple experimental groups.
5. To analyze a multiple-group experiment, you first have to conduct an F-test.
6. An F-test is a ratio of between groups variance to within groups variance.
7. The following table summarizes the mathematics of an F-table.

Source of Variance (SV)	Sum of Squares (SS)	degrees of freedom (df)	Mean Square (MS)	F
Treatment (T)	SST	levels of T − 1	$\frac{SST}{df\ T}$	$\frac{MST}{MSE}$
Error (E) also known as within groups variance	SSE	subjects − df T − 1	$\frac{SSE}{df\ E}$	
Total	SS Total	Subjects − 1		

8. If you get a significant F, you know the groups are not all the same. To find out which groups are different, you need to do post hoc tests.

KEY TERMS

analysis of variance (ANOVA)
between groups variance (mean square treatment, mean square between)
confounding variables
curvilinear
functional relationship
grand mean

hypothesis guessing
levels of the independent variable
linear trend
post hoc test
trend analysis
within groups variance (mean square within, mean square error, error variance)

EXERCISES

1. A researcher randomly assigns a statistics class to two groups. In one group, each subject is assigned a tutor. The tutor is available to meet with the student twenty minutes before each class. The other group is a control group not assigned a tutor.

   Suppose the researcher finds the tutored group scores significantly better on exams.

a. Can the researcher conclude the experimental group students learned statistical information in tutoring sessions that enabled them to perform better on the exam? Why or why not?

b. What changes would you recommend in the study?

2. Suppose people living in homes for the elderly were randomly assigned to two groups: a no-treatment group and a transcendental meditation (TM) group. Transcendental meditation involves more than sitting with eyes closed. The technique involves both a "mantra, or meaningless sound selected for its value in facilitating the transcending or settling down process and a specific procedure for using it mentally without effort again to facilitate transcending" (Alexander, Langer, Newman, Chandler, & Davies, 1989). Thus, the TM group was given instruction in how to perform the technique, then "they met with their instructors one-half hour each week to verify that they were meditating correctly and regularly. They were to practice their program twenty minutes twice daily (morning and afternoon), sitting comfortably in their own room with eyes closed and using a timepiece to ensure correct length of practice" (Alexander et al., 1989).

Suppose the TM group performed significantly better than other groups on a mental health measure.[5]

a. Could the researcher conclude it was the transcendental meditation that caused the effect?

b. What besides the specific aspects of TM could cause the difference between the two groups?

c. What control groups would you add?

d. Suppose you added these control groups and then got a significant F for the treatment variable. What could you conclude? Why?

3. Assume you want to test the effectiveness of a new kind of therapy. This therapy involves screaming followed by hugging people in group sessions followed by individual meetings with a therapist. What control group(s) would you use? Why?

4. Assume a researcher is looking at the relationship between caffeine consumption and sense of humor.

a. How many levels of caffeine should the researcher use? Why?

b. What levels would you choose? Why?

c. If a graph of the data suggests a curvilinear relationship, can the researcher assume the functional relationship between the independent and dependent variables is curvilinear? Why or why not?

d. Suppose the researcher **ranked** subjects based on their sense of humor. That is, the person that laughed most got a score of "1," the next person got a "2," etc. Can the researcher use these data to do a trend analysis? Why or why not?

e. Suppose the researcher used the following four levels of caffeine: 0 mg, 20 mg, 25 mg, 26 mg. Can the researcher do a trend analysis? Why or why not?

---

[5]A modification of this study was actually done. The study included appropriate control groups.

f. If a researcher used four levels of caffeine, how many trends can the researcher look for? What is the treatment degrees of freedom?

g. If the researcher used three levels of caffeine and thirty subjects, what are the degrees of freedom for the treatment? The degrees of freedom for the error term?

h. Suppose the F is 3.35. Referring to the degrees of freedom you obtained in your answer to "g" (above) and to table e.3 in appendix E, are the results statistically significant? Can the researcher look for linear and quadratic trends?

5. A computer analysis reports that $F(6,23) = 2.54$. The analysis is telling you the F-ratio is 2.54 and the degrees of freedom for the top part of the F-ratio are 6 and the degrees of freedom for the bottom part are 23. Is this result statistically significant at the .05 level (refer to table e.3 in appendix E)? How many groups did the researcher use? How many subjects were in the experiment?

6. How is the top part of the F-ratio like the top part of the t-ratio? How is the bottom part of the F-ratio like the bottom part of the t-ratio?

7. A computer analysis computes the following Fs. On what basis would you want these Fs rechecked?
   a. $F(2,63) = .10$, not significant
   b. $F(3,85) = -1.70$, not significant
   c. $F(1,120) = 52.8$, not significant
   d. $F(5,70) = 1.00$, significant
   e. $F(15,2) = 3.68$, not significant

8. Complete the following table. Please note that the researcher randomly assigned subjects to one of three groups.

Source of Variance (SV)	Sum of Squares (SS)	degrees of freedom (df)	Mean Square (MS)	F
Treatment (T) three levels of treatment	SST = 180	—	—	—
Error (E) also known as within groups variance	SSE = 80	8	—	
Total	SS Total = 260	Subjects − 1 = —		

9. Complete the following table.

Source of Variance (SV)	Sum of Squares (SS)	degrees of freedom (df)	Mean Square (MS)	F
Treatment (T)	50	5	—	
Error (E) also known as within groups variance	100	—	—	
Total	—	30		

10. A study compares the effect of having a snack, taking a ten-minute walk, or getting no treatment on energy levels. Sixty participants are randomly assigned to a condition and then asked to rate their energy level on a zero (not at all energetic) to ten (very energetic) scale. The mean for the "do nothing" group is 6.0, for having a snack 7.0, and for walking 7.8. The F-ratio is 6.27.

   a. Graph the means.
   b. Are the results statistically significant?
      (1) If so, what conclusions can you draw? Why?
      (2) If not, what would you conclude?
   c. How would you extend this study?

7 EXPANDING THE SIMPLE EXPERIMENT: FACTORIAL DESIGNS

OVERVIEW

In chapter 5, you learned how the logic of the simple experiment enables it to be internally valid. However, you also learned it was limited: with it, you could only study two values of a single independent variable.

In chapter 6, you learned the basic logic behind the simple experiment could be extended to design experiments that study three or more values of a single independent variable. You saw that such multiple-group experiments could possess impressive internal, external, and construct validity.

In this chapter, you will learn how to extend the basic logic of the simple experiment to study the effects of two or more independent variables in a single experiment. But beyond learning how to design and interpret the results of such experiments, you will learn why you should want to study the effects of two or more independent variables in a single experiment.

THE 2 × 2 FACTORIAL DESIGN

To illustrate how you can study two independent variables in a single experiment, suppose you wanted to know the effect of both caffeine and exercise on the appetite. You want to use two levels of caffeine (0 mg and 20 mg) and two levels of exercise (no exercise and fifty minutes of exercise). To examine these variables with one experiment, you would randomly assign subjects to the following four groups:

1. No exercise, no caffeine
2. No exercise, 20 mg caffeine
3. Fifty minutes of exercise, no caffeine
4. Fifty minutes of exercise, 20 mg caffeine

In technical terminology, you would be using a **factorial experiment**: an experiment that examines the effects of two or more independent variables (**factors**) on *one* dependent variable. Specifically, because the exercise factor has two levels and the caffeine factor has two levels, you have a 2 (no exercise/50 min exercise) × 2 (no caffeine/20 mg caffeine) factorial experiment.

HOW ONE EXPERIMENT CAN DO AS MUCH AS TWO EXPERIMENTS

Of course, if you wanted to study the effects of exercise and caffeine on appetite, you would not have to do a factorial experiment. Instead, you could do two simple experiments. One simple experiment would look at caffeine's effects on appetite. The other

TABLE 7.1 How Three Cells of A 2 × 2 Experiment Contain the Information of Two Simple Experiments

SIMPLE EXPERIMENT #1

Control group	Caffeine group

Simple experiment #2

Control group
Exercise group

THREE OF THE FOUR CELLS OF A 2 × 2 EXPERIMENT

Control group	Caffeine group
Exercise group	The extra group?

would look at exercise's effects on appetite. To visualize the difference between doing a single 2 × 2 factorial experiment or doing two simple experiments, look at table 7.1.

As you can see by looking at table 7.1, the first three cells of the 2 × 2 experiment have every group the two simple experiments have. The three cells of the 2 × 2 incorporate the two simple experiments.

If the two simple experiments have four groups, how can the 2 × 2 do the same work with three groups? A close look at table 7.1 shows that although the two simple experiments have four groups, they only have three different groups. That is, two of those groups do the same thing—serve as a control group. By not duplicating the control group, three cells of the 2 × 2 can contain the three different groups the two simple experiments have.

By getting double duty out of the control group, the three cells of the 2 × 2 incorporate the two simple experiments. Consequently, three cells of the 2 × 2 experiment can do everything the two simple experiments do. Specifically, by comparing the two groups in the first column of the 2 × 2 (the control group and the exercise group), you would get a *simple main effect for exercise*—just as you would if you had done simple experiment #2. By comparing the two groups in the first row of the 2 × 2 (the control group and the caffeine group), you would get a *simple main effect for caffeine*—just as you would have gotten if you had done simple experiment #1.

HOW ONE EXPERIMENT CAN DO MORE THAN TWO EXPERIMENTS

If the 2 × 2 can do everything two simple experiments can do with only three groups, why do we have the fourth group? We have the fourth group so we can discover things we could not have discovered had we used two simple experiments.

Four Simple Main Effects

As you can see from table 7.2, because of the fourth group, the 2 × 2 incorporates four simple experiments. That is, if we used the appropriate statistical techniques, we could use the 2 × 2 to find four simple main effects:

1. the simple main effect for caffeine in the no-exercise conditions,
2. the simple main effect for caffeine in the exercise conditions,
3. the simple main effect for exercise in the no-caffeine conditions, and
4. the simple main effect for exercise in the caffeine conditions.

We should stress that psychologists do **not** do factorial experiments with the primary aim of detecting these four simple main effects. Usually, analysis of factorial experiments does **not** begin with looking for these simple main effects. Often, no analysis is done to look at these simple main effects. Indeed, in most undergraduate research design texts, students are **not** told how to test for these simple main effects.

One reason individual simple effects are not emphasized is thatthe strength of

---

TABLE 7.2 How the 2 × 2 Experiment Contains the Information of Four Simple Experiments

	SIMPLE EXPERIMENT #1 (EFFECT OF EXERCISE WHEN NO CAFFEINE IS PRESENT)	SIMPLE EXPERIMENT #2 (EFFECT OF EXERCISE WHEN CAFFEINE IS PRESENT)
	Control group	Caffeine group
	Exercise group	Caffeine + Exercise group

Simple experiment #3 (effect of caffeine for subjects who do not exercise)	Control group	Caffeine group
Simple experiment #4 (effect of caffeine for subjects who do exercise)	Exercise group	Caffeine + Exercise group

This row contains simple experiment #3	Control group	Caffeine group
This row contains simple experiment #4	Exercise group	Caffeine + Exercise group
	This column contains simple experiment #1	This column contains simple experiment #2

the factorial experiment is its ability to examine relationships that cannot be studied by individual simple experiments. To reiterate, the strength of the 2 × 2 is not that it could be used to test four separate simple effects. Instead, its strength is that it allows the researcher to obtain two *pairs* of simple effects. In the next section, you will see there are two primary advantages to having two pairs of simple main effects (a pair of caffeine simple main effects and a pair of exercise simple main effects).

Two Overall Main Effects

First, researchers average each pair of simple main effects to find out what the average effect for that variable is. Taking the *average* of a variable's two simple main effects yields the variable's **overall main effect.** In the caffeine-exercise study, the researcher would average the two caffeine simple main effects to get an *overall main effect* for caffeine. Likewise, the researcher would average the two exercise main effects to get an *overall main effect* for exercise.

One reason for the focus on overall main effects is convenience. It is easier to talk about one overall main effect than about two simple main effects individually. However, a much more important advantage of averaging the two simple main effects into an overall main effect is it allows us to make more general statements about that variable's effects. For example, consider the advantage of averaging the two simple main effects of caffeine. Because we have combined two simple main effects, we are not confined to saying that caffeine has an effect if you exercise fifty minutes a day. Instead, we can say, on the average, in a study that varied exercise levels, caffeine has an effect. Therefore, we can be more confident the effect of caffeine generalizes across a variety of exercise levels.

Interactions

But what if the effect of caffeine is different in the exercise condition than in the no-exercise condition? Then you should not make a general statement about the effect of caffeine without mentioning the fact that the effect changes depending on how much exercise one does. That brings us to the second thing researchers can do with pairs of simple main effects: compare each factor's two simple main effects to see if they **differ.** If the simple main effects of caffeine differ **depending** on the level of exercise, there is an **interaction** between caffeine and exercise (see table 7.3).

Interactions are a fact of life and a fact of psychology (see table 7.4). We are always finding out that the effect of an action depends on other factors. In everyday life, the meaning of almost everything we do depends on the context. For example, telling someone "congratulations" will have a good effect if they have just been promoted, a bad effect if they have just been fired. Similarly, many experiments find a treatment will have one effect on one group of subjects, but a different effect on another group. For instance, if you have a group of subjects who believe they have no control over the noise level in the room, increasing the noise level seriously harms performance. However, for subjects who believe they could control the noise level, increasing the noise level does not harm performance. Thus, noise level interacts with perceived control (Glass & Singer, 1972). Because of this interaction, you cannot simply say noise hurts performance. You have to say the effect of noise level on performance depends on perceived control. In other words,

TABLE 7.3 Simple Main Effects, Overall Main Effects, and Interactions

Simple main effects	Definition: Effects of one independent variable at a specific level of a second independent variable
	How estimated: An effect that could have been obtained by doing a simple experiment
	Question addressed: (What is the effect of caffeine in the fifty-minute exercise condition?)
Overall main effect	Definition: Effect of one independent *variable*, averaged over all the levels of a second independent variable, a general rule about the variable's effect in the study
	How estimated: Averaging a variable's simple main effects
	Question addressed: (What is the *average* of the caffeine effect in the no-exercise condition and the caffeine effect in the fifty-minute exercise condition?)
Interaction	Definition: The general rule (the average effect of the variable) is not consistent across conditions
	How estimated: Looking at differences between simple main effects
	Question addressed: (Is there a *difference* between caffeine's effect in the no-exercise condition and caffeine's effect in the fifty-minute exercise condition?)

rather than stating a simple rule about the effects of noise, you have to state a more complex rule. This complex rule puts qualifications on the statement that noise hurts performance. Specifically, the statement that noise hurts performance will be qualified by some word or phrase such as "depending on," "but only if," "however, that holds only under certain conditions."

As psychology has progressed, psychologists have focused increasingly more attention on interactions. Part of the reason psychologists focus on interactions is because psychologists have already discovered the main effects of many variables. We know how many individual variables act in isolation. Now, it is time to go to the next step—addressing the question "What is the effect of combining these variables?" Put another way, once we learn what the general effect of a variable is, we want to find out what specific conditions may modify this general, overall effect.

Another reason psychologists focus on interactions is because they realize both that (1) individuals rarely are exposed to one and only one variable and (2) interactions are common. Consequently, psychologists now frame general problems and issues in terms of interactions. That is, rather than saying "what is the (main) effect of personality and what is the (main) effect of the situation?", psychologists are now asking "how do personality and the situation interact?" Asking this question has led to research indicating some people are more influenced by situational influences than others (Snyder, 1974). Similarly, rather than looking exclusively at the main effects of heredity and the main effects of environment, many scientists are looking at the interactions between heredity and environment. The results of looking for interactions often provide revealing new insights. For example, psychologists have found certain children may benefit from an environment

TABLE 7.4 Ways of Thinking about Interactions

VIEWPOINT	HOW IT RELATES TO INTERACTIONS
Chemical reactions	Lighting a match, in itself, is not dangerous. Having gasoline around is not, in itself, dangerous. However, the *combination* of lighting a match in the presence of gasoline is explosive. Because the explosive effects of combining gas and lighting a match are different from simply adding their separate, individual effects, gasoline and matches interact.
Personal relationships	John likes most people. Mary is liked by most people. *But,* John dislikes Mary. Based only on their individual tendencies, we would expect John to like Mary. Apparently, however, like gasoline and matches, the combination of their personalities produces a negative outcome.
Sports	The whole is not the same as the sum of the parts. That is, a team is not the sum of its parts. The addition of a player may do more for the team than the player's abilities would suggest—or the addition may help the team much less because the team "chemistry" is upset. In other words, the interaction between the player's skills and personality may interact with those of the other players on the team or with the team's strategy. Sometimes, the result is that adding the player will help the team more than what would be expected by knowing only the team's characteristics and the player's characteristics. Sometimes, adding the player will help the team less than what would be expected if one only knew the team's characteristics and the player's characteristics. Knowing the interaction between the team and the player—how the two will mesh together—may be almost as important as knowing the player's abilities.

Good pitchers get batters out. Poor hitters are easier to get out than good hitters. *However,* sometimes a poor hitter may have a good pitcher's "number" because the pitcher's strengths match the hitter's strengths. Similarly, some "poor" pitchers are very effective against some of the league's best batters. Managers who can take advantage of these interactions can win more games than would be expected by knowing only a team's talents. |
| Prescription drugs | Drug A may be a good, useful drug. Drug B may also be a good, useful drug. But, taking drugs A and B together may result in harm or death. Increasingly, doctors and pharmacists have to be aware not only of the effects of drugs in isolation, but their combined effects. Ignorance of these interactions can result in deaths and in malpractice suits. |

TABLE 7.4 Continued

VIEWPOINT	HOW IT RELATES TO INTERACTIONS
Making general statements	Interactions indicate you cannot make a general, simple statement that one variable always has a specific effect. You cannot talk about the effects of one variable without mentioning the effect of the variable depends on a second variable. Therefore, if you have an interaction, when discussing a factor's effect, you need to say "but," "except when," "depending on," or "only under certain conditions." Indeed, you often will see results sections say the main effect was "qualified by a ___ interaction" or "the effect of the ___ variable was different depending on the level of (the other) variable."
Overall main effect	If you do *not* have an interaction, the overall main effect should be similar to all the individual simple main effects making up that overall main effect. If, on the other hand, you do have an interaction, you cannot safely talk about the variable's average effect without mentioning the effect differs depending on the level of a second variable.
Simple main effects	In the 2 × 2, you have two simple main effects for each variable. If the two simple main effects for a variable are very different, you probably have an interaction. For example, if the simple main effect for caffeine in the no-exercise conditions is large, but the simple main effect for caffeine in the exercise conditions is zero, you probably have an interaction.
Visually	If you graph an interaction, the lines will not be parallel. That is, the lines either already cross or, if they were extended, they would eventually cross.
Mathematically	If you have an interaction, the effect of combining the variables is *not* the same as adding their two effects together. Rather, the effect is better captured as the result of multiplying the two effects. That is, when you add 2 to a number, you know the number will increase by 2, regardless of what the number is. However, when you multiply a number by 2, the effect will depend on the other number. When doubling a number, the effect is quite different when the number to be doubled is 2 than when it is 1000 or when it is −40. To take another example of the effect of multiplication, consider the multiplicative effects of interest rates on your financial condition. If interests rates go up, that will have a big, positive effect on your financial situation if you have lots of money in the bank; a small, positive effect if you have little money in the bank; and a negative effect on your finances if you owe money to the bank (you will have to pay more interest because you have a negative amount of money in the bank).

that would be detrimental to children who had inherited a different genetic predisposition (Plomin, 1989). Eventually, such research may lead to parents identifying their child's genetic predispositions and then altering their parenting strategies to fit that predisposition.

Example of Questions Answered by the 2 × 2 Factorial Experiment

Now that you have a general understanding of main effects and interactions, let us apply this knowledge to a specific experiment. If you were to do the caffeine and exercise experiment we described earlier, you would look for three different kinds of effects:

1. the average or main effect of caffeine,
2. the average or main effect of exercise, and
3. the interaction between caffeine and exercise.

The main effect of caffeine would be calculated by averaging the simple main effects of caffeine. Likewise, the main effect of exercise would be calculated by *averaging* the two simple main effects of exercise. The interaction, on the other hand, would be calculated by *subtracting* the simple main effects from each other. If both pairs of caffeine main effects are the same (they do not differ) and if both pairs of exercise main effects are the same, you do not have an interaction. Thus, a significant main effect for caffeine would mean caffeine had an effect, a significant main effect for exercise would mean exercise had an effect, and a significant interaction would mean the *combination* of exercise and caffeine produces an effect that is not simply the sum of their two separate effects (see table 7.5).

As you can imagine, significant interactions force scientists to answer such questions as "Does caffeine increase calorie consumption?" by saying, "Yes, but it depends

---

TABLE 7.5 Questions Addressed by a 2 × 2 Experiment

EFFECT	QUESTION ADDRESSED
Overall main effect for exercise	On the average, does varying exercise levels have an effect? (Is the average of the two exercise simple main effects significantly different from zero?)
Overall main effect for caffeine	On the average, does varying caffeine levels have an effect? (Is the average of the two exercise simple main effects significantly different from zero?)
Interaction between caffeine and exercise	Does the effect of varying caffeine *differ depending on* how much exercise subjects get? Put another way: does the effect of varying exercise *differ depending on* how much caffeine subjects get? (Do the two caffeine simple main effects differ significantly? Do the two exercise simple main effects differ significantly?)

on. . . ." or "It's a little more complicated than that." Psychologists do not give these kinds of responses to make the world seem more complicated than it is.

On the contrary, psychologists would love to give simple answers. Like all scientists, they love parsimony. Therefore, they would love to report main effects that are not complicated, qualified, or interfered with by interactions. They would like to say exercise is always good, drinking caffeine is always bad. However, if interactions occur, scientists have the obligation to report them—and in the real world, interactions abound. Only the person who says, "Give me a match, I want to see if my gas tank is empty," is unaware of the pervasiveness of interactions. Time and time again, you learn that when variables combine, the effects are different than you would expect from knowing only their independent effects.

Because we live in a world where we are exposed to a variety of variables and because these variables interact, you may be compelled to do experiments that capture some of this complexity. But how would you describe the results from a complex study?

POTENTIAL RESULTS OF A 2 × 2 EXPERIMENT

There are eight basic patterns of results you could obtain with a 2 × 2 experiment. These patterns are listed in table 7.6.

If you did a study, how would you know which of these patterns of results you obtained? The first step would be to calculate the mean response for each group and then make a table of those means.

A Main Effect and No Interaction

Suppose you obtained the results displayed in table 7.7. From the first row, you can see that when there was no caffeine, exercise had no effect. Obviously, this finding could have been discovered by doing a simple experiment. Looking at the next row, you see exercise had no effect in the 20 mg of caffeine group. Again, this effect could have been

TABLE 7.6 Eight Potential Outcomes of a 2 × 2 Factorial Experiment

	MAIN EFFECT FOR VARIABLE 1	MAIN EFFECT FOR VARIABLE 2	INTERACTION
1	Yes	No	No
2	No	Yes	No
3	Yes	Yes	No
4	Yes	Yes	Yes
5	No	No	Yes
6	Yes	No	Yes
7	No	Yes	Yes
8	No	No	No

TABLE 7.7 Main Effect for Caffeine, No Interaction

	No exercise	50 min exercise	EXERCISE SIMPLE MAIN EFFECTS	EXERCISE OVERALL MAIN EFFECT
No caffeine	2000 cal	2000 cal	2000 − 2000 = 0 *Simple main effect of exercise for no-caffeine conditions*	
				(0 + 0)/2 = 0
20 mg caffeine	2200 cal	2200 cal	2200 − 2200 = 0 *Simple main effect of exercise for 20-mg caffeine conditions*	
MAIN EFFECTS OF CAFFEINE	2200 − 2000 = 200 *Simple main effect for caffeine in no-exercise conditions*	2200 − 2000 = 200 *Simple main effect for caffeine in exercise conditions*		

Overall caffeine main effect = 200
(200 + 200)/2

Note: The average, overall caffeine main effect (200) is just the average of caffeine's two simple main effects. In this case, you know you do not have an interaction between caffeine and exercise because the simple main effect for caffeine in the no-exercise condition (200) is the same as the simple main effect for caffeine in the exercise condition (200).

discovered by doing a simple experiment. Averaging the effect of exercise over both the 0 and 20 mg of caffeine conditions, you find that exercise's average (overall) effect was zero. Thus, there was no main effect for exercise.

Looking at the columns tells you about the effect of caffeine. You see that when there is no exercise, the subjects consume two hundred more calories in the 20-mg caffeine condition than in the no-caffeine group. This simple main effect of caffeine could have been discovered by using a simple experiment. Looking at the second column, you learn that in the fifty-minute condition, the 20-mg caffeine group also consumes two hundred more calories than the no-caffeine group. Thus, it appears there is an overall main effect for caffeine.

There is no interaction because the effect of caffeine is unaffected by the level of exercise. As table 7.7 demonstrates, the effect of caffeine is independent of the amount of exercise.

Instead of having no interaction and a main effect for caffeine, you could have no interaction and a main effect for exercise. This pattern of results is shown in table 7.8. From the first row, you can see that when there was no caffeine, exercise increased calorie consumption by five hundred. Looking at the second row, you see exercise also increased

TABLE 7.8 Main Effect for Exercise, No Interaction

	No exercise	50 min exercise	EXERCISE SIMPLE MAIN EFFECTS	EXERCISE OVERALL MAIN EFFECT
No caffeine	2000 cal	2500 cal	2500 − 2000 = 500 *Simple main effect of exercise for no-caffeine conditions*	
				(500 + 500)/2 = 500
20 mg caffeine	2000 cal	2500 cal	2500 − 2000 = 500 *Simple main effect of exercise for 20-mg caffeine conditions*	
MAIN EFFECTS OF CAFFEINE	2000 − 2000 = 0 *Simple main effect for caffeine in no-exercise conditions*	2500 − 2500 = 0 *Simple main effect for caffeine in exercise conditions*		
	Overall caffeine main effect = 0 (0 + 0)/2			

Note: Overall exercise main effect (500) is just the average of exercise's two simple main effects. In this case, you know you do not have an interaction between caffeine and exercise because the simple main effect for exercise in the no-caffeine condition (500) is the same as the simple main effect for exercise in the caffeine condition (500).

calorie consumption by five hundred in the 20 mg of caffeine conditions. By averaging the effect of exercise over both the 0- and 20-mg caffeine conditions, you find exercise's average effect (the overall main effect of exercise) was five hundred.

Looking at the columns tells you about the effect of caffeine. You see that when there is no exercise, the subjects in the 20-mg caffeine condition consumed the same number of calories as subjects in the no-caffeine condition. Looking at the second column, you learn that in the fifty minutes of exercise condition, the 20-mg caffeine group consumes the same number of calories as the no-caffeine group. Thus, it appears there is no main effect for caffeine.

You also know there is no interaction because the effect of exercise is unaffected by the level of caffeine. As table 7.8 demonstrates, exercise increases food consumption by 500 calories regardless of the amount of caffeine consumed.

Although making tables of means is a useful way to summarize your data, perhaps the easiest way to interpret the results of your experiment is to graph the data. Get a piece of paper and plot your four means. Then, draw a straight line between the means in the first row of the table. Draw a second line between the means in the second row. Your graph should look something like figure 7.1.

The graph confirms what you saw in the table. Exercise increased calorie consumption as shown by the fifty minutes of exercise line being above the no-exercise line. Caffeine did not increase calorie consumption as shown by the fact that both lines stay perfectly level as they go from no caffeine to 20 mg caffeine. Finally, there is no interaction between exercise and caffeine on calorie consumption, as shown by the fact that the lines are parallel. The lines are parallel because exercise is having the same effect on the no-caffeine groups as it is on the 20-mg groups. Thus, if you graph your data, you only need to look to see whether the lines are parallel to see whether you have an interaction. To reiterate, if your lines do not cross and if they would not cross even if you extended them, then you do *not* have an interaction.

Two Main Effects and No Interaction

Table 7.9 reflects another pattern of effects you might obtain. From the first row, you can see that when there was no caffeine, exercise increased calorie consumption by five hundred. Looking at the second row, you see that in the 20-mg groups, exercise also increased calorie consumption by five hundred. Averaging the effect of caffeine over all caffeine conditions, you find that the average effect of exercise (the overall main effect of exercise) was to increase calorie consumption by five hundred.

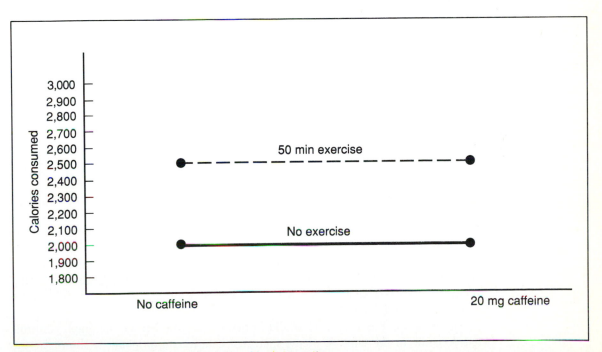

FIGURE 7.1 Main Effect for Exercise, No Interaction

TABLE 7.9 Main Effects for Caffeine and Exercise, No Interaction

			EXERCISE SIMPLE MAIN EFFECTS	EXERCISE OVERALL MAIN EFFECT
	No exercise	**50 min exercise**		
No caffeine	2000 cal	2500 cal	2500 – 2000 = 500 *Simple main effect of exercise for no-caffeine conditions*	
				(500 + 500)/2 = 500
20 mg caffeine	2200 cal	2700 cal	2700 – 2200 = 500 *Simple main effect of exercise for 20-mg caffeine conditions*	
MAIN EFFECTS OF CAFFEINE	2200 – 2000 = 200 *Simple main effect for caffeine in no-exercise conditions*	2700 – 2500 = 200 *Simple main effect for caffeine in exercise conditions*		
		Overall caffeine main effect = 200 (200 + 200)/2		

Note: You know you do not have an interaction between caffeine and exercise because the simple main effect for caffeine in the no-exercise condition (200) is the same as the simple main effect for caffeine in the exercise condition (200). Likewise, the simple main effect for exercise in the no-caffeine condition (500) is the same as the simple main effect for exercise in the caffeine condition (500).

Looking at the columns tells you about the effect of caffeine. You see that when there is no exercise, the subjects consume two hundred more calories in the 20-mg caffeine condition than in the no-caffeine group. Looking at the second column, you learn that in the fifty-minute condition, the 20-mg caffeine group consumes two hundred more calories than the no-caffeine group. Thus, it appears, in addition to the exercise main effect, you have a caffeine main effect. That is, it increases consumption by 200 calories in both the exercise and the no-exercise conditions.

Finally, there is no interaction because the effect of caffeine is unaffected by the level of exercise. As table 7.9 demonstrates, the effect of caffeine is independent of the amount of exercise. That is, it increases consumption by 200 calories in both the exercise and the no-exercise conditions.

If you graph the means, as we did in figure 7.2, you can see the graph confirms what you saw in the table. Caffeine increased calorie consumption as shown by the caffeine line going above the no-caffeine line. Similarly, exercise increased calorie

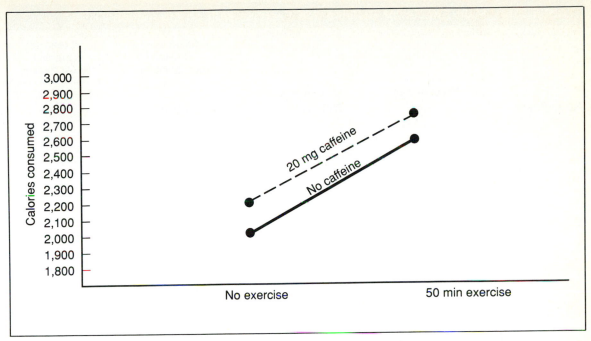

FIGURE 7.2 Main Effects for Caffeine and Exercise, No Interaction

consumption as shown by both lines sloping upward as they go from no exercise to exercise. Finally, the graph tells you there is no interaction between exercise and caffeine on calorie consumption because the lines are parallel.

Two Main Effects and an Interaction

Now imagine you got a very different set of results from your study. For example, suppose you found the results in table 7.10.

As table 7.10 shows, you have main effects for both exercise and caffeine. The average effect of caffeine is to increase calorie consumption by 500 and the average effect of exercise is to increase calorie consumption by 500. However, the effect of caffeine varies depending on how much exercise subjects get. In the no-exercise condition, caffeine increases calorie consumption by 200. In the exercise condition, on the other hand, caffeine increases consumption by 800 calories. Because the effect of caffeine varies depending on the amount of exercise, you have an interaction. The interaction is also revealed in figure 7.3, by the fact that the lines are no longer parallel.

Interaction Without Main Effects

You have seen you can have main effects without interactions, but can you have interactions without main effects? Consider the data in table 7.11 and figure 7.4.

In figure 7.4, you notice the lines are not parallel. Therefore, you have an inter-

TABLE 7.10   Main Effects for Caffeine and Exercise with an Interaction

	No exercise	50 min exercise	EXERCISE SIMPLE MAIN EFFECTS	EXERCISE OVERALL MAIN EFFECT
No caffeine	2000 cal	2200 cal	2200 − 2000 = 200 *Simple main effect of exercise for no-caffeine conditions*	
				(200 + 800)/2 = 500
20 mg caffeine	2200 cal	3000 cal	3000 − 2200 = 800 *Simple main effect of exercise for 20-mg caffeine conditions*	
MAIN EFFECTS OF CAFFEINE	2200 − 2000 = 200 *Simple main effect for caffeine in no-exercise conditions*	3000 − 2200 = 800 *Simple main effect for caffeine in exercise conditions*		

Overall (average) caffeine main effect
(200 + 800)/2 = 500

Note: Here you know you do have an interaction between caffeine and exercise because the simple main effect for caffeine in the no-exercise condition (200) is different from the simple main effect for caffeine in the exercise condition (800).

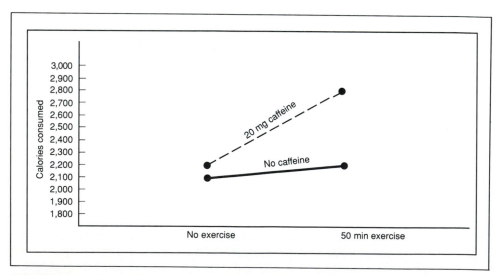

FIGURE 7.3 Main Effects for Caffeine and Exercise with an Interaction

TABLE 7.11 No Overall Main Effects for Caffeine or Exercise with an Interaction

	No exercise	50 min exercise	EXERCISE SIMPLE MAIN EFFECTS	EXERCISE OVERALL MAIN EFFECT
No caffeine	2000 cal	2500 cal	2500 − 2000 = +500 *Simple main effect of exercise for no-caffeine conditions*	
				(500 + −500)/2 = 0
20 mg caffeine	2500 cal	2000 cal	2000 − 2500 = −500 *Simple main effect of exercise for 20-mg caffeine conditions*	
MAIN EFFECTS OF CAFFEINE	2500 − 2000 = +500 *Simple main effect for caffeine in no-exercise conditions*	2000 − 2500 = −500 *Simple main effect for caffeine in exercise conditions*		

Overall caffeine main effect = 0
(500 + −500)/2

Note: In this case, you know you have an interaction between caffeine and exercise because the simple main effect for caffeine in the no-exercise condition (+500) is very different from the simple main effect for caffeine in the exercise condition (−500).

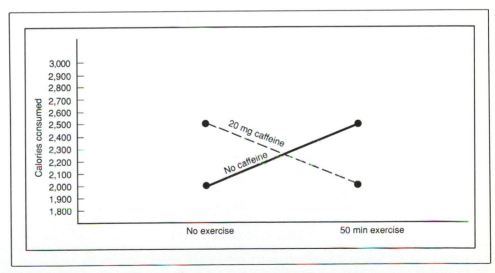

FIGURE 7.4 No Main Effects for Caffeine or Exercise with an Interaction

action. But note you do not have a main effect for caffeine or exercise: On the average, there is no effect for exercise or caffeine on calorie consumption (see table 7.11). However, you would not say caffeine and exercise are unrelated to hunger. Instead, you would say either (1) caffeine has an effect, but its effect depends on the level of exercise; or (2) exercise has an effect, but the kind of effect it has depends on the amount of caffeine consumed. Note that no matter whether you emphasize the effect of caffeine (as in statement 1) or the effect of exercise (as in 2), you cannot talk about the effect of one variable without talking about the other. Whenever the effect of one variable depends on the other, there is an interaction.

One Main Effect and an Interaction

If you can have (1) no main effects and an interaction and (2) two main effects and an interaction, can you also have (3) one main effect and an interaction? Certainly. Such a pattern of results is listed in table 7.12 and graphed in figure 7.5.

As table 7.12 reveals, the average effect for caffeine is zero. Exercise's average effect is to increase calorie consumption by 250. However, exercise's effect is uneven. In the

TABLE 7.12 Main Effect for Exercise and an Interaction

	No exercise	50 min exercise	EXERCISE SIMPLE MAIN EFFECTS	EXERCISE OVERALL MAIN EFFECT
No caffeine	2000 cal	2500 cal	2500 − 2000 = 500 *Simple main effect of exercise for no-caffeine conditions*	
				(500 + 0)/2 = 250
20 mg caffeine	2250 cal	2250 cal	2250 − 2250 = 0 *Simple main effect of exercise for 20-mg caffeine conditions*	
MAIN EFFECTS OF CAFFEINE	2250 − 2000 = +250 *Simple main effect for caffeine in no-exercise conditions*	2250 − 2500 = −250 *Simple main effect for caffeine in exercise conditions*		
	Overall caffeine main effect = 0 (250 + −200)/2			

Note: You know you have an interaction between caffeine and exercise because the simple main effect for caffeine in the no-exercise condition (+250) is very different from the simple main effect for caffeine in the exercise condition (−250).

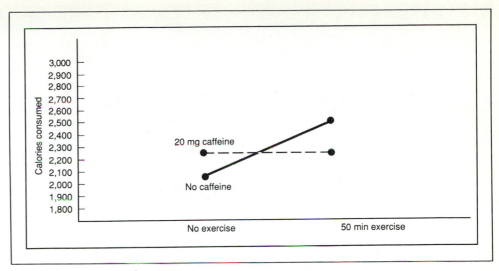

FIGURE 7.5 Main Effect for Exercise only and an Interaction

no-caffeine condition, exercise increases consumption by 500 calories. However, in the twenty mg of caffeine conditions, exercise has no effect on calorie consumption. Thus, the effect of exercise is qualified by caffeine level.

You would reach the same conclusion if you looked at a graph of the data. Looking at figure 7.5, you realize there may be an interaction because the lines are not parallel. If you mentally combine the two lines, you would see the lines slope upward, indicating a main effect for exercise. You can also see the midpoint of both caffeine lines is at the same place (2,250), indicating there is no main effect for caffeine.

No Main Effects and No Interaction

The last pattern of results you could obtain is to get no statistically significant results. That is, you could fail to find a caffeine effect, fail to find an exercise effect, and fail to obtain an interaction between caffeine and exercise. An example of such a dull and dreary set of findings is listed in table 7.13 and graphed in figure 7.6.

ANALYZING THE RESULTS FROM A 2 × 2 EXPERIMENT

You can now graph and describe the eight possible patterns of results from a 2 × 2 experiment, but how do you analyze your results? How do you know whether a main effect or an interaction is statistically significant?

As with the multiple-group experiment, you would use analysis of variance (ANOVA) to analyze your data. However, instead of testing for one main effect, you will be testing for two main effects and an interaction. Thus, your ANOVA summary table might look like this:

TABLE 7.13 No Main Effects and No Interaction

	No exercise	50 min exercise	EXERCISE SIMPLE MAIN EFFECTS	EXERCISE OVERALL MAIN EFFECT
No caffeine	2500 cal	2500 cal	2500 − 2500 = 0 *Simple main effect of exercise for no-caffeine conditions*	
				(0 + 0)/2 = 0
20 mg caffeine	2500 cal	2500 cal	2500 − 2500 = 0 *Simple main effect of exercise for 20-mg caffeine conditions*	
MAIN EFFECTS OF CAFFEINE	2500 − 2500 = 0 *Simple main effect for caffeine in no-exercise conditions*	2500 − 2500 = 0 *Simple main effect for caffeine in exercise conditions*		

Overall caffeine main effect = 0
(0 + 0)/2

Note: You know you do not have an interaction between caffeine and exercise because the simple main effect for caffeine in the no-exercise condition (0) is the same as the simple main effect for caffeine in the exercise condition (0).

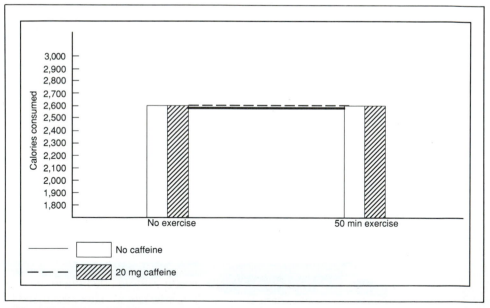

FIGURE 7.6 No Main Effects and No Interaction

Source of Variance	Sum of Squares	df	Mean Square	F
Exercise main effect (A)	900	1	900	9.00
Caffeine main effect (B)	200	1	200	2.00
Interaction (A × B)	100	1	100	1.00
Error term (within groups)	3600	36	100	
Total	4800	39		

Despite the fact this ANOVA table has two more sources of variance than an ANOVA for a multiple-group experiment, most of the rules that apply to the multiple-group ANOVA table apply to the table for a factorial design. For example, the number of treatment levels is one more than the treatment's degrees of freedom. Since the ANOVA summary table tells us the degrees of freedom for exercise is 1, we know the study used two levels of exercise. Likewise, since the degrees of freedom for caffeine is 1, we know the study used two levels of caffeine. In addition, as was the case with the multiple-group experiment, the total of the degrees of freedom is one less than the number of subjects. Therefore, the ANOVA table tells us there were forty subjects in the experiment ($40 - 1 = 39$). For more advice about how to tap the information in an ANOVA summary table, consult box 7.1.

The only new thing you need to figure out is the degrees of freedom for the interaction term. To calculate the degrees of freedom for the interaction term, multiply

BOX 7.1 The Mathematics of an ANOVA Summary Table for Between Subjects Factorial Designs

1. Degrees of freedom (df) for a main effect equal one less than the number of levels of that factor. If there are three levels of a factor (low, medium, high), that factor has 2 df.

2. Degrees of freedom for an interaction effect are equal to the product of the df of the factors making up that effect. If you have an interaction between a factor that has 1 df and a factor that has 2 df, that interaction has 2 df ($1 \times 2 = 2$).

3. To get the df for the error term, add up the df for all the main effects and interactions. Then, subtract that total from the total number of subjects. Finally, subtract one from that number.

4. To get the mean square for any effect, get the sum of squares for that effect, then divide by that effect's df. If an effect's sum of squares was 300 and its df was 3, its mean square would be 100.

5. To get the F for any effect, get its mean square and divide it by the mean square error. If an effect's mean square was 100 and the mean square error was 50, the F for that effect would be 2.

the degrees of freedom for the main effects making up that interaction. For a 2 × 2 experiment, that would be 1 (*df* for first main effect) × 1 (*df* for second main effect) = 1. For a 3 × 2 experiment, the interaction term's degrees of freedom would be 2 (because 2 × 1 = 2).

INTERPRETING THE RESULTS OF AN ANOVA TABLE

To determine whether an effect was significant, you compare the F for that effect to the value given in the F-table under the appropriate number of degrees of freedom. If your obtained F is larger than the value in the table, the effect is significant. Generally, you will want to start your inspection of the ANOVA results by first looking to see if any of your main effects are significant. Then, if you have a significant main effect, you will want to know whether this main effect was qualified by an interaction.

Main Effects without Interactions

If the interaction was not significant, your conclusions are simple and straightforward. Having no interactions means there are no "ifs" or "buts" about your results. That is, you have not found anything that would lead you to qualify your results by saying the main effect occurs only under certain conditions. For instance, if you have a main effect for caffeine and no interactions, that indicates caffeine had the same kind of effect throughout your experiment—no matter what the level of exercise was.

INTERACTIONS

If you find a significant interaction, your results are not as easy to interpret. Having an interaction means caffeine has a different effect depending on the level of exercise the subject received. In other words, the simple main effect of caffeine in the no-exercise condition is different from the simple main effect of caffeine in the exercise condition. Thus, to understand the main effect, you must understand the simple main effects that make up the overall main effect.

The easiest way to understand the pattern of the simple main effects—and thus understand the interaction—is to graph those simple effects.[1] If the lines in your graph cross each other, a variable has one kind of effect in one condition and the *opposite* kind of effect in another condition. This kind of interaction is called a **cross-over** or a **disordinal interaction.** You would have a cross-over interaction if caffeine increased

---

[1]Interactions suggest that the simple main effects making up the overall main effect differ from the overall main effect. Therefore, one way to understand the interaction is to do statistical analyses on the individual simple main effects. The computations for these tests are relatively simple. However, because there are some relatively subtle issues involved in deciding which test to use, most undergraduate research design texts do not discuss these tests.

calories consumed in the no-exercise condition, but decreased calorie consumption in the fifty minutes of exercise condition (see figure 7.4).

If the lines do not cross and are not sloping in opposite directions, you have an **ordinal interaction.** An ordinal interaction reflects the fact that a factor **appears** to have more of an effect in one condition than in another condition. An ordinal interaction would occur if caffeinated subjects consumed 200 more calories than no-caffeine subjects in the no-exercise condition, but consumed 800 more calories than no-caffeine subjects in the exercise condition (see figure 7.3).

We say **appears** to have more of an effect because it is not easy to determine whether a variable had more of a psychological effect in one condition than in another. For example, to state the difference between 2200 calories and 2000 calories is less than the difference between 3000 calories and 2200 calories, you must have interval scale data.

Obviously, in this case, you have interval scale data—**if you are interested in number of calories consumed.** However, if you are using calories consumed as a measure of how hungry people felt, then your measure may not be interval. You may not have a one-to-one correspondence between number of calories consumed and degree of hunger. It may take the same increase in **perceived hunger** to make a person who normally eats 2000 calories consume an additional 200 calories as it does to get someone who would eat 2200 calories to eat an additional 800 calories. In other words, the ordinal interaction may be due to your measure of hunger yielding ordinal rather than interval data.

To see how you might get an ordinal interaction even when the effect of combining two variables produces nothing more than the sum of their individual effects, consider figure 7.7. In figure 7.7a, the lines are not parallel and thus indicate an interaction. Now, look at figure 7.7b, **which is a graph of the same data.** In figure 7.7b, the lines are parallel, indicating no interaction. Why does one graph yield an interaction whereas the other does not? The first graph yields an interaction because it **assumes** the data are interval. Thus, the psychological distance between two and three is depicted as being the same as the psychological distance between seven and eight. If this were true, caffeine makes subjects feel hungrier in the exercise condition than it does in the no-exercise condition. The second graph shows what can happen if we do not buy the assumption of the data being interval. Specifically, the graph shows what happens when the psychological distance between rating a "7" and rating an "8" is greater than the psychological distance between a "2" and "3." In that case, at the psychological level, caffeine's effect on the subjective state of "feeling hungry" is the same in the exercise condition as it is in the no-exercise condition. Thus, even though there is an interaction at the statistical level, there is not an interaction at the psychological level: caffeine has the same psychological effect in both conditions.

As you have seen, ordinal interactions may be nothing more than an artifact of not having interval data. Because you can rarely be sure you have interval data, you should be cautious when interpreting ordinal interactions. However, there are two basic situations that should lead you to be especially cautious in interpreting ordinal interactions—(1) when ceiling effects are likely and (2) when floor effects are likely.

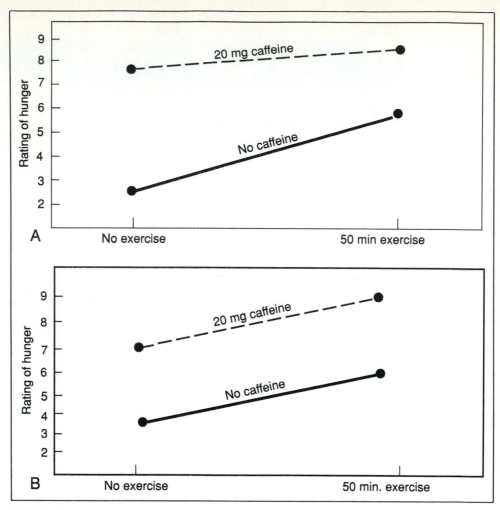

FIGURE 7.7 How an Ordinal Interaction May Not Be a True Interaction

Ceiling Effects

Both ceiling and floor effects are due to dependent measures that do not tap the full range of the variable being measured. In the case of ceiling effects, the measure does not allow subjects who are extremely high on the variable to score as high as they should. For example, imagine an extremely easy knowledge test in which half the class scores 100 percent. The problem with such a test is that we are unable to differentiate between those students who knew the material fairly well and students who knew the material extremely well. The test's "low ceiling" did not allow very knowledgeable students to show they knew more than less knowledgeable students.

To see how a ceiling effect can create an ordinal interaction, consider the following experiment. An investigator wants to know how information about a specific person affects the impressions people form of that person. The investigator uses a 2 (information about a stimulus person's traits—no information versus extremely positive information) × 2 (information about a stimulus person's behavior—no information versus extremely positive information) experiment. For the dependent measure, subjects rate the stimulus person's character on a three-point scale (1 = below average, 2 = average, and 3 = above average).

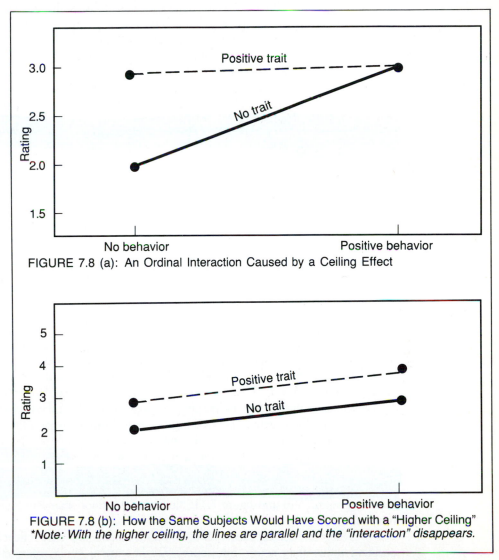

FIGURE 7.8 (a): An Ordinal Interaction Caused by a Ceiling Effect

FIGURE 7.8 (b): How the Same Subjects Would Have Scored with a "Higher Ceiling"
*Note: With the higher ceiling, the lines are parallel and the "interaction" disappears.

FIGURE 7.8 How a Ceiling Effect Can Create an Ordinal Interaction

As you can see from figure 7.8, the investigator obtains an ordinal interaction. The interaction suggests that getting information about a specific person's behavior has less of an impact if subjects already have information about that person's traits. In fact, the interaction suggests that if subjects already know about the stimulus person's traits, information about the person's behavior is worthless.

The problem in interpreting this interaction is that the results could be due to a ceiling effect. That is, even if getting additional favorable information about the stimulus person raises subjects' opinion of that person, subjects cannot show this increased respect. That is, subjects may feel that a person with a favorable trait is a "3" (above average) and a person with both a favorable trait and a favorable behavior is a "4" (well above average), but they cannot rate the person a "4." The highest rating they can give a person is a "3." The highest rating (above average) or "ceiling" response is not high enough. By not allowing subjects to rate the stimulus person as high as they wanted to, the investigator did not allow subjects to rate the positive trait/positive behavior person higher than either the positive trait/no behavior person or the positive behavior/no trait person. Thus, the investigator's ordinal interaction was due to a **ceiling effect**: The effect of a treatment or combinations of treatments is underestimated because the dependent measure is not sensitive to psychological states above a certain level. The interaction is due to the dependent measure placing an artificially low ceiling on how high a response can be. As you can see from figure 7.8 and figure 7.9, "raising the ceiling" would eliminate some ordinal interactions.

Floor Effects

Just as ceiling effects can account for ordinal interactions, so can their opposites—floor effects. For example, suppose the investigator uses the same three-point rating scale as before (1 = below average, 2 = average, and 3 = above average). However, instead of using no information and extremely positive information, the investigator uses no information and extremely *negative* information. The investigator might again obtain an ordinal interaction. Again, the interaction would indicate that adding behavioral information to trait information has little effect on subjects' impressions. This time, however, the interaction could be due to the fact subjects could not rate the stimulus person lower than a "1." The bottom rating or "floor" is too high. By not allowing subjects to rate the person as low as they wanted to, the investigator did not allow subjects to rate the negative trait/negative behavior stimulus person lower than the negative trait/no behavior person or the negative behavior/no trait person. Thus, this time, the investigator's ordinal interaction was due to a **floor effect**: the effects of the treatment or combination of treatments is underestimated because the dependent measure places too high of a floor on what the lowest response can be. As you can see from figure 7.10 and figure 7.11, "lowering the floor" can eliminate some ordinal interactions.

As floor and ceiling effects show, an ordinal interaction may reflect a measurement problem rather than a true interaction. So, be careful when interpreting ordinal interactions (see figure 7.11).

"Headed" for trouble—Coaching doesn't help Larry's performance in the pole vault condition. Maybe if Larry could vault outdoors or in a building with a higher ceiling things would be different.

FIGURE 7.9 Ceiling Effects Can Cause Headaches

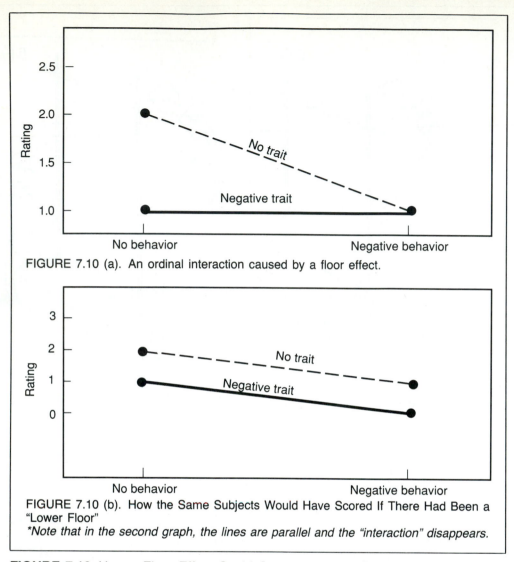

FIGURE 7.10 (a). An ordinal interaction caused by a floor effect.

FIGURE 7.10 (b). How the Same Subjects Would Have Scored If There Had Been a "Lower Floor"

Note that in the second graph, the lines are parallel and the "interaction" disappears.

FIGURE 7.10 How a Floor Effect Could Cause Us to Underestimate the Combined Effects of Knowing Both Negative Traits *and* Negative Behaviors on the Impressions We Form

PUTTING THE 2 × 2 TO WORK

You now understand the logic behind the 2 × 2 design. In the next sections, you will see how you can use the 2 × 2 to produce research that is more interesting and has greater construct validity, external validity, and power than research produced by a simple experiment.

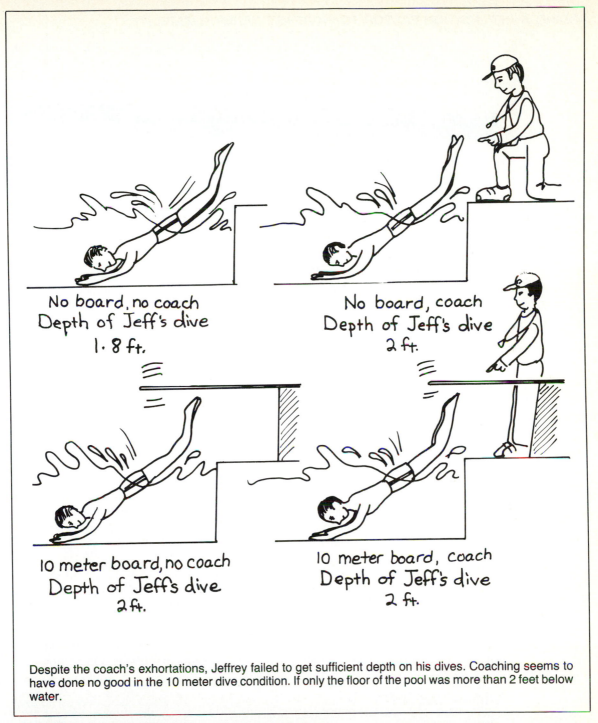

No board, no coach
Depth of Jeff's dive
1·8 ft.

No board, coach
Depth of Jeff's dive
2 ft.

10 meter board, no coach
Depth of Jeff's dive
2 ft.

10 meter board, coach
Depth of Jeff's dive
2 ft.

Despite the coach's exhortations, Jeffrey failed to get sufficient depth on his dives. Coaching seems to have done no good in the 10 meter dive condition. If only the floor of the pool was more than 2 feet below water.

FIGURE 7.11 Floor Effects Can Cause Headaches

ADDING A REPLICATION FACTOR TO INCREASE GENERALIZABILITY

The generalizability of results from a single simple experiment can always be questioned. Critics ask questions such as "Would the results have been different if a different experimenter had performed the study?" and "Would the results have been different if a different manipulation had been used?" The researcher's answer to these critics is to do a **systematic replication:** a study that varies from the original only in some minor aspect, such as using different experimenters or different manipulations.

For example, Morris (1986) found students learned more from a lecture presented in a rock-video format than from a conventional lecture. However, Morris only used one lecture and one rock video. Obviously, we would have more confidence in his results if he had used more than one of each lecture format. Morris plans to replicate his experiment using another lecture and another rock video.

As you can see, Morris would have benefited from doing a 2 × 2 experiment. Since the 2 × 2 factorial design is like doing two simple experiments at once, he could have obtained his original findings and replicated them in a single 2 × 2 experiment. Specifically, in addition to manipulating the factor of presentation type, he could also have manipulated the factor of **stimulus sets:** the particular stimulus materials used in the experiment. Thus, he could have done a 2 (presentation type—conventional lecture versus rock video format) × 2 (stimulus sets—material about Shakespeare versus material about economics) study. Because psychologists often want to show the manipulation's effect can occur with more than just one particular stimulus set, experimenters routinely include stimulus sets as an experimental factor.[2]

Similarly, it is not unusual to have more than one experimenter run a study and use experimenter as a factor in the design. Some investigators use experimenter as a factor to show the generality of their results. Specifically, they want to show that certain experimenter attributes (gender, attractiveness, status) do not affect the outcome of the experiment. Other investigators use experimenter as a factor to ensure that experimenters are not intentionally or unintentionally influencing the results. For example, Ranieri and Zeiss (1984) did an experiment in which subjects rated their mood by filling out a self-rating form. Ranieri and Zeiss were worried that experimenters might unintentionally influence subjects' responses. Therefore, they used three experimenters and randomly assigned subjects to experimenter. If they had found different experimenters achieved different patterns of results, they would suspect the results might be due to experimenter effects rather than to the manipulation itself.

USING AN INTERACTION TO FIND AN EXCEPTION TO THE RULE: LOOKING AT A POTENTIAL MODERATING FACTOR

Thus far, we have discussed instances where the investigator's goal in using the factorial design was to increase the generalizability of the experimental results. Often, however, you may read a research report and say to yourself, "But I bet that would not happen

[2]Whether traditional, fixed effects analysis of variance should be used to analyze such studies is a matter of debate (Clark, 1973; Coleman, 1979; Kenny & Smith, 1980; Richter & Seay, 1987; Wickens & Keppel, 1983; Wike & Church, 1976).

TABLE 7.14 Strategies for Dealing with an Extraneous Situational Variable

Problem: You are interested in social loafing—people exerting less effort when working in groups than when working alone. However, you are concerned that the situation one is in will also affect social loafing. Specifically, you believe that how hard the task is (task difficulty) will affect the degree to which subjects will work hard. What do you do? You have three basic choices: (1) keep the task difficulty constant, (2) do not control task difficulty, or (3) systematically vary the degree of task difficulty.

In other words, you can hold the relevant variable constant, allow it to vary randomly, or systematically vary it. What are the consequences of using these different strategies?

STRATEGY	CONSEQUENCE
Hold situational variables as *constant* as possible. Be sure each subject encounters the same exact situation.	Gain power—no random variations in task difficulty to hide the social loafing effect you are looking for.
	You do not learn anything about the effect of task difficulty on how hard individuals or groups work.
	You do not know whether you would find the same social loafing effect if you had used harder or easier tasks.
Allow situational variables to *vary randomly*.	Lose power—random variations in the task difficulty may hide social loafing effects.
	You do not learn anything about the effect of task difficulty on how hard individuals or groups work.
	If you get a main effect for group size, you know, across a wide variety of situations, the average effect of group size is to decrease effort.
	But you do not know whether groups loaf more on some tasks than others. It may even be, in some cases, group size increases effort. However, you would not know that because you have no way of finding out how or whether group size interacts with situational variables, such as task difficulty. You do not know the effects of different combinations of group size and tasks.
Systematically vary the situation (e.g., vary the task difficulty).	Have power—some of the variability due to situations is now accounted for. That is, task difficulty variability, rather than contributing to random error that might mask or hide the effects of group size, is now an independent variable.
	You know the effect of the situational factor (task difficulty). You varied it and assessed its effect.
	You learn whether the group size effect generalizes across different situations (different levels of task difficulty).
	You learn whether the group size effect interacts with the situational variable. That is, does adding co-workers increase loafing as much in the easy task conditions as in the difficult task conditions?

under _____ conditions." In that case, you should do a study in which you essentially repeat the original experiment, except you add what you believe will be a moderating factor (see table 7.14).

To see how a moderating factor experiment would work, let us look at a study by Jackson and Williams (1985). Jackson and Williams were aware of the phenomenon of social loafing: People are less productive in tasks when they work in groups than when they work alone. But they felt social loafing would not occur on extremely difficult tasks. Therefore, they did a study which, like most social loafing studies, manipulated whether or not subjects worked alone or in groups. In addition, they added what they thought would be a moderating factor—whether the task was easy or difficult.

As expected, and as other studies had shown, social loafing occurred. However, social loafing only occurred when the task was easy. When the task was difficult, the reverse of social loafing occurred: subjects worked better in groups than alone (see figure 7.12). This interaction between task difficulty and number of workers confirmed their hypothesis that task difficulty moderated social loafing.

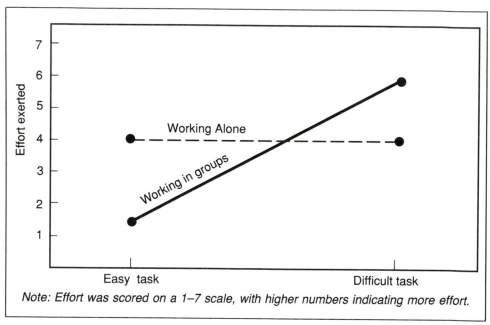

Note: Effort was scored on a 1–7 scale, with higher numbers indicating more effort.

FIGURE 7.12 Interaction Between Task Difficulty and Number of Coworkers on Effort

USING INTERACTIONS TO CREATE NEW RULES

Although we have discussed looking for an interaction to find an exception to an existing rule, some interactions do more than complicate existing rules. Some interactions reveal new rules. Consider Barbara Tversky's (1973) 2 × 2 factorial experiment. Dr. Tversky randomly assigned students to one of four conditions:

1. expected a multiple-choice test and received a multiple-choice test,
2. expected a multiple-choice test and received an essay test,
3. expected an essay test and received a multiple-choice test, or
4. expected an essay test and received an essay test.

She found an interaction between test expected and test received. Her interaction showed subjects did better when they got the same kind of test they expected. That is, they did better when the test **matched** their expectations. Similarly, a researcher might find an interaction between mood (happy, sad) at the time of learning and mood (happy, sad) at the time of testing. The interaction might reveal that recall was best when subjects were in the **same** mood at the time of testing as they were at the time of recall. As you can see, the 2 × 2 experiment may be useful for you if you are interested in assessing the effects of similarity.

USING INTERACTIONS TO PINPOINT WHAT YOU ARE MANIPULATING

Similarity is not the only construct that interactions help you tap. Often, interactions can help you get a more specific idea of what constructs you are manipulating. For example, suppose you manipulated negative ion concentration and found the higher the concentration of negative ions, the better mood people were in. You might conclude that negative ions improve mood. However, this conclusion would be wrong. A study by Baron, Russell, and Arms (1985) shows that although higher negative ion concentrations improve mood for people who have not been provoked, higher negative ion concentrations cause negative shifts in moods for people who have been provoked. Thus, the interaction between provocation and negative ion concentration suggests that negative ions intensify mood rather than improve it.

Similarly, Johnson (1985) looked at the effects of smell on sexual arousal. In his experiment, heterosexual female subjects viewed slides of males. He found that when subjects smelled androstenol (a male hormone), their brain-wave reaction to the photographs was stronger than when they did not smell androstenol. But how did he know androstenol was really increasing sexual arousal? Couldn't the brain-wave pattern simply reflect the fact subjects were aroused by androstenol?

Johnson anticipated this question. Therefore, he not only manipulated androstenol, but also whether the pictures were of males or of females. He found that when females smelled androstenol while viewing a picture of a female subject, androstenol did not increase the brain-wave activity. In fact, in this condition, androstenol actually reduced the brain-wave activity.

The interaction between photo (same sex or opposite sex) and androstenol (no androstenol/androstenol) shows androstenol did not merely increase arousal. Because of this interaction, Johnson can make a convincing argument that androstenol increases **sexual** arousal in heterosexual females.

STUDYING NONEXPERIMENTAL VARIABLES

Rather than converting a simple experiment into a 2 × 2 experiment by adding a second experimental factor, you could convert a simple experiment into a 2 × 2 design by adding a nonexperimental factor. The nonexperimental factor could be any variable that you cannot randomly assign, such as age, sex, or personality type. In such a 2 × 2 design, you could make causal statements about the effects of the experimental factor, but you *could not make any causal statements regarding the nonexperimental factor* (see table 7.15).

If you cannot make causal statements about the nonexperimental factor, why would you want to add a nonexperimental variable to your simple experiment? The most obvious and exciting reason is you are interested in that nonexperimental variable. To see how adding a nonexperimental variable (age of subject, sex of subject, introvert-extrovert, etc.) can spice up a simple experiment, consider the following simple experiment: Subjects are either angered or not angered in a problem-solving task by a confederate who posed as another subject. Later, subjects get an opportunity to punish or reward the confederate. Obviously, we would expect subjects would punish the confederate more when they had been angered. This simple experiment, in itself, would not be very interesting.

Holmes and Will (1985) added a nonexperimental factor to this study—whether subjects were Type A or Type B personalities. The results of this study were intriguing: If subjects had not been angered, Type A subjects were more likely to punish the confederate than Type B subjects; however, if subjects had been angered, Type A and Type B subjects behaved about the same.

TABLE 7.15   The Hybrid Experiment

	Female	Male	DIFFERENCES BETWEEN GROUPS NOT CAUSED BY TREATMENT	
No stress	2000 cal	3000 cal	Simple main "effect" of gender in no stress = 1,000	Overall main "effect" of gender = 1,750 (1,000 + 2,500)/2
Stress	1500 cal	4000 cal	Simple main "effect" of gender in stress = 2500	
EXPERIMENTAL EFFECTS: EFFECTS CAUSED BY TREATMENT	Simple main "effect" of stress for the female groups is −500	Simple main effect of stress for the male groups is +1000		
	Overall main *effect* of stress is 250 (−500 + 1000)/2			

Note: the hybrid 2 × 2 answers two questions that the simple experiment does not: (1) Do male and female subjects differ on the dependent variable? and (2) Is the effect of stress different in our sample of males than in our sample of females?

Similarly, Hill (1991) could have done a relatively uninteresting simple experiment. He could have determined whether research participants are more likely to want to talk to a stranger if that stranger is supposed to be "warm" than if the stranger supposedly lacks warmth and empathy. The finding that people prefer to affiliate with people who are nice would have hardly been startling. Fortunately, Hill conducted a more interesting study by adding another variable: need for affiliation. He found participants who were high in need for affiliation were very likely to want to interact with an allegedly "warm" stranger, but very unlikely to want to interact with a stranger who allegedly lacked warmth. For low need for affiliation subjects, on the other hand, the warmth of the stranger made little difference.

You can add a nonexperimental variable to a simple experiment for most of the same reasons you would add an experimental variable: to increase the generalizability of the findings, to look for a similarity effect, and to look for a moderating factor. In addition, you can use a nonexperimental variable to improve your study's power.

Increasing Generalizability

You could increase the generalizability of a simple experiment that used only males as subjects by using males and females as subjects and making sex of subject a factor in your design. This design would allow you to determine whether the effect held for both males and females.

Studying Effects of Similarity

If you were interested in similarity, you might include some subject characteristic (sex, status, etc.) as a factor in your design, while manipulating the comparable experimenter or confederate factor. For example, if you were studying helping behavior, you could use style of dress of the subject (dressed-up/casual) and style of dress of the confederate as factors in your design. You might find this interaction: dressed-up subjects were more likely to help confederates who were dressed-up, but casually dressed subjects were more likely to help confederates who were dressed casually. This interaction would suggest that similarity of dress influences helping behavior.

Finding an Exception to the Rule

If you thought intelligence would be a moderating variable for the effectiveness of programmed instruction, you might use intelligence as a factor in your design. To do this, you would first give your subjects an IQ test and then divide them into two groups (above average intelligence and below average intelligence). Next, you would randomly assign half the high-intelligence group to programmed instruction and half to group instruction. You would do the same for the low-intelligence group. This study might reveal some interesting findings. For instance, suppose you found programmed instruction vastly improves learning for low-IQ children, but slightly decreases learning for high-IQ children. If you had done only a simple experiment, you might have found a significant positive effect for the new teaching technique. On that basis, you might have recommended using this technique with all school children. What a terrible mistake!

Increasing Power: The Blocked Design

The only difference between blocked design and other 2×2 studies that include a nonexperimental factor is its purpose. In the blocked design, you are not interested in the nonexperimental variable. You only include it to improve the power of your design (see table 7.16).

TABLE 7.16 Strategies of Dealing with Differences Between Subjects

STRATEGY	CONSEQUENCES
Hold between subject variables as *constant* as possible by using a homogeneous group of subjects (subjects of same age, gender, genetic background).	May not be able to hold subject variables constant.
	Gain power—provided you do not decrease the number of subjects in your study. That is, if you get homogeneity simply by excluding subjects from your study, you may lose power.
	You do not learn anything about the relationship of the subject variable to the dependent measure.
	You do not know whether the treatment effect will generalize to other levels of the subject variable (other types of subjects).
Allow between subject variables to *vary randomly.*	You know what the effect of the treatment variable is averaged across several levels of the subject variable. If you get a main effect, you know, as a general rule (across several levels of the subject variable), the treatment has an effect.
	You do not learn anything about the relationship between the subject variable and the dependent measure.
	You may lose power if individual differences mask your treatment effect.
	You do not know if the subject variable interacts with treatment variable. That is, you do not know whether the treatment's effect is the same at all levels of the subject variable.
Block on the subject variable so you can account for variation due to subject differences.	You know, as a general rule, whether the treatment has an effect over the range of the subject variable.
	You learn about the correlation between the subject variable and the dependent measure.
	You have power.
	You know if the subject variable interacts with treatment variable.

To see why you might use a blocked design, suppose you want to find out whether the programmed learning method is more effective than the lecture method. Your subjects are 60 fourth graders at a local elementary school. As you are planning your study, you discover the students vary widely in terms of their intelligence. Half of the students seem to be well above average, the other half seem to be well below average.

This wide range of individual differences concerns you because this means you will have a great deal of error variance. This error variance may prevent you from detecting the treatment effect. That is, with all these individual differences in learning ability, it will be hard to detect the effect of different instructional techniques. Specifically, your mean square error may be so large that only enormous treatment effects will reach significance.

What can you do? You might eliminate the intelligent students from the experiment. That would give you a more homogeneous group and would reduce error variance due to individual variability.

However, the costs of this solution are high. You are obeying one rule of increasing power—reduce error variance. However, you are reducing error variance by breaking another rule of increasing power—increase the number of subjects. Put another way, although eliminating the extreme subjects should reduce the amount of random error variance in your data, reducing the number of subjects reduces the opportunities for random error to balance out. In a sense, you are robbing Peter to pay Paul (see table 7.17). Another cost of your strategy of limiting who can be in the experiment is you are limiting the generalizability of your results. Obviously, your results would not apply to extremely intelligent children.

Fortunately, there is a solution that allows you to use all your subjects and reduce

---

TABLE 7.17 Ways to Increase Power by Reducing the Mean Square Error

The higher the F-ratio for an effect, the more likely the effect is to be significant. As you may recall, the F-ratio is a ratio of the mean square treatment divided by mean square error. Consequently, the smaller the mean square error, the bigger the *F*. For example, if the mean square treatment is 10 and the *MSE* is 10, *F* will be 1.0. However, if the mean square treatment is 10 and the *MSE* is 2, *F* will be 5. Therefore, if you can shrink the size of the mean square error, you can increase power. Fortunately, there are two ways you can decrease the size of the mean square error. Both ways take advantage of the fact that $MSE = SSE/df$.

FORMULA FOR *MSE*	STRATEGY TO REDUCE *MSE*	HOW TO IMPLEMENT STRATEGY
$MSE = SSE/df$	Decrease *SSE*.	Use a homogeneous group of subjects.
		Divert variance due to subjects away from *SSE* into sum of squares for the blocking factor.
$MSE = SSE/df$	Increase degrees of freedom (*df*).	Having more subjects in your study.

error variance at the same time. Before the experiment starts, divide your subjects into two groups (or blocks): the high-IQ group (block) and the low-IQ group (block). Next, randomly assign each member of the high-IQ group to instruction condition, thus ensuring that half the high-IQ subjects are assigned to the programmed instruction group and that half the high-IQ subjects are assigned to the lecture condition. Then randomly assign each member of the low-IQ block to instruction condition. In other words, the solution is to do exactly the same study we discussed under the moderating factor study.

The difference between doing this blocked design and the moderating factors study we described earlier is not what you are doing, but *why* you are doing it. If you are using a blocked design, you do not care about intelligence and you do not care about the interaction between intelligence and instruction. You only care about getting enough power to find a significant instruction effect.

To see how the blocked design can improve your study's power, let us look at an analysis of variance summary table for this experiment. As you can see, you have a 2×2 study where instructional technique is the experimental factor and intelligence is the nonexperimental factor.

		SS	df	MS	F
Instruction condition	(C)		1		
Intelligence	(I)		1		
Interaction	(C × I)		1		
Error			56		
Total			59		

Note how this analysis differs from a table of a sixty-subject experiment on the effects of instructional technique that does not include intelligence as a factor.

	SS	df	MS	F
Instruction condition (C)		1		
Error		58		
Total		59		

The most obvious difference between the two tables is the error term in the blocked design has *56* degrees of freedom whereas the error term in the regular experiment has *58* degrees of freedom. What is the significance of losing those two degrees of freedom?

The loss of two degrees of freedom (df) in the error term may increase your mean square error (MSE). It might increase MSE because MSE = SSE *divided by* df *error.* That is, if both studies yielded the same SSE, the second study would yield the smaller MSE because dividing by 58 produces a smaller number than dividing by 56. For example, if SSE was 112 in both studies, the mean square error will be bigger in study 1 (112/56 = 2.0) than it would be in study 2 (112/58 = 1.9).

Why do you care that losing those two degrees of freedom could increase your

MSE? Because the reason you decided to use a blocked design was to reduce MSE. You knew the larger your estimate of random error, the larger the differences would have to be among your groups to reach statistical significance. With a large estimate of random error, even a moderate treatment effect could be shrugged off as being due to random error. Conversely, with a small estimate of random error, even a small difference between your groups might be statistically significant. In short, you were concerned about reducing MSE because you knew a large MSE would shrink your F-ratio (because F = Treatment effect/MSE).

Therefore, if the blocked design does increase the size of your MSE, then using the blocked design would backfire. Blocking would actually decrease your chances of finding a significant difference. This point will become clear if you compare the two ANOVA tables in table 7.18.

In this case, the loss of 2 df hurt power—the blocked design gave us a smaller F than the simple experiment. Usually, however, blocked designs will increase the size of your F-ratio. Blocked designs increase the size of the F-ratio by reducing error variance.

To understand how blocked designs reduce error variance, remember what error variance is—variability that cannot be accounted for. Thus, in a simple experiment, there is no way to account for individual differences in intelligence. Therefore, individual variability in intelligence is a source of error variance. By making intelligence a factor in your design, you are removing that variability due to intelligence from your error term. You are soaking up that variability. Instead of variability contributing to error variance, it is contributing to your intelligence main effect. As a result of accounting for intelligence, you will end up with a smaller error term. Consequently, as you can see in table 7.19, you have made your treatment effect easier to spot.

In this case, the F for intelligence is much higher in the blocked analysis (F = 10) than in the simple experiment (F = 2.6). The larger F is due to a sum of square's error (SSE) of 28 in the blocked design versus 112 in the simple experiment. Why was the SSE 84 units smaller in the blocked design? Those 84 units were soaked up by the blocking factor—intelligence.

TABLE 7.18 When Blocking Backfires

Source	BLOCKED EXPERIMENT SS	df	MS	F
Instruction condition (C)	5	1	5.0	2.5
Intelligence (I)	0	1	0.0	
Interaction (C × I)	0	1	0.0	
Error (S/CI)	112	56	2.0	

Source	SIMPLE EXPERIMENT SS	df	MS	F
Instruction Condition (C)	5	1	5.0	2.6
Error (S/CI)	112	58	1.9	

TABLE 7.19   When Blocking Improves Power

Source	SS	df	MS	F
SIMPLE EXPERIMENT				
Instruction condition (C)	5	1	5.0	2.6
Error (S/CI)	112	58	1.9	

Source	SS	df	MS	F
BLOCKED EXPERIMENT				
Instruction condition (C)	5	1	5.0	10.0
Intelligence (I)	84	1	84.0	168.0
Interaction (C × I)	0	1	0.0	0.0
Error (S/CI)	28	56	0.5	

You have seen that blocking can increase or decrease your study's power. If the blocking variable does not account for enough variance, the blocked design will have less power than a simple experiment. If, on the other hand, the blocking variable accounts for enough variance, the blocked design will have more power than the simple experiment. But how much variance is enough? Traditionally, statisticians have argued the correlation between the blocking variable and the dependent variable should be at least .30 (a small to moderate relationship). Otherwise, you have not only wasted time and energy on measuring everyone on the blocking variable, but you have also decreased your chance of finding an effect for the experimental factor. Therefore, if the correlation between the blocking variable is not at least .30 you should not use a blocked design.

To reiterate, the term **blocked design** is a technical one: it means you know the blocking variable is related to the dependent measure, but you are not interested in studying the blocking variable. Instead, you are only using the blocking variable to siphon off error variance so you can find an effect for the experimental factor.

EXPANDING THE 2 × 2

As you have seen, the 2 × 2 design's complexity makes it extremely versatile. However, we can make the 2 × 2 more complex. We have already suggested that you can expand a 2 × 2 by adding more levels to one or both variables. For instance, if you were examining the effects of exercise and caffeine on hunger, you could use three levels of exercise and three levels of caffeine. This 3 × 3 factorial experiment would combine the advantages of a factorial experiment (looking at more than one variable at a time), with the advantages of a multi-level experiment (having more than two levels of each variable). That is, such an experiment would not only allow you to look at the interaction between caffeine and exercise, but it would also allow you to map two functional relationships: (1) the functional relationship between caffeine and hunger and (2) the functional relationship between exercise and hunger.

Similarly, suppose you wanted to know if a factor's effect generalized to different stimulus sets. Rather than just look at two stimulus sets, you might look at four. Thus, instead of a 2 × 2, you would have a 2 × 4.

In addition to adding levels to the 2 × 2, you can expand it by adding variables. You could do a 2 × 2 × 2 or even a 2 × 2 × 2 × 2. Imagine, you could study four variables at once! Unfortunately, as you add factors, you add groups. Adding groups causes you to need more subjects and causes your results to be more difficult to interpret.

To illustrate, contrast a 2 × 2 design with a 2 × 2 × 2 design. In the 2 × 2, you only need four groups of subjects. With the 2 × 2 × 2 design, you need eight groups of subjects. Thus, to keep the same number of subjects per group, you would need twice as many subjects in a 2 × 2 × 2 than in a 2 × 2. In addition to needing twice as many subjects, you need twice as many cells to summarize your results. That is, whereas you could represent all four groups of a 2 × 2 design in a single 2 × 2 table, you need two 2 × 2 tables to represent all eight groups of the 2 × 2 × 2.

Increasing the number of cells also increases the number of interactions and main effects you can find. For instance, suppose you have a 2 × 2 that examines the effects of exercise and caffeine on hunger. If your study involved forty subjects (ten per group),[3] your F-table would look like this:

	SS	df	MS	F
Exercise		1		
Caffeine		1		
Interaction of exercise and caffeine		1		
Error		36		

However, suppose you had a 2 × 2 × 2, looking at the effects of exercise, caffeine, and temperature on hunger. If your study used eighty subjects (ten per group), your F-table would look like this:

	SS	df	MS	F
Exercise		1		
Caffeine		1		
Temperature		1		
Interaction of exercise with caffeine		1		
Interaction of exercise with temperature		1		
Interaction of caffeine with temperature		1		
Interaction of exercise with caffeine with temperature		1		
Error		72		

[3]As you may recall from chapter 5, having only ten subjects per group provides very little power. Most experts would recommend at least thirty subjects per group and some would want at least sixty-five subjects per group.

As you can see from the ANOVA summary tables, the 2×2 can only yield two main effects and an interaction. The $2 \times 2 \times 2$, on the other hand, may yield three main effects and four interactions. Three of the $2 \times 2 \times 2$'s interactions involve *two* variables and are therefore called **two-way interactions.** You are familiar with two-way interactions from the 2×2 design. You know that with a two-way interaction, the effect of the first variable depends on the level of the second variable. However, you are not familiar with one of the $2 \times 2 \times 2$'s interactions—its three-way interaction. A **three-way interaction** is an interaction involving three variables. That is, combining the three variables yields an effect that could not be predicted even if you knew both the individual effects of the three variables as well as all the two-way interactions among those three variables. Put another way, with a three-way interaction, the effect of one variable depends on the level of a second variable *and* the level of a third variable.

Perhaps the easiest way to visualize a three-way interaction is to imagine a chemistry experiment that includes three independent variables (see table 7.20): (1) presence or absence of oxygen, (2) presence or absence of hydrogen, and (3) presence or absence of a flame.

In this study, it is only when you combine oxygen, hydrogen, and a flame that you produce water (H_2O). Because you need the right combination of all three factors to produce the reaction, you have a three-way interaction. Having only two of the factors present accomplishes nothing. Combining flame and hydrogen produces nothing, combining flame and oxygen produces nothing, and combining oxygen and hydrogen produces nothing.

Another way of looking at the three-way interaction is it limits the statements we can make about the two-way interactions. Specifically, in this example, you have a two-way interaction between hydrogen and oxygen. In general, when hydrogen and oxygen are present, they interact to form water. However, this interaction only occurs in the flame condition. In the no-flame condition, hydrogen and oxygen do not interact to form water. Thus, in this three-way interaction, the two-way interaction between hydrogen and oxygen *depends* on the level of the third variable—the flame.

There are two advantages to viewing three-way interactions as moderators of two-way interactions. First, this viewpoint may help you generate hypotheses involving three-way interactions. To understand how, remember that you could generate research hypotheses involving two-way interactions by thinking of conditions that might moderate a main effect. If you could think of situations that would either strengthen, weaken, or reverse a main effect, you could generate a two-way interaction. For example, suppose you read that people would be more persuaded by videotaped messages than by written messages. By thinking about when this relationship would hold true and when it might not, you would develop a hypothesis involving a two-way interaction. Thus, you might hypothesize that videotaped messages would be more persuasive than written messages, but only when the messages are easy to understand. When the messages are hard to understand, written messages might be more persuasive. Consequently, in the "easy message" conditions, you would hope to replicate the original main effect: videotaped messages should be more persuasive. However, in the "difficult message" conditions, you would hope to find a different relationship between medium and messages. Specifically, you would hope the written messages would be more persuasive. In other words, you are

TABLE 7.20   Three-way Interaction Involving a Chemistry Experiment

	No hydrogen	Hydrogen	HYDROGEN MAIN EFFECTS (COMPARING HYDROGEN TO NO HYDROGEN)
No oxygen	0 drops of water	0 drops of water	0 − 0 = 0 Simple main effect of hydrogen for no-oxygen conditions
Oxygen	0 drops of water	0 drops of water	0 − 0 = 0 Simple main effect of hydrogen for oxygen conditions
MAIN EFFECTS OF OXYGEN	0 − 0 = 0 Simple main effect for oxygen in no-hydrogen conditions	0 − 0 = 0 Simple main effect for oxygen in hydrogen conditions	

No-flame condition

	No hydrogen	Hydrogen	HYDROGEN MAIN EFFECTS (COMPARING HYDROGEN TO NO HYDROGEN)
No oxygen	0 drops of water	0 drops of water	0 − 0 = 0 Simple main effect of hydrogen for no-oxygen conditions
Oxygen	0 drops of water	20 drops of water	20 − 0 = 20 Simple main effect of hydrogen for oxygen conditions
MAIN EFFECTS OF OXYGEN	0 − 0 = 0 Simple main effect for oxygen in no-hydrogen conditions	20 − 0 = 20 Simple main effect for oxygen in hydrogen conditions	

Flame condition

hypothesizing a two-way interaction between medium of message (videotape or written) and message difficulty (easy to understand or hard to understand).

Just as you could create a two-way interaction by finding a situation where the main effect does not hold, you can create a three-way interaction by finding a situation where a two-way interaction does not hold. For instance, consider the two-way interaction we just discussed: videotaped messages are more persuasive than written messages, but only when the messages are easy to understand. When messages are difficult to understand, written messages are more persuasive (Chaiken & Eagly, 1976).

What factors might alter this relationship? What exceptions could you find? What could decrease the extent of this relationship? Can you think of anything that might cause easy-to-understand, videotaped messages to be less persuasive than easy-to-understand, written messages? One factor that might moderate the interaction is the quality of the arguments. For example, suppose the original study used good, strong arguments. With strong arguments, we might expect the interaction that Chaiken and Eagly (1978) found. Specifically, if the message was hard to understand and made some good points, people would be more persuaded if they read it than if they saw it on videotape. But would this interaction follow the same pattern if the message contained very weak arguments? Possibly not. Subjects might be slightly persuaded by a videotaped message containing difficult to understand, but weak arguments because subjects would not be able to detect the arguments' flaws. However, subjects that read the weak arguments would see the arguments' weaknesses and not be persuaded. As you can see from figure 7.13, we would hope to replicate the original two-way interaction in the "strong" argument conditions, but hope to find a different pattern in the "weak" argument conditions.

To reiterate, to think of hypotheses involving three-way interactions, think of conditions that would alter a two-way interaction. For example, remember the two-way interaction that indicated people were more likely to help people who were dressed similarly to themselves? Are there any factors that might modify that relationship? We can think of several:

1. Attractiveness of the person to be helped
2. Gender of subject (women may be more attuned to dress style than men)
3. Whether subjects had just heard a lecture on the value of trying to relate to people who seem to have different views, ideas, or backgrounds
4. Whether the person needing help had done something embarrassing

Any of these factors might alter the two-way interaction. For instance, if the similarly dressed person had done something embarrassing, the similarly dressed subjects might want to show that they are different from that other person and thus be even less likely to help than a person who dresses differently. Such a relationship is illustrated in figure 7.14 which shows the previously described two-way interaction in the "no-embarrassment" condition, but the reverse pattern in the "embarrassment" condition.

The graphs in figure 7.14 illustrate the second advantage of thinking of three-way interactions as moderating two-way interactions: it allows you to easily spot potential three-way interactions. For example, consider figure 7.15. From that graph, you should instantly suspect a three-way interaction. How? The two-way interaction between caffeine

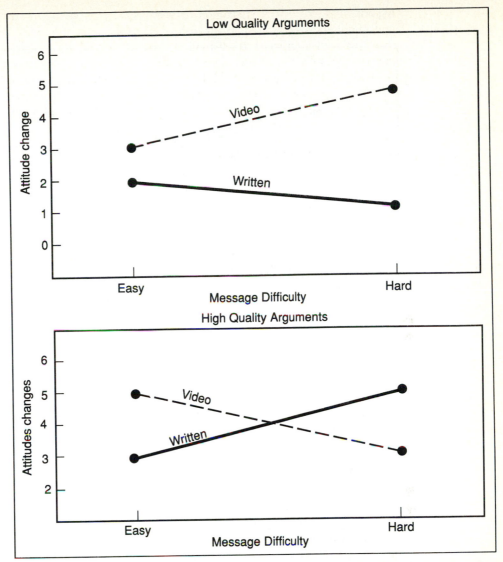

FIGURE 7.13 Three-Way Interaction Between Message Difficulty, Medium of Message, and Quality of Arguments on Persuasiveness

and exercise follows a very different pattern in the low-temperature condition than in the high-temperature condition. Put another way, the interaction relationship between caffeine and exercise appears to *depend* on temperature.

The disadvantage of thinking about three-way interactions as modifying two-way interactions is you may have a tendency to think you must have a two-way interaction to have a three-way interaction. This is not the case. Just as you can have two-way interactions without main effects, you can have a three-way interaction without any

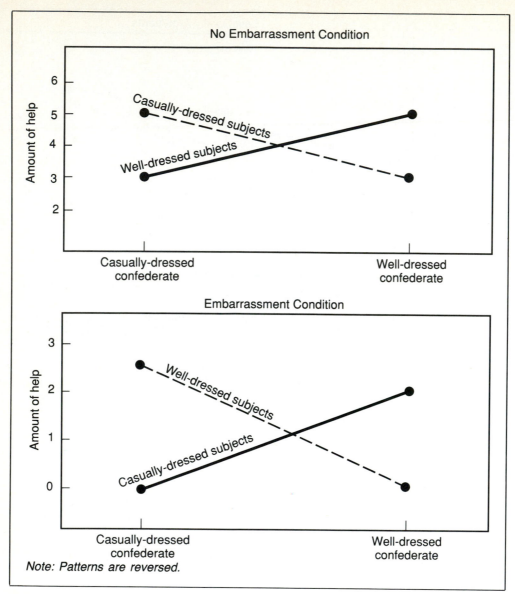

FIGURE 7.14 Three-Way Interaction Between Dress Style of Confederate, Dress Style of Subject, and Embarrassment

two-way interactions. Indeed, you can have a significant three-way interaction without any main effects and without any other interactions.

We have discussed adding variables **or** adding levels to the 2 × 2. Of course, you can also expand the 2 × 2 by adding both levels **and** variables. If you wanted to, you could do an 8 × 2 × 4 × 3 × 6 experiment. But, as you can imagine, the more complex your

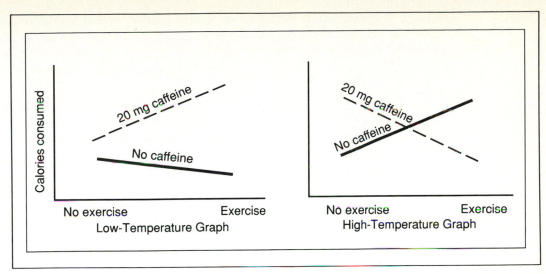

FIGURE 7.15 Graphing a 2 × 2 × 2

design, the more subjects you have and the more difficult your results may be to interpret. With a three-factor experiment, you may have to try to interpret three-way interactions; with a five-factor experiment, you may have to try to interpret five-way interactions. You must walk the fine line between getting a great deal of useful information from an experiment and getting a great deal of uninterpretable information. For most novice experimenters, that fine line is the 2 × 2 experiment.

CONCLUDING REMARKS

In this chapter, you have seen the benefits of using the 2 × 2 experiment. Your awareness of this design opens up new possibilities for research. Just as importantly, your understanding of this commonly used design increases your ability to read, understand, and evaluate the research of others. Therefore, you now have the ability to discover new paths for research that radiate from the research of others. In the next two chapters, you will refine this ability.

SUMMARY

1. Factorial experiments allow you to look at more than one variable or factor at a time.
2. The simplest factorial experiment is the 2 × 2 experiment.

3. The 2 × 2 allows you to study two independent variables in one experiment **and** it lets you see the effects of combining different levels of your two independent variables.

4. Whenever independent variables combine to produce an unexpected effect, you have an interaction.

5. Interactions can most easily be observed by graphing your data. If your two lines are not parallel, you have an interaction.

6. If your lines cross, you probably have a cross-over (disordinal interaction). If your lines do not cross, you have an ordinal interaction.

7. Ordinal interactions may be the result of ceiling effects or floor effects. That is, ordinal interactions may reflect a measurement problem rather than the fact two variables combine in an unexpected manner.

8. A significant interaction usually qualifies main effects. Thus, a significant interaction means you cannot talk about your main effects with referring to the interaction.

9. Sometimes the interaction in the 2 × 2 represents another variable. For instance, in a 2 × 2 with place of learning and place of testing as factors, an interaction may reveal it is best to be tested in the **same** place you learned the information.

10. You can use the 2 × 2 to refine a simple experiment by adding a replication factor to increase generality, adding a potential moderating factor, or examining the relationship between your dependent variable and a personality variable.

11. You can also improve the power of a simple experiment by using a blocked design. Your hope is the blocked factor will absorb enough random error to make an otherwise nonsignificant result statistically significant.

12. Factorial designs can be as complicated as you desire. However, the more complex the design, the more difficult it is to analyze the data.

KEY TERMS

blocked design
ceiling effect
cross-over (disordinal) interaction
factorial experiment

floor effect
interaction
main effect (overall main effect)
ordinal interaction

replication factor
simple main effect
stimulus set
systematic replication

EXERCISES

1. Half the subjects receive a drug that blocks the effect of endorphins, half receive a placebo. Half of the placebo group and half of the drug group get acupuncture. The

subjects are then asked to rate the pain of various shocks on a 1 (not at all painful) to 10 (very painful) scale. The results are as follows:

GROUP	AVERAGE RATING
Placebo, no acupuncture	7.2
Placebo, acupuncture	3.3
Drug, no acupuncture	7.2
Drug, acupuncture	3.3

    a. Graph the results.

    b. Describe the results in terms of main effects and interactions (tabling the data may help).

    c. What conclusions would you draw?

2. Below is the ANOVA summary table of a study looking at the effects of similarity and attractiveness on liking. How many subjects were used in the study? How many levels of similarity were used? How many levels of attractiveness were used? Complete the table.

SV	SS	df	MS	F
Similarity (S)	10	1	—	—
Attractiveness (A)	—	2	20	—
$S \times A$ Interaction	400	2	200	—
Error	540	54	—	
Total	990	59		

3. A professor doing a simple experiment finds students who are given lecture notes do better than those who are not given lecture notes. Replicate this study as a 2 × 2 factorial. What is your second variable? What predictions do you make? Does your prediction involve an interaction? Why or why not?

4. A lab study on motivation yielded the following results:

GROUP	PRODUCTIVITY
No financial bonus, no encouragement	25%
No financial bonus, encouragement	90%
Financial bonus, encouragement	90%
Financial bonus, no encouragement	90%

    a. Describe the results in terms of main effects and interactions.

    b. What is your interpretation of the findings?

5. A memory researcher looks at the effects of processing time and rehearsal strategy on memory.

GROUP	PERCENT CORRECT
Short exposure, simple strategy	20
Short exposure, complex strategy	15
Long exposure, simple strategy	25
Long exposure, complex strategy	80

a. Describe the results in terms of main effects and interactions.

b. What is your interpretation of the findings?

6. Suppose a researcher wanted to know which was more effective for learning basic facts—the lecture style or group discussion? Therefore, the researcher did a study and obtained the following results.

SOURCE OF VARIANCE	SS	df	MS	F
Teaching (T)	10	1	10	5
Intraversion/ Extraversion (I)	20	1	20	10
$T \times I$ interaction	50	1	50	25
Error	100	50	2	

a. What does the interaction seem to indicate?

b. Even if there had been no interaction between teaching and extraversion, would there be any value in including the intraversion-extraversion variable? Explain.

c. What, if anything, can you conclude about the effects of intraversion on learning?

d. List another factor that might interact with teaching style. Describe your hypothesis about how the two variables interact. If you were to study that variable would you use a 2 (teaching style) × 2 (your variable) or would you use a 2 (teaching style) × 2 (intraversion-extraversion) × 2 (your factor)? Why?

7. Brown and Smart (1991) first had participants complete a self-esteem test. Based on scores on that scale, participants were classified as low or high on self-esteem. Then, Brown and Smart had research participants take a test (an alleged test of integrative orientation). The participants who received the success manipulation were led to believe they had done very well on the test. The participants who were assigned to the failure manipulation were led to believe they had done very poorly on the test. After being told they had failed or succeeded on the test, assume participants either rated themselves on adjectives related to achievement (intelligent, smart, competent, unwise, unimaginative, incompetent) or on adjectives related to social qualities (sincere, loyal, kind, insensitive, inconsiderate, insincere). The results are tabled below:

Self-descriptiveness for social attributes and achievement attributes as a function of prior outcome (success or failure) and self-esteem

| | SOCIAL ATTRIBUTE | | ACHIEVEMENT ATTRIBUTE | |
ESTEEM	SUCCESS	FAILURE	SUCCESS	FAILURE
Low	5.93	5.33	5.49	5.27
High	5.82	6.29	6.27	6.22

Note: Values can range from one to seven; higher scores indicate more positive evaluations of self.

Reproduced from Brown, J. D., & Smart, S. A. (1991). The self and social conduct: Linking self-representations to prosocial behavior. *Journal of Personality and Social Psychology, 60,* 368–375. Used with the kind permission of Jonathon D. Brown and the American Psychological Association.

a. Graph the data.

b. Do your graphs suggest the presence of a three-way interaction? Why or why not?

c. If the three-way interaction were significant, what would it mean?

d. Discuss any ethical concerns you would have about this experiment. How might these concerns be dealt with?

8 Matched Pairs and Within Subjects Designs

In chapters 5, 6, and 7, you learned you could perform an internally valid experiment by independently and randomly assigning subjects to groups. Although you understand the logic of randomly assigning subjects to groups, you may still have two basic reservations about between subjects designs.

First, you may believe between subjects designs are wasteful in terms of the number of subjects they require. For example, in the simple experiment, the subject is either in the control group *or* in the experimental group. Clearly, it would seem more efficient if each subject was in both the control group *and* in the experimental group. One subject would do the job of two.

Second, you may be concerned that between subject designs are not powerful enough. You may believe that if we use each subject as their own control, we could detect differences that would not be detected if we were comparing subjects with one another. Your concern is based on the fact between subject differences may hide the treatment's effect. For example, suppose you use a simple experiment to examine a treatment that produces a small effect. The treatment's small effect might be discounted as being due to random differences between the two groups. If, on the other hand, we use each subject as his or her own control, the treatment's effect cannot be dismissed as being due to differences between the two groups. Consequently, the treatment's effect might be detected and found to be statistically significant.

You are rightfully concerned about the twin weaknesses of between subjects experiments: they require many subjects and have relatively little power. Therefore, in this chapter, you will learn some alternatives to pure between subjects designs. These alternatives require fewer subjects and often have more power than between subjects experiments.

You will begin by learning about matched pairs designs. In matched pairs designs, you first reduce between subject differences by matching pairs of subjects on a key characteristic. Then, you let randomization take care of the effects of the few remaining uncontrolled variables.

Next, you will learn about pure within subjects designs. In these designs, you try to eliminate between subjects differences by using subjects as their own controls. Then, you let randomization take care of the effects of the few remaining uncontrolled variables. By limiting the nonexperimental variables that randomization has to account for, the pure within subjects design—like the matched pairs design—often has impressive power.

After learning about pure within subjects designs, you will learn about mixed designs. Mixed designs have aspects of both between and within subjects designs. Specifically, mixed designs are factorial designs in which at least one factor is a between subjects factor and at least one factor is a within subjects factor. That is, different subjects get different levels of the between subject factor(s), but all subjects get all levels of the within subjects factor(s).

Finally, you will learn how to weigh the tradeoffs involved in choosing among various experimental designs. Thus, by the end of this chapter, you will be better able to choose the best experimental design for your research problem.

MATCHED PAIRS DESIGNS

If you do not have enough subjects to do a powerful simple experiment, you might use a design that requires fewer subjects, such as a matched pairs design (see table 8.1). As you will see, the matched pairs design combines the best aspects of matching and randomization: it uses matching to reduce irrelevant variables and randomization to establish internal validity.

PROCEDURE

In the matched pairs design, you first measure your subjects on a variable that correlates with the dependent measure. For example, if you were measuring memory, your matching variable could be education, IQ, or scores on a memory test. After measuring all your subjects on the matching variable, you would form **matched pairs**: pairs of subjects that have similar scores on this measure. Thus, if you were doing a memory experiment using a matched pairs design, you might first give all your subjects a memory test. Next, you would rank their scores on this memory test from lowest to highest. Then, you would pair the two highest scorers, the next two highest scorers, and so on. This would give you pairs of subjects with similar scores. Finally, you would randomly assign one member of each pair to the control group and the other member to the experimental group.

CONSIDERATIONS IN USING MATCHED PAIRS DESIGNS

You now have a general idea of how to conduct a matched pairs experiment. But should you use a matched pairs design? When considering a matched pairs design, you should address the following four questions:

1. How do you select a matching variable?
2. How important is it that you have a powerful design?
3. Will matching harm external validity?
4. Will matching harm construct validity?

TABLE 8.1 Comparing the Matched Design with the Simple Experiment

MATCHED DESIGN	SIMPLE EXPERIMENT
First, *match* subjects on a key characteristic.	*No matching.*
Then, *randomly assign* each member of pair to a condition.	*Randomly assign* subjects to a condition.

Using an Effective Matching Variable

As we intimated earlier, you can only make effective use of the matched pairs design if you can match subjects on a variable that correlates strongly with the dependent measure. Sometimes, you can match subjects on the basis of earlier performance on the dependent measure task. Thus, in a memory experiment, subjects could be matched based on scores on an earlier memory test; in a maze-running experiment, subjects could be matched based on earlier maze-running performance. If you cannot match on some kind of pretest, you may have to consult the research literature to find a matching variable (see appendix B). Consulting the literature will not only tell you what matching variables other researchers have used, but also tell you what variables correlate with your dependent measure. Unfortunately, after doing your library research, you may find (a) there are no variables that have a strong, documented relationship with performance on the dependent measure or (b) there are good matching variables, but for ethical or practical reasons you cannot use them.

Power

You want to find an appropriate matching variable so your study will have adequate power. Indeed, the reason you may choose a matched pairs design is to avoid the problems that plague researchers using simple experiments or other between subjects design. As you may recall, those researchers lose power because individual differences between subjects hide treatment effects. With between subjects designs, researchers often do not know whether a difference between groups is due to the treatment or to the groups being different before the experiment began.

To combat the risk that between subjects differences may obscure a treatment effect, some between subjects experimenters try to reduce differences between their subjects by using a homogeneous group of subjects. For example, one researcher may only use subjects who are eighteen years old, white, American, female, and have IQs between 115–120. Another researcher may only use male lab rats that are between 180 and 210 days of age.

Usually, matching reduces random error more than limiting who can be in the experiment. If matching succeeds in reducing random error, the matched pairs design will give you more power than the simple experiment. The same difference that would not be statistically significant with a simple experiment may be significant with a matched pairs design.

How is this possible? Because your t-value will be higher with the matched pairs design. Remember, the t-value is the difference you observe divided by an estimate of random error (the standard error of the difference). With less random error, the t-value becomes larger. For example, if the standard error of the difference for a simple experiment is 6, then a difference of six seconds between conditions would yield a nonsignificant t-value of 1.00 (6/6). However, if a matched pairs design reduced random error so much that the standard error of the difference was only 1.0, then that same difference of six seconds would yield a highly significant t-value of 6.00 (6/1). In other words, if matching reduces the impact of individual differences, you may be able to find relatively small effects.

But what if matching fails to reduce random error? For example, suppose a researcher matched participants on shoe size. Then, the matched pairs design may be less powerful than the simple experiment. Why? Because by using a matched pairs design instead of a simple experiment you lose half your degrees of freedom. For instance, if you used twenty subjects in a simple experiment, you would have 18 degrees of freedom (two fewer than the number of subjects). But in a twenty-subject, matched pairs design, you have only 9 degrees of freedom (one fewer than the number of pairs). Losing degrees of freedom can hurt your power. As you know from looking at the t-table in appendix E, the fewer degrees of freedom you have, the larger your t-value must be to reach significance. In our example, with 18 degrees of freedom (what you would have if you tested twenty subjects in a simple experiment), you would only need a t-value of 2.101 for your results to be statistically significant. On the other hand, with 9 degrees of freedom (what you would have if you tested twenty subjects—ten pairs of subjects—in a matched pairs experiment), your t-value would have to be at least 2.262 to be statistically significant.

Thus, if you got the same t-value with the matched pairs design as you would have with a simple experiment, the matched pairs design cost you power. However, if your matching is any good, you should not get the same t-value with a matched pairs design as with a simple experiment. Instead, you will almost always get a larger t-value with a matched pairs design because you have reduced a random error due to subject differences (remember, t = treatment effect/estimate of random error). Usually, the increase in the size of the t-value will more than compensate for the degrees of freedom you will lose.

External Validity

Power is not the only consideration in deciding to use a matched pairs design. You may either use or avoid matching for reasons of external validity.

For example, a matched pairs design may have more external validity than an equally powerful between subjects design. Why? Because the between subjects design may get you power by limiting what type of subject can participate (male, albino rats between the ages of 180–185 days of age), whereas the matched pairs gets you power without limiting the kind of subject you can have. Since you can reduce random error by matching subjects rather than limiting the kinds of subjects you have, the matched pairs design may allow you to generalize your results to a broader population.

However, if subjects drop out of the study between the time they are tested on the matching variable and the time they are to perform the experiment, matching will reduce the generalizability of your results. For instance, you might start off with twelve matched pairs, but end up with only ten pairs. Although you are not losing enough subjects to seriously damage your study's power, you are hurting your experiment's external validity: You cannot generalize your results to individuals resembling the subjects who dropped out of your experiment.

Whether or not subjects drop out, matching reduces the ability to generalize your results to individuals who were not pretested. To illustrate, suppose an experimenter uses a matched pairs design to examine the effect of caffeine on anxiety. In the experiment, the subjects receiving caffeine become more anxious that those not receiving caffeine. Can the investigator generalize his results to people who have not taken an anxiety test before consuming caffeine? No, it may be that caffeine only increases anxiety if it is consumed after taking an anxiety test—taking the anxiety test makes subjects so concerned about their level of anxiety that they interpret any increase in arousal as an increase in anxiety. Because of the anxiety test, the arousal produced by caffeine—which might ordinarily be interpreted as invigorating—is interpreted as anxiety.

Construct Validity

In the caffeine study we just discussed, taking the anxiety test before and after the treatment might make subjects aware the experimenter was looking at the effects of a drug on anxiety. However, the fact subjects are guessing the hypothesis does not, in itself, ruin the experiment's construct validity.

For instance, if you used a treatment condition and a placebo condition, it does not matter if subjects think the drug is supposed to increase anxiety. Because both groups have the same hypothesis ("The drug I took will increase my anxiety"), knowing the hypothesis would not cause the treatment group to differ from the placebo group. A significant difference between groups would have to be due to the treatment.

If, on the other hand, your independent variable manipulations have low construct validity, matching will make your manipulation's weaknesses more damaging. For instance, if, in the caffeine study, an empty control group was used (nothing was given to control subjects), matching might seriously threaten construct validity. In this case, the two groups would have different hypotheses. The experimental group subjects would hypothesize that the drug should affect their anxiety level. Because control subjects were not given anything resembling a drug, they would not form such a hypothesis. Consequently, a significant effect might be due to the two groups acting on different hypotheses.

ANALYSIS OF DATA

But how do you know whether you have a significant effect? As we have already suggested, you cannot use a regular, between subjects t-test. Instead, you should analyze the results of a matched pairs design by using the dependent groups t-test.[1] Although you must go through several steps to compute the dependent groups t-test, the steps themselves are so simple that this is one of the easiest tests to perform. To learn how to do this simple statistical test, look at the example in box 8.1.

SUMMARY OF THE MATCHED PAIRS DESIGN

The matched pairs design's weaknesses stem from matching. If matching alerts subjects to the purpose of your experiment, matching can cost you the naivete of your subjects. If subjects drop out of the experiment between the time they are measured on the matching

---

[1]We are assuming you have ratio or interval scale data. If you only have ordinal data, you should use the sign test.

BOX 8.1 Calculating a Dependent Groups t-Test in Seven Easy Steps

Step 1: Subtract condition 1 score from condition 2 score for each subject or for each matched pair.

PAIR OR SUBJECT	CONDITION 1 SCORE	CONDITION 2 SCORE	DIFFERENCE
1	3	2	1
2	4	3	1
3	5	4	1
4	2	1	1
5	3	2	1
6	5	2	3
7	5	2	3
8	4	3	1
9	3	4	−1
10	5	6	−1

Step 2: Sum up the differences, then divide by the number of pairs of scores to get the average difference.

PAIR OR SUBJECT	CONDITION 1 SCORE	CONDITION 2 SCORE	DIFFERENCE
1	3	2	1
2	4	3	1
3	5	4	1
4	2	1	1
5	3	2	1
6	5	2	3
7	5	2	3
8	4	3	1
9	3	4	−1
10	5	6	−1

Total difference = 10

Average difference = 10/10 = 1

Step 3: Calculate the variance for the differences by subtracting each difference from the average difference. Square that difference and divide by one less than the number of pairs of scores.

Pair or Subject	Average Difference (AD)	Observed Difference (D)	AD − D	AD − D Squared
1	1	1	0	0
2	1	1	0	0
3	1	1	0	0
4	1	1	0	0
5	1	1	0	0
6	1	3	−2	4
7	1	3	−2	4
8	1	1	0	0
9	1	−1	2	4
10	1	−1	2	4

Total sum of squares = 16
Variance of differences = 16/9 = 1.77

Step 4: Take the square root of the variance of the differences to get the standard deviation of the differences.

Standard deviation of the differences = $\sqrt{1.77}$ = 1.33

Step 5: Get the standard error of the difference by dividing the standard deviation of the differences by the square root of the number of pairs of scores.

$1.33/\sqrt{10} = 0.42$

Step 6: Set up the t-ratio by dividing the average difference by the standard error of the difference.

$t = 1/0.42 = 2.38$

Step 7: Calculate the degrees of freedom by subtracting one from the number of pairs of scores. In this example, because we have ten pairs of scores, we have 9 degrees of freedom. Then, look up the t-value in the t-table in appendix E.

variable and the time they are to be given the treatment, matching costs you the ability to generalize your results to the subjects who dropped out. Furthermore, even if subjects do not get suspicious and do not drop out, matching still costs you time and energy.

Although matching has its costs (see table 8.2), matching offers one big advantage: power without restricting your subject population. Matching makes the matched pairs design very powerful, while random assignment makes the matched pairs design internally valid. Because of its power and internal validity, this design is hard to beat when you can only study a few subjects.

TABLE 8.2 Advantages and Disadvantages of Matching

ADVANTAGES	DISADVANTAGES
More power because matching limits between subjects differences.	Matching makes more work for researcher.
	Matching may alert subjects to experimental hypothesis.
Power is not bought at the cost of restricting the subject population. Thus, results may, in some cases, be generalized to a wide variety of subjects.	Results cannot be generalized to subjects who drop out after matching task.
	Generalizing results to individuals who have not been exposed to the matching task may be risky.

PURE WITHIN SUBJECTS DESIGNS

The within subjects design is very similar to the matched pairs design. In fact, if you conduct both kinds of experiments, you will end up doing very similar things for the same reasons. Although the logic behind both designs is very similar, the two designs' similarities are most apparent when you look at the "nuts and bolts" of carrying out the two kinds of studies.

PROCEDURE

The procedural differences between the two-condition, within subjects experiment and matched pairs experiment stem from a single difference: in the within subjects experiment, you get a pair of scores from a single subject, whereas in the matched pairs design, you get a pair of scores from a pair of subjects. The matched pairs researcher randomly determines, for each *pair,* who will get what treatment. In some pairs, the first member will get treatment A; in other pairs, the first member will get treatment B.

The within subjects researcher randomly determines, for each *individual,* the order in which subjects will get each treatment. For some individuals, the first treatment will be treatment A; for other individuals, the first treatment will be treatment B. Whereas the matched pairs experimenter randomly assigns members of pairs to treatments, the within subjects experimenter randomly assigns individual subjects to orders of treatments. For example, Hilton and Fein (1989) had participants read information about college students. After reading the information, participants were to rate the assertiveness of each of these students on a nine-point scale ranging from very passive to very assertive. For eight of the students, participants were given clearly irrelevant information (Bob found twenty cents in a pay phone in the student union when he went to make a phone call). For eight of the students, the information was "pseudorelevant" (Bill has a 3.2 GPA and is thinking about majoring in psychology). The order of presenting the information was randomized. They found the students about which there was "pseudorelevant" information were judged to be more assertive than those about which there was "clearly irrelevant" information. Hilton and Fein (1989) concluded that even irrelevant information may affect our judgments about people.

CONSIDERATIONS IN USING A WITHIN SUBJECTS DESIGN

Now that you have a general idea of how to conduct a within subjects experiment, you are in a position to decide whether you should conduct one (see table 8.3). As you intuitively realize, a main advantage of within subjects designs is their power. By comparing subjects with themselves, even subtle treatment effects may be statistically significant. However, as you also may intuitively realize, there are problems with comparing subjects with themselves. Because subjects change from day to day, from hour to hour, and even from minute to minute, a change in a subject may not be due to the treatment. Indeed, as we shall see, how a subject behaves after being exposed to a treatment sometimes depends on *when* the subject receives the treatment. That is, the order in which events unfold matters. For example, the lecture that might have been scintillating had it been the first lecture you heard that day may only be tolerable if it is your fourth class of the day. Because order affects responses, if a subject reacts differently to the first treatment than to the last, we have a dilemma: Is it an order effect or is it a treatment effect?

Power

Despite the problems with order effects, the within subjects design is often used. Perhaps the major reason for the within subjects design's popularity is power. The within subjects design increases power in two ways.

The first way is similar to how the matched pairs design increases power—by reducing random error. As you may recall, the matched pairs experimenter tries to reduce

TABLE 8.3 Contrasting Three Designs		
BETWEEN SUBJECTS	**MATCHING DESIGN**	**WITHIN SUBJECTS**
Randomly assign subjects to treatment condition	Randomly assign members of each pair to treatment condition	Randomly assign order of treatment conditions
Allow random assignment to account for individual differences between treatment conditions	Reduce subject differences by matching, then use random assignment to deal with the effects of individual differences	Eliminate the effects of subject differences by comparing subjects against themselves

random error by reducing individual differences. Therefore, the matched pairs experimenter compares similar subjects with one another. Within subjects experimenters are even more ambitious: they want to *eliminate* random error due to individual differences. Therefore, they do not compare one subject with another subject; instead, they compare each subject's score under one condition with that same subject's score under another condition. For example, Hilton and Fein (1989) did **not** compare how one group of participants rate students about which there is "pseudorelevant" information with how another group of participants rate students about which there is "clearly irrelevant" information. They did not want to risk the possibility that individual differences in how participants rate (some people tend to give high ratings, some low, some neutral) might have hidden the effect. Therefore, Hilton and Fein (1989) compared each participant's ratings of the students described by "pseudorelevant" information with that same participant's ratings of students described by "clearly irrelevant" information.

The second way the within subjects design increases power is by increasing the number of observations. As you know, the more observations you have, the more random error will tend to balance out and the more power you have. With the designs we have discussed up to now, the only way to get more observations is to get more subjects (because with those designs, you can only get one score per subject). But in a within subjects experiment, you get at least two scores out of each subject. In the simplest case, your subjects serve double duty by being in both the control and experimental conditions. In more complex within subjects experiments, your subjects might do triple, quadruple, or even octuple duty. Thus, Hilton and Fein (1989) also increased their power by getting at least two scores from each research participant—an average rating of students described by "pseudorelevant" and an average rating of students described by "clearly irrelevant" information.

The Order Problem

Although getting more observations per subject improves power, this tactic has drawbacks. To get a general sense of these drawbacks, imagine being a subject in a within subjects experiment where you take a drug, play a video game, take a second drug, and play the video game again.

If you perform differently on the video game the second time around, can the experimenter say the second drug has a different effect than the first drug? No, because the conditions did not differ simply in that in one case you took drug 1 and in the other case you took drug 2 (see table 8.4). In the first case, before you played the game, you took drug 1. However, in the second case, before you played the game, you (1) took drug 1, (2) played the video game, and then (3) took drug 2. Put another way, the only treatment you got before you played the video game the first time was drug 1. But before you played the video game the second time, you were exposed to three "treatments": the first drug, playing the video game, and the second drug.

In the next few sections, you will see how being exposed to "treatments" other than the second drug can hurt the internal validity of your study. That is, you will see how your video game performance following the second treatment could be affected by factors other than the second treatment. We will start by looking at an obvious reason you may perform

TABLE 8.4 Unlike the Simple Experiment, There Are Several Differences between the Drug 1 Condition and the Drug 2 Condition

EVENTS HAPPENING BEFORE PLAYING THE VIDEO GAME THE *FIRST* TIME	EVENTS HAPPENING BEFORE PLAYING THE VIDEO GAME THE *SECOND* TIME
Get drug 1	Get drug 1
	Play video game
	Get drug 2

differently on the task after the second treatment—you are performing the task for the second time. Clearly, the second time you play the game you may score differently than you did the first time. Next, we will look at another reason you may score differently after the second treatment—you are experiencing some lingering effects of the first drug. Then, we will look at a final reason you may score differently after getting the second treatment—learning the experimental hypothesis. Thus, by the end of the next few sections, you will understand how the **order** in which you get the treatments may affect the results. Specifically, you will know how treatment A may **appear** to have one kind of effect when it comes first, but **appear** to have a different kind of effect if it comes second.

Practice and Fatigue Effects

If you perform better after the second treatment than you did after the first treatment, your improvement may simply reflect the effects of **practice** on the video game. Subjects often perform better as they warm up to the experimental environment and get used to the experimental task.

Even if your performance is not affected by practice, it may be affected by **fatigue**.[2] You may do worse on later trials merely because you are getting tired or less enthusiastic as the experiment goes on. Unfortunately, a researcher might interpret your fatigue as a treatment effect.

Treatment Carry-over Effects

Practice and fatigue effects have nothing to do with any of the treatments subjects receive. Often, these effects are simply due to getting more exposure to the dependent measure task. Thus, in the video game example, performance may improve as you learn the game or worsen as you get bored with the game. However, exposure to the dependent measure is not the only thing that can affect performance in later trials. A treatment may also affect responses in later trials. The effects or side effects of an earlier treatment on responses in later trials are called **treatment carry-over effects**. To illustrate treatment carry-over effects, suppose on trial 1, the researcher gave you marijuana. Then, the researcher measured your video game performance. On trial 2, the researcher gave you alcohol and

---

[2]Fatigue effects could be viewed as cases in which performance is hurt by practice whereas practice effects could be viewed as cases in which performance is improved by practice.

measured your video game performance. On trial 3, the researcher gave you a placebo and measured your video game performance. If your performance was worst in the placebo (no drug) condition, the researcher might think the drugs helped your performance. However, the researcher could be wrong. Your poor performance in the placebo condition may be due to carry-over effects from the previous treatments.

Clearly, the carry-over effect will depend on the type of treatments used and the order in which those treatments occur. Thus, you cannot say "all subjects will have carry-over effects on the second trial." For example, if a subject's first treatment was a placebo, there will be no carry-over effects on the second trial. If, on the other hand, the subject's first treatment was marijuana, there could be enormous carry-over effects on the second trial.

Sensitization

In addition to practice, fatigue, and treatment carry-over effects, the fourth factor that might cause you to perform differently after the second treatment is *sensitization*. Sensitization occurs if, after getting several different treatments and performing the dependent variable task several times, subjects realize (become sensitive to) what the independent and dependent variables are. Consequently, during the latter parts of the experiment, you might guess the experimental hypothesis and play along with it. Certainly, by the third trial, you should realize the experiment had something to do with the effects of drugs on video game performance. Thus, the results from the third trial would probably have no construct validity.

DEALING WITH THE ORDER PROBLEM

You have seen that because of fatigue, practice, carry-over, and sensitization, the order in which subjects get the treatments could affect the results. Practice effects might cause a subject to do better on the last trial, even though none of the treatments had an effect. Alternatively, fatigue effects might cause a subject to do worse on the last treatment condition, even though none of the treatments had an effect. If carry-over occurs, a subject could appear to be affected by treatment C, a treatment that has no effect, because the subject is still being affected by a previous treatment.

Finally, you have seen how sensitization could cause an order effect. The subject is most naive about the experimental hypothesis when receiving the first treatment, least naive when receiving the last treatment. Thus, the ability of the subject to play along with the hypothesis increases as the study goes on. Changes in the ability to play along with the hypothesis may create order effects which could masquerade as treatment effects.

Minimizing Each of the Individual Threats

Fortunately, there are steps you can take to minimize these threats. To minimize the effects of practice, you can give subjects extensive practice before the experiment begins. For example, if you are studying maze running and you have the rats run the maze one hundred times before you start administering treatments, they have probably learned as much from practice as they can. Therefore, it is unlikely the rats will benefit greatly from the limited practice they get during the experiment. You can reduce fatigue effects by making the experiment interesting, brief, and not too taxing.

You can reduce carry-over effects by lengthening the time between treatments. For instance, if you were looking at the effects of drugs on maze-running performance, you might space your treatments a week apart (e.g., marijuana, wait a week, alcohol, wait a week, placebo).

You can reduce sensitization by using treatments that seem so similar to one another that subjects will not notice you are varying anything (Greenwald, 1976). For example, suppose you were studying the effects of different levels of full-spectrum light on typing performance. There are three ways you could reduce sensitization problems. First, you could use very similar levels of the treatment in all your conditions. By using slightly different amounts of full-spectrum light, subjects may not realize you are actually varying amount of light. Second, you could change the level of the treatment so slowly that subjects do not notice. Thus, between trials you change lighting level watt by watt until it reaches the desired level. Third, you might be able to reduce sensitization effects by using good placebo treatments. That is, rather than using darkness as the control condition, you use light from a normal bulb as the control condition.

You can also reduce order effects by reducing the number of experimental conditions—the fewer conditions, the fewer opportunities for practice, fatigue, carry-over, or sensitization. To illustrate this fact, compare a within subjects experiment that has eleven conditions with one that has only two conditions. In the eleven-condition experiment, subjects have ten opportunities to practice on the dependent measure task before they get the last treatment; in the two-condition experiment, subjects only have one opportunity for practice. The eleven-condition subjects have eleven conditions to tire them out; two-condition subjects only have two. In the eleven-condition experiment, there are ten treatments that could carry-over to the last trial; in the two-condition experiment there is only one. Finally, in the eleven-condition experiment, subjects have eleven chances to figure out the hypothesis; in the two-condition experiment, they only have two chances (see table 8.5).

Randomization

Although you can take steps to reduce the impact of order, you can never be sure you have eliminated its impact. Therefore, if a subject scores differently after receiving the second treatment than she did after receiving the first treatment, you will never know whether this difference is due to differences in the treatment or due to differences in the order in which the treatments were given.

Because the order of treatments will probably affect your results, you should not give each subject the treatment in the same order. Instead, you should assign subjects to get the treatment in different orders. You can do this by randomly determining, for each subject, which treatment they get first, which treatment they get second, and so on. Randomization should ensure that subjects get the treatments in different orders.

Unfortunately, randomization does not always balance out the effects of order. For example, if you randomly assign each of 24 subjects to a different order, you probably will not find that exactly 12 subjects got treatment A first and exactly 12 subjects got treatment B first. In fact, you may find that 16 of the 24 got treatment A first.

TABLE 8.5 Order Effects and How to Minimize their Impact

EFFECT	EXAMPLE	WAYS TO REDUCE IMPACT
Practice effects	Getting better on task due to being more familiar with the task or the research situation.	Give extensive practice and warm-up prior to introducing treatment.
Fatigue effects	Getting tired as study wears on.	Keep study brief and interesting. Use few levels of treatment.
Carry-over effects	Effect of one treatment lasting long enough to affect responses on other trials.	Allow sufficient time between treatments for treatment effect to wear off. Do not use many treatment levels.
Sensitization	As a result of getting many different levels of the independent variable, the subject—during the latter part of the study—becomes acutely aware of what the treatment is and what the hypothesis is.	Use subtly different levels of treatment. Gradually change treatment levels. Use few treatment levels.

SUMMARY AND ANALYSIS OF PURE WITHIN SUBJECTS DESIGNS

The within subjects design and the matched pairs design are very similar. In terms of procedures, the only real difference is the matched pairs experimenter randomly assigns members of pairs to treatments, whereas the within subjects experimenter randomly assigns individual subjects to orders of treatments. In terms of analysis, the two designs are virtually identical. In fact, to analyze data from the two-condition within subjects design, you can use the same dependent groups t-test (see box 8.1) you used to analyze matched pairs designs. The only difference is, instead of comparing one member of a pair against the other, you compare each subject with him or herself. Specifically, instead of comparing, for each pair, the member who got one treatment with the member who got the other treatment, you compare, for each subject, the subject when he or she got the treatment with the same subject when he or she got the other treatment.

The two designs share similar strengths. Both designs have impressive power because they reduce the effects of between subjects differences. Because of the power of these two designs, both should be seriously considered if subjects are scarce.

The unique strengths and weaknesses of the within subjects design stem from the fact the within design collects more than one observation per subject (see table 8.6). Because it uses subjects (rather than matched pairs) as their own controls, the within design is the more powerful of the two designs. Because it uses subjects as their own controls, the within design is also more useful if you want to generalize your results to real-life situations in which individuals get more than one "treatment." Thus, if you were

TABLE 8.6 Comparing the Matched Pairs Design with the Within Subjects Design

MATCHED PAIRS DESIGN	WITHIN SUBJECTS DESIGN
Powerful	More powerful
No concern about order effects	Order effects are a serious problem
Use random assignment to balance out between subjects differences	Use randomization to balance out order effects
Useful for assessing variables that vary *between* subjects in real life	Useful for assessing variables that vary *within* subjects in real life

studying persuasion, you might use a within design because a person is likely to be exposed to many types of persuasive messages (Greenwald, 1976).

Although there are benefits to collecting more than one observation per subject, there is one big drawback: you have to contend with order effects. To deal with order effects, you can try to minimize the effects of practice, fatigue, carry-over, and sensitization; and then hope randomization will balance out the order of your treatments.

COUNTERBALANCED DESIGNS

Instead of hoping chance might balance out the order of your treatments, why not make sure? That is, why not use a counterbalanced design? In a **counterbalanced design,** like the within subjects design, each subject gets more than one treatment; however, unlike the within subjects design, subjects are randomly assigned to systematically varying orders of conditions in a way that ensures *routine* order effects are balanced out. Thus, if you were studying two levels of a factor, the counterbalanced design would ensure that half your subjects got treatment A first and half got treatment B first. Now that you understand the main objective of counterbalancing, let us look at an example to see how counterbalancing achieves this goal.

PROCEDURE

If you were to use a counterbalanced design to study a two-level factor, you would randomly assign half your subjects to receive treatment A first and treatment B second, while the other half would receive treatment B first and treatment A second. By randomly assigning your subjects to these counterbalanced orders, most order effects will be neutralized. For example, if subjects tend to do better on the second trial, this will *not* help treatment A more than treatment B because both occur in the second position equally often.

THE ADVANTAGES AND DISADVANTAGES
OF COUNTERBALANCING

By using a counterbalanced design, you have not merely balanced out routine order effects, you have also added another factor to your design—a counterbalancing factor. Adding this factor has one disadvantage and several advantages.

The disadvantage of adding the two-level between subjects factor of counterbalancing is you now need more subjects than you did when you were planning to use a pure within subjects design. You need two groups of subjects to test your two-level between subjects factor of counterbalancing; you only needed one group when you were using a pure within subjects design. In effect, by going from a within subjects design to a counterbalanced design, you are going from having zero levels of a between subjects factor to having two levels of a between subjects factor. As you recall from our discussion of multi-level experiments, the more levels of a between subjects factor you have, the more subjects you need.

The disadvantage of needing more subjects is sometimes offset by being able to discover more effects. By adding the two-level factor of counterbalancing, you not only increased the number of subjects you needed, but you also converted the two-condition experiment into a 2 × 2 experiment. The treatment is a within subjects factor (all subjects get all levels of the treatment), and counterbalancing is a between subjects factor (different subjects get the treatments in different sequences). This 2 × 2 experiment gives you more information than the simple, two-condition experiment. With the two-condition experiment, you only obtain a single main effect (treatment main effect) so you can only find out whether the treatment had an effect.

With the 2 × 2, you obtain two main effects and an interaction (see table 8.7). As a

TABLE 8.7 A 2 × 2 Counterbalanced Design

The first group gets a list of words, is asked to form a sentence with those words, and is asked to recall those words. Then, they get a second list of words, are asked to form images of those words, and are asked to recall the words.

The second group gets a list of words, is asked to form images of those words, and is asked to recall the words. Then, they get a second list of words, are asked to form a sentence with those words, and are asked to recall those words.

GROUP 1

First task	Second task
Form images	Form sentences

GROUP 2

First task	Second task
Form sentences	Form images

Questions this study can address:

1. Do people recall more when asked to form sentences than when asked to form images?
2. Do people do better on the first list of words they see than on the second?
3. Do group 1 subjects recall more words than group 2 subjects? Such a finding might suggest that one should do imagery before forming sentences.

result, you find out three things. First, you find out whether the treatment had an effect (treatment main effect). Second, you find out whether subjects getting the treatments in one sequence did better than subjects getting the other sequence (counterbalancing main effect). Finally, you find out whether there is an order effect. That is, you find out whether subjects score differently the second time they respond to the dependent measure. If subjects tend to get higher scores after the second treatment—regardless of what the second treatment is—there will be a treatment by counterbalancing interaction.

To understand what these three effects represent, let us look at a memory experiment. In this study, subjects learned lists of words using two different rehearsal strategies. In one condition, they made a sentence out of the list; in the other, they formed mental images. Subjects were randomly assigned to two different counterbalanced sequences. Half the subjects formed sentences for the first list, then formed images to recall the second list. The other half formed images to recall the first list, then formed sentences to recall the second list. The means for that study are listed in table 8.8 and the results of the analysis of variance are summarized in table 8.9.

By looking at table 8.9, we see the main effect for counterbalancing is not significant. As table 8.8 shows, both groups recalled about the same amount. Next, we see

TABLE 8.8 Table of Means for a Counterbalanced Memory Experiment

| | MEMORY STRATEGY | | |
Group's Sequence	Images	Sentences	Effect
Group 1 (images 1st, sentences 2d)	8.0	7.0	+ 1.0
Group 2 (sentences 1st, images 2d)	7.0	8.0	− 1.0
		Strategy main effect = 0	

Counterbalancing main effect = 0
  Both groups remembered fifteen words.
  Put another way, group 1 did better in the image condition (8.0 to 7.0), but this was balanced out by group 2 doing better in the sentence condition (8.0 to 7.0).
Order effect = + 1.0
  Subjects remember first list better.
  They averaged 8.0 words on the first list and 7.0 on the second.
  Order effect revealed by *interaction* involving counterbalancing *group and* rehearsal *strategy.* That is, group 1 did better in image condition (8.0 to 7.0), but group 2 did better in the sentence condition (8.0 to 7.0).
Strategy effect = 0
  Average recalled in image condition was 7.5—(8.0 + 7.0)/2.
  Average recalled in sentence condition was 7.5—(7.0 + 8.0)/2.

TABLE 8.9 ANOVA Summary Table for a Counterbalanced Design

ANALYSIS OF VARIANCE TABLE

Source	SS	df	MS	F	p
Group sequence (counterbalancing)	0	1	0	0	n.s.*
Error term for between subjects factor	44	22	2		
Memory strategy	0	1	0	0	n.s.
Interaction between memory strategy and group sequence (effect of order—1st versus 2d list)	10	1	10	10	< 0.01
Within subjects error term	23	23	1		

*n.s. is abbreviation for not statistically significant.

Note: p indicates the probability the researcher could get those results even if the variables were not related. Thus, the smaller the p-value, the more likely the variables are related.

the memory strategy factor also failed to reach significance. Thus, we have no evidence that one strategy is superior to the other. Finally, we find we have a significant interaction of memory strategy and group sequence. By looking at table 8.8, we see this interaction is caused by the fact that group 1 does best using images whereas group 2 does best by making sentences. In other words, subjects do better on the first list than on the second.

What does this order effect mean? If the researchers were not careful in their selection of lists, the order effect could merely reflect the first list being made up of words that were easier to recall than the second list. However, we would hope the researcher would counterbalance lists so that across subjects, each list occurred equally often under each instructional condition. Therefore, if the experiment were properly conducted, the order effect must reflect either the effects of practice, fatigue, treatment carry-over, or sensitization. In this case, it probably reflects the fact that recalling the second list is hurt by the practice subjects got on the first list. This negative practice effect is not considered a nuisance by psychologists. On the contrary, this negative practice effect is one of the most important and most widely investigated facts of memory—interference.

Now that you understand the three effects you find with a counterbalanced design, let us look at an experiment where all three effects are of interest to the researcher. Mary Jones, a politician, produces two commercials: an emotional commercial and a rational commercial. She hires a psychologist to find out which commercial is most effective so she'll know which one to give more air time. The researcher uses a counterbalanced design to address the question (see table 8.10).

By looking at the treatment main effect, the researcher is able to answer the original question "Which ad is more effective?" By looking at the counterbalancing main effect, the researcher is able to find out whether one sequence of showing the ads is better than another. He is able to answer the question "Should we show the emotional ad first or the rational ad first?" Finally, by looking at the ad by counterbalancing interaction, the researcher is able to determine whether there is an order effect. He is able to answer the question "In terms of increasing the candidate's popularity, do the two ads seem to build

TABLE 8.10   Effects Revealed by a 2 × 2 Counterbalanced Design

GROUP 1	
First Ad	*Second Ad*
Emotional ad	Rational ad

GROUP 2	
First Ad	*Second Ad*
Rational ad	Emotional ad

Questions addressed by design:

1. Is the rational ad more effective than the emotional ad? (main effect of the within subjects factor of ad)
2. Is it better to show the emotional ad and then the rational ad or is it better to show the rational ad and then the emotional ad? (main effect of between subjects factor of counterbalancing)
3. Are attitudes more favorable to the candidate after seeing the second ad than after seeing the first? (ad by counterbalancing interaction)

on one another?" Obviously, he would expect the ads to build on one another. Therefore, he would expect voters would rate the candidate higher after seeing the second ad than they did after the first ad.

But what if he does not find an order effect? Then, because there is no obvious benefit of showing both ads, he might suggest the candidate show only one ad. Or, what if he got an order effect such that people always rated the candidate worse after the second ad? In that event, he would take a long, hard look at the ads. It may be that both ads are making people dislike the candidate or it may be that the combination of these two ads does not work. Seeing both ads may reduce liking for the candidate by making her seem inconsistent. For example, one ad may suggest that she is for military spending while the other may suggest that she is against military spending.

Thus, if either order or sequence effects are of interest to you, the counterbalanced design is your best bet. Perhaps order effects are of most interest to you when you can control the order of real-life treatments. In that case, you would like to know how to order the treatments to your advantage. Thus, you might be interested in using a counterbalanced design to find out whether it is best to be the first or the last person interviewed for a job. Or, if you want to do well in one particular course (research design, of course), you might like to know whether you would do better in that particular course if it were the first subject you studied or whether you would do better if it were the last subject you studied. To find out about these order effects, you would need to rely on a counterbalanced design.

Similarly, sequence effects will probably be of the most interest if you can control the sequence of real-life treatments. There are probably many situations in which you may ask yourself, "If I do these tasks in one sequence, will that lead to better outcomes than if I do these tasks in a different sequence?" For instance, will studying your courses in one sequence give you a 2.8 GPA, whereas if you studied them in a different order you would get a 3.2? Or, if you are going to compliment and criticize a friend, would you be better off to criticize and then praise or to praise and then criticize?

In conclusion, the counterbalanced design not only balances out routine order effects, but also tells you about the impact of order and about the effects of sequence. Knowing what kind of order and sequence effects exist is sometimes of interest because real life is often a series of treatments (Greenwald, 1976). That is, most of us are not assigned to receive either praise or criticism, ads for a candidate or against a candidate, success or failure, pleasure or pain, etc. Instead, we receive both praise and criticism, ads for and against a candidate, success and failure, and both pleasure and pain. Counterbalanced designs allow us to understand the effects of different patterns of receiving these "treatments."

CHOOSING DESIGNS

If you want to compare two levels of an independent variable, you have several designs you can use: matched pairs, within subjects designs, counterbalanced designs, and the simple between subjects design. To help you choose among these designs, we will briefly summarize the ideal situation for using each design.

THE TWO-CONDITIONS CASE

The matched pairs design is ideal when (1) you can readily obtain each subject's score on the matching variable without arousing their suspicions about the purpose of the experiment, (2) the matching variable correlates highly with the dependent measure, and (3) subjects are scarce.

The pure within subjects design is ideal when (1) sensitization, practice, fatigue, or carry-over are not problems, (2) you want a powerful design, (3) subjects are hard to get, and (4) you want to generalize your results to real-life situations, and in real-life, individuals tend to be exposed to both levels of the treatment.

The 2 × 2 counterbalanced design is ideal when (1) you want to balance out the effects of order or you are interested in learning the nature of any order or sequence effects, (2) you have enough subjects to meet the requirement of a counterbalanced design, and (3) you are not concerned that being exposed to both treatment levels will alert subjects to the purpose of the experiment.

The simple experiment is ideal when (1) you think fatigue, practice, sensitization, or carry-over could affect the results, (2) you have access to a relatively large number of subjects, and (3) you want to generalize your results to real-life situations, and in real-life, individuals tend to receive either one treatment *or* the other, but not both. (For a summary, see table 8.11.)

TABLE 8.11 Ideal Situations for Different Designs

SIMPLE EXPERIMENT	MATCHED GROUPS	WITHIN SUBJECTS	COUNTER-BALANCED DESIGN
Subjects plentiful	Subjects very scarce	Subjects very scarce	Subjects somewhat scarce
Order effects could be a problem	Order effects could be a problem	Order effects not a problem	Want to assess order effects or order effects can be balanced out
Power not vital	Power vital	Power vital	Power vital
In real life, people usually only get one or the other treatment, rarely get both	In real life, people usually only get one or the other treatment, rarely get both	In real life, people usually get both treatments, rarely get only one or the other	In real life, people usually get both treatments, rarely get only one or the other
Multiple exposure to dependent measure will tip subjects off about hypothesis	Exposure to matching variable will *not* tip subjects off about hypothesis	Multiple exposure to dependent measure will *not* tip subjects off about hypothesis	Multiple exposure to dependent measure will *not* tip subjects off about hypothesis
Exposure to different levels of the independent variable will tip subjects off about hypothesis	Exposure to different levels of the independent variable will tip subjects off about hypothesis	Exposure to different levels of the independent variable will *not* tip subjects off about hypothesis	Exposure to different levels of the independent variable will *not* tip subjects off about hypothesis
	Matching variable easy to collect and correlates highly with the dependent measure		

WHEN YOU HAVE MORE THAN TWO LEVELS OF THE INDEPENDENT VARIABLE

If you want to study two levels of an independent variable, you know what designs are available and how to choose among those designs. But what if you want to study three or more levels of an independent variable? Your four options are basically extensions of your two-condition options, namely:

1. a multi-level between subjects design,
2. a matched group design (matched trios, matched quadruplets, etc.),
3. a complex counterbalanced design, or
4. a multi-level within subjects design.

Which of these basic options should you use? To decide on which option, you might be tempted to use the same criteria you used when choosing among designs in the two-condition case. Therefore, if you would pick a within or counterbalanced design when investigating two levels of the factor, you might think you should use the same design if you were studying more than two levels of the factor. However, this is not necessarily the case. In fact, there are three reasons why you may not want to go beyond studying two levels of a variable with either a completely within subjects design or with a counterbalanced design.

First, when you are using the two-condition within subjects design, you are using the within design least vulnerable to order effects. As you add levels, you multiply the risk that practice, fatigue, carry-over, or sensitization will contaminate your results. Order effects can be so tricky that even counterbalancing may not totally control for them.

Second, after you go beyond two levels, you cannot use the dependent group's t-test. Instead, you must use a within subjects analysis of variance.[3] The computations for this kind of analysis of variance are so complex that you really should use a computer program to do it—and not all statistical packages will do it. Furthermore, by using multiple levels, you are setting yourself up for doing tests to determine which conditions differ from each other. For example, if you get a significant result, you may want to know which specific conditions differed from each other or you may want to know the shape of the relationship between the variables. Doing such tests is usually easier if you have a between subjects than if you have a within subjects design.

Third, by adding levels you complicate counterbalancing, and complicating counterbalancing leads to problems. Ironically, one thing that is not a problem is actually figuring out the correct counterbalancing. As you can see from box 8.2, counterbalancing complex designs is simple. The problems are as follows:

1. With more than two conditions, you need more subjects because you have more groups.

2. With more than two conditions, your counterbalancing may not include every possible sequence of conditions. Consequently, you may have difficulty generalizing your results to individuals who get the treatments in a sequence you did not test.

3. With more conditions, order and sequence effects are harder to figure out. To analyze the effect of order when you have two levels of an independent variable, you need to interpret a 2×2 interaction. To analyze the effect of order when you have four levels of a factor, you have to interpret a 4×4 interaction.

With more levels, you not only have to interpret more complex interactions, but you also allow more complex effects to occur. With four levels of a factor, for example, you can have very complex order and sequence effects. You could have any combination of linear, quadratic, and cubic interactions and sequence main effects. (If you are having trouble understanding these terms, you probably want to stick to a two-condition experiment). With two conditions, on the other hand, you can have only two kinds of significant order effects: either the first is better than the second or the second is better than the first. Similarly, with two conditions, you can have only two kinds of significant sequence effects: either it is better to get treatment A and then treatment B or it is better to get treatment B and then treatment A.

[3]Some experts recommend an even more sophisticated analysis—MANOVA (multivariate analysis of variance).

BOX 8.2   The ABCs of Counterbalancing Complex Designs

You have seen an example of the simplest form of counterbalancing in which one group of subjects gets treatment A followed by treatment B (A-B) and a second group gets treatment B followed by treatment A (B-A). This simple form of counterbalancing is called A-B, B-A counterbalancing. Note that even this simple form of counterbalancing accomplishes two goals.

First, it guarantees every condition occurs in every position, equally often. Thus, in A-B, B-A counterbalancing, A occurs in both the first and last position. The same is true for B.

Second, each condition precedes every other condition just as many times as it follows that condition. That is, in A-B, B-A counterbalancing, A precedes B once and follows B once. This symmetry is called **balance.**

Although achieving these two objectives of counterbalancing is easy with only two conditions, with more conditions, counterbalancing becomes more complex. For example, with four conditions (A,B,C,D) you would have four groups. To determine what order the groups will go through the conditions, you would consult the 4 × 4 Latin Square.

| | **POSITION** | | | |
	1	2	3	4
Group 1	A	B	D	C
Group 2	B	C	A	D
Group 3	C	D	B	A
Group 4	D	A	C	B

In this 4 × 4 complete Latin Square, treatment A occurs in all four positions (1st, 2d, 3rd, and 4th), as do treatments B, C, and D. In addition, the square has balance. As you can see from looking at the square, every letter precedes every other letter twice and follows every other letter twice. For example, if you just look at treatments A and D, you see that A comes before D twice (in groups 1 and 2) and follows D twice (in groups 3 and 4).

Balance is relatively easy to achieve for two, four, six, eight or even sixteen conditions. But, what if you have three conditions? Immediately you recognize that with a 3 × 3 Latin Square, A cannot precede B the same number of times as it follows B. Condition A can either precede B twice and follow it once or precede it once and follow it twice. Thus, with an uneven number of conditions, you cannot create a balanced Latin Square.

One approach to achieving balance when you have an uneven number of treatment levels is to add or subtract a level so you have an even number of levels. However, adding a level may greatly increase the number of sequences and groups you need. Subtracting a level, on the other hand, may cause you to lose vital information. Therefore, you may not wish to change levels. Fortunately, you can achieve balance with an uneven number of treatment levels by using two Latin Squares.*

For instance, consider the 3 × 3 squares below.

	SQUARE 1				SQUARE 2		
	Position				Position		
	1	2	3		1	2	3
Group 1	A	B	C	Group 4	C	B	A
Group 2	B	C	A	Group 5	A	C	B
Group 3	C	A	B	Group 6	B	A	C

If you randomly assign subjects to six groups, as outlined above, you ensure balance. See for yourself that if you take any two conditions, one condition will precede the other three times, and will be preceded by the other condition three times.

---

*Another option is to use incomplete Latin Square designs. However, the discussion of incomplete Latin Square designs is beyond the scope of this book.

In conclusion, if you want to study several levels of an independent variable, you may be better off—at this point in your life—using a between subjects design instead of using a within subjects design (see table 8.12). However, if you have a computer program or statistical consultant (preferably both), you may decide to use a within subjects or counterbalanced design if (1) you need power, (2) you want to generalize your results to real-life situations where people are bound to get more than two levels of the treatment, or (3) you believe order effects are not a problem.

WHEN YOU HAVE MORE THAN ONE INDEPENDENT VARIABLE

Thus far, we have discussed the case where you were studying the effects of a single variable. Often, however, you may want to investigate the effects of two or more variables.

As you may have inferred from our discussion of counterbalancing with multiple levels, counterbalancing becomes less attractive as the design becomes more complicated. Thus, as a general rule, beginning researchers who plan on manipulating two independent variables usually are choosing between a two-factor within subjects design and a two-factor between subjects design. In many respects, this choice is similar to choosing between a multi-level within subjects design and a multi-level between subjects design. Specifically, you should use a pure within subjects design if (1) you can handle the statistics; (2) sensitization, practice, fatigue, and carry-over are not problems; (3) you are

TABLE 8.12 Complications Due to Going Beyond Two Levels of the Independent Variable

Between Subjects Designs	Matched Designs	Pure Within Designs	Counter-Balanced Designs
Need more subjects	Need more subjects		Need more subjects
	Harder to find four matched people than two	More order effects are possible	More order effects possible, may not be able to control
			Probably won't test all possible orders
Statistics become more complex	Statistics become much more complex	Statistics become much more complex	Statistics become much more complex

concerned about power; and (4) in real-life situations, people are exposed to all levels of the treatment.

On the other hand, you should use a between subjects design if (1) you are worried about the statistics of a complex within design; (2) you are worried about order effects; (3) you are not worried about power; and (4) in real-life situations, people are exposed to either one treatment condition *or* the other.

Sometimes, however, you will find choosing between a totally within and a totally between design difficult (see table 8.13). For example, consider the following two cases.

Case 1: You are studying the effects of brain lesions and practice on how well rats run mazes. On the one hand, you do not want to use a totally within subjects design because you consider brain damage to occur "between subjects" in real life. On the other hand, you do not want to use a totally between subjects design because you think practice occurs "within subjects" in real life.

TABLE 8.13 Should a Factor be a Between Subjects Factor or a Within Subjects Factor?

Ideal Situation for Making a Factor Between or Within	
Make Factor Between	*Make Factor Within Subjects*
Order effects pose problems	Order effects not a problem
Lack of power is *not* a concern	Lack of power is a serious concern
Want to generalize results to situations where subjects receive either one treatment or another	Want to generalize results to situations where subjects receive all levels of the treatment

Case 2: You are studying the effects of subliminal messages and marijuana on creativity. You expect that if subliminal messages have any effect, it will be so small that only a within subjects design could detect it. However, you feel oral ingestion of marijuana should not be studied in a within design because of huge carry-over effects.

Fortunately, in these cases, you are not forced to choose between a totally within subjects factorial and a totally between subjects factorial. As you know from our discussion of counterbalanced designs, you can do a study in which one variable is within and one is between. Such designs are called **mixed designs.**

In the two cases we just discussed, the mixed design is an ideal solution. For example, in case 1, we could make brain lesion a between subjects variable by randomly assigning half the subjects to get lesions and half not. That way we do not have to worry about carrry-over effects. We could make practice a within subjects variable by having each subject run the maze three times. Consequently, we have the power to detect subtle differences due to practice (see table 8.14 and figure 8.1).

Note that in this lesion experiment, the interesting statistical effects might have little to do with the two main effects. That is, we would not be terribly surprised to find a main effect for lesion. We would expect brain-lesioned rats to perform worse—especially if the control rats got no operation at all. Nor would we be surprised to find a main effect of practice. We would expect subjects to improve with practice. However, we would be interested to know about the practice $\times$ lesion interaction. A significant practice by lesion interaction would tell us that one group of rats was benefiting from practice more than the other.

Similarly, we could investigate the hypotheses in case 2 using a mixed design. We would randomly assign subjects so that half ingested marijuana and half did not. This random assignment would allow us to avoid carry-over effects. Then, we would expose all subjects to a variety of subliminal messages. Some of these would be designed to encourage creativity, some of these messages would be neutral. By comparing the average overall creativity scores from the marijuana group to that of the no-marijuana group, we

TABLE 8.14 Analysis of Variance Summary Table for a Mixed Design

SOURCE OF VARIANCE	df	SS	MS	F	p
Brain lesion	1	52.083	52.08	10.06	0.0068
Between subjects error	14	72.416	5.17		
Trials	2	26.660	13.33	11.10	0.0003
Lesions X Trial interaction	2	13.722	6.86	5.71	0.0083
Within subjects error	28	33.612	1.20		

Note: The mean square error for the within subjects term is much smaller than the between subjects error term (1.2 to 5.17), giving the design tremendous power for detecting within subjects effects. This table corresponds to the graph in figure 8.1.

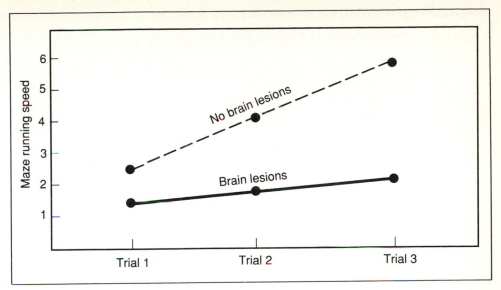

FIGURE 8.1 An Interaction in a Mixed Design

could assess the effect of marijuana. By comparing subjects' scores following the "creative" subliminal messages to their scores following "neutral" subliminal messages, we could even detect rather subtle effects of subliminal messages. Finally, by looking at the interaction between marijuana and messages, we could determine whether the marijuana group was more influenced by the subliminal messages.

As you have seen, in case 1 and in case 2, the mixed design is the ideal solution for two reasons. First, the mixed design allows you to examine the effects of two independent variables and their interaction. Second, instead of trading off the needs of one variable for the needs of another variable, you are able to give both variables the design they need. Because of its versatility, the mixed design is one of the most popular experimental designs.

CONCLUDING REMARKS

You are now familiar with most of the basic experimental designs. You know what they are, how to perform them, how to analyze them, how to interpret their results, and how to choose among them. (See box 8.3 for notes on computer analysis of your design.) Therefore, you should be very comfortable reading the write-up of any kind of experiment. If you are not, by the time you finish reading the next chapter, you will be.

BOX 8.3   Making Sure the Computer Understands Your Design

If you use a two-factor design, you will probably have a computer analyze your data for you. Fortunately, most computers can analyze data from any kind of design: totally between subjects, totally within subjects, or mixed. Unfortunately, if you are not careful, the computer may analyze data from your design as if it were from another kind of design. To ensure the computer understands your design, check your printout carefully.

If you used a totally between subjects design, your printout should include only one error term. If you take the MS for any treatment or interaction and divide it by your one and only MSE, you will get the F for that effect.

If, on the other hand, you used a totally within subjects design, your printout will contain several error terms. Specifically, each main effect and each interaction will have its own error term. Thus, if you have three effects (two main effects and an interaction effect), you will have three error terms.

The degrees of freedom for an effect's error term will equal the degrees of freedom for the effect multiplied by one less than the number of subjects. Thus, if you used twenty-one subjects in a 4×3 design, it is easy to correctly match the error term to the effect. The four-level factor has 3 degrees of freedom (remember, the formula for all main effects is number of levels minus one). So, its error term will be the one that has 60 df (3×20). The three-level factor has 2 degrees of freedom so its error term has 40 df (2×20). The interaction term will have 6 degrees of freedom (remember, you calculate the interaction df by multiplying the df of the factors that make it up. In this case, $3 \times 2 = 6$). Therefore, the error term for the interaction will have 120 df ($6 \times 20 = 120$). (It is no accident the procedure for determining the error term df seems similar to the way you calculate df for an interaction. The error term is the interaction between subjects and the effect you are testing.)

Rarely would the computer analyze a within design as a between design or vice-versa. More commonly, the computer will get mixed up when you use a mixed design. The computer sometimes fails to realize which factors are within subjects factors and which are between. So, if you do a mixed design, scrutinize your computer printout carefully.

Start with the between factors. All between factor main effects should be tested against a single error term. This error term is also used to test any interactions that involve between factors only. To make sure this is the case, divide the MS for each between factors main effect or exclusively between factors interaction by the MS for the between subjects error term. In every case, you should get the same F that is reported in the printout.

To double-check the computer correctly identified all the between subjects variables, add up the degrees of freedom for all the between subjects main effects, the df for the interactions that involved only between subjects, and the df for the between subjects error term. The total of these degrees of freedom should be one fewer than the number of subjects.

Next, check the within factors. As in the within subjects design, each within subjects main effect and each interaction that involves only within subjects factors should be tested against a different error term.

Finally, look at interactions involving both within and between factors. To find the appropriate error term for these interactions, ignore the between subjects factor. Attend only to the within subjects factors. If A is a within factor and B is a between factor and you see an A × B interaction, this interaction should be tested against the same error term that A is tested against. If A is a within factor and B and C are between factors, the error term for the A × B × C interaction should still be the same error term that was used for testing A. If it is not, the computer does not understand your design.

SUMMARY

1. The matched pairs design uses matching to reduce random error and randomization to establish internal validity.

2. Because the matched pairs design gives you power without limiting the kind of subject you can use, you may be better able to generalize your results to a broader population (i.e., it may have greater external validity) than if you use a simple experiment.

3. The matched pairs design's weaknesses stem from matching: Matching may sensitize subjects to your hypothesis and subjects may drop out of the study between the time of the matching test and the time the experiment is performed.

4. The two-condition within subjects design gives you two scores per subject.

5. The within subjects design increases power by eliminating random error due to individual differences and by increasing the number of observations.

6. Because of practice effects, fatigue effects, carry-over effects, and sensitization, the order in which a subject gets the treatments may affect the results.

7. To reduce the effects of order, you should randomly determine the order in which each subject will get the treatments.

8. In the counterbalanced design, subjects are randomly assigned to systematically varying orders of conditions to ensure that routine order effects are balanced out. Counterbalancing tells you about the impact of order and the effects of sequence.

9. Because you must include the between subjects factor of counterbalancing in your analyses, counterbalanced designs need more subjects than pure within subjects designs.

10. In counterbalanced designs, subjects will be exposed to several treatments. Consequently, subjects may be sensitized to the hypothesis.

11. If you want to compare two levels of an independent variable, you can use matched

pairs, within subjects designs, counterbalanced designs, and simple between subjects designs.

12. Mixed designs have both a within and a between subjects factor.

KEY TERMS

carry-over
counterbalanced
dependent groups t-test
fatigue effects
matched pairs design

mixed designs
practice effects
sensitization
within subjects designs

EXERCISES

1. A researcher uses a simple experiment involving ten subjects to examine the effects of memory strategy (repetition versus imagery) on memory. Do you think the researcher will find a significant effect? Why or why not? What design would you recommend?

2. If the researcher had used a matched pairs study involving ten subjects, would the study have more power? Why? How many degrees of freedom would the researcher have? What matching task would you suggest? Why?

3. An investigator wants to find out whether hearing jokes will allow a person to persevere longer on a frustrating task. The researcher matches subjects based on their reaction to a frustrating task. Of the thirty subjects, five quit the study after going through the "frustration pretest." Beyond the ethical problems, what problems are there in using a matched pairs design in this situation?

4. What problems would there be in using a within subjects design to study the "humor-perseverance" study? Would a counterbalanced design solve these problems?

5. Why are within subjects designs more powerful than matched pairs designs?

6. Two researchers hypothesize that spatial tasks will be performed more quickly when the tasks are seen in subjects' left visual fields than when the tasks are seen in subjects' right visual fields (because messages seen in the left visual field go directly to the right brain which is often assumed to be better at processing spatial information). Conversely, they believe verbal tasks will be performed more quickly when the tasks are shown to subjects' right visual fields than when the tasks are shown to subjects' left visual fields. What design would you recommend? Why?

7. A student hypothesizes that alcohol level will affect sense of humor. Specifically, the more people drink, the more they will find slapstick humor funny. However,

the more people drink, the less funny they will find other forms of humor. What design would you recommend the student use? Why?

8. In a study using a mixed design, one mean square error is 12, the other mean square error is 4. Which mean square error is probably the between subjects error term? Why?

9. You want to determine whether caffeine, a snack, or a brief walk has a more beneficial effect on mood. What design would you use? Why? How?

10. An investigator wanted to examine the effects of three treatments on pain perception: hypnosis, acupuncture, and distraction. The researcher used a counterbalanced design, randomly assigning the twelve paid volunteers to one of three orders of treatment:

hypnosis	acupuncture	distraction
acupuncture	distraction	hypnosis
distraction	hypnosis	acupuncture

Participants were exposed to a treatment, received a mild shock to the wrist, rated their level of discomfort, and then received the next treatment.

a. What order effects was the design trying to balance out? Be specific.
b. Was this counterbalancing effective in that goal? Why or why not?
c. What design would you have used? Why?
d. Below are the results of the ANOVA for the study. Please interpret the results. What recommendations would you make?

SOURCE OF VARIANCE	df	SS	MS	F	p
Counterbalancing (c)	2	205.712	102.856	64.833	.0000
Error	9	14.278	1.586		
Treatment (t)	2	1.145	.573	.812	.4595
C × T interaction	4	6.728	1.682	2.387	.0895
Error	18	12.687	.705		

9

Critically Reading Research

Overview

Reading for Understanding

Reread the Article Looking for Weaknesses

Developing Research Ideas from Existing Research

Concluding Remarks

Summary

Key Terms

Exercises

"The best way to get a good idea is to steal one."
Abe Burrows

—*How to Succeed in Business Without Really Trying*

OVERVIEW

In this chapter, you will learn how to benefit from reading other people's research. You will start by learning how to make sense of a research article. Then, you will learn how to spot flaws and limitations in research. Finally, you will learn how you can get research ideas by reading research. Thus, the aim of this chapter is to make you an intelligent consumer *and* producer of research.

READING FOR UNDERSTANDING

You would not find a "how to" manual about how to fix a Volkswagen very useful unless you were reading it while you were fixing a Volkswagen. Similarly, you will find this "how to read an article" chapter little more than a review of what you already know, unless you read it while you are reading an article. Therefore, you need to choose an article.

CHOOSING AN ARTICLE

But do not choose just any article. Because critically evaluating means *actively* applying what you have learned about research design, select an article that will motivate you to actively apply what you know about research design. Specifically, choose an article that uses a design you are familiar with and that deals with an area you find interesting.

To start your quest for such an article, you could do one of the following:

1. Glance at the table of contents of journals, looking for titles that sound interesting;
2. Look at sections of books you find particularly interesting and look up the articles they reference (for example, you might want to look up a study referenced in this text, such as the study by Wilson and Schooler on when thinking about why we like something hurts our ability to know how much we like it, or the study by Linville and Fischer about whether people prefer to experience two negative events on the same day or on different days);
3. Consult some of the resources described in table 9.1.

CHOOSING A JOURNAL

Before you choose your article, some would argue you should choose what journal the article will be in. Not all journals are alike (see table 9.1). Not only do they cover different

TABLE 9.1 A Look at Selected Journals

JOURNAL	RELEVANCE TO YOU
Psychological Bulletin	Publishes articles that review existing work on either a research area or on a research/statistical technique.
Psychological Review	Publishes work that compares and criticizes existing theories.
American Psychologist	Publishes theoretical articles, review articles, and empirical articles. Although articles are often written by distinguished scholars, they are written to a broad audience and are thus relatively easy to understand.
Psychological Science	Publishes theoretical articles, review articles, and empirical articles. Although articles are often written by distinguished scholars, they are written to a fairly broad audience and are thus relatively easy to understand. You may find the articles slightly harder to understand than those in the *American Psychologist.*
Contemporary Psychology	Contains reviews of recent books, is easy to read, and covers a wide range of topics.
Psychological Abstracts	Presents brief summaries of most published articles in psychology and is a good browsing or reference tool. The abstracts are indexed by both author and topic.
Psych/Scan	Like *Psychological Abstracts,* contains summaries of recent articles. There are six different *Psych/Scans* for six different content areas: (1) developmental, (2) clinical, (3) learning disorders and mental retardation, (4) applied psychology, (5) applied experimental and engineering, and (6) psychoanalysis.
American Journal of Psychology	Primarily contains original research in basic psychological science; not as competitive as *JEP* (see below).
Journals of Experimental Psychology (JEP)	Usually publishes original experimental studies concerning basic mechanisms of perception, learning, motivation, and performance. There are four different journals—*JEP: General; JEP: Animal Behavior Processes; JEP: Learning, Memory, and Cognition; and JEP: Human Perception and Performance.*
Behavioral Neuroscience	Emphasizes biological basis of behavior. Because of the interdisciplinary nature of the journal, you may find some of the articles hard to understand if you do not have the necessary background in chemistry or endocrinology.
Journal of Comparative Psychology	Articles may include both laboratory and field observation of species. Emphasis is on relating findings to the theory of evolution.
Bulletin of the Psychonomic Society	Articles cover any area of general experimental psychology. Good source of short articles describing relatively simple studies. Articles do not undergo peer review.
Journal of Applied Behavior Analysis	Articles report a sizeable effect on an important behavior, usually employing a single-subject design.
Psychological Record	Articles discuss theory or report experiments. Average article is relatively brief.
Psychological Reports	Good source of brief articles in general psychology.
Journal of Consulting and Clinical Psychology	Wide range of articles and brief reports dealing with theory and research in counseling; some use of the case study method.
Psychological Assessment: A Journal of Consulting and Clinical Psychology	Contains studies assessing the validity of a variety of tests and measures.

Journal of Counseling Psychology	Publishes research articles evaluating the effectiveness of counseling, studies on the effectiveness of selecting and training counselors, theoretical articles, and other articles relating to counseling.
Journal of Abnormal Psychology	Occasionally reports experimental studies on humans or animals related to emotion or pathology and some studies that test hypotheses derived from psychological theories.
Psychology and Aging	Reports research on physiological and behavioral aspects of aging during older adulthood; fairly easy to read.
Developmental Psychology	Primarily publishes research relating to development; some experiments, some cross-cultural studies, some correlational studies.
Journal of Educational Psychology	Contains research and theoretical articles relating to teaching and learning; fairly easy to read.
American Education Research Journal	Publishes research in education. Single study papers are accepted.
Journal of Applied Psychology	Reports research relating to industry, government, health, education, consumer affairs, and other applied areas.
Journal of Personality and Social Psychology	Contains three sections: (1) attitudes and social cognition, (2) interpersonal relations and group processes, and (3) personality and individual differences. Primarily reports articles involving several studies or fairly complex designs. Discussions may suggest follow-up studies that could be performed.
Journal of Experimental Social Psychology	Almost all articles report the results of experiments.
Journal of Social Psychology	Source of fairly simple studies.
Personality and Social Psychology Bulletin	Contains short articles that are often easy to understand.
Representative Research in Social Psychology	One of the few journals to publish studies that have nonsignificant results.

topics and favor different designs, but they also differ in how hard it is to get published. To be published in a "prestige" journal, an article must first be approved by an editor and one or more expert reviewers. This process is called *peer review*. Reviewers may reject the study for being methodologically flawed, being theoretically unimportant, not adequately citing previous research and theory, not making a contribution to the field, only involving a single study, not using a complex design, or a host of other reasons. Because of all the reasons an article can be rejected, you should not be surprised to learn the vast majority of studies submitted to "prestige" journals will be rejected.

However, not all journals are "prestige" journals. To illustrate this point, realize that in 1978 there were 8,062 scientific journals. However, between 1979 and 1988, *29,621* new scientific journals were founded (Sykes, 1990). The quantity of good research did not quadruple during those eight years, and scientists did not start reading four times as many journals. Clearly, not all of these new journals are "prestige" journals that expose articles to rigorous peer review. Indeed, some of them accept virtually any article submitted.

Your professor may advocate you read only articles from "prestige" journals, such as *Journal of Experimental Psychology* or *Journal of Personality and Social Psychology*. The "better" journals usually contain more theoretically meaningful and more methodologically sound research than those contained in less prestigious journals.

However, we are not saying only inferior research is published in less competitive and less prestigious journals, such as *Bulletin of the Psychonomic Society* or *Journal of Social Psychology*. Admittedly, less prestigious journals sometimes may rely on "leftovers" or "rejects" from "prestige" journals, but these rejects are not necessarily poor articles. Indeed, many good articles must be rejected because there are simply many more good articles submitted than can be accepted. To illustrate that good articles are rejected, Peters and Ceci (1982) took articles that had been accepted in a journal and then resubmitted those articles to the same journals. Almost all were rejected! Peters and Ceci's (1982) study brings up a second problem with "prestige" journals: they depend on a less than perfect process—peer review.

What are the problems with peer review? As Peters and Ceci's study suggests, and as Lindsey (1978) documented, peer reviewers disagree much of the time. One reason for this lack of objectivity is reviewers have their individual biases. For example, Mahoney (1977) found peer reviewers are much more likely to accept research studies that produce research results supporting the reviewer's point of view. Specifically, Mahoney found that if a study reported results that supported a reviewer's beliefs, the study would be proclaimed "methodologically sound." However, if the same study reported results conflicting with those beliefs, the study would be rejected as "methodologically flawed." Consequently, studies that challenge existing views may be less likely to appear in "prestige" journals (Karon, 1990; Kuhn, 1970; Mahoney, 1977).

Not only do reviewers have their own individual biases, but "establishment" peer reviewers tend to share three other biases. First, reviewers of elite journals tend to be prejudiced against nonsignificant results. For some reviewers, null results are grounds for rejection (Fiske & Fogg, 1990). Furthermore, studies reporting null results will rarely be published in prestige journals (Greenwald, 1975). Second, reviewers for "prestige" journals are prejudiced against articles that replicate previous research (Fiske & Fogg, 1990)—even though replication is essential to firmly establishing scientific fact. Third, reviewers for elite journals may be prejudiced against studies that use new measures (Fiske & Fogg, 1990; Karon, 1990).

You have seen that tough competition for limited space in journals and problems with peer review may cause a good article to be rejected and thus end up in a "lesser" journal. However, we should stress not all research articles appearing in less competitive journals are rejects from "prestige" journals. Some good research may appear in a less prestigious journal because the researcher did not submit the article anywhere else. For example, the researcher may mistakenly believe the article would not be accepted by the "best" journal or the researcher may want the article published faster than would be possible with peer review.

Yet, despite these qualms with elite journals and peer review, the vast majority of psychologists would agree, articles in "prestige" journals are usually better than those in "lesser" journals. Does this mean you should not read articles in "lesser" journals? No. In fact, there are at least two advantages to choosing an article in a "lesser" journal. First, compared to articles in less prestigious journals, articles in "prestige" journals tend to be more heavily based on previous research and theory, tend to involve more studies, and tend to involve more complex designs—all factors that may make the article harder for you to read. Second, if you want to do a research project based on improving an existing study, it may be easier to improve on a study you find in a less prestigious journal.

To this point, we have described the differences between "elite" and "lower level" journals (see table 9.2 for a review). You may have noticed we have danced around the issue of which type of journal you should use. We have danced around that issue primarily because choosing a journal depends on your goals. If you want to know the latest, conventional thinking on a topic, then you should probably read an article from a "prestige" journal. Such journals will tend to provide you with models of how articles should be written, as well as ideas about how to expand and extend the researcher's work.

TABLE 9.2 Selected Differences between "Prestigious" and "Less Prestigious" Journals

LESS PRESTIGIOUS JOURNAL	MORE PRESTIGIOUS JOURNAL
As a general rule, *not affiliated* with a national or international society of professionally trained scientists, such as APA (American Psychological Association) or APS (American Psychological Society).	As a general rule, *affiliated* with a national or international society of professionally trained scientists, such as APA (American Psychological Association) or APS (American Psychological Society).
Few of the articles submitted are rejected. In some cases, if you pay the publication fee, your article will be published.	Articles are reviewed by experts in the field. These experts decide whether your study should be published. (This process is called "peer review.")
	Most of the articles submitted are rejected.
More likely to be methodologically flawed.	Less likely to be methodologically flawed.
May involve a single study that involves a very simple design. Study may even be a pilot study.	Probably involves several studies or one very complex study.
Probably fairly short.	May be relatively long.
Less likely to be theoretically important.	More likely to be theoretically important.
May be easier to read.	May be harder to read.
Methodological flaws easier to spot.	Methodological flaws harder to spot (although some may be conceded by the author as a condition of getting study published).
Articles may stimulate research to verify study's results or correct methodological flaws. May want to repeat with improved design, procedures, or stimulus materials. Alternatively, may want to extend study by using a more complex design.	Articles may stimulate research ideas designed to build and extend on that research. May want to extend study by looking at effect of additional variables. May choose to make different tradeoffs than the researcher did. May want to do studies suggested in article's discussion section.

If, on the other hand, you want a relatively easy-to-read article, a less conventional way of thinking about a topic, you may want to read an article from a "lesser" journal. Such journals may stimulate you to improve the study by replicating it with improved procedures, stimulus materials, or designs, or give you ideas about how to extend the study using a more complex design. However, note these are general rules: Great research may be published in even the least selective of journals and terrible research be published in even the best journals. Because the journal's reputation does not guarantee quality, rather than worrying about what journal to use, your best bet may be to simply find an article you find interesting.

Your first clue to whether the article is interesting is its title. Usually, the title identifies the key variables in the study. For example, in articles describing an experiment, the independent variable(s) and the dependent variable may be in the title. In some cases, the title may hint at what the hypothesis was or even what the main findings were. Once you find a promising title, locate the article and look at the first page. Right under the title, you will see a paragraph that stands apart from the rest of the article. Although unlabeled, this one-paragraph summary of the study is called the abstract.[1] This abstract summarizes the purpose, methodology, and results of the research.

READING THE ABSTRACT

By reading the abstract, you should get a general sense of what the researchers' hypotheses were, how they tried to test those hypotheses, and whether the results supported those hypotheses. But most importantly, you will get an idea about whether you want to read the article.

Because reading the abstract can be so informative, you may want to start your literature search by skimming the *Psychological Abstracts*. The *Psychological Abstracts* contain abstracts from a wide variety of journals and can be searched by year of publication, topic of article, or author. (See table 9.1 and appendix B for more information on how to use the *Psychological Abstracts*.)

READING THE INTRODUCTION

Once you find an article that has an interesting title and abstract, you are ready to start reading the rest of the article. For the beginning student, the best place to start reading an article is at the beginning. Although unlabeled, the beginning of the article is called the introduction. The introduction is the most difficult and the most important part of the article to understand. You must understand the introduction because it is where the authors tell you the following:

1. How they came up with the hypothesis, including reasons why they think the hypothesis will be supported;

[1]Some older articles do not have an abstract but do contain a summary placed at the end of the article.

2. Reasons why the hypothesis might not be correct;
3. Why the hypothesis is important;
4. Why the authors' way of testing the hypothesis is the best way to test the hypothesis (see figure 9.1).

One way of thinking of the introduction is as a commercial for the article. The authors try to sell you on the importance of their research. They may try to sell you on their study by claiming that, relative to previous research ("our competitor's brands"),

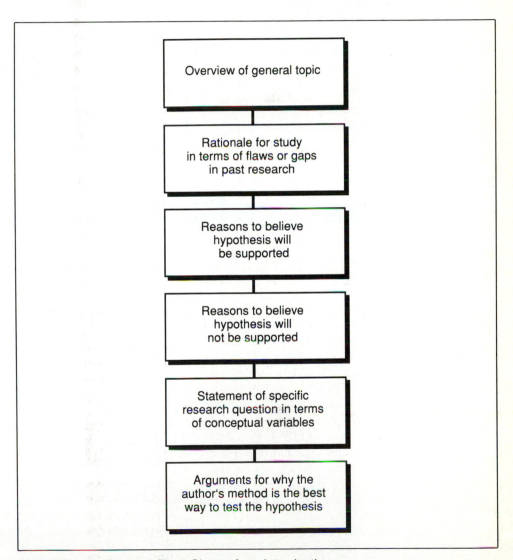

FIGURE 9.1: General Flow Chart of an Introduction

their methodology is "clearly superior" because it has a "better formula." "Better formulas" usually mean a better measure, a better manipulation, better control groups, or a more powerful design.

Alternatively, they may try to sell you on their study by telling you that, relative to previous hypotheses, their hypothesis is "new and improved." They will try to get you to say "It's incredible that people have done all this other, related research, but not tested this hypothesis! Why didn't anyone else think of this?" Generally, they are trying to excite you about a study that extends existing research by

1. Using a different sample than previous research (women versus men);
2. Looking at a different behavior (gait instead of facial expression, gambling rather than bar-pressing);
3. Looking at a variable that might moderate or alter a previously discovered relationship;
4. Looking at cognitive or physiological variables that may mediate the relationship;
5. Testing a competing explanation for the effect; or
6. Attempting to reconcile studies that have produced apparently conflicting results.

A second way of looking at the introduction is as a preview to the rest of the article. The author starts by giving you a general overview of the research area. Next, the author gives the rationale for the study. Usually, the rationale is either that the research fills a gap in past research or that it fixes a flaw in past research. Then, the authors may explicitly state the research question in terms of conceptual variables. Finally, the authors may explain why their method for testing the hypothesis is the best way (see figure 9.1). For example, they may justify their choice of design, their choice of measures, and their choice of subjects. Consequently, if you understand the introduction, you should be able to anticipate what will be said in the rest of the article.

Unfortunately, understanding the introduction is not always easy. The main reason the introduction may be hard for you to understand is that the authors are not writing it with you in mind. Instead, they are writing it to other experts in the field. Their belief that the reader is an expert has two important consequences for how they write up their research. First, because they assume the reader is an expert in the field, they do not think they have to give in-depth descriptions of the published articles they discuss. In fact, authors often assume that just by mentioning the authors and the year of work (e.g., Miller & Smudgekins, 1956) the reader will instantly recall the essentials of that article. Second, because they assume the reader is an expert in the field, they do not think they have to define relevant concepts or theories.

Because you are not an expert in the field, the authors' failure to fully describe studies and define concepts may make it difficult to fully understand what they are trying to say. Fortunately, you can compensate for not having the background the authors think you have by doing two things. First, read the articles the authors refer to. Second, look up unfamiliar terms or theories in a psychological dictionary, advanced textbook, or other sources listed in table 9.3.

To encourage yourself to look up all relevant terms and theories, make a photocopy

TABLE 9.3 Deciphering Journal Articles

Even experts may need to read a journal article several times to fully understand it. One way to help discipline yourself and to show you are making progress is to photocopy the article. Next, highlight any terms or concepts you do not understand. That shows you what you do not understand (if you highlight the entire article, maybe you should find another article). Once you know what you do not understand, simply use one of the techniques tabled below to decipher those terms.

TO DECIPHER HIGHLIGHTED TERMS

Consult introductory psychology text
Consult advanced psychology text
Consult psychological dictionary
Consult professor
Consult general sources such as *Psychological Bulletin, Annual Review, American Psychologist, Psychological Science*
Consult other articles referenced in article

---

of your article. On this copy, use a yellow marker to highlight any terms or concepts you do not understand (Brewer, 1990). Then, do some background reading and reread the introduction. This time through the article, highlight any terms or concepts you do not understand with a pink magic marker. Do some more background reading to get a better understanding of those terms. Then, reread the introduction using a green marker to highlight terms you still do not understand.

By the third time you read the introduction, you should see much less green than yellow, visually demonstrating that you are making progress. However, even if you know all the individual terms, how do you know you understand the introduction? One test is to try to describe the logic behind the hypothesis in your own words. A more rigorous test is to design a study to test the hypothesis and then describe the impact of those results for current theory and further research.

To reiterate, do not simply skim the introduction and then move on to the method section. The first time through the introduction, ask yourself two questions: (1) What concepts do I need to look up? and (2) What references do I need to read?

Then, reread the introduction. Do not move on to the method section until you can answer the following questions:

1. What variables are they interested in?
2. What is the hypothesis involving these variables? (What is being studied?)
3. Why does the prediction make sense?
4. Why is the authors' study a reasonable way to test this hypothesis?
5. Does the study correct a weakness in previous research? If so, what was that weakness? Where did others go wrong?
6. Does the study fill a gap in previous research? If so, what was that gap? What did others overlook?

READING THE METHOD SECTION

After you are clear about what predictions are being made, why those predictions are being made, and why the study provides a good test of those predictions, read the method section. The method section describes the basic characteristics of the research participants, what was done to those participants, and what measures were used. More precisely, the method section is usually subdivided into at least three subsections: subjects, apparatus, and procedure. Some method sections will also describe the research design. For example, they often tell you whether the design was a between subjects design, a within subjects design (often referred to as a *repeated measures* design), or a mixed design.

The method section should be easy to understand for two reasons. First, the only thing the method section is trying to do is to tell you what happened in the experiment—who the subjects were, how many subjects there were, and how they were treated. Like a good recipe, the method section should give you enough information that you could repeat the study yourself.

Second, the method section should be easy to understand because the introduction should have foreshadowed how the author planned to test the hypothesis.[2] Therefore, the only trouble you may have in understanding a method section is if you are unfamiliar with some task (e.g., a Stroop task) or piece of equipment (e.g., tachistiscope) the researchers used. If you run into unfamiliar apparatus, look up that apparatus in the index of either an advanced text or a laboratory equipment catalog. If that fails, ask your professor. If you run into an unfamiliar measure, find a source that describes the measure in detail. Such a source should be referenced in the original article's bibliography. If it is not, look up the measure in the index of one or more texts. If that fails, look up the concept the measure is claiming to assess in *Psychological Abstracts*. The *Abstracts* should lead you to an article that will describe the measure.

After reading the method section, take a few minutes to think about what it would have been like to be a subject in each of the experiment's conditions. Then, think about what it would have been like to be the researcher.

Do not go on to the results section until you understand what happened well enough that you could act out the roles of both researcher and subject. More specifically, do not go on to the results section until you can answer the following questions:

1. Who were the subjects?
2. How were they obtained?
3. What was done to the subjects?
4. What tasks or actions did the subjects perform?
5. What was the design?

---

[2]We do not mean to say that all method sections are easy to read. We mean that authors *should* be able to write a clear, understandable method section. Unfortunately, authors sometimes do not write coherent method sections. So, if you do not understand a method section, it is probably not your fault. It is probably the fault of the author and editor.

READING THE RESULTS SECTION

Now, turn to the results section and find out what happened. At the beginning of the results section (if they did not do so in the method section), the authors will briefly explain how they got the numbers they analyzed. That is, they will describe how they scored subjects' responses. Often, these scores are fairly straightforward. For example, researchers may say, "The data were the number of correctly recalled words." Or, they may say, "The number of anagrams solved by each subject was divided by the total number of anagrams used in the study to obtain a percentage solved. These percentages were analyzed in a one-way ANOVA." Occasionally, computing a score for each subject involves a little more work. For example, in one study, researchers were looking at whether subjects believed a person to be normal or pathological (Hilton & von Hippel, 1990). To measure these beliefs, the researchers had subjects answer two questions. First, subjects answered either "yes" or "no" to a question about whether the person had a pathology. Then, researchers had subjects rate, on a 1–9 scale, how confident subjects were of their decision. How did the researchers turn these two responses into a single scale? "In creating this scale, a value of −1 was assigned to "no" responses and a value of +1 was assigned to "yes" responses. The confidence ratings were then multiplied by these numbers. All ratings were then converted to a positive scale by adding ten to the product. This transformation led to a scale in which "1" indicates a high degree of confidence that the person is normal and "19" represents a high degree of confidence that the person is pathological."

Do not merely glance at the brief section describing the scores to be used. If you do not understand what the numbers being analyzed represent, you will not be able to understand the results of analyses based on those numbers.

After explaining how they got the scores for each subject, the authors may explain how those scores were analyzed. For example, they may say "these data were subjected to a 2 (attractiveness) $\times$ 2 (type of crime) analysis of variance (ANOVA)." Of course, both the kind and the number of analyses will depend on the study. Depending on the study, the authors will usually report anywhere from one to four kinds of results.

Basic Descriptive Statistics

This section, which is often omitted, usually starts off by summarizing the sample's scores on one or more measures. Typically, they will describe the average score, the range of scores (or the standard deviation), and the degree to which the scores were normally distributed. For instance, they may report: "Overall, recall was fairly good ($M = 12.89$, $SD = 2.68$) and recall scores were normally distributed." Knowing the data are normally distributed is useful because many statistical tests, such as the t-test and ANOVA, assume data are normally distributed. If the data are not normally distributed, the researcher may perform some mathematical operation on the scores to get a more normal distribution (see figure 9.2). Occasionally, this transformation is relatively simple. For instance, rather than analyze how much *time* it took subjects to scan a word, a researcher may analyze the scanning *speed.* The time to speed transformation involves inverting the time scores.

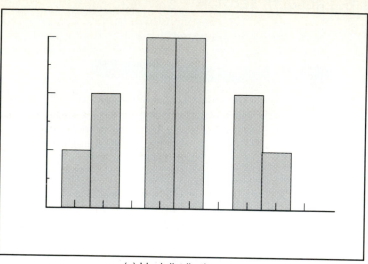

(a) Ideal distribution

Many statistical tests require that data be normally distributed like the data above. However, your data may not be so cooperative. For example, you might get data like the reaction time scores below.

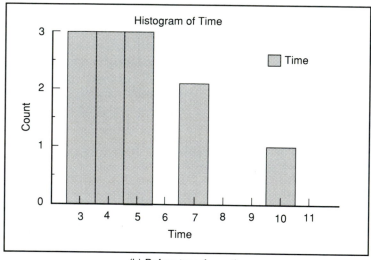

(b) Before transformation

Fortunately, such "non-normal" data can often be rescued by transforming the data. For example, the graph below represents the same data as in the graph above. The difference is that whereas the data above are reaction times, the data below are reaction speeds.

FIGURE 9.2: How Transforming Scores can Cause Scores to Become Normally Distributed

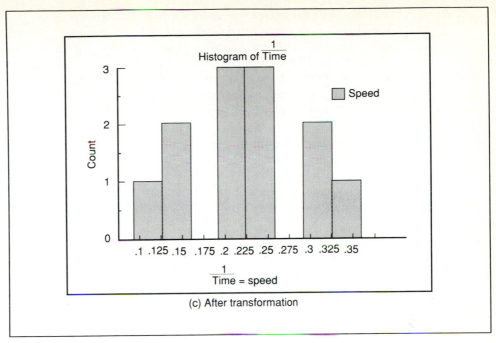

(c) After transformation

FIGURE 9.2: Continued

Thus, a scanning time of 1/2 second per word may become a speed of two words per second (2/1).

If a new measure is used, the authors may report evidence of the measure's reliability or internal consistency. For example, if a scale was very reliable, they might report that the scale had a "coefficient alpha of .91." Similarly, they may write "Interobserver reliability computed for overall stopwatch readings was .98" or "Inter-rater reliability was extremely high ($r = .98$)."

Results of the Manipulation Checks

The next section that may appear will report the results of the manipulation check. Usually, these results will be statistically significant and unsurprising. For example, if a study manipulates attractiveness of defendant, the researchers will probably report "Subjects rated the attractive defendant ($M = 6.2$ on a 1–7 scale) as more attractive than the unattractive defendant ($M = 1.8$), $F(1,44) = 11.56$, $p < 0.01$." Once they have shown you that they manipulated the factor they said they manipulated, they are ready to discuss the effects of that factor.

Results Relating to Hypotheses

The next findings the authors would discuss are the findings every author discusses—those that relate to the hypotheses. The authors try to clearly connect the results to the hypotheses so the reader can easily tell how the hypotheses fared. For example, if a hypothesis was that attractive defendants would receive lighter sentences than unattractive defendants, the author would report what the data said about this hypothesis: "The hypothesis that attractive defendants would receive lighter sentences was not supported. Attractive defendants received an average sentence of 6.1 years whereas the average sentence for the unattractive defendants was 6.2 years. This difference was not significant, $F(1,32) = 1.00$, n.s."

Other Significant Results

After reporting results relating to the hypotheses (whether or not the results are statistically significant), authors will dutifully report any other statistically significant results. Even if the results are unwanted and make no sense to the investigator, significant results must be reported. Therefore, you may read things like "There was an unanticipated interaction between attractiveness and type of crime. Unattractive defendants received heavier sentences for violent crimes whereas attractive defendants received heavier sentences for nonviolent crimes, $F(1,32) = 18.62$, $p < 0.05$." Or, you may read "There was also a significant four-way interaction between attractiveness of defendant, age of defendant, sex of subject, and type of crime. This interaction was uninterpretable." Typically, these results will be presented last. Although an author is obligated to report these unexpected and unwelcomed findings, an author is not obligated to emphasize them.

In conclusion, depending on the statistics involved, reading the results section may be difficult. The first time through you may not understand everything. However, you should be able to answer the following questions before moving on to the discussion section:

1. What are the scores they are putting into the analysis?
2. What are the average scores for the different groups? Which types of subjects score higher? Lower?
3. Do I understand all the tables and figures that contain descriptive statistics, such as tables of means, percentages, correlations, etc.?
4. Do the results appear to support the authors' hypotheses? Why or why not?
5. What type of statistical analysis did the authors use?

READING THE DISCUSSION

Finally, read the discussion. The discussion should hold few surprises. In fact, before reading the discussion, you could probably write a reasonable outline of it. All you would have to do is (1) jot down the main findings, (2) relate these findings to the introduction, and (3) speculate about the reasons for any surprising results.

Because many discussion sections follow this three-step formula, if the authors get the results they expect, the discussion is mostly a reiteration of the highlights of the introduction and results sections. If, on the other hand, the results are unexpected, the discussion section is usually an attempt to reconcile the introduction and results sections.

Thus, by the time you finish the discussion section, you should be able to answer these four questions:

1. How well do the authors think the results matched their predictions?
2. How do they explain any discrepancies between their results and their predictions?
3. Do the authors admit their study was flawed or limited in any way? If so, how?
4. What additional studies, if any, do the authors recommend?

REREAD THE ARTICLE LOOKING FOR WEAKNESSES

Now that you understand the ideas and arguments the authors are trying to sell, you are ready to challenge their claims. You are ready to apply what you have learned in the previous eight chapters (see table 9.4). Engage your powers of critical reasoning by thinking about how you would have studied the same problem. Once you are in a critical frame of mind, systematically scrutinize each section of the article starting with the introduction.

CRITIQUING THE INTRODUCTION

Read the introduction with the same skepticism you would read an advertisement—because the introduction is an ad. It is an unusual ad, but an ad nonetheless. Instead of using emotional appeals or endorsements from famous people, the introduction tries to get you to buy through using arguments that appear logical and by making the authors seem to be experts. Instead of trying to get you to buy hamburgers, the introduction is trying to get you to buy several ideas:

1. Testing the hypothesis is vital;
2. The hypothesis follows logically from theory and intuition;
3. The authors have found the perfect way to test the hypothesis.

You can question all of these notions. The first idea, that testing this particular hypothesis is vital, is certainly a matter of opinion. What one scientist feels is important, another may feel is worthless. Admittedly, scientists usually agree research that tests theory or builds on existing work is more important than research unrelated to previous work. However, even this rule has exceptions. If it did not, new research areas would never be pioneered.

The second notion, the hypothesis follows logically from theory or intuition, is slightly less open to interpretation. If you have become familiar with the theories, concepts, and articles the authors mention, you are now in a position to decide whether the authors' interpretation of these studies and theories is accurate.

The third notion, the authors have found the perfect way to test their hypothesis, is

TABLE 9.4   Lessons on Journal Reading from Previous Chapters

CHAPTER	LESSONS
1	Question every study's internal, construct, and external validities. Even the best of studies may not have internal, external, *and* construct validities. Science advances by verifying other people's findings and building on those findings.
2	More than one explanation may account for a set of results. Look for variables that may moderate or mediate a relationship.
3	There is often a gap between the conceptual variables one tries to measure and operational definitions. Evaluate the measure's validity, reliability, sensitivity, reactivity, and scales of measurement. Researchers make tradeoffs between these different characteristics.
4	Question cause-effect statements. Factors that may promote internal validity may hurt external validity.
5	People may misinterpret nonsignificant results. Nonsignificant results are inconclusive. With more power, statistical significance might have been achieved. Attempts to get power may hurt external and construct validities. Type 1 errors occasionally occur. If the data do not meet the assumptions of the statistical test, the statistical test will not be valid.
6	Confounding due to poor manipulations or inadequate control groups may make treatment effects hard to interpret. Using several levels of the treatment variable may reduce problems due to confounding and help determine the function relationship between variables. Multi-group experiments require post hoc tests to determine which means differ from one another. However, post hoc tests should only be done if the overall effect is statistically significant. Beware of people doing multiple statistical tests without correcting for the fact that their reported alpha level is only valid if they are doing only a single test. For example, if one does one hundred t-tests, five could turn out significant by chance alone.
7	You can use a factorial design to see whether other factors moderate an observed relationship. Ceiling and floor effects can obscure relationships.
8	The right design may increase a study's power and generalizability. Between subjects designs have less power but are not vulnerable to order effects and are applicable when subjects tend to receive one, but not both, levels of the treatment. Within subjects designs can be vulnerable to order effects. Appropriate counterbalancing may control for order effects.

definitely open to question. Because measures are not perfect and executing a study involves making a series of decisions, all of which involve tradeoffs, no study is perfect.

In short, when reading the introduction, a healthy dose of skepticism is vital. Specifically, you should ask the following questions:

1. Are the studies the authors cite as limited and flawed as the authors claim?
2. Do the predictions really follow from theory or previous research? Could the same research or theory be used to make the opposite prediction?
3. Would another theory make the same predictions?

4. Will the study provide a good test of these predictions?
5. Are the reasons for choosing the measure clear and convincing?
6. How could you use a different approach to test the same hypothesis?

When you get to the method section, you can begin your critiquing in earnest. The method section gives you enough specific information so that you can critique the study's construct, external, and internal validity.

CRITIQUING THE SUBJECTS SECTION

You can begin your critique by looking at the subjects section. The subjects section gives clues as to the study's internal validity, power, external validity, and construct validity.

Looking for Internal Validity Problems

The study's internal validity should be questioned if

1. The subjects were not randomly assigned or there are other reasons to suspect the different groups of subjects were not equivalent before the study began;
2. Subjects' responses were not independent, as would be the case if subjects were able to influence one another's responses or if the treatment group subjects were tested in one session and the control group in a second session; or
3. Mortality was a problem—many more subjects dropped out of the experimental group than the control group.

Looking for Problems with Power

The subjects section may also tip you off to a problem with the study's power. If there were not enough subjects per condition, the researchers might be unable to find an effect. For example, assume the researchers are studying a medium-sized effect. If they have a two-group experiment that uses twenty subjects per group, their chances of establishing that this effect is statistically significant is only one in three. Even with thirty subjects per group, their chances of discovering the effect is less than fifty-fifty (Cohen, 1990).

Not only could you determine whether there were enough subjects, but you also could determine whether the subjects were sufficiently homogeneous. If the subjects are very different from each other, power will be low. Even large differences between groups of subjects may not be regarded as due to treatment effects but rather as due to random differences between subjects.

Looking for External Validity Problems

The subjects section can also alert you to problems with the study's external validity. Specifically, looking at the subjects section should prompt you to ask "Would the results have been the same if a different population of subjects had been studied?" To address this question, start by asking two others. First, ask yourself "Do the subjects represent a unique or unusual population?" For example, the results from a study using an unusual population—such as rats, drug addicts, or people responding to a newspaper ad—may not hold for the general population. Second, ask yourself if the subjects fail to represent some segment of the population. That is, "Are the subjects too homogeneous?" For instance, do they only represent white males between the ages of eighteen and nineteen who go to elite colleges? Then, ask the key question "Do the subjects fail to represent some group for whom I believe the results would not hold?" To emphasize the importance of this last question, suppose the "attractive defendant" study had used only male subjects. If you point out women were not included, that might raise a question about the study's external validity. However, your concerns about the study's external validity would carry much more weight if you had specific reasons for why the results would not hold for female subjects.[3]

Clearly, it is important to look at the kinds of subjects who were recruited into the study. However, do not focus exclusively on the kinds of subjects the researchers recruited. Also, look at which participants stayed in and which dropped out. If mortality is high, the results may apply only to a very narrow population—those who stayed in the study.

Looking for Construct Validity Problems

Finally, the subjects section may even provide some clues about potential threats to the study's construct validity. If, for example, rather than being naive, subjects are junior and senior psychology majors, you might worry that the subjects may have figured out the hypothesis. Similarly, if the study was run over a period of months at a very small school, you might be concerned that the research hypothesis spread across the campus.

CRITIQUING THE PROCEDURE SECTION

Although the subjects section may give you some clues about the study's validity, the procedure section provides you with even more information about the study's potential weaknesses. The procedure section is an especially useful source of information about the study's construct validity.

Looking for Construct Validity Problems

Start by thinking about whether the results might be due to subjects guessing the hypothesis and then playing along with it. Imagine being a researcher and ask yourself how you might have unintentionally influenced subjects or tipped them off to the hypothesis. Next, pretend to be a subject, and ask yourself whether you could have guessed the hypothesis. Then, ask yourself these specific questions:

[3]Concerns about external validity also carry more weight if you show why external validity is important. In some cases, as Mook (1983) has shown, external validity is irrelevant or unnecessary. That is, in some cases, generalizing to another subject population is not important. For example, in the famous Harlowe monkey experiments, Harlowe's goal was not to generalize his results to say human babies reared with a wire mother would do better than human babies reared with cloth mothers.

1. Was the hypothesis an easy one to figure out? That is, was it simple and intuitive?
2. Did the study have **research realism**: was the task interesting enough that subjects were psychologically engaged in the task, rather than merely playing the role of research subject?
3. Was an empty control group (a group that got no treatment at all, not even a placebo treatment) used? Subjects in such a group might guess they were in the control group.
4. Were double-blind procedures used? If the experimenter is not blind to knowing what condition the subject is in, then the experimenter might overtly or covertly influence the subject to behave in a manner that supports the hypothesis.
5. Was the study standardized to avoid researcher bias?
6. Was the dependent measure an obtrusive or an unobtrusive measure? If the subject is unaware of the behavior being recorded, the subject probably will not fake the behavior.
7. Was the dependent measure a self-report question or did it require subjects to engage in a public behavior? Subjects may be less likely to play along with the hypothesis when it involves changing their behavior than when it involves making a mark on an anonymous rating scale.
8. Were subjects exposed to pretesting, several levels of treatment, or any other factor that would make them aware of the hypothesis?
9. Were subjects debriefed and asked not to tell other people about the study?
10. Was there any attempt to find out what subjects were thinking when they were in the experiment? For example, subjects could be probed during debriefing about what they thought the hypothesis was, what they thought when they encountered the manipulation, and what they thought when they encountered the dependent measure.
11. Was a cover story used so subjects would not guess the researchers' hypothesis? If you were a subject, would you find the cover story convincing?

Next, question the treatment's construct validity. Remember, no manipulation is perfect. Ideally, the authors would have (1) given a good rationale for their manipulation in the introduction—this rationale might include demonstrating how the manipulation follows from theory and citations demonstrating the manipulation had been used in other studies—and (2) performed a manipulation check or questioned subjects about how the subjects interpreted the manipulation.

Even if the authors provided this information, you should still look for weaknesses in the measure. One way to find weaknesses in a manipulation is to imagine you are a subject and think about how you might misinterpret a manipulation. For example, if you were reading a study about the effects of defendant attractiveness, put yourself in the subject's place. By looking at the photos of the defendants, you may find that you would have perceived the attractive defendants as better dressed and more affluent than the unattractive defendants. Thus, the "attractiveness" manipulation might really be a status manipulation. Or, you might find that the unattractive defendants seem bigger and stronger than the attractive defendants.

When thinking about the validity of a manipulation, do not overlook the control condition. Often, the weakness of the manipulation is in the control conditions. Either there are too few control groups or the groups are inadequate, as in the case of an empty control group. Playing the role of subject will help you spot these inadequate control groups. For instance, suppose the researchers used a photo of an attractive person in the attractive conditions, but used a no-photo condition as their control group. By playing the role of subject, you would immediately be aware that the results might not be due to level of attractiveness but to the presence or absence of attractiveness information. That is, merely knowing what the defendant looks like—regardless of whether the defendant is attractive or unattractive—might reduce the length of sentence imposed.

Pretending to be a subject might be even more helpful when questioning the dependent measure's validity. Think about what factors would influence your response on your measure. If the authors argue the length of sentence is a measure of forgiveness, think about what things other than forgiveness might lead you to give a very short or a very long sentence. For example, subjects might give lenient sentences because they are uncertain about the defendant's guilt, they do not want the defendant to appeal the sentence, or they think the defendant is too frail to survive a long sentence.

Pretending to be a subject should allow you to detect certain flaws in the measure. For example, you will probably think of problems with measures that rely on recall or self-report. In addition, you may realize that a measure does not tap certain aspects of the construct.

To fully evaluate the measure, however, you need more information. The authors should give you a rationale for why their measure is the best to use. This rationale may include citing studies that show the measure

1. correlates with other measures of that construct,
2. does not correlate with measures of unrelated constructs,
3. is reliable,
4. can be scored relatively objectively (high interobserver correlations),
5. is commonly used in research, and
6. follows from the definition of the construct.

If the studies cited indicate the measure has low reliability or validity, you should question the measure's validity. If the authors fail to cite evidence for the measure, you should do a literature search to determine what evidence exists that either supports or refutes the measure's validity.

Looking for External Validity Problems

As you have seen, examining the procedure section can give you insight into potential problems with the study's construct validity. In addition, questioning the procedure can help you uncover any problems about the study's external validity. One question to ask is whether the study is high on **mundane realism**: that is, are the tasks similar to what would be done in real life? However, realize many studies that lack mundane realism have tremendous external validity (Banaji & Crowder, 1989). The more important question is whether the research setting differs from real life in *specific* ways you believe will cause the results not to hold in real life. That is, you are able to postulate an interaction between the treatment and some real-life variable that was not included in the study. In essence, you are asking whether the results would hold if other factors had been varied. For example, you might have a reason to expect the results of a brief laboratory study would not hold for a long trial. Specifically, you might hypothesize that during a long trial jurors would focus much more attention on the attractive defendant than on the less attractive defendant. Because subjects spend more time thinking about the attractive defendant and her crimes, they may be more likely to give her a heavy sentence.

In addition to thinking about whether the results would generalize to situations where other factors were present, you also might consider whether the results would generalize to different levels of the treatment. For example, if the authors used two levels of an independent variable (e.g., very attractive/very unattractive), you might wonder whether a defendant who was extremely attractive would fare better than a defendant who was slightly above average.

Looking for Internal Validity Problems

Looking at the procedure section can also help you in critiquing a study's internal validity. For instance, the procedure section could show you subjects' responses were not independent. Similarly, the procedure section could show you whether the researchers had appropriately dealt with extraneous variables. That is, you could tell whether the researchers had controlled for variables that, if left uncontrolled, might lead to falsely concluding the independent variable had an effect. Basically, extraneous variables should be dealt with in one of three ways: (1) keeping those factors constant, (2) allowing random assignment to balance those factors out, or (3) counterbalancing those factors.

For example, you might find all the experimental group subjects were tested by one researcher, in a certain room, at a certain time of day, but all the control group subjects were tested by a different researcher, in a different room, at a different time of day. Failure to deal with extraneous factors is almost the norm when amateur scientists do research. For instance, several years ago, some studies "showed" that people preferred Pepsi to Coke, whereas other studies "showed" that people preferred Coke to Pepsi. The discrepancy was due to two uncontrolled variables. First, in some studies, Pepsi was *always* on the subject's right. Thus, people may have been showing a preference for things on their right. Second, in some studies, Coke was *always* labeled "L" and the Pepsi cup was always labeled "M." Thus, subjects may have been showing their preference for the letter "L" over "M" rather than their preference for Pepsi over Coke. Clearly, randomization or counterbalancing could have helped the internal validity of these studies.

Looking for Problems with Power

Lastly, the procedure section may hint at some problems with the study's power. Start by considering whether the procedures seem sufficiently standardized. Each time researchers run a control subject, they should follow the same exact procedures. Each time they run an experimental condition, they should follow the same exact procedures. To the extent that they do not, they will introduce random error into the study that may obscure a treatment effect. Therefore, try to decide whether the instructions are clear enough and whether they are specific enough.

Next, look at the manipulation. Is it strong enough to produce a moderately large effect or should the researchers have used more intense levels of the treatment? If the independent variable is manipulated via instructions, are the instructions clear? How likely is it the subject would misinterpret or ignore the instructions?

Finally, look at the measure. Is it sufficiently reliable? Was there much error due to random observer differences? Did the measure allow subjects to express a range of responses so subtle differences between subjects could be detected? Was the measure so indirect that it might be insensitive? For example, suppose a researcher wanted to know whether an ad made people feel more positive toward a product. To test this hypothesis, the researcher distributed advertising flyers to some randomly selected apartment complexes. However, instead of directly asking people about their attitudes, the researcher went through an apartment complex's trash to determine whether the residents seemed to be buying more of the advertised product. In this case, the researcher used an insensitive (and ethically questionable) measure.

CRITIQUING THE DESIGN SECTION

After critiquing the subjects and procedure sections, you may be finished with the method section. However, some method sections include a design section. Often, the design section gives you one last chance to critique how the study was conducted.

Generally, the design section gives you an opportunity to evaluate the study's internal validity. For example, if the researchers are trying to establish cause-effect without using an experimental design, be very skeptical.

In terms of construct validity, the main question to ask is whether they had sufficient control groups. That is, could the control groups rule out alternative explanations for a difference between the treatment group and the other groups? For example, suppose rats injected with an experimental drug run the maze faster than the control rats. With adequate control groups, you would know the only reason the experimental group ran faster was because of the drug. If, however, the control groups were inadequate, the experimental rats might be running the maze faster because they were the only ones getting a shot. That is, rather than being aroused by the drug, they were aroused by being held and stuck with a needle.

The most complex judgment you have to make about a design section is whether the researchers made the right decision in terms of using a between subjects design, a repeated measures (within subjects) design, or a mixed design (see table 9.5 and table 9.6). As we mentioned in chapter 8, within subjects designs usually have more power. Furthermore, if, in real life, people encounter more than one level of a certain factor, making that factor a within subjects variable may produce results that are more generalizable to real life.

However, within subjects designs are not without their problems. If the effect of an earlier treatment lingers to affect subjects' responses following a later treatment, the study's internal validity will suffer. That is, the researchers may mistakenly think the

TABLE 9.5 · What Can Go Wrong with a Between Subjects Experiment

False cause-effect statements	Not using random assignment Violation of independence Mortality (attrition) Type 1 errors
Insufficient power	Too few subjects Large individual differences between subjects Insensitive dependent measure Weak manipulation of independent variable
Lack of external validity	Used homogeneous subjects Used very simple, controlled testing environment Artificially high levels of treatment were used In real life, individuals are exposed to both levels of the treatment
Lack of construct validity	Used empty control group Task did not psychologically engage subjects Dependent measure vulnerable to subject biases
Analyses	Representing null results as proof there is no effect Representing differences between means as real even though results were not significant Doing a post hoc test even though the overall effect was not significant In a multiple-group experiment, specifying which groups differed without doing post hoc test to verify group differences In a multiple-group experiment, describing functional relationship without doing post hoc test trend analysis Failing to realize an ordinal interaction may simply be the result of a floor or ceiling effect Doing analyses when assumptions of test were violated—that is, doing an F- or T-test without having independent random assignment or without having at least interval scale data

second treatment has an effect when the subject is really responding to a carry-over effect of the first treatment. Furthermore, seeing different levels of the treatment variable and repeatedly doing the dependent measure task may sensitize subjects to the hypothesis. Consequently, within subjects designs may have poor construct validity. Finally, with complex within subjects designs, analysis becomes more complicated.

CRITIQUING THE RESULTS SECTION

After finishing with the method section, you are ready for the results section. When examining the results section, you will be looking primarily to see if the statistical conclusions are valid. Specifically, you will be asking

TABLE 9.6 What Can Go Wrong in a Within Subjects Design

False cause-effect statements	Not randomly assigning subjects to different orders, thereby allowing practice or fatigue effects to be mistaken for treatment effects Carry-over effects resulting in violation of independence Type 1 errors
Insufficient power	Insensitive measures Weak manipulation of treatment Strong order effects could obscure treatment effect
Lack of external validity	Used homogeneous subjects Used very simple, controlled testing environment Artificially high levels of treatment were used In real life, individuals are exposed to only one level of the treatment
Lack of construct validity	Sensitization occurred as a result of repeated exposure to the independent variable and the dependent measure task; sensitization is especially a problem when differences between treatment conditions are obvious as is the case when using "empty control" condition or subjects are exposed to many levels of the treatment Task did not psychologically engage subjects Dependent measure vulnerable to subject biases
Analyses	Representing null results as proving there is no effect Representing differences between means as real even though results were not significant In a multiple-condition experiment, specifying which conditions differed without doing specific tests (contrasts) to establish which conditions differ In a multiple-condition experiment, describing functional relationship without doing trend analysis Failing to realize an ordinal interaction may simply be the result of a floor or ceiling effect

1. Did the data meet the assumptions of their statistical tests?
2. Were Type 1 errors likely?
3. Were the right conditions being compared?
4. Were appropriate follow-up tests done?
5. Were the statistical tests done correctly?
6. Were the results of the tests interpreted correctly?
7. If the authors report a null result, were Type 2 errors likely?

Ironically, however, the first thing you may find out from the results section bears on the construct validity of the study's manipulations and measures. If observers gave subjects scores, the results section should report some measure of interobserver reliability. If the measure involves several scales, the authors should report some measure of the degree to which (1) the items within a scale are correlated and (2) the scales are correlated with each other. Finally, if a novel manipulation is used, you would hope the researcher gives you manipulation check data, allowing you to have some empirical reason to believe in the manipulation's validity. Some reviewers perceive the authors' failure to provide data about the manipulation or measure as a serious flaw (Fiske & Fogg, 1990).

Shortly before or after looking at the validity data, you may have an opportunity to learn about the nature and the distribution of the scores to be analyzed. The distribution of scores may inform you about two potential problems. First, you may be alerted to potential ceiling or floor effects. For example, if subjects were to recall 12 items and the mean recall was almost 12, then this ceiling effect would probably obscure any treatment effect. Thus, null results and ordinal interactions must be interpreted in light of either ceiling or floor effects. Second, the distribution of scores may indicate that certain statistical tests are inappropriate. For example, t-tests and analysis of variance assume the data are normally distributed. If the data do not approximate a normal distribution and the authors use relatively few subjects, their analyses might be more accurate if they mathematically transformed their data to make it more normal. Failing that, they should use a **"distribution-free" test**: a test that does not require that data be normally distributed.

In addition to looking at the distribution of the scores, you should also carefully consider the scores themselves. As you may recall from chapters 5 and 6, conventional wisdom says researchers should only do t-tests and ANOVA if they have interval or ratio scale data.[4] If, however, the researchers have ranked data (the highest score is "1," second highest is "2," etc.) or qualitative data ("1" = cautious, "2" = concerned, "3" = cooperative, "4" = competitive, and "5" = anxious), the researchers should not use a t-test or ANOVA. Put another way, if it does not make sense to take the mean of the scores, then the researchers cannot legitimately do a t-test or ANOVA on those scores.

In our example where different numbers stood for different categories, computing a mean makes no sense. How do you add "cautious" and "concerned" to get an average? It would be like assigning the number "1" to the category "Eskimo," the number "2" to the category "Caucasian–non-Hispanic," "3" to the category "African-American," "4" to the category "Hispanic," "5" to the category "American Indian" and then saying your average subject was a 2.4.

Similarly, if numbers represent ranks, computing the means would be a mistake. To illustrate, imagine we assign a "1" to the highest test score, a "2" to the second highest test score, etc. Then we average these ranks. For example, we average the highest score ("1") and the ninth highest ("9") to get a mean of "5." Then, we average the second and third highest scores, to get a mean rank of 2.5. However, we cannot legitimately say 2.5 is higher than 5. To understand why, imagine the distribution of test scores was as follows: 100, 50, 49, 48, 47, 46, 45, 44, 42. The average of the first and ninth scores would be 71 ([100 + 42]/2), whereas the average of the second and third scores would be 49.5.

---

[4] Conventions may be changing. Many statisticians now argue that scales of measurement should not dictate the choice of statistical test. That is, some statisticians argue that one can do ANOVA, Pearson r's, and even t-tests on nominal data. On the other side of the coin, some statisticians argue that not only do these tests require interval scale data but such tests require data that have been unquestionably proved to be interval. These statisticians argue that most psychological data have not been proved to be interval. Therefore, they argue that psychologists should not use ANOVA, Pearson r's, t-tests, etc. People holding either of these positions tend to feel strongly about their position. Consequently, if your professor disagrees with conventional wisdom, your professor will definitely let you know about the "right" position on this issue.

However, it could be the 2.5 really does represent a much higher score than the 5. For instance, suppose the scores were distributed as follows: 100, 99, 98, 48, 47, 46, 45, 44, 22. In this case, the average of the first and ninth scores would be 61 ([100 + 22]/2). However, the average of the second and third ranks would be 98.5. Thus, this time the mean rank of 2.5 is higher than the mean rank of 5. Note, however, if you had only the ranks, you would not know when 2.5 is higher than 5. In short, because a mean rank of 2.5 could be higher or lower than a mean rank of 5, taking the mean of ranked scores makes no sense (see table 9.7).

To assure you they did the right analysis, the authors will often justify why they did the analysis. If the data are clearly interval scale data and the analysis parallels the design, the authors may not give an extensive rationale for their analysis. Thus, if they used a matched pairs design and used a paired groups t-test, they may not explain their analysis. However, if their analysis is complex or not typical of the analyses published in that journal, the authors may cite textbooks or articles that claim the analysis is proper in this situation. Occasionally, the authors may cite other studies that have used the same analysis on similar data.

Why should the authors establish the analyses they reported were appropriate and relevant to their hypotheses? Primarily because doing the wrong analysis or doing too many analyses will increase the chance of Type 1 errors: a random pattern of results being declared statistically significant. For example, in a multiple-group study, using a series of t-tests rather than ANOVA would greatly increase the risk of a Type 1 error. Similarly, doing a post hoc analysis even though the overall effect was not significant will greatly increase the odds of declaring a chance difference significant. Some would also argue that declaring results significant even though they do not reach conventional levels of significance ("significant at the .07 level" or "significant at the .13 level") not only increases the odds of declaring a chance difference "significant" but also constitutes using an improper analysis.

You can easily catch authors who are running a high risk of making Type 1 errors by

TABLE 9.7 Type of Data Dictates Type of Statistic that Should Be Used			
SCALE OF MEASUREMENT	EXAMPLE	SUMMARY STATISTIC (AVERAGE)	TYPICAL STATISTICAL ANALYSIS
Nominal	When numbers represent categories, such as 1 = Democrat, 2 = Republican, 3 = independent	Mode (most common score) or simply describe percentage of subjects in each category	Chi-Square
Ordinal	Ranks	Median (middle score)	Mann-Whitney "U" test, Kruskal-Wallis, Friedman test
Interval	Rating scales	Mean	t-test, ANOVA
Ratio	Height, magnitude estimation	Mean	t-test, ANOVA

using improper analyses or unconventionally lenient significance levels. But how can you determine when the authors are using too many statistical tests? It is hard to say for certain, but there are two questions you can ask. First, are they performing tests that seem to have little to do with their predictions?[5] If they are, this suggests they are "going on a fishing expedition" by casting a wide net out across the sea of results, having a good chance of catching something by blind luck. Second, are they performing many statistical tests? If so, realize about five out of one hundred tests (1/20) should be significant by chance alone. In short, if you read an article where it looks like the authors looked at around 100 correlations and they only point to the four that were statistically significant at the $p < .05$ level, suspect a Type 1 error.

Once you are comfortable with the general analyses being used, you then should be sure the correct comparisons are being made. At the very least, the statistical tests being performed should correspond to the predictions made in the introduction. Thus, if the hypothesis is group A will score higher than group B, the test should directly compare group A against group B. Unfortunately, sometimes authors will not report such a comparison. Instead, they will report (1) group A was significantly greater than some value; (2) group B was not significantly greater than that value; (3) therefore, group A was significantly greater than group B.

Do not accept these indirect comparisons. If group A is supposed to be bigger than group B, insist on a direct comparison between group A and group B.

Sometimes, the reason the authors are verbally describing a comparison they did not actually make is they failed to do the appropriate contrasts or post hoc tests. For instance, they may do a five-group experiment and find a significant effect. On that basis, they conclude group 1's scores are significantly higher than group 3's scores. Remember, they cannot make that statement unless they directly compared group 1 to group 3. If they had predicted a difference between groups 1 and 3 before the study began, they could report the results of a "planned comparison" between the two groups. If, however, they did not have a specific prediction regarding groups 1 and 3, they should report the results of a post hoc test that directly compared group 1 with group 3. Similarly, if they report the shape of the functional relationship between the variables (linear, quadratic, etc.), they should have done a trend analysis to directly test their assertion the data followed a linear or quadratic trend. Finally, the authors may interpret a statistical interaction for you without statistically testing their claims. For example, they may say the interaction was due to scores being very different in one condition. However, to make this statement they should verify this by comparing that condition against the other groups. If they predicted that group to be vastly different from the other groups, they could do a planned comparison. If, on the other hand, they did not expect the interaction, they should do a post hoc test to see if the condition differs significantly from the other groups. For the same reasons, if the authors say "The interaction was due to the memory manipulation only having an effect in the low arousal condition," they should test that claim. Specifically, they are claiming (1) the simple main effect for memory in the low-arousal condition is significant and (2) the simple main effect for memory in the high-arousal

[5]Be especially concerned if their method section indicates they measured many variables but only report analyses incorporating a handful of these variables.

condition is not significant. Clearly, such claims would be more convincing if they had actually tested the two simple main effects.

If the authors reported the proper follow-up tests, the next question is whether they performed those tests correctly. Usually, it will be difficult to determine whether they made a calculation error. However, there are three basic clues you can look for.

First, do their analyses appear to conflict with the descriptive statistics? For example, suppose the group means for one variable are all the same, but the results are statistically significant. For a second variable, on the other hand, the groups are not statistically significant even though the group means differ greatly. In this case, you might suspect the authors have mislabeled their variables.

Second, determine whether the degrees of freedom make sense. You know that if they used forty subjects in a between subjects design, their total degrees of freedom should be 39. If there are three levels of a variable, the degrees of freedom for that variable should be 2. Any deviation from these patterns should alert you to a problem.

Third, you can be on the alert for values that rarely or never occur. For example, a negative F or a correlation of $+3.0$ signal a serious problem.

Once it appears the appropriate tests have been done correctly, your final task is to determine the tests have been properly interpreted. Often, this simply involves looking at the means to verify a significant effect was in the direction the authors thought it was. For example, beginning researchers may assume significant treatment effects indicate the results supported their hypothesis; i.e., that the treatment improved performance. However, significant results could indicate the treatment **hurt** performance. Even experienced researchers may occasionally misinterpret a significant main effect. For instance, if authors misremember how their treatment levels or measures were scored, they may conclude that a treatment increased performance when it actually decreased performance.

You may also want to be sure the authors did not mistake an F- or a t-value for a p-value. We have seen very bright beginning researchers believe they had a significant effect because t was nearly zero. They are distressed to learn that a t of zero does not indicate their results are very unlikely to be due to chance. On the contrary, such a t indicates the results could very easily be due to chance and thus carry a very large p-value. (Remember, p indicates the probability the researcher could get those results even if the variables were not related. Thus, the larger the p-value, the less likely the variables are related.)

A more common problem is interpreting significant interactions. Beginning authors mistakenly may talk about an interaction as though it were a main effect. For instance, they may say the interaction between attractiveness and crime severity is due to the fact attractive defendants received more lenient sentences than less attractive defendants. One way to avoid being confused by interactions is to keep your eyes on the relevant means.

Even when the authors keep track of the relevant means, they may misinterpret significant interactions. Specifically, they may misinterpret ordinal interactions. They may fail to realize such interactions may be due to the scale of measurement being ordinal rather than interval. As we mentioned in chapter 7, ordinal interactions may be artifacts of ceiling or floor effects. Thus, before accepting the authors' interpretation of an ordinal interaction, look at the distribution of scores and entertain the possibility that the interaction is simply an artifact of having ordinal scale data.

Although significant effects are occasionally misinterpreted, the most frequently misinterpreted results are nonsignificant or null results. As you know, nonsignificant results are inconclusive. However, some authors will merrily discuss nonsignificant differences between the means as though the differences were real, but merely not significant. Other authors may argue that the null results indicate the treatment has absolutely no effect. However, you realize the null hypothesis cannot be proved. Therefore, before entertaining the possibility that null results indicate the treatment has either no effect or a small effect, determine whether the null results might be due to a ceiling or floor effect. Then, question the study's power. See if the authors did a power analysis of their study. Determine the size of the difference between the conditions. Is this difference large enough that it would have been significant with a more powerful design? Then, go back to the method section and find out whether:

1. The different conditions were different enough on the independent variable
2. The dependent measure was as sensitive as it could have been
3. The study was sufficiently standardized
4. Enough subjects were used (at least 64 per group)[6]
5. The subjects were homogeneous enough that random individual differences would not have obscured a genuine effect
6. The most sensitive design was used
7. The length of time between treatment and measurement was short enough so that the effect of the treatment would not wear off by the time the effect was being measured

CRITIQUING THE DISCUSSION

In rereading the discussion, be very careful. You must be careful because in the discussion section—unlike in the method and results sections—the authors are allowed to speculate. Consequently, it is sometimes hard to distinguish between fact and speculation.

Are the Conclusions Warranted by the Data?

One of the first things to check is whether the authors have accurately described the results. Sometimes, authors blatantly state conclusions that are not warranted by data. Therefore, comparing the discussion section with the results section will often lead you to find some interesting discrepancies. For example, you may discover a finding that was reported as "not statistically significant" in the results section is discussed as though it were significant in the discussion section. Similarly, the authors may act as though their hypotheses were overwhelmingly supported when only a few of the results support their hypotheses. That is, they may ignore the findings that failed to support their hypotheses. Occasionally, in an article reporting multiple studies, authors may fail to discuss the fact that whereas one study supported a certain hypothesis, the other did not.

[6]According to Cohen (1990).

Although discussion sections that contradict results sections are more common than you might think, an even more common problem is discussion sections that discuss analyses that were not reported in the results section. For example, the authors may say group 1 performed better than group 3, even though the results section has no mention of any test comparing group 1 against group 3. Or, they may claim the correlation between intelligence and school achievement was higher than the correlation between intelligence and social skills, but they never reported any analysis comparing the two correlations. Because authors sometimes make claims that are not substantiated, do not leave the discussion section before making sure all comparisons discussed in the discussion section correspond with statistical comparisons reported in the results section.

Are There Alternative Explanations?

Even if the data do support the conclusions, the data may also support other conclusions. Therefore, ask yourself "Is the authors' way the only way to interpret the results?" Usually, you will find two basic kinds of alternative explanations: (1) explanations due to statistical/methodological problems and (2) explanations due to competing theories or hypotheses.

Clearly, you should be able to develop alternative explanations when authors make cause-effect statements *without* using an experimental design. As you know from chapters 1, 2, 4, 5, and 7, merely because two factors are related, we cannot presume the first factor causes the second. Thus, finding a relationship between income and happiness is not sufficient grounds for saying money causes happiness. It may be that higher income people make more money because they are happier. That is, happiness could lead to better productivity or increased popularity, either of which could translate into being promoted into better paying jobs. Alternatively, happiness and income may not affect each other. For instance, some other factor, such as education, may cause both happiness (due to fully developing one's intellectual development) as well as increased earnings.

Almost as easy to catch as careless cause-effect statements are statements that appear to accept the null hypothesis. For example, the authors might report the "treatment had no effect." As we have already mentioned in chapter 5, you can only reject or fail to reject the null hypothesis; you cannot accept the null hypothesis. You cannot accept it because null (nonsignificant) results may simply reflect a lack of power (see table 9.8). If the study had used a more sensitive measure, more subjects, more homogeneous subjects, different levels of the treatment, a more powerful design, or more standardized procedures, the results might have been statistically significant. That is, null results may simply reflect a lack of power. Therefore, if the authors discuss null results, check to see if the authors report any data about their design's power. For instance, do they report their probability of making a Type 2 error? In addition, as you saw from chapters 3 and 7, a nonsignificant result may be due to a ceiling or floor effect. Therefore, if the authors discuss a null result, check the results section to see if there is any evidence of a ceiling or floor effect.

Just as Type 2 errors make it very risky to discuss the absence of a relationship, Type 1 errors make it somewhat risky to discuss the presence of a relationship. Fortunately, most of the time a relationship is reported, it exists. However, you should always entertain the possibility that a reported relationship may be the result of a Type 1 error. Realize this possibility is greatest when the researchers (1) are discussing relationships that are signifi-

TABLE 9.8	Possible Reasons for Not Getting a Statistically Significant Result

1. Not enough subjects
2. Subjects were too heterogeneous
3. A within subjects design should have been used rather than a between subjects design
4. A more sensitive measure should have been used to examine the measure's reliability, ability to produce a range of scores, vulnerability to floor and ceiling effects and "directness": number and riskiness of inferences involved
5. Too weak a manipulation or poor choice of levels
6. Lack of standardization and lack of control over testing environment created too much error variance

cant at a level less stringent than .05, such as .07 or .20; (2) have done many statistical tests even though they appeared to have very few hypotheses; or (3) are reporting a finding that conflicts with existing literature.

As you have seen, it is relatively easy to discover alternative possibilities for cause-effect statements. But, whereas it is easy to challenge a study's internal validity, it is more difficult to challenge a study's construct validity. This is unfortunate because, as you learned in chapters 1 and 3, establishing construct validity is extremely difficult.

To assess the degree to which the study really manipulated and assessed the variables it claimed to assess, there are four things you can do. First, go back to the introduction and see if their rationale for their choice of measures was clear and convincing. In addition, scan the method and results sections to see if the authors provide any statistical evidence of the measure's validity, reliability, and objectivity. Second, go to the method section and try to determine how likely it would be the results might be due to subjects playing along with the hypothesis. Consider the naivete of the subjects, whether the design would lead to sensitization, the quality of the control conditions, the degree to which procedures were standardized, how involving the task was, and how vulnerable the measure was to social desirability and reactivity biases. Third, in the method section, look at the difference between the different conditions. Is there only one difference between the experimental and the control condition? Are there enough control groups? Fourth, look at the results sections to see if the authors performed a manipulation check. Did the manipulation strongly affect what it should have? Did it fail to affect irrelevant measures? For example, the "attractive" defendants should be rated as more attractive than the "low-attractiveness" defendants, but they should not be rated as wealthier.

In addition to methodological/statistical explanations for the findings, competing theories or hypotheses may be able to explain the relationship. For example, memory failures may be due to encoding, storage, or retrieval problems. Slips of the tongue may be due to interference, attention problems, or unconscious desires (Freudian slips). The serial position effect may be due to having a short-term memory and a long-term memory or due to interference. The fact that women tend to prefer wealthy men could be explained by evolutionary theory or by social learning theory. Many of the predictions derived from information-processing theory could also be derived from classical memory theory. Therefore, whenever the authors argue that their explanation is the only one that can account for the results, play devil's advocate. Think of another explanation for their results. In considering other possibilities, you may find yourself thinking of a study that will allow the data to decide between "their" explanation and "your" alternative explanation.

After vigorously debating what the authors said, turn your attention to what the authors failed to say. Authors are most likely to fail to say one of two things: (1) to properly qualify their results or (2) to interpret complex or conflicting findings.

Because no study is perfect, the results of any study should be qualified. In some cases, the authors' results may be limited because of questionable external validity. That is, they may have used an unusual subject population. In most cases, the authors should mention some limits to their study's construct validity. For example, since few measures are perfect, the authors should probably advocate replicating the study using different measures.

In addition to looking at whether the authors fully explain the limitations of their study, you should determine whether they fully explain their findings. The most serious omissions are when the authors do not explain findings that are either inconsistent with previous literature or inconsistent with their original hypothesis. It is unfortunate when researchers do not tie their findings in with previous research, because science is a cumulative enterprise. That is, science does not advance because of one individual working in isolation but because scientists build on one another's work. It is unfortunate when authors disregard results that are inconsistent with their explanation for the findings because science's strength is looking at all good data. Therefore, when reading the authors' explanation for their "main" findings, ask yourself (1) What significant results are they not discussing? and (2) If this explanation is true, what other results should they have obtained? Did they obtain those results?

Finally, turn your attention to results the authors admitted they were unable to explain. For example, suppose the authors could not explain why attractive defendants got stiffer penalties for minor crimes. You might say that for the minor crimes used in the study (e.g., prostitution, embezzlement), subjects might be likely to believe an attractive person committed these crimes. However, subjects might doubt whether an ugly person could pull these crimes off. Then, try to develop a study to test your explanation. (For a summary of questions to ask when critiquing a study, see box 9.1.)

DEVELOPING RESEARCH IDEAS FROM EXISTING RESEARCH

As you can see, any study can be questioned. To document or destroy a study's findings, additional studies must be done. Thus, familiarity with research breeds more research.

THE DIRECT REPLICATION

Whenever you read a study, one obvious research idea always comes to mind: repeat the study. That is, do a direct replication.

BOX 9.1   Questions to Ask of a Study

Questions about Construct Validity

1. Was the manipulation valid?
2. Was the measure valid?
3. Did the subjects play along with the hypothesis?
   a. Did the experiment lack experimental realism?
   b. Was an empty control group used?
   c. Did the researcher fail to make the study a double-blind study?
   d. Did the lack of standardization make it easy for researchers to bias the results?
   e. Was the dependent measure too obtrusive?
   f. Was the dependent measure a rating scale measure?
   g. Were any procedures used that might sensitize subjects to the hypothesis (matching on dependent variable, a within subjects design, etc.)?
   h. Was a cover story used?
   i. Could subjects have learned about the study from former subjects?

Questions about External Validity

1. Would results apply to the average person?
   a. Were subjects human?
   b. Are subjects distinct in any way?
   c. Is there any specific reason to suspect the results would not apply to a different group of subjects?
2. Would the results generalize to different settings?
   a. Was the study done in a lab?
   b. Did the study have mundane realism?
   c. Can you pinpoint a difference between the research setting and a real-life setting and give a specific reason why this difference should prevent the results from applying to real life?
3. Would the results generalize to different levels of the treatment variable?
   a. What levels of the treatment variable were included?
   b. What levels of the treatment variable were excluded?
   c. How many levels of the treatment variable were used?

Questions about Internal Validity

1. Was an experimental design used? If so, internal validity should not be a problem unless the following questions have negative answers:
   a. Was independence established and maintained?
   b. Was mortality a problem?
   c. If a within subjects design was used, did order effects pose a serious threat?

2. If a nonexperimental design was used, did the researchers account for history, maturation, mortality, instrumentation, testing, selection, selection by maturation interactions, and regression effects?

Questions about Power
1. If null results were obtained, ask:
   a. Were measures sensitive enough?
   b. Was the study sufficiently standardized?
   c. Were enough subjects used?
   d. Did conditions differ enough on treatment or predictor variable?
   e. Were subjects homogeneous enough?
   f. Was the design sensitive enough?
   g. Was the length of time between treatment and measurment of effect too long? Too short?

Clearly, one reason to do a direct replication is for educational purposes. Many professors—in chemistry, biology, physics, as well as in psychology—have their students repeat studies to help students develop research skills.

But, from a research standpoint, isn't repeating a study fruitless? Isn't it inevitable you will get the same results the author reported? Not necessarily. A direct replication may turn out differently than the original study either because the researchers made erroneous statements about the relationship between the variables or because the researchers' results have limited generalizability.

Changing Times: "You wouldn't find that today"

It is possible that the results of a study done in a different time would not generalize to today. Thus, because times have changed, the results of a 1932 study that examined the effects of race and sex of the defendant on jury verdicts may not hold today. Although psychologists believe certain classic findings will hold today, tomorrow, and forever, we have a duty to test this assumption.

Effects May Not Generalize to Different Locations: "Not in my town"

Similarly, you may get different results because the study's results do not generalize to your subjects. For example, a study done at a French university may turn out differently at your school.

Suspicion of Fraud

Until now, we have discussed reasons why the relationship between the variables would not generalize. This assumes, of course, there was such a relationship to begin with. Unfortunately, there are at least three reasons why the relationships reported in the original study may never have existed: fraud, Type 1 errors, and Type 2 errors.

Although fraud is very unusual, it does occur. Researchers may cheat for personal fame or simply because they believe their ideas are right even though their results fail to reach the .05 level of significance.

Because thousands of researchers want to be published and many are under great pressure to publish, why is cheating so uncommon? Because if other scientists cannot replicate your results, you are in trouble. Thus, the threat of direct replication keeps would-be cheats in line. However, some scientists are beginning to worry that science's fraud detectors are not as effective as they once were because people are not doing replications as often as they used to (Broad & Wade, 1982).

Suspicion of Type 1 Errors

Although fraud is one reason some findings in the literature are probably inaccurate (Broad & Wade, 1982), perhaps more common sources of nonreplicable findings are Type 1 and Type 2 errors. Partly because of psychologists' concerns about Type 1 and Type 2 errors, some journals solicit and accept studies that replicate—or fail to replicate—previously published research.

To understand how the original study's results may have been significant because of a Type 1 error, imagine you are a crusty journal editor who only allows simple experiments that are significant at the .05 level to be published in your journal. If you accept an article, the chances are less than five in one hundred the article will contain a Type 1 error. Thus, you are appropriately cautious. But, what happens once you publish one hundred articles? Then you may have published five articles that have Type 1 errors.

In fact, you may have many more Type I errors than that. How? Because people do not send you nonsignificant results. They may have done the same experiment eight different times, but it only came out significant the eighth time. Thus, they only send you the results of the eighth replication. Or, let us say twenty teams of investigators do the same experiment, only the team that gets significant results (the team with the Type 1 error) will submit their study to your journal. For example, while serving as editor for the *Journal of Personality and Social Psychology*, Dr. Anthony Greenwald received an article that found a significant effect for ESP. Because Dr. Greenwald was aware many other researchers had done ESP experiments that were not significant, he asked for a replication. The authors could not replicate their results.

Suspicion of Type 2 Errors

Just as studies that find significant effects may be victimized by Type 1 errors, studies that fail to find significant effects may be victimized by Type 2 errors. Indeed, there are reasons to expect Type 2 errors may be even more common than Type 1 errors. Realize, in a typical study, the chance of a Type 1 error is usually about 5 percent. However, in most studies, the chance of a Type 2 error is much higher. Dr. Cohen, a person who has championed planning studies with adequate power, suggests setting the chance of a Type 2 error about 20 percent. However, few researchers conduct studies that come close to having that much power. For example, Cohen (1990) reports that, even in some highly esteemed journals, the studies published are ones that ran more than a 50 percent chance of making a Type 2 error. Similarly, when reviewing the literature on the link between attributions and depression, Robins (1988) found only eight of eighty-seven published analyses had the level of power that Cohen recommends. No wonder some studies found relationships between attributions and depression whereas others did not! Thus, when a study fails to find a significant effect, do not assume that a direct replication would also fail to find a significant effect. The study may bear repeating (see table 9.9).

THE SYSTEMATIC REPLICATION

However, rather than merely repeating the study, you could do a systematic replication: a study that varies in some systematic way from the original study. Generally, systematic replications fall into two categories. First, the systematic replication refines the design or methodology of the previous study. For example, the systematic replication may use more subjects, more standardized procedures, or more objective methods of coding behavior than the original research. Second, the person doing the systematic replication may make different tradeoffs than the original researcher. That is, whereas the original researcher traded construct validity for power, the replicator may trade power for construct validity. Because you can always make different tradeoffs than the original researcher and because most sudies can be improved, you can almost always do a useful systematic replication.

In conclusion, there are two basic advantages of doing a systematic replication. First, because the systematic replication is similar to the original study, the systematic replication, like the direct replication, can help verify that the results reported by the original author would hold today. Second, because the systematic replication changes the original study in some way, the systematic replication may have more power, more external validity, or more construct validity than the original.

Improving Power by Tightening-up the Design

As we suggested earlier, if a study obtains null results, you may want to repeat the study, adding a few minor refinements to increase power (see table 9.10). You might improve power by increasing standardization. For example, you might have researchers follow a very detailed script or have instruments (such as a computer) present stimuli. You might improve power by using more subjects than the original study and choosing subjects who were more homogeneous than those used in the original study. Alternatively, you might increase power by using a more sensitive measure or by using more extreme levels of the treatment or predictor variable. Finally, you might replicate the experiment using a more sensitive design. For instance, if the authors used a simple experiment and found no effect

TABLE 9.9 Direct Replications: Why and How	
PURPOSE	**How**
To verify findings are not due to fraud, Type 1 errors, or Type 2 errors	Repeat any study
To establish study's external validity	Repeat a study done many years ago or repeat a study done in a foreign land

TABLE 9.10 How to Devise a Systematic Replication that Will Have More Power than the Original Study

1. Improve standization of procedures
2. Use more subjects
3. Use more homogeneous subjects
4. Use more extreme levels of treatment or predictor variable
5. Use more sensitive dependent measure
6. Use more powerful design (within or blocked design) rather than simple between groups design

for a mnemonic strategy on recall, you might replicate the experiment with a blocked design (blocking subjects by IQ) or with a repeated measures (within subjects) design.

Improving External Validity

If the study has adequate power, this power may come at the expense of other valued characteristics (see table 9.11), such as external validity. Note that many of the things you were doing to improve power reduce the generalizability of the results. If the researcher

TABLE 9.11 Tradeoffs Involving Power

Power versus construct validity	Using an empty control group, but not controlling for placebo effects.
	Using a sensitive measure despite its vulnerability to reactivity and/or self-report biases.
	Using a within subjects design despite serious sensitization problems.
	Using a matched design despite the fact matching alerts subjects to the hypothesis.
Power versus external validity	Using a restricted sample of subjects to reduce random error due to subject differences.
	Using a simple, controlled environment to reduce random error due to uncontrolled situational variables.
	Using a within subjects design even though in real life individuals rarely receive more than one level of the treatment.
	Maximizing the number of subjects per group by decreasing the number of groups. That is, choosing to do simple experiment rather than multilevel or factorial. Consequently, degree to which results generalize to various levels of treatment or across different factors is hard to assess.
Power versus internal validity	Using a within subjects design even when carry-over, fatigue, and practice effects are likely.
	Increasing risk of Type 1 error to increase power.

uses a homogeneous group of subjects to reduce power, the researcher may not be able to generalize the results to other kinds of subjects. What applies to this particular group of subjects (e.g., white, middle-class, first-year college students) may not apply to other groups of people (e.g., poor, uneducated, elderly).

If a study was done in a laboratory to reduce error variance, you do not know if the results would generalize outside of this artificial environment. If you measure the dependent variable immediately after the subject gets the treatment to maximize your chances of obtaining a significant effect, you do not know whether the treatment's effects will last.

To increase a study's generalizability, there are at least four things you can do (see table 9.12). First, you can systematically vary the kinds of subjects used. If the study used all male subjects, you might use all female subjects. Second, you can change a lab experiment into a field experiment. By moving the defendant study to the field you might be able to use real jurors as subjects rather than college students. Third, you can wait awhile before collecting the dependent measure to see whether the effects last. Fourth, you can use different levels of the independent variable to see whether the effects would generalize to different levels of the independent variable. In the defendant study, researchers only compared attractive versus unattractive defendants. Therefore, you might replicate the study to see whether extremely attractive defendants have an advantage over moderately attractive defendants.

Improving Construct Validity

Finally, you might do a systematic replication to improve a study's construct validity. Often, you can make some minor changes that will reduce the threat of hypothesis guessing (see table 9.13).

To illustrate, imagine a two-group experiment where one group gets caffeine (in a cola), whereas the other group gets nothing. You might want to replace this empty control group with a placebo treatment (a caffeine-free cola). Or, you might keep the empty control group, but add a treatment condition in which subjects get a very small amount of caffeine. This will give you three levels of the treatment variable. If both treatment conditions differ from the control group, but do not differ from one another, you might suspect that subject and experimenter expectancies were responsible for the treatment effect. Because of the advantage of using three levels of the treatment variable, you may wish to replicate a 2×2 study as a 3×2 or as a 3×3.

TABLE 9.12 How to Devise a Systematic Replication that Will Have More External Validity than the Original Study

1. Use more heterogeneous group of subjects or use a subject group (e.g., females) that was not represented in the original study
2. Repeat as a field study
3. Delay measurement of the dependent variable to see whether treatment effect persists over time
4. Use more levels of the independent or predictor variable

TABLE 9.13 How to Devise a Systematic Replication that Will Have More Construct Validity than the Original Study

1. Replace empty control group with placebo treatment group
2. Use more than two levels of the independent variable
3. Alter study so it is a double-blind study
4. Add or improve cover story
5. Replicate as a field study

Besides adding or improving levels of the independent variable, there are three other minor alterations you can do to make it harder for subjects to figure out the hypothesis. First, you could replicate the study as a double-blind experiment. Second, you could mislead the subjects regarding the purposes of the study by giving them a clever cover story. Third, you could do the study in the field: If subjects do not know they are in a study, they probably will not guess the hypothesis.

THE CONCEPTUAL REPLICATION

Suppose you think there were problems with the original study's construct validity. However, you believe these problems cannot be solved by making minor procedural changes. Then you should perform a **conceptual replication**: a study that is based on the original study but uses different methods to better assess the true relationships between the treatment and dependent variables. In a conceptual replication, you might use a different manipulation or a different measure.

Because there is no such thing as a perfect measure or manipulation, virtually every study's construct validity can be questioned. Because the validity of a finding is increased when the same basic result is found using other measures or manipulations, virtually any study can benefit from conceptual replication. Therefore, you should have little trouble finding a study you wish to conceptually replicate.

There are many ways to go about a conceptual replication (see table 9.14). One way is to use another way of manipulating the treatment variable. Remember, the more manipulations of a construct that find the same effect, the more confident we can be that the construct actually has that effect. Indeed, you might use two or three manipulations of your treatment variable and use the type of manipulation as a factor in your design. For instance, suppose a study used photos of a particular woman dressed in either a "masculine" or "feminine" manner to manipulate the variable "masculine versus feminine style." You might use the original experiment's photos for one set of conditions, but also add two other conditions that use your own photos. Then your statistical analysis would tell you whether your manipulation had a different impact than the original study's manipulation.

Of course, you are not limited to using the same type of manipulation as the original study. Thus, instead of manipulating "masculine" versus "feminine" by dress, you might manipulate "masculine" versus "feminine" by voice (masculine- versus feminine-sounding voice).

TABLE 9.14 How to Devise a Conceptual Replication that Will Have More Construct Validity than the Original Study

1. Use different manipulation of treatment variable and add manipulation check
2. Use different dependent measure
   a. More behavioral, therefore less vulnerable to demand characteristics, self-report biases, and social desirability biases
   b. Less obtrusive and thus less subject to reactivity biases

Although varying the treatment variable for variety's sake is worthwhile, changing the manipulation to make it better is even more worthwhile. One way of improving a treatment manipulation is to make it more consistent with the definition of the construct. Thus, in our previous example, you might feel the original picture manipulated "fashion sense" rather then "masculine/feminine style." Therefore, your manipulation might involve two photos: one photo of a woman who was fashionably dressed in a feminine way, one of a woman who was fashionably dressed in a masculine manner. You also might want a manipulation check to get more evidence as to the validity of the manipulation. Thus, you might ask subjects to rate the masculine and feminine photos in terms of attractiveness, fashion sense, and masculine-feminine.

Because no manipulation is perfect, replicating a study using a different treatment manipulation is valuable. Similarly, because no measure is perfect, replicating a study using a different measure is valuable. Often, you can increase the construct validity of a study by replicating it with a measure that is more behavioral or less obtrusive than the measure used in the original study. Such manipulations may be less vulnerable to demand characteristics and self-report biases.

THE VALUE OF REPLICATIONS

Replications are important to the advancement of psychology as a science. Direct replications are essential for guaranteeing that the science of psychology is rooted in solid, documented fact. Systematic replications are essential in making psychology a science that applies to all people. Conceptual replications are necessary for psychology to go beyond knowing about the effects of specific operations on specific measures to knowing about broad, universal constructs.

In addition to replicating previous research, systematic and conceptual replications extend previous research. Consider, for a moment, the conceptual replication that reveals that the original investigators were not measuring the constructs they thought they were measuring; the conceptual replication that uses more relevant behavior as the dependent variable; the systematic replication that shows the finding occurs in field settings or in other countries; the systematic replication that determines the duration of the effect; and the systematic replication of a simple study by using a multi-level experiment that illuminates the functional relationship between the treatment and dependent variables. Clearly, conceptual and systematic replications can transcend the original research.

EXTENDING RESEARCH

In addition to systematic and conceptual replications, there are two easy ways of extending published research. First, you could both replicate and extend research by repeating the original study while adding a variable you think might moderate the observed effect. For instance, if you think being attractive would hurt a defendant if the defendant had already been convicted of another crime, you might add the factor of whether or not the defendant had been previously convicted of a crime. Second, you could extend the research by doing the follow-up studies that the authors suggest in their discussion section or by doing studies based on the problems you found in the authors' discussion section. For a more extensive list of ways to extend research, see table 9.15.

In short, much of the work done by scientists is a reaction to reading other scientists' work. Sometimes, the reaction is excitement: the researcher thinks the other person is on

TABLE 9.15 Extending Research

1. Replicate the research but add a factor (subject or situational variable) that may moderate the effect. That is, pin down under what situations and for whom the effect is most powerful.
2. Conduct studies suggested by authors in their discussion section.
3. Look for variables that may mediate the relationship. That is, look for cognitive or physiological factors that may be the underlying causes for the effect.
4. Look for related treatments that might have similar effects. For example, if additional time to rehearse is assumed to improve memory by promoting the use of more effective rehearsal strategies, you might consider other variables that might promote the use of more sophisticated rehearsal strategies such as training in the use of sophisticated strategies.
5. See if the effects last in the long term. For example, many persuasion and memory studies only look at short-term effects.
6. Use a less global measure to pinpoint exactly what the effect of the variable is. For example, if the original study used a general measure of memory, replicating the study with a measure that could pinpoint what aspect of memory (encoding, storage, or retrieval) was being affected would allow a more precise understanding of what happened.
7. If the study involves basic (nonapplied) research, see if the finding can be applied to a practical situation. For example, can a memory effect demonstrated in the lab be used to help students on academic probation?
8. If the study describes a correlational relationship between two variables, do an experiment to determine if one variable causes the other. For example, if you find teams wearing black are most likely to be penalized, do an experiment to find out if wearing black causes one to be more violent.
9. Do a study to test a competing explanation for the study's results. For example, if the researchers argue people wearing black are more likely to be violent, you might argue there is an alternative explanation: People wearing black are more likely to be perceived as violent. Similarly, researchers might argue the serial position curves reflect the fact there is a short-term memory and a long-term memory, whereas you might claim the curve only reflects the effects of interference.

to something special and wants to follow-up on that work. Sometimes, the reaction is anger: the researcher thinks the other person is wrong and designs a study to prove it. Regardless, the outcome is the same: The publication of an article not only communicates information but it also creates new questions. As a result of scientists reacting to each other's work, science progresses. Because this exchange is so vital, some professionals skim the reference section before reading an article. If they find that the author has not cited the relevant work in the field, they decide not to waste their time reading the article. Therefore, if you want your research to be meaningful, critically read the relevant research before conducting your study. If you want your report to be read, thoroughly reference the relevant research in your report.

CONCLUDING REMARKS

You not only know how to criticize research but also how to improve it. Thus, every time you read an article, you should get at least one research idea.

Once you have a research idea, the next step is to test it. If you are ready for this step, then you are ready for chapter 13—"Getting Started."

SUMMARY

1. In the introduction, the authors tell you what the hypothesis is, how they came up with it, why it is important, and justify their method of testing it.

2. To understand the introduction, you need to refer to theory and previous research.

3. The method section tells you who the subjects were, how many subjects there were, and how they were treated.

4. Three kinds of results may be presented in the results section: results of manipulation checks, results of hypotheses, and other statistically significant results.

5. The discussion section either reiterates the introduction and results sections or tries to reconcile the introduction and results sections.

6. When you critique the introduction, question whether testing the hypothesis is vital, the hypothesis follows logically from theory and intuition, and the authors have found the best way to test the hypothesis.

7. When you critique the method section, question the construct validity of the independent and dependent variables, determine if subjects may have played along with the hypothesis, and evaluate external and internal validity.

8. When you look at the results section, question any null results.

9. In the discussion section, question the authors' interpretation of the results, try to explain results the authors have failed to explain, and note any weaknesses the authors concede.

10. The possibility of Type 1 error, fraud, or lack of generalizability may justify doing a direct replication.

11. You can do a systematic replication to improve power, external validity, or construct validity.

12. Conceptual replications are mandated when problems with a study's construct validity cannot be ameliorated through minor changes.

13. Replications are vital for the advancement of psychology as a science.

14. Reading research should stimulate research ideas.

KEY TERMS

mundane realism
research realism
conceptual replication

direct replication
systematic replication

EXERCISES

1. Using box 9.1, complete the critique of the journal article you selected.

2. What are the *major* weaknesses you found in your article?

3. Design a direct replication based on the article you critiqued. Do you think your replication will yield the same results as the original? Why?

4. Design a systematic replication based on the article you critiqued. What problems in the original study does your systematic replication correct? How?

5. Design a conceptual replication based on the article you critiqued. What problems in the original study does your conceptual replication correct? How?

10

Beyond Randomized Lab Experiments: Field Experiments, Single-Subject Experiments, and Quasi-Experiments

Overview

Inferring Causality in Randomized Laboratory Experiments

Establishing covariation
Establishing temporal precedence
Controlling for irrelevant factors without keeping everything constant

The Field Experiment

Advantages of doing the field experiment
Limitations of the field experiment
Special problems with doing field experiments using intact groups

An Alternative to Randomization and Statistical Tests: Single-Subject Experiments

Keeping nontreatment factors constant: The A-B design
Variations on the A-B design
Evaluation of single-subject experiments
Conclusions about single-subject experiments

Quasi-Experiments

The problem: accounting for nontreatment factors
The pretest-posttest design
Time series designs
The nonequivalent control group design
Tactics for studying age
Conclusions about quasi-experimental designs

Concluding Remarks

Summary

Key Terms

Exercises

OVERVIEW

To this point, we have shown you only one way to infer causality—by using random assignment in a laboratory experiment. In this chapter, you will learn how to infer causality without the benefit of both random assignment and a laboratory setting.

After reviewing how randomized experiments done in the lab meet the requirements for establishing causality, you will see that the requirements for causality can be met using randomized experiments that are not done in the lab. Then, you will examine two types of designs that attempt to meet these requirements without random assignment: single-subject experiments and quasi-experiments.

In short, after reading this chapter, you should be well prepared if anyone should ask you to design a study to determine if a treatment causes an effect. Specifically, you will know a variety of techniques, as well as the advantages and disadvantages of these techniques.

INFERRING CAUSALITY IN RANDOMIZED LABORATORY EXPERIMENTS

Whether you use a randomized laboratory experiment or any other technique, you must satisfy three criteria if you are to infer that one variable (smiling at others) causes a change in another variable (others helping you). Specifically, you must establish covariation, temporal precedence, and control of irrelevant factors.

ESTABLISHING COVARIATION

First, you must establish **covariation**: that the cause and effect change together. Therefore, to show smiling causes people to help you, you must prove people are more helpful to you when you smile than when you do not.

In the randomized lab experiment, you establish covariation by comparing the average scores for your different conditions. If your conditions are significantly different from one another, then you know that changes in the independent variable are accompanied by changes in the dependent variable: covariation. Thus, in a randomized experiment involving smiling and helpfulness, you would compare the amount of help you got when you smiled with the amount of help you got when you did not smile.

ESTABLISHING TEMPORAL PRECEDENCE

Second, you must show that the causal variable comes before the effect: **temporal precedence**. That is, you would have to show that you smile at others *before* they help you. Otherwise, it may be that you smile after people help you.

In a randomized experiment, you automatically establish that the cause comes before the effect (temporal precedence) by manipulating the independent variable. You always present the independent variable (smiling) *before* you present the dependent measure task (giving subjects an opportunity to help).

CONTROLLING FOR IRRELEVANT FACTORS WITHOUT KEEPING EVERYTHING CONSTANT

Third, you must show that the causal factor is the only thing that is varying. Therefore, to show that your smiling causes others to be nice to you, you must show that everything is the same during the times that you smile and the times that you do not smile, except for your smiling.

It is difficult to prove the *only* difference between the times when you get help and times when you do not is your smile. But without such proof, you cannot say your smiling causes people to be more helpful. Why? Because you might be smiling more when the weather is nicer, when things at school are more relaxed, or when you are with your friends. These same conditions (being with friends, nice weather) may be the reason you are getting help—your smile may have nothing to do with it. If you cannot be sure everything else was the same, then the relationship between smiling and helpfulness may be **spurious**: due to other variables.

In the randomized lab experiment, you do not keep everything constant, except for the treatment variable. Instead, you use random assignment to convert systematic error into random error and statistical tests to subtract out the random error.

As you learned in chapter 5, random assignment ensures uncontrolled variables do not vary systematically. Your conditions will be equivalent except for the effects of the independent variable and the chance impact of random variables. Therefore, as a result of randomization, only random variables stand in the way of keeping irrelevant variables constant.

If you could remove those random variables, you would be able to keep everything constant. But, of course, you cannot remove them. But you can use statistics to estimate their effects: If the difference between groups is greater than the estimated effects of random error, the results are declared "statistically significant."

If you find a statistically significant effect for your independent variable, you can argue that your independent variable causes a change in the dependent variable. However, you may be wrong. You may have underestimated the amount of random error and falsely identified a chance difference as a treatment effect. That is, you may have made a Type 1 error. Fortunately, thanks to statistics, before you do the study you establish what your chances are of making a Type 1 error. Usually, most investigators make the chances of making a Type 1 error fairly remote. Specifically, most investigators set the probability of mistaking chance variation as a genuine treatment effect at less than five in one hundred ($p < 0.05$).

We have just explained what allows a randomized laboratory experiment to establish causality. It is not a sterile lab filled with fancy equipment. Indeed, it is not the lab at all—it is random assignment.

Obviously, you do not need a lab to randomly assign subjects to groups. Therefore, if you do not want to do your experiment in a lab, you could conduct a **field experiment**: an experiment performed in a natural setting.

ADVANTAGES OF DOING THE FIELD EXPERIMENT

Why would you want to leave the comfort of the lab to do a field experiment? The four major reasons for leaving the lab are as follows:

1. The desire to generalize your results to different settings
2. The desire to generalize your results to a different group of people
3. The desire to ensure that subjects are reacting to the treatment rather than feigning the reaction they think will please you
4. The desire for more power

External Validity

First, you might want to generalize your results beyond the laboratory setting. The controlled, isolated lab is a far cry from the chaotic, crowded world that we live in. Consequently, some people question whether an effect found in a lab would hold in a real-world setting. The field experiment lets you find out.

Second, you might want to generalize your results to people other than those who volunteer to be in psychology experiments. In most lab experiments, subjects are students in introductory psychology courses. These students are probably not typical of the average person. In the field experiment, on the other hand, your subjects can be anyone.

Construct Validity

Third, you might want to avoid lab experiments because volunteers for these experiments know they are in an experiment. Because they know the treatments are not real, their responses may be more of an act than an honest reaction to the treatment. Thus, rather than reacting to the treatment as they naturally would, they may act the way they think you want them to act. In other words, they may act to confirm your hypothesis.

To field experiment subjects, on the other hand, the treatment is real. These subjects are not trying to confirm your hypothesis. In fact, they do not even know you are doing an experiment on them. Because of their naivete, they are more likely to give natural responses.

Power

Fourth, you might leave the lab because you do not have enough volunteer subjects. As you may remember from chapter 5, the more subjects you have, the more able you are to find significant effects. When confronted with having only a few people who might agree to come to the lab for your experiment, and a world of potential subjects waiting for you outside the lab, you may decide to go where the subjects are.

LIMITATIONS OF THE FIELD EXPERIMENT

Although the field experiment *may* give you more power, more construct validity, and greater external validity, the field experiment is not an automatic cure-all. The field experiment may lack external, construct, and internal validities. Furthermore, field experiments may lack power, be unethical, and demand more time and energy than you would ever suspect.

Is it Ethical?

The first problem to consider is an ethical one. According to the American Psychological Association's "Ethical Principles of Psychologists" (1981), all subjects for an experiment should be volunteers. Not only should subjects be volunteers but you should get their **informed consent** prior to their participation. That is, subjects should have a good idea of what is going to happen to them and should give their written permission before the experiment begins. Furthermore, after the experiment, subjects should be **debriefed**: informed about what they have just done and why.

These ethical guidelines may conflict with your research goals. You may not want to use volunteers because volunteers are atypical, but the guidelines suggest you use volunteers. If you were forced to use volunteers, you might not want to tell them what the experiment was about so they would not play along with your study. However, the guidelines recommend that human subjects know what they are volunteering for. Finally, you may not want to debrief your subjects for fear your subjects might tell other potential subjects about the study. The ethical guidelines, on the other hand, recommend you debrief subjects so subjects get some benefit from their participation and so you can remove any harm you may have inadvertently caused.

What is the solution to these thorny ethical issues? Unfortunately, there are no easy answers. Your desire for valid information must be weighed against subjects' rights to privacy. Because you may not be able to fairly weigh subjects' rights against your desires, you should consult informed individuals (e.g., your research design professor) before doing a field experiment. In addition to consulting with your professor, you also may have to get your experiment approved by your institution's ethics committee.

Perhaps the easiest way to deal with ethical problems is to avoid violating the guidelines. For example, you might do a field experiment, but ask for volunteers, give informed consent, and debrief your subjects. Under these conditions, you have lost some advantages of field experimentation, but you *may* still get subjects that are more "typical" than laboratory subjects and you *do* get to see whether your results generalize to a real-world setting.

A more controversial approach is to perform a field experiment on unsuspecting volunteers while they think they are waiting for an experiment to begin. For example, Latane and Darley (1968) had subjects witness a theft while they were in a waiting room ostensibly waiting to start a laboratory experiment.

The "experiment in the waiting room" is a compromise between ethical principles and research goals. To meet the ethical guidelines requesting the use of volunteer subjects, you lose the ability to get subjects who are more like "real people" than volunteer subjects and you lose the ability to overcome a shortage of volunteer subjects.

To meet the research goal of seeing whether the effect would occur outside the lab and seeing whether the effect would occur with naive subjects, you violate the ethical guidelines for informed consent. Because subjects signed up for one experiment, but ended up in another study, this kind of study raises serious ethical questions.

External Validity Is Not Guaranteed

If you think that by doing a field experiment you will get subjects who represent the average person, you may be disappointed. In the "waiting room" study we just described, the subjects are the same college sophomores who would participate in a lab study. Even doing an experiment in the field (e.g., a shopping mall), will not ensure that your subjects will represent "the average person." In fact, in many field experiments, you may not know whom your subjects represent. Sometimes, the only thing you can say is subjects "represented people who used the telephone booth at the Tarfield Mall between 2:00 P.M. and 4:00 P.M. during March 1994." Consequently, you may not be surprised by what Dipboye and Flanagan (1979) found when they examined published research in industrial psychology. They found field research typically dealt with a rather narrow range of subjects and generally had no more external validity than the lab studies.

Construct Validity Is Not Guaranteed

Similarly, if you want to study naive subjects, the field experiment may let you down. Former subjects or talkative bystanders may talk about the experiment to potential subjects and ruin everyone's naivete. To illustrate this point, consider a field experiment conducted by Shaffer, Rogel, and Hendrik (1975) in the Kent State University library. A confederate of the researchers sat down at a table occupied by a naive subject. After several minutes of studying, the confederate walked away from the table leaving behind several personal items. Sometimes the confederate asked the naive subject to watch his belongings (request condition), other times he said nothing (no-request condition). Shortly after the confederate left the table a "thief" appeared, went through the confederate's belongings, discovered a wallet, and quickly walked away with it. The dependent variable was whether subjects tried to stop the thief. Results showed that 64 percent of the subjects in the request condition tried to stop the thief, compared to only 14 percent in the no-request condition.

Imagine you were a subject in this experiment. After watching a thief steal a man's wallet, perhaps after trying to foil a robbery attempt, would you tell any one about it? Let us say you told a friend about the incident and that friend says she has heard of a similar incident. One night, she goes to the library to study. Shortly after she sits down, she finds herself approached by the same victims he has heard about and witnessing the very crime you told her about. Not only has she lost her naivete but when she tells her friends about this, the whole school will know about the experiment.

Or, put yourself in the place of a curious bystander, say the reference librarian. You are working at the reference desk and out of the corner of your eye you observe two students sitting at a table. One student gets up and walks away leaving behind his books and several personal items. You go about your work. But then you notice a different man go up to the pile of belongings, rummage through them, pocket a wallet, and walk hurriedly away. What would you do? As a responsible employee, you would try to stop the thief. At the very least, you would report the incident to the authorities. The campus police arrive to get your statement, perhaps even to make an arrest. To stop the police investigation, the researcher explains that it is only an experiment. Students in the library strain to overhear the conversation with the police, and students question you endlessly about the incident. Soon, everyone on campus knows about the experiment.

Thus, a field experiment may end up having no more construct validity than a laboratory study *unless you take appropriate precautions*. Therefore, if you were doing Shaffer, Rogel, and Hendrik's study, you would try to collect all the data in one night to reduce the chances of subjects talking to potential subjects. Furthermore, to reduce the chance of innocent bystanders destroying subjects' innocence, you might inform the library staff about the experiment.

Internal Validity Is Not Guaranteed

A carelessly conducted field experiment may not only lack external and construct validity, but internal validity as well. Although all field experiments should have internal validity, some do not because of failure to randomly assign subjects to groups and because of mortality: subjects dropping out of the study.

Failure to Randomly Assign

All the designs we have discussed so far rely on independent random assignment for their internal validity. Unfortunately, random assignment is much more difficult in the field than in the laboratory. Random assignment is especially difficult when you are manipulating an important, real-life treatment. Often, real-world subjects and their representatives do not believe people should be randomly assigned to important treatments. Instead, they believe people should be able to choose their own treatment.

To imagine the difficulties of random assignment in the field, suppose you wanted to study the effects of television violence on children's behavior. You approach parents and tell them you want some children to watch certain nonviolent television programs (e.g., "Mr. Rogers" or "Sesame Street") and other children to watch violent television programs, such as TV wrestling, boxing, and specific action/adventure shows. You may find that few parents will let you randomly assign their child to *either* condition. If you say, "I want to be able to assign your child to either one of these conditions," many parents will object. Some will say, "You can show my child 'Sesame Street,' but you're not going to make my kid watch violence and trash!" Other parents will say, "You can make my kid watch wrestling. I watch it all the time anyway. But not those other shows. They're on the same time as my shows. You're not going to make me sit around and watch kiddie junk!" However, the hassles with the parents may be nothing compared with the hassles of getting the children themselves to agree to random assignment.

Yet, with enough persistence (and enough money), you could probably get people to agree to random assignment. But once you have done that, you face a huge problem: how do you know subjects will watch the television shows you assigned? You cannot go to everyone's house. You cannot trust young children to carry out your instructions. You cannot trust parents to supervise the children because they may be busy with other tasks. The children are too young to be trusted to implement the treatment program. Therefore, the prospect of using random assignment to determine children's television diets seems intimidating.

In fact, the idea of randomly assigning children to television viewing seems so intimidating that most investigators researching the effects of TV have often avoided field experiments. This is unfortunate because such experiments would provide the strongest evidence about the effects of viewing violent television shows.

Have these researchers given up too soon? Cook and Campbell (1979) claim researchers often give up on random assignment faster than they should. Cook and Campbell argue that random assignment can often be used in the field—if the researcher is creative.

In the case of researching the impact of television on children's behavior, researchers may have given up too soon. Perhaps researchers should approach a nursery school. If the nursery school would cooperate and get informed consent from the parents and children, the television viewing could take place at the school as part of the children's ordinary routine. In this way, you would know subjects were getting the treatment they were assigned to.

Mortality

Unfortunately, even after you assign your subjects to condition, they may not stay assigned. Mortality may raise its ugly head. That is, subjects may drop out of your experiment before you collect the dependent measure. For example, suppose you are doing the television violence experiment with nursery school children. As the study progresses, you find subjects are dropping out of the violent television condition (perhaps the kids are getting too violent or the parents are having second thoughts). However, subjects are not dropping out of the nonviolent condition. The fact subjects in one group are more likely to quit than subjects in the other group threatens the study's internal validity. That is, if the violent television group is more aggressive, we cannot say whether this is due to the less aggressive children dropping out of the violent television group or to television violence causing children to be aggressive.

Usually, losing more subjects from one group than the other is due to one of two reasons. First, the treatment is too intense. In such cases, the treatment should be toned down or eliminated. To use a manipulation that leads to such a high drop-out rate is often unethical. To take an extreme case of using an unethical level of treatment, suppose the television these children were watching was X-rated violence. In that case, mortality from the treatment group would be high (although we would hope an ethics committee would prevent such a study from being conducted). Second, mortality from the treatment group will be higher than from the control group if the control group is left alone to engage in their normal activities. For example, if the experimental group was to watch a prescribed set of programs at home whereas the control group was simply allowed to do whatever they normally did at home, mortality would be higher in the experimental group. Therefore, the control group should always get some kind of treatment, even a placebo treatment.

Power May Be Inadequate

Not only is it easier to create an internally valid experiment in the lab than in the field, but it is also easier to create a powerful experiment in the lab than in the field. In the lab, you can have impressive power by reducing random error and by using sensitive dependent measures. By leaving the lab, you may lose your ability to reduce random error and your ability to use sensitive measures.

Random Error

In the laboratory, you can reduce random error by minimizing the degree to which irrelevant variables vary. You can reduce unwanted variation due to individual differences by using a homogeneous group of subjects. You can reduce unwanted variation in the environment by running subjects under identical conditions. You can reduce unwanted variation due to subjects being distracted by putting subjects in a soundproof, simple, virtually distraction-free environment. You can reduce unwanted variation in your procedures by rigidly standardizing your experiment. Thus, if you do your study in the laboratory, you can use many tactics to stop irrelevant variables from varying.

By leaving the lab, you may lose your ability to stop these variables from fluctuating. Sometimes you willingly give up the opportunity to control these variables so you can generalize your results to the real world. For example, you may do a field experiment to get access to a heterogeneous group of subjects. The advantage of having a wide range of subjects is you can generalize your results to a wide range of people. The disadvantage is you are giving individual differences a chance to account for a sizeable difference between your groups. Therefore, your treatment's effect might be obscured by these individual differences.

Sometimes, however, you unwillingly give up the ability to control irrelevant variables. For instance, you always want to standardize your procedures. However, it is hard to follow the same procedure every time if you have to conduct your study (1) on the run (perhaps even approaching subjects and saying, "Excuse me, may I talk to you for a moment?"); (2) without the benefit of equipment; (3) in a noisy, crowded environment.

Furthermore, even if you succeed in administering the treatment in the same, standard way, your subjects may fail to perceive the treatment in the same, standard way. That is, distractions in the environment may prevent all your subjects from attending to your entire manipulation. Indeed, a manipulation that is overpowering in the lab may seem almost invisible when taken to the field.

Insensitive Measures

You have seen that, in the field, you cannot always administer the same manipulations with the same degree of standardization as you could in the lab. Because your measures are less standardized and less effective, your experiment is less powerful. Unfortunately, the same factors that impede your ability to administer your manipulations may also hurt your ability to use sensitive, powerful measures. To illustrate, let us say you are interested in whether getting an unexpected gift will increase happiness. In the lab, you would probably measure happiness by having subjects rate how happy they are on a one to seven scale. Even if you were to use a more indirect behavioral indicator of happiness, such as helping, you would measure helping with a high degree of precision. For example, you would measure either exactly *how long* it took subjects to help a person or *how much* they helped the person.

In the field, measuring happiness is much more difficult. You probably will not be able to have subjects fill out a rating scale. Therefore, you will probably have to use a less sensitive behavioral measure, such as helping. Furthermore, you may not even be able to measure helping with any degree of precision. Unlike in the lab, you cannot merely sit in your chair, gaze through a one-way mirror, and record how much or how long subjects help. Instead, you must inconspicuously peer around the corner, filter out the dog barking, the traffic sounds, and other people to see whether your subjects help. Under these conditions, you are lucky to see whether subjects help, much less to see how much they help. Thus, in the field, you may be too busy to collect anything other than dichotomous (two-valued) variables. Clearly, asking whether someone responded gives you less information than asking how long it took the person to respond or to what extent the person responded.

But you do not have to settle for less sensitive measures when you go to the field. One way to avail yourself of more sensitive measures is to use a second experimenter who does nothing but record data. This leaves you free to put quarters (unexpected gifts) in phone booths, hide until a subject finds it, and make yourself a convenient person "in need" for your unsuspecting subjects to demonstrate their goodwill. This second experimenter could observe and record things like how quickly subjects responded and to what extent they responded. If you do not have a second experimenter, let such equipment as videotape cameras, tape recorders, and stopwatches do the recording for you.

For example, Milgram, Bickman, and Berkowitz (1969) had confederates look up at a tall building. Their independent variable was how many confederates looked up at the building. Their dependent measure was the proportion of people walking by who also looked up. Actually, the confederates were looking up at a videotape camera. After the experiment was over, they were able to count the number of people looking up by replaying the videotape. (The pros and cons of conducting field experiments are summarized in table 10.1.)

SPECIAL PROBLEMS WITH DOING FIELD EXPERIMENTS USING INTACT GROUPS

Some field experimenters try to regain the power lost due to having high levels of random error and insensitive measures by using a large number of subjects. To get large numbers of subjects, some researchers do field experiments on intact groups. For example, they might use a few large classes or a work group.

TABLE 10.1 Pros and Cons of Field Experiments

PROS	CONS
Power may be enhanced by access to many subjects.	The increase in subjects may be more than negated by the inability to control random variables and the inability to use the most sensitive of measures.
Like randomized lab experiment, has internal validity because subjects were randomly assigned.	Random assignment is sometimes difficult in the field. Mortality may harm internal validity.
External validity may be enhanced by studying a wide variety of settings and subjects.	Often, field experiments do not study a wider range of subjects than those in the lab. It may take more effort to do a field experiment than a lab experiment. Ethical questions may arise, especially in terms of informed consent.
Construct validity may be enhanced by using subjects that are not playing the role of subject.	Construct validity may be harmed if people learn of the study. Not telling subjects about the study raises ethical questions.

Failure to Establish and Maintain Independence

Unfortunately it is hard to independently assign subjects from intact groups, and once they are assigned, it is hard to maintain independence. For example, suppose a nursery school was willing to help you out with your study on the effects of watching prosocial television. Then you would have a large, convenient sample. However, there might be a catch: the nursery school might insist you keep the classes intact. Thus, although you might want to assign each student independently, you may have to assign one class to one condition and another class to the other condition. Consequently, no matter how many people are in your study, you only have two independent units—the two classes. Because any two classes will obviously differ from one another in many ways, your experimental and control groups would be very different before the experiment began.

Even if you are able to independently assign subjects, you may be unable to *maintain* independence because subjects interact with one another, thereby influencing each other's responses. If the children in the group influence each other, you do not have independent responses from sixty individuals. Instead, you have responses from two mobs. For example, suppose there is one very aggressive child in the control group. As any teacher knows, one misbehaving child can cause virtually everyone in the group to misbehave.

Violation of independence, whether due to faulty assignment or failure to maintain independence of responses, can have one of two consequences—bad or worse. The worst consequence happens if the researcher does not realize independence has been violated. In that case, he would conduct his statistical tests as if he had more individual units than he has. He would think that because each group is made up of thirty randomly assigned subjects, the groups should be fairly equivalent. He would believe that because he has so many independent units, chance differences between groups should be minimal. However, because in reality he has only two independent units, chance could easily be responsible for substantial differences between groups. Therefore, he is very likely to misinterpret a difference that is due to chance as a treatment effect.

The bad consequence occurs if the researcher realizes he has only two independent units. In that case, the good news is, because he realizes even large differences might be due to chance, he probably will not mistake chance differences for treatment differences. However, the bad news is, because he realizes even large differences may be due to chance, he will tend to dismiss real treatment effects as being due to chance. In other words, his study will be powerless.

Threats to Construct Validity

You can remedy the problem of too few independent units by using more classes. For example, you might have ten classes in one group and ten classes in the other group. However, violation of independence is only one problem with using intact groups. Using intact groups exposes your study to three serious threats to construct validity: demoralization, compensation, and diffusion of treatment.

Demoralization

Your study's construct validity starts the moment the classes talk to each other and find out about their differential treatment. Do not be surprised if the no-television group becomes demoralized. They may vent their frustration about missing out on television by being violent. As a result, the television-watching group may be better behaved, even though watching television did not improve their behavior. In this case, it is not that watching television reduces violence, it is that feeling deprived increases violence.

Compensation

On the other hand, upon learning of the experimental group's good fortune, *compensation* could occur. That is, the no-television class might pull together and behave as best as they could so that they would be allowed to watch television. As a result of their efforts, the no-television group might behave better than the television group. Again, you would see a difference between your groups, but the difference would not be due to the effects of the treatment.

Diffusion of Treatment

Finally, you might not observe any effect for treatment because of *diffusion of treatment:* both your groups are getting the treatment. In your television study, members of the no-television class might be watching television. For example, their teacher may succumb to their begging to "watch television like the other class" and thus borrow the television from the other teacher. Or, if the classes are held in the same room, pupils in the no-television group might watch or overhear the other class's television shows. Consequently, the impact of the television shows would diffuse to the no-television group.

Minimizing Threats to Construct Validity

How can you minimize demoralization, compensation, and diffusion of treatment? The steps to take are obvious once you realize that these threats usually result from subjects finding out that their treatments differ (see table 10.2). With this in mind, the first step is to make your conditions resemble one another as much as possible. Never use a treatment group and a no-treatment group. Instead, use a treatment group and a placebo treatment group or two different kinds of treatment.

In the television study, you could have one group watch one kind of television program (e.g., violent) while the other watched another kind of program (e.g., nonviolent). Or, you could be sneakier and show both groups the same shows—the only difference is that in one condition you have edited out some of the violence. In this way, subjects would not notice that their conditions differ.

The second step is to give subjects fewer opportunities to talk. For example, shorten the time between giving the treatment and collecting the dependent measure. Obviously, the longer the time between the introduction of treatment and collecting the dependent measure, the more likely the group are to talk. Therefore, you might conduct the entire study in one day rather than having it last for several months.

If you want to look at long-term effects of the treatment, you could reduce opportunities for subjects to talk to one another by using subjects who will not run into another. Thus, in the television study, rather than assigning different classes in the same schools to different conditions, you could assign different schools to different conditions. The chances of a toddler from Busy Bee Day Care comparing curriculum with a child from Lazy Larry's Day Camp are remote.

TABLE 10.2 Dealing with Problems Caused by Studying Intact Groups

PROBLEMS	PARTIAL REMEDIES
Groups are not independent.	Use many groups. In analyzing data, do not consider each subject as an individual unit. Instead, consider each unit as an independent unit. Thus, for the purposes of analysis, rather than have three hundred subjects, you may only have ten classes.
Demoralization (no-treatment group being depressed they were not in treatment group).	Use placebo treatments. Minimize opportunities to talk by doing study in short time span and using groups that do not come into contact with one another very often.
Compensation (no-treatment group working harder to compensate for being denied the treatment).	Use placebo treatments. Minimize opportunities to talk by doing study in short time span and using groups that do not come into contact with one another very often.
Diffusion of treatment (no-treatment group getting access to the treatment).	Use placebo treatments. Minimize opportunities to talk by doing study in short time span and using groups that do not come into contact with one another very often.

AN ALTERNATIVE TO RANDOMIZATION AND STATISTICAL TESTS: SINGLE-SUBJECT EXPERIMENTS

You have seen that the field experiment does the same thing the randomized lab experiment does. Specifically, the randomized lab experiment and field experiment both (1) establish that the cause comes before the effect, (2) establish that changes in the treatment coincide with changes in the dependent measure, and (3) show that the changes in the dependent measure are due to the treatment rather than to some uncontrolled factor.

Like all experimental designs, randomized experiments establish that the cause comes before the effect by manipulating the independent variable (smiling) before presenting the dependent measure task (helping). Like all experimental designs, randomized experiments establish covariation by comparing the different treatment conditions (comparing smiling versus no-smiling conditions). However, unlike all experimental designs, randomized experiments use randomization and statistical tests to rule out the effects of nontreatment factors.

The single-subject experiment, for example, strives to control, rather than to estimate, nontreatment factors. Instead of letting nontreatment variables vary and then accounting for the effects of those variables, single-subject experimenters stop nontreatment factors from varying (see table 10.3).

KEEPING NONTREATMENT FACTORS CONSTANT: THE A-B DESIGN

To understand how single-subject experimenters keep nontreatment factors constant, let us examine the simplest single-subject design, the A-B design. In the A-B design, as in all single-subject designs, the experimenter studies a single subject. The experimenter makes sure the subject's behavior on the dependent measure task (pecking) occurs at a consistent rate. This is called establishing a **stable baseline**. This first step is designated as A. Next, the experimenter introduces the treatment. The experimenter then compares posttreatment behavior (B) with baseline (A).

The A-B design strives to keep nontreatment factors constant by eliminating the two basic sources of nontreatment variables: nontreatment effects due to between subjects variability and nontreatment effects due to within subjects variability.

Between subjects variability is obviously not a problem for the single-subject design. Differences between individuals cannot account for differences between conditions because the same subject is in all conditions. Experimenters using between subjects designs have to be concerned that differences between conditions may be due to the fact that different individuals are in the different conditions. In other words, between subjects experimenters worry that individual difference variables may be responsible for the differences between treatment conditions. The single-subject experimenter has no such worries.

However, the single-subject experimenter does have to deal with random within subjects variability. With or without treatment, a subject's behavior may vary. How does

TABLE 10.3 How Different Experimental Designs Establish Causality

REQUIREMENT	LAB AND FIELD EXPERIMENTS	A-B SINGLE-SUBJECT DESIGN
Temporal precedence (treatment came before changes in scores).	Introduce treatment *before* there is a change in the dependent variable.	Introduce treatment *before* there is a change in the dependent variable.
Covariation (different treatment conditions score differently on measure).	Observing difference between treatment and control conditions.	Observing difference between conditions A (baseline) and B (posttreatment behavior).
Accounting for irrelevant variables (the treatment and the scores are not both effects of some other factor).	1. Independent random assignment to make sure all irrelevant factors vary randomly rather than systematically. 2. Then, use statistics to account for effects of these random factors. If difference between groups greater than would be expected as a result of these random factors, difference assumed to be the effect of the one nonrandom, systematically varied factor: the treatment.	1. Eliminate between subjects variables by using only one subject. 2. Control relevant environmental factors. Demonstrate effect of control by establishing stable baseline. Then, introduce treatment. If change occurs, assumed to be due to treatment.

the single-subject experimenter know that the treatment is responsible for the change in the subject's behavior?

The single-subject experimenter is confident the difference between no-treatment and treatment conditions is not due to random within subjects variability because he has collected a stable baseline. The baseline shows the subject's behavior is not varying.

But how does a single-subject experimenter obtain a stable baseline? After all, behavior is variable. To obtain a stable baseline, the single-subject experimenter must control all relevant environmental variables. That is, the single-subject experimenter strives to hold constant all those variables that might affect the subject's responses.

If the experimenter does not know what the relevant variables are, the experimenter tries to keep the subject's environment as constant as possible. For example, the researcher might perform the experiment under highly controlled conditions in a sound-proof laboratory. If the experimenter knows what the relevant variables are, then the experimenter only needs to control those relevant variables. Thus, if an experimenter knew that parental praise was the only relevant variable in increasing studying behavior, the experimenter would need only to control that one variable. However, the experimenter usually does not know what variables can be safely ignored. Psychology has not advanced to the state where we can catalog what variables affect and do not affect every possible response.

After attempting to control variables, the experimenter checks to see whether he has succeeded by looking at the baseline. If the baseline is not stable, the experimenter continues to control variables until the behavior becomes stable.

But what if a researcher cannot achieve a stable baseline? Then, the researcher cannot use the A-B single-subject design. This is often the case. If the organism is complex and therefore affected by many variables, if the behavior is complex and therefore affected by many variables, or if the environment is extremely complex, the researcher usually cannot control all the relevant variables. Consequently, you will rarely see the A-B single-subject experiment investigating the creativity of an executive in a business setting. More often, researchers using the A-B design have a simple organism (pigeon, rat, planarium, neuron) perform a rather simple behavior (pecking) in a simple environment, such as in a Skinner box.

Thus far, we have seen how the single-subject experimenter using an A-B design can hold individual difference variables and relevant environmental variables constant. But how does the experimenter know that the difference between conditions is not due to maturation: natural biological changes in the organism such as those due to development or fatigue?

The single-subject experimenter may hold maturation constant by choosing an organism that he knows will not mature during the course of the study. Thus, he might use a pigeon or a rat because the extent of their maturation as it relates to certain tasks (barpressing and pecking) is well documented.

Or, as you will soon see, the experimenter may use a design that will allow him to account for maturation. Before looking at a design that accounts for maturation, let us look at an example of the A-B design, the simplest of single-subject designs.

Howard Blough (1957) wanted to study the impact of LSD on a pigeon's visual perception. His first step was to place the pigeon in a highly controlled environment, a Skinner box, equipped with a light that could illuminate a spot on the stimulus panel at different intensities. On the wall of the Skinner box were two disks—"1" and "2." As an index of visual threshold, the pigeon was conditioned to peck at disk 1 when the spot was visible and to peck at disk 2 when the spot was not visible.

Before Blough began to manipulate his independent variable (LSD), he had to make sure that no other variables were influencing the pigeon's behavior. To do this, he had to keep all the relevant variables in the pigeon's environment constant. Therefore, he placed the pigeon in the Skinner box and carefully observed the pigeon's behavior while it performed the visual perception task. If he had succeeded in eliminating all nontreatment variables, the pigeon's behavior would be relatively stable—the relationship between pecking and illumination would be constant. If he had failed, he would observe fluctuations in the pigeon's behavior (e.g., erratic increases and decreases in pecking).

Once the pigeon's behavior was stable, Blough was ready to introduce the independent variable: LSD. After administering the LSD, Blough compared the pigeon's behavior before the treatment (A) to its behavior after the treatment (B). Blough found that after taking the LSD the pigeon's threshold for visual perception increased. Specifically, the pigeon pecked at disc 2 (cannot see spot) under a level of illumination that—prior to treatment—led to a peck at disc 1. Because Blough had ensured that nontreatment variables were not influencing the pigeon's behavior, he concluded that the LSD was the sole cause of the increase in visual ability.

Howard Blough's study was exceptional because he knew that the pigeon's behavior on this task normally would not change much over time. However, in studies with other kinds of subjects or tasks, the researcher would not know whether subjects would change, develop, or learn over a period of time. Therefore, most experimenters are not so confident that they have controlled all the important variables. They know that two potentially important nontreatment variables have changed from measurement at baseline (A) to measurement after administering the treatment (B).

First, because the posttest comes after the pretest, subjects have had more practice on the task when performing the posttest than they had when performing the pretest. Thus, their performance may have improved as a result of testing: the effects of doing the dependent measure task on subsequent performance on that task. For example, the practice a subject gets doing the task during the A phase may help the subject do better during the B phase. Second, because the posttest occurs after the pretest, time has passed from pretest to posttest. Consequently, changes from pretest to posttest may be due to maturational effects such as fatigue, boredom, or development.

VARIATIONS ON THE A-B DESIGN

Because psychologists want to assess the effects of testing and maturation, single-subject experimenters rarely use the A-B design. Instead, they use variations on the A-B design, such as the reversal design, psychophysical designs, or the multiple-baseline design.

The Reversal Design

In the reversal design, also known as the A-B-A design, the experimenter measures behavior (A), then administers the treatment and measures behavior (B), then withdraws the treatment and measures behavior (A).

To see why the A-B-A design is superior to the A-B design, consider one in a series of single-subject experiments performed by Ayllon and Azrin (1965; 1968). They worked with a group of psychotics in a mental hospital to see if a token economy was an effective way of increasing socially desirable behavior. In a typical experiment, Ayllon and Azrin first identified a desirable behavior (e.g., feeding oneself). Next, the experimenters collected baseline behavior for a patient (A). They then attempted to reinforce this behavior with a token. Like money, the token could be exchanged for desirable outcomes such as candy, movies, social interaction, or privacy. Thus, they gave the patient tokens for each instance of the socially desirable behavior and measured the behavior (B). The patient performed more socially desirable behaviors once the tokens were introduced. Great! A token economy increases socially desirable behavior. Right?

If Ayllon and Azrin's study had ended here they could not be confident in their answer. Remember, with an A-B design, you do not know whether the increase in socially desirable behavior is due to maturation, testing, or the treatment.

However, they expanded the A-B design to an A-B-A design by withdrawing the treatment and continuing to observe their patient's behavior. Consequently, they were able to determine that the treatment (tokens) increased socially desirable behavior. If, after withdrawing the treatment, socially desirable behavior had continued to increase, they would have concluded that the increase in socially desirable behavior was *not* due to the treatment. Instead, they would have concluded that the increase was due to maturation and/or testing.

What made them conclude that the tokens were responsible for the effect? Their conclusion was based on finding that socially desirable behavior (1) increased when tokens were introduced and (2) fell back to near-baseline level when the tokens were withdrawn.

But if tokens caused the effect, shouldn't their withdrawal cause the behavior to fall to baseline rather than *near* baseline? Ideally, you would like to see the dependent measure (socially desirable behavior) fall back to baseline level. However, do not insist that you will not make a causal inference unless the behavior returns to baseline. The behavior probably will not return to baseline. Most behaviors do not return to baseline after you withdraw the treatment because of maturation effects, testing effects, and carry-over effects—the treatment's effects persisting after the treatment has been removed.

Because of these effects, you can infer causality as long as there is a substantially higher (or lower) level of the dependent variable during treatment than during either pretreatment or posttreatment.

Certainly, you can be logically justified in inferring causality if treatment behavior is substantially different from both pretreatment and posttreatment behavior. Unfortunately, justified or not, you could be wrong if you infer causality based on such an apparent treatment effect.

How could you be wrong? You would be wrong if the effects of practice and/or maturation are cyclical. For instance, suppose performance was affected by menstrual cycles. Thus, performance might be good during the pretreatment phase (before menstruation), poor during the treatment phase (during menstruation), and good during the posttreatment phase (after menstruation). Although such an unsteady effect of maturation or testing would be unlikely, it is possible.

To rule out the possibility that apparent treatment effects are due to some simple cyclical pattern involving either maturation or practice, you might extend the A-B-A design. For example, you might make it an A-B-A-B design. Ayllon and Azrin did this and found reintroduction of the token rewards led to an increase in the socially desirable behavior. By adding even more measurements, you could use an A-B-A-B-A design to rule out the possibility of even more complicated maturational or practice cycles. Obviously, the more measurements you collect, the less likely it is that time or practice can explain apparent treatment effects. Imagine trying to explain how maturation or testing effects could explain apparent treatment effects in an A-B-A-B-A-B-A-B-A-B design!

Psychophysical Designs

Psychophysical experiments extend the A-B-A-B-A design. In psychophysical experiments, subjects are asked to judge stimuli. For example, they may be asked to rate whether one light is brighter than another, one weight is heavier than another, or one picture is more attractive than another. The idea is to see how variations in the stimulus relate to variations in judgments. Because the dependent variable is *psychological* judgment and the independent variable is often some variation of a stimulus's *physical* characteristic (loudness, intensity, etc.), the name psychophysics is apt.

Because a subject can make these judgments quickly, subjects can be asked to make many judgments. Indeed, in a few exceptional cases, subjects have been asked to make 67,000 judgments!

With so many judgments, you might worry about maturation effects. For example, subjects might get tired as the experimental session goes on and on.

In addition, you might be concerned about carry-over effects. Specifically, you might worry that earlier stimuli may affect ratings of later stimuli. For instance, suppose you were rating how heavy a fifty-pound weight was. If the last ten weights you had judged were all about one hundred pounds, you might tend to rate fifty pounds as light. However, if the last ten weights had all been around 10 pounds, you might tend to rate 50 pounds as heavy. Similarly, if you were judging how wealthy a person making $50,000 was, your rating would be affected by whether the previous people you had judged had been multi-millionaires or poverty-stricken (Parducci, 1984).

To deal with these order effects, researchers do three things, all of which follow from the ideas of one of the earliest pioneers in psychophysics, Gustav Fechner. First, have subjects rate each stimulus more than once. Second, randomize the presentation of stimuli. Do not simply have subjects start by rating the most intense stimulus, then the next most intense stimulus, etc. Third, counterbalance the order of presentation of stimuli. That is, like the reversal design, vary the order of B and A. Do not always present A before B. Instead, only present A before B half of the time; the other half of the time, present B before A (Fechner, [1860] 1966). By using these three techniques, maturation, testing, and carry-over should not be problems.

The Multiple-Baseline Design

Another single-subject experimental design that rules out the effects of maturation, testing, and carry-over is the multiple-baseline design. In a typical multiple-baseline design, you would collect baselines for several behaviors. For example, you might collect baselines for a child making her own bed, putting her toys away, washing her hands, and vacuuming her room. Then, you would reinforce one of the behaviors. If the behavior being reinforced increases, you would suspect reinforcement is causing the behavior to increase.

But the effects might be due to being observed or to the child becoming more mature. To see whether the child's improvement in behavior is due to maturation or testing, you would look at her performance on the other tasks. If those tasks are still being performed at baseline level, then maturation and testing are not improving performance on those tasks. Because maturation and practice have no effect on the other behaviors, maturation and practice probably are not increasing the particular behavior you decided to reinforce. Therefore, you would be relatively confident the improvement in that behavior was due to reinforcement.

To be even more certain that reinforcement is causing the change in behavior, you would reinforce a second behavior and compare it against the other nonreinforced behaviors. You would continue the process until you had reinforced all the behaviors. You would hope to find that when you reinforced hand washing, hand washing increased—but that no other behavior increased. Similarly, when you reinforced tooth brushing, you would hope tooth brushing—and only tooth brushing—increased. If increases in behavior coincided perfectly with reinforcement, you would be very confident that reinforcement was responsible for the increases in behavior.

EVALUATION OF SINGLE-SUBJECT EXPERIMENTS

You have now examined some of the more popular single-subject designs. Before leaving these designs, let us see how they stand up on three important criteria: internal, external, and construct validity.

Internal Validity

The single-subject experimenter uses a variety of strategies to achieve internal validity. Like the physicist, the single-subject experimenter keeps many relevant variables constant. For example, the single-subject experimenter holds individual difference variables constant by studying a single subject and may hold environmental variables constant by placing that subject in a highly controlled environment (imagine a rat in a soundproof Skinner box).

Like the within subjects experimenter, the single-subject experimenter must worry that subjects may have changed as a result of being measured or as a result of time passing. Thus, both kinds of experimenters may adapt similar strategies to deal with the threats of maturation and testing. Both experimenters may try to reduce maturation by shortening the length of their study. Both experimenters may try to reduce the effects of practice (testing) by giving subjects extensive practice on the task prior to beginning the study. By giving extensive pre-experimental practice on the task, they reduce the likelihood that subjects will benefit from any additional practice they get during the experiment. Single-subject experimenters, in particular, like to make sure the subject's response rate is stable before the treatment is introduced.

We do not mean to say that within subjects and single-subject experimenters always use the same methods to eliminate threats to validity. Indeed, their primary methods of dealing with these threats are fundamentally different. That is, whereas the within subjects experimenter relies primarily on randomization to rule out practice and fatigue effects, the single-subject experimenter relies on introducing and removing the treatment in a systematic order.

Both the single-subject and the within subjects experimenter must also be concerned about carry-over effects. Because of carry-over, investigators using an A-B-A design frequently find subjects do not return to the original baseline. Of course, the problems of carry-over multiply when you use more levels of the independent variable and/or when you use more than one independent variable. To minimize carry-over's complications, most single-subject experimenters use only two levels of a single independent variable.

Construct Validity

The single-subject researcher and the within subjects experimenter have even more in common when they attack threats to construct validity (see table 10.4). For both researchers, sensitization poses a serious problem and both researchers use the same solution. Specifically, both can reduce the effects of sensitization by (1) making the difference between the treatment conditions so subtle subjects do not even realize anything has changed (e.g., gradually varying the loudness of a stimulus); (2) using placebo treatments, or (3) using very few levels of treatment. Researchers' concerns about sensitization may account for the popularity of the A-B-A design over more complicated single-subject designs. That is, the A-B-A design is more popular than the A-B-A-B-A-B-A-B-A-B or A-B-C-D-D-C-B-A designs.

External Validity

At first glance, the single-subject experiment seems to have less external validity than other designs. How can the results from one subject be generalized to others? Further-

TABLE 10.4 Similarities Between Within Subjects Experiments and Single-subject Experiments

PROBLEM	SINGLE-SUBJECT EXPERIMENT	WITHIN SUBJECTS DESIGN
Practice effects may harm internal validity	Give extensive practice before introducing treatment	Give extensive practice before introducing treatment
Fatigue or maturation may harm internal validity	Keep study brief	Keep study brief
Assorted order effects may harm validity	Counterbalance order	Counterbalance order and randomly assign subjects to different orders
Carry-over effects may harm internal validity	1. Use few levels and few variables 2. Have a long period between treatments	1. Use few levels and few variables 2. Have a long period between treatments
Subjects may learn what study is about (sensitization), thus harming construct validity	1. Use placebo treatments 2. Use few levels of treatment 3. Gradually increase or decrease intensity of treatment or use very similar levels	1. Use placebo treatments 2. Use few levels of treatment 3. Gradually increase or decrease intensity of treatment or use very similar levels

more, how can the results from an experiment conducted in such a highly controlled setting be generalized to other settings? Although it seems as if other designs must have more external validity than the single-subject experiment, things are not always as they seem.

Whether you use one subject or one thousand subjects, you can only *infer* that your results will apply to individuals who were not in your study. In other words, you are assuming that no other individual difference variables interact with your treatment to reverse or negate its effects. Because single-subject experiments tend to investigate processes that are well understood and known to occur in all organisms, the results of such experiments may be generalized to other members of the same species. Thus, the results of psychophysical and operant conditioning experiments performed on a single member of a species can often be generalized to other members of that species.[1]

In addition to having strong generalizability because they study universal processes (such as reinforcement), single-subject experiments may have strong generalizability *because* they only study a single subject. To see why this apparent weakness could be a strength, consider the situation in which you have a treatment that makes half your subjects get better and half your subjects get worse. On the surface, this situation would seem to be tailor-made for a randomized experiment. After all, if you do a single-subject experiment, the results would only generalize to half the population.

But, what if you did use a traditional between subjects design? Then, the positive effects from subjects who improved would be cancelled out by the negative effects from subjects who got worse. As a result, the average treatment effect would be zero. You would conclude that the treatment had no effect even though the treatment had an effect for every single subject. Your results, based on many subjects, would not generalize to anybody (just as national surveys show that the average American family has 2.3 children, although no American family has 2.3 children). Thus, the single-subject experiment, although only generalizing to half the population, would apply to many more people than the between subjects experiment. Furthermore, replicating the single-subject experiment would be more informative than replicating the between subjects experiment. Replicating the between subjects experiment might just give you the same null results every time. Replicating the single-subject experiment, on the other hand, might reveal that the treatment helps some subjects, but harms others. As a result of continued replications of the single-subject experiment, you might be able to isolate the variable that determines whether subjects are harmed or helped by the treatment.

You have seen that results based on a highly controlled study of a single subject can often be generalized to other subjects. But can the results of an experiment conducted under such controlled conditions be generalized to other settings? Yes, especially when the single-subject experiment investigates universal phenomena that are relatively unaffected by setting (e.g., sensation). Even when single-subject investigators cannot generalize their results to all settings, their detailed knowledge of the phenomena may allow them to be specific about which settings their results would generalize to.

---

[1]For a dissenting view, see Brewer (1974) who argues that there is no convincing evidence for operant conditioning in humans.

CONCLUSIONS ABOUT SINGLE-SUBJECT EXPERIMENTS

Not coincidentally, the single-subject experiment bears a close resemblance to physics and chemistry experiments. As is the case with experiments in the physical sciences, the single-subject experiment is most easily interpreted when the potential causal variables have been identified and controlled. Furthermore, just as universal physical laws (e.g., gas laws) allow the results of chemistry experiments done on a few hydrogen molecules to be generalized to all hydrogen molecules, universal laws (e.g., psychophysical laws, laws of operant conditioning) may allow experiments done on a single member of a species to be generalized to all members of the species. Finally, like the physics or chemistry experiment, when much is known about the variables that affect a given phenomenon, scientists can accurately predict the extent to which the results of a highly controlled study can be applied to other settings.

QUASI-EXPERIMENTS

Another popular alternative to the randomized experiment is the quasi-experiment. According to Cook and Campbell (1979), quasi-experiments are "experiments that have treatments, outcome measures, and experimental units, but *do not use random assignment* to create the comparisons from which treatment-caused change is inferred." Quasi-experiments are useful when researchers want to establish a causal relationship, but random assignment is impossible or impractical. For example, when it comes to letting one group of individuals have a certain type of therapy, drug, training, social program, or technology, organizations want to be the ones who decide who gets what treatment. Government agencies and business are often quite resistant to the idea of using random assignment to determine who gets the treatment. Consequently, often the only way to determine the effect of a treatment is to use a quasi-experimental design.

Because quasi-experimental designs are so useful for assessing the effects of real-life treatments, we will devote the remainder of this chapter to these designs. We will begin by discussing the general logic behind quasi-experimental designs. Then, we will take a more detailed look at some of the more popular quasi-experimental designs.

THE PROBLEM: ACCOUNTING FOR NONTREATMENT FACTORS

Like experiments, quasi-experiments establish temporal precedence by ensuring that the treatment comes before the outcome. Like experiments, quasi-experiments assess covariation by comparing treatments versus nontreatment conditions. However, unlike experiments, quasi-experiments are unable to account for nontreatment factors through either randomization or control.

Identifying Nontreatment Factors: The Value of Campbell and Stanley's Spurious Eight

Thus, the challenge in doing quasi-experiments is to rule out the effects of nontreatment variables without the aid of random assignment or control of nontreatment variables. The first step to meeting this challenge is to be aware of all the variables that might account for a relationship between the treatment and the effect. Once you have identified these variables, you will try to demonstrate that these variables did not account for the relationship.

To be aware of all the variables that might account for the relationship between the treatment and the effect is a tall order. Fortunately, however, all possible nontreatment factors fall under the eight threats to internal validity you learned about in chapter 4, namely:

1. History: apparent treatment effects being due to events in the outside world that are unrelated to the treatment.

2. Maturation: apparent treatment effects being due to natural biological changes.

3. Mortality: apparent treatment effects being due to subjects dropping out of the study. For instance, subjects might drop out shortly after entering the treatment condition.

4. Testing: apparent treatment effects being due to subjects having experienced the pretest.

5. Instrumentation: apparent treatment effects being due to changes in the measuring instrument. For example, the researcher may use a revised version of the measure on the retest.

6. Selection: apparent treatment effects being due to comparing groups that are different (comparing apples and oranges).

7. Statistical regression: apparent treatment effects being due to regression to the mean (the tendency for subjects who receive extreme scores on the pretest to receive less extreme scores on the posttest).

8. Selection-maturation interaction: apparent treatment differences between two groups that scored similarly in the pretest being the result of the groups naturally maturing at different rates. In other words, just because two groups scored similarly at the beginning of the study, you cannot assume they would have scored identically at the end of the study.

Using Logic to Combat the Spurious Eight

Once you have identified the threats to internal validity, you must determine which threats are ruled out by the design and which threats you can eliminate through logic (see table 10.5). Whereas experimental designs rule out threats to validity automatically, quasi-experimental designs vary in their ability to automatically rule out threats. Yet, even with a quasi-experimental design that does not automatically rule out threats, you may occasionally be able to infer causality.

TABLE 10.5 Ways of Preventing Threats to Internal Validity

THREATS	PRECAUTIONS
History	Isolate subjects from external events during the course of the study.
Maturation	Conduct the study in a short period of time to minimize the opportunities for maturation. Use subjects who are maturing at slow rates.
Testing	Only test subjects once. Give subjects extensive practice on task prior to collecting data so they will not benefit substantially from practice they obtain during the study. Know what testing effects are (from past data) and subtract out testing effect. Use different versions of same test to decrease the testing effect.
Instrumentation	Administer same measure, same way, every time.
Mortality	Use rewards, innocuous treatments, and brief treatments so subjects do not drop out of study. Use placebo treatments or subtly different levels of the treatment so more subjects do not drop out of one condition than out of another. Make sure subjects understand instructions so subjects are not thrown out for failing to following directions.
Regression	Do not choose subjects on basis of extreme scores. Do not match groups on variables on which they are fundamentally different.
Selection	Use random assignment. Match on all relevant variables. Do not use designs that involve comparing one group of subjects with another.
Selection Interactions	Match on all relevant variables, not just on pretest scores. In addition, use tips from earlier in this table to reduce the effects of variables—such as history and maturation—that might interact wtih selection. In other words, reducing the effect of maturation will also tend to reduce selection by maturation interactions.

THE PRETEST-POSTTEST DESIGN

To illustrate the potential usefulness of quasi-experimental designs, we will start by looking at a design that many would not even consider to be in the same class as a quasi-experimental design: the pretest-posttest design. The pretest-posttest design is very similar to the single-subject A-B design. But rather than compare one subject's behavior before treatment with that same subject's behavior after treatment, you use several subjects. That is, in a pretest-posttest study you would test one group of subjects, administer a treatment, and then retest them.

This design does not rule out many threats automatically. Hence, its low status as a design. However, because you are testing individuals against themselves, you do not have to worry about selection or selection-maturation interactions.

Although you do have to worry about mortality, instrumentation, regression, maturation, history, and testing, you may be able to rule out these threats on the grounds they are extremely improbable. If nobody dropped out of your study, mortality is not a problem. Similarly, if you were careful enough to use the same measure and administer it in the same way, instrumentation is not a problem. You might be able to rule out regression by arguing that people were not in the study because their scores were extreme. To support your argument, you might show that subjects were not in your study because they had "hit bottom" or were experiencing an unusually good or bad period in their lives. Furthermore, you might show that their pretest scores were not extreme. If there is a very short time between pretest and posttest, maturation is unlikely. About the only maturation that could occur in a short period of time would be boredom or fatigue. Obviously, you could rule out boredom and fatigue, and thus maturation, if performance was better on the posttest than on the pretest. If there were only a few minutes between the pretest and posttest, then history is unlikely.

Thus far, in this particular study, you have been able to rule out every threat except testing. And, you might even be able to rule out testing. For instance, if your measure was an unobtrusive one, testing might not be a problem. Or, if you used a standardized test, you might know how much people tend to improve when they take the test the second time. If your subjects improved substantially more than these norms, you could rule out the testing effect as an explanation for your results.

As you have seen, the pretest-posttest design eliminates very few threats to internal validity. However, by using your wits, you may be able to rule out the remaining threats and thereby infer causality (see table 10.6 for a review). Furthermore, as you will soon see, by extending the pretest-posttest design, you can create a quasi-experimental design that does eliminate most threats to internal validity—the time series design.

TABLE 10.6 How to Deal with the Threats to Internal Validity if You Must Use a Pretest-posttest Design

THREAT	HOW DEALT WITH
Selection	Automatically eliminated because subjects are tested against themselves.
Selection by maturation	Automatically eliminated because subjects are tested against themselves.
Mortality	Not a problem if subjects do not drop out. Conduct study over short period of time and use "undemanding" treatment.
Instrumentation	Standardize the way you administer the measure.
Regression	Do not select subjects based on extreme scores. Use a reliable measure.
Maturation	Minimize the time between pretest and posttest.
History	Minimize the time between pretest and posttest.
Testing	Use an unobtrusive measure. Have data from previous studies about how much subjects tend to change on retest.

Just as the complex single-subject design is an extension of the basic A-B design, the time series design is an extension of the basic pretest-posttest design. Like the pretest-posttest design, the time series design tests and retests the same subjects. Thus, it is not threatened by selection biases. However, unlike the pretest-posttest design, the time series design does not use a single pretest and a single posttest. Instead, the time series design uses several pretests and posttests. Thus, you could call time series designs "pre-pre-pre-pre-post-post-post-post" designs.

To illustrate the differences between the pretest-posttest design and the time series design, suppose you are interested in seeing if disclosing a professor's marital troubles affects how students evaluate him. With a pretest-posttest design, you would have a class evaluate the professor before he tells them about his marital problems, then have them rate him after he discloses his problems. If you observed a difference between pretest and posttest ratings, you would be tempted to say the difference was due to the disclosure. However, the difference might really be due to history, maturation, testing, mortality, instrumentation, or regression. Because you have no idea of how much of an effect history, maturation, testing, mortality, and instrumentation may have had, you cannot tell whether you had a treatment effect.

Estimating the Effects of Threats to Validity with a Time Series Design

But what if you extended the pretest-posttest design? That is, what if you had students rate the professor after every lecture for the entire term, even though the professor would not disclose his marital problems until the fifth week? Then, you would have a time series design.

What do you gain by all these pretests? From plotting the average ratings for each lecture, you know how much of an effect maturation, testing, instrumentation, and mortality tend to have (see table 10.7). In other words, when you observe changes from pretest to pretest, you know those changes are not due to the treatment. Instead, those differences must be due to maturation, testing, history, instrumentation, or mortality. For example, suppose ratings steadily improve at a rate of 0.2 points per week during the five-week, pre-disclosure period. If you then found an increase of 0.2 points from week five to six (when the professor made the marital disclosure), you would not attribute that increase to the disclosures. Instead, you would view such a difference as being due to the effects of history, maturation, mortality, testing, or instrumentation. If, on the other hand, you found a much greater increase in ratings from week five to week six than you found between any other two consecutive weeks, you would suspect the professor's disclosures about his marital problems improved his student evaluations (see figure 10.1).

Problems in Estimating Effects of Nontreatment Factors

Yet, your suspicions could be wrong. That is, you are *assuming* you can correctly estimate the effects of history, maturation, mortality, testing, and instrumentation during the time the treatment was administered. On the surface, this seems a safe assumption. After all,

TABLE 10.7 How Pretest-Posttest Designs and Time Series Designs Stack up in Terms of Dealing with Campbell and Stanley's Threats to Internal Validity

	TYPE OF DESIGN	
Threat to Validity	Pretest-Posttest Design	Time Series Design
Selection	A	A
Selection by Maturation	A	A
Mortality	C	C
Instrumentation	C	C
Maturation	P	E
Testing	P	E
History	P	E
Regression	P	D

Key: A = automatically eliminated by design; C = can be eliminated by using common sense; D = the design allows you to determine whether this factor is a plausible explanation for the apparent treatment effect; E = design allows you to estimate and then subtract out the effects of this factor—however, estimates may be wrong if the factor exerts an inconsistent effect; P = this factor is a real threat with this design.

for the pretest period, you know what the effects of those variables were. Thus, you may feel safe assuming that the effects of those variables were the same during the treatment period as they were during the pretest period. However, this assumption is only correct if the effects of history, maturation, mortality, instrumentation, and testing are relatively consistent over time. In other words, your suspicions could be wrong if there is a sudden change in any one of these variables.

Inconsistent Instrumentation Effects

Obviously, sudden changes in these variables are possible. Variables that have had negligible effects can suddenly have large effects. Suppose you administered the same rating scale in the same way for the first five weeks. Your measurements from weeks one through five would not be affected by instrumentation. As a result, your estimate for the amount of change to expect between week five and week six would not include any effect for instrumentation. However, what if you ended up handing out a refined version of your rating scale during week five—the same week the professor started telling his class about his marital problems? In that case, you could mistake an instrumentation effect for a treatment effect.

Inconsistent Mortality Effects

Likewise, if mortality does not follow a consistent pattern, you might mistake mortality's effects for treatment effects. For example, what if the last week to drop the course was the same week the professor started to tell the class about his problems. In that case, a disproportionate number of students who did not like the professor might drop out during that week. Consequently, the professor's ratings might improve because of mortality rather than because of his disclosures. Admittedly, you might discount some of this

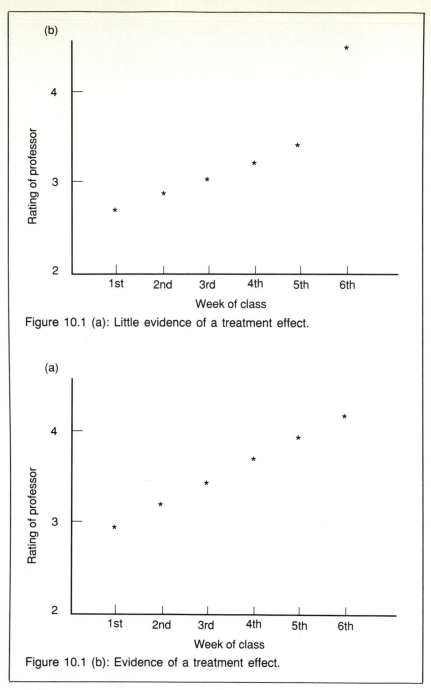

Figure 10.1 (a): Little evidence of a treatment effect.

Figure 10.1 (b): Evidence of a treatment effect.

FIGURE 10.1 Two Very Different Patterns of Results in a Time Series Design in Which the Treatment was Introduced after the Fifth Week

mortality effect if mortality was gradually causing ratings to improve during weeks one through five. However, the sudden rash of mortality will create an effect much greater than the data from weeks one through five would lead you to expect. Consequently, you might believe you have a treatment effect, when you really have a mortality effect.

Inconsistent Testing Effects

In this study, the effect of testing should be gradual and consistent. However, the effect of testing will not be consistent in every study. For example, in some studies, subjects might develop insight into the task. As a result of discovering the rule behind the task, their performance may increase dramatically. Even when subjects are not aware of having insight, practice does not always lead to steady improvement. As you know from experience, after weeks of practice or study with little to show for it, you may suddenly improve greatly.

Inconsistent Maturation Effects

Similarly, maturation's effect may sometimes be discontinuous. For instance, suppose you measure young children every three months on a motor abilities test. Then, you expose them to an enriched environment and measure them again. Certainly, you will see a dramatic change. But is this change due to the treatment or due to the children jumping to a more advanced developmental stage (e.g., learning to walk)?

Unfortunately, you cannot escape sudden, sporadic maturation by studying adults. Even in our teacher evaluation study, subjects might mature at an inconsistent rate. That is, first-year students might mature rapidly after getting their first exams back, students might suddenly develop insight into the professor's lecturing style, or the professor might suddenly develop insight into how the students like to have the class conducted. If this sudden development occurred the same week the professor started to disclose his marital problems, maturation could masquerade as a treatment effect.

History

Although you can often reasonably assume that the effects of testing, instrumentation, mortality, and maturation are consistent across time, history is less predictable. There are many specific events that could affect performance on the posttest. For instance, ratings of the professor might change as a result of students getting the midterm back, the professor getting ill, or the professor reading a book on teaching. Unlike the single-subject design, the time series design does not control all these history effects. Indeed, you could argue that the time series design's lack of control over history, and thus its vulnerability to history, prevent it from reaching experimental design status.

Although history is the one threat to which the time series is vulnerable, you can try to reduce its effects. One strategy is to have a very short interval between testing sessions. With an extremely short interval, you give history fewer opportunities to have an effect.

In addition to reducing the effects of history, you can also try to do a better job of estimating its effects. Because intimately knowing the past should enhance your ability to predict the future, you might collect an extensive baseline. Ideally, you would collect baseline data for several years. This baseline will help you identify any historical events or patterns that tend to repeat themselves regularly. For instance, your baseline would alert you to cyclical patterns in student evaluations, such as students being very positive toward the professor during the first two weeks of the term, more negative toward the professor after the midterm examination, then becoming more favorable during the last week of the term. Thus, your baseline would prevent you from mistaking these cyclical fluctuations for a treatment effect.

The Threat of Regression

To this point, we have discussed threats to validity that might be expected to change steadily from week to week (see table 10.8). But what about regression? Because regression is due to chance measurement error, regression will not change steadily from week to week. Therefore, you cannot use a time series design to measure regression's effect. However, you can use time series designs to determine whether regression is a likely explanation for your results. Specifically, you should be concerned about regression if the ratings immediately before the treatment are extremely high or extremely low relative to the previous ratings.

Eliminating, Rather Than Estimating, Threats to Validity

You have seen that the time series design can rule out certain threats to validity by estimating the effects of those threats. When using these designs, however, do not focus so much on estimating the impact of the threats to validity that you do not try to eliminate those threats (see table 10.9). For example, try to eliminate the threat of instrumentation by using the same measuring instrument each time and administering it the same way. For our student evaluation study, we would give students the same rating scales and the same instructions each time.

Likewise, try to eliminate mortality, whenever possible. Thus, if you had students sign their rating sheets, you could eliminate mortality by only analyzing data from students who had perfect attendance. If the ratings were anonymous, you could eliminate mortality by analyzing ratings from days when attendance was perfect.

Furthermore, try to reduce the effects of maturation and history by keeping the interval between pretest and posttest short. Finally, minimize the likelihood of regression occurring by choosing the time you will administer the treatment well in advance—do not introduce the treatment as an immediate reaction to extremely bad ratings.

Types of Time Series Designs

Now that you are familiar with the basic logic behind the time series design, you are ready to see how it can be extended. One simple way of extending a time series design is to

---

TABLE 10.8 Threats to Time Series Designs

History
Regression
Inconsistent effects
    Inconsistent instrumentation effects
    Inconsistent mortality effects
    Inconsistent testing effects
    Inconsistent maturation effects

TABLE 10.9 How Time Series Designs Deal With Threats to Internal Validity

THREAT	APPROACH
Selection	Automatically eliminated because testing and retesting same subjects.
Selection by maturation	Automatically eliminated because testing and retesting same subjects.
Instrumentation	If effects are constant, effects can be estimated. In addition, try to give same instrument in the same way every time.
Mortality	If effects are constant, effects can be estimated. In addition, if no subjects drop out, mortality is not a problem.
Testing	If effects are constant, effects can be estimated.
Maturation	If effects are constant, effects can be estimated. In addition, study slowly maturing subjects or make sure the time between last pretest and the posttest is very brief.
Regression	Regression unlikely if ratings prior to introducing the treatment were not extreme and did not differ greatly from previous ratings.
History	Try to collect extensive pretest data to predict history's effects. In addition, *may* try to make sure (1) time between last pretest and the posttest is brief and (2) subjects are isolated from outside events.

increase the number of pretest and posttest measurements you take. The more measurements you take, the easier it will be to estimate the combined effects of maturation, history, mortality, testing, and instrumentation. In addition, the more measurements you have, the less likely that an unusual history, maturation, mortality, testing, or instrumentation effect will occur at the same time you administer the treatment. For example, suppose you only measure student evaluations on the fourth, fifth, and sixth weeks. You administer the treatment between the fifth and sixth weeks. Would it be an unusual coincidence if history, maturation, mortality, testing, or maturation had more of an effect between the fifth and sixth weeks than between the fourth and fifth weeks? No. Consequently, a threat to validity might easily imitate a treatment effect. However, what if you had students evaluate the teacher from week one to week twelve? Then it would be quite a coincidence for a threat to have an extraordinarily large effect between the fifth and sixth week (the same week you gave the treatment), but not have such an effect between any of the other weeks.

Reversal Time Series Designs

You can also extend your time series design by administering *and* withdrawing the treatment. That is, you can imitate the single-subject experimenter's reversal design. For example, you might pretest, administer the treatment, posttest, withdraw the treatment, and test again. You might even withdraw and introduce the treatment several times.

To see the beauty of this reversal design, imagine you were able to get increases each time the professor tells his class about his marital problems, then decreases when he stops talking about his problems, followed by increases when the professor again tells the class about his marital woes. With that pattern of results, you would be very confident the disclosures made a difference.

Despite the elegance of this reversal design, there are cases when you should not use it. In some situations, you cannot ethically withdraw the treatment after you have administered it (e.g., psychotherapy, reinforcement for wearing seatbelts).

In other situations, withdrawing and readministering the treatment may alert subjects to your hypothesis. However, you may be able to prevent subjects from guessing the hypothesis or becoming resentful when you withdraw the treatment by using placebo treatments or multiple levels of the treatment. Thus, if you were to use this design for your student evaluations study, you might have a placebo condition in which the professor discloses innocuous facts about his marriage. Alternatively, you might use several levels of disclosure ranging from innocuous to intimate.

Two-Group Time Series Design

A final way of extending the time series design is to collect time series data on two groups. One group, the control group, would not get the treatment. The advantage of using a control group is that it allows you to rule out certain history effects. In your disclosure study, the control group might be another section of the same professor's class. If, after the treatment was administered, the ratings went down only in the treatment group, you could rule out general history effects (midterm blues, spring fever) as an explanation of the results. However, you cannot rule out every history effect because the two classes may have different histories (see figure 10.2). For example, the professor may have gotten mad at one class and not the other. To better understand the problems and strengths of using a time series with control group design, let us look at the parent of this design: the nonequivalent control group design.

THE NON-EQUIVALENT CONTROL GROUP DESIGN

The non-equivalent control group design is the simple experiment without randomization. Because of the non-equivalent control group design's similarity to the simple experiment, it has many of the simple experiment's strengths.

For example, because every subject is only tested once, the non-equivalent control group design, like the simple experiment, is not bothered by maturation, testing, or instrumentation. Furthermore, because of the control group, the non-equivalent group design, like the simple experiment, can successfully deal with the effects of history, maturation, and mortality.

But because this design does not use random assignment, the control and treatment groups are not equivalent. Because the control and treatment groups are not equivalent, comparing them may be like comparing apples and oranges. Thus, with the non-equivalent control group design, the threat of selection is serious.

To address the selection threat, some investigators match subjects. That is, they try to make sure that each subject in one treatment group is identical in several key respects to a subject in the other group. Subjects may be matched on a few background variables

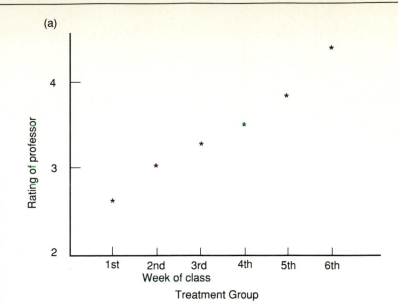

(a)

Figure 10.2 (a): Right after week 5, the treatment is introduced. Since ratings improve after getting the treatment, there is some suggestion that the treatment had an effect.

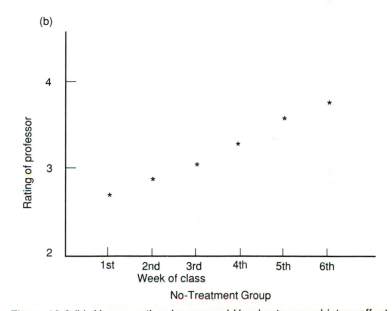

(b)

Figure 10.2 (b): However, the change could be due to some history effect. Thus, we use a no-treatment comparison group. In this case, the no-treatment group does not increase dramatically after week 5. Thus, we are more confident that the treatment has an effect.

FIGURE 10.2 The Two-Group Time Series Design

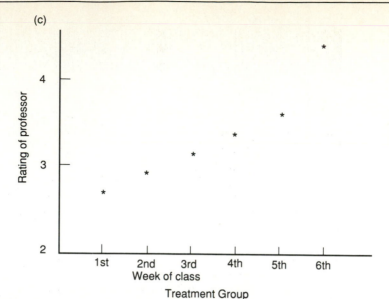

(c)

Figure 10.2 (c): Right after week 5, the treatment is introduced. Since ratings improve after getting the treatment, there is some suggestion that the treatment had an effect.

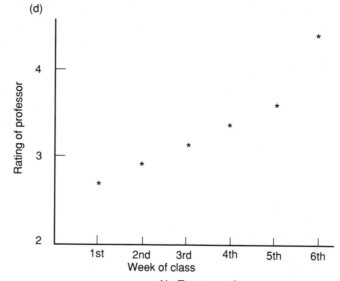

(d)

Figure 10.2 (d): However, the change could be due to some history effect. Thus, we use a no-treatment comparison group. In this case, the no-treatment group does increase dramatically after week 5. Consequently, we are now suspicious that the apparent treatment effect was just a history effect.

FIGURE 10.2 Continued

TABLE 10.10 How Two Non-equivalent Control Group Designs Stack up in Terms of Dealing with Threats to Internal Validity

Threat to Validity	Type of Non-equivalent Control Group	
	Unmatched	*Matched*
Selection	P!!!!	p
Selection by maturation and other interactions with selection	p	p
Mortality	C	C
Instrumentation	C	C
Maturation	A	A
Testing	A	A
History	A	A
Regression	p	P

Key: A = automatically eliminated by design; C = can be eliminated by using common sense; p = this factor is a threat to this design; P = this factor is a very serious and likely threat to this design's internal validity.

(age, gender, IQ) that may be expected to correlate with task performance or subjects may be matched on actual task performance (pretest scores). Although matching seems effective (see table 10.10), realize two important points about matched subjects: (1) matched subjects are *only* matched on a *few* variables and (2) matched subjects are matched on **observed scores** (observed scores are not the same as true scores).

Just because two groups are matched on a few variables, you should not think they are matched on all variables. They are not. The unmatched variables may cause the two groups to score differently on the dependent measure. For instance, suppose you decide to use a non-equivalent group design to test your hypothesis about the effect of marital disclosure. You want two classes that are similar so you match the classes on IQ scores, grade-point average, proportion of psychology majors, proportion of females and males, and proportion of sophomores, juniors, and seniors. Unfortunately, you have not matched them in terms of when classes meet (morning versus afternoon), interest in going on to graduate school, number of times they had taken classes from this professor before, and a few other hundred variables that might affect their ratings of the professor. These unmatched variables, and not the treatment, may account for the difference between your treatment and control groups.

Because investigators realize they cannot match subjects on every single factor that may influence task performance, some investigators try to match subjects on task performance (pretest scores). Yet, even when groups are matched on pretest scores, unmatched variables can cause the groups to score differently on the posttest. That is, just because two groups of students start out with the same enthusiasm for a course, you cannot be sure they will end the term with the same enthusiasm for the course. For example, one group may end the term with more enthusiasm because that group had a clearer understanding of what the course would be like, what the tests would be like, and how much work was involved. Consequently, although both groups might rate the professor the same at first, the groups may differ after they get the first exam back. That is, because the naive group had misconceptions about how the professor tested, they may rate the professor more harshly than the experienced group. Although this change in student attitudes toward the professor might appear to be a treatment effect, it is not. Instead, the difference between the two groups is due to the fact that subjects changed over time in different ways because of variables they were not matched on. Technically, there was a selection by maturation interaction. Because of interactions between selection and other variables, even matching on pretest scores does not free you from selection problems.

What can be done about interactions between selection and other variables? One approach is to **assume** that nature prefers simple, direct main effects to complex interactions. Thus, if an effect could be due to either a treatment main effect or an interaction between selection and maturation, assume the effect is a simple treatment main effect. Be aware, of course, that your assumption may be wrong.

If you want to go beyond merely assuming selection interactions are unlikely, you can make them less likely. One way to make selection interactions less likely is to make the groups similar on as many selection variables as possible. That is, not only can you match the groups on pretest scores but also on other variables. Because there would be fewer variables on which the groups differed, there would be fewer selection variables to interact with maturation, testing, history, etc. Hence, you would reduce the chance of these interactions occurring.

You have seen one way to reduce interactions between selection variables and other variables—reduce differences between groups that might contribute to selection. The other way to reduce interactions between selection and other variables is to eliminate those other variables. For instance, you can reduce the chances of the most common selection interaction, the selection by maturation interaction, by minimizing opportunities for maturation. After all, if neither group can mature, you cannot have a selection-maturation interaction. To do this, you should present the posttest as soon after the pretest as possible so that maturation has very little time to occur.

Another problem with matching is that subjects must be matched on **observed** scores, rather than on true scores. Unfortunately, observed scores are not the same as true scores. Observed scores are merely imperfect reflections of true scores because they are contaminated by measurement error. As a result of this measurement error, two groups might appear to be similar on certain variables when, in fact, they are actually very different on these same variables.

To illustrate this point, suppose a researcher wanted to examine the effect of a drug on treating clinical depression. The practitioner/researcher has received approval and patients' permissions to give the drug to the ten clinically depressed patients at his small psychiatric facility. However, he realizes if the participants improve after getting the drug, it proves nothing. Maybe the patients would get better anyway. He wants to have a comparison group that does not get the drug. After getting a phone call asking him to give a guest lecture at a nearby college, he gets an idea. He could use some college students as his comparison group. After testing hundreds of students, he obtains a group of ten college students who **score** the same on the depression scale as the group of ten mental patients. But are the two groups equal in terms of depression?

Probably not. The college students' scores are extremely depressed relative to the average college student. This is important because extreme scores tend to have an extreme amount of random error. Thus, when the students are tested again, their scores will be less extreme because their scores will not be as dramatically swayed by random error. That is, on the posttest, the college student subjects will score more like average college students—less depressed. Thus, because of the regression effect, it may appear that the drug hurts recovery from depression.

How can you stop from mistaking such a regression effect for a treatment effect? The obvious approach is to reduce regression. Because regression takes advantage of random measurement error, you can reduce regression by using a measure that is relatively free of random measurement error: a reliable measure. In addition, because extreme scores tend to have more random error than less extreme scores, do not select subjects who have extreme pretest scores.

A trickier approach to combat regression is to obtain results that regression cannot account for. In our depression example, regression would tend to make it look as if the college students had improved in mood more than the mental patients. Thus, if the college students improved more than mental patients, the results might be due to regression. However, if you found the opposite results—mental patients improving in mood more than college students—regression would not be an explanation for your results. So, the key is to get results exactly opposite from what regression would predict.

Unfortunately, there is no way to guarantee that your effect will be in exactly the opposite direction of the way regression is pushing the scores. Furthermore, even if the effect is in the opposite direction of what would be expected by regression, regression may overwhelm the effect. For example, even though your treatment had a positive effect, the scores—because of regression—may still decline.

When regression and selection by maturation are both pushing scores in the opposite direction of the treatment, the effect of even a moderately effective treatment may be hidden. Perhaps the researchers who have been most victimized by the double-team of both regression and selection by maturation are those that have tried to determine the effect of social programs. Sometimes, these researchers have tried to look at the effect of a social program by matching a group that participates in the program with individuals who are not eligible. For example, the researchers might match children who participated in Head Start with an upper-income group of children who had the same test scores. Unfortunately, they would have to choose the lowest scorers from that upper-income group, thereby setting themselves up for regression. Furthermore, the upper-income group would be expected to mature at a higher rate due to having a more enriched home environment. Thus, not surprisingly, some early studies of Head Start that failed to take regression and selection by maturation into account made it look as if Head Start harmed rather than helped children.

Although regression to different means and interactions with selection are formidable problems, they are not the only problems you can have when you match (see table 10.11). You may also have practical problems with matching. For example, suppose you have only one person who scored an "86." You could drop this subject from your study. But, if you drop every subject that does not have an exact match, you may end up

TABLE 10.11 Problems With Matching

PROBLEM	IMPLICATION
Cannot match on all variables.	Selection by maturation interactions possible.
Cannot match on true scores. Have to match on observed scores, which are not totally accurate.	May have regression effects.
Do not have subjects with identical scores.	If groups are not equal on matching variable, have selection problem.
	If need to throw out subjects to get groups to match, results may not generalize to subjects dropped from study.

dropping several subjects from the study. Because of all the subjects you eliminate, you may have trouble generalizing your results.

Therefore, you might try to use all your subjects. So, you might match the "86" with the next closest score, "92." This approach uses all your subjects, but, unfortunately, does not match them perfectly. As a result, you might not know whether your results were due to poor matching or to the treatment.

TACTICS FOR STUDYING AGE

To study the effects of age, developmental psychologists have cleverly modified several quasi-experimental designs. They modify those designs so that instead of looking at treatment effects, they are looking at age effects—what quasi-experimenters call maturation effects. Thus, the quasi-experimenter's threat to validity, maturation, becomes the age-researcher's variable of interest.

Cross-sectional Designs

One of the most common modifications of a quasi-experimental design is the cross-sectional design: a modification of the non-equivalent control group design. As with the non-equivalent control group design, the cross-sectional design involves at least two groups. However, instead of having two different treatment groups (a treatment group and a no-treatment group), the cross-sectional design includes two or more different age groups.

Like the non-equivalent control group design, the main threat to validity is selection (see table 10.12). That is, although you hope the age groups will be identical except for age, they may be different on other variables, such as education level or income. As with the nonequivalent control design, the best way to avoid the threats of these non-age variables is to match on as many variables as possible. However, even with extensive matching, you cannot rule out the possibility that what you call the effects of age are really

TABLE 10.12 The Non-equivalent Control Group Design and the Cross-sectional Design Share Similar Weaknesses

THREATS TO THE VALIDITY OF THE NON-EQUIVALENT CONTROL GROUP DESIGN	THREATS TO THE VALIDITY OF THE CROSS-SECTIONAL DESIGN
Selection	Selection
	Cohort effects (being exposed to a different history than the other groups)

the effects of growing up in a different generation: what developmental psychologists call cohort effects. That is, no matter how you match, you cannot give different generations the same histories. Thus, the cohort of people who were eighteen during the Vietnam War may have a different view of war than those who were eighteen during the war on Iraq. Thus, a change in attitudes toward war might not be the result of aging, but of different experiences. Similarly, younger individuals may score better on IQ tests simply because their cohort's education exposed to them to more of the material and vocabulary covered on IQ tests than the older cohort's did (Schaie, 1988). Again, without considering cohort effects, one might mistakenly overestimate the impact of aging on intelligence. Despite the cross-sectional design's vulnerability to selection and cohort effects, the cross-sectional design is very popular because it is less time-consuming than other designs.

Longitudinal Designs

Another popular method of studying age-related changes is the longitudinal design. The longitudinal design involves taking multiple measurements of each individual over a period of time. Sometimes this period of time can be fifty years!

In effect, the longitudinal design is a variation of the time series design (see table 10.13). As you will recall, the purpose of multiple measurements in the time series design is to assess the *combined* effects of maturation, instrumentation, mortality, and testing. Although longitudinal researchers use basically the same design, they want to assess the effects of only one of these variables: maturation. Unfortunately, longitudinal researchers cannot measure maturation in isolation. Instead, they must measure the combined effects of maturation, instrumentation, mortality, and testing. Thus, the researchers' task is to rule out instrumentation, mortality, and testing effects. They may rule out the effects of instrumentation by consistently using the same measure. They may rule out the effects of mortality by including only subjects who make it through the entire length of the study.

Ruling out the effects of testing is more difficult, but might be done by using unobtrusive measures or by using tests in which practice does not affect performance. As a last resort, researchers might use tests in which the effects of practice are well known and subtract out that effect. However, even if you rule out mortality, instrumentation, and testing, you still have to worry about the time series' old nemesis: history.

TABLE 10.13 The Time Series Design and the Longitudinal Design Share Similar Weaknesses

THREATS TO THE VALIDITY OF THE TIME SERIES DESIGN	THREATS TO THE VALIDITY OF THE LONGITUDINAL DESIGN
History!	History!
Mortality	Mortality
Testing	Testing
Instrumentation	Instrumentation
Maturation	

Sequential Strategies

In an attempt to disentangle cohort, age, and history effects, Baltes (1968) proposed two additional methods: the cross-sectional sequence and the longitudinal sequence. These two hybrids are most appropriate when your objective is to describe, rather than explain, age and cohort changes.

Both the cross-sectional and longitudinal sequences parallel the multiple-group time series design by combining the cross-sectional design with the longitudinal design. To get a better idea of how these hybrid designs work, imagine you have an age effect for the cross-sectional aspect of the design. If you have a group of twenty-five-year-olds who behave differently from a group of twenty-year-olds, this "age" effect could be a selection effect. For example, the older group might come from rural areas whereas the younger group comes from Philadelphia. However, an age effect for the longitudinal aspect of the design (twenty-five-year-olds behave differently than when they were twenty) cannot be explained by selection. In a sense, because the two designs that make up the sequential design have different weaknesses, they cover for each other. Therefore, a researcher finding an age effect for both the cross-sectional and longitudinal aspects of the design, would probably conclude age caused the observed effect.

The Cross-sectional Sequence

With the cross-sectional sequence, you simultaneously study different age groups (as in the cross-sectional design), but retest them after a period of time has passed (as in the longitudinal design). To understand the design, suppose you wanted to know when age changed people's attitudes toward their parents. In that case, you might measure attitudes of a group of fifteen-years-olds, a group of twenty-year-olds, and a group of twenty-five-year-olds. Five years from now, you would measure their attitudes again.

The Longitudinal Sequence

In the longitudinal sequence, you would conduct the study by measuring the attitudes of a group of fifteen-year-olds this year. Five years later, you would retest that group (when they are twenty) and test a new group of fifteen-year-olds. Five years later, you would retest both groups. Five years, later you would retest them again. Thus, you would have information on two different cohorts (cross-sectional) when they were both fifteen, twenty and twenty-five years old (longitudinal).

Evaluation of Sequential Strategies

Although the sequential strategies are welcomed improvements over the cross-sectional and longitudinal designs, critics point out that sequential designs presume to disentangle cohort, age, and history effects by assuming that history has little or no effect. This is a very big assumption.

CONCLUSIONS ABOUT QUASI-EXPERIMENTAL DESIGNS

Quasi-experiments ensure temporal precedence and assess covariation. However, quasi-experiments do not automatically rule out the effects of nontreatment factors.

Therefore, quasi-experimenters use a variety of tactics to compensate for the limitations of their designs. They may combine quasi-experimental designs, using one design to cover for another's weaknesses. For example, they may use a time series design to rule out selection biases and then use a non-equivalent control group design to rule out history effects. They may follow specific procedures to prevent certain threats. For instance, they may eliminate instrumentation biases by administering the same measure, the same way, every time. Finally, they may eliminate some threats by arguing that the particular threat is not a likely explanation for the effect. That is, they may argue that mortality was low and therefore not a threat or that scores were not extreme and so regression is not a problem.

When arguing that nontreatment factors are unlikely explanations for their results, quasi-experimenters often invoke the law of parsimony. The law of parsimony is the assumption that the simplest explanation is the most likely. Thus, the time series researcher argues that the simplest assumption to make is that the effects of maturation, instrumentation, testing, and mortality are consistent over time. Therefore, a dramatic change after introducing the treatment should not be viewed as a complex, unexpected maturation effect but as a simple, straightforward treatment effect.

You have seen that quasi-experimenters use the law of parsimony to suggest that simple, straight-line relationships among variables are more likely than complex, curvy, cyclical relationships. Quasi-experimenters also use the law of parsimony to suggest that main effects are more likely than interactions. For instance, suppose a researcher uses a non-equivalent control group design, but matches subjects on pretest scores to reduce the threat of selection. Such a design would still be vulnerable to selection-maturation interactions. Thus, the results might be explained as either a treatment main effect or a selection-maturation interaction. However, the treatment main effect is a simpler explanation than the selection-maturation interaction. Therefore, the researcher would—on the basis of the law of parsimony—argue that the results should be interpreted as a treatment main effect.

Clearly, the quasi-experimenter's job is a difficult one, requiring much creativity and effort. But there are rewards. Quasi-experimenters can often study the effects of treatments that could not be studied with conventional experimental designs. For example, quasi-experimenters can study treatments that could not—or should not—be randomly assigned. Furthermore, because quasi-experimenters often study real-life treatments, their studies sometimes have more external validity than traditional experimental designs.

CONCLUDING REMARKS

If you want to infer causality, the methods you learned about in this chapter are extremely useful. But what if you do not want to infer causality? What if you want to describe or predict behavior? Then, you will want to use one of the methods discussed in chapters 11 and 12.

SUMMARY

1. To infer that a treatment causes an effect, you must show that changing the amount of the treatment has an effect (covariation), that changes in the treatment come before changes in the effect (temporal precedence), and that no other variables are responsible for the effect.

2. By comparing treatment and nontreatment conditions, you can see whether the cause and the effect covary.

3. When you manipulate the treatment, you make sure the cause comes before the effect, ensuring temporal precedence.

4. Randomization is an effective way of ruling out the likelihood that nontreatment effects may be responsible for the effect.

5. Like the experiments we discussed in chapters 5, 6, 7, and 8, field experiments rely on random assignment to ensure that the treatment factor is the only factor that systematically varies. The main difference is that instead of using random assignment in a laboratory setting, the field experiment uses random assignment in a natural, real-life setting.

6. Field experiments may be useful when you want to increase power, generalize results to different settings or subjects (increase external validity), or increase construct validity.

7. The field experiment is not a cure-all. Using it does not guarantee enhanced power, external validity, or construct validity. In some cases, the field experiment may have less power and validity than the lab experiment. Furthermore, sometimes doing a field experiment may be unethical.

8. Although random assignment is difficult in the field, many researchers prematurely abandon the idea of using field experiments.

9. Field experiments that use intact groups often fail to establish or maintain independence, thus harming their internal validity. Furthermore, they may be vulnerable to three threats to construct validity: demoralization, compensation, and diffusion of treatment.

10. Like randomized experiments, single-subject experiments manipulate the treatment to ensure temporal precedence and compare conditions to assess covariation.

11. Single-subject experimenters try to identify the important, nontreatment variables. Once identified, they try to keep those variables constant.

12. Single-subject experimenters keep relevant individual difference variables constant by using a single subject.

13. Single-subject experimenters often keep relevant environmental variables constant by keeping the subject in a highly controlled environment.

14. The A-B-A, or reversal design, and the multiple-baseline design are used by single-subject experimenters to control for the effects of maturation and testing.

15. When it comes to construct validity, the single-subject experimenter and the within subjects experimenter are very similar. To prevent subjects from becoming sensitized to the hypothesis, both experimenters may use (1) few levels of the independent variable, (2) placebo treatments, and (3) gradual variations in the levels of the independent variable.

16. Unlike single-subject experimenters, quasi-experimenters do not know what all the relevant variables are and cannot exercise control over those variables.

17. Quasi-experimenters must explicitly rule out the eight threats to validity: history, maturation, testing, instrumentation, mortality, regression, selection, and interactions with selection.

18. Instrumentation can be ruled out simply by using the same measure, the same way, every time.

19. Mortality can be eliminated merely by keeping subjects in your study.

20. You can rule out regression if subjects were not chosen on the basis of their extreme scores or if your measuring instrument is extremely reliable.

21. The time series design is very similar to the single-subject design. The main difference is the time series design does not isolate subjects from history the way the single-subject design does. As a result, the time series Achilles' heel is history.

22. The non-equivalent control group design resembles the simple experiment. However, because subjects are not randomly assigned to groups, selection is a serious problem in the non-equivalent control group design.

23. Although the cross-sectional and longitudinal designs are more common among age researchers, the sequential strategies are most useful because they are more effective in disentangling the effects of cohort, age, and history.

24. Although quasi-experimental designs are not as good as experimental designs for inferring causality, they are more versatile.

A-B design
A-B-A reversal design
baseline
cohort effects
covariation
cross-sectional design
debrief
compensation
demoralization
field experiment
history

informed consent
instrumentation
longitudinal design
maturation
mortality
multiple-baseline design
non-equivalent control
   group design
pretest-posttest design
quasi-experiments

selection
selection-maturation
   interaction
sequential designs
single-subject designs
spurious
statistical regression
time series design
temporal precedence
testing

1. Compare and contrast how single-subject experiments and randomized experiments account for nontreatment factors.
2. What arguments can you make for generalizing results from the single-subject experiment?
3. How do single-subject designs and time series designs differ?
4. Design a quasi-experiment that looks at the effects of presidential assassinations on the stock market. What kind of design would you use? Why?
5. An ad depicts a student who has improved his grade-point average from 2.0 to 3.2 after a stint in the military. Consider Campbell and Stanley's "spurious eight." Is the military the only possible explanation for the improvement?
6. What problems are there in determining the effects of age?
7. In a field experiment, one work group is given a training program, the other is not. Productivity is then assessed.
   a. What problems might afflict this design?
   b. When productivity is assessed, the researchers find both groups are significantly more productive than the average worker. What might account for this result?
   c. What if both groups were significantly more productive than the average, but they were **not** significantly different from each other? What would you conclude?
8. According to one study, holding students back a grade harmed students. The evidence: Students who had been held back a grade did much worse in school than students who had not been held back.
   a. Does this evidence show that holding students back harms their performance? Why or why not?

b. If you were a researcher hired by a department of education to test the assertion that holding students back harms them, which of the designs in this chapter would you use? Why?

c. Design a study to test the hypothesis that holding children back harms their academic performance.

9. Design a study to determine whether electroconvulsive shock is an effective treatment for depression. Evaluate your study in terms of:

a. being ethical

b. having internal validity

c. having external validity

d. having construct validity

11

Descriptive Methods

In this chapter, you will be introduced to methods of describing behavior. Descriptive research is relatively straightforward because to describe behavior, all you need to do is measure variables.

In fact, at the most primitive level of describing behavior, you only have to measure a single variable, such as counting how many times something happens. Thus, the earliest research on "date rape" involved finding out how frequently women were raped by their dates.

At a more sophisticated level of description, you would measure your original variable and several other variables to see if they are related. Thus, research on date rape evolved from counting the number of date rapes to looking at variables that might be associated with being a date rapist or victim. For example, researchers studied whether date rapists exhibited aggressive tendencies prior to raping their victim and whether certain situations were more likely to lead to a date rape (e.g., a blind date).

As you see, descriptive research quickly progresses from describing a single variable to describing relationships among variables. Almost as soon as researchers had estimated the number of date rapes, they were finding factors that related to date rape. Because descriptive research almost always involves determining how variables *co*-vary, or how variables *relate* with one another, descriptive research methods are also called **correlational** methods.

USES FOR DESCRIPTIVE METHODS

When you use descriptive methods, you gain the ability to study virtually any variable in virtually any situation. You can use descriptive methods without manipulating variables. You can even use descriptive methods without limiting or accounting for the effects of extraneous variables. In short, with descriptive methods, you are free to discover whatever relationships exist between whatever variables you care to explore.

DESCRIPTIVE RESEARCH AND CAUSALITY

But this flexibility comes at a cost. Without being able to manipulate variables or account for the effects of extraneous variables, you cannot infer causality. As a result, you cannot determine the reason for the relationships you find. Thus, if you find a relationship between low self-esteem and people who have been raped, you cannot say *why* low self-esteem and rape are related. Certainly, you cannot say low self-esteem causes one to be raped.

Why not? First, because you do not know rape victims had low self-esteem *before* they were raped. It may be that prior to being raped, rape victims had high self-esteem but that being raped led to low self-esteem. Instead of low self-esteem being the cause of rape, it may be an effect of rape.

Second, you have not controlled for or accounted for variables that might be responsible for the relationship between self-esteem and rape. Many factors might lead one to have low self-esteem and to be raped. For example, being short may lead to low self-esteem and decrease one's ability to fight off an attacker. Or, having a low income may lead to low self-esteem and also make one more vulnerable to rape because low-income people may live in more dangerous neighborhoods (see figure 11.1).

To repeat a very important point, correlational methods do not establish causality.

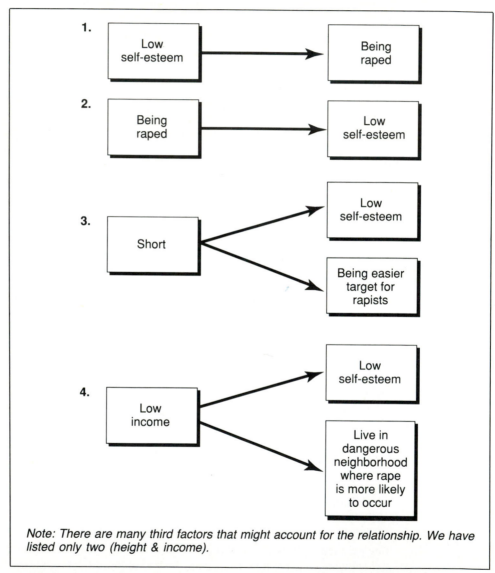

Note: There are many third factors that might account for the relationship. We have listed only two (height & income).

FIGURE 11.1: Three Basic Possibilities for an Observed Relationship

When you use a correlational method to find a relationship between two variables, you do not know whether the relationship is due to (1) changes in the first variable causing the second variable to vary, (2) changes in the second variable causing the first variable to vary, or (3) a third variable causing both variables to vary.

Stimulating Causal Hypotheses

Although correlational methods do not allow you to infer causality, they may stimulate causal hypotheses. As you can see from table 11.1, there are two ways that correlational methods may stimulate causal hypotheses.

First, if you find a relationship between two variables, you may want to do an experiment to determine whether the relationship is a causal relationship. For instance, knowing there was a correlation between smoking and lung cancer led to experiments that tested whether smoking caused lung cancer.

Second, even if you find that two related factors are *not* causally related, you may try to find out why they are related. That is, you may try to find out what third factor accounts for the relationship. For example, the finding that students who study more have lower grade-point averages might stimulate you to see if some studying strategies are less effective than others.

In summary, descriptive research does not allow you to infer causality (see table 11.2). However, descriptive research may stimulate research that will allow you to infer causality: Once you know what happens, you can try to find out why it happens.

DESCRIPTION FOR DESCRIPTION'S SAKE

By hinting at possible *causal* relationships, descriptive research can indirectly help psychologists achieve two goals of psychology—explaining behavior and controlling behavior. But the main purpose of descriptive research is to achieve another important goal of psychology—describing behavior.

But is description really an important, scientific goal? Yes, in fact, description is a major goal of every science. What is chemistry's famed periodic table, but a description of

TABLE 11.1 Generating Causal Hypotheses from Correlational Data

For each correlational finding listed below, develop an experimental hypothesis.
1. The correlation between studying and good grades is −.1, indicating some of the people who study the longest do below average in school.
2. People report being more persuaded by newspaper editorials than by television editorials.
3. People with high self-esteem believe vigilantes should not be arrested.
4. People are more depressed around holidays.
5. First-born children are less curious than their younger siblings.
6. The more people drink, the higher they tip.
7. Couples that laugh at the same things like each other more.

TABLE 11.2 Questions that Need To Be Answered to Establish that Two Variables Are Causally Related

Is there a relationship between the two variables in the sample?
 Did the researchers accurately measure the two variables?
 Did the researchers accurately record the two variables?
 Did the researchers accurately perceive the degree to which the variables were related?

If the variables are related in the sample, are the variables related in the population?
 Is the sample a random sample of the population?
 Even if the sample is a random sample of the population, is the sample big enough—and the relationship strong enough—that we can be confident the relationship really occurs in the population?

If the variables are related, did the predictor variable cause changes in the criterion?
 Is it possible that the "criterion" variable caused the predictor variable? That is, are we confusing cause and effect? Do we know which variable came first?
 Do we have data that suggest to us which came first? For example, high school records might provide information about self-esteem before being victimized. If there is no difference between victims' and non-victims' self-esteem before the attack, we would be more confident the attacks came before the lowered self-esteem.
 Can we logically rule out the possibility one variable preceded the other? For example, if height and being a victim were correlated, we can make a good case that the person's height was established before they were attacked. (Posture might be affected, but we would rely on accurate measurement to correct for this.)
 Is it possible that a third variable could be responsible for the relationship? That is, neither variable may directly affect (cause) the other. Instead, the two variables might be related because they are both effects of some other variable.
 Were all other variables kept constant or randomized? (This only happens in experimental designs.)
 Does the researcher know what the potential third variables are? If so, the researcher may be able to statistically control for those variables. However, it is virtually impossible to know and measure all the potential third variables.

the elements? What is biology's system of classifying plants and animals into kingdom, phyla, genus, and species, but a way of describing living organisms? What is astronomy, but a description of outer space? What is science, but systematic observation and measurement? Thus, one reason psychologists like descriptive methods is because description is the cornerstone of science.

DESCRIPTION FOR PREDICTION'S SAKE

Psychologists also like descriptive methods because knowing what is happening helps them predict what will happen. In the case of suicide, for example, psychologists discovered that certain signals (giving away precious possessions, abrupt changes in personality) were associated with suicide. Because past behavior is a good predictor of future behavior, psychologists realize that people sending out those signals are more likely to attempt suicide than people not behaving this way.

WHY DO WE NEED SCIENCE TO DESCRIBE BEHAVIOR?

Certainly, describing behavior is an important goal of psychology. But do we need to use scientific methods to describe what is all around us? Yes! Intuition alone cannot objectively measure variables, keep track of these measurements, measure the degree to which variables are related, and determine the generalizability of these results (see figure 11.2).

We Need Scientific Measurement

We need scientific methods to accurately measure the variables we want to describe. As you saw in chapter 3, objective, reliable, valid, and sensitive measurement of psychological variables is not automatic. If you are to observe psychological variables in a systematic and unbiased way, you must use scientific methods. Imagine using intuition to measure the number of sexist remarks, level of motivation, intelligence, or some other psychological variable!

We Need Systematic, Scientific Record Keeping

Even if your intuition gave you *accurate* measurements of psychological variables, you could not rely on your memory to keep track of your observations. Memory is, after all, "that strange deceiver." Therefore, if you are to accurately describe behavior, you need to systematically record your observations so your conclusions are not biased by memory's selectivity.

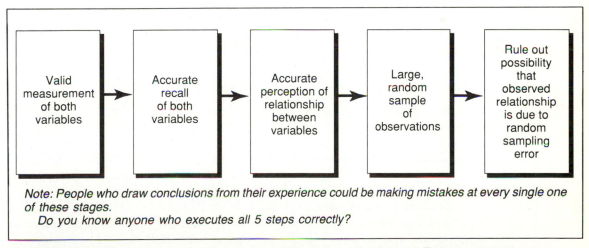

Note: People who draw conclusions from their experience could be making mistakes at every single one of these stages.
Do you know anyone who executes all 5 steps correctly?

FIGURE 11.2 Steps Involved in Determining That There Really Is a Relationship Between Two Variables

We Need Objective Ways to Determine Whether Variables Are Related

Obviously, if you are poor at keeping track of observations of one variable, you are going to be even worse at keeping track of two variables and the relationship between them. Therefore, you cannot rely on your judgment to determine whether or not two things are related.

People seem so anxious to see relationships that they see variables as being related even when they are not. In several experiments (Chapman & Chapman, 1967; Ward & Jenkins, 1965), researchers gave participants data that did not follow any pattern and did not contain any relationship among variables. However, participants usually "found" patterns in the data and "found" relationships between variables. Out of the lab, we know people "see" systematic patterns in the stock market, even though the stock market behaves in an essentially random fashion (Shefrin & Statman, 1986). Many people also believe that the interview is an invaluable selection device, even though research shows that interviews have virtually no validity (Schultz & Schultz, 1990).

Even when there is a relationship between two variables, the relationship people see between two variables may be exactly opposite of the relationship that exists. For example, basketball players and coaches swear (both literally and figuratively) that if a player makes a shot, that player will be more likely to make the next shot. In fact, as Tversky (1985) discovered, a shooter is less likely to make the next shot if he has made the previous shot. Many people are aware of the famed "*Sports Illustrated* Jinx"—the "fact" that a team or person on the cover of *Sports Illustrated* will perform worse. The belief in the "jinx" is so strong that many fans hate to see their favorite team on the magazine's cover. But fans need not fear—the truth is players and teams do better after appearing on the cover of *Sports Illustrated*.

Of course, sports fans are not the only ones to totally misperceive relationships. Many Americans think terrorism has increased since the late 1970s; in fact, terrorism has declined fairly steadily since the late 1970s. Many bosses and parents swear that rewarding people does not work while punishment does, even though research shows that rewards are more effective than punishments. And many students swear that cramming for exams is more effective than studying consistently, even though research contradicts this claim.

We Need Scientific Methods to Generalize From Experience

But even if you accurately describe your own experience, how can you generalize the results of that experience? After all, your experience is a limited and small sample of behavior. The problem with small samples is that they may cause you to overlook a real relationship. Thus, it is not surprising that one man wrote to "Dear Abby" to inform her that lung cancer and smoking were not related: He knew many smokers and none had lung cancer.

In addition to our experiences being so limited that we do not have an opportunity to see a relationship, we may fail to see that our experiences represent the exception rather than the rule. That is, the relationship you observe may simply be due to a coincidence. For example, if we go by some people's experiences, playing the lottery is a financially profitable thing to do. Whereas scientists can use statistics to determine the likelihood that a pattern of results is due to a coincidence, how can you intuitively discount the role of coincidence?

To discount the role of coincidence, you need to do two things. First, you need to have a random sample of behavior. Second, you need to use probability theory to determine the likelihood that your results are due to random error. Thus, even if you were an intuitive statistician, you would still face one big question: What's to say that your experience is a random sample of behavior? Your experience may be a biased sample of behavior. Results from such biased samples are apt to be wrong. For example, several years ago, George Bush beat Michael Dukakis by one of the biggest margins in the history of United States presidential elections. However, right up to election eve, some ardent Dukakis supporters thought Dukakis would beat George Bush. Why? Because everyone they knew was voting for Dukakis.

CONCLUSIONS ABOUT THE NEED FOR DESCRIPTIVE RESEARCH

As you can see, we need descriptive research if we are to accurately describe how people behave. Fortunately, descriptive research is relatively easy to do. To describe a single variable, you only need a way to accurately record a single variable from a representative sample of behavior. To describe how two variables are related, you need to get a representative sample of behavior, accurately measure both variables, and then objectively assess the association between those variables. Thus, the bottom line in doing descriptive research is getting measurements of a representative sample of behavior.

In the next few sections, we will look at several ways to get accurate measurements of samples of behavior. We will start by examining ways of making use of data that have already been collected, then move on to creating our own data.

SOURCES OF DATA

One possible source of data for descriptive research is the data you have already collected. For example, you might have done an experiment looking at the effects of time pressure on performance on a verbal task. At the time you did the study, you may not have cared about the age, gender, personality type, or other personal characteristics of your participants. For testing your experimental hypothesis, these individual difference variables were just nuisance variables because they caused unwanted random error. However, like saving money for a rainy day, you collected this information anyway.

EX POST FACTO RESEARCH: USING DATA YOU HAVE ALREADY COLLECTED

After the experiment is over, you might want to go back and look for relationships between these "nuisance variables" and task performance. This kind of research is called **ex post facto research**: research done after the fact.

External Validity

Suppose your ex post facto research revealed that women did better than men on the verbal task. Although this finding is interesting, you should be careful about generalizing your results. Unless the males and females in your study are a random sample drawn from the entire population of males and females, you cannot say females do better at this verbal task than males do. Your effect may simply be due to sampling males of average intelligence and females of above average intelligence. This sampling bias could easily occur, especially if your school was one that had higher admissions standards for women than for men. (Some schools did this when they switched from being an all women college to a coeducational institution.)

You could have a bit more confidence that your results were not due to sampling error if you had included a mathematical task and found that although the women did better than the men on the verbal task, men did better on the mathematical task. If, in this case, your results are due to sampling error, they are not due to simply having sampled women who are above average in intelligence. Instead, your sampling error would have to be due to something rather strange such as sampling women who were better than the average woman in verbal ability *and* who were worse than the average woman in mathematical ability. Although such a sampling bias is possible, it is not as likely as having merely sampled women who are above average in intelligence. Therefore, with this pattern of results, you would be a little more confident that your results were not due to sampling error.

Construct Validity

Even if you could show that your results are not due to sampling error, you could not automatically conclude that women had greater verbal ability than men. To make this claim, you would have to show that your measure was a valid measure of verbal ability **and** that the measure was just as valid for men as it was for women.

Internal Validity

Through careful random sampling and choice of measures, you might be able to determine that women had better verbal ability than men. However, you could not say *why* women had superior verbal ability. Remember, correlational methods are not useful for inferring causality. Therefore, you could not say whether the difference in men's and women's verbal ability was due to inborn differences between men and women or due to differences in how men and women are socialized.

Conclusions about Ex Post Facto Research

In summary, ex post facto research takes advantage of data you have already collected. Therefore, the quantity and quality of ex post facto research depends on the quantity and quality of data you collected during the original study. The more information you collect about your participants' personal characteristics, the more ex post facto hypotheses you can examine. The more valid your measures, the more valid your conclusions. The more representative your sample of participants, the more external validity your results will have. Therefore, if you are doing a study, and there is any possibility that you will do ex post facto research, you should prepare for that possibility by using a random sample of participants and/or collecting a lot of data about each participant's personal characteristics.

ARCHIVAL DATA

Rather than use data that you have collected, you can use **archival data**: data that someone else has already collected. Basically, there are two kinds of archival data: coded data and uncoded data.

Collected and Coded Data

Coded data are data that have been collected and tabulated by others. Market researchers, news organizations, behavioral scientists, and government researchers are all collecting and tabulating data. How much data? To give you some idea, over five thousand Americans are surveyed every day—and surveys are just one way these researchers collect data.

If you can get access to archival research, you can often look at data that you could never have collected yourself. Unfortunately, much of these data you never would have wanted to collect because they were collected and coded in a way that is inappropriate for your research problem.

Collected but Uncoded Data

If you want to code data yourself, but you do not want to collect your own data, you can use the second kind of archival data: data that have been recorded, but are uncoded. Records of behavior range from letters to the editor to transcripts of congressional hearings to videotapes of "The People's Court" to baseball statistics to ads in the personal columns for a husband or a wife.

The primary advantage of using records of data is that the data have already been collected for you. All you have to do is code it. And you can code it as best suits your needs.

The disadvantage of this kind of data is that you have to code it. As we mentioned in chapter 3, a useful way to code behavior is **content analysis.** Content analysis has been used to categorize a wide range of free responses—from determining whether a threatening letter is from a terrorist or a prankster to determining whether someone's response to an ambiguous picture shows they have a high need for achievement.

To use content analysis to categorize behavior, you first must carefully define your categories. Next, you should provide examples of each category. Finally, train yourself and your raters to use these categories.

A primary aim in content analysis is to define your categories as objectively as possible. Some researchers define their categories so objectively that all the coder has to do is count the number of times certain words come up. For example, to get an indication of America's mood, a researcher might count the number of times words like "war" or "fight" appear in *The New York Times*. These word-counting schemes are so easy to use that even a computer can use them. In fact, researchers have invented a computer program that can tell genuine suicide notes from fake ones (Stone, Dunphy, Smith, & Ogilvie, 1966).

Unfortunately, objective criteria are not always so valid. To get totally objective criteria, you often have to ignore the context—yet the meaning of behavior often depends on the context. For example, you might use the number of times the word "war" appears in a newspaper as a measure of how eager we are for war. This method would be objective, but what if the newspaper was merely reporting wars in other countries? Or, what if the newspaper was full of editorials urging us to avoid war no matter what the cost? In that case, our measure would be objective, but invalid.

For measuring some variables, context is so important that totally objective scoring criteria are virtually impossible. Whether a remark is sarcastic, humorous, or sexist may depend more on when, where, and how the statement is made than on what is said.

To illustrate both the advantages and disadvantages of archival research, suppose you wanted to know whether people were more superstitious when they were concerned about the economy. As your measure of concern about the economy, you use government statistics on unemployment. As your measure of how superstitious people are, you have the computer count the number of key words such as "magic," "superstition," and "Ouija board" that appear in local newspapers and then divide this number by the total number of words in the newspaper. This would give you the percentage of superstitious words in local newspapers.

Internal Validity

Once you had your measures of the economy and of superstition, you would correlate the two. Suppose you found the higher unemployment was, the more superstitious words were used in the newspaper. Because you have done a correlational study, you cannot say why the two variables are related. That is, you do not know whether (1) the economy caused people to become superstitious, (2) superstitious beliefs caused the downfall of the economy, or (3) some other factor (a bad freeze or drought ruining crops) is responsible for both an increase in superstitious beliefs and a decline in the economy.

Construct Validity

In addition to the normal problems associated with correlational data, you have several problems specific to archival data. You are using measures of a construct, not because they are the best but because they are the only measures that someone else bothered to collect. Although you are using unemployment records as an index of how insecure people felt about the economy, you would have rather asked people about how they felt about the economy. To the degree to which the relationship between how many people were unemployed and how people felt about the economy is questionable, your measure's construct validity is questionable.

Even if there is a strong relationship between unemployment and concerns about the economy, your measure may lack construct validity because it may not even assess unemployment. It may have poor construct validity because of **instrumentation bias:** the criteria for who is considered unemployed changing over time. Sometimes this change in criteria is planned and is formally announced. For example, the government may change the definition from "being unemployed" to "being unemployed and showing documentation that he or she looks for three jobs every week." Other times, the change may not be announced. For instance, computerization and unemployment compensation make current unemployment statistics more complete than they were in the early 1900s. Or, because the people who would collect unemployment statistics—social workers and other government workers—are sometimes laid off during hard economic times, unemployment statistics might be less complete during periods of high unemployment. Or, more sinisterly, politicians or administrators may distort unemployment data to make things seem better than they are.

Of course, the construct validity of your measure of superstition is also questionable. Is the number of times superstitious terms are mentioned in newspapers a good index of superstition? Perhaps these articles sell papers, and major newspapers only stoop to using these articles when sales are very low. About the only advantage of this measure over having results of some nationwide survey that questioned people directly about their superstitious beliefs is that your measure is **nonreactive**: your collecting it does not change participants' behavior.

External Validity

Because you can collect so much data so easily, your results should have good external validity. In some cases, your results may apply to millions of people because you have data from millions of people. For example, you can easily get unemployment statistics for the entire U.S. Furthermore, because you can collect data for a period of years rather than for just the immediate present, you should be able to generalize your results across time.

The Limits of Aggregate Data

Gaining access to group data (e.g., the unemployment rate for the entire U.S. for 1931) is convenient and may aid external validity. However, as psychologists, we are interested in individuals and what individuals do. Therefore, we want individual data. Consequently, even if we find a correlation between unemployment for the nation as a whole and superstition for the nation as a whole, we are still troubled. We do not care about knowing about the nation as a whole, we care about individual behavior. Are the people who are unemployed the ones who are superstitious? Or, are the superstitious ones the people whose friends have been laid off? Or, do the rich become superstitious? With aggregate data, we cannot say.

Conclusions about Archival Research

By using archival data you can get access to a great deal of data that you did not have to collect. Having access to these data may allow you to test hypotheses you would otherwise be unable or unwilling to test. Furthermore, because these data often summarize the behavior of thousands of people, your results may have impressive external validity.

Unfortunately, relying on others to collect data has its costs. You may find that data were not collected as carefully and as consistently as you would have collected them. You may find that others used measures that have less construct validity than the measures you would have used. You may find that you have data about groups, but no data about individuals. As a result of these problems with archival data, you may decide that the best way to get data is to get it yourself.

OBSERVATION

One way to collect your own data is through observation. As the name implies, observation involves simply watching behavior. As such, observation is often incorporated in many research methods. For example, observation is sometimes used to measure behavior in experiments.

Observation is also of interest for its own sake. Describing behavior is a vital concern of every field of psychology. Developmental psychologists use observation to describe child-parent interactions, social psychologists to describe cults, clinical psychologists to describe abnormal behavior, counseling psychologists to describe human sexual behavior, and comparative psychologists to describe animal behavior.

Types of Observational Research

Basically, there are two kinds of observation: naturalistic observation and participant observation. In **naturalistic observation,** you try to unobtrusively observe the participant, adopting a detached attitude. In **participant observation,** on the other hand, you actively interact with your participants. In a sense, you become "one of them."

Which method is better? It depends on who you talk to. Advocates of participant observation claim you get more "inside" information by using participant observation.

Advocates of naturalistic observation counter that the information you get through participant observation may be tainted. As a participant, you are in a position to influence (bias) what your participants do. Furthermore, as an active participant, you may be unable to sit back and record behavior as it occurs. Instead, you may have to rely on your (faulty) memory of what happened.

Problems with Observation

Whether you use participant or naturalistic observation, you face two major problems. First, if participants know they are being watched, they may not behave in their normal, characteristic way. Second, even if participants act "natural," you may not objectively record their behavior. That is, your personality and motives may affect what things you ignore and how you interpret what you do pay attention to.

Effects of the Observer on the Observed

There are two basic strategies you can use to minimize the degree to which you change behavior by observing it. First, you can observe participants unobtrusively. For example, you might want to observe participants through a one-way mirror.

If you cannot be unobtrusive, you may try the second strategy: become less noticeable. There are two basic strategies for becoming less noticeable. First, you can observe participants from a distance, hoping they will ignore you. Second, you can let participants become familiar with you, hoping they will eventually habituate to you. Once participants are used to you, they may forget you are there and revert back to normal behavior.

Difficulties in Objectively Coding Behavior

Of course, while you are observing behavior, you will be recording it. As is the case with archival data, one problem with observation is different coders may code data differently. As is also the case with archival data, the solution is to develop a content analysis scheme. You need to do the following:

1. Define your categories
2. Develop a set of criteria to determine whether or not a given behavior meets that criteria
3. Develop a check sheet to mark off each time a target behavior is exhibited
4. Train your raters to use your check sheet

Training and motivating your raters is even more important in observational research than in archival research for two reasons. First, in observational research, the rater not only codes the data but also collects the data. Second, in observational research, there usually are no permanent records of data. Because there are no permanent records, unmotivated or disorganized raters do not get a second chance to rate a behavior they missed—there is no instant replay. Furthermore, because there are no permanent records, you cannot check or correct a rater's work.

Training should involve at least three steps. First, you should spell out what each category means, giving both a definition of each category and some examples of behaviors that do and do not belong in each category. Second, you should have raters judge several videotapes, then explain why their ratings are right or wrong. Third, you should continue the training until each rater is at least 90 percent accurate.

TESTING

If you do not want to rely on observers, you may decide to use tests. Tests are especially useful if you want to study personality variables. For instance, you might correlate scores on an ability to delay gratification test with scores on an intelligence test or with scores on a social adjustment test.

External Validity

As is the case with ex post facto research, the external validity of your findings depends on the representativeness of your sample. You cannot generalize your results to a population unless you have a random sample of that population. Therefore, you cannot say women are more extroverted than men unless you have a random sample of all men and women. Similarly, you cannot say extroverts are more intelligent than introverts unless you have a random sample of all introverts and extroverts.

Internal Validity

As is the case with all correlational research, if you find a relationship, it is not necessarily a causal relationship. This is important to keep in mind because many researchers try to show genetic basis for some characteristic (career preferences, schizophrenia, introversion, etc.) by showing a correlation between identical twins on that trait. However, identical twins could be similar on the trait because they share a similar environment or because they have influenced one another.

Even when researchers show that twins reared apart score similarly on tests, it does not necessarily mean heredity accounts for the similarity. Identical twins reared apart tend to live in similar environments. Why? Because great care is taken to select parents that are as similar to their natural parents as possible. Because twins have the same natural parents, they tend to be reared in similar environments.

Conclusions about Testing

By using tests, you can take advantage of measures that other people have spent years developing. As a result, construct validity is usually less of a problem than if you had devised your own measures. Furthermore, tests are often easier to use than other measures. Because of these advantages, tests are often used in experimental as well as nonexperimental research. However, when tests are used in nonexperimental research, this research has the same weaknesses as other correlational research: It does not allow you to establish causality, and the generalizability of your results will be only as good as the representativeness of your sample. (For a comparison of correlational methods, see table 11.3.)

TABLE 11.3 Comparing Different Correlational Methods

VALIDITY	EX POST FACTO	ARCHIVAL	OBSERVATION	TESTS
Construct validity	Fair	Fair to poor	Fair to poor	Fair to good
Objective—avoids observer bias	Good	May be good	May be poor	Good
Non-reactive—avoids subject biases	Often a problem	Often good	Can be poor	Reactive—but steps taken to control for subject biases
Operational definition fits definition of construct	Fair to poor	Often poor	Fair	Good
External validity	Depends on sample	Depends on sample	Depends on sample	Depends on sample
Ease of getting large, representative sample	Depends on original study	May be easy	Hard to do	May be easy
Internal validity	Poor	Poor	Poor	Poor

DESCRIBING YOUR DATA

Once you have coded your data, you want to compile and summarize them. You want to know what the data "looks like." To find out what patterns there are in the data, you have two basic options: graph the data or compute descriptive statistics.

GRAPHING

Usually, one of the first things you should do after collecting your scores is to graph them. Start by labeling the *x*-axis (the horizontal axis) with one of your variables and labeling the *y*-axis (the vertical axis) with the other variable. Then, plot each observation.

For example, suppose we were looking at the relationship between impulsivity and grade-point average. Figure 11.3 shows the beginning of such a graph. As you can see, we have plotted the score of our first participant, a student who has a grade-point average of 2.0 and a score of "4" on the impulsivity scale. For reasons that will be obvious after we plot all our data, this graph is called a **scatterplot.**

There are four basic relationships the scatterplot could reveal. First, the scatterplot could reveal a pattern like the one shown in figure 11.4. The figure indicates that the more impulsive one is, the higher one's grade-point average is likely to be. Put another way, the less impulsive one is, the lower one's grade-point average. This kind of relationship is called a **positive correlation.** One common example of a positive correlation is the relationship between height and weight: the taller you are, the more you are likely to weigh.

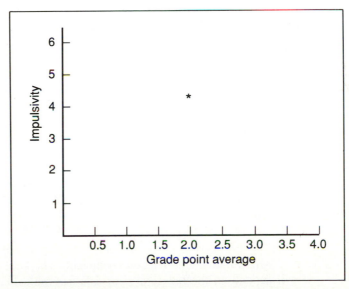

FIGURE 11.3: The Beginning of a Scatterplot

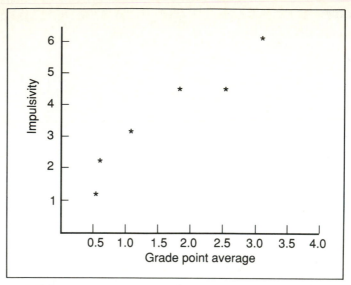

FIGURE 11.4: A Scatterplot Revealing a Positive Correlation

Second, the scatterplot could reveal a pattern like the one shown in figure 11.5, where the more impulsive one is, the lower one's grade-point average. Put another way, the less impulsive one is, the higher one's grade-point average. This relationship is called a **negative correlation.** Many variables are inversely or negatively related. One common example of a negative correlation is the relationship between exercise and weight: the more you exercise, the less you tend to weigh.

Third, the scatterplot might reveal no relationship between impulsivity and grade-point average. This pattern is depicted in figure 11.6.

Fourth, you could have a nonlinear relationship between impulsivity and grade-point average. As you can see from figure 11.7, in a complex, nonlinear relationship, the relationship between impulsivity and grade-point average may vary, depending on the level of the variables. Thus, in the low ranges of impulsivity, impulsivity may be positively correlated with grade-point average, but in the high ranges, impulsivity may be negatively correlated with grade-point average.

CORRELATION COEFFICIENTS: WHEN A NUMBER MAY BE WORTH ONE THOUSAND POINTS

Although a graph gives a good picture of your data, you may want to summarize your data with a single number: a **correlation coefficient.** The kind of correlation coefficient you use will depend on the nature of your data (see table 11.4).

Like all correlation coefficients, the Pearson r summarizes the relationship de-

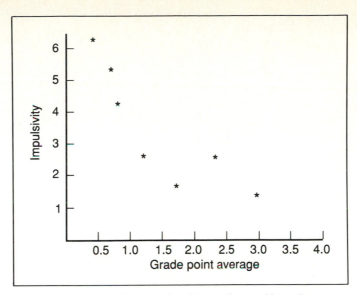

FIGURE 11.5: A Scatterplot Revealing a Negative Correlation

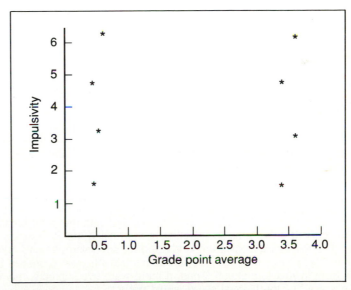

FIGURE 11.6: A Scatterplot Revealing a Zero Correlation

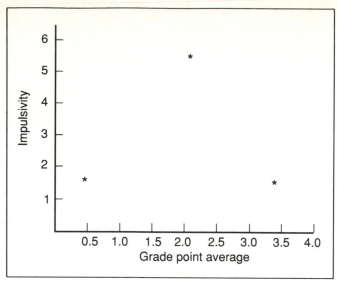

FIGURE 11.7: A Scatterplot Revealing a Nonlinear Relationship

---

TABLE 11.4   Different Kinds of Correlation Coefficients

In reading the literature, you may come across correlation coefficients other than the Pearson r. In addition, you may be called on to compute correlations other than the Pearson r. This table should help you understand the distinctions between these different coefficients.

NAME OF COEFFICIENT	USES
Pearson r	When both variables are interval (height with weight)
Point biserial	When one variable is interval, the other nominal (weight with gender)
Spearman's rho	Data are ordinal—ranked data (high school rank with military rank)
Phi coefficient	Both variables are nominal (gender with race, race with learning style)

As Cohen and Cohen (1983, 38–39) point out, the Pearson r, the point biserial, the phi coefficient, and Spearman's rho can all be computed using the same formula. That formula is the formula for the Pearson r (see box 11.1).

If all these correlations can use the same formula, then why do they have different names? One reason is, when people had to calculate these correlations without the aid of computers, they wanted the shortest computational formula available. It turns out that with the point biserial, phi, and rho, there are easier ways to compute the correlation coefficient than using the Pearson formula. A second reason is to sensitize people to the fact that different kinds of data are being plugged into the equation. If, for example, you use Spearman's rho, you do not use participants' raw scores in the formula, but their ranks (ranking them from lowest to highest). Thus, if there were five subjects, the lowest score on the first variable would get a "1," the highest score would get a "5."

---

scribed in your scatterplot with a single number. Like most correlation coefficients, the Pearson r ranges from −1 to +1.

Also, like most correlation coefficients, the Pearson r should corroborate your scatterplot. If your scatterplot indicates a positive correlation between the two variables, your correlation coefficient should also be positive. If the scatterplot indicates your variables are not related, then your correlation coefficient should be near zero. Finally, if your variables are negatively related, then the correlation coefficient should be negative.

The Logic Behind the Pearson r

Although box 11.1 shows you how to compute the Pearson r, it does not explain the logic behind the Pearson r. Basically, there are two ways to think about that logic: in terms of the definition of correlation and in terms of a scatterplot of the data.

As you know, the correlation coefficient is a measure of the degree to which two variables go together. If the variables are positively correlated, then, when one variable is above average, the other is usually above average. In addition, when one variable is below average, the other tends to be below average. If the variables are negatively correlated, the reverse happens: when one is above average, the other is usually below average.

To see how the Pearson r mathematically matches that description, suppose we have the scores of several students on two variables: how well they learned definitions of

---

BOX 11.1 Calculating the Pearson r

As we mentioned in the text, the Pearson r is an index of the degree to which two variables vary together. Thus, you will not be surprised to find that in computing the Pearson r, each pair of scores is multiplied together.

We also mentioned that correlations may be negative if X and Y are inversely related. However, if X and Y are both always positive (height and salary), how can we obtain a negative number? The answer is by subtracting an estimate of what the product of the two sets of scores would be if the numbers were totally unrelated. Thus, if the numbers are truly unrelated, the correlation will be 0. If the numbers are inversely related, their product will be smaller than this estimate, resulting in a negative correlation.

Finally, we mentioned that correlations cannot be smaller than −1 nor larger than +1. Therefore, you realize the product of all the pairs of scores is divided by two things that will keep the Pearson r from getting too large: the number of pairs of scores and a measure of variability of the scores of each of the two variables.

Because the product of scores is divided by these two factors, the correlation will range between −1 and +1, regardless of whether you compute a correlation based on five or five thousand and regardless of whether the participants' raw scores range from 1.5 to 1.6 or from 200 to 200,000.

Specifically, one formula for the Pearson r is:

$$\frac{\Sigma XY - (\Sigma X \cdot \Sigma Y/N)}{N \cdot sdX \cdot sdY}$$

To see this formula in action, imagine you collected data from five students at your school on impulsivity (X) and grade-point average (Y). Furthermore, assume impulsivity and grade-point average are interval scale variables. To see if the variables were related, you would use the following steps to compute a Pearson r:

Step 1: List each pair of scores in the following manner:

	SCORE FOR *X*	SCORE FOR *Y*	*X · Y*
1st pair	1	1	1
2d pair	2	2	4
3rd pair	3	2	6
4th pair	4	4	16
5th pair	5	3	15
Step 2: Sum the scores in each column.	15	12	42

Step 3: Calculate the means for variables X and Y. Mean of X: 15/5 = 3. Mean of Y: 12/5 = 2.4.

Step 4: Calculate the sum of squares (SS) for variables X and Y.

$(X - \bar{X})^2$	$(Y - \bar{Y})^2$
$(1 - 3)^2$	$(1 - 2.4)^2$
$(2 - 3)^2$	$(2 - 2.4)^2$
$(3 - 3)^2$	$(2 - 2.4)^2$
$(4 - 3)^2$	$(4 - 2.4)^2$
$(5 - 3)^2$	$(3 - 2.4)^2$
10	5.2

Step 5: Calculate the variance for X and Y (variance = SS/N). Variance for X: 10/5 = 2.0. Variance for Y: 5.2/5 = 1.04.

Step 6: Calculate the standard deviations (sd) for variables X and Y (sd = square root of variance). sdX: $\sqrt{2.0}$ = 1.41. sdY: $\sqrt{1.04}$ = 1.02.

Step 7: Multiply the sum of X by the sum of Y and divide by the number of pairs: (15 · 12)/5 = 180/5 = 36.

Step 8: Subtract this term (36) from the sum of X · Y (42): 42 − 36 = 6.

Step 9: Divide this term (6) by the number of pairs times the standard deviation of X times the standard deviation of Y: 6/(5 · 1.41 · 1.02) = .83.

certain words and how well they picked up on nonverbal cues.[1] To see if student learning is correlated with sensitivity to nonverbal cues, we convert those scores in the following way. If a student scores below the average in terms of recalling the definitions, the student gets a negative score on learning (a score of "−1"). If the student recalls more than the average student in the study, then the participant gets a positive score (a score of "+1"). We do the same thing for students' scores on reading nonverbal cues: a score of "−1" indicates the participant is below average, a score of "+1" indicates the participant is above average.

After recoding the data, we multiply each pair of scores. Thus, if someone is above average in both learning and sensitivity to nonverbal cues, we multiply +1 × +1. If someone is below average in both amount learned and nonverbal sensitivity, we multiply −1 × −1. We then add up all the results of these and divide by the number of research participants. This will give us a number between −1 and +1.

This number will be positive if there is a positive correlation between amount learned and nonverbal sensitivity. That is, people who are high in both amount learned and nonverbal sensitivity will contribute +1s (because +1 × +1 = +1), as will people who are low in both amount learned and nonverbal sensitivity (because −1 × −1 = +1). Thus, if the variables are positively correlated for most people, most of the scores will be +1s. Consequently, the average will be positive. The greater the percentage of people who are high on both variables or low on both variables, the closer the average will be to +1.

Conversely, if participants who are above average on one variable (+1) are usually below average on the other variable (−1), we will end up with a negative correlation. Indeed, if everyone who is high on one variable is low on the other, our average will be −1 (because +1 × −1 = −1).

Finally, consider the case where there is no relationship between the variables. In that case, half the participants who are above the average in nonverbal sensitivity are above the average in amount learned. However, half of the participants who are above the average in nonverbal sensitivity are below average on amount learned. In other words, half those participants are contributing a +1 (because +1 × +1 = +1), whereas half are contributing a −1 (because +1 × −1 = −1). The +1s and the −1s cancel each other out, summing to 0. Likewise, half the participants who are below average on nonverbal sensitivity are below average on amount learned, whereas half are above average on amount learned. Therefore, half of those participants are contributing a +1 (because −1 × −1 = +1), whereas half are contributing a −1 (because −1 × +1 = −1). The +1s and the −1s cancel each other out, summing to 0. Because half the time we end up with a +1 and half the time a −1, our coefficient will end up being 0.

Mathematically, the Pearson r is a little more complex than this. However, this is the basic logic behind it.

We have discussed how the Pearson r could be mathematically derived from the verbal definition of correlation. However, as we mentioned earlier, the Pearson r can also be viewed as deriving from a visual representation of correlation.

---

[1]For a published example of a Pearson r calculated on these two variables, see Bernieri, F. J. (1991). Interpersonal sensitivity in teaching interactions. *Personality and Social Psychology Bulletin, 17*, 98–103.

Pearson r can be calculated by drawing a straight line through the points in your scatterplot. If the line slopes upward, the correlation is positive. If the line slopes upward and every single point in your scatterplot fits on that line, you have a perfect correlation of +1. Usually, however, there are points that are not on the line. For each point that is not on the line, the correlation coefficient is made closer to zero by subtracting a value from the coefficient. The farther the point is from the line, the larger the value that is subtracted. Once all the misfit points are accounted for, you end up with the correlation coefficient.

If the line that fits the points slopes downward, the correlation is negative. If every single point fits on that line, you have a perfect negative relationship, thus your correlation coefficient equals −1. However, perfect negative relationships are rare. Therefore, many points probably are not on that line. For each point that is not on the line, the correlation coefficient is made closer to zero by adding a value to the coefficient. The farther the point is from the line, the larger the value that is added. After all the misfit points are accounted for, you end up with the correlation coefficient.

As you can see, the correlation coefficient describes the nature of the linear relationship between your variables. However, it ignores nonlinear relationships, such as the one depicted in figure 11.7.

The fact that the correlation coefficient only examines the degree to which variables are linearly related is not as severe a drawback as you may think. Why? First, because totally nonlinear relationships among variables are rare. Second, even if you encounter a nonlinear relationship, you would know you had such a relationship by looking at your scatterplot.

The Coefficient of Determination

The sign of the correlation coefficient tells you the kind of relationship you have (positive or negative). However, you may want to know not only what kind of relationship you have, but how strong this relationship is.

The strength of the relationship has nothing to do with the *sign* of the correlation coefficient. To emphasize this point, realize that to find out how closely two variables are associated, many scientists square the correlation coefficient. Thus, if they had a +.80 correlation, they would get +.64—just as they would if they had a correlation of −.80. Squaring the correlation coefficient not only gets rid of the sign, but yields the **coefficient of determination.** The coefficient of determination, as the name suggests, tells the degree to which knowing one variable helps you know *(determine)* the other. The coefficient of determination can range from 0 (knowing a participant's score on one variable is absolutely no help in guessing what their score on the other variable will be) to +1 (if you know a participant's score on one variable, you will know exactly what their score is on the other variable).

So, if you have a correlation of +1 (+1 × +1 = +1), you have a coefficient of determination of +1. This means if you know one variable, you can predict the other one with 100 percent accuracy. The same would be true if you had a correlation coefficient of −1 (because −1 × −1 = +1).

Essentially, the coefficient of determination tells you the amount of scatter in your scatterplot. If the coefficient of determination is near $+1$, there is little scatter in your scatterplot. If you draw a line through your scatterplot, most of the points would be on or near that line. If, on the other hand, the coefficient of determination is near zero, there is a lot of scatter in your scatterplot. If you draw a line through the scatterplot, few of the points will be close to that line.

SUMMARY OF DESCRIBING CORRELATIONAL DATA

You now have two ways to summarize data from a correlational study. First, you can visually summarize your data with a scatterplot. Second, you can use two numbers that summarize the essence of your scatterplot: the correlation coefficient and the coefficient of determination.

MAKING INFERENCES FROM DATA

As figure 11.8 shows, accurately characterizing relationships in a given sample is an accomplishment. Therefore, once in a while, a person may want only to describe what happened in a particular sample. For example, a professor may find that in one of her courses, there was a relationship between self-esteem and grade-point average. And that may be all she is interested in. She does not care what happens in other classes, she just wants to describe what happened in that particular class during that particular term. In that case, the only thing she should do is describe data. Thus, scatterplots and correlation coefficients are all she needs.

Most of the time, however, you are interested in generalizing the results obtained in a limited sample to a larger population. You know what happened in this sample, but you want to know what would happen in future samples. To generalize your results to a larger population, you first need a random sample of that population. If you want to generalize results based on observing a few students in your class to all the students in your class, then the participants you examine should be a random sample of class members. If you

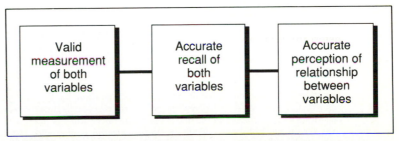

FIGURE 11.8: Steps Involved in Accurately Describing the Relationship That Exists Between Two Variables in a Sample

want to generalize the results based on measuring a few people to all Americans, you must have measured a random sample of Americans. If you want to generalize results based on observing two rats for one hour a day to all the times the rats are awake, then the times you observe the rats must be a random sample from the rats' waking hours.[2]

Of course, random samples are not perfect samples. Even with a random sample, you are going to have sampling error (see figure 11.9). Thus, if you studied a random sample of sophomores at your school and you found a correlation of −.30 between grade-point average and self-esteem, you cannot say that if you had studied all sophomores at your school, you would have obtained a negative correlation coefficient.

To convince yourself that what happens in a sample does not necessarily mirror what happens in the population, you could conduct the following study. Simply have people flip a coin four times. Record each person's height and the number of heads the person flipped. Do this for ten "samples" of four people. Graph each sample of four persons separately. Some of your graphs will reveal a positive correlation, others will reveal a negative correlation. The true relationship, of course, is no relationship.

ANALYSES BASED ON CORRELATION COEFFICIENTS

As you have seen, even if the two variables are not related, they will be related in some samples. That is, a relationship that exists in a particular sample may not exist in the population. Consequently, if you observe a relationship, you will want to know if you have observed a real pattern that is characteristic of the population (see figure 11.10).

Fortunately, there is a way to determine whether what is true of your sample is true

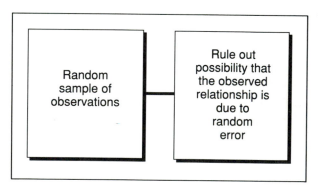

FIGURE 11.9: Necessary Ingredients for Generalizing a Sample's Results Beyond That Sample

[2]Many researchers do not randomly sample from a population, but they still generalize their results. How? They argue their sample could be considered a random sample of an unknown population. Then, they use statistics to determine whether the results are due to sampling error or whether the results hold in the larger population. If their results are statistically significant, they argue the results hold in this unspecified population. (The "unspecified population" might be "subjects I would study at my institution.") Although you might see some problems with generalizing to an unspecified population, they argue significant results indicate that if they repeated the study, they would probably obtain the same pattern of results.

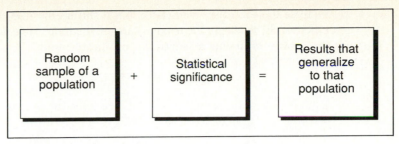

FIGURE 11.10: Necessary Ingredients for Producing Generalizable Results

of the population: inferential statistics. Inferential statistics will allow you to determine how likely it is that the relationship you saw in your sample could be due to random error. Specifically, inferential statistics allow you to ask the question "Can I get this size of correlation coefficient in this big a random sample if there is no relationship in the population?" If the answer to this question is "no," then you can be confident the correlation coefficient in the population is not zero. To use proper terminology, you would say your correlation coefficient is significantly different from zero.

How you determine whether a correlation coefficient is statistically different from zero depends on what kind of correlation coefficient you have. If you have a Pearson r, a point biserial, or a Spearman's rho, you can use the formula described in box 11.2. Traditionally, if you have nominal data, you should use a chi-square test (see box 11.3). Regardless of what test you use, the test will rely on two principles.

First, the further the sample's correlation coefficient is from zero, the less likely the

---

BOX 11.2   How to Determine the Significance of a Pearson r

If your data on self-esteem and grade-point average were collected from a random sample of students at your school, you could use that data to determine whether there is a relationship between impulsivity and grade-point average for the entire school. All you would have to do would be to determine whether the observed Pearson r is significantly different from zero by following the steps listed below. In this case let us suppose the Pearson r $(r) = +.58$ and the number of subjects $(N) = 5$.

Step 1: Compute a t-value, using the formula:

$$t = \frac{r \cdot \sqrt{(N - 2)}}{\sqrt{[1 - (r \cdot r)]}}$$

Note that, all other things being equal, the bigger N is, the bigger t will be. Also, note that the bigger r is, the bigger t will tend to be. Not only does a larger r increase the size of the numerator, but it shrinks the size of the denominator. In other words, the larger the relationship and the more subjects you have, the greater the chance of finding a statistically significant result.

$$t = \frac{.58 \cdot \sqrt{(5-2)}}{\sqrt{1-(.58 \cdot .58)}}$$

$$t = \frac{.58 \cdot 1.73}{\sqrt{1-.34}}$$

$$t = \frac{1.00}{.81} = 1.23$$

Step 2: After computing the t-value, look the value up in the t-table under 3 degrees of freedom (N − 2) for the .05 level of significance. That value is 3.182. Because 1.23 does not reach that value, you would conclude the correlation failed to reach significance.

Note that playing with this formula *before* you conduct a study may be very useful. For example, suppose you thought you would find a correlation of .58. Playing with the formula would show you that to have any realistic shot at getting significant results, you would need to have at least fifteen participants. How could you figure this out?

You know you need a t-value that will be significant when you obtain a correlation of .58. That is, you know that

$$\frac{.58 \cdot \sqrt{(N-2)}}{\sqrt{1-(.58 \cdot .58)}} > \text{critical value of } t$$

By plugging in enough values, you would eventually stumble onto the right one.

Or you could use some algebra to realize the formula can be reduced down to:

$$\sqrt{N-2} > \frac{\text{critical value of } t \cdot \sqrt{1-(r \cdot r)}}{r}$$

or $N > \{[\text{critical value of } t \cdot \sqrt{1-(r \cdot r)}]/r\}^2 + 2$.

In this case, if we put our desired t-value at 2.5, we find that

$$N > \frac{2.58 \cdot .81}{.58} \cdot \frac{2.58 \cdot .81}{.58} + 2$$

In other words, N > 14.

Note, because of random error, even if the real r in the population is .58, you would not obtain an r of .58 all the time. Specifically, because of random error, about half the random samples will yield an r below .58. Thus, if the real r was .58 and you used fifteen subjects, you would only have about a fifty percent chance of getting statistically significant results. If you wanted to have a ninety-five percent chance of getting a significant result, you would need not 15, but **34** subjects.

BOX 11.3 **Computing a 2 × 2 Chi Square and the Phi Coefficient**

Suppose you asked men and women whether they believed homosexuals deserved the same employment opportunities as heterosexuals. If you wanted to know if there was a gender difference in their responses, you could find out by calculating a chi-square using the following steps.

Step 1: Set up a table like the one below.

	FEMALE	MALE	TOTAL
Yes	(A) 20	(B) 15	35
No	(C) 55	(D) 10	65
Total	75	25	(N) 100

Step 2: Multiply B and C. Then multiply A and D.

$$B \cdot C = 15 \cdot 55 = 825$$
$$A \cdot D = 20 \cdot 10 = 200$$

Step 3: Plug in the appropriate numbers in the following formula:

$$X^2 = \frac{N(BC - AD)^2}{(A + B) \cdot (C + D) \cdot (A + C) \cdot (B + D)}$$

$$X^2 = \frac{100(825 - 200)^2}{35 \cdot 75 \cdot 75 \cdot 25}$$

$$X^2 = \frac{100 \cdot 390625}{4265625} = \frac{39062500}{4265625} = 9.16$$

Step 4: Turn to the chi-square table in appendix E and find the row corresponding to 1 degree of freedom. (For a 2 × 2, your degrees of freedom will always be 1; df equals the number of rows minus one, times the number of columns minus one.)

Step 5: Determine whether your chi-square is one-tailed or two-tailed. You should be able to decide based on your hypothesis. For example, if you just predicted there would be a difference between the genders in views toward homosexuals' employment rights, you have a two-tailed test. However, if you predicted men were less likely to think homosexuals should have equal employment opportunities, then you have a one-tailed test. A one-tailed test is more powerful than a two-tailed test.

Step 6: If you have a two-tailed test with a value of 3.84 or more, your test is significant at the .05 level. If your two-tailed test value is at least 5.41, then your test is significant at the .02 level. If you have a one-tailed test, you are in even better shape. The significance level for a one-tailed test is one-half of the probability of a two-tailed test. Thus, to be significant at a .05 level, you need only a value of 2.71. A value of 5.41 will be significant at the .01 level.

To compute the phi coefficient, simply use the following formula:

$$\frac{BC - AD}{\sqrt{(A + B) \cdot (C + D) \cdot (A + C) \cdot (B + D)}}$$

In this case,

$$\frac{825 - 200}{\sqrt{4265625}} = .30$$

population coefficient is zero. Thus, a correlation coefficient of .80 is more likely to be significantly different from zero than a correlation coefficient of .20.

Second, the larger the sample, the less the sample will be influenced by random error. Thus, a correlation coefficient of .30 is more likely to be significantly different from zero if it comes from a sample of one hundred observations than if it comes from a sample of ten observations.

Admittedly, the most popular test of correlations is testing to see if the coefficient is statistically significant from zero. Significant results allow the researcher to conclude that the two variables are related. However, it is just one kind of test you can perform on your correlation coefficients. You could, for example, ask the following questions:

1. Is the correlation between self-esteem and grade-point average higher among women than among men?
2. Is the relationship between self-esteem and grade-point average greater than the correlation between impulsivity and grade-point average?

If you wish to ask these kinds of questions, consult Cohen and Cohen's (1983) book on correlational analysis.

ANALYSES NOT INVOLVING CORRELATION COEFFICIENTS

You do not have to use correlations to analyze data from correlational research. That is, if you are trying to see if there is a relationship between gender and scores on a self-esteem test, you do not have to calculate the correlation between gender and scores. Instead, you could compute the mean test score for men and the mean test score for women. You could then compare the differences between means, using a t-test or ANOVA. Doing a t-test to see if the differences between the group means is greater than zero is the same as testing to see if the correlation between the variables is greater than zero (see box 11.4). In both cases, a significant result would indicate gender and self-esteem are correlated in the population.

To do a t-test, however, you need two groups. But what if you do not have two groups? For example, what if you have a bunch of people's self-esteem scores and their

BOX 11.4 The Similarities Between a t-test Between Means, an F-test, and Determining Whether a Correlation is Significantly Above Zero When Analyzing the Results of a Two-group Study

When you only have two groups, doing a t-test, an F-test, and an analysis of correlation is the same. Thus, in the simple experiment, the three procedures are essentially identical. In all three cases, you are seeing if there is a relationship between the treatment and the dependent variable. The only difference is that in one case, you are using the difference between means as your measure of covariation; in one case, you are using the variance between means as the measure of covariation; and in one case, you are using a correlation coefficient as the measure of covariation. Consequently, regardless of which technique you use to analyze the results of a simple experiment, significant results will allow you to make causal statements. Furthermore, regardless of which technique you use to analyze the results of a correlational study, significant results will *not* allow you to make causal statements.

T-TEST ANALYSIS

Group	N	Mean
1	59	9.429
2	58	8.938

Standard Error of the difference = .565

$$\frac{9.429 - 8.938}{.565} = \frac{.491}{.565} = .87$$

df = 115; t-value = .87; prob. = .3859.

ANALYSIS OF VARIANCE

SOURCE	df	SS	MS	F	p
Treatment	1	4.155	4.155	.758*	.3859
Error	115	630.768	5.485		
Total	116	634.923			

CORRELATIONAL ANALYSIS

Count = 117; *R* = .081.
Using the formula from box 11.3, we find that

$$t = \frac{r\sqrt{(N-2)}}{\sqrt{[1-(r \cdot r)]}} = \frac{.081 \cdot \sqrt{115}}{\sqrt{.993}} = \frac{.868}{.996} = 0.87, \quad p = .3859$$

---

*Note that if you square the t-value (.87), you get the F-value (.758). Thus, if you want to check your work, you can do a t-test and an F-test on the same data. If the square root of the F-test is different from the t-value you have a problem. An even easier way to check your work is to see whether the p-values produced by the two analyses are the same.

grade-point averages. In that case, you could create two groups by dividing your participants into high scorers or low scorers depending on their test score. Then, you would compare the average grade-point average of "high" scorers (participants with above average self-esteem) with the average grade-point average for "low" scorers. The procedure of dividing participants into two groups depending on whether they scored above or below the median (the middle score) is called a **median split.**

The median split is a popular technique. You will see it reported in the finest journals. However, rather than doing a median split and then computing a t-test, you might be better off simply determining whether the correlation is statistically significant. Why? Because using a t-test based on median splits reduces your ability to find relationships (Cohen & Cohen, 1983). You are less able to find relationships because you have less information to work with. Put another way, you have less ability to find differences because you are recoding data in a way that hides differences (see table 11.5). That is, instead of using participants' specific scores, you are using the median split to lump together all the participants who scored above average. Thus, a participant that scores one point above average gets the same score as a participant that scores fifty points above average. Similarly, you are lumping together everyone who scored below average, despite the differences in their scores. In a sense, you are deliberately throwing away information about participants' actual scores. Not surprisingly, some researchers object to this waste. For example, Cohen (1990) argues that researchers should not lose power and information by "mutilating" variables. Instead of "throwing away" the information regarding participants' specific score by doing a median split, Cohen believes researchers should do correlational analyses that use participants' actual scores.

Rather than breaking your participants down into two groups (top half, bottom half), you might decide to break your participants into three or more groups. You could then compare the different groups by doing an ANOVA.

With a multiple-group ANOVA, your analysis includes more detail about participants' scores than if you did just a t-test (see figure 11.11). For instance, rather than coding that a participant scored in the top half, you might code that the participant scored

---

TABLE 11.5   Advantages and Disadvantages of Using a t-Test Based on a Median Split to Analyze Results of Correlational Research

ADVANTAGES	DISADVANTAGES
The t-test is a convenient way to analyze data.	Before one can do t-test, may have to recode scores based on median split.
	"Convenience" also costs power. Has less power than correlational analysis because not using actual scores. Instead, using much less detailed information. Instead of actual score, only recording whether score is in top half or bottom half of distribution.
Familiar way to analyze data.	Because it is a familiar way to analyze *experimental* data, may *falsely* conclude significant results indicate one variable causes the other.

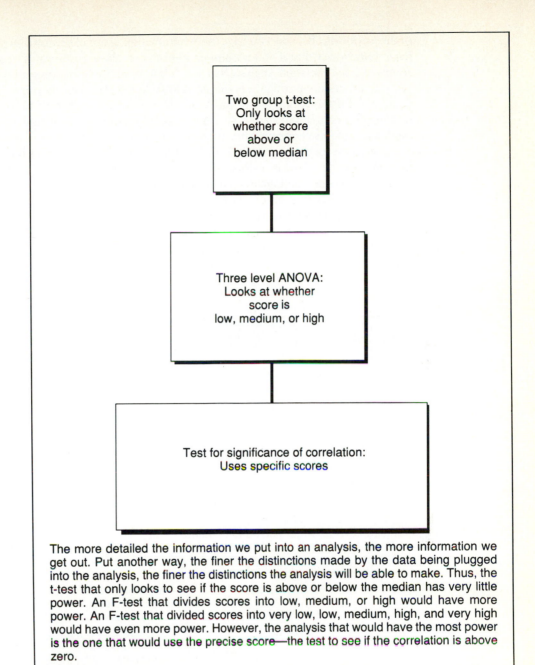

The more detailed the information we put into an analysis, the more information we get out. Put another way, the finer the distinctions made by the data being plugged into the analysis, the finer the distinctions the analysis will be able to make. Thus, the t-test that only looks to see if the score is above or below the median has very little power. An F-test that divides scores into low, medium, or high would have more power. An F-test that divided scores into very low, low, medium, high, and very high would have even more power. However, the analysis that would have the most power is the one that would use the precise score—the test to see if the correlation is above zero.

FIGURE 11.11 Tests That Use More Information Have More Power

in the top fourth. Because you have more information about participants' scores, you may have more power. But if you want more information about participants' scores, why not simply use a correlation analysis that will allow you to use everyone's precise score?

The reason you might choose an ANOVA is so you can do one of two types of analyses.[3] First, you might use an ANOVA to determine whether the relationship is nonlinear. For example, an ANOVA between the groups might find the group with moderately high self-esteem got better grades than the groups with very high or very low self-esteem. Second, you could use an ANOVA to examine the relationships among three or more variables. That is, with an ANOVA, you could look at the relationship between self-esteem, gender, and grade-point average. Specifically, an ANOVA would allow you to compare the average group points of (1) women with low self-esteem, (2) women with high self-esteem, (3) men with low self-esteem, and (4) men with high self-esteem. As a result, you might find high self-esteem is related to high grade-point averages for women, but high self-esteem is related to low grade-point averages for men. (A summary of the advantages and disadvantages of using an ANOVA to analyze correlational research is presented in table 11.6.)

TABLE 11.6 Advantages and Disadvantages of Using ANOVA to Analyze Results of Correlational Research

ADVANTAGES	DISADVANTAGES
Allows a variety of easy analyses to be performed. Can do more than look at the simple relationships between two variables. Instead, can look at the relationship between three or more variables at once. Could determine whether the relationship between variables is nonlinear.	Has less power because it doesn't use actual scores. Instead, uses much less detailed information. If using two-level ANOVA, only records whether score is in top half or bottom half of distribution.
Can avoid problem of losing detail by dividing scores into more groups. Not limited to just looking at top half versus bottom half. Instead, might compare 1st fifth vs. 2d fifth vs. 3rd fifth vs. 4th fifth vs. 5th fifth. Because uses fairly detailed information, has reasonable power.	However, still does not have as much detail and power as if used actual scores.
Convenient way to analyze data.	May not be so convenient if unequal number of subjects in each group. Often have to do unbalanced ANOVAs by hand.
Familiar way to analyze data.	Because it is a familiar way to analyze *experimental* data, may *falsely* conclude significant results indicate that one variable causes the other.

[3]These analyses can be done using sophisticated correlational analyses. However, such sophisticated correlational analyses may be more difficult for you to perform than ANOVA.

INTERPRETING SIGNIFICANT RESULTS

No matter what statistical tests you use, remember what a statistically significant result means (see table 11.7). It means the relationship you observed is probably not due to random error. Instead, the relationship you observed in the sample probably also exists in the population from which you randomly sampled.

Keep in mind that statistical significance does *not* mean the variables are causally related. As we said earlier in this chapter, to infer causality, you must do much more than establish that your variables are statistically related. For example, to infer self-esteem caused low grade-point averages, you would have to show not only that self-esteem and grade-point average are related, but also that no other differences between your high- and low-self-esteem individuals could account for this relationship (there were no differences between groups on ability to delay gratification, IQ, parental encouragement, etc.) and the student had low self-esteem *before* they got low grades.

Also keep in mind that if you use the conventional $p < .05$ significance level, you are saying there is less than five chances in one hundred that the particular statistical test will be significant by chance alone. That is fine if you are only testing a single relationship. However, because correlational data are often easy to obtain, some researchers correlate hundreds of variables with hundreds of other variables. If they do hundreds of statistical tests, many results will be significant by chance alone.

Therefore, we urge you to resist temptation. Do not go wild and compute every possible correlation coefficient. Decide what hypotheses you have and test those correlations.

If you are doing more than one statistical test, make your significance level more conservative than .05. Use a .01 or even a .001 level. Or, repeat your study with another random sample of participants to see if the correlations that were significant the first time are still significant the second time around.

INTERPRETING NULL RESULTS

If your results are not significant, it means you failed to show that your results were not due to sampling error. It does not mean your variables are not related, it means only that

TABLE 11.7 The Different Meanings of Statistical Significance	
MEANING OF A SIGNIFICANT RESULT IN A CORRELATIONAL STUDY	**MEANING OF A SIGNIFICANT TREATMENT EFFECT IN AN EXPERIMENT**
Variables are related. Do not know whether predictor variable caused change in criterion variable because subjects may differ from each other in many ways other than just the two variables being correlated and you do not know which variable came first.	Variables are related. Know treatment variable caused changes in dependent variable because experimental design guaranteed that treatment is only systematic difference between treatment conditions and treatment came before change in dependent variable.

you did not establish that they were related. There are several reasons why you may get null results, even though a relationship exists between your variables.

First, you may not have had enough observations. Even if you observed a fairly strong relationship in your sample, it is hard to say your relationship is not a fluke unless you have enough observations.

Second, your measures might be insensitive measures of your variables. As a result, the true relationship is obscured by measurement error.

Third, your variables may be related in a nonlinear way. This would be a problem because your statistical tests are most sensitive to linear relationships. You could tell if this is the problem by looking at a scatterplot of your data. Thus, if a graph of your data revealed a definite U-shaped curve or some other clear pattern that deviated sharply from a straight line, you would know that a conventional correlation coefficient would greatly underestimate the strength of the relationship between the variables.

Fourth, you may have failed to find a significant relationship because of **restriction of range**: you sampled from a population where everyone scores similarly on one of the variables. You see, to say that two variables vary together, you need both variables to vary. If they do not, you have problems. For example, suppose you were looking at the relationship between IQ and grade-point average, but everyone in your sample scored between 125 and 130 on the IQ test. In this case, the correlation between IQ and grade-point average would be pretty small. Consequently, the correlation might not be significant. However, if your participants' IQ had ranged from 85 to 185, you probably would have a sizable and statistically significant correlation between IQ and grade-point average.

A Look Ahead

In this chapter, you have been introduced to the logic of descriptive research. However, you have not learned about the most common method of doing descriptive research: asking questions. Therefore, the next chapter is devoted to showing you how to conduct surveys, perform interviews, and write questionnaires.

SUMMARY

1. Descriptive research allows you to accurately describe behavior. The key to descriptive research is to precisely measure and record your variables using a representative sample.
2. Although descriptive research cannot tell you whether one variable causes another, it may stimulate causal hypotheses.
3. Description is an important goal of science for description's sake. It is also useful because description paves the way for prediction.
4. Ex post facto research uses data you collected before you came up with your hypothesis.
5. Archival research uses data collected and sometimes coded by someone else.

6. With both ex post facto and archival research, data may not have been measured, collected, or coded in a way appropriate for testing your hypothesis.

7. Observational research is equally applicable to correlational and experimental research.

8. In both naturalistic observation and participant observation, the researcher must be careful that the observer does not affect the observed and that objective coding is used.

9. Using preexisting, validated tests in your correlational research will not only increase the validity of your study, but save you from having to develop your own (a time-consuming endeavor). As with all research, external validity is dependent on the representativeness of your sample.

10. Using a scatterplot to graph your correlational data will tell you the direction of the relationship (positive or negative) and give you an idea of the strength of the relationship.

11. Correlational coefficients give you one number that represents the direction of the relationship (positive or negative).

12. A positive correlation between two variables means that if a subject scores high on one of the variables, the subject will probably score high on the other.

13. A negative correlation between two variables means that if a subject scores high on one of the variables, the subject will probably score low on the other variable.

14. By squaring the correlation you get the coefficient of determination which tells you the strength of the relationship.

15. If your results are based on a random sample, you may want to use inferential statistics to analyze your data.

16. Remember, statistical significance only means that your results can be generalized to the population from which you randomly sampled. Statistical significance does not mean you have found a causal relationship.

17. You may obtain null results even though your variables are related. Common culprits are: insufficient number of observations, insensitive measures, nonlinear relationships, and restriction of range.

18. Beware of doing too many tests of significance. Remember, if you do one hundred tests and use a .05 level of significance, five of those tests might be significant by chance alone.

KEY TERMS

archival data	ex post facto research	nonreactive
content analysis	instrumentation bias	participant observation
coefficient of determi- nation	median split	positive correlation
	naturalistic observation	restriction of range
correlation coefficient	negative correlation	scatterplot

1. Steinberg and Dornbusch (1991) found there is a positive correlation between class-cutting and hours of week adolescents work. In addition, they found a negative correlation between grade-point average and number of hours worked.
   a. Describe, in your own words, what the relationship is between class-cutting and hours of week adolescents work.
   b. Describe, in your own words, what the relationship is between grade-point average and hours of week adolescents work.
   c. What conclusions can you draw about the effects of work? Why?
   d. If you had been analyzing their data, what analysis would you use? Why?

2. Steinberg and Dornbusch (1991) also reported the correlation between hours of employment and interest in school was statistically significant. Specifically, they reported $r(3,989) = -.06$, $p < .001$. (Note that the r (3,989) means they had 3,989 subjects in their study.) Interpret this finding.

3. Brown (1991) found a measure of aerobic fitness correlated $+.28$ with a self-report measure of how much people exercised. He also found the measure of aerobic fitness correlated $-.41$ with resting heart rate. Is resting heart rate or self-report of exercise more closely related to the aerobic fitness measure?

4. In the same study, sex was coded as 1 = male, 2 = female. The correlation between sex and aerobic fitness was $-.58$, which was statistically significant at the $p < .01$ level.
   a. In this study, were men or women more fit?
   b. What would the correlation have been if sex had been coded as 1 = female and 2 = male?
   c. From the information we have given you, can you conclude that one gender tends to be more aerobically fit than the other? Why or why not?

5. Suppose you wanted to see whether the magazine *Psychology Today* became more psychological after the American Psychological Association took it over in 1984. Your strategy might be to count the number of articles that dealt with psychology. But, to determine whether an article was psychological or not, you would want to set up a content analysis system. How would you operationalize "psychological"? How would you sample the articles?

6. A physician looked at twenty-six instances of crib death in a certain town. The physician found some of these deaths were due to parents suffocating their children. As a result, the physician concluded most crib deaths in this country are not due to problems in brain development, but to parental abuse and neglect. What problems do you have with the physician's conclusions?

7. A thirty-six-year prospective study examined the relationship between child rearing practices when the child was five and how socially accomplished the person was at forty-one (Franz, McClelland, & Weinberger, 1991). They concluded that having a warm and affectionate father or mother was significantly associated with "adult social accomplishment."

a. What are the advantages of using a prospective study rather than asking forty-one-year-olds to reflect back on their childhood?
b. How would you measure "adult social accomplishment"?
c. How would you measure "parental warmth"? Why?
d. Assume, for the moment, that the study clearly established a relationship between parenting practices and adult social accomplishment. Could we then conclude that parenting practices account for (cause) adult social accomplishment? Why or why not?
e. Imagine they had failed to find a significant relationship between the variables of adult social accomplishment and parental warmth. What might have caused their results to fail to reach significance?

12

Asking Questions: An Introduction to Surveys, Interviews, and Questionnaire Construction

If you want to know what people are thinking, feeling, or doing, you could survey them. You might survey them orally through an interview. Or, you might give them a questionnaire survey by having them read your questions and write their answers.

Because asking questions seems easy, survey research is the most common method of tapping people's attitudes, beliefs, and behaviors. Because conducting surveys is not as easy as it seems, the survey method is also the most abused research method.

Good survey research is at least as difficult to conduct as other research methods. Careful planning, execution, and analysis are vital for reliable and valid information. In addition, practice and skill are necessary for writing and sequencing survey questions. In this chapter, you will learn the methods and skills necessary to conduct sound survey research.

APPLICATIONS AND CONSIDERATIONS FOR SURVEY RESEARCH

The most obvious—but least asked—question in survey research is, "Why should I use a survey to answer my research question?" To appropriately respond to this question, you must understand the strengths and weaknesses of survey research.

APPLICATIONS

With a survey, you can gather information from a large sample of people with less effort and expense than most other data-gathering techniques. Surveys are used most often to assess people's beliefs, attitudes, and self-reported behaviors. Researchers use surveys to describe behavior and to develop causal hypotheses that can be tested in experiments. Finally, researchers can incorporate surveys into experimental and quasi-experimental designs. That is, after manipulating the treatment, the researcher may use surveys to assess people's beliefs, attitudes, or moods. If the researcher finds a difference in survey responses between the treatment and no-treatment groups, the researcher may be able to conclude the treatment had an effect.

Describing Behavior

As a main research tool, a survey can yield a lot of descriptive data on your variables. It is especially useful if you want to know about people's attitudes, values, beliefs, experiences, and intentions. For example, the Gallup Poll asks people all over the country about their attitudes toward political candidates. Similarly, market researchers ask people about products they buy or might buy.

These surveys can tell us more than how many people support a particular position.

They also can tell us who supports what kinds of positions. For example, they can tell us men tend to be more in favor of war than women and people who oppose legalized abortion are more likely to favor the death penalty.

Stimulating Causal Hypotheses

Describing relationships among variables may lead to a hypothesis about the reason for that relationship. Thus, a survey could be followed up by a more controlled study that would enable you to determine causality among certain variables. For example, if you conducted a survey that demonstrated a relationship between professors who use computers and sympathy toward students, you might hypothesize that using computers causes professors to understand the problems of learning new material, thereby causing them to be more sympathetic toward students. This hypothesis could lead to an experiment where professors are randomly assigned to either a computer- or non-computer-using condition and then measured on sympathy toward students.

Measuring Behavior in an Experimental Design

In addition to stimulating ideas that can be tested in experiments, surveys can be an important element of experiments. In all experiments, participants' behavior must be measured. Sometimes a machine can measure this behavior, as in the case of a blood pressure monitor. Sometimes, participants' behaviors are observed by trained observers. Often, participants' behaviors are measured by using questionnaires, tests, or interviews.

Surveys are most likely to be used if the researcher is trying to manipulate beliefs, attitudes, or moods. For example, suppose a researcher wants to know if commercials aired during shows that encourage people to be skeptical, such as "60 minutes," are less effective than ads shown during other shows. The researcher might have one group see an ad for an IBM computer spliced into a videotape of "60 minutes," whereas the other group sees the same ad spliced into a videotaped section of the "Today Show." To determine the effect of context, the participants of both groups might be asked to fill out a survey about their attitudes toward IBM computers.

CONSIDERATIONS

If you do survey research, you must be concerned with the following five questions:

1. What is my hypothesis?
2. Will I know what to do with the data after the survey is finished?
3. Am I only interested in describing and predicting behavior, or do I want to infer causality?
4. Are my respondents answering accurately?
5. Do my results apply only to those people who responded to the survey, or do the results apply to a larger group?

Know Your Hypothesis

The first question to ask is "What is my hypothesis?" Because good research begins with a good hypothesis, you might think everyone would ask this question. Unfortunately, many inexperienced researchers try to write surveys without clear research questions. What they have not learned is you cannot ask pertinent questions if you do not know what you want to ask. Therefore, before you write your first survey question, make sure you have a clear hypothesis to base your questions on.

Ask Pertinent Questions and Ask Few Questions

If you do not focus your questions on your hypothesis, you may end up with an overwhelming amount of data—and still not find out what you wanted to know. For example, the now defunct United States Football League spent millions of dollars on surveys to find out whether they should be a spring or fall league. Despite the fact it took over twenty books to summarize the survey results, the surveys did not answer the research question (*USA Today*, 1984). So, do not be seduced by how easy it is to ask a question. Instead, ask questions with a purpose.

We take two steps to make sure we ask useful questions. First, we determine what analyses we plan to do before we administer the questionnaire. If we do not plan on doing any analyses involving responses to a specific question, we get rid of that question. Then, with the remaining questions, we imagine participants responding in a variety of ways. If we find that no pattern of answers to a question would give us useful information, we eliminate that question.

Do Not Try to Establish Causality

Usually, if your questions focus on the research hypothesis, your survey will be able to address your research question. However, there is one big exception to this rule: when you have a *causal* hypothesis. Like all correlational methods, surveys cannot, *by themselves,* establish causality.

We do not mean to imply that if you see a study that uses a questionnaire, interview, test, or survey, you will know that no causal statements can be made. If the survey is simply part of an experimental design, then causal statements can be made. For example, suppose people are randomly assigned to one of two conditions (Freedman & Fraser, 1966): being asked to donate one hour of their time to help out at an orphanage or being asked their opinions about orphans. Then, all participants would be surveyed. As part of the survey, participants would be asked if they would be willing to volunteer a total of forty hours to the orphanage. If the group that had originally been asked to donate an hour of their time is significantly more willing to donate time, we could conclude that being asked to perform a small favor causes people to be more likely to comply with a larger request. However, note it is the experimental design—not the survey—that would allow us to make this causal statement.

To illustrate why you cannot make causal inferences from pure survey research, let us return to the computer and sympathy study. If you find that professors who use computers are more sympathetic toward students, you cannot say using computers causes student sympathy. Because correlational methods do not establish temporal precedence, you have not ruled out the possibility that sympathy toward students causes professors to use computers. Furthermore, you have not eliminated the possibility that some other factor (e.g., open-mindedness) causes both computer usage and sympathy toward students.

Do Not Accept Respondents' Answers as Gospel

Even people who realize the weaknesses of correlational methods want to use survey methods to establish causality. They argue that all they have to do is ask people **why** they behaved in a certain manner. Certainly, respondents can give reasons for their behavior, but these reasons may not be accurate. For example, Nisbett and Wilson (1977) reported that if people are shown a row of TV sets, they will prefer the TV furthest to the right. Yet, when asked why, nobody says "I like that TV because it's the furthest to the right."

This example illustrates a general problem with the survey: people's answers may not reflect the truth. There are numerous reasons why respondents' answers may be inaccurate. In the example we just mentioned, the participants did not know the truth. This is often the case. People do not know why they do everything they do. For example, we do not know why we dislike liver or why we find some comedians funnier than others. People do not know everything that goes on in their heads. For instance, we do not know what goes through our mind that allows us to regain control of our car after it starts skidding on the ice or what causes us to think of a particular joke. The moral: Although asking people questions about why they behave the way they do is interesting, do not accept their answers at face value.

As Nisbett and Wilson's (1977) study showed, when people do not know the real cause, they make up a reason—and they believe that reason. Similarly, even though people have forgotten certain facts, they may still think they remember. For example, obese people tend to under-report what they have eaten, and students tend to over-report how much they study. Both groups are surprised when they actually record their behavior (Williams & Long, 1983). Because memory is fallible, you should be very careful when interpreting responses that place heavy demands on participants' memories. If you are not careful in interpreting those responses, your critics will be. Indeed, one of the most commonly heard criticisms of research is "The results are questionable because they are based on retrospective self-report."

Although respondents may think they know when they really do not know, people are sometimes aware of their ignorance. Unfortunately, some surveys do not allow the participants to say they do not know. For example, an immigrant to the U.S. might be asked "Yes or No. Ronald Reagan did a good job of handling domestic issues." Chances are this newcomer does not have enough information to answer. Therefore, you should allow participants to say they do not know.

To this point, we have discussed honest mistakes that respondents make. Sometimes, respondents deliberately distort the truth, giving you the answer that will impress you the most. For example, to impress you, they may exaggerate the amount of money they give to charity. Or, they may give you the answer you want to hear. Their behavior may be very similar to yours when, after having a lousy meal, the server asks you, "Was everything okay?" That is, rather than telling the server everything was lousy and ruining his day, you say what you think he wants to hear, "Yes, everything was okay."

Occasionally, rather than shading the truth, participants will lie. Participants are most likely to lie if your questions are extremely personal (e.g., Have you cheated on your taxes?). Therefore, do not ask personal questions unless they are crucial to your study.

To Whom Do Your Results Apply?

Even if you have a good set of questions centered around your hypothesis and can get accurate answers to those questions, your work is probably not done. Usually, you want to generalize your results beyond the people who responded to your survey. For example, you might survey a couple of classes at your university, not because you want to know what those particular classes think but because you think those classes are a representative sample of your college as a whole. But are they? Unfortunately, they probably are not. Instead, they probably are a biased sample.

Even if you start out with an unbiased sample, your sample may be biased by the end of the study. Why? People often fail or refuse to respond to a questionnaire. In fact, if you do a mail survey, do not be surprised if only 10 percent of your sample returns the survey. Is this 10 percent typical of your sample? Probably not, it is very likely they feel more strongly about the issue than non-respondents.

Summary

In summary, a survey can be a relatively inexpensive way to get information about people's attitudes, beliefs, and behaviors. With a survey, you can collect a lot of information on a large sample in a short period of time.

Although surveys are useful, use them with care. You must watch out for the inaccuracy of self-report data, obtaining too much data to analyze, and biased samples. Finally, you should be aware that you cannot use a survey design to make causal inferences.

THE ADVANTAGES AND DISADVANTAGES OF MAJOR KINDS OF SURVEYS

After weighing the advantages and disadvantages of the survey method, you may decide that a survey is the best approach for your research question. In that case, you need to decide whether to use a questionnaire or an interview.

QUESTIONNAIRES

If you are considering a questionnaire survey, you have two basic options: self-administered and investigator-administered. In this section, we will discuss the advantages and disadvantages of both types of questionnaires.

Self-Administered Surveys

A self-administered survey is a questionnaire filled out by participants in the absence of an investigator. Self-administered surveys are used by behavioral scientists, as well as manufacturers, business people, special interest groups, and magazine publishers. You probably have seen some of these surveys in your mail, at restaurant tables, in newspapers or magazines, or attached to stereo warranties.

Self-administered surveys have several advantages. First, self-administered surveys are easily distributed to a large number of people. Second, self-administered surveys are relatively inexpensive to conduct. Third, self-administered surveys allow anonymity. Allowing respondents to be anonymous may be important if you want honest answers to highly personal questions.

Although self-administered surveys can yield reliable data with ease and economy, there are some major drawbacks to this method. First, self-administered surveys usually have a low return rate. Because the few individuals who return the questionnaire may not be typical of the people you tried to survey, you may have a biased sample.

Second, because the researcher and the respondent are not interacting, errors or oversights in the questionnaire cannot be corrected. Thus, if the survey contains an ambiguous question, the researcher cannot help the respondent understand the question and the respondent probably will not let the researcher know the question is ambiguous. For example, see question 14 in box 12.1, "College students work hard." One respondent might think this question refers to a job a student might hold down in addition to school. Another respondent might interpret this to mean students work hard at their studies. Still, another might interpret this item to mean students are serious about life. Because respondent and researcher are not interacting, the researcher will have no idea that these three respondents are answering three different questions.

Third, just as you have no way of knowing whether respondents are correctly interpreting your questions, you have no way of knowing whether respondents object to your question format. For example, if fixed-alternative items are used, respondents may object that their attitudes are not represented by the alternatives. On the other hand, if you use open-ended questions, respondents may resist spending the time to write a response. In either case, if potential respondents are annoyed by the question format, they probably would not bother to respond. If they do bother to respond, they may vent their annoyance by giving superficial or misleading or even hostile answers.

Investigator-administered Questionnaire

The investigator-administered questionnaire is filled out in the presence of a researcher. Answers may be recorded by either the respondent or the investigator.

Investigator-administered surveys share many of the advantages of the self-administered survey. With both methods, many respondents can be surveyed at the same time. Both methods can be administered in a wide variety of times and places.

But, because the investigator must be present, the investigator-administered survey is slightly more limited in terms of where and when it can be administered. Still, investigator-administered surveys can be conducted in a variety of locations, including the lab, the street, in class, over the phone, or at respondents' homes.

A major advantage of having an investigator present is the investigator can clarify questions for the respondent. In addition, the investigator's presence encourages participants to respond. As a result, investigator-administered surveys have a higher response rate than self-administered.

Unfortunately, the investigator's presence may do more than just increase response rates. The investigator-administered questionnaire may reduce perceived anonymity. Because respondents feel their answers are less anonymous, respondents may be less candid.

Psychological Tests

An extremely refined form of the investigator-administered questionnaire is the psychological test. Psychological tests have several advantages over questionnaires because they are validated, standardized, and checked for reliability. Whereas questionnaires are often developed in a matter of days or hours, psychological tests are painstakingly developed over months, even years. Tests, such as the Wechsler Adult Intelligence Scale (WAIS), have been extensively pilot-tested. Furthermore, they have been validated against behavior and other tests. Psychological tests commonly control for the effects of social desirability by incorporating "lie detector" items such as "Have you ever told a lie?" Psychological tests also control for the effects of "nay" sayers (people who always respond no, regardless of the question) and "yea" sayers (people who always respond yes) by asking a question in more than one way: "How much do you love your mother?"; "How much do you hate your mother?"

To see that the distinction between questionnaires and tests is sometimes blurred, you only need to look at research involving questionnaires. You will find questionnaires often incorporate items from psychological tests. For example, in a study on people's concern about body weight, Patricia Pliner and her colleagues (1990) incorporated two psychological tests in their questionnaire: the Eating Attitudes Test (Garner & Garfinkel, 1979), and the Feeling of Social Inadequacy Scale (Janis & Field, 1959).

Even if you do not include a test as part of your survey, your questionnaire should try to emulate the characteristics of good tests. That is, in developing your questionnaire, you should use as many principles from chapter 3 as you can. Specifically, you should consider doing as much of the following as possible:

1. Standardize the way you administer the survey.
2. Strive for objective scoring by using "objective" items, such as multiple-choice questions, that do not require the person scoring the test to interpret the participant's response; by having a detailed scoring key for responses that do require the scorer to interpret responses; and not letting scorers know the identity of the respondent. For example, if the hypothesis is male respondents will be more aggressive, do not let coders know whether the respondent is male or female. If the hypothesis is people scoring high on introversion will write more expressively, do not let the coders scoring the essay know the respondents' introversion score. In short, to enhance objectivity, you may have to have different coders score different sections of the questionnaire.

3. Try to balance out the effects of response biases, such as "yea" saying and "nay" saying by re-asking the same question in a variety of ways.
4. Attempt to validate your measure by the following:
   a. Correlate it with other measures of the same variable. Often, this will involve correlating a self-report measure with an objective measure. For example, Steinberg and Dornbusch (1991) justified using self-reported grade-point average rather than actual grade-point average by establishing that previous research had shown school-reported and self-reported grade-point average were highly correlated. Similarly, Moorehouse (1991) argued the validity of asking teachers about children by pointing out the questionnaire correlated with promotion, achievement test scores, and IQ.
   b. Determine that all the items making up a scale seem to be assessing the same thing. Presumably, if all the items are tapping the same construct, responses to the individual questions making up the scale should correlate with each other.
   c. Show your survey is reliable by resurveying respondents a month or so later and showing they score similarly both times. Finding a strong, positive correlation between the two times of measurement will suggest you are measuring some stable characteristic rather than merely assessing random error.
   d. Show that your scale does not correlate with variables that it should not correlate with. For example, investigators sometimes correlate scores on their scale with the Crowne-Marlowe scale of social desirability (Crowne & Marlowe, 1960). If they can establish the correlation between their scale and social desirability is near zero, the researchers can argue the scale is not vulnerable to the social desirability bias. Similarly, Gibb (1990) showed that the Hope Scale did not correlate highly with self-consciousness, and Irving et al. (1990) showed that Hope Scale scores did not correlate with a measure of IQ.

INTERVIEWS

On the surface, the questionnaire and the interview are very similar. However, in an interview, the investigator *orally* asks respondents a series of questions and the *interviewer records* responses. As subtle as these differences seem to be, they have important consequences. One important consequence is interviews are more expensive than questionnarires. Interviews are more expensive partly because you cannot legitimately interview more than one person at a time. To interview more than one person at a time would prevent you from getting independent responses. That is, participants might go along with the group rather than give their true opinions. Because you can only interview one person at a time, interviews are more time-consuming and thus more expensive than questionnaires. Interviews are also more expensive because it takes more energy and personal involvement to administer an interview than a questionnaire.

What does the added expense of the interview buy you? Basically, the expense buys you more interaction with the participant. Because of this interaction, you can clarify questions the respondents do not understand. You can follow up on ambiguous or interesting responses—a tremendous asset in exploratory studies where you have not yet identified all the important variables. Finally, this personal touch may increase your response rate.

Unfortunately, the personal nature of the interview creates two major problems. First, there is the problem of **interviewer bias:** the interviewer may influence respondents' answers by verbally or nonverbally encouraging and rewarding "correct" responses. Second, because participants are interviewed by the investigator, they may be more apt to give socially desirable responses than if they were merely writing their answers on an anonymous questionnaire.

Telephone Interviews

Psychologists have found a certain kind of interview is less affected by demand characteristics and interviewer bias than the personal interview. Furthermore, this method generates such a high response rate that it is less vulnerable to sampling bias than any other method: the telephone interview.

Because the telephone interviewer cannot see the respondents, the interviewer cannot bias respondents' answers via subtle visual cues. Furthermore, by monitoring and tape-recording all the interviews, you can discourage interviewers from saying anything that might bias responses. For example, you could prevent interviewers from changing the wording or order of questions or from giving more favorable verbal feedback for expected answers.

The telephone survey also appears to reduce the effects of demand characteristics by giving participants a greater feeling of anonymity (Groves & Kahn, 1979). This feeling of anonymity is partly responsible for the fact telephone surveys have a higher response rate than personal interviews. Thus, thanks to anonymity, the telephone survey is less vulnerable to both response bias and sampling bias than other survey methods.

How to Conduct a Telephone Interview

In the following section we will discuss the general things you should consider when planning any survey—whether it is a telephone survey, a mail survey, or whatever. But, at this point, we would like to give you a few words of advice that apply only to the unique situation of conducting a telephone survey.

Your first step is to determine what population you wish to sample and figure out a way of getting all of their phone numbers. Often, your population is conveniently represented in a telephone book, membership directory, or campus directory. Once you obtain the telephone numbers you are ready to draw a random sample from your population by following the instructions given later in this chapter.

When you draw your sample, pull more names than you actually plan to survey. You will not be able to reach everyone you attempt to phone so you will need some alternate names. Usually we draw 25 percent more names than we actually plan on interviewing.

Once you have followed the advice in the "Planning a Survey" section, you are ready to practice your survey. You might practice by interviewing a friend on the phone or having someone read the interview to you. Often you will need to improve your questions to make them *sound* more understandable. Remember there are differences between the spoken word and the written word. Make your questions short and concise, and keep your voice clear and slow. Be careful not to bias your interview through inflection. Tape yourself reading the questions and play it back. Is your voice hinting at what answer you want participants to give? If not, you are ready to begin calling participants.

If you get a busy signal or a phone is not answered, try again later. A good rule of thumb is to phone a person three or four times at different times of the day before replacing them with an alternate name or number.

When you do reach a person, identify yourself and ask for the person on the list. As with any study, informed consent is a necessary ingredient. Therefore, after you identify yourself, give a brief description of what the survey is about and ask the person if he or she is willing to participate.

Then, ask the questions slowly and clearly. Be prepared to repeat questions or clarify questions.

Once the survey is completed, thank your respondent. Then, volunteer to answer any questions they have. Often, you may give them the option of being mailed a detailed debriefing or a summary of the survey results.

Conclusions about Telephone Interviews

You have seen that the telephone survey is superior to the personal interview for reducing response biases, interviewer biases, and sampling biases. However, the main reason for the popularity of the telephone interview is practicality: the telephone survey is more convenient, less time-consuming, and cheaper than the personal interview.

Although there are many advantages to using the telephone interview, you should be aware of its limitations. First, as with any survey method, there is the possibility of a biased sample. Even if you followed proper random sampling techniques, telephone interviews are limited to those households with phones. Although this may not seem serious, not everyone has a telephone. Furthermore, some people will not be available to answer their phones or choose to screen their calls through an answering machine. A recent study reported that 25 percent of men between the ages of twenty-five and thirty-four screen all their calls (*Marketing News*, 1990).

Even when a person does answer the phone, they may refuse to answer your questions. In fact, some people get very angry when they receive a phone call regarding a telephone survey. The authors have been yelled at on more than one occasion by people who believe telephone interviews are a violation of their privacy.

With telephone surveys, you are limited to asking very simple and short questions. Often, participants' attention spans are very short. Realize that, rather than answering your questions, their interest may be focused on the television show they are watching, the ice cream that is melting, or the baby who is crying.

Finally, by using the telephone survey, you limit yourself to only learning what participants tell you. You cannot see anything for yourself. Thus, if you want to know what race the respondent is, you must ask. You do not see the respondent or the respondent's environment, and the respondents know that. Therefore, a seventy-year-old bachelor living in a shack could tell you he is a thirty-five-year-old millionaire with a wife and five kids. He knows you have no way of verifying his fable.

PLANNING A SURVEY

All research requires careful planning. The survey is no exception. In this section, we will show you the necessary steps in developing and executing your survey.

WHAT IS YOUR HYPOTHESIS?

As with all psychological research, the first step in designing a survey is to have a clear research question. You need a hypothesis to guide you if you are to develop a cohesive and useful set of survey questions. Writing a survey without a hypothesis to unify it, is like writing a story without a plot—in the end, all you have is a set of disjointed facts that tell you nothing.

Not only do you want a clear research question, you want an important one. Therefore, before you write your first survey item, write down in your research proposal why your study is important. As you will learn in chapter 13, to establish the importance of any study, you need to conduct a thorough literature review. You must demonstrate your research question builds on existing work. You must either show how your survey will contribute to the field of psychology or how your survey will contribute to solving an applied problem. That is, you should be able to answer at least one of these questions:

1. What useful information about human behavior will your survey provide?
2. What would be the practical implications of your survey results?

FORMAT OF QUESTIONS

Once you have decided your research question is appropriate and what kind of survey will give you the best information, you are ready to decide what types of questions to use.

Fixed Alternative

A fixed-alternative question resembles an item on a multiple-choice test. With this type of question, respondents are given several choices. Fixed alternatives usually yield two basic kinds of data: nominal data (e.g., do you belong to _____ category?) and interval scale data (e.g., strongly agree, agree, disagree, strongly disagree).

Nominal-dichotomous Data

Dichotomous questions—questions that only allow two responses (usually yes or no)—give you *qualitative* data. That is, they ask whether or not a person has a given *quality*. Often, respondents are asked whether they are a member or non-member of a category (e.g., "are you employed?" or "are you married?").

Sometimes, several dichotomous questions are asked at once. For example, "Are you African-American, Hispanic, Asian, or Caucasian (non-Hispanic)?" Although this seems like one question, it can be rephrased as several dichotomous questions: "Are you African-American?" (yes or no), "Are you Hispanic?" (yes or no), etc. Thus, the information is still dichotomous—either participants claim to belong to a category or they do not. Consequently, the numbers you get from these kinds of questions are on a nominal scale: if you get numbers from these questions, these numbers are just stand-ins for words (e.g., 1 = yes, 2 = no). In other words, different numbers stand for different types *(qualities),* rather than for different amounts (quantities).

There are several advantages to nominal-dichotomous items. Well-constructed nominal items can be easier to answer and score than other types of questions. Specifically, it is a lot easier for respondents to decide between two alternatives (e.g., "Are you for or against animal research?") than five (e.g., "Rate how favorably you feel toward animal research on a five-point scale."), or a potentially infinite number of alternatives (open-ended questions). Furthermore, because there are only two—usually very different—options, there is a greater chance respondents and investigators will have similar interpretations of the items. Therefore, a well-constructed dichotomous item can be a highly reliable and valid measure.

Although there are many advantages to nominal-dichotomous items, there are some disadvantages. One problem with nominal-dichotomous items is some respondents will resist the fixed-alternative nature of the question. To illustrate, consider this question: "Do you approve or disapprove of abortion?"

1. Approve
2. Disapprove

Many respondents may want to say, "It depends. Is the mother's life in danger? Was rape or incest involved? Will the baby be born with severe birth defects?" Yet, the fixed alternatives do not allow for any of these conditions.

Another problem is some respondents may not think their viewpoint is represented by the two alternatives given. For example, how would people who are neutral toward abortion respond? What about those who are fervently opposed to abortion?

If you have artificially limited your respondents to two alternatives, your respondents may not be the only ones irritated by the fact your alternatives prevent them from accurately expressing their opinions. You too should be annoyed. By depriving yourself of information about subtle differences among respondents, you deprive yourself of **power:** the ability to find relationships among variables.

Likert-type and Interval Items

On a Likert-type scale, participants usually respond to a statement by checking either "strongly agree" (scored a "5"), "agree" (scored a "4"), "undecided" ("3"), "disagree" ("2"), or "strongly disagree" ("1"). Traditionally, most psychologists have assumed a participant who "strongly agrees" (a "5") and a participant who merely "agrees" (a "4") differ by as much as a participant who is "undecided" (a "3") differs from someone who "disagrees" (a "2"). In other words, Likert-type scales are assumed to yield interval data: there is an equal psychological interval between each consecutive number. Questions 9 through 14 in box 12.1 are examples of Likert-type, interval scale items.

Likert-type items are extremely useful in questionnaire construction. Whereas dichotomous items only allow respondents to agree or disagree, Likert-type items give respondents the freedom to: strongly agree, agree, be neutral, disagree, or strongly disagree. Thus, Likert-type items yield more information than nominal-dichotomous items. Furthermore, because Likert-type items yield interval data, responses to Likert-type items can be analyzed by more powerful statistical tests than nominal-dichotomous items.

The major disadvantage of Likert-type items is respondents may resist the fixed-alternative nature of the question. In an interview you can get around this by reading the question as if it were an open-ended question. Then, you would record the answer under the appropriate alternative. In fact, all the questions in box 12.1 can be read like open-ended items. Another tip, for either an interview or questionnaire, is to have a "don't know," "undecided," or "neutral" option. This way, respondents will not feel forced into an answer that does not reflect their true position.

Summating Scores   If you have several Likert-type items that are designed to measure the same variable (e.g., student sympathy), you can sum each respondent's answers to these questions. For example, the possible answers for questions 9–14 in box 12.1 are based on the same five-point interval scale, where strongly agree = 1, agree = 2, undecided or neutral = 3, disagree = 4, and strongly disagree = 5. Once each response has been transformed into a number that ranges from one to five, the answers for questions 9–14 can be added (summed) to produce a summated score. Thus, suppose we obtained the following pattern of responses:

Question   9 = "1"
Question 10 = "2"
Question 11 = "1"
Question 12 = "3"
Question 13 = "1"
Question 14 = "2"

Then, the summated score (total score for liking students) would be 10 because 1 + 2 + 1 + 3 + 1 + 2 = 10.

There are two statistical advantages to using summated scores. First, just as a fifty-question multiple-choice test is more reliable than a one-question test, a score based on several questions is more reliable than a single question. Second, analyses are often simpler for summated scores. If we summed the responses for the six Likert-type items in box 12.1, we could compare computer users and nonusers on student sympathy by doing one t-test. Without a summated score, you would have to perform six separate t-tests and then correct the t-test for the effects of having done multiple analyses.[1]

Open-ended Questions

Whereas fixed-response items resemble multiple-choice items, open-ended questions resemble short-answer or essay questions. That is, rather than having respondents choose

---

[1]Or, you could use a more complex analysis, such as multivariate analysis of variance (MANOVA).

BOX 12.1 Sample Telephone Survey

Hello my name is _____. I am conducting a survey for my research design class at Bromo Tech. Your name was drawn as a part of a random sample of university faculty. I would greatly appreciate it if you would answer a few questions about your job and your use of computers. The survey should take only five minutes. Will you help me?

DEMOGRAPHICS	#	%

1. Gender (Don't ask)*
___ Male   1 ___   ___
___ Female   ___   ___

2. What is your position at Bromo Tech?
___ Instructor   2 ___   ___
___ Assistant professor   ___   ___
___ Associate professor   ___   ___
___ Professor   ___   ___
___ Other (If other terminate interview)

3. How long have you been teaching college?
___ 0–4 years   3 ___   ___
___ 5–9 years   ___   ___
___ 10–14 years   ___   ___
___ 15–19 years   ___   ___
___ 20 or more years   ___   ___

4. What department do you teach in?
___ Anthropology   4 ___   ___
___ Art   ___   ___
___ Biology   ___   ___
___ Business   ___   ___
___ Chemistry   ___   ___
___ English   ___   ___
___ History   ___   ___
___ Math   ___   ___
___ Physical Education   ___   ___
___ Physics   ___   ___
___ Political Science   ___   ___
___ Psychology   ___   ___
___ Sociology   ___   ___

5. What is the highest academic degree you have earned?

_____ B.A.   5 _____   _____

_____ M.A./M.D.   _____   _____

_____ Ph.D./Ed.D.   _____   _____

6. How old are you?

_____ ≤25   6 _____   _____

_____ 26–34   _____   _____

_____ 35–44   _____   _____

_____ 45–54   _____   _____

_____ 55–64   _____   _____

_____ ≥65   _____   _____

End of demographics

7. Do you use computers?

_____ Yes   7 _____   _____

_____ No (skip to 9)   _____   _____

8. How many hours a week do you estimate you use computers?

_____ ≤1 hour   8 _____   _____

_____ 2–4 hours   _____   _____

_____ 5–9 hours   _____   _____

_____ 10–14 hours   _____   _____

_____ 15–19 hours   _____   _____

_____ ≥20 hours   _____   _____

Please indicate how much you agree or disagree with the following statements. State whether you strongly agree, agree, disagree, strongly disagree, or are undecided.

9. I like college students.	SA	A	U	D	SD
10. College is stressful for students.	SA	A	U	D	SD
11. Colleges need to spend more time on students' emotional development.	SA	A	U	D	SD
12. Colleges need to spend more time on students' physical development.	SA	A	U	D	SD
13. College students should be allowed to postpone tests when they are sick.	SA	A	U	D	SD
14. College students work hard.	SA	A	U	D	SD

Thank you for your help.

*Questions 2–8 can be read like open-ended questions.

between several researcher-determined response options, participants are free to respond in their own words. This format gives respondents more freedom about how they answer questions than fixed-alternative and scaled items. This flexibility makes open-ended questions a useful exploratory device because it allows unexpected, but important, responses.

Open-ended questions also enable you to find out how much participants know about the survey topic. This will give you insight into whether your respondents really have the information you are seeking and why they give the answers they do. For example, one professor may respond to question 9 in box 12.1, "I like college students" with an "undecided" because he is new to the college and does not know. Another professor may give the same rating because he has mixed feelings about students. Asking open-ended questions would allow you to see that these two respondents have different reasons for giving the same response.

Although there are numerous advantages to open-ended questions, these are tempered by some potentially serious disadvantages. First, open-ended questions take more time to ask and record than other question formats. This not only places greater demands on you, it also requires more from your respondents. Participants will often skip open-ended questions because of the difficulty of generating their own responses.

You should also be aware that it takes some skill to ask open-ended questions. For example, you have to be very careful not to bias respondents' answers through inflection and nonverbal behavior. Often, respondents will be looking at you for signs of whether they are answering the question correctly. Your nonverbal behavior may guide them, whether you are aware of it or not.

It will also take some skill to accurately and sufficiently record responses to open-ended interview questions. If you do not take shorthand, you might consider video-recording or tape-recording the interview.

But perhaps the biggest disadvantage of open-ended questions, whether in an interview or questionnaire, is that they are difficult to score. Answers may be so varied you will not see an obvious way to code them. Often the coding strategy you finally adopt will be arbitrary. To help you come up with a logical and systematic method of coding open-ended questions, try to come up with a content analysis scheme (see chapter 3 and chapter 11) *before* you start collecting data.

Once you have done a content analysis, you may convert the information from your open-ended questions into nominal or interval data where appropriate. For example, if you ask people how old they are, you would analyze these quantitative data as interval data. If you ask participants what gender they are, you would analyze these qualitative, categorical data as nominal data.

FORMAT OF SURVEYS

The format of your questions will largely determine your survey format. In this section, we will discuss the three survey formats: structured, semi-structured, and unstructured.

Structured

The structured survey is the kind most often used in psychological research. In a structured survey, all respondents are asked a standard list of questions in a standard order.

The structured format will ensure each participant is asked the same questions and has the same response options (e.g., yes or no). Furthermore, by using a standard list of questions, the risk of interviewer bias is reduced. Thus, by controlling the questions and limiting the response range, you can obtain accurate and easily interpretable responses.

Of course, once you have developed your structured questions, you need to pretest them. Again, questions may look fine on paper but have weaknesses that only come out when given to your actual study population. Thus, when you pretest your questions, ask respondents how they interpreted each question and why they answered the way they did.

Semi-structured

A semi-structured survey is constructed around a core of standard questions. However, unlike the structured survey, the interviewer may expand on any question in order to explore a given response in greater depth. Like the structured questionnaire, the semi-structured questionnaire can yield accurate and comprehensive data. In addition, it has the advantage of being able to probe for underlying factors or relationships that may be too elusive for the structured survey.

Unfortunately, these advantages may be outweighed by two major disadvantages. First, data from an unstructured survey may be hard to interpret. It is difficult to compare participants' responses when different participants are asked different follow-up questions. Second, in giving the interviewer more freedom to follow up on answers, you may be giving the interviewer more freedom to bias the results. Which answers are probed and how they are probed may affect subsequent answers to fixed items.

The semi-structured questionnaire is best when you are examining uncharted waters. It provides enough standard information so you can make meaningful interpretations. In addition, it provides you with new information that may be useful for future studies.

As with structured questions, you should pretest any unstructured questions. How will potential respondents interpret the question? What kinds of follow-up questions are likely? What are common responses to these follow-up questions?

Unstructured

Unstructured surveys are very popular in the media, in the analyst's office, and with the inexperienced researcher. In the unstructured survey, interviewers have objectives which they believe can be best met without an imposed structure. Therefore, there is no set of standard questions. The interviewer is free to ask what she wants, how she wants, and the respondent is free to answer how he pleases. Without standardization, the information is extremely vulnerable to interviewer bias and is usually too disorganized for analysis.

Because of these problems, the unstructured interview is best used as an exploratory device. As a research tool for reaping meaningful and accurate information, the unstructured survey is limited.

Although it is important to decide how participants should respond to questions (open-ended, Likert-type, dichotomous), it is more important to ask good questions. Although asking questions is a part of everyday life, asking good survey questions is not. In this section, you will learn the criteria for good questionnaire construction. By adhering to these criteria, you will get the most out of your surveys.

Framing Questions

Accurate communication is the major goal in questionnaire construction. To accurately communicate, your questionnaire must adhere to several criteria.

Use words a third-grader would understand. Your task is **not** to impress respondents with your command of vocabulary and technical jargon; your task is to make sure respondents understand you. Therefore, use basic vocabulary and avoid jargon.

Use words and terms that will not be misinterpreted. There are several steps you can take to make sure participants know *exactly* what you are talking about. First, avoid slang terms. Slang terms often have different meanings to different groups. Thus, if you want to know people's attitudes toward marijuana, use the word "marijuana" rather than a slang term like "dope." Dope may be interpreted as meaning marijuana, heroin, or all drugs. Second, be specific. If you want to know how people feel about college students, do not ask "How do you feel about students?" Finally, you can avoid misinterpretations through extensive pretesting. Often, the only way to find out a question or term will be misinterpreted is by asking people what they think the question means. For example, through extensive pretesting, you might find that a seemingly straightforward question such as "Should Pittsburgh increase coke production?" may be interpreted in at least five different ways:

1. Should Pittsburgh increase cocaine production?
2. Should Pittsburgh increase coal production?
3. Should Pittsburgh increase steel production?
4. Should Pittsburgh increase soft-drink production?
5. Should Pittsburgh increase Coca-Cola production?

Avoid personal questions unless you really need the information. Personal questions tend to arouse suspicion and resistance.

Make sure your sample has the information you seek. Obviously, respondents cannot give you accurate answers if they do not know the answer. Therefore, you should avoid asking questions like, "How much marijuana do your children smoke a month?" If you suspect some participants will not know the answer to a question you have decided to ask, allow participants to say they do not know the answer. Such a question might read, "I spent _____ hours advising students on personal matters last year: less than 20; between 20–40; between 40–60; between 60–80; more than 80; don't know."

Avoid leading questions. Remember, your aim is to get accurate information, not to get conformity. Therefore do not ask "You disapprove of the horrible way television presents graphic violence, don't you?" Instead, ask "How much do you approve or disapprove of television's presentation of violence?"

Avoid questions that are loaded with social desirability. Do not ask questions that have a socially correct answer (e.g., "Do you donate money to student causes?"). Generally, the answers to such questions cannot be trusted because participants will respond with the socially desirable answer. Furthermore, such questions may contaminate participants' responses to subsequent questions because such questions may arouse respondents' suspicions. For instance, the respondent may think, "They said there were not right or wrong answers. They just wanted my opinion. But obviously, there are right and wrong answers to this survey after all." Or, the respondent may think, "They know I would give that answer. Anyone would give that answer. This survey is starting to feel like one of those 'surveys' used by people who try to sell you something or convert you to a religion. What are they trying to sell?"

Avoid double-barreled questions. You would not think of asking a respondent more than one question at the same time. But that is exactly what happens when you ask a double-barreled question: several questions packed into a single question (e.g., "How much do you agree with the following statement: 'Colleges need to spend more time on students' emotional *and* physical development.' "). The responses to this question are uninterpretable because you do not know whether participants were responding to the first statement ("Colleges need to spend more time on students' emotional development"), the second statement ("Colleges need to spend more time on students' physical development"), or both statements.

As you can see, the conjunction "and" allowed this question to be double-barreled. Almost all double-barreled questions are joined by "and" or some other conjunction. So when looking over your questions, look suspiciously at all "ands," "ors," "nors," and "buts."

Keep questions short and concise. This will help you avoid ambiguity, confusion, and double-barreled questions. Remember, short questions are easier to understand. A useful rule of thumb is to keep most of your questions under ten words (one line) and all your questions under twenty words.

Choose response options carefully. From your experiences with multiple-choice tests, you are keenly aware the response options are part of the question. Not only should you carefully consider the wording of each option but you should also carefully consider how many options there are and how different the options should be.

As a general rule, the more options, the greater your ability to detect subtle differences between participants. For example, according to the rule, using a 1–3 scale may not find differences between groups, whereas a 1–7 scale would. However, like most rules, this one has exceptions. If you present too many options, your respondents may be overwhelmed. Likewise, if the options are too similar, participants may be confused. The easiest way to determine how many options are appropriate is to pretest your questions.

A related problem is to determine the psychological distance between your options. Usually, you should try to keep equal distances between your options. Keeping equal distances will allow you to compute means and use standard, familiar statistical tests. For example, if you are asking respondents about their grade-point averages, do not have

$1 = 0.00–0.99$, $2 = 1.0–1.69$, $3 = 1.7–2.29$, $4 = 2.30–2.70$, $5 = 2.8$ and above. With this system, averaging respondents' answers is meaningless. A better choice of options would be $1 = 0.00–0.99$, $2 = 1.0–1.99$, $3 = 2.00–2.99$, and $4 = 3.00–4.00$.[2]

Avoid negations. The appearance of a negation in a questionnaire item increases the possibility of misinterpretation. Furthermore, it takes more time to process and interpret a negation than a positively stated item. To illustrate, compare these two statements: "Don't you not like it when students don't study?" versus "Do you like it when students study?"

Avoid irrelevant questions. Be sensitive to the relevancy of a questionnaire item for your population and your research question. For example, "Do you eat fondue?" is irrelevant to the research question "Are professors who use computers more sympathetic to students?"

Although there are many obvious reasons for not including irrelevant questions, the most important reason is irrelevant questions irk respondents. If you ask an irrelevant question, many respondents will conclude you are either incompetent or disrespectful. Because they have lost respect for you, they will be less likely to give accurate answers to questions. In fact, they may even refuse to continue with the survey.

Finally, you should *pretest the questionnaire* in a pilot study to eliminate weaknesses.

Sequencing Questions

Once you have developed a good set of questionnaire items, you need to decide what order to ask them in. Ordering questions is important because the sequence of questions can influence results (Krosnick & Schuman, 1988). To appropriately order questions, follow these four general rules.

Put innocuous questions first, personal questions last. Participants are often tense or anxious at the beginning of a survey. They do not know what to expect. They do not know whether they should continue the survey. The questions you ask at the beginning of the survey set the tone for the rest of the survey. Thus, if the first question is extremely personal, participants may decide to withdraw from the survey. Even if they do not withdraw, they will be very defensive throughout the survey. If, on the other hand, your initial questions are innocuous, participants may relax and feel comfortable enough to respond frankly to personal questions.[3]

Putting the most sensitive questions at the end of your survey will not only increase the number of candid responses, it will also yield more data. To illustrate, suppose you have a twenty-item survey in which all but one of the questions are relatively innocuous.

[2]Probably the best thing to do would be to simply ask subjects for their grade-point average. However, some investigators are so eager to get their data on multiple-choice forms that can be computer scored, they insist every question to be answered as a, b, c, d, or e.

[3]Not everyone agrees with this rule. Dillman (1978) suggests the survey should start with questions that hook the respondents' interest. If you have trouble with subjects starting—but not completing—the survey, you might consider Dillman's advice. However, we have found that by carefully explaining the purpose of the survey before administering it (in accordance with the principle of informed consent), participants will conscientiously answer the questions.

If you put the sensitive item first, respondents may quit the survey immediately. Because this item was the first question you asked, you have gathered no information whatsoever. If, on the other hand, you put the sensitive item last, respondents may still quit. But, even though they quit, you still have their responses to nineteen of the twenty questions.

Qualify early. If people must meet certain qualifications to be included in your sample or to be asked certain questions, find out if they qualify before you ask them those questions. In other words, do not ask people questions that do not apply to them. There is no need to waste their time, and yours, by collecting useless information. Participants do not like saying, "No, doesn't apply" ten times. Box 12.1 has two qualifying questions. The first is question 2, "What is your position at Bromo Tech?" This question establishes the presence of two qualifications for the survey: (1) the person is a professor and (2) the person teaches at Bromo Tech. If people do not meet these qualifications, the survey is terminated at the start of the interview, not at the end. This saves time and energy. Can you identify the second qualifying question?

Be aware of response sets. If all your questions have the same response options, people sometimes get locked into one answer. For example, if each question has the alternatives "strongly agree, agree, undecided, disagree, or strongly disagree," respondents may answer each question with the same alternative (e.g., "undecided"). The undecided response allow them to get the questionnaire over with as soon as possible. To avoid the undecided response set, you may want to eliminate the undecided option. Of course, the undecided response set is not the only response bias. You will also encounter the "yea sayers" and the "nay sayers" that you read about in chapter 3.

One of the most common ways of dealing with response styles is to alternate the way you phrase the questions. That is, you might ask respondents to strongly agree, agree, disagree, or strongly disagree to the statement "Students are hard working." Then, later in the questionnaire ask them to strongly agree, agree, disagree, or strongly disagree to the statement "Students are lazy."

Keep similar questions together. There are several reasons why you get more accurate responses when you keep related questions together. First, your participants perceive the survey to be organized and professional. Therefore, they take the survey seriously. Second, participants do not get confused about what your questions apply to as they do when surveys constantly skip between topics. Third, by asking all the related questions together, participants are already thinking about the topic before you ask the question. Because they are already thinking about the topic, they can respond quickly and accurately. If respondents are not thinking about the topic before you ask the question, it may take some respondents a while to think of the answer to the question. At best, this makes for some long pauses. At worst, respondents will avoid long pauses by saying they do not know or by making up an answer.

Add Demographic Questions

In addition to writing items that directly address your research question, you should ask some questions that will reveal your sample's **demographics**: characteristics such as age, gender, and education level. Thus, in our survey of college professors (see box 12.1), we asked six demographic questions. By comparing our sample's responses to these demographic questions with the population's demographics, we can see how representative our sample is. That is, we can look in the catalog or go to the personnel office to find out what percentage is male. Then, we can compare our sample demographics to these population demographics. If we found 75 percent of the faculty were male, but only 25 percent of our sample was male, we would know that our sample was not representative of faculty.

Note that we put the demographic questions first (questions 1–6). Why? We put our demographic questions first because they were relatively innocuous. Thus, these questions would put our respondents at ease before we asked more personal questions.

Putting the Final Touches on Your Questionnaire

Once you have written your questions, carefully sequenced them, and pretested them, you should carefully proof and pretest your questionnaire to make sure it is accurate, easy to read, and easy to score.

Obviously, subjects are more likely to take your research seriously if your questionnaire looks professional. Therefore, your final copy of the questionnaire should be free of smudges and spelling errors. The spaces between questions should be uniform.

Even though the questionnaire is neatly typed, certain key words may have been scrambled or omitted. At best, these scrambled or missing words could cause embarrassment. At worst, they would cause you to lose data. Therefore, not only should you proof the questionnaire to ensure the form of the questionnaire looks professional, you should also pretest the questionnaire to ensure the content is professional.

Once you have thoroughly checked and rechecked both the form and the content of the questionnaire, you should code your pretest of subjects' responses. After coding your pretest of participants' responses, you should consider ways of making coding easier. Basically there are four strategies you can use to facilitate coding:

1. Line up responses in either the far right or far left margin. This will allow you to score each page quickly because you can go straight down the page without shifting your gaze from left to right or filtering out extraneous information. If you put information in the far left margin, you are less likely to miscode items because the number of the item is right next to the relevant answer.

2. Have respondents put their answers on an answer sheet. With an answer sheet, you do not have to look through and around questions to find the answers. The answer sheet is an especially good idea when your questionnaire is more than one page long because the answer sheet saves you the trouble of turning pages.

3. Have participants put their responses on a coding sheet that can be scored by computer. Computer scoring is more accurate than hand scoring. Besides, computers like dull, time-consuming tasks, so why not let them code responses?

4. If you really want to employ computers, you could have the computer administer the questionnaire, print out the responses, and even score the questionnaire. (See appendix C for more information on computer applications.)

SAMPLING

Once you have decided what questions you will ask and how you will ask them, you need to decide **who** you will ask. To decide who you will ask, you first have to decide **exactly** what population you want to study. If your population is extremely small (all art history teachers at your school), you may decide to survey all members of your population. Usually, however, your population is so large that you cannot survey everyone. Therefore, instead of surveying the entire population, survey a sample of people from that population. Whether you acquire your sample by random sampling, stratified random sampling, convenience sampling, or quota sampling, your goal is to get a sample that is representative of your population.

RANDOM SAMPLING

In random sampling, each member of the population has an equal probability of being selected. Furthermore, the selection of respondents is independent. In other words, the selection of a given person has no influence on the selection or exclusion of other members of the population from the sample.

To select a random sample for a survey, you would first identify every member of your population. Next, you would go to a random numbers table and assign each member of the population a number. Then, you would rank order each member from lowest to highest based on their random number. Thus, if a person were assigned the random number 00000, that person would be the first person on the list, whereas a person assigned the number 99999 would be the last person on the list. You would select your sample by selecting names from the beginning of this list until you got the sample size you needed. Thus, if you needed one hundred respondents, you would select the first one hundred names on the list.

As you can imagine, random assignment can be very time consuming. First, you have to identify every member of the population. That can be a chore, depending on your population. If you are interested in a student sample, then a trip to the registrar's office should yield a list of all currently enrolled students. In fact, some schools can generate a computerized random sample of students for you. If you are interested in sampling a community, the local telephone company is a good place to start. Or, if you are willing to spend the money, you can buy census tapes from the government or from marketing research firms.

After you have identified the population, you have to assign random numbers to your respondents. Just the first step—assigning random numbers to all members of a population—can be cumbersome and time-consuming. Imagine assigning 1,000,000 random numbers to names! But after that is done, you have to rank order the names based on these numbers to determine who you will sample. Fortunately, many of the headaches of random sampling can be computerized if you have a computerized list of your population.

Despite the hassles involved with random sampling, people are willing to put up with it because random sampling allows you to generalize the results of your study to a larger population. Remember, you can use inferential statistics to infer the characteristics of a population from a *random* sample of that population.

Determining Sample Size for Random Samples

As you know, your random sample may differ from the population by chance. That is, although your population may have 51 percent females, your random sample may have 49 percent females. You also know that you can reduce random sampling error by increasing your sample size. In other words, a sample of 10,000 will tend to more accurately reflect the population than a sample of 10. However, surveying 10,000 people may cost more time and energy than the added accuracy it buys. To figure out how many people you will need to survey if you use random sampling, consult table 12.1.

STRATIFIED RANDOM SAMPLING

With pure random sampling, you leave everything up to chance. You count on using a large sample size so the effects of chance will be small. With stratified random sampling,

TABLE 12.1   Required Sample Size as a Function of Population Size, Desired Accuracy (within 5, 3 or 1%), and Level of Confidence

CONFIDENCE LEVEL: SAMPLING ERROR: Size of Universe	95% 5%	90% 5%	85% 5%	80% 5%	95% 3%	90% 3%	85% 3%	80% 3%	95% 1%	90% 1%	85% 1%	80% 1%
50	44	42	40	39	48	47	46	45	50	50	50	49
100	79	73	167	63	92	88	85	82	99	99	98	98
200	132	116	102	92	169	159	148	140	196	194	193	191
500	217	178	147	126	343	302	268	242	476	466	456	447
1,000	278	216	172	145	521	434	365	319	907	873	838	809
2,000	322	242	188	156	705	554	447	380	1661	1550	1443	1357
5,000	357	261	199	163	894	664	516	429	3311	2897	2545	2290
10,000	370	268	203	166	982	711	545	448	4950	4079	3414	2970
20,000	377	272	205	168	1033	737	560	459	6578	5124	4117	3488
50,000	381	274	207	168	1066	754	569	465	8195	6055	4697	3896
100,000	383	275	207	169	1077	760	573	467	8926	6445	4929	4054
1,000,000	384	275	207	169	1088	765	576	469	9706	6842	5157	4207
100,000,000	384	275	207	169	1089	765	576	469	9800	6389	5134	4225

Example of use of table: If you are sampling from a universe of fifty people and you want to be 90 percent confident your results will be within 5 percent of the true percentage in the population, you need to randomly sample forty-two people.
Note: Table provided by David Van Amburg of Market Source, Inc.

on the other hand, you do not leave everything up to chance. Instead, you make sure the sample is similar to the population in certain respects. For example, if you know the population is 75 percent male and 25 percent female, you make sure your sample is 75 percent male and 25 percent female. You would accomplish this goal by dividing your population (stratum) into two sub-populations, or sub-strata. One sub-stratum would consist of male members of the population, the other sub-stratum would consist of female members. Next, you would decide on how many respondents you would sample from each sub-stratum (e.g., seventy-five from the male stratum, twenty-five from the female stratum). Finally, you would draw random samples from each sub-stratum, following the same basic procedures you used in random sampling. The only difference is you are collecting two samples from two sub-strata, rather than one sample from the main population.

By using stratified random sampling, you have all the advantages of random sampling, but you do not need to sample nearly as many people. As a result, the Gallup Poll can predict the outcome of presidential elections based on samples of only three hundred people. Furthermore, a stratified random sample ensures your sample matches the population on certain key variables.

CONVENIENCE SAMPLING

In convenience sampling, you simply sample people who are easy to survey. Convenience surveys are very common. Newspapers ask people to mail their responses to a survey question, and radio stations ask people to call in their reactions to a question. Even television stations have gotten into the act, asking people to call one number if they are in favor of an issue, another number if they are opposed to the issue.

To see how you would get a convenience sample, suppose you were given one week to get one thousand responses to a questionnaire. What would you do? You might go to areas where you would expect to find lots of people, like a shopping mall. Or, you might ask your professors if you could survey their classes. Or, you might put an ad in the newspaper, offering people money if they would respond to a questionnaire.

As you can see, the convenience sample can provide you with a lot of data. Unfortunately, you do not know whether the sample represents your population. Your best bet is that it does not. In fact, if your respondents are actively volunteering to be in your survey, you can bet your sample is extremely biased. The average person does not call in to radio shows, write letters in response to questions in the newspaper, or respond to ads asking for people to be in a survey.

QUOTA SAMPLING

Quota sampling is designed to make your convenience sample more representative of the population. Like stratified random sampling, quota sampling is designed to guarantee your sample matched the population on certain characteristics. For instance, you might make sure 25 percent of your sample was female or 20 percent of your sample was Hispanic.

Unlike stratified random sampling, however, quota sampling does not involve random sampling. Consequently, even though you met your quotas, your sample may not reflect the population at all. For example, you may meet your 20 percent quota of Hispanics by hanging around a hotel where a national convention of high school Spanish teachers is being held. Obviously, the Hispanics in your survey are not representative of the Hispanics in your community.

CONCLUSIONS ABOUT SAMPLING TECHNIQUES

To get samples that represent your population, we recommend you use either random sampling or stratified random sampling. However, no sampling technique is totally free of sampling bias because, ultimately, respondents choose the sample. That is, you can sample them, but they may not answer you. As a result, your sample will not represent members of the population who choose not to respond.

There are two things you can do about the bias caused by nonresponse. First, you can try to have a very low nonresponse rate. Some investigators have 97 percent response rates by using fairly brief telephone surveys. Second, keep detailed records on the people who refused. If possible, unobtrusively record their gender, race, and estimated age.

ADMINISTERING THE SURVEY

You have your survey questions. You have carefully sequenced your questions and determined your sampling technique. You have had your study approved by your professor and any appropriate ethical review committees. Now it is time for you to actually administer your survey. Basically, you are going to follow the same advice you received for administering experiments, quasi-experiments, and other correlational studies. That is, you must follow the American Psychological Association's (APA) "Ethical Principles of Psychologists" (APA, 1990), and you must conduct yourself professionally in every step of the survey (see appendix A and chapter 13).

For example, participants should always be greeted. An investigator does not have to be present for participants to be greeted. Thus, a mail questionnaire should always be accompanied by a cover letter—a written greeting. Just like a personal greeting, in a cover letter you should introduce yourself, explain the nature of your study, and request their help.

Participants should always be given clear instructions. As with any other study, an important part of these instructions is making it clear that participation is entirely voluntary. In an interview, the instructions are oral. In a questionnaire, they are written. Of course, if an investigator is administering the questionnaire, any written instructions can be backed up with oral ones.

After participants complete a survey, they should be debriefed and thanked. Thus, at the end of a mail questionnaire, you should write a debriefing, thank your participants, and give them any additional instructions. For example, "Please mail your questionnaire in the enclosed envelope. To find out more about the survey, put a checkmark in the upper left-hand corner of the questionnaire and we will send you a summary of the results once the survey is completed."

Finally, as in all studies, you should be careful to ensure your participants' confidentiality. This means you should not only be careful when collecting data (e.g., by using a cover page and spreading subjects out so they do not see each other's responses) but also when storing data as well as when disposing of data (see appendix A and chapter 13).

ANALYZING SURVEY DATA

Once you have collected your survey data, you need to analyze them. In this section, we will show you how to summarize your data and which statistical tests to use.

SUMMARIZING DATA

The first step in analyzing survey data is to determine what data are relevant to your hypotheses. Once you know what data you want, you need to summarize that data. How you summarize your data will depend on what kind of data you have.

The type of data you have will depend on the type of questions you ask. When you ask rating-scale questions or when you ask people to quantify their behavior ("How *many* hours a week do you use a computer?"), then you can probably assume your data are interval scale data. If you ask questions where people have to answer either "yes" or "no" ("Do you use a computer?"; "Do you like students?") or questions where people have to classify themselves ("Are you male or female?"; "Are you a sophomore, junior, or a senior?"), then you have nominal data.

Summarizing Interval Data

If you simply want to know the typical response to an interval scale question ("How many hours do people in the sample use computers?"), then you need only to calculate the mean for that question. More often, however, you will be interested in the relationship between one or more variables. In that case, you will probably want to construct tables of means that reflect these relationships. In our example, we expected there would be a relationship between computer use and sympathy for students. Therefore, we compared computer users' average sympathy for students (see table 12.2). In addition, we were interested in seeing whether male or female professors were more sympathetic to students (see table 12.2). To supplement your tables of means, you may want to compute a correlation coefficient to get an idea of the strength of the relationship between your two variables.

TABLE 12.2 Table of Means and Interactions

TABLE OF MEANS FOR COMPUTER USAGE ON QUESTION 9: "I LIKE COLLEGE STUDENTS"

Computer Usage	
Yes	No
4.0	3.0

Average score on a 1 (strongly disagree) to 5 (strongly agree) scale.

TABLE OF MEANS FOR GENDER ON QUESTION 9: "I LIKE COLLEGE STUDENTS"

Gender	
Male	Female
3.25	3.75

Average score on a 1 (strongly disagree) to 5 (strongly agree) scale.

INTERACTION FOR GENDER BY COMPUTER USAGE ON QUESTION 9: "I LIKE COLLEGE STUDENTS"

	Computer Usage	
Gender	Yes	No
Male	3.5	3.0
Female	4.5	3.0

Average score on a 1 (strongly disagree) to 5 (strongly agree) scale.

Looking at Complex Relationships

Thus far, you have seen how to describe the relationship between pairs of variables (e.g., computer use and sympathy, gender and sympathy, gender and computer use). Sometimes, however, you may want to see how three or more variables are related. The easiest way to compare three or more variables is to construct a table of means, as we have done in table 12.2. As you can see, this 2 × 2 table of means allows us to look at how both computer use and gender are related to sympathy.

Summarizing Ordinal or Nominal Data

If your data are not interval scale data, do not summarize your data by computing means. For example, if you code 1 = male, 2 = female, do not say the mean sex in your study was 1.41.

Similarly, if you are having participants rank several choices, do not say the mean rank for option B was 2.2. To understand why, imagine five persons rate option A "2-2-2-2-2" and option B 1-1-3-3-3. The mean rank for option A is 2.0, the mean rank for option B is 2.2 (Semon, 1990). Thus, according to the mean, A is assumed to be better liked. However, the mean is misleading. The mean gives the edge to A because the mean assumes the difference between being a second choice and being a third choice is the same as the difference between being a first choice and being a second choice. As you know, this is not the case. The psychological distance between first and second is often much farther than the difference between second and third (Semon, 1990). That is, when judging what people prefer, there is usually a considerable drop-off between their favorite and their second choice, but not such a great difference between their second and third choices. For example, you may find an enormous drop-off between your liking of your favorite opposite sex friend and your second favorite opposite sex friend or between your favorite football team and your second favorite football team. Because we like "the best" much better than second best and because two people ranked B best and nobody ranked A first, Semon (1990) would say option B was more liked. Yet, if we had computed the mean, we would have led people to believe that option A was better liked (Semon, 1990). Therefore, if you do not have interval data, do not use means. Instead, use percentages to summarize your data (table 12.3).

To look at relationships among variables, use tables of percentages to compare different groups' responses. These tables are called **crosstabs** (or **crosstabulations**) because they allow you to compare across groups. As you can see in table 12.3, crosstabs are a powerful way to graphically display similarities and differences between groups.

If you want to compute a measure to quantify how closely two variables are related, you can calculate a correlational coefficient called the **phi coefficient** (see box 12.2). Like most correlation coefficients, phi ranges from –1 (strong negative correlation) to +1 (strong positive correlation).

Looking at Complex Relationships

If you want to look at how three or more variables are related, do not use the phi coefficient. Instead, construct two tables of percentages, as we have done in the lower half of table 12.3. These 2×2 tables of percentages does for our ordinal data what the 2×2 table of means did for our interval data—allowed us to look at three variables at once.

USING INFERENTIAL STATISTICS

In addition to using descriptive statistics to describe the characteristics of your sample, you may wish to use inferential statistics. Inferential statistics may allow you to generalize the results of your sample to the population it represents.

There are two reasons why you might want to use inferential statistics. First, you

Table 12.3 Contingency Tables

COMPUTER BY GENDER

Use computers	Gender	
	Male	Female
Yes	(A) 20	(B) 15
No	(C) 55	(D) 10

THE RELATIONSHIP AMONG COMPUTER USE, GENDER, AND ACADEMIC DEPARTMENT

Use Computers	GENDER		Use Computers	GENDER	
	Male	Female		Male	Female
Yes	10	10	Yes	20	20
No	80	0	No	40	20
	Physical Science Professors			Social Science Professors	

might want to use inferential statistics to estimate certain **parameters:** characteristics of the population, such as the population mean. Thus, if you wanted to estimate the average amount of time students spend using computers, you might want to use inferential statistics. This use of inferential statistics is called **parameter estimation.**

Second, you might want to determine whether the relationship you found between two or more variables would hold in the population or whether the observed relationship is merely due to sampling error. For example, you might want to determine whether using computers and grade-point average are related in the population. Because you are deciding whether or not to reject the null hypothesis that the variables are not related in the population, this use of inferential statistics is called **hypothesis testing.**

Despite the obvious value of parameter estimation and hypothesis testing, you should carefully consider whether or not to use these techniques. Remember, you can only use inferential statistics if you can assume you have randomly sampled from a given population. *Therefore, if you cannot assume your sample represents a random sample from a given population, do not use inferential statistics.*

Even if you can assume your sample is a random sample, be wary of doing too

BOX 12.2 Computing the Phi Coefficient

Once you have drawn your crosstabs, the phi coefficient is extremely easy to calculate. The formula is:

$$\text{phi coefficient} = \frac{BC - AD}{\sqrt{(A + B) \times (C + D) \times (A + C) \times (B + D)}}$$

Thus, for our crosstabs between computer usage and gender (see table 12.3), the computations would be as follows:

$$\text{phi coefficient} = \frac{(15 \times 55) - (20 \times 10)}{\sqrt{(20 + 15) \times (55 + 10) \times (20 + 55) \times (15 + 10)}}$$

$$= \frac{825 - 200}{\sqrt{35 \times 65 \times 75 \times 25}}$$

$$= \frac{625}{\sqrt{4265625}} = \frac{625}{2065.34} = .30$$

many analyses. Remember, if you use the .05 level of significance, but you do one hundred separate analyses, five of your analyses are likely to be significant by chance alone.

Parameter Estimation with Interval Data

One reason for using statistics would be to estimate population parameters. For example, from our survey of computer usage and student sympathy, we might want to estimate the amount of sympathy the average professor has.

You can establish 95 percent confidence intervals for any population mean from the sample mean, if you know the standard error of the mean. (If you do not have a computer or calculator that will compute the standard error of the mean for you, see chapter 5.) You establish the lower limit of your confidence interval by subtracting two standard errors from the sample mean. Then, you establish the upper limit of your confidence interval by adding two standard errors to the sample mean. Thus, if the average sympathy rating for all the professors in our sample was 4.0 and the standard error was 0.5, we could be 95 percent confident the true population means is somewhere between 3.0 and 5.0.

Hypothesis Testing with Interval Data

You can also use statistics to see if there are significant differences between groups. For example, we might want to know if the differences we observe in our sample also apply to the population at large. Through a t-test, we could test whether the differences in sympathy we observed between computer users and nonusers was too large to be due to sampling error and thus probably represented a true difference.

The t-test between means is not the only way to determine whether there is a relationship between computer usage and student sympathy. We could also determine whether a relationship exists between computer usage and student sympathy by determining whether the correlation coefficient between those two variables was significant. (To do this test, consult box 11.2.)

If you were comparing more than one pair of variables, you could do several t-tests or test the significance of several correlations. In either case, you should correct for doing more than a single statistical test by using a more stringent significance level than the conventional .05 level. For example, if you looked at five comparisons, you might use the .01 level; if you looked at fifty comparisons, you might use the .001 level.

Relationships Among More than Two Variables

If you wanted to look at more than two variables at once (computer usage and gender on sympathy, table 12.2), you might use analysis of variance (ANOVA). If you perform multiple ANOVAs, you should correct your alpha level for the number of ANOVAs you computed, just as you would if you use multiple t-tests.

More Complicated Procedures

You should be aware that we have just scratched the surface of how interval data from a survey can be analyzed. Factor analysis, multivariate analysis of variance, and multiple regression are all techniques that could be used to analyze survey research data. However, these statistical techniques are beyond the scope of this book.

Using Inferential Statistics with Nominal Data

Just as statistical tests can be performed on interval data, they can be performed on nominal data. The difference is that tests based on nominal data tend to be less powerful than those using interval scale data.

Estimating Overall Percentages in Population

If you select your sample size according to table 12.1, you are 95 percent confident your sample percentages are within 5 percent of the population's percentages. Thus, if you found 35 percent of your participants were female, you would be 95 percent confident that between 20–40 percent of your population was female.

Relationships Between Variables

With nominal data, you can use significance tests to determine whether differences between sample frequencies reflect differences in population frequencies. But instead of using t-tests, as you would with interval data, you would use the chi-square test (see box 12.3).

If you are performing more than one chi-square test, you should correct for the number of analyses performed. Just as with the t-test, you should raise your significance level to compensate for doing multiple analyses. Thus, if you are comparing five chi-squares, you should use a .01 significance level rather than a .05.

BOX 12.3 Computing a 2 × 2 Chi-square

You have already completed your first step in computing a chi-square. That is, you have arranged the data in a 2 × 2 contingency table. To complete the rest of the calculation, just follow the steps outlined below.

Step 1: Add up the frequencies in cells A and C, B and D, A and B, then C and D.

DO YOU USE COMPUTERS?

	MALE	FEMALE	TOTAL
Yes	(A) 20	(B) 15	35
No	(C) 55	(D) 10	65
Total	75	25	100

Step 2: Multiply B and C. Then multiply A and D.

$$B \times C = 15 \times 55 = 825$$
$$A \times D = 20 \times 10 = 200$$

Step 3: Then plug the appropriate numbers in the following formula.

$$X^2 = \frac{N(BC - AD)^2}{(A + B) \times (C + D) \times (A + C) \times (B + D)}$$

Thus,

$$X^2 = \frac{100(825 - 200)^2}{35 \times 75 \times 75 \times 25} = \frac{100(390625)}{4921875} = \frac{39062500}{4265625}$$

$$X^2 = 9.16$$

Step 4: Turn to table E.2 in appendix E and find the row corresponding to 1 degree of freedom. (For a 2 × 2, your degree of freedom will always be 1. *df* equals the number of rows minus one, times number of columns minus one.)

Step 5: Then, see if the number you calculated (in this case, 9.16) exceeds the value listed in the table under the appropriate two-tailed significance level. Thus, if your significance level had been .05, your calculated value would have to exceed 3.84 to be significant. If your significance level had been .02, your calculated value would have to be at least 5.41 to be significant.

CONCLUDING REMARKS

In this chapter, you learned the essence of good survey research. Early in the chapter, you were introduced to the applications and limitations of survey research. You saw the advantages and disadvantages of different survey formats, as well as the strengths and weaknesses of different kinds of questions. After learning how to write a survey, you learned how to administer a survey and how to score and analyze survey data.

Now that you know the basics of survey research, you are ready to apply your knowledge. Experience will make you even more aware of the need for careful planning, execution, and analyses. Through direct application of the principles you learned in this chapter, you will become a skillful survey researcher.

SUMMARY

1. Surveys can help you describe what people are thinking, feeling, or doing.
2. Surveys allow you to gather information from a large sample with less effort and expense than most other data-gathering techniques.
3. In a survey, it is important to ask only pertinent questions. Otherwise, your research question could be lost in a lot of irrelevant information.
4. Do not accept respondents' answers as gospel. People do not always tell the truth.
5. Know who you want to generalize your results to before you start your study.
6. Remember, surveys only yield correlational data. You cannot determine causality.
7. There are several drawbacks to self-administered questionnaires: they have a low return rate, respondents may misinterpret questions, and participants may object to question format.
8. Investigator-administered questionnaires have a higher response rate than self-administered questionnaires.
9. Interviews are especially useful for exploratory studies.
10. Telephone surveys have higher response rates, are easier to administer, and offer greater anonymity than personal interviews.
11. Your first step in survey research is to have a hypothesis.
12. There are three basic question formats: nominal-dichotomous, Likert-type, and open-ended.
13. Structured surveys are generally more useful than unstructured.
14. Asking good questions is the key to good survey research.
15. Be sure to edit your questions according to our ten major points.
16. Careful attention should be placed on sequencing questions. Keep similar questions together, qualify early, and put personal questions last.
17. Be aware of response sets.

18. Some time spent deciding how to code your questionnaire can save time in the end.

19. Random and stratified random sampling allow you to make statistical inferences from your data.

20. Participants in survey research should be treated with the same respect as participants in any other kind of study.

KEY TERMS

chi-square
convenience sampling
crosstabs (also known as
  crosstabulations)
demographics
double-barreled question
fixed-alternative items
hypothesis testing
interval data
interviewer bias

Likert-type items
leading question
nominal items
open-ended items
parameters
parameter estimation
phi coefficient
quota sampling
random sampling

response set
self-administered
  questionnaire
semi-structured
  questionnaire
stratified random
  sampling
structured questionnaire
summated scores

EXERCISES

1. Develop a hypothesis that can be tested by administering a survey.

2. Is a survey the best way to test your hypothesis? Why?

3. Is an interview or a questionnaire the best way to test your hypothesis? Why?

4. List the advantages and disadvantages of the three basic question formats: nominal-dichotomous, Likert-type, and open-ended.

5. Based on your hypothesis, write three nominal-dichotomous questions.

6. Based on your hypothesis, write three Likert-type items.

7. Based on your hypothesis, write three open-ended questions.

8. Edit your questions using the ten points presented in this chapter.

9. Why can you make statistical inferences from data based on random sampling and stratified random sampling?

13 Putting It All Together

"What it boils down to is that you've got to know the bottom line."

—*Body Heat*

"An ounce of prevention is worth a pound of cure."

OVERVIEW

Your research should be carefully planned before you run your first subject. Without such planning, you may fail to have a clear hypothesis or you may fail to properly test your hypothesis. In short, poor planning leads to poor execution.

Poor execution is unethical. At best, it wastes subjects' time; at worst, it harms subjects. Therefore, the purpose of this chapter is to help you avoid unethical research by showing you how to plan, implement, and report the results of your study. If you follow our advice, your research should be humane, valid, and meaningful.

AIDS TO DEVELOPING YOUR IDEA

In this section, you will learn about two major research tools: the research journal and the research proposal. Many scientists regard the research journal and the research proposal as essential to the development and implementation of sound, ethical research.

THE RESEARCH JOURNAL

We recommend that you keep a **research journal**: a diary of your research ideas and your research experiences. Keeping a journal will help you in at least three ways. First, you will not have to rely on memory to explain why and how you did what you did. Second, writing to yourself helps you think through design decisions. Third, the research journal can help you in preparing a research proposal.

Because the journal is for your eyes only, your journal does not have to be neatly typed and free of spelling and grammatical errors. What is in the journal is much more important than how it is written.

What should you put in your journal? Every idea you have about your research project. So, at the beginning of the research process, when you are trying to develop a research hypothesis, use your research journal for brainstorming. For example, write down any research ideas you think of and indicate what stimulated each idea. As you narrow down your choices, explain why you eliminated certain ideas and chose to focus on others. When you decide on a given idea, explain why you decided on that particular research idea. When reading related research, summarize and critique it in your journal.

Remember to write down the authors, year, title, and publisher for each source. This information will come in very handy when you write your research proposal.

In short, whenever you have an insight, find a relevant piece of information, or make a design decision, record it in your journal.

THE RESEARCH PROPOSAL

Like the research journal, the purpose of the research proposal is to help you think through each step of your research project. In addition, the research proposal will let others (e.g., friends and professors) think through your study so they can give you advice on how to improve your study. Thus, by writing the proposal, you will have the opportunity to try out ideas and explore alternatives without damaging a single subject. The process of writing the proposal will help you make intelligent and ethical research decisions.

Although the research proposal builds on the research journal, the research proposal is much more formal than the journal. In writing the proposal, you will have to go through several drafts. The end result of this writing and rewriting will be a proposal that is not only clear but also conforms in content, style, and organization to the guidelines given in the American Psychological Association's (APA) *Publication Manual* (1983).

We want to emphasize that it is not enough to have good ideas. You must present them in a way that people will receive them. History is full of examples of people who had ideas, but got little credit because they expressed them poorly. Conversely, some people have become famous more for how well they expressed their ideas rather than the originality of their ideas. If you write a research proposal or article that is not in APA format, many people will not even bother to look at the content. They feel that if you cannot follow the format, you certainly are incapable of doing good research. Thus, to reiterate, following APA format is important. Indeed, one of the most well-known professors of research design, Dr. Charles Brewer, cites learning APA format as one of the most important things students learn from his design class (Brewer, 1990).

Of course, there is more to writing the research proposal than following APA format. There is also content. Specifically, in your research proposal, you will state the following:

1. Why your general topic is important
2. What your hypothesis is
3. How you arrived at your hypothesis
4. How your study fits in with existing research
5. How you define and operationalize your variables
6. Who your subjects will be
7. What procedures you will follow
8. How you will analyze your data
9. What implications you hope your results will have for theory, real life, or future research

Thus, the introduction and the method sections you write for your research proposal should be a highly polished draft of the introduction, method, and reference sections of your final report. Furthermore, parts of the research proposal will serve as preliminary rough drafts of your abstract, results, and discussion sections. In short, writing the research proposal lays the groundwork for both the study and the final report.

WRITING THE INTRODUCTION TO YOUR RESEARCH PROPOSAL

Now that you know what a research proposal is, it is time for you to begin writing one. We will first show you how to write your introduction.

THE ELEMENTS OF AN INTRODUCTION

The purpose of the introduction is to demonstrate to your readers that you have read the relevant research and thoroughly understand your research question. Once you have articulated the reasoning behind your hypothesis, you will explain what you plan to do and why you plan to do it. After reading the introduction, your reader should know (1) why your research area is important, (2) what your hypothesis is, (3) why your predictions make sense, and (4) why your study is the best way to test the hypothesis.

Establishing the Importance of Your Study

To convince people your study is important and interesting, you must first let them know exactly what you are studying. You must define your concepts. Once you have explained what your concepts are, then you can explain why the concepts are important. In this section, we will discuss three common strategies for establishing the importance of concepts: (1) presenting statistical or other evidence of the problem's prevalence, (2) presenting a case study or other arguments to illustrate the concept's relevance, and (3) demonstrating historical precedence.

Demonstrate the Concept's Prevalence
One strategy for showing your concept is important is to show it is a common or frequent part of real life. You might document the prevalence of the concept by presenting *statistical evidence.* Thus, if you are studying widowhood, you might present statistics on the percentage of people who are widowed. In the absence of statistics, you could use quotations from influential people or organizations (e.g., APA) to stress the prevalence of your concept. Occasionally, the frequency of an event is so obvious (e.g., the prevalence of stress), that you may be able to simply assert that your concept is a prevalent problem.

Demonstrate the Concept's Relevance to Real Life
Rather than emphasizing the concept's prevalence, you might emphasize its relevance. For example, you might stress the practical problems that might be solved by understanding the concept. Alternatively, you might demonstrate the problem's relevance by pre-

senting a **case study**: a real-life situation where your concept is in action. Giving an example of the concept is a very good way to simultaneously define the concept and provide a vivid picture of its importance.

Demonstrate Historical Precedence

Finally, you might show there is *historical precedence* for your study. You could emphasize the great minds that have pondered the concept you will study, the number of people through the ages who have tried to understand the behavior, or merely the length of time the concept has existed. Generally, you will also want to show the problem has—or should have—been important to both researchers and theorists. (For a summary of how to establish a study's importance, see table 13.1.)

The Research Summary

Clearly, one way of establishing historical precedence is to do a research summary. Citing a quantity of research not only informs your reader about the concept, it shows that the field considers these concepts important. That is, if the field did not consider these concepts important, investigators would not be researching these areas and their findings would not be published. Thus, it is not uncommon for introductions to include statements like "The focus of research for years. . . ." or "Research emphasized. . . ."

However, even if you do not use the research summary to establish the importance of the general concepts, you will still want to write a research summary. To reiterate, all introductions should contain a research summary.

The research summary shows how your particular research study fits in with existing work. In other words, whereas there are several ways to show that the general concepts are important, there is only one way to show that your particular research study is important: the research summary. Without a thorough research summary, the reader will not be convinced that your study has not been done before or that you understand the important issues.

Goals of the Research Summary

Because the research summary is designed to "sell" your particular study, you need to do more than merely summarize previous work. You also must use the summary to set the stage for your study. You will set the stage for your study by either showing that your study corrects a weakness in previous research or showing that your work builds on and extends work of previous researchers.

As you can see, you have to set the stage for your research by showing that existing research is in some way deficient. That is, you need to make the reader feel there is a *need* for more research. Table 13.2 lists some common ways of getting the reader to believe previous research raises some questions that must be answered.

Deciding Which Research to Summarize

We have addressed the goals of the literature review. Now let us talk about what you will review. When citing research, review several older, classic works as well as recent research (see appendix B about how to find articles to review). Critiquing—rather than merely summarizing—these articles will show that you have thought about what you have read. By critiquing a number of recent and seminal articles, you will establish you have done your homework.

TABLE 13.1 Ways of Showing that the General Topic is Important

1. Show that it is common in real life

    "_____ is a prevalent problem in the United States."

    "There are many occasions in everyday life when we _____."

    "We are struck by the number of times in our daily life that _____."

    "A large proportion of everyday _____ behavior is _____. For example. . . ."

    "The evidence is that _____ is indeed quite prevalent; estimates suggest that x% of _____ have _____."

2. Show that it is relevant to real life

    "Suppose that you are doing _____ and _____ happens. How do you react?"
    "For instance, consider the following scenario. . . ."

    "This story about _____ raises several important questions."
    "Many of us can recall a time when. . . ."

    "Few experiences in life are capable of producing more _____ than _____."

    "The potential practical applications of _____ are far reaching."

    "Some of the most important events ____ in people's lives are the result of ____."

3. Show historical precedence
    a. Concern to all people
    "For centuries, people have contemplated _____."
    b. Concern to theorists

    "_____ is a core assumption of _____ theory."

    "So's (1991) theory posits _____."

    "_____ theorists have emphasized _____."

    c. Concern to researchers

    "_____ has been the focus of research for years."

    "Over _____ studies have examined _____."

    "There has been much recent interest in the area of _____."

    "A growing literature concerns the effects of _____ on _____."

    "To date, numerous studies have examined _____."
    "At least two literatures in psychology address these issues."

    "The question of _____ has attracted increasing interest among psychologists in recent years."

TABLE 13.2 Common Complaints About Existing Research

- Methodological weaknesses
    - Lack of power
        - Used inadequate sample sizes
        - Used insensitive measures
    - Artificial task
    - Inadequate controls
    - Has not controlled for self-selection
    - Has not controlled for demand characteristics
    - Has not used valid measures
        - Relies on retrospective reports
        - Failed to use objective measures
        - Measures failed to tap construct
        - Has not used valid manipulations
- Conflicting findings
- Has not looked at how the effect is moderated by _____ factor
- Has made the untested assumption that _____ is true
- Has been limited to one kind of experimental paradigm; paradigm may be limited in that has not studied _____ population
- Has not used an experimental hypothesis even though they are hypothesizing that one variable causes changes in another
- Has not looked at what mediates the relationship
- Has only used global measures rather than specific measures that would give a more detailed picture of what is going on
- Failed to determine which of several possible explanations for their results was the correct one

Although critiquing these original articles may establish yourself as a scholar, realize that your goal is not simply to establish your credibility. Instead, your primary goal is to show how your study follows from existing research.

You may find these two goals conflict. On the one hand, you want to establish you know what you are talking about. Therefore, you may feel you should cite all research ever done in the field. On the other hand, you want to use the literature review to set up your research study. Consequently, you only want to cite and analyze those studies that bear directly on your study. There are three things you can do to address the apparent conflict between these two goals.

First, realize that your main goal is to set up your study. Thus, you will be offering in-depth critiques only of those studies that directly bear on your study.

Second, realize that introductions begin by talking about the general area and then start to focus on the specific research question. Thus, seminal research and basic, established findings that only bear indirectly on your work should probably only be cited in the first paragraph or two.

Third, before you start writing, group the studies that seem to have something in common together. Thus, if you have summaries of all your studies on large index cards, you might put all the ones that obtained one kind of finding in one pile and all those that obtained the opposite finding in another pile. Then, for each pile, write a sentence summarizing what all the cards have in common. Each pile's sentence could be the topic sentence, with the rest of the pile providing evidence and citations for the statement made in that sentence (Kuehn, 1989).

Once you have finished a draft of your research summary, reread it. Your research summary should do more than evaluate other people's work. It also should set the stage for your study (see table 13.3 and table 13.4). For example, the measure you praise will be in

---

TABLE 13.3   Ways of Showing that Your Research Stems from Weaknesses in Previous Work

•Methodological weaknesses
>   Lack of power
>>   Used inadequate sample sizes
>>   Used insensitive measures
>   Artificial task
>   Inadequate controls
>   Has not controlled for self-selection
>   Has not controlled for demand characteristics
>   Has not used valid measures
>>   Relies on retrospective reports
>>   Failed to use objective measures
>>   Measures failed to tap construct
>   Has not used valid manipulations

• Conflicting findings

>   "The findings with respect to _____ (this particular problem) have been inconsistent. There are a number of methodological and theoretical issues that have contributed to the contradictory findings, including. . . ."

>   "The few studies that have done this have yielded inconsistent findings."

>   "Research relating _____ to _____ has yielded equivocal results. For example. . . . It was hypothesized that the inconsistent findings were due in part to the neglect of the importance of _____."

• Assumption not tested

>   "Unfortunately, almost all research in this area makes several untested assumptions."

>   "Despite growing research in _____, all researchers implicitly assume that _____."

• Failure to eliminate alternative explanations for the findings

>   "The basic finding is _____. This has been explained in terms of _____. However, there is an alternative explanation."

>   "An often overlooked explanation for these findings is. . . ."

TABLE 13.3   Continued

- Failure to distinguish between two or more theoretical explanations of a phenomenon

  "Existing research still fails to distinguish between _____ explanation and _____ explanation."
- Failure to properly define concepts

  "However, the definition of _____ in some of these studies is open to question."
- Failure to directly test a hypothesis

  "However, _____ study did not allow a direct test of this hypothesis because

  _____. To more directly test this hypothesis, we . . ."

  "However, So and So (1992) did not directly test this hypothesis."

  "Nevertheless, as yet there have been no studies directly evaluating the effect of

  _____ on _____."
- Failure to use experimental design to test causal hypothesis

  "To date, existing research has been correlational. Thus, it has not been possible to

  determine whether _____ and _____ are causally related."
- To follow up on a finding that another investigator obtained but had difficulty explaining

TABLE 13.4   Showing How Your Research Extends Previous Research

- Study suggested by other author
- Related variable not investigated (a variable that is similar to the treatment variable might be expected to have the same effect as the treatment; consequently, the effect of this variable might be tested)
- Test generality of findings

  "However, the generality of this effect requires further verification."

  "We argue that this (limited subject population, artificiality of task, etc.) may impose serious constraints on the generality of the findings obtained from that research."
  1. Extend to a practical, real-life problem
  2. Search for moderating factors (factors that might interact with the treatment factor)

  "Current versions of _____ theory have not been concerned with _____.

  However, our review of the research leads us to propose that _____ may

  moderate _____."

  "_____ and _____ have been studied separately, but previous research has

  never examined how they operate together to affect _____."

  "What is striking, however, is the extent to which the data revealing _____ dif-

  ferences derives almost exclusively from _____ (a limited sample, a limited

  setting, a single research paradigm)."

    a. A different subject population
       "The question is whether there are gender differences. So's (1993) study was restricted to women."
    b. A different task
    c. A different setting
    d. Time—does effect wear off or intensify over time?
  3. Use different levels of the treatment variable (less extreme, more moderate)

    "Almost all previous _____ research has assumed a linear relationship be-

    tween _____ and _____."

- Search for mediating variables (cognitive or physiological factors that come between the stimulus and the response).
  "Inspection of various studies (So & So, 1991; Them, 1990) shows that typically

  there was no direct assessment of _____."
  "However, what mediates this effect is unknown."
- Studying something that other researchers have somehow overlooked

  "However, systematic research on _____ is lacking."

  "With one notable exception, there have been no studies of _____."

  "Studies of _____, for the most part, have not involved _____. In the present

  study, _____ will be studied."

  "Little research has been done on _____."
  1. A related variable that should have a similar effect

     "There is much research on _____. In contrast, no research has explored the

     effect of _____ (a related factor)."
  2. The other side of the coin" (other studies had looked at subjects "high" on the variable but not "lows" or had looked only at negative consequences rather than potential positive consequences

     "Thus, there has been extensive work on the effects of _____ on _____.

     However, there does not appear to be any corresponding body of work on the

     effects of _____ on _____ (the opposite aspect)."
- Use specific, rather than global measures, to pinpoint the effect

  "However, prior studies used global measures of _____. These diffuse measures

  make it impossible to distinguish changes in _____ from changes in _____."
- Determine if the treatment had an effect on related measures
  "Because So and So's (1993) study was limited, a number of variables were not measured."

  "_____ (a treatment variable) has been shown to affect a wide variety of _____ -related measures."

your study; the manipulation you attack will not. Furthermore, just from reading your research summary, a very astute reader could guess what your hypothesis is and how you plan to test it.

Of course, you will not make people guess the rationale for your hypothesis and for your study. After summarizing the relevant research carefully, spell out, step-by-step, the reasoning that led to your hypothesis. Be so explicit that your readers will know what your hypothesis is before you actually state it.

Stating Your Hypothesis

Even though your readers may have guessed your hypothesis, leave nothing to chance: *State your hypothesis* (see table 13.5). To emphasize a point that cannot be emphasized

---

TABLE 13.5 General Strategies for the Latter Part of the Introduction: Explaining the Rationale for the Hypothesis, Stating the Hypothesis, and Setting Up the Study

RATIONALE FOR THE HYPOTHESIS

"Subjects high in _____ (the predictor or treatment variable) should _____.

Consequently, they will score (low, high) on _____ (the dependent measure). In contrast, subjects low in _____ (the predictor or treatment variable) should

_____. Therefore, they should score (low, high) on _____ (dependent variable)."

"We believe this is so, and an analogy may serve to explain why. . . ."

"At least two lines of reasoning would lead one to predict that _____. First. . . . Second. . . ."

"Although there is no well-articulated theoretical view asserting that _____ (the hypothesis is true), a few studies in the literature suggest that this may be the case."

"There is some theoretical reason to believe that _____ (the hypothesis is true).

In considering derivations from _____ theory, So and So (1992) suggested that

_____ (the hypothesis is true)."

"Some indirect support for the hypothesis that _____ can be found in a study done by So and So (1990)."

"Unfortunately, So and So (1992) did not directly test this hypothesis."

"The currently available evidence bearing on this hypothesis is rather limited. Admittedly, the findings of one study seem to support the hypothesis. However, this study

was _____ (limited or flawed) because _____ (low power, measures were not objective, should have used between subjects design, should have used within subjects design, poor counterbalancing, demand characteristics, poor measures, poor manipulations, poor sample, subjects were unusual, the treatment variable was confounded with _____)."

"The same principles that affect _____ (a related concept) should also affect _____ (this concept)."

"For these and other reasons, subjects low in _____ should behave like _____, whereas subjects high in _____ should behave like _____."

"In short, there are sound reasons to believe that. . . ."

Occasionally, to heighten the drama, authors will give reasons why their prediction might be wrong.

"Contrary to this view. . . ."

"On the other hand, _____ (research by _____ or _____ theory) might suggest that. . . ."

"Although there are some reasons to predict _____, there are also reasons to predict _____ (the opposite)."

"Despite its plausibility, several questions can be raised."

"The conventional line of thinking is that. . . . An alternative possibility is that. . . ."

State the Hypothesis

"It was therefore hypothesized that. . . ."

"The existing data, although very limited and somewhat flawed, lead us to believe that. . . ."

"We hypothesized that. . . ."

"Thus, we predicted that. . . ."

"The following hypotheses were tested. . . ."

"In summary, there is reason to expect that. . . ."

"It is expected, then, that. . . ."

"The prediction based on (the finding, the argument made earlier) is that. . . ."

"The hypotheses of the present study were that. . . ."

"Model 1 predicts x, model 2 predicts y, and model 3 predicts z."

Set Up the Study

"This is the objective of the research reported here—to show that _____."

"One way to address this question is. . . ."

"To examine this hypothesis, we. . . ."

"In the present study. . . ."

"To determine if there was a (causal) relationship between _____ and _____. . . ."

"The purpose of this study to is conduct a more systematic investigation of _____."

"We conducted a study to test the following hypotheses."

"Most previous research in this area has consisted of laboratory studies or self-ratings of _____ not tied to specific behavior. By way of contrast, this investigation was a field study conducted in a real-life situation. . . . Participants were therefore unaware that they were research participants. The present study allows a test of the hypothesis in a natural setting."

enough, state your hypothesis boldly and clearly so readers cannot miss it. Let them know what your study is about by writing, "The hypothesis is. . . ."

When you state your hypothesis be sensitive to whether you will be testing it with an experiment or a correlational study. If you will be directly manipulating the predictor variable (the treatment), you will be conducting an experiment. Only with an experiment may you use the word "cause" ("A sedentary lifestyle causes depression."). If you do not plan on directly manipulating your predictor variable then you have a correlational study—you can only test whether two or more variables "relate" ("A sedentary lifestyle is related to depression.").

Once you have stated your hypothesis, you need to convince people that your study is the best way to test your hypothesis. Thus, you must describe what you are going to do and why you are going to do it.

Justifying Your Manipulations and Measures

You should justify your method of testing your hypothesis with the same care you took in justifying the hypothesis itself. Early in the introduction, foreshadow your choice of procedures. Near the end of the introduction, carefully build on what you already said, spelling out your reasons for choosing your methods and procedures.

For example, suppose your justification for using a set of procedures, manipulations, or measures is that these procedures are commonly used and accepted. Then, when you summarize the relevant research, let your readers know about the procedures and about how well accepted they are.

But what if you are using novel procedures or measures? In that case, when you review the relevant research, let your readers know you are dissatisfied with existing measures. Point out problems with existing measures or emphasize that there are no existing measures. Later in the proposal, when you justify your procedures, you will draw on your earlier criticisms to show why your methods are best. For instance, if you are using a new measure, you will refer to your definition of the concept and point out how your measure captures the essence of this definition. Then, you will remind your readers of the weaknesses you spotted in other measures and point out that your measure avoids these weaknesses.

Overview of the Introduction

We have given you some general advice on how to write an introduction (see table 13.6). You have seen the importance of clearly defining your concepts, critically summarizing research, explicating your hypothesis, and justifying your way of testing the hypothesis.

JUSTIFYING SPECIFIC TYPES OF STUDIES

Thus far, you have only been given general advice because the specific way you will justify your study will depend on the kind of study you are doing. In the next section, you will learn how to justify six common kinds of studies:

TABLE 13.6 Checklist for the Introduction

1. Did you cite relevant, recent research?
2. Did you read and cite primary (original) sources rather than second-hand accounts (summaries of studies in texts)?
3. Have you critically commented on the limitations of that research? What were the weaknesses of that work? Are critiques of past research accurate?
4. Is it clear how the work you have cited relates to your hypothesis or study? Is it clear how this study will build on previous work? How does this study fit in the context of past research?
5. Have you cited enough sources?
6. Is your hypothesis clear? If you are including a variable, but have no hypothesis relating to this variable, this may indicate a problem. Your hypothesis should concern a relationship between two or more variables. Note that (a) those variables should be carefully defined and (b) those variables should be measurable.
7. Is the reason for making the hypothesis clear? Why are you making this prediction? Is that logic clear? Why might previous research or theory make that prediction? Note that to make such arguments you may have to clearly define relevant concepts and theories.
8. Does it seem as if the hypothesis could be tested?
9. Is it clear why your research hypothesis should be tested? Is it clear why the problem is important?
10. Is it clear that your study intends to test the hypothesis? Is it clear why your study is the best way to test this hypothesis?
11. Do ideas follow logically? Or does it appear to jump around? If ideas seem to jump around, try
    a. Outlining your introduction.
    b. Grouping together studies that seem to "go together." Then, write a sentence describing the main conclusion or similarity shared by these studies. This will be your topic sentence. Write your topic sentence and then use the studies to provide evidence or support for that sentence (Kuehn, 1989).
    c. Using subheadings.
    d. Summarizing the point you are trying to make before moving on to your next

    point (e.g., "Thus, the evidence suggests that ____. However, existing research can

    be criticized for ____.")
12. Can the reader anticipate the rest of your paper from your introduction?

METHOD OR INTRODUCTION

1. Is it clear why you used the measures you used? Do you have evidence they are valid, well accepted, or follow from how the concept is defined?
2. Is it clear why you used the task you used?
3. Is it clear why you used the design you used? Is it clear that this study is the best way to test the hypothesis?

---

1. Exploratory
2. Direct replication
3. Systematic replication
4. Conceptual replication
5. Replication and extension
6. Theory-testing

The Exploratory Study

In introducing an **exploratory study**, a study investigating a new area of research, you must take special care to justify your study, your hypothesis, and your procedures. You must compensate for your readers' lack of knowledge about your research area.

New Is Not Enough

Unlike most introductions, you cannot state your research area is important merely by showing the area has inspired a lot of research. It has not—that is why your study is an exploratory study. To justify an exploratory study, do not merely state your research question has been ignored. Many dull research areas have been ignored. Convince your readers that your research question deserves top priority. After all, it is a tragedy that your research question has been overlooked. This wrong must be righted to help psychology advance as a science.

One approach you can use to justify your exploratory study is to discuss hypothetical or real-life cases that could be solved or understood by answering your research question. For example, consider how Latane and Darley (1966) opened their pioneering work on helping behavior. They did not stop at saying that helping behavior had not been extensively investigated. Instead, they referred to the case of Kitty Genovese. Ms. Genovese was brutally attacked for more than half an hour in the presence of over 30 witnesses—none of whom intervened. Thus, Latane and Darley effectively convinced readers that understanding why people fail to help is an important research area.

To reiterate, your first step in justifying an exploratory study is to show that the area is important. Once you have convinced your readers that the research area is important, you can further excite them by emphasizing that you are exploring new frontiers, going where no investigators have gone before.

Spell Out Your Reasoning

In an exploratory study, as in all studies, you must spell out the rationale for your hypothesis. Because you are studying an unexplored dimension, you must give your readers the background to understand your predictions. Therefore, be extremely thorough in detailing the logic behind your predictions—even if you think your predictions are just common sense. Not everyone will share your common sense.

How do you detail the logic behind "common sense" predictions? Even common sense predictions can often be justified by theory or research on related variables. For example, suppose you are interested in seeing how low-sensation seekers and high-sensation seekers differ in their reactions to stress. You might argue that differences would be expected based on the arousal optimization theory—the theory that we all have an ideal level of arousal. Thus, you might argue that high-sensation seekers like stress because it increases their arousal levels, whereas low-sensation seekers hate stress. In addition, you could argue that introversion-extroversion and sensation seeking are related concepts. Because introversion and sensation seeking are related, and stress has different effects on introverts and extroverts, stress should also have different effects on low-sensation seekers versus high-sensation seekers.

Defend Your Procedures

Finally, in an exploratory study you may be studying variables that have never been studied before. In that case, you cannot use other people's measures and manipulations of your concepts. Explain why your manipulations and measures are valid.

The Direct Replication

When doing a direct replication (a repetition of an original study), you must be very clear about why you are repeating the study. If you are not careful, the reader may think you performed the study before you realized that someone else had already done your study. Even if you do spell out why you repeated the study, some journal reviewers will find the fact that you did a direct replication a legitimate reason to reject the paper for publication (Fiske & Fogg, 1990). However, there is a two-pronged strategy you can use to convince people your study is worth doing.

Document the Original Study's Importance

To justify a direct replication, you should show first that the original study was important. To establish the study's importance, discuss its impact on psychology. To get some objective statistics that support your opinion, note the number of times the study has been cited using the *Social Science Citation Index* described in appendix B.

Explain Why the Results Might Not Replicate

After establishing the study's importance, convince your readers that the study's results might not replicate. That is, argue the original study was flawed, the findings would not occur today, the findings contradict other published work, or Type 1 or Type 2 error occurred.

For instance, if the results from the original study were barely significant, you can justify a direct replication by arguing that a Type 1 error may have occurred. On the other hand, if the original study reported null results, you might argue that a Type 2 error occurred by claiming random error or poor execution of the study may have hidden real differences. If the original study's findings seem to conflict with several other published papers, you have a compelling rationale for replicating the study.

Finally, you can justify a direct replication if you think the study would not come out the same today. For example, you might want to replicate a conformity study because you feel people are no longer as conforming as they were when the original study was conducted. Regardless of what approach you take, you must present a compelling rationale for any study that is merely a rerun of another study.

The Systematic Replication

As you may recall from chapter 9, the systematic replication involves making a minor modification in the original study. As such, the systematic replication accomplishes everything the direct replication does and more. Therefore, every reason for doing a direct replication is also a reason for doing a systematic replication. In addition, you can justify a systematic replication by showing that modifying the procedures would improve the original study's power, construct validity, or external validity.

Improved Power

If you thought the original study's null results were due to a Type 2 error, you might make a minor change in procedure to improve power. For example, you might use more subjects, more extreme levels of the predictor variable, or a better way of collecting the dependent measure (e.g., a more accurate stopwatch) than the original study.

Improved Construct Validity

You also might want to modify the original study if you thought the original study's results were biased by demand characteristics. Thus, you might repeat the study using a double-blind procedure to reduce subject and researcher bias.

Improved External Validity

If you are systematically replicating a study to improve external validity, you should explain why you suspect the results may not generalize to different stimulus materials, levels of the treatment variable, or subjects. Even if it seems obvious to you why a study done on rats might not apply to humans, why a study done on college students may not apply to factory workers, why a study done on males may not apply to females, or why the results would not hold if different levels of the treatment were used—*spell out your reasons* for suspecting the results will not generalize.

The Conceptual Replication Study

Most of the reasons for conducing a systematic or direct replication are also relevant for introducing and justifying a **conceptual replication**: a study that is based on the original, but uses different methods in order to better assess the true relationships between the variables being studied. In addition, the conceptual replication has several other unique selling points, depending on how you changed the original study.

Using a Different Measure

Your conceptual replication might differ because you used a different way of measuring the dependent measure than the original authors did. In that case, you should support your operationalization by showing how your measure is more reliable, sensitive, or valid than the original measure. To make the case for your measure, you may want to cite other studies that used your measure. As in the legal arena, precedent carries weight in psychology. If someone else published a study using a given measure, then the measure automatically gains some credibility.

Using a Different Manipulation

Instead of trying to use a different measure of a construct, you may want to use a different manipulation of a construct. If you use a different manipulation, you should start by defining the variable you are trying to manipulate. Next, you should discuss weaknesses of previous manipulations. Then, show why your manipulation avoids these weaknesses. Conclude by showing that your manipulation is consistent with definitions of the concept you are trying to manipulate.

Using a Different Design

If you are changing the original study's design, explain why. If you are replicating a between subjects design using a within subjects design to improve power, tell your readers. If you are converting a within subjects design to a between subjects design because you feel subjects will be less likely to guess the hypothesis in a between subjects design, tell your readers. Your readers will *not* instantaneously realize the advantages of using a different design.

The Replication and Extension Study

Your study may go beyond a conceptual replication to looking at additional factors or measures. In that event, your introduction would not only contain everything a conceptual replication would but also a rationale for the additional factors or measures.

Rationale for Additional Factors or Measures

For example, suppose the original author found people loaf in groups. You might think of a situation (e.g., a group where all members were good friends) where social loafing would not occur. Thus, you might include friendship as a factor in your design. Be sure to justify your reasoning for including the factor, defend your manipulation of that factor, and state your predictions regarding the factor.

Rationale for Additional Dependent Measures

Instead of adding a predictor variable to a study, you might add a dependent measure. Your purpose would be to discover the process behind the effect. Thus, in social loafing, you might collect measures of participants' perceptions of others to find out the cognitive processes responsible for social loafing (e.g., perceptions that their efforts are not being noticed). Or, you might record their interactions with others to find out the behavior responsible for social loafing (e.g., working being punished, socializing being rewarded). Or, you might monitor arousal levels in an attempt to discover the physiological reasons for social loafing (e.g., lower physiological arousal in a group setting).

The tricky part about writing an introduction to a "process" study is to convince your readers that you really are measuring the underlying causes of a phenomenon. You must do more than merely show that these "processes" occur before the phenomenon. These "processes" could be incidental side effects of the treatment. For instance, a fever comes before you get ill and intensifies as you get ill, but a fever does not cause you to be ill. It is just a side effect of your illness. In the same way, a dependent measure may correlate with a phenomenon, but not cause that phenomenon.

The Theory-Testing Study

If you are testing a prediction from a theory, there is good news and bad news. The good news is you will not have to spend much effort justifying your study's importance. Almost everyone assumes testing a theory is important.

The bad news is not everyone will agree your predictions follow from the theory. To protect yourself, you must clearly spell out how your predictions follow from theory. By being clear, everyone will follow your logic, and some may even agree with it.

PLANNING YOUR PROCEDURES

You have reviewed the literature, developed a hypothesis, operationalized your variables, and stated your reasons for testing your hypothesis. However, your preliminary work is still not done. You must now decide exactly what specific actions you will take. In other words, although you have probably decided on the general design (e.g., a 2 × 2), your plan is not complete until each minute detail has been thought through and written down.

In your journal, specify *exactly* what procedures you will follow. For example, what instructions will participants be given? Who will administer the treatment? Where? Will subjects be run in groups or individually? How should the researcher interact with subjects? Although your answers must be accountable to issues of validity and reliability, your paramount concern must always be ethics. You do not have the right to harm another.

ETHICAL CONSIDERATIONS: HUMAN RESEARCH

Ethics should be the foundation of your research plan. Therefore, you should read appendix A ("Ethics") before conducting a study.

In addition to reading appendix A, you must be extremely careful not to harm your participants. Ideally, your participants should feel just as well when they leave the study as they did when they began the study. Unfortunately, even in the most innocuous studies, protecting your participants from discomfort is much easier said than done.

Weighing the Risks

Realize that any experience may be traumatic to some participants. Trauma can occur from things you would never think of as being traumatic. Because any study has risks and you cannot know all of the risks, *do not run a single subject without your professor's permission.*

To begin to sensitize yourself to the risks involved in your proposed study, list the 10 worst things that could possibly happen to subjects. If you are using human participants, be aware that not all participants will react in the same way. Some may experience trauma because the study triggers some painful memory. Some participants may feel bad because they did poorly. Other participants may feel bad because they felt their behavior ruined your study. Realize that some of your participants may be mentally unbalanced and any attack on their self-esteem might lead to disastrous consequences. Because participants are so fragile, you should list some serious consequences in your worst case scenario.

Reducing Risks

Because any study has the potential for harm, the possibility of severe consequences does not mean your professor will not allow you to do the study. However, you and your professor should think about ways to minimize the risks.

Screening Participants

One method of minimizing risks is to screen out "vulnerable participants." For instance, if there is any reason to believe your study may increase heart rate or blood pressure, you may want to make sure that only people in good health participate in your study. If your study might harm people with very low self-esteem you may want to use only participants who are well adjusted and have high levels of self-esteem. Therefore, you might give a measure of self-esteem to potential participants to eliminate those with low self-esteem.

Informed Consent

Not only should you screen participants, but you should also let participants screen themselves. That is, participants should be volunteers who give their **informed consent:** know what the study is about before volunteering for it.

How informed is informed consent? Very informed, when it comes to telling participants about any unpleasant aspect of the study. If participants are going to get shocked, exposed to loud noises, or extreme cold, they should be informed of this before they volunteer. Consequently, if your study does involve unpleasantness, you may have difficulty getting participants to volunteer.

Informed consent is considerably less informed when it comes to more innocuous aspects of the study. After all, the study would be ruined if participants knew everything that would happen (and why it happened) before it happened. So, although participants are usually told the truth, they are not always told the whole truth. For example, a memory experiment's description would mention that participants have to memorize words, but might omit the fact the researcher is looking at the order in which facts are recalled or that there is a surprise recall of all the lists at the end of the study.

Because participants are not fully informed about your study, there may be some things about it they dislike (e.g., the task may be too hard for them). Had they known about these features, they would not have participated. What can you do about the problem of participants disliking something you did not warn them about because you did not think it would bother them? For example, suppose a participant finds it upsetting to try the surprise recall tasks. What can you do?

One protection against these unexpected problems is to make sure participants understand they can quit the study at any time. So, before the participants begin your study, tell them that if they find any aspect of the study uncomfortable, they can and **should** escape this discomfort by quitting the study. Assure them it is their duty to quit if they experience discomfort. Furthermore, tell them that if they quit, they will still get full credit for participating.

Modifying the Study

You have seen that you can minimize ethical problems by letting participants know what they are getting in for and by letting participants gracefully withdraw from the study. You should also minimize harm by making your study as humane as possible. You can make your study more ethical by reducing the strength of your treatment manipulation, carefully selecting stimulus materials, and by being a conscientious researcher.

Reducing the Treatment Strength

Although using extreme levels of your predictor variable may help you get a significant change in the criterion variable, extreme levels may harm your participants. For example, 24 hours of food deprivation is more likely to cause hunger than 12 hours. However, 24 hours of deprivation is more stressful to the participant. If you plan an unpleasant manipulation, remember your participants' welfare and minimize the unpleasant consequences as much as possible. Consider using levels of the predictor variable that are less severe than you originally intended.

Modifying Stimulus Materials

By modifying your stimulus materials, you may be able to prevent them from triggering unpleasant memories. For instance, if you were interested in the effects of caffeine on memory for prose, you would not want the prose passage to cover some topic like death, divorce, alcoholic parents, or rape. Instead, you would want to use a passage covering a less traumatic topic, such as sports. If the sports article referred to someone's death or hospitalization, you might want to delete that section of the article.

The Conscientious Researcher

Often, it is not the study that is unethical, it is the researcher's arrogance. Although we know of a few participants who were hurt as a direct result of a research manipulation, we know of many more who were hurt because the researcher treated them like dirt.

To ensure you are sensitive, courteous, and respectful to all of your human participants, you should do two things. First, when scheduling your research sessions, make sure you leave a ten-minute gap between the end of one session and the beginning of the next session. Some investigators believe that, like a physician, they should efficiently schedule people one after another. Their "efficiency" results in participants having to wait for the investigator, the investigator having to rush through the formalities of greeting participants, or—even worse—the investigator rushing through debriefing. Thus, the "efficient" investigator, like the efficient physician, is seen as unconcerned. Although this conduct does not become physicians, it is intolerable for psychological researchers!

After a research participant has given an hour of his or her time, you should be more than willing to answer any questions the participant has. Furthermore, if you rush through greeting or debriefing the participant, the participant will see you as uncaring. Consequently, they will be less likely to tell you about any psychological discomfort they felt and less likely to accept any aid you might offer. Therefore, we advise that you walk, not run, subjects through your study.

Second, give the participants power. That is, allow participants to rate your study on a scale such as the one in table 13.7. Give each participant's rating sheet to your instructor. Following this simple procedure helps you to appreciate each participant's individuality.

TABLE 13.7 Sample Debriefing Rating Scale*

Being a participant in psychology studies should provide you with a first-hand look at research. On the scale below, please indicate how valuable or worthless (in terms of whether the experience was personally or educationally valuable) you found today's study by circling a number from +3 to −3.

Worthless: −3 −2 −1 +1 +2 +3 :Valuable

If you wish to explain your rating or to make comments on this study, either positive or negative, please do so below.

*For more detailed information on debriefing scales and procedures, please see appendix A.

Debriefing

Although you should try to anticipate and prevent every possible bad reaction a participant may have to being in your study, you will not be successful. Inevitably, your procedures will still cause some unpleasantness. After the study is over, you should try to remove this unpleasantness by informing them about the study, reassuring them that their reactions were normal, and expressing your appreciation for their participation.

You also should listen to participants and be sensitive to any unexpected, unhappy reactions to your study. By being a good listener, you should be able to undo any damage you have unwittingly done. This process of informing your participants about the study and removing any harm done is called **debriefing**. Occasionally, ordinary debriefing will not undo the harm caused to the research participant. In those cases, there are several steps you may take to alleviate distress. For participants who are upset with their responses, you should ask them if they want you to destroy their data. For participants you cannot calm down, you should take them to talk to a professor, counselor, or friend.

In summary, you should be very concerned about ethics. Because ethics involve weighing the costs of the study against the potential benefits, you should do everything you can to minimize the risk of your participants experiencing discomfort. If, despite your efforts, a participant experiences discomfort, you should try to reduce that discomfort during debriefing.

ETHICAL CONSIDERATIONS: ANIMAL RESEARCH

With animal subjects, you incur the same responsibilities that you did with human subjects—you must protect animal subjects from undue stress and discomfort. In many ways, you have even more responsibility to animal subjects because they are dependent on you for their mere existence. You keep them fed, clean, warm, and comfortable—twenty-four hours a day. To fulfill your responsibility to animal subjects, you must follow the APAs guidelines for proper housing, food and water, and handling (see appendix A).

Furthermore, because your animal subjects do not have the power to give their informed consent, nor the power to quit the study, you must carefully question the value of your study. Ask yourself and your professor this question: "Is the potential knowledge gained from the study worth the cost to the animals?" Finally, if you must euthanize (kill) your animal subjects at the end of your study, follow APA's guidelines to ensure this is done in the most humane way.

MAXIMIZE THE BENEFITS: THE OTHER SIDE OF THE ETHICS COIN

We have discussed ways of minimizing harm to subjects. However, minimizing harm is not enough to ensure your study is ethical. For your study to be ethical, the potential benefits must be greater than the potential harm. Thus, an extremely harmless study can be unethical if the study has no potential benefits. So, just as you owe it to your subjects to reduce potential harm, you owe it to your subjects to maximize the potential benefits of your study. You maximize that potential by making sure your study provides accurate information. To provide accurate information, your study needs to have power and validity.

Power Is Knowledge

One of the most serious obstacles to obtaining accurate information is lack of power. Remember, null results do not prove the null hypothesis. They only make people wonder about the study's power. There is no point in doing a study that is so powerless that it will lead to inconclusive, null results.

To have power, you should use a strong manipulation, a sensitive dependent measure, well-standardized procedures, homogeneous subjects, a sensitive design, and enough subjects.

Sample Size: There is Power in Numbers

Perhaps your most important obstacle to finding a significant effect is a lack of subjects. As a rule of thumb, you should have at least 16 subjects in each group.[1] Of course, the number of subjects you need in each group will be affected by the sensitivity of your design, the heterogeneity of your subjects, the number of observations you get from each subject, the size of the difference you expect to find between conditions, and the sensitivity of your dependent measure.

If you have a within subjects design, a reliable and sensitive criterion variable, and expect a rather large difference between your conditions, you may be able to use fewer than 16 subjects per group.

If, on the other hand, you are using a simple between subjects design, heterogeneous subjects, a manipulation that may have little effect, and a relatively insensitive dependent measure, you may want at least 100 subjects per condition.

---

[1]Of course, the more subjects, the more power. Indeed, some (Cohen, 1990) would consider 64 subjects per group to be a reasonable minimum. In some cases, however, a researcher might use a design that is so powerful that even the smallest of effects, no matter how practically and theoretically insignificant would be statistically significant. Having a design that is too powerful is rarely a problem for novice researchers.

Hunting For Participants

How are you going to get all the volunteer participants you need to conduct a powerful study? The threat of death is not ethical.

The Draft   Some researchers rely on "captive" samples. For example, many colleges "volunteer" students in introductory psychology courses for the research draft. In fact, most of the research strength of modern psychology has been built using this research draft. If your school has such a draft, count yourself among the blessed. All you have to do is ask your professor how to become a recruiter.

Enlisting Volunteers   If your school does not have a draft, an effective way of getting participants is to ask professors to request volunteers from their classes. Many professors will gladly do this. Some will even give volunteers extra credit as an incentive for participating in your study.

Non-college Samples   But what if you do not want to use college students in your study? For example, suppose you want to study children or retirees? Or, suppose you agree with the skeptics who claim results from studies done on college students cannot be applied to "normal people." Then, you would look beyond college classrooms for participants. A note of caution: You may find getting "real-world" participants takes as much work and creativity as planning your study.

Children   If you want to study children, you may be able to take advantage of the "captive" audience approach. After all, most children have to go to school. However, obtaining access to those children may turn into a nightmare of red tape. You will have to obtain permission from all or many of the following: the school board, the superintendent, principal, teacher, parent, child, your professor, and university. If you are going to get these permissions in time for your study, you will need to plan ahead—and be very lucky.

Adults   Finding adult participants can be even more challenging than finding children. For example, one of your text's authors wanted an adult population for her doctoral dissertation. Her first thought was to contact a major company and gain access to its employees. This tactic failed. Next, she tried to run a newspaper ad asking for volunteers. One newspaper refused to print it. Another would only run it in the "Personal" section. Thus, her appeal for participants appeared with ads for astrological advice, massage services, and people wanting dates. Although a few "volunteers" called, most wanted either a date or an obscene conversation. We do not recommend newspaper ads—especially if your goal is to get a representative sample of the adult population.

Older Adults   The authors have had greater success recruiting elderly participants. Nutrition centers, retirement communities, friendship networks, and nursing homes have been fruitful sources of participants. In addition, we recommend the "grandmother connection": having an older relative or friend introduce you to other prospective participants.

Obviously, finding human participants will take planning, perseverance, and luck. Once you contact prospective participants, you should explain your study to them and have them sign a permission form. The permission form will protect both you and your participants. Basically, it states that you have explained the study to the volunteers and they agree to participate (see table 13.8). If minors are participating in your study, you need to have separate forms for both the participants and their parents.

Animal Subjects Our experience with recruiting human participants might have increased your enthusiasm for animal research. In many ways, animals are better subjects than humans. You do not have to worry about permission slips, extra credit, or obscene phone calls. Consult with your instructor about obtaining animals for your research. Often schools will provide animals for student research.

Reducing Threats to Construct Validity

After ensuring your study has adequate power, we would like to be able to tell you that you can take it easy and relax. Unfortunately, however, you cannot relax. Power is not your only concern when conducting psychological research. You must also ensure the construct validity of your results is not destroyed by (1) researchers failing to conduct your study in an objective, standardized way; or (2) participants reacting to how they think you want them to react to the treatment, rather than reacting to the treatment itself.

Researcher Effects
If you use more than one investigator, you may be able to detect researcher effects by simply including researcher as a factor in your design. In other words, randomly assign

---

TABLE 13.8 Sample Informed Consent Form

Students taking PSY 455, Research Design, are investigating the effects of noise and sleep deprivation on anxiety.

If you participate in this study, you will be deprived of sleep for two nights and exposed to common city noise for one hour. During the hour, you will be asked to fill out two questionnaires, and your pulse and blood pressure will be measured several times.

You will be asked to spend two nights in a special dorm room so that your sleep can be monitored. In addition, it will take ninety minutes for the noise treatment and measures to be completed.

You will receive $20 for participating in the study.

Physical injury, psychological injury, or deception are not part of this study. In addition, all your responses and answers will be held confidential. No one other than the investigators will see information about your particular responses.

Any questions you have regarding this project should be addressed to the investigators or to Dr. _____, faculty supervisor.

If you agree to participate in this study, please sign the following statement.

I have read the above Consent Form and understand the proposed project. I consent to participate in this study. I understand that I can quit the study at any time. Finally, I will be paid $20 whether or not I complete the study.

Signature   Date

---

subjects to condition and to researcher. If you have two researchers and two treatment conditions (A and B), you would have four conditions: A1, B1 (conditions run by researcher 1), and A2, B2 (conditions run by researcher 2). Then, do an ANOVA using researcher as a factor to see whether different researchers got different results.[2]

However, using ANOVA to detect researcher effect is not the solution to reducing researcher effects for two reasons. First, this statistical approach will only tell you if one researcher is getting different results than other researchers. If all your researchers are biased, you may not get a significant researcher effect. Of course, if you are the only researcher, you cannot use researcher as a factor in an ANOVA. Second, and more importantly, detecting researcher effects is not the same as preventing researcher effects.

To prevent researcher effects, you must address the three major causes of researchers failing to conduct studies in an objective and standardized manner. What are these causes? First, researchers may not know how to behave because the procedures for how the researchers should conduct the study have not been spelled out. Second, researchers may not follow the instructions. Third, the researchers may strongly expect or hope for subjects to behave in certain ways.

Loose Protocol Effect: The Importance of Developing a Protocol Often, the researchers are not behaving in an objective and standardized way because of the **loose protocol effect:** the instructions are not detailed enough. Fortunately, the loose protocol effect can be avoided.

Before you start your study, carefully plan everything out. As a first step you should write out a set of instructions that chronicles the exact procedure for each subject. These procedures should be so specific that, by reading and following your instructions, another person could run your subjects the same way you do.

To make your instructions specific, you might want to write a computer program based on these instructions. Because computers do not assume anything, writing such a program forces you to spell out everything down to the last detail. If you cannot program, just write the script as if a robot were to administer the study. Write out each step, including the actual words that researchers will say to the participants. The use of such a script will help standardize your procedures, thus reducing threats to validity.

Once you have a detailed draft of your protocol, give it a test run. For example, to ensure you are as specific as you think you are, pretend to be a participant and have several different people run the study using *only* your instructions. See how the different individuals behave. This may give you clues as to how to tighten up your procedures. In addition, you should run several practice participants. Notice if you change procedures in some subtle way across participants. If so, adjust your instructions to get rid of this variability.

At the end of your test runs, you should have a detailed set of instructions that you and any co-investigator can follow to the letter. To double-check your protocol, see table 13.9.

Inspiring the Troops to Avoid Researcher Effects Unfortunately, even if you write out your protocol (procedures) in detail, you or your co-investigators may still fail to follow

---

[2]You may want to consult with your professor as to the type of ANOVA you should use. There is some debate as to whether conventional ANOVA should be performed or whether a "random effects" model should be used.

TABLE 13.9 Protocol Checklist

How will you manipulate your treatment variables?

How will you measure your dependent (criterion) variables?

How many subjects will you need?

Do you have your professor's permission?

Do you have a suitable place to run your subjects?

How will you get your subjects?

If you are using animals, how will they be cared for?

What will you do with your animals after the study?

If you are using human participants, how will you make your sign-up sheets available to potential participants?

Have you included a description of the study on the sign-up sheet?

Will participants be rewarded for volunteering to be in your study (e.g., money or extra credit)?

If you are conducting an experiment, how will you assign subjects to a condition?

Have you written out a detailed research protocol?

If you are using human participants, have you developed a consent form?

If you are using human participants, have you written out the oral instructions you will give your participants?

If you are using human participants, have you written out what you will say during debriefing?

If you use volunteers from college classes, how will you notify professors about which students will participate?

Will you inform participants about the outcome of your study? How?

that protocol. To avoid the **researcher failure to follow protocol effect,** you need to make sure that (1) all investigators know the procedures and (2) everyone is motivated to follow the procedures.

To make sure investigators learn the procedures, you should hold training sessions. Supervise investigators while they practice the procedures on each other and on practice participants.

Once researchers know the right way to run the study, the key is to make sure they are motivated to run the study the same way every time. To increase researchers' motivation to be consistent, you might have them work in pairs. While one researcher runs the participants, the other will listen in through an intercom or watch through a one-way mirror. You may even wish to record research sessions.

If your researchers still have trouble following procedures, you may need to automate your study. For instance, you might use a computer to present instructions, administer the treatment, or collect the dependent measure. Computers have the reputation for following instructions to the letter, so using a computer may help standardize your procedures. Of course, computers are not the only machine that might help you. Some of the machines that could help you give instructions and present stimuli include automated slide-projectors, tape recorders, and videotape players. Countless other devices can be used to record your data accurately, from electronic timers and counters to noise-level meters.

Researcher Expectancy Effect   The final source of researcher bias is the **researcher expectancy effect**: researchers' expectations are affecting the results. You can take three steps to prevent the researcher expectancy effect:

1. Be very specific about how investigators are to conduct themselves. Remember, researcher expectancies probably affect the results by changing the investigator's behavior rather than by causing the investigator to send a telepathic message to the participants.
2. Do not let the investigators know the hypothesis.
3. Do not let investigators know what condition the subject is in—making the investigator blind. Although making investigators blind is easiest in drug experiments where subjects take either a placebo or the real drug, you can make investigators blind in non-drug experiments. For example, if you present stimuli in booklets, you can design your booklets so that booklets for different conditions look very similar. In that way, an investigator running a group of subjects might not know what condition each subject is in. For some studies, you may be able to use a second investigator who does nothing except collect the dependent measure. This second investigator could easily be kept in the dark as to what condition the subject was in.

Review of Researcher Effects

Whether you are the only investigator or one of a team of investigators, researcher effects may bias your results. Therefore, you should always try to prevent the loose protocol effect, the failure to follow protocol effect, and the researcher expectancy effect.

Subject Effects

Unfortunately, in psychological research, you must beware not only of researcher effects but also of **subject effects**: participants may see through the study and try to play along with what the investigator wants. Fortunately, there are various ways of preventing participants' expectancies from biasing your results.

Preventing Subjects' Expectancies   For starters, you might make your researcher "blind" to reduce the chance the participant will get any ideas from the researcher. In experimental investigations, you might use a between subjects design rather than a within subjects design because participants who are exposed only to one treatment condition are less likely to guess the hypothesis than participants who are exposed to all treatment conditions.

Placebo Treatments   A related tactic is to prevent participants from knowing whether they are in the comparison or treatment condition. Therefore, if you have comparison condition(s), use placebo treatment(s) rather than "no-treatment" condition(s). That way, all groups think they are in the treatment condition. Thus, any treatment effect you find will not be due to participants changing their behavior because they expect the treatment to have an effect.

Unobtrusive Recording   Participants are less likely to know the hypothesis if they do not know what you are measuring. Obviously, if they do not even know they are being observed—as in some field studies—they will not know what you are measuring. Thus, if your hypothesis is an obvious one, you may try to do a field study. (But make sure you are not invading participants' privacy!)

Although field studies lend themselves to unobtrusive recording, unobtrusive recording can even occur in a laboratory study. That is, participants will assume that if you are not in the room with them, you are not observing them. However, thanks to one-way mirrors and intercoms, you can monitor participants' behavior from the next room.

Unobtrusive Measures   Even if the participant knows you are watching, the participant does not have to know what you are watching. That is, you can use unobtrusive measures. For example, you might put the participant in front of a computer and ask the participant to type an essay. Although the participant thinks you are measuring the essay's quality, you may have the computer programmed to monitor speed of typing, time in between paragraphs, number of errors made, and times a section was rewritten. In addition, you might also have tape-recorded and videotaped the participant, monitoring his or her facial expressions, number of vocalizations, and loudness of vocalizations.

Research Realism   Rather than trying to obscure or confuse participants as to the purpose of the study, you may try to prevent participants from even thinking about the purpose of the study. How? By designing a study that has a high degree of **research realism**: a study that involves participants in the task. Research realism means participants are not constantly saying to themselves "What does the researcher really want me to do?" or "If I were a typical person, how would I behave in this situation?" Note that research realism does not mean the study is like real life; it means participants are engrossed in the task. In this age of video games, even a fairly artificial task can be very high in research realism.

ETHICS SUMMARY

Before reading this chapter, you might have been surprised to see research realism and other strategies for reducing subject effects in a section on ethics. However, you now know that planning an ethical study involves taking many factors into account. Not only must you ensure the safety of your subjects but you also must demonstrate the validity of your methods. To avoid overlooking an important ethical consideration, consult table 13.10, appendix A, and your professor.

WRITING THE METHOD SECTION

Once you have thoroughly thought out each step of your study, you are ready to write the method section of your proposal. This is the *how* section—here you will explain exactly how you plan to conduct your study. However, just like the introduction, the method

TABLE 13.10 Research With Human Participants: An Ethics Checklist

- Is a physically unpleasant stimulus going to be used in your study? If so:
  1. Is this fact clearly stated
     a. on the sign-up sheet?
     b. on the consent form?
  2. Have you considered alternatives that would be less unpleasant?
  3. Have you limited the intensity of this stimulus?
  4. Have you taken steps to reduce potential harm to your subjects caused by a physically unpleasant stimulus?
- Are you going to use stress of some sort (e.g., sense of insecurity or failure, assault upon values, fatigue, or sleep deprivation) in your study? If so:
  1. Is this fact clearly stated
     a. on the sign-up sheet?
     b. on the consent form?
  2. Have you considered alternatives that would be less stressful?
  3. Have you limited the intensity of this stimulus?
  4. Have you taken steps to reduce potential harm to your subjects caused by a psychologically unpleasant stimulus?
- What will you do if participants exhibit signs of harm (e.g., crying, disoriented behavior)?
- Are you prepared to describe the purpose and nature of your study to your participants during debriefing?
- Will you use deception in your study? If so, what will you tell them during debriefing?
- Are you aware that participants can quit your study at any time? If a participant does drop out, will you give your participants credit for participating? Is this fact stated on the informed consent form? Is this fact part of your instructions to the participants?
- What educational gain do you think participants will obtain from participating in your study?
- How will you ensure the confidentiality of each participant's data?

section is written on two levels. As you will recall, at one level, the introduction summarizes existing research. But, at another level, the introduction sells the need for your study by pointing out deficiencies in existing research. Similarly, on one level, the method section tells the reader what you did. However, at another level, it sells the reader on the idea that what you did was correct. Although the introduction already set this section up by pointing out which subjects should be studied, which measures should be used, and what variables should be controlled for, do not hesitate to remind your reader again. Thus, in the method section, you may mention that your measure is valid, that your manipulation is widely accepted, or that you did something a certain way to reduce demand characteristics, researcher biases, random error, or some other problem.

In short, selling the value of a research strategy is a never-ending job. If possible, you should sell your strategy in each of the method section's subsections: subjects, design, apparatus, and procedure.

SUBJECTS

In the subjects section, you will describe the general characteristics of your subjects: how many subjects you plan to have, how many will be male, how many will be female, their ages, and how you plan to obtain or recruit them. In addition, include any other relevant information (e.g., what strain of rat). You also should indicate when and where they will be tested and whether they will be tested individually or in groups. If they will be tested in groups, you should state the size of the groups. If you plan to exclude data from some subjects, state the precise criteria for exclusion (e.g., scores above 16 on a depression inventory) and your reasons for excluding those individuals from your study.

The subjects section is written in a straightforward and somewhat mechanical fashion. In fact, it is so mechanical you can use the "fill-in-the-blanks" example in table 13.11 to write most subjects sections.

DESIGN

The design section is also easy to write. Merely describe the design of your study. For an experiment, state the number of levels for each independent variable, whether the variable is a between or within subjects variable, and the dependent variable. Because the design section is so straightforward, you can probably write your design section by using the "fill-in-the-blanks" example in table 13.11.

APPARATUS AND MATERIALS

In the apparatus and materials section, describe the equipment and materials you plan to use. This includes laboratory equipment, tests, computers, etc.

If you plan to use equipment made by a company, list the brand name and the make of the product. If you designed your equipment, briefly describe it. You need to give enough detail so readers will have a general idea of what it looks like. In the appendix, include a photo or diagram of your apparatus.

If you used a test or questionnaire, reference the source of the test and give at least one example of a typical item. This gives readers a feel for what the subjects will see. In the appendix, include a copy of your measure.

PROCEDURE

As the name suggests, your procedure section will be a summary of your protocol. The $64,000 question is: "How much detail should you include?" To help you answer this question, we offer two suggestions. First, include any methodological wrinkles you believe are critical to the study's internal, external, and construct validities. Second, read the procedure sections of several related studies and mimic their style. Do not worry if

TABLE 13.11   **Fill-in-the-blank Subjects Sections**

Subjects

Participants were ____ (#) (____ male, ____ female) undergraduates who participated in the ____ (study, experiment)

     a. to receive extra credit for introductory psychology
     b. to fulfill a course requirement
     c. for money
     d. other

during the (Fall, Winter, Spring, Summer) of 19 ____.

     Subjects were tested (individually, in groups of ____).
If appropriate add:

     Subjects were randomly assigned to ____ (#) conditions.

     Data from ____ (#) subjects were not analyzed because
     a. they did not follow instructions
     b. they quit the study
     c. their data were lost
     d. other

____ (#) subjects were in the ____ condition and ____ (#) subjects were in the ____ condition.
Or, if doing animal research, your subjects section might follow this format:
Subjects

     Subjects were (# male, # female)
     a. rats
     b. pigeons
     c. other

They were ____ days old at the start of the experiment and were maintained at ____% of their free-feeding weight. They were randomly assigned to condition.

FILL-IN-THE-BLANK DESIGN SECTION

Design

     The design was a ____ (name of the treatment variable and/or brief description of levels) X ____ (name of the treatment variable and/or brief description of levels) ____ (within subjects, between subjects) design. The dependent measure was ____.

your procedure section seems too brief. You will be including your complete protocol in the appendix of your proposal.

PUTTING THE METHOD SECTION TOGETHER

When you type up your method section, place it directly after the introduction. Identify the start of the method section with a centered heading labeled "Method" one double-spaced line below the last line of the introduction. On the next double-spaced line, label your subjects section. The word "Subjects" should be left-justified and underlined. The text for the subjects section should start on the next line (see table 13.12). The design, apparatus, and procedure sections should be presented in the same fashion as the subjects section. That is, their headings should be left-justified, underlined, and the text for each section should start on the line below the heading. (See table 13.13 for a checklist of material to be covered in the method section.)

TABLE 13.12   Sample Method Section

METHOD

Subjects

Forty Clarion University undergraduate women enrolled in an introductory psychology course served as subjects. Each received course credit for participation and each was randomly assigned to a condition. We included women only in this research because of their greater availability in the subject pool. One person was dropped from the analysis because she misunderstood the instructions.

Measures

The _____ is a self-report measure of _____ based conceptually on So and So's (1992) theory of _____. The measure consists of 7-point, bipolar rating scales. Characteristics rated included submissive-dominant, irritable-easygoing, sneaky-direct, and very unsexy–very sexy. Scoring is objective and thus highly reliable. The _____ has been used in well over 500 studies and has extensive and well-established construct validity. For example, test-retest reliability is _____, internal consistencies range from .85 to .94 for the various subscales, and So and So (1993) showed that the measure correlated with teacher and peer ratings of _____.

Procedure

After receiving an overview of the study, participants read and signed a consent form that explained the procedures. All participants signed the consent form and agreed to participate.

Then, following procedures used by _____ (1991), subjects were. . . .
Finally, subjects were debriefed and dismissed.

TABLE 13.13   Method Section Checklist

SUBJECTS

1. Is it clear how many subjects you studied? How many were men and how many were women?
   "Subjects were 62 undergraduates (42 women and 20 men). . . ."

2. Is it clear how subjects came to be in your study and how they were compensated?
   "Enrolled in general psychology classes, each participant received course credit for participation."

   "We recruited _____ (number of) participants by _____ (putting an ad in the newspaper). Participants received $5 for their participation."

3. How they were assigned to condition?
   ". . . and each was randomly assigned to experimental condition."

   "Following So and So (1992), subjects who scored below _____ on the _____ test were classified as. . . ."

4. How many were eliminated? Why?
   "One subject was dropped from the study because a friend had told her the hypothesis."
   "Two subjects were dropped from the study because they failed to follow instructions."

5. Did you follow the models in tables 13.10 and 13.11?

PROCEDURE

1. Is it written in chronological order (what happened to the subjects first, second, third, etc.)? In other words, is the procedure a step-by-step description of how subjects were run? Usually, you should write the procedure from the subjects' viewpoint. This makes it easier for readers to put themselves in the subjects' shoes and to understand what really happened.

2. Is it clear what the stimuli were that subjects were exposed to?

3. Is it clear how control or comparison groups ruled out alternative explanations? You probably foreshadowed the value of these controls in your introduction. "To control for _____, we _____."

4. Is there any evidence of the validity of your measure?
   a. Reliability?
      "Test-retest reliability is .92."
   b. Validity?

      "The measure correlates .70 with _____, an accepted measure of the construct."

      "_____ correlates with behavioral measures of the _____ construct."

      "_____ is considered to have the best psychometric properties of all available measures (Them, 1991)."
   c. Objectivity?
      "Correlations between the two raters ranged from .91 to .96."
   d. Consistency with definition of construct?
   e. How it avoids problems with biases, such as self-report biases?

5. If your measure is commonly used, have you cited evidence to that effect?

   "_____ measure is the most commonly used measure (So & So, 1992)."

TABLE 13.13 Continued

6. Is it clear what subjects were doing? What was the task? If using a paper-and-pencil measure, did you list example items? That is, is it clear what your measure is? You may want to have a separate measures section.

   "The measure of _____ was the response, on a scale ranging from 1 to 5, to the following question. . . ."

7. Do you describe any procedures used to avoid demand characteristics?

8. If you are using a commonly used procedure, do you cite this fact?
   "The procedure, adapted from So and So (1993), involved. . . ."

   "Following a procedure frequently used by _____ researchers (cf. So & So, 1991), we. . . ."

9. Is it clear what design you are using? If you have a complicated design, you may want a separate design section. *Note:* You may want to combine information about your design and your participants into one subjects and design section.

10. Does the reader have a general idea of instructions given to participants? Key instructions, such as those that differentiate between conditions, should be included verbatim. Include your complete instructions in an appendix.

11. Could someone repeat your study based on reading the method section?

WRITING THE RESULTS SECTION

In your proposal's results section, you should state how you plan to analyze your data. As was the case with the method section, your goal is not only to tell the reader what you are going to do but also to sell the reader on the idea that you are doing the right thing. Thus, it is important to be clear not only about what analysis you are going to do but why. Ideally, your proposal should answer the following four questions:

1. What data will be analyzed? That is, how will a subject's behavior be converted into a score?

2. What statistics will be used on those scores?

3. Why can that statistical test be used? At this point, you might show that the data meet the assumptions of the statistical test or you might cite a text or article that supports the use of the test under these conditions.

4. Why should the analysis be done? Usually, you will remind the reader of the hypothesis you want to test. However, sometimes your purpose is to demonstrate the validity of a measure. To emphasize the value of the analysis, you may want to describe what results of an analysis would support your hypothesis and what outcomes would not. You might even plug in imaginary outcomes of your study to give the reader a concrete example of how your analyses correspond to your hypotheses.

To illustrate how a results section might accomplish these goals, look at the following sample results section:

Results

Manipulation Check

Our intention in manipulating _____ (the treatment variable) is to expose subjects to _____ (stimuli) that differ in _____ (the treatment variable). To determine whether the _____ (treatment) manipulation works, participants will rate _____ (the degree to which the stimulus possesses the characteristic we are trying to manipulate) on a 7-point scale ranging from low _____ to high _____. An analysis of variance will be performed to assess the effect of _____ manipulation on self-reported _____ (perceptions of the characteristic that we are trying to manipulate). I expect that participants in the high _____ (level of treatment) condition will perceive the _____ (stimulus, themselves) as more _____ (credible, expensive, concrete, happy, attractive, or some other adjective referring to the quality the researcher is trying to manipulate) ($M =$ _____), $F(1,65) =$ _____, $p < .05$ than participants in the low _____ (level of treatment) condition ($M =$ _____).

Hypothesis Tests

Participants will respond to the two items we think might be affected by the (independent variable). We will sum their responses to these two items to come up with a score for each participant which will range from 2 (very low) to 10 (very high). Such scores are assumed to be interval (Winer, 1972). Consequently, those scores will then be subjected to a 2 × 2 analysis of variance.

It will be recalled that _____ subjects are expected to differ from _____ subjects on _____ (our measure). If the results turn out as I predict, _____ (treatment group) subjects ($M =$ _____) will score higher on _____ (the dependent measure) than _____ (control group) subjects ($M =$ _____), $F(1,80) =$ _____ $p < .05$. This significant main effect would indicate that the hypothesis _____ was supported.

In terms of format, your results section should immediately follow the methods section. Center the title "Results" one double-spaced line below the last line of the method section.

WRITING THE DISCUSSION SECTION

Once you have decided how you will analyze your data, you are ready to discuss how you will interpret them. If your hypothesis is supported, how will this information relate to the literature and arguments you covered in the introduction? How will you interpret results that do not confirm your hypothesis?

In addition, the discussion is the place to present the limitations of your study and to speculate about what research should be done to follow up on your study.

Writing the discussion section of the proposal is difficult because you do not know how the study will turn out. Probably the easiest thing to do is to imagine your study turned out as you expected. In that case, your discussion can be primarily a rehash of the introduction. To be more specific, your discussion should probably devote a paragraph to each of the following four points:

1. Relating the predicted results to the hypothesis ("Consistent with our predictions, . . .")

2. Relating the predicted results to previous research and theory discussed in the introduction ("This study joins others in showing. . . ." or "The findings are consistent with _____ (a theory, previous research).")

3. Discussing future research that would build on the present study ("Future research might consider _____ (testing the generality of the effect, other variables that may produce similar effects, mediating variables).")

4. Stressing the importance of remembering or building on the major findings ("To summarize, we found _____. This finding suggests that _____ (the treatment should be more widely used, more people should know about this finding, _____ theory must be revised to account for, no _____ research should be conducted without first considering these findings, we have taken an enormous step toward understanding _____, etc.). However, future research is required to _____.")

In terms of format, your discussion section will come directly after the results section. Once again, the title "Discussion" should be centered one double-spaced line below the last line of the results section.

PUTTING THE FRONT AND BACK ON

You have written the introduction, method, results, and discussion sections. Now it is time to return to the beginning of your proposal. Specifically, it is time to type the title page and the abstract.

TITLE AND THE TITLE PAGE

The title is the first thing readers will see. Your title should be simple, direct, honest, and informative. Ideally, your title should be a brief statement about your predictor and criterion variables.

Avoid being too cute or obscure. If there is some catchy saying or title that you must include, use a colon to add this extra title to the simpler title. Such a title might be, "The effect of eating sugar on anxiety: A bittersweet effect."

The title should appear centered on a separate piece of paper. Two lines below the title, center your name. Two lines below your name, center the name of the course (e.g., PSY 250: Research Methods).

The title should also appear, centered, at the top of the first page of your introduction. Thus, in a sense, the title takes the place of the heading "Introduction."

ABSTRACT

Once they have read your title, readers will continue to the next section—the abstract. In your abstract, you will give them a short, one-page summary of your research proposal.

Jolley, Murray, and Keller (1984) give six basic sentences that can be used to write most abstracts. The first sentence describes the general research topic (e.g., Love is a common topic in popular music.). The order of the next five sentences often varies. However, there should be a sentence that gives the number of subjects and their treatment (e.g., 16 participants will listen to love ballads for one hour, while 16 control participants will sit in a quiet room for one hour.). In a third sentence, you should explain how you plan to collect the dependent measure (e.g., Participants will fill out the Reuben love-like scale 10 minutes after treatment.). You should describe the hypothesis in a fourth sentence (e.g., It is hypothesized that listening to love ballads will raise scores on the love-like scale.). The final sentence will be reserved for your research report. In this sentence, you will describe the main results—the results that relate to your hypothesis (see table 13.14).

In terms of format, the abstract should appear on a separate sheet of paper following the title page. The heading "Abstract" should appear centered at the top of the page. The text of your abstract should begin one double-spaced line below the heading.

REFERENCES

Now that you have the title and abstract written, it is time to write your reference list. To help you organize your references, we suggest you write each reference on an index card and alphabetize the cards. If you have more than one reference for an author, put the cards for that author in chronological order. By writing them on cards before you type them up, you reduce the chances of making two common errors: (1) omitting a reference and (2) typing your references in the wrong order.

TABLE 13.14   Sample Abstracts and Checklist

ABSTRACT ONE

We examined the effect of _____ (independent variable) on _____ (dependent variable). Sixty female undergraduates ranging in age from 18 to 22 performed _____ task. As hypothesized, we found that _____. Implications of the results for _____ theory and for practical situations are discussed.

ABSTRACT TWO

The present study was designed to test the hypothesis that _____. In a simple between subjects design, 80 male subjects read either _____ or _____. Subjects than _____ (made some response). Results showed that, consistent with the hypothesis, _____ group scored higher than _____ group. The results are interpreted in light of _____ theory.

   Note: Some authors use the first sentence of the abstract to summarize previous research ("Previous research has shown that. . . ." "An unexpected finding that has surfaced in research on _____ is _____."). To keep their abstract short, they may then omit information about the subjects, especially if the subject population is not relevant to their research problem.

ABSTRACT CHECKLIST

   Does your abstract describe
   1. the hypothesis (what you studied and why, the essence of your introduction)?
   2. who the subjects were (the essence of your subjects section)?
   3. what you did, what subjects did (in very general terms)? (the essence of your procedure section)
   4. whether the data supported the hypothesis? (the essence of your results section)
   5. your general strategy for interpreting the results? (the theory, research literature, or practical areas for which your results have implications; the general approach your discussion section will take)

You should use the reference style given in the American Psychological Association's *Publication Manual* (1983). For examples of proper referencing, see table 13.15.

References should be typed on a separate sheet of paper and appear at the end of your proposal.

BEYOND THE PROPOSAL: THE PILOT STUDY

Even after you have carefully designed your study, modified it based on comments from your instructor, and been given your professor's "go ahead" to run it, you may still want to

TABLE 13.15 Sample References

EDITED VOLUME AND MULTIPLE AUTHORS
Etzold, T. H., & Gaddis, J. L. (Ed.). (1978). *Containment: Documents on American policy and strategy, 1945–1950* (pp. 25–41). New York: Columbia University Press.
ARTICLE IN AN EDITED VOLUME
Gaddis, J. L. (1978). The strategy of containment. In T. H. Etzold & J. L. Gaddis (Eds.), *Containment: Documents on American policy and strategy, 1945–1950* (pp. 25–41). New York: Columbia University Press.
JOURNAL ARTICLE
Hatch, O. G., (1982). Psychology, society, and politics. *American Psychologist, 42,* 29–33.
UNPUBLISHED MANUSCRIPT
Hilgard, E. (1945, September). *Psychological problems of the coming peace.* Unpublished manuscript, SPSSI Archives, University of Akron, Akron, OH.
BOOK
Lifton, R. J. (1968). *Death in life.* New York: Random House.

run several participants (friends, family members, other members of the class) just for practice. By running practice subjects, you will get some of the "bugs" out of your study. Specifically, by running and debriefing practice subjects, you will discover

1. whether participants perceived your manipulation the way you intended,
2. whether you can perform the study the same way every time or whether you need to spell out your procedures in more detail,
3. whether you are providing the right amount of time for each of the research tasks and whether you are allowing enough time in between tasks,
4. whether your instructions were clear,
5. whether your cover story was believable,
6. whether you need to revise your stimulus materials,
7. how participants like the study, and
8. how long it takes you to run and debrief a participant.

In short, running practice subjects helps you to fine-tune your study. Because running practice subjects is so useful, many professional investigators run enough practice subjects to constitute a small study—what researchers call a **pilot study.**

CONDUCTING THE ACTUAL STUDY

The dress rehearsal is over. Final changes in your proposal have been made. Now you are ready for the real thing—you are ready to run your study! This section will show you how.

ESTABLISHING RAPPORT

As you might imagine, your prospective participants may be apprehensive about the study. Participants often are not sure whether they are in the right place or even whether the researcher is a Dr. Frankenstein.

To put your participants at ease, let them know they are in the right place and be courteous. You should be both friendly and business-like. The expert investigator greets the participant warmly, pays close attention to the participant, and seems concerned that the participant knows what will happen in the study. The expert investigator is obviously concerned that each participant is treated humanely and that the study is done professionally.

Being professional does not hurt how participants view you. Why? First, most participants like knowing they are involved in something important. Second, some will view your efficiency as a way of showing you value their time—which you should.

So, how can you exude a professional manner? Some novice investigators think they appear professional when they act aloof and unconcerned. Nothing could be less professional. Participants are very turned off by a disinterested attitude. They feel that you do not care about the study and you do not care about them.

To appear professional, you should be neatly dressed, enthusiastic, well organized, and prompt. *Prompt* may be an understatement. You should be ready and waiting for your participants at least 10 minutes before the study is scheduled to begin. Once your participants arrive, concentrate exclusively on the job at hand. Never ask a participant to wait a few minutes while you socialize with friends.

What do you lose by being a "professional" investigator? Problem participants. If you seem enthusiastic and professional, your participants will also become involved in doing your study—even if the tasks are relatively boring. Thus, if you are professional in your manner and attitude, you will probably not even have to ask the participants to refrain from chatting throughout the study. Similarly, if you are professional, participants will stop asking questions about the study if you say, "I'll explain the purpose at the end of the study."

After you have established rapport, you need to give your participants instructions. To get participants to follow instructions to the letter, you might do one or more of the following:

1. Be repetitive
2. Have participants read the instructions and then they should orally paraphrase those instructions
3. Run participants individually
4. Ask participants to ask questions
5. Have participants demonstrate they understand the instructions by quizzing them or by giving them a practice trial before beginning the study

Once the study has begun, try to follow the procedure to the letter. Do not let participants change your behavior by reinforcing or punishing you. For instance, imagine you are investigating long-term memory. You want to expose participants to information and then see what they can write down. However, if you do this, participants may be writing down information that is in short-term memory. Thus, you would not be assessing long-term memory. Therefore, you add a counting backwards task that should virtually eliminate all of the information from short-term memory. Specifically, in your memory study, participants are exposed to information, are supposed to count backwards by threes for twenty seconds, and then are asked to recall the information. Ideally, their recall will represent only what they have in long-term memory. Unfortunately many participants will find the counting task unpleasant, embarrassing, or simply an unwanted nuisance. Consequently, some participants will thank you for telling them they can stop; others will plead nonverbally for you to stop. Clearly, you cannot let any of these strategies affect how long you have them count backwards. If you vary your procedures from participant to participant based on each participant's individual whims, your study will have questionable validity.

DEBRIEFING

Once the study is over, you should debrief your participants. In debriefing, you first should try to find out whether the participants suspected the hypothesis. Simply ask participants what they thought the study was about. Then, you should explain the purpose of your study.

If you deceived your participants, you need to make sure they are not upset about the deception. You also need to make sure they understand why deception was necessary. Participants should leave the study appreciating the fact there was one and only one reason you employed deception: it was the only way to get good information about an important issue.

Making sure participants accept your rationale for deception is crucial for three reasons. First, you do not want your participants to feel humiliated or angry. Second, if they get mad, they may not only be mad at you but also at psychologists in general. Perhaps the anger or humiliation will stop them from visiting a psychologist when they need help. Third, the unhappy participant may spread the word about your deception, ruining your chances of deceiving other participants.

After explaining the purpose of the study, you should answer any questions the participants have. Although answering questions may sometimes seem like a waste of time, you owe it to your participants. They gave you their time, now it is your turn.

After participants' questions and doubts have been dealt with, give them an opportunity to rate how valuable they felt the study was. These ratings (1) encourage you to be courteous to your participants, (2) let you know if your study is more traumatic than you originally thought, and (3) make participants feel you respect them because you value their opinions.

After the rating, you should assure participants their responses during the study will be kept confidential. Tell them that no one but you will know their responses. Then, ask the participants not to talk about the study because it is still in progress. For example, you might ask them not to talk about the study until next week. Finally, you should thank your participants, escort them back to the waiting area, and say goodbye.

PROTECTING DATA: CONFIDENTIALITY

You might think that once a participant leaves the study, your responsibilities to that participant end. Wrong! You are still responsible for guaranteeing that participant's privacy. Knowledge about a given participant is between you (the investigator) and the participant—*no one else.* Never violate this confidentiality. To ensure confidentiality, you should take the following precautions:

1. Assign each participant a number; when you refer to a given participant, always use the assigned number, never that participant's name.
2. Never store a participant's name and data in a computer—this could be a computer hacker's delight.
3. If you have participants write their names on booklets, tear off and destroy the cover of the booklet after you have analyzed the data.
4. Store a list of participants and their numbers in one place and the data with the participants' numbers on it in another place.
5. Watch your mouth. There is rarely a reason to talk casually about a participant's behavior. Even if you do not mention any names, other people may guess or think they have guessed the identity of your participant.

ANALYZING DATA

After you have finished running participants and made plans to protect the data, you are ready to start a new phase—analyzing and interpreting data. If you have planned your analyses in your research proposal, data analysis may be fairly straightforward. If you need additional help, consult the chapter in this book that corresponds to the design you selected. In addition, see the "Writing the Results" section which appears later in this chapter.

WRITING THE FINAL REPORT

Much of the work on your research report has already been done. Essentially, your research proposal was the first draft of your research report. To complete your research report, follow the advice in this section.

WHAT STAYS THE SAME OR CHANGES VERY LITTLE

The title page, introduction, and references from your proposal can be transferred to your research report without any changes. You will need to make three changes in the method section.

First, you will need to change the method section to reflect any changes you made in the procedures. Generally, the procedures you initially proposed are not the ones you ended up following. Sometimes, after reading your proposal, your professor will ask you to make some modifications. Sometimes, an ethics committee may mandate some changes. Usually, after running some practice subjects, you will make some changes.

Second, you will probably have to make some minor changes in the subjects section. Prior to actually running the study, you can rarely anticipate who your subjects will be and how many you will have to exclude.

Third, you need to rewrite the method section in the *past tense.* In the proposal, you told people what you were going to do; in the report, you tell them what you did.

Like your method section, your abstract only needs slight changes. Specifically, you need to add a sentence to describe the main results.

In contrast to the other sections, the results and discussion sections cannot always be transferred to the final report. Often, you will have to extensively revise these sections before you can put them in your final report. Indeed, if your results are totally un-expected, you may have to ignore your proposal and start over from scratch. Because these sections change the most from proposal to final report, the rest of this chapter will be devoted to these two sections.

WRITING THE RESULTS SECTION

There are two main purposes of the results section: to show the reader you competently analyzed the data and to tell the reader what you found. To accomplish these goals, you will report anywhere from one to five kinds of results: (1) results describing the distribution of your measure, (2) results supporting the validity of your measure, (3) results of the manipulation check, (4) results relating to your hypothesis, and (5) other statistically significant results.

Results Describing the Distribution of Scores

At the beginning of your results section, you might include a section that describes the distribution of scores on your dependent variable. Thus, you might give the mean and the standard deviation (or range) of scores.[3] For example, you might report "The scores on

_____ (the dependent measure) were normally distributed ($M = 75$, range $= 50–100$)." This section is often omitted. If you do include this section, it will probably be for one of the following reasons:

1. To make a case that the sample is representative of some population by showing that the *distribution* of scores *in the sample* are very similar to the population's distribu-tion of scores
2. To argue that the data meet the assumptions of the statistical tests by showing that the scores were normally distributed or the different groups had similar variances

[3]If the data are not normally distributed, you may want to provide a graph of the raw scores.

3. To show the data had to be transformed or that the data could not be analyzed by a certain statistical test because the data were not normally distributed

4. To argue there should be no problems due to ceiling effects, floor effects, or restriction of range by demonstrating there was a wide range of scores and scores were normally distributed

5. Because the distribution of scores is of interest in its own right, as would be the case if reporting percentage of sample who had attempted suicide

Results Supporting the Measure's Validity

Like the section describing the distribution of scores, the section supporting the measure's validity is often omitted. If you are using an accepted, validated measure, you will probably omit this section. If you choose to include this section, you will probably stress the results that emphasize the measure's

1. test-retest or alternate forms reliability, indicating the measure is not unduly influenced by random error as shown by the fact subjects get the same score from one day to the next;

2. interobserver reliability, indicating the measure is objectively scored because different observers give the subjects the same scores; and

3. internal consistency, indicating the items of a test or subscale are all measuring the same thing because the items correlate with each other (people that get a high score on one item will tend to get a high score on the other test items).

Results of the Manipulation Check

If you used a manipulation check, you should put these findings near the beginning of the results section. Although these results will usually be statistically significant and unsurprising, it is important to demonstrate you manipulated what you said you would manipulate. Thus, reporting the outcome of your manipulation check is a good lead into discussing results relating to your hypothesis. That is, once you have shown the reader you manipulated the variable you planned to manipulate, the reader is ready to know whether that variable had the effects you expected.

Results Relating to your Hypothesis

As you introduce the results relating to your hypothesis, clearly connect the results to that hypothesis. Make it very easy for your readers to tell how the hypothesis fared. For example, if a hypothesis was that people who own cats are less likely to hit their children, report what the data said about this hypothesis: "The hypothesis that people who own cats are less likely to hit their children was supported. Cat owners hit their children on the average 2.3 times a month per child, whereas people who did not own cats hit their children on the average 4.6 times, $F(1,64) = 18.2$, $p < .05$."

Other Significant Results

After reporting results relating to your hypothesis (whether or not the results were significant), you should report any other statistically significant results. Even if the results are unwanted and make no sense to you, significant results must be reported. Therefore, you might report "There was an unanticipated relationship between gender of the child and cat ownership. Parents of girls were more likely to own cats, $F(1,64) = 20.1$, $p < .05$."

Tips on Writing the Results Section

Now that you are familiar with the general parts of the results section, it is time to start writing the results section. One thing to always keep in mind is the results section is where you tell readers what you found out. It is here that they find out whether your hypothesis was supported or refuted.

You may find it useful to think of this section as an "analysis of results" section. That is, instead of just giving the reader your raw data, you are reporting your analysis of that data. Thus, just as you would not simply include every subject's score, you would not merely stick the reader with the computer printout of all the statistical tests. If you did that, the reader would be completely lost. You do not want to lose the reader. Instead, you want to guide the reader through this section. You should give the reader a clear picture of the following:

1. How the subjects' behavior was converted into a score.
2. Why these scores are being analyzed. Usually, this question can be answered by explaining what hypothesis is being tested.
3. What happened? That is, was the hypothesis supported?
4. What statistical test was used to find this out?
5. What were the results of that test (value of the statistic and the probability value)?
6. How did subjects actually score? That is, include descriptive statistics (means, percentages, etc.) to help readers see for themselves whether the pattern of your results supports the hypothesis. The means (or other summary statistics, such as medians or percentages) help readers understand the direction of the relationship and get some indication of its strength. You may choose to use tables or graphs to show these means, especially if there are many means or the relationship is complex.

In short, you should try to make your results section as clear and understandable as possible. Your general approach to making the results section clear is to do two things. First, start off by discussing simple or general findings and then move to more specific tests. For example, report main effects before interactions, and report the results of the overall F-test before talking about the results of more specific follow-up tests. Second, ask yourself if the reader will understand your results section. Specifically, will the reader leave the results section knowing whether the results supported your hypothesis? Focusing on this question will cause you to do many of the things we mentioned above: be clear about what scores are being analyzed, explain why those scores are being analyzed, explain how the results of the statistical test support—or fail to support—the hypothesis, and show that the pattern of means seems to support—or fails to support—the hypothesis. If you focus your results section on your hypothesis and you consult table 13.16 and table 13.17, you should be able to write an understandable and useful results section.

TABLE 13.16 Essentials of a Results Section

- Tell the reader *what* data you are analyzing and *how* you are going to analyze that data (what statistical test you will use)

  "A _____ index (alpha = .98) was constructed by adding the scores from questions 1 to 30. The results of this _____ index were analyzed by a two-factor analysis of variance (ANOVA)."

  "These readings were averaged to create a _____ score, which was submitted to _____ (analysis of variance, t-test, etc.)."

  "For data analysis, we calculated a score by _____. These scores were then subjected to _____ (analysis of variance, t-test, etc.)."

  "To analyze the data, subjects' responses on _____ (a task) were _____ (averaged, summed). These scores were then analyzed using a between subjects analysis of variance."

  "The dependent variable in this study was _____. Scores on this variable were analyzed using a between groups t-test."

- Remind them of *why* you are doing the analysis. That is, remind them of the predictions you made.

  "It will be recalled that _____ subjects were expected to differ from _____ subjects on measures of _____."

  "To provide a test of the hypothesis that . . ., we conducted _____ analysis."
  "In order to examine the hypothesis that . . ., we. . . ."

  "To assess _____, we _____ (did a certain analysis)."

  "To evaluate the _____ (treatment's) effectiveness, a 2 (independent variable 1) × 2 (independent variable 2) analysis of variance was performed on _____ (the dependent measure)."

- Tell them whether the prediction was supported. Use descriptive statistics *and* significance tests to emphasize prediction. If you are worried that putting so many numbers in text may confuse your readers, put your means in a table or on a graph.
  "As predicted. . . ."
  "Consistent with the prediction that. . . ."
  "Consistent with the hypothesis. . . ."
  "The results present a very clear picture. . . ."

  "_____ results support this assertion."

  "The analysis of variance revealed that _____."

  "As table 1 shows, the predicted effect was obtained: High _____ scored differently than low _____ $F(1,36) = 35.43$, $p < .001$."

"As expected, subjects who _____ scored higher on _____ (the dependent measure) ($M = 5.0$) than subjects who _____ ($M = 4.0$), $F(1, 80) = 17.45$, $p < .05$. This indicates that the hypothesis that _____ was supported."

"The analysis of variance on _____ (the dependent measure) showed that, as predicted, _____ (the treatment had an effect). Specifically, the _____ (treatment group) scored significantly higher than the _____ group ($Ms = 58.5$ vs. 37.3), $F(1,36) = 12.43$, $p < .005$."

"Strong support was found for the major hypothesis that _____ (scores on the dependent measure) would be higher for _____ (a particular group) than for _____ (the other group). The significant main effect for _____ (independent variable), $F(1,235) = 200.00$, $p < .001$, indicates that _____'s (the treatment group's) scores on the measure ($M = 5.46$) were higher than those for _____ (the control group) ($M = 3.98$)."

"A main effect for _____ (the treatment) was obtained, $F(1,30) = 15.00$, $p < .001$; overall, the _____ (treatment group) scored higher than the _____ (control group) ($Ms = 9.30$ vs. 2.77)."

"When given an opportunity to sample feedback regarding any of their attributes, did participants prefer feedback pertaining to their best characteristic? Yes. The means displayed in table 1 reveal that participants were much more interested in receiving feedback regarding their best attribute than their worst attribute. A within subjects (best vs. worst attribute) analysis of variance (ANOVA) of the average ranks assigned, corroborated this conclusion, $F(1,19) = 37.17$, $p < .001$."

- After talking about general effects, move to interactions or to unexpected results.
  "The results also revealed that . . . ."

  "They also rate themselves as more _____ than the other group, $F(1,60) = 40.00$, $p < .001$ ($Ms = 4.3$ and 1.5; 7-point scale)."

  "Men were also more likely to choose red than blue $\times$ 2 $(1,N = 80) = 6.80$, $p < .01$."

  "This main effect was qualified, however, by the predicted _____ $\times$ _____ interaction, $F(1,36) = 5.16$, $p < .01$."

- After presenting an interaction, show the means that make up that interaction. You can sometime have a table do the work for you if you wish.
  "As table 2 shows. . . ."

  "A significant _____ (first independent variable) $\times$ _____ (second independent variable) interaction, $F(1,60) = 27.42$, $p < .001$, revealed the expected pattern: Relative to _____ (subjects low on variable 1), _____ (subjects high on variable 1) scored higher in the _____ (low level of variable 2) conditions ($Ms = 10.0$ vs. 4.0), but lower in the _____ (high level of variable 2) conditions ($Ms = 3.0$ vs. 8.0)."

TABLE 13.17 Checklist for the Results Section

1. Is it clear what data were used? In other words, is it clear how subjects' behaviors or responses were converted into scores?

2. Is it clear what analysis was used on these scores?

3. Is the analysis justifiable?

   a. Do data meet the assumptions of the test (observations independent, appropriate scale of measurement)?

   b. Have others used or recommended that test in similar circumstances? If so, you might cite their work.

4. Is it clear why the analysis was done? That is, what hypothesis is being tested by the analysis? You will often want to remind the reader of your hypothesis. After reading the method section, the reader may have forgotten the hypothesis described in the introduction. Furthermore, sometimes an analysis is not done to test a hypothesis. For example, an analysis might be done to show the measure or manipulation is valid or the data meet the assumption of the test. In such cases, you should clearly explain why you are doing that analysis. For example, you might write, "To determine whether the mood manipulation did change subjects' moods, an analysis of variance was done to assess the effect of mood manipulation on self-reported mood."

5. Does your presentation of results follow this general format?

   a. Statement of hypothesis or relationship to be discovered.

   b. Statement of whether hypothesis was supported or relationship uncovered.

   c. Report of statistical significance, indicating whether proof of relationship was found. After reporting whether result was significant, should report statistic (f, t, X^2, etc.), value of statistic, and probability value ($p < .05$).

   d. Means, percent, or other summary, descriptive statistics to give better understanding of relationship. The means help reader understand direction of the relationship and give some indication of its size. You may choose to use tables or graphs to convey this information, especially if there are many means or the relationship is complex.

6. Are the degrees of freedom correct?

7. Is it clear how the results relate to the hypothesis? The results should provide a clear "scorecard" for the hypothesis. That is, do the results tell a story about how much support the hypothesis got? Or, is the reader simply bombarded with statistics?

8. Do you do more than just state that a result is significant? That is, do you include summary statistics (means, percentages, etc.) to help the reader see the pattern of your results? That is, saying the results were significant, does not tell us who did better.

9. Are tables or graphs needed to make the pattern of results easier to understand? Tables and graphs are probably necessary to help the reader understand any interactions you have.

10. Are there relationships that you hypothesized but did not report? There should not be!

11. Did you do and report appropriate follow-up tests?

12. Did you confuse the value of your test statistic (F, t, r) with the p-value? Remember, the p-value refers to how likely it is that your results could be obtained by chance. If the results were extremely unlikely to be due to chance, you would conclude the variables are really related. Thus, if you got a p-value of .001, you would be relatively confident your results are not due to chance. Note that if you have a large F, t, or r, you will probably have a small p-value (because that would indicate a big relationship in your sample, and having a big relationship in your sample is unlikely if there is really no relationship). Conversely, a small r-, F-, or t-value will probably be accompanied by a large p-value (because a small relationship in the sample could quite easily be due to chance).

WRITING THE DISCUSSION SECTION

If the results matched your predictions, the discussion section you wrote for your proposal might work as the discussion section for the final report. However, there are two reasons why the discussion section you wrote for your proposal will probably have to be substantially modified. First, you may not get the results you expected. Second, during the course of conducting the research or writing the paper, you will probably think of problems or implications that you did not think of when you wrote your proposal.

The examples in table 13.18 will give you some ideas about how to write your discussion section. As you can see from those models, in the discussion section, you should do the following:

1. Briefly review the research question or hypothesis.
2. Briefly summarize the results, relating them to the hypothesis.
3. Interpret the results in light of the arguments made in your introduction.

TABLE 13.18   Example of Strategies to Use for the Discussion Section

• Brief summary of results—put findings in context of hypothesis

"Do _____ (subjects in the treatment group, subjects high on some variable)

score differently than _____ (subjects in the control group, subjects low on that variable)? Yes. . . ."
"Consistent with our predictions. . . ."
"In general, the findings support the hypothesis. . . ."

"Contrary to our hypothesis, _____ did not differentially affect _____. In other words. . . ."
• Interpretation of results—put findings in context of the research and theory discussed in the introduction
"Consistent with this view (a view described in the introduction). . . ."

"The findings are consistent with _____ (previous research, so & so's theory)."
"For the most part, the findings replicate previous research."
"This study joins others in showing. . . ."
"Our findings converge with those of. . . ."

"As has been found with _____. . . ."
"As So and So (1992) argue. . . ."
"Several explanations can be offered to account for the discrepancy between the present findings and So and So's (1993)."
• Discuss and try to rule out alternative explanations, but admit weaknesses
"An alternative possibility is. . . . However, we think this is highly unlikely because. . . ."
"This alternative explanation is not plausible for several reasons. . . ."

"The low average levels of _____ in this sample suggest that this is not a ceiling effect but a genuine finding."

TABLE 13.18 Continued

"Because the data used in this study are correlational, it is always possible that the results reported represent a spurious joint association of the variables examined to some unassessed third variable. Thus, it may well be that _____ does not cause _____."

"Our failure to find a significant relationship between these variables may be due to lack of power. For example, our sample size was relatively small."

- Meaning of results

  "Of what consequences are the differences revealed here on _____ (our society, theory, interpreting past research)?"

  "Thus, researchers examining _____ theory should consider these findings before conducting further research."

  "Thus, researchers using _____ research paradigm should consider these findings before conducting further research."

  "We propose that _____ theory should be modified to incorporate these results."
  "Hence, the results suggest the need to broaden the theoretical framework within which _____ is understood."

  "The findings of this study support a _____ theory interpretation of _____. They do so in several ways. . . ."

- Discussion or speculation about unexpected results
  "We obtained two unexpected differences. . . ."
  "Two findings were difficult to interpret. . . ."
  "One curious aspect of data deserves attention."
  "Another possibility for this unexpected finding is. . . ."
  "These findings may reflect. . . ."
  "Perhaps these findings are due to. . . ."

  "It is interesting to consider this pattern of results in light of _____ (some theoretical view; So & So's study)."
  "It is interesting to note that research consistent with this finding was obtained by So and So."

  "The finding that _____ is puzzling."

- Future research—deals with limitations of study and dealing with unexpected findings
  1. Extending the research
     "Future research needs to explore. . . ."
     "An exciting avenue for future research is. . . ."
     "Future research might explore. . . ."
     a. Improvements in design: Increasing power by using more subjects, more homogeneous subjects, within subjects design, more standardized procedures, and/or more sensitive measures
        Using a design that will establish causality (experimental rather than correlational)
        Different, more involving tasks

More complex, realistic, or more carefully designed stimulus materials
More objective measures to rule out subject or researcher biases
More valid measures
More specific measures of the construct to pinpoint the exact effect of the treatment (a global measure of memory being replaced with a measure of encoding and a measure of retrieval)
More valid manipulations
Placebo conditions and double-blind conditions to rule out demand characteristics
More specific measures

    b. Longer-term consequences
    c. Whether related factors have the same effect
    d. The extent to which the results generalize to different levels of the treatment variable to different age groups, genders, situations, tasks, settings, and/or a broader sample
    e. Research applying the finding to an applied problem
    f. Manipulations that might moderate the observed relationship between the variables
    g. Possible mediating factors, usually cognitive or physiological variables that intervene between stimulus and response

2. Ruling out alternative explanations for the findings or for competing explanations of an unexpected finding

"Unfortunately, we do not currently have data to test these alternative possibilities. Research should be done to test our hypothesis about the reasons for these unexpected results."

"Research designed to distinguish between these two explanations (our explanation and an alternative one for the results) should be done."

• Final Paragraph—summarize major findings and stress their importance

    1. Brief description of major findings
        "To summarize. . . ."

    2. Importance of findings to theory, research, or practice
        "If our results hold, this raises a serious concern."

"To summarize, _____ (theory, findings) can be applied to _____ (this population, an applied problem). The findings suggest that _____ (some treatment should be applied on a wider scale or that people should be made aware of this principle). However, future research is required to _____ (specify exactly how this should be done)."

"It would be interesting to extend this research to real-life situations in order to assess the extent to which the findings are generalizable."

"We now have a clearer, more detailed picture of this phenomena. This is an important step in understanding _____."

"This research suggests that we need a new theory of _____."

"This research suggests the need for more work to find out when _____ theory applies."

"The results presented here, in conjunction with _____ (the work of other researchers, the work of others, or changes in our society), should lead us to take a serious look at _____ and its potential impact on society."

"The timeworn contention that errors in the laboratory have no consequences in the real world may, in fact, prove to be more than a harmless optimism. Our human history of conflict and carnage attests to both the ubiquity and the virulence of social misunderstanding; if we fail to acknowledge that the roots of these events lie in ourselves, and not in our stars, then we may be doomed to witness their endless repetition. (Gilbert & Osborne, 1989, p. 947)."

4. Acknowledge alternative explanations for your results, trying to dismiss these alternatives if possible.

5. Discuss unexpected findings and speculate on possible reasons for them.

6. Discuss, in general terms, future research. What would you do if you were to follow up on this research (assume an unlimited budget). This research might focus on improving the methodology of your study, exploring unexpected findings, trying to rule out alternative theoretical explanations for your findings, testing the generality of your findings, looking for practical implications of the findings, looking for variables that might have similar effects, mapping the shape of the relationship, or looking for mental or physiological factors that mediate the relationship.

7. Discuss the practical or theoretical implications of your findings.

For more guidance on writing the discussion, please refer to the checklist in table 13.19. Once you have written your discussion section, you are nearly finished. However, as with most papers, you will need to write several drafts before you have a polished paper. To help you edit your paper so that it conforms to APA format, check your "next-to-final draft" against the checklist in table 13.20. In addition, because having a model is often useful, you will probably want to compare your paper to the sample paper in appendix F.

TABLE 13.19   Checklist for the Discussion Section

1. Did you briefly summarize results? Is the first paragraph closely tied to the results? Do nonsignificant results stay nonsignificant?

2. Are all the comparisons you make (group 1 > group 5) backed up by analyses specifically testing these comparisons? Do you confuse the meaning of main effects and interactions? That is, do you say, "The elaborative rehearsal group did better than the rote rehearsal group, as shown by the rehearsal by type of information interaction?"

3. Did you relate results to your hypothesis and to the points you made in the *introduction*? That is, do they have relevance for previous theory or research? Have you connected your results and your study back to the problems stated in the introduction?

4. Have you answered the question "What are the implications of this study?"
   a. Theoretical?
   b. Practical?
   c. Future research?

5. Are there alternative interpretations for your results? Remember, there are always many explanations for null results. Discuss these alternatives.

6. Do you try to explain unexpected findings?

7. Are there other studies that should be done?
   a. To address alternative interpretations?
   b. To improve the study (if it were to be redone, what would you do differently)?
   c. To extend the research by using different types of subjects, additional variables, or additional levels of variables?

8. Is it evident that you have given some thought to your results? That you have tried to make them meaningful?

TABLE 13.20   Format Checklist

TITLE

1. Is there a separate title page?
2. Is title centered?
3. Is the title simple and to the point? Does it include the names of the relevant variables (e.g., the independent and dependent variables)?
4. Is your name
   a. two lines below the title?
   b. centered?
5. Is your institution's affiliation
   a. two lines below your name?
   b. centered?
6. Near the bottom of the title page, do you have the words "Running head:" followed by a shortened (four- to six-word) form of your paper's title?
7. Is the running head centered?
8. On the top right-hand corner do you have
   a. a short, two- or three-word "mini-title" of your paper? (This "mini-title" is simply the first two or three words of your title; it is *not* the running head.)
   b. below the "mini-title," the number "1," indicating this is page one?

ABSTRACT

1. Is it on a separate page?
2. Is the heading "Abstract" centered at the top of the page?
3. Is the text one double-spaced line below the heading?
4. Is it less than 150 words?
5. Is it a single paragraph?
6. Is the beginning of the abstract *not* indented? That is, the entire abstract (other than the title "Abstract") should look like a single block, with all lines beginning at the left margin.
7. Is it numbered page "2"?

INTRODUCTION

1. Does it begin on a separate page ("3")?
2. Is the title of the article centered at the top of the first page of the introduction?
3. Remember you do *not* label the introduction with the label "introduction."
4. If you are citing several articles within one set of parentheses, are the articles listed in alphabetical order?
5. If you are discussing a paper with three or more authors, mention all the authors the first time you cite that paper. Only after you have referred to all the authors, can you—in subsequent citations—use the first author's name, followed by et al. (e.g., Glick et al., 1990).
6. When citing people, did you avoid footnotes? Citations should be in parentheses. If you mention the authors in the sentence, simply put the date in parentheses. For example, "Jolley and Mitchell (1990) argued that. . . ." If the authors' names are not part of the sentence, put their name and the date in parentheses. Separate the names and the dates with a comma. For example, "Some have argued that . . . (Jolley & Mitchell, 1990)."

TABLE 13.20   Continued

METHOD SECTION

1. Is it written in the past tense?
2. Is the heading "Method" centered and one double-spaced line below the last line of the introduction?
3. Is the word "Subjects" one double-spaced line below "Method"?
4. Is the label "Subjects" on the left margin and underlined?
5. Does the text for the subjects section begin on the line below the "Subjects" heading?
6. If you started a sentence with a number (e.g., "Twenty undergraduates served as subjects," did you write out the number? Note, you can say "Subjects were 20 undergraduates," but you cannot say "20 undergraduates were subjects." Instead, you must say "Twenty undergraduates were subjects."
7. Is the word "Procedure" on the left margin and underlined?
8. Is it one double-spaced line below the the last line of the previous section?
9. Does the text for the procedure section start on the line below the "Procedure" heading?
10. If you used standard laboratory equipment, did you identify the manufacturer and model number?

RESULTS SECTION

1. Does it immediately follow the method section?
2. Is the title "Results" centered? Is it one double-spaced line below the last line of the method section?
3. Is it written in the past tense?
4. When you report the result of a statistical test, did you give the statistic, the degrees of freedom for the test, the value of the statistic, and the level of significance (the p-value)? The format, except for the spacing, should follow that shown below:

STATISTIC	df	NUMERICAL VALUE OF THE TEST	PROBABILITY
$\underline{F}$	(2,46) =	3.85,	$\underline{p} < .05$
$\underline{t}$	(24) =	3.0	$\underline{p} < .001$
$\underline{r}$	=	.71,	$\underline{p} < .01$
X^2	(6,$\underline{N}$ = 80) =	11.48,	$\underline{p} < .05$

(Note that you need to underline the statistic (F, t, r, etc.) and the "p." Also note that with chi-square (X^2), you need to report degrees of freedom and sample size (N).)

5. If you have tables, do you refer to those tables in the text of your paper (e.g., "As Table 1 indicates. . . .")? Are tables numbered sequentially as they appear in the text of your paper?
6. Are all tables and graphs at the end of your report?
7. Have you referred to all graphs as figures (figure 1, not graph 1)? Did you label both axes? Give each graph an informative heading?
8. Have you indicated where each table or figure would be inserted, if you were to place it in the results section? Generally, you will sandwich this information between the first paragraph that mentions the table or figure and the next paragraph. Centered between these two paragraphs type "Insert Table (number or table) about here." Thus, for the first table you refer to in text, you would type "Insert Table 1 about here." For the first graph you refer to, you would type "Insert Figure 1 about here."

9. Do the tables adhere to the format illustrated below?

Table 1
Correlations Between Body Concept and Self-Esteem for Females and Males

| | Body Concept | |
Gender	Attractiveness	Fitness
Female	.65***	.50**
Male	.35*	.70***

*p < .05, **p < .01, ***p < .001

Table 2
Analysis of Variance: Exercise and Self-esteem

Source	SS	df	MS	F
Between (treatment)	499.41	2	249.71	9.75
Within (error)	145.76	57	2.56	

DISCUSSION

1. Does it immediately follow the results section?
2. Is the title "Discussion" centered? Is it one double-spaced line below the last line of the results section?

REFERENCES

1. Do they start on a separate piece of paper?
2. Is the word "References" on the top of the page, centered?
3. Is everything double-spaced?
4. Are they alphabetical?
5. Does the first line of every reference start at the margin? The first line of a reference should *not* be indented.
6. If a reference takes up more than one line, are the additional lines of that reference *indented three spaces?*
7. Do your individual references follow the format in table 13.15?
8. Are all the references in this section also cited in your paper? Your reference section should only include those references you actually cited. All works cited in the reference section must also be cited in the body of the paper.
9. Are all the references cited in your paper also listed in this section? All works cited in your paper should also be listed in your reference section. It is considered sloppy to fail to reference a paper that you cited.

GENERAL FORMAT

1. Is everything double-spaced? Nothing should be single-spaced!
2. Are the first two or three words of the title on the top right-hand corner of every page?
3. Is the page number on the top right-hand corner of every page (below the first two or three words of the title)?
4. Did you start every paragraph by indenting five spaces (except for the abstract)?
5. Have you avoided sexist and racist language?
6. Have you avoided passive sentences as much as possible?
7. Is the paper's appearance professional?

Concluding Remarks

Well, you've done it! If you carefully followed the advice in this book, you should have just completed a carefully planned, meaningful, and ethical research project. Congratulations and best wishes for your continued success as a researcher!

SUMMARY

1. The research journal and proposal will help you do the planning necessary for conducting ethical and valid research.

2. The research proposal is more formal than the journal and should conform to the *Publication Manual* (1983) of the American Psychological Association.

3. In the introduction of your proposal, you need to summarize and critique relevant research. This critique should set up the reasons you think your hypothesis (a) will be supported, (b) should be tested, and (c) should be tested the way you are going to test it.

4. In the introduction, state your hypothesis, explain why your predictions make sense, and explain why your study will provide a valid test of your hypothesis.

5. Before writing the method section, you should carefully plan out each step of your study.

6. In planning your procedures, ethics should be your primary concern. There are two aspects of ethics: minimizing harm and maximizing potential benefits.

7. To minimize harm in human research, you should anticipate potential problems, use detailed informed consent forms, and thoroughly debrief your participants.

8. If a manipulation is potentially harmful, you may want to screen participants, weaken the manipulation, or use a different manipulation.

9. When using animal subjects, you must plan for twenty-four-hour care of the animals.

10. To maximize the benefits of your study, you should take steps to be sure your study has power and construct validity.

11. Once you have planned out every detail of your study, you should formalize your plan in the method, results, and discussion sections in your proposal.

12. The method section is the "how" section, where you explain how you plan to conduct your study.

13. In the results section, you will plan your statistical analyses.

14. In the discussion section, you will explore the implications of your anticipated research findings for theory, future research, or real life.

15. Once you finish the body of the proposal, write the abstract (a brief summary of the proposal), the title page, and the reference section.

16. The pilot study is a good way to get the "bugs" out of your proposal before running the real study.

17. In addition to a well-developed research plan, being courteous and professional are essential to being a good researcher.

18. Remember to keep all data confidential.

19. Make sure your data conform to the assumptions of the statistical test you plan to use.

20. Much of your final report will be based on your proposal—provided you wrote a good proposal.

21. The title page, introduction, and reference sections of your proposal can be transferred directly to your final report. After you change the method section to the past tense, it also may be transferred (with only minor modifications) to the final report.

22. Try to make the results section as understandable as possible. Tell the reader what you are trying to find out by doing the analysis and what you found out from doing the analysis.

23. In the results section, be sure to stress whether the results supported or failed to support your hypothesis.

24. In the discussion section, summarize the main findings of your study and relate these to the points you made in the introduction.

25. Writing involves a great deal of rewriting.

KEY TERMS

abstract
conceptual replication
debriefing
direct replication
exploratory study

failure to follow protocol
  effect
informed consent
loose protocol effect
pilot study
research effects

researcher expectancy
  effect
research realism
systematic replication
subject effects

APPENDIX

A   Ethics

In chapter 1, we introduced you to the main ethical principles of research. In chapter 13, we showed you how to apply ethical principles to research. In short, throughout this text, we have mentioned the importance of conducting research in an ethical manner. Thus, you may wonder why we have an appendix on ethics. The main reason is so you can have quick access to APA's specific ethical principles.

HUMAN RESEARCH

Although we have included APA's guidelines on ethical human research in this appendix, we will first highlight the main principles. The first thing a researcher should do is to try to foresee the risks of conducting a study. Knowing the risks can help in devising safeguards, in deciding whether the study should be conducted, and in letting participants decide whether to participate. After evaluating the risks, the researcher should decide whether the research would put participants at "minimal risk" or "at risk" (APA, 1990). Typically, a study that involves "minimal risk" involves no deception, no assault of values or other psychologically noxious stimulus such as making participants feel they had done poorly on a task and no physical stress (unpleasant noise, mild shocks, etc.). To the naive person, a study that involves "minimal risk" would seem to involve no risk. However, psychologists realize that whenever research involves humans, there is always some risk.

If the proposed study would put participants "at risk" or violate APA guidelines, the researcher must seek out the advice of others to determine whether the study should be done. (As a student researcher, you should do this even if you think the study involves virtually no risk.) That is, the researcher should ask other researchers and, perhaps, submit their research to an ethics committee or an internal review board. In consulting other people, the researcher may end up filling out a form like the one in box A.1.

The point of consulting others is three-fold. First, consulting others will help you look at alternatives. That is, others will ask, "Are there ways of answering the research question that would induce less stress or put participants at less risk?" Second, consulting with others may generate some insights about how to protect the participants. Third, consulting with others may help you decide whether to do the study. For example, other people may see risks you did not see, or they may be more objective than you when it comes to weighing the risks to the participants against the potential gain. As a result of seeing and weighing the risks, other people may argue—or demand—that the study not be done.

544

BOX A.1   The Clarion University Psychology Department's Human Participants Review Form

DIRECTIONS: Please type and submit in triplicate.

1.   A. Name of submitter _____

B. Date _____

C. Title of study: _____

2. Brief description of procedures to be used. (If doing a study that uses a questionnaire, you must attach a copy of that questionnaire.)

3. Where will this study be conducted: _____

4. A. Is a physically noxious stimulus to be employed in this study?
      YES   NO
   B. Is a psychologically noxious stimulus or stress of some sort (sense of insecurity or failure, assault upon values, fatigue, or sleep deprivation) to be used in this study?   YES   NO
   C. If answering yes to either A or B,
      1. Describe the nature of the stress induced and/or the noxious stimulus or stimuli employed.
      2. Describe the precautions you have taken with regards to any stress induced and/or any noxious stimulus employed.
   D. Is deception to be used in this study?   YES   NO
      If yes, (1) What is the nature of this deception?
   E. Have provisions been made for debriefing and any potentially necessary subject follow-up?   YES   NO
   F. I will use the psychology department's debriefing scale?
      YES   NO
      If not, why not?
   G. Describe, in detail, any risks to participants that were not addressed by the previous parts of this question. Also specify how you plan to minimize these risks.

5. What will you do if participants exhibit signs of harm (e.g., crying, disoriented behavior)?

6. Will your participants be limited to students at CUP?   YES   NO
   If no, fill in the following so that we know more about the characteristics of your participants.

   A. Sex   Male_____ Female_____ Both_____

   B. Age group(s) _____

   C. Special ethnic group _____

D. General state of health _____

E. Source of participants _____

7. How many participants will you need?

8. What educational gain do you think the participants will obtain from being in this study?

9. State briefly what you can tell the participants about the study's significance:

10. How will you ensure the confidentiality of each subject's data? Address the following five phases:
    A. When collecting it
    B. When coding it
    C. When storing it
    D. When analyzing it
    E. When disposing of raw data

11. I have enclosed a copy of the informed consent form and the sign-up sheet?   YES   NO
    If no, why not?

12. All participants will fill out a written informed consent form before they begin the study?   YES   NO
    If no, why not?

13. My responsibilities as a researcher are clear to me?   YES   NO

Type the name of each researcher under the corresponding signature line. All researchers must sign.

_____
                                    Date.

_____
                                    Date.

_____
                                    Date.

_____
                                    Date.

IF PEOPLE OTHER THAN A FULL-TIME (12-HOUR TEACHING LOAD OR EQUIVALENT) FACULTY MEMBER IN THE PSYCHOLOGY DEPARTMENT WILL BE RUNNING PARTICIPANTS, A FULL-TIME MEMBER OF THE DEPARTMENT MUST RESPOND TO ITEM 14.

14. I have personally discussed the proposed study with the researcher(s) and I approve of the study and will provide close supervision of procedures and ethical standards. Furthermore, these individuals have been informed of their responsibilities as a researcher; namely that:

(a) they should not lightly miss sessions for which subjects have signed up;

(b) they should be prepared to describe the purpose and nature of the study to subjects at the completion of the study if the subject wishes;

(c) the subject has the right to terminate the session at any point;

(d) even if the subject doesn't terminate the session, the researcher should terminate the session if the subject shows signs of extreme discomfort;

(e) if a subject becomes distraught, comforting the subject takes priority over all other tasks;

(f) subjects' privacy is to be respected;

(g) subjects fill out the informed consent form before they participate in the study.   YES   NO

_____

(Signature of research   Date
advisor who must be a
full-time member of
the Psychology
Department)

_____

Name of Research Advisor, typed

_____

Debriefing Scale

This scale is designed to assess your reactions to the study so that we can find out whether any procedures need to be improved or eliminated.

1. I found participating in this study to be (circle the appropriate number):

    UNPLEASANT: –3   –2   –1   +1   +2   +3 :PLEASANT

2. I found the researcher to be (circle the appropriate number):

   UNPROFESSIONAL: –3   –2   –1   +1   +2   +3 :PROFESSIONAL

3. Would you be willing to volunteer (in exchange for money or credit) to participate in another study?

   DEFINITELY NOT: –3   –2   –1   +1   +2   +3 :DEFINITELY

4. Serving as a subject in a psychological study should provide people with an informative, first-hand look at research. On the scale below, please indicate how valuable or worthless you found the experience of participating in today's study to be.

    WORTHLESS: –3   –2   –1   +1   +2   +3 :VALUABLE

If you wish to explain your rating or to make any comments on this study, either positive or negative, please do so below.

INFORMED CONSENT FORM

I have been informed that the study in which I am about to participate is investigating (following section to be filled out by researcher) _____

I have also been informed that I will be asked to (following section to be filled out by researcher)

_____

I understand that the responses I give will be kept confidential and that no names will be used.

I will be free to ask any questions about the study and I may withdraw from the study at any time without prejudice.

1. Name (printed) _____

2. I hereby give my written consent to participate in this investigation.

   Signature _____

   Date _____

3. Signature of person obtaining consent

   _____

                                                           Date

_____

_____

SIGN-UP SHEET

KINDS OF PARTICIPANTS WANTED:

DESCRIPTION OF STUDY:

POTENTIALLY UNPLEASANT EVENTS THAT MAY OCCUR TO PARTICIPANTS DURING THE STUDY:

TIME REQUIRED:

WHERE STUDY WILL BE CONDUCTED:

NOTE: PARTICIPATION IN A RESEARCH STUDY IS ENTIRELY VOLUNTARY.

YOU MAY WITHDRAW FROM A STUDY AT ANY TIME.

IF YOU FIND YOU CAN'T MAKE THE TIME YOU SIGNED UP FOR, PLEASE CALL 226-2295 AS SOON AS POSSIBLE.

IF YOU HAVE ANY COMPLAINTS ABOUT A STUDY THAT YOU PARTICIPATED IN, PLEASE CALL 226-2295.

Even if the research is approved by a review board, the bottom line is the investigator is still the one person who is responsible for any harm done to the participants. To help minimize this harm, the researcher should have participants sign an informed consent form prior to participating in the study (see box A.2). The form should stress

1. any foreseeable risks or discomforts that might cause the participant to decide not to participate,
2. that the subject's participation is totally voluntary,
3. that the participant can quit the study at any time—the participant does not have to explain why they want to leave and there is no penalty for leaving, and
4. that participants' responses will be confidential (if responses will not be confidential, this should be explained).

In regard to the last step (maintaining confidentiality), there are two steps you can take. First, do not use names. Second, if you must use names, use code names or numbers. Store the data with the code name in one place, store the names and the code names in a different place.

BOX A.2 Sample Informed Consent Form

INFORMED CONSENT FORM

I have been informed that the study in which I am to participate is investigating personnel decision-making. I have also been informed that I will be asked to read personnel files of two job applicants and then asked to decide which of the two individuals I would be more likely to hire. I also understand that I will be asked to justify my decision.

I understand that the responses I give will be kept confidential and that no names will be used.

I will be free to ask any questions about the study and I may withdraw from the study at any time and still receive full credit for participating.

Name (printed) _____

I hereby give my written consent to participate in this investigation.

Signature   _____

Date   _____

Signature of person obtaining consent

_____   Date: _____

After the participant has filled out the consent form and participated in your study, you should debrief the participant. During this *debriefing,* you should

1. correct any misconceptions the participant may have about the research;
2. try to detect and remove any harm that may have been produced by the study;
3. give a summary of the study in nontechnical terms (many departments believe this summary should be both written and oral, the written part being about one full-page typed, describing the hypothesis, why the procedures were used, and why the study was important);
4. provide participants an opportunity to ask whatever questions they may have (some departments want you to provide a number for participants to call so research participants can ask follow-up questions);
5. thank the participant for participating; and
6. explain why deception was necessary (if deception was used).

Debriefing is a good time to assess the degree to which you and your co-investigators are conducting the study in an ethical manner. To do so, ask participants to complete an anonymous questionnaire that assesses their perceptions of the study. Such a question-naire might include the following questions:

1. Could you quit the study at any time?
2. Were you given enough information to decide whether you wanted to participate? If not, what should you have been told before you took part in the study?
3. What was the purpose of this research?
4. Were you treated with respect?
5. Was the researcher polite?
6. Did you have all your questions answered?
7. Were you deceived in any way? If so, did the researcher provide justification for the deception? Are you satisfied with that justification?
   Why or why not?
8. Did you experience more discomfort than you would in your day-to-day activities? If so, did the researcher provided sufficient justification for discomfort? What caused this discomfort?
9. Will your responses be kept confidential?

In conclusion, the ideal study would not involve stress or deception. Participants would choose whether to participate only after reading an accurate description of the study. After the study was done, all data would be kept entirely confidential and participants would be completely debriefed. However, on occasion, ethical guidelines may be violated. A study may involve unpleasantness of some kind, it may involve deception. Occasionally, participants may participate without the benefit of informed consent or they may not be completely debriefed.

When these guidelines are violated, it can be for only one of two reasons. First, the guidelines may be violated if the potential benefits of the study justify such a violation. However, even in this case, alternatives to the study *must* be considered and other people should be consulted. Second, the guidelines may be violated if upholding one guideline means harming the participant. For example, suppose a participant's response was bizarre and unusual. Telling a participant their behavior was bizarre might meet the guideline of giving a complete debriefing. However, such a disclosure might upset and harm the participant. For a closer look at ethical guidelines for human research, see box A.3.

ANIMAL RESEARCH

Conducting animal research in an ethical manner is vital. Unethical treatment of animals is inhumane and, in many cases, illegal. However, we have not spent much time on ethics in animal research for two basic reasons.

First, the basic concepts that govern human research also govern animal research. That is, pain and discomfort should be minimized. Furthermore, any study that inflicts stress must be justifiable on the basis that the study is likely to produce some benefit that outweighs the risks and there is no other way to get that potential benefit.

Second, because humane treatment of animals is so important, APA has tried to make sure you will not do animal research unethically. Specifically, APA has taken the following three steps to almost guarantee that you cannot do animal research without knowing its ethical standards:

1. If you conduct research with animal subjects, you must be trained in the humane care, handling, and maintenance of animals.
2. As a student, you cannot conduct research with animals unless you are supervised by someone who is well trained in both animal research and in how to handle, care, and maintain animals.
3. A copy of the guidelines for how you are to conduct research must be posted in the animal lab.

Because you will be shown how to take care of the animals, because you will be supervised, and because the guidelines will be posted in the lab, you will probably not violate ethical principles out of ignorance. However, because violating ethical procedures in animal research may violate federal law, you should be very careful. If you are conducting research with animals, you should consult APA's *Ethical Principles Governing the Care and Use of Animals for Research* (1990) at the end of this appendix (see box A.4). In addition, you should work closely with your research supervisor. Finally, figure out some strategy so you do not forget to take care of your animal. Unless you have a routine or a system, it is easy to forget to check on your animal during the weekend. However, animals need food, water, gentle handling, and a clean living environment *every single day.*

BOX A.3 American Psychological Association's Ethical Principles Governing the Treatment of Human Participants*

A. In planning a study, the investigator has the responsibility to make a careful evaluation of its ethical acceptability. To the extent that the weighing of scientific and human values suggests a compromise of any principle, the investigator incurs correspondingly serious obligation to seek ethical advice and to observe stringent safeguards to protect the rights of human participants.

B. Considering whether a participant in a planned study will be a "subject at risk" or a "subject at minimal risk," according to recognized standards, is of primary ethical concern to the investigator.

C. The investigator always retains the responsibility for ensuring ethical practice in research. The investigator is also responsible for the ethical treatment of research participants by collaborators, assistants, students, and employees, all of whom, however, incur similar obligations.

D. Except in minimal-risk research, the investigator establishes a clear and fair agreement with research participants, prior to their participation, that clarifies the obligations and responsibilities of each. The investigator has the obligation to honor all promises and commitments included in that agreement. The investigator informs the participants of all aspects of the research that might reasonably be expected to influence willingness to participate and explains all other aspects of the research about which the participants inquire. Failure to make full disclosure prior to obtaining informed consent requires additional safeguards to protect the welfare and dignity of the research participants. Research with children or with participants who have impairments that would limit understanding and/or communication requires special safeguarding procedures.

E. Methodological requirements of a study may make the use of concealment or deception necessary. Before conducting such a study, the investigator has a special responsibility to (i) determine whether the use of such techniques is justified by the study's prospective scientific, educational, or applied value; (ii) determine whether alternative procedures are available that do not use concealment or deception; and (iii) ensure that the participants are provided with sufficient explanation as soon as possible.

F. The investigator respects the individual's freedom to decline to participate in or to withdraw from the research at any time. The obligation to protect this freedom requires careful thought and consideration when the investigator is in a position of authority or influence over the participant. Such positions of authority include, but are not limited to, situations in which research participation is required as part of employment or in which the participant is a student, client, or employee of the investigator.

G. The investigator protects the participant from physical and mental discomfort, harm, and anger that may arise from research procedures. If risks of such consequences exist, the investigator informs the participant of that fact. Research procedures likely to cause serious or lasting harm to a participant are not used unless the failure to use these procedures might expose the participant to risk of greater harm, or unless the research has great potential benefit and fully informed and voluntary consent is obtained from each participant. The participant should be informed of procedures for contacting the investigator within a reasonable time period following participation should stress, potential harm, or related questions or concerns arise.

H. After the data are collected, the investigator provides the participant with information about the nature of the study and attempts to remove any misconceptions that may have arisen. Where scientific or humane values justify delaying or withholding this information, the investigator incurs a special responsibility to monitor the research and to ensure that there are no damaging consequences for the participant.

I. Where research procedures result in undesirable consequences for the individual participant, the investigator has the responsibility to detect and remove or correct these consequences, including long-term effects.

J. Information obtained about a research participant during the course of an investigation is confidential unless otherwise agreed upon in advance. When the possibility exists that others may obtain access to such information, this possibility, together with the plans for protecting confidentiality, is explained to the participant as part of the procedure for obtaining informed consent.

Note.* From *American Psychologist*, 1981, 36, pp. 633–638. Copyright 1981 by the American Psychological Association. Reprinted by permission. Also, note that these guidelines are consistent with the APA's 1989 guidelines printed in *American Psychologist*, 1990, 45, 394–395.

BOX A.4 American Psychological Association's Ethical Principles Governing the Care and Use of Animals

I. General
  A. The acquisition, care, and use of all animals must be in compliance with relevant federal, state, and local laws and regulations and with international conventions to which the U.S. is a party.
  B. Psychologists working with animals must be familiar with Principle 10 (Care and Use of Animals) of the "Ethical Principles of Psychologists" of

the APA (*American Psychologist*, 1981, 36, 633–638) and research must be conducted in a manner consistent with that principle.*

C. The guidelines shall be conspicuously posted in every laboratory, teaching facility, or other setting in which animals are maintained and used by psychologists and their students.

D. Considerations limited to the time convenience or expense of a procedure do not justify violations of any of the principles included in this document.

E. Violations of these guidelines should be reported to the facility supervisor whose name is appended at the end of this document. If not resolved on the local level, allegations of violations of these guidelines or Principle 10 of the Ethical Principles of Psychologists should be referred to the APA Ethics Committee, which is empowered to impose sanctions.

F. Psychologists may consult with the Committee on Animal Research and Experimentation at any stage preparatory to, or during, a research project for advice about the appropriateness of research procedures or ethical issues related to experiments with animals. Individuals with any questions concerning these guidelines should consult with the Committee on Animal Research and Experimentation.

G. Psychologists are strongly encouraged to become familiar with the ethical principles of animal research. To facilitate this, the Committee on Animal Research and Experimentation will maintain a list of appropriate references.

II. Personnel

A. A supervisor, experienced in the care and use of laboratory animals, shall closely monitor and be responsible for the health, comfort, and humane treatment of all animals within the particular facility.

B. A veterinarian shall be available for consultation regarding housing, nutrition, animal care procedures, health, and medical attention. The veterinarian should conduct periodic inspections of the facility at least twice a year.

C. Psychologists shall ensure that all individuals using animals under their supervision have received explicit instruction in experimental methods and in the care, maintenance, and handling of the species being studied. Responsibilities and activities of all individuals dealing with animals shall be consistent with their respective competencies, training, and experience.

D. It is the responsibility of the psychologist to be cognizant of and to comply with all federal, state, city, or local laws pertaining to the acquisition, care, use, and disposal of animals. Investigators should also be fully familiar with the "*NIH Guide for the Care and Use of Laboratory Animals.*"

---

*An investigator of animal behavior strives to advance understanding of basic behavioral principles and/or to contribute to the improvement of human health and welfare. In seeking these ends, the investigator ensures the welfare of animals and treats them humanely. Laws and regulations notwithstanding, an animal's immediate protection depends upon the scientist's own conscience.

E. It is the responsibility of the supervisor of the facility to ensure that adequate records of the utilization and disposition of animals are maintained.

F. It is the responsibility of the supervisor of the facility to ensure that all personnel involved in the care, maintenance, and handling of animals be familiar with these guidelines.

III. Facilities

A. The facilities housing animals shall be designed to conform with specifications in the "NIH Guide for the Care and Use of Laboratory Animals" and in relevant legislation.

B. Investigators are encouraged to seek accreditation of their facilities from such organizations as the American Association for Accreditation of Laboratory Animal Care (AAALAC).

C. Research may not be conducted until it has been reviewed by a local institutional committee to ensure that procedures are appropriate and humane. The committee should have representation from within the institution and, when possible, from the local community.

IV. Acquisition of Animals

A. When appropriate, animals intended for use in the laboratory should be bred for that purpose.

B. Animals not bred in the researcher's facility must be acquired lawfully from reliable sources. The U.S. Department of Agriculture (USDA) may be consulted for information regarding suppliers.

C. Animals taken from the wild should be trapped in a humane manner and in accordance with local, state, and federal laws.

D. Investigators should ensure that those responsible for transporting animals to the research facility provide adequate food, water, ventilation, and space and impose no unnecessary stress on the animals.

E. Endangered species or taxa should be utilized only with full attention to required permits and ethical concerns not covered by legislation. Information can be obtained from the Office of Endangered Species, U.S. Department of the Interior, Fish and Wildlife Service, Washington, DC 20240. Similar caution should be used in work with threatened species.

V. Care and Housing of Animals

Responsibility for the conditions under which animals are kept, both within and outside of the context of active experimentation or teaching, rests jointly upon the investigator or instructor and those individuals appointed by the institution to administer animal care. Housing must be consistent with all relevant laws and standards and, when feasible, should enable the animals to express their natural behavior. Animals should be provided with humane care and healthful conditions during their entire stay in the facility.

VI. Justification of the Research

A. Research should be undertaken with a clear scientific purpose. There should be a reasonable expectation that the research will

1. increase our knowledge of the processes underlying the evolution, development, control, or biological significance of behavior;
2. increase understanding of the species under study in the research; or
3. provide results that benefit the health or welfare of humans or other animals.

B. The contributions to knowledge or to health expected to result from the research should be sufficient to benefit as to outweigh any distress to the animals used.

C. The psychologist should monitor the animals' welfare throughout the course of an investigation in order to ensure continued justification for the research.

VII. Experimental Design

A. The investigator should consider the possibility of using alternatives to animals in research and teaching whenever appropriate.

B. Humane considerations should constitute one of the major sets of factors that enter into the design of research. In particular, several relevant considerations should be noted:

1. The species chosen for study should be well suited to answer the question(s) posed. When the research involves procedures that are likely to cause pain or discomfort to the animal and when any of several species are equally appropriate to answer the scientific questions asked, the researcher should employ the species that appears likely to experience least distress.

2. The number of animals utilized in a study should be sufficient to provide a clear answer to the question posed. Care should be exercised to use the minimum number of animals consistent with sound experimental design, especially where the procedures might cause pain or discomfort to the animals.

VIII. Experimental Procedures

Humane consideration for the well-being of the animal should be incorporated into the design and conduct of all procedures involving animals.

A. Procedures which involve no pain or distress to the animal, or in which the animal is anesthetized and is euthanized before regaining consciousness, are acceptable if the investigator abides by the principles enunciated in these guidelines.

B. Experiments involving pain that is not relieved by medication or other acceptable methods should be undertaken only with justification as noted above (Section VI).

C. An animal observed to be in a state of severe distress or pain which cannot be alleviated should be euthanized immediately, using a humane, approved method.

D. The use of aversive stimuli should be undertaken only with justification as noted above (Section VI). Care should be taken to adjust the parameters of aversive stimulation to levels that appear minimal, though compatible with the aims of the research. Investigators are encouraged and should be able to control the effects of acute experimental pain (e.g., by escape or avoidance behavior).

E. Procedures involving food or water deprivation should be used only when less stressful procedures are inappropriate to the design and purpose of the experiment. Minimal levels of deprivation consistent with the goals of the research should be used.

F. Prolonged physical restraint should be used only after less stressful procedures are inappropriate to the design and purpose of the experiment. Minimal levels of deprivation consistent with the goals of the research should be used.

G. Procedures that entail extreme environment conditions, such as high or low temperatures, high humidity, modified atmospheric pressure, etc., should be undertaken only with justification as noted above (Section VI).

H. Studies entailing prey killing or intensive aggressive interactions among animals should be fully justified and conducted in a manner that minimizes extent and duration of pain.

I. Procedures entailing the deliberate infliction of trauma should be restricted and used only with very strong justification. Animals used in such experiments should be anesthetized.

J. Procedures involving the use of paralytic agents without reduction in pain sensation require particular prudence and humane concern. Utilization of muscle relaxants or paralytics alone during surgery or other invasive procedures, without general anesthesia, is unacceptable, and should not be used for surgical restraint.

K. Surgical procedures, because of their intrusive nature, require close supervision and attention to humane considerations by the investigator.

  1. All surgical procedures and anesthetization should be conducted under the direct supervision of a qualified scientist who is competent in the use of the procedure.

  2. If the surgical procedure is likely to cause greater discomfort than that attending anesthetization, the animals should be rendered incapable of perceiving pain and maintained in that condition until the experiment or procedure is ended.

  3. Sound post-operative care and monitoring must be provided to minimize discomfort, prevent infection, and other untoward consequences of the procedure.

  4. As a general rule, animals should not be subjected to successive surgical procedures unless this is required by the nature of the research. However, there may be occasions when it is preferable to carry out more than one procedure on a few animals than to carry out a single procedure on several animals. The alternatives must be carefully weighed, and the guiding principle is to cause the least possible distress on the fewest possible animals.

IX. Field Research
   A. Field workers should disturb their populations as little as possible. Investigators should make every effort to minimize potential harmful effects of the study on the population and on other plant and animal species in the area.
   B. Research conducted in populated areas should be done in a manner that is in accordance with all laws and with respect for the property and privacy of the inhabitants of the area.
   C. Particular justification is required for the study of endangered species. Such research should not be conducted unless all requisite permits are obtained.

X. Educational Use of Animals
   A. When animals are used solely for educational rather than research purposes, the consideration of possible benefits accruing from their use versus the cost in terms of animal distress must take into account the fact that no new knowledge is likely to be acquired and some of the procedures which can be justified for educational purposes.
   B. Classroom demonstrations involving animals should be used only when instructional objectives cannot effectively be achieved through the use of videotapes, films or other alternatives. Careful consideration should be given to the question of whether the type of demonstration is warranted by the anticipated instructional gain.
   C. Student projects involving pain or distress to animals should be undertaken judiciously and only when the training objectives cannot be achieved in any other way. Greater justification is required if there is no anticipated new scientific knowledge but only learning or practice of established procedures by students.
   D. Demonstrations of scientific knowledge in such contexts as exhibits, conferences, or seminars do not justify the use of painful procedures or multiple surgical interventions. Audio-visual alternatives should be considered.

XI. Disposition of Animals
   A. When an animal is no longer needed, alternatives to euthanasia should be considered.
      1. Animals may be distributed to colleagues who can utilize them. Care should be taken that such a procedure does not expose the animal to excessive surgical or other invasive or painful procedures. The investigator donating animals should be assured that the proposed use by the recipient colleague has the approval of or will be evaluated by the appropriate institutional animal care committee and that humane treatment will be continued. It may sometimes be feasible to return wild-trapped animals to the field. This should be done only when there is reasonable assurance that such release will not detrimentally affect the fauna and environment of the area and when the ability of the animal to survive in nature has not been seriously impaired.

Unless conservation efforts dictate otherwise, release should normally occur within the same area from which animals were originally trapped. Animals reared in the laboratory generally should not be released; either they cannot survive or they may survive and disrupt the natural ecology.

B. When euthanasia constitutes the most humane form of disposition of an animal at the conclusion of an experiment:
   1. Euthanasia must be carried out in compliance with all federal, state, city, and local laws.
   2. Euthanasia must be accomplished in such a humane manner, appropriate for the species under anesthesia, or in such a way as to ensure immediate death in accordance with procedures approved by the institutional care committee.
   3. No animal is to be discarded until its death is verified.
   4. Disposal of euthanized animals should be accomplished in a manner that is in accord with all relevant legislation; consistent with health, environmental, and aesthetic concerns; and approved by the institutional animal care committee.

Note. Reprinted from "New animal guidelines." (1985, April). APA *Monitor*, p. 6. Used with the permission of the American Psychological Association.
Also note. These guidelines are consistent with APA ethical principles as amended June 2, 1989.

APPENDIX

B

Library Resources

Library research is a necessary and useful component of any research project. Library research can help you come up with your basic research question, refine that question into a hypothesis, and inform you about research and theories that relate to your hypothesis. Once you have refined and justified your hypothesis, a literature review can help you design your study. Specifically, a thorough search through your library's resources can save you from wasting time and effort in at least two ways. First, searches can help by directing your attention to measures and manipulations that other researchers have found fruitful. Second, searches can help you by directing your attention away from measures and manipulations that other researchers have found fruitless.

To conduct a literature review, there are nine basic steps you can take.

1. Consult general sources
   a. Introductory psychology texts
   b. Specialized texts (texts on your general topic (e.g., memory)—these texts may be targeted at juniors, seniors, or even graduate students)
2. Consult books or chapters written for experts in the field; you may be able to find these texts by
   a. Looking in *Books In Print*
   b. Looking at *Psyc BOOKS: Books & Chapters in Psychology*, set of volumes especially designed to help individual psychologists locate recent books and chapters that are relevant to their specific interest area
   c. Looking at the *Annual Review of Psychology*
   d. Consulting the card catalog
3. Track down articles referenced in those books
4. Read those articles and their reference sections; track down research they reference
5. To see if the authors have done more recent research, look them up in the author index of *Psychological Abstracts*
6. Look up topic in subject index of *Psychological Abstracts*
7. See what recent articles have referenced your key articles by consulting the *Social Science Citation Index*
8. Scan recent issues of journals where you have found previous articles related to your topic or that are general in scope (*Psychological Bulletin, American Psychologist, Psychological Science, Psych Scans, Current Contents*)
9. Do a computerized search of the literature

The first five steps of the literature search are fairly straightforward. The remaining steps are not. Therefore, the rest of this appendix is devoted to making those steps more manageable.

PSYCHOLOGICAL ABSTRACTS

Many people start their literature search with the *Psychological Abstracts*. The *Psychological Abstracts* include brief summaries of a wide range of work in psychology and related fields. To get a sense of what a rich resource the *Abstracts* are, consider that they summarize articles from hundreds of journals, as well as summarizing books and doctoral dissertations.

The inclusiveness of the *Abstracts* means they probably include any relevant article you might want. However, the inclusiveness also poses a problem: How do you find the articles you want from among the thousands of articles summarized in the *Abstracts*? Reading the *Abstracts* from cover to cover is probably not a practical option. Fortunately, because the *Abstracts* are well organized, there are more practical alternatives.

Searching by Subject

Because the *Abstracts* are organized and indexed by topic, the first step is to find out what topics you want to look up. At the very least, you will probably want to look up your dependent measure and the general subject you are investigating.

Using the Thesaurus

Looking under these topics might give you some information, but you might miss some important references. Why? Because psychologists may have other names for your concepts. To find out about those names, look at the *Psychological Thesaurus*. The *Thesaurus* will tell you other subject titles that your criterion variable might be listed under. For example, "self" is also called identity, personality, and ego. Because the *Psychological Thesaurus* is so useful for searching the *Abstracts*, it will usually be located with the *Abstracts*.

Once you have looked up the concepts you are planning to investigate in the *Thesaurus*, you are armed with the terms you need. You are now ready to tackle the *Abstracts*.

Current Issues of *Psychological Abstracts*

If you are trying to find current references, locate the *Abstracts'* issues for this year. The *Abstracts* published this year will be found in several soft bound issues that share the same volume number. For example, all of the issues published in 1992 are classified as Volume 79.

Once you have rounded up all the issues for this year, the rest of your job is simple. Simply look up your terms in the subject index in the back of each issue. The index will give you the *numbers* of the abstracts relating to that term. For example, if next to your term you saw "1029," that would tell you that the abstract is number 1029, the 1029th abstract of that volume. (Each abstract has a number. Like page numbers, abstract numbers go in order. Thus, 1000 is right after abstract number 999 and right before number 1001. At first, you might think it would be better to give page numbers rather than abstract numbers. However, abstract numbers are more useful because there could be 20 abstracts on a single page. Thus, the numbers tell you exactly where to look. Consequently, after using the *Abstracts* for just a few minutes, you will appreciate the value of using an abstract's specific number.)

After recording the numbers of all the potentially important abstracts, you can go through the issue locating those abstracts. The only hassle is, because each index only covers that issue, you will have to look up your terms several times. That is, you have to look up "self" in the January issue index as well as in the March issue.

Hard-Bound Issues

To help people avoid the hassle of looking up the same term again and again, most libraries bind together the previous year's issues. Specifically, they bind all the issues of the *Abstracts* that bear the same volume number. For example, all of the issues published in 1991 are probably bound together with a hard-bound cover and labelled Volume 78. However, they do not bind the indexes with the *Abstracts*. Instead, the subject and author indexes are bound separately. Thus, for each of the hard-bound volumes there is a hard-bound subject index and a hard-bound author index. The indexes will have the same volume number as the *Abstracts* they refer to. Thus, the 1991 *Abstracts*, the 1991 subject index, and the 1991 author index are all labelled Volume 78.

In short, if you want to locate references for previous years, find the hard-bound indexes that correspond to the years you are interested in. Look up your terms in the subject index. Write down both the volume number of the index and the abstract numbers. Then, go to that volume of the *Abstracts*.

Looking Up References by Author
If you know the names of investigators who have done research relating to your study, you may want to see if they have done more recent work. In that case, simply look up their names in either an issue or volume index.

Browsing Through the Abstracts
In a given volume, all abstracts that are on the same topic are located together. Thus, once you find an abstract that addresses your topic, look at the surrounding abstracts.

Finding the Original Resource
After reading an abstract of the study, you will have a good idea whether you want to read the original source. If so, you will find a reference for the original publication with the abstract. Go to your library's catalogue files to locate the original source. If your library does not own it, try inter-library loan.

SOCIAL SCIENCES INDEX

A source that is like the *Abstracts*, but even more inclusive, is the *Social Sciences Index*. This index is a comprehensive source for journal references in all the social sciences. In addition to psychology, such fields as anthropology, sociology, social work, and geography are included. Because psychologists are not the only people who conduct behavioral research, the *Social Sciences Index* can help you locate useful references published in non-psychological journals.

Like *Psychological Abstracts*, several issues are published each year. Also, like the *Abstracts*, the issues for a particular year are identified by the same volume number and bound together in hardback. Finally, like the *Abstracts*, the most recent indexes will probably be in several soft-bound issues that bear the same volume number.

In the front of each index, you will find a list of abbreviations for the journals indexed, a list of addresses for those journals, an explanation of other abbreviations used in the index, and a sample entry. These lists and examples will help you interpret the references given under your topic.

As was the case with searching the *Psychological Abstracts*, the key is to have the appropriate subject heading. One key to assuring that you have the appropriate terms is to look up your concepts in the *Psychological Thesaurus* (it should be located with the *Psychological Abstracts*). Once you have found the appropriate terms, look up your topic under the appropriate subject heading. Under your topic, you should find several references. These references will be organized in the following order: title, author, brief description, journal, volume number, pages, month, and year.

Because much of this information is presented in abbreviated form, you will need to look at the guides presented at the beginning of each index. Otherwise, you may be unable to interpret these abbreviations. For example, a reference might read

Reactivity of adults in timed tests. M. Davis,
bibl. J. Gent.P. 19:907–14, D, '85.

In this example, the "bibl." means it is a bibliography—you have hit a gold mine! In other words, this is a list of references on your topic. The article was published in the *Journal of Genetic Psychology*, Volume 19, pages 907–914, in December of 1985.

As you can see, the *Social Sciences Index*, compared to the *Abstracts*, has several advantages and several disadvantages. The advantages are it includes sources outside of psychology and it is simpler. You do not have to look in the index to find a number and then track down that number in a different part of the issue or in a different book. Instead, once you look it up in the index, you have found your reference. Unfortunately, these advantages carry two disadvantages. First, the *Social Sciences Index* does not provide summaries of the articles referenced. Thus, you will often have to find the original article to determine if it is at all relevant to your work. Second, the *Social Sciences Index* only allows you to search for articles in one way—by topic.

SOCIAL SCIENCES CITATION INDEX

Unlike the *Social Sciences Index*, the *Social Sciences Citation Index (SSCI)* gives you several different ways to locate references. Specifically, the *SSCI* gives you three ways to find a reference: by topic, by who wrote it, and by who referenced it. The *SSCI* is able to do this because it consists of three separate but related indexes: a subject index, an author index, and a citation index. Each index covers the same journal articles. They all index over 70,000 articles that appear in more than 2,000 journals. The difference is in how they index those articles. The fact that they all cover the same articles has two important implications.

First, you can start your search using any of the indexes. Where you start will probably depend on what you already know. If you only know the topic, you will use the subject index. If you know a researcher that does work in this area, you may start with the author index. If you know of a classic study in your area, you may want to find articles that cite that study. Therefore, you would start your search in the citation index.

Second, you may get information in one index that will give you leads you can follow up in another index. For instance, in searching the subject index, you may repeatedly find the name of a certain author. Therefore, you may choose to look up that author in the author index.

The Permuterm Subject Index

The *SSCI* refers to its subject index as the "Permuterm Subject Index" (PSI). In the PSI, every major word from the title of an article is paired with every major word in that title. For example, if an article were titled "Sex differences in the effect of television viewing on aggression," the article would be indexed under Sex Differences and Aggression; Sex Differences and Television Viewing; and Television Viewing and Aggression. These *permuted* (arranged in all possible ways) pairs are alphabetically listed as two-level indexing entries and linked to the names of the authors who used them in the titles of their articles. For example:

Aggression	
Sex differences	Eron M
Television viewing	Bunker A
Sex differences	
Aggression	Eron M
Television viewing	Mutin SS
Television viewing	
Aggression	Bunker A
Sex differences	Mutin SS

Thus, the PSI tells you that during the period indexed, the authors Bunker and Mutin used the words shown opposite their name ("Television Viewing and Aggression" and "Television Viewing and Sex Differences," respectively).

To use PSI, simply think of words and word pairs that are likely to appear in the titles of articles related to your study. By looking up these words, you will discover the names of authors who have used the words in the titles of their articles. Once you find the names of authors, look them up in the "*Source Index*."

The Source Index

The "Source Index" is a straightforward author index to the articles covered each year. For each article indexed, you are given the language it is written in (if it is not English), its title, authors, journal, volume number, page numbers, year, the number of references cited in the article, and the journal issue number. In addition, beginning with the

May–August, 1974 issue, references contained in each indexed article are listed. To facilitate reprint requests and other correspondence, a mailing address is often provided for each first author. Following is a sample entry of the "Source Index." As the entry's third line reveals, the entry comes from an article published in the *Journal of Applied Psychology*, volume 25. It begins on page 9, was published in 1987, has 20 references, and is in issue number 3.

BUNKER, A
    THE RELATIONSHIP OF AGGRESSION AND TV VIEWING
    J APPL PSY   25 09 87 20R N3
CTR FOR REHABILITATIVE CHANGE, CENTER AVENUE
NEW MEXICO, MEXICO

The Citation Index

The final index included in the *SSCI* is the "Citation Index." This index looks at what references authors cite in their papers. The "Citation Index" is based on two related assumptions. First, if a paper cites an article, then the paper is on the same topic as the older (cited) reference. Second, papers that refer to (cite) the same article, usually address the same topic. For example, if a bunch of papers cite an article on the effects of chlorpromazine on the sexual behavior of rats, many of these papers probably investigate the effects of drugs on the sexual behavior of rats.

To start a search in the "Citation Index," look up the name of an author who published material relevant to your topic. If anything the author has written was cited during the indexing period, the names of the publications that were cited will be listed. This feature is useful in at least two ways. First, if you are not completely familiar with the author's work, you may find out about other interesting articles by that author. Second, if nobody cited the paper you are interested in, you will know instantly—the article will not appear.

If the article you are interested in was cited, the "Citation Index" will include the name of that article. Next to the article name will be the names of the authors who cited the publication. Now that you know who referenced the publication, you need to find out in what journal and in what article they referenced it. To find out this out, look up their names in the "Source Index."

In summary, the *Social Sciences Citation Index* allows you to do at least three basic types of searches. If you know of a classic study in your area of research, you can do a citation search. If you do not know of an earlier, relevant paper, you can do a search by looking up the variables you are studying in a permuterm (subject) search. Finally, when you know the name of a researcher who has recently published on your topic (or learn of such a person as a result of a permaterm or citation search), do an author search.

CURRENT CONTENTS

In contrast to the sources we described earlier, *Current Contents* is very easy to use. *Current Contents* simply lists the table of contents for several journals. Because you can often figure out whether an article is relevant to your topic from its title, this reference can be very useful. Thus, by looking at titles you can determine which articles you want to find and read. Although you might prefer the articles were organized by topic rather than by journal, you will soon find that most journals only cover certain topics. That is, if you are looking for a measure of aggression, you would not look at the contents for *The Journal of Memory and Cognition*. To get a better idea of what journals you should scan, see table B.1.

COMPUTER SEARCHES

The quickest way to locate references is to do a computer search. We will discuss two types of computer searches: on-line and cd-rom searches.

With an on-line search, you use a computer terminal to gain access to databases stored on a computer at some other location. These databases contain all of the indexes and abstracts we have just discussed and more. Two popular databases used by behavioral scientists are *PsycINFO* and *ERIC*. Access to these databases is purchased through computer vendors. For example, PsycINFO is available through DIALOG and BRS/After Dark (APA, 1989). In other words, the computer terminal in your library connects, via phone line, to a computer operated by one of these vendors. The library (or you!) is charged for the amount of time you spend "on-line" searching the vendor's database. In addition, there may be a long-distance phone charge.

As an alternative to "on-line" searches, some libraries purchase PsycLIT on cd-rom discs. Rather than connect to a computer at some distant location, with PsycLIT you use a microcomputer equipped with a cd-rom disc drive. The databases contained in PsycLIT are very similar to PsycINFO (both are produced by the American Psychological Association). If your library has purchased PsycLIT, it is probably available to you without charge.

Whereas it might take you hours to search through all the resources we discussed in this appendix to find the references you need, computer searches can condense that time into minutes. Why not let the computer do the searching so you can have more time to plan and execute your study?

One way that computer searches save you time is by cross-referencing two or more variables. To cross-reference variables on a computer search, you must first come up with the variables. Once you have your research idea this should not be very difficult. For example, if your topic is aggression in food-deprived monkeys, the computer will find only those references that concern "aggression" in "food-deprived" "monkeys." If you were using just an abstract or index, you could only look up one (two at the most) of these variables at a time. Thus, if you looked up aggression, you would have to read through all the references concerning aggression in humans, rats, birds, and lions to find ones that dealt with monkeys. You would then have to sort through all the scattered monkey listings to find "food-deprived" monkeys.

Although computer searches can save time, you will only save time if you have some knowledge about how to conduct a computer search. To help you plan your search, APA publishes two workbooks called *Search PsycINFO* intended to provide this training. One workbook is for students, the other for instructors. Both can be purchased from APA's order department. Additional help may be obtained from your reference librarian.

TABLE B.1 A Look at Selected Journals

JOURNAL	RELEVANCE TO YOU
Psychological Bulletin	Publishes articles that review existing work on either a research area or on a research/statistical technique.
Psychological Review	Publishes work that compares and criticizes existing theories.
American Psychologist	Publishes theoretical articles, review articles, and empirical articles. Although articles are often written by distinguished scholars, they are written to a broad audience and are thus relatively easy to understand.
Psychological Science	Publishes theoretical articles, review articles, and empirical articles. Although articles are often written by distinguished scholars, they are written to a fairly broad audience and are thus relatively easy to understand. You may find the articles slightly harder to understand than those in the *American Psychologist.*
Contemporary Psychology	Contains reviews of recent books, is easy to read, and covers a wide range of topics.
Psychological Abstracts	Presents brief summaries of most published articles in psychology, is a good browsing or reference tool, and the abstracts are indexed by both author and topic.
Psych/Scan	Like *Psychological Abstracts,* contains summaries of recent articles. There are six different *Psych/Scans* for six different content areas: (1) developmental, (2) clinical, (3) learning disorders and mental retardation, (4) applied psychology, (5) applied experimental and engineering, and (6) psychoanalysis.
American Journal of Psychology	Publishes primarily original research in basic psychological science; not as competitive as *JEP* (see below).
Journals of Experimental Psychology (JEP)	Usually contains original experimental studies concerning basic mechanisms of perception, learning, motivation, and performance. The four different journals are *JEP: General; JEP: Animal Behavior Processes; JEP: Learning, Memory, and Cognition;* and *JEP: Human Perception and Performance*
Behavioral Neuroscience	Emphasizes biological basis of behavior. Because of the interdisciplinary nature of the journal, you may find some of the articles hard to understand if you do not have the necessary background in chemistry or endocrinology.
Journal of Comparative Psychology	Articles may include both laboratory and field observation of species. Emphasis is on relating findings to the theory of evolution.
Bulletin of the Psychonomic Society	Articles cover any area of general experimental psychology. This is a good source of short articles describing relatively simple studies; articles do not undergo peer review.
Memory and Cognition	A good source of articles in human experimental psychology. See also *Cognitive Science, Cognitive Psychology,* and *JEP: Learning, Memory, and Cognition.*
Journal of Applied Behavior Analysis	Publishes articles reporting a sizable effect on an important behavior, usually employing a single-subject design.

JOURNAL	RELEVANCE TO YOU
Psychological Record	Contains articles discussing theory or reporting experiments; average article is relatively brief.
Psychological Reports	Publishes articles in general psychology; is a good source of brief articles.
Journal of Consulting and Clinical Psychology	Publishes a wide range of articles and brief reports dealing with theory and research in counseling and some use of the case study method.
Psychological Assessment: A Journal of Consulting and Clinical Psychology	Contains studies assessing the validity of a variety of tests and measures.
Journal of Counseling Psychology	Publishes research articles evaluating the effectiveness of counseling, studies on the effectiveness of selecting and training counselors, theoretical articles, and other articles relating to counseling.
Journal of Abnormal Psychology	Occasionally reports experimental studies on humans or animals related to emotion or pathology and some studies that test hypotheses derived from psychological theories.
Psychology and Aging	Publishes research reporting on physiological and behavioral aspects of aging during older adulthood; is fairly easy to read.
Developmental Psychology	Primarily publishes research relating to development and some experiments, cross-cultural studies, and correlational studies. See also, *Child Development, Merrill Palmer Quarterly,* and *Psychology and Aging.* In addition, can track down related work by consulting *Psych Scan/Developmental.*
Journal of Educational Psychology	Publishes research and theoretical articles relating to teaching and learning, is fairly easy to read.
American Education Research Journal	Publishes research in education; single-study papers are accepted.
Journal of Applied Psychology	Reports research relating to industry, government, health, education, consumer affairs, and other applied areas.
Journal of Personality and Social Psychology	Contains three sections: (1) Attitudes and Social Cognition, (2) Interpersonal Relations and Group Processes, and (3) Personality and Individual Differences. Primarily reports articles involving several studies or fairly complex designs. Discussions may suggest follow-up studies that could be performed.
Journal of Experimental Social Psychology	Almost all articles published report the results of experiments.
Journal of Social Psychology	A good source of fairly simple studies.
Personality and Social Psychology Bulletin	Contains short articles that are often easy to understand.
Representative Research in Social Psychology	One of the few journals to publish studies that have nonsignificant results.

APPENDIX

C

Using the Computer to Help You Conduct Your Study

There are numerous advantages to using a computer to run subjects. Most of these advantages stem from the fact that the computer will do exactly what it is told.

Because you must tell the computer exactly what to do, you are forced to think through every detail of your procedure before you run a single subject. Then, you must write out (program) each step. By comparing the programs for the different conditions, you can readily observe every single difference between your various treatment conditions. Thus, you can easily see whether all differences between conditions are relevant to the treatment variable. If there are any nontreatment differences between conditions, you can try to eliminate these treatment-irrelevant differences. Consequently, programming can help you make your treatment manipulation as pure as possible.

Another consequence of having to program every step of the procedure is that you become aware of the decisions you are making at each step. By forcing you to become more aware of the details of the procedure and by forcing you to consciously make decisions about procedures, programming may improve your procedures. In addition, this keen awareness of what the procedure is and why it is the way it is should make writing the method section easier.

Although you get some benefits from writing a program, the major benefits come from having the computer use your program. Because the computer follows instructions to the letter, a computerized study is the ultimate in standardization: Everyone receives the same instructions and stimuli; procedures are not inadvertently changed as the study goes on. This high degree of standardization reduces error variance, thereby increasing your study's power.

This high degree of standardization also ensures that subjects are not reinforced for responding in a way that supports the hypothesis. Although a human experimenter might nod and smile for "correct" answers and frown for "incorrect" answers, the computer responds the same way, no matter how the subject responds. Therefore, a computerized study reduces experimenter bias.

Finally, because the program is so detailed, you have a detailed record of your procedure. This is useful for writing up the method section of your study and for replicating your study. Indeed, anyone who has a copy of your program can replicate your study.

In addition to standardizing the presentation of instructions and stimuli, programming can also help you collect data. Computers have three advantages over humans when it comes to collecting data. First, computers can sometimes collect data more unobtrusively than a human can. The computer can stealthily monitor how fast the subject is typing or how fast the subject is answering questions. Second, computers do not get as bored as humans. Thus, the computer can tirelessly record hours of bar pressing and/or physiological responses. Third, computers record without bias. Because computers are blind to the hypothesis, they never deliberately change a response or interpret an answer to make the data more consistent with the hypothesis.

Beyond being consistent about presenting stimuli and collecting data, computers can also motivate subjects to attend to the task. Some subjects are more impressed with a study if it is on computer. They think to themselves, "If it's computerized, it must be scientific." Others are motivated by a computer study because the computer interacts with the subject: it reacts immediately to the subjects' responses. To capitalize on the motivating aspect of the computer's responsiveness, some investigators program the computer to call the subject by name. Other investigators go even farther by making their study resemble a video game.

Of course, all this programming takes time and effort. But once it is done, you may save time and effort. For example, you may save time by running several subjects at once if you have more than one computer. You may also save time by running fewer subjects because your high degree of standardization has reduced error variance. Finally, running subjects on a computer should be less draining. The computer, by presenting and recording data, is doing your job for you!

Fortunately, you can take advantage of the computer's ability to run subjects, even if you know nothing about programming. How? You can take advantage of "user-friendly" programs specifically designed to run subjects—if you are lucky enough to have access to one of these programs.[1] If you are not that fortunate, you can quickly learn the rudiments of programming. In two hours, you can learn enough to program a computer to help you run subjects for certain kinds of studies. Although you may have heard that learning programming is like learning another language, most of the commands you will need do not sound very foreign. That is, the commands "print," "end," "go to," "if," and "clear screen" should all have a familiar ring.

We do not mean to say that in two hours you will know enough to make the computer randomly assign subjects to condition, present instructions, present stimulus materials, record and store data, debrief subjects, and analyze your data. You won't.

But having the computer do everything is not necessary. In fact, for both ethical and practical reasons, we do not believe researchers should have computers do everything.

For ethical reasons, we feel you should not have the computer debrief subjects. Instead, you should personally debrief subjects. Why? Beyond the obvious arguments that subjects may have questions they would not ask a computer or questions that a computer could not answer, we feel that to debrief subjects by computer is dehumanizing.

---

[1]One such program is Micro Experimental Laboratory (abbreviated MEL). As its manual says, "MEL assumes no prior computer programming experience. . . . MEL allows you to run . . . experiments without bothersome programming."

For practical reasons, we feel you should not have the computer do anything that could be done just as well by other means. For example, you may find it may be better to have instructions written down on a piece of paper than on the computer screen because the instructions written on paper may be easier to read.

In general, we urge you to fight the urge to "overprogram." The most common "overprogramming" error is to have the computer store the data for all the subjects in the study. We know of many researchers who wrote—or paid professional programmers to write—programs that ended up incorrectly storing data. Only after the study was over, did these researchers realize they did not have any data they could analyze. In some cases, they had no data. In other cases, they had data, but could not establish which data belonged to which experimental condition (e.g., control or experimental group). Therefore, we urge that you have the computer print out each subject's data right after the subject has been debriefed, check whether the data correspond to the participant's experimental condition, and regularly back up the data on a second diskette.

One way to fight the urge to overprogram is to realize you do not have to program the whole study to reap enormous benefits. That is, you can dramatically improve your study by programming only a small aspect of it. For example, if you had a program that only presented stimuli, you would standardize your procedures and reduce researcher bias. In addition, such a program might eliminate the time and expense of other ways of presenting stimuli. For example, if you were going to present your stimuli in a booklet, computer presentation would save you the trouble of duplicating, collating, and stapling together booklets. Finally, and most importantly, such a program would force you to think through your procedures very carefully before you ran the study. As a result, writing the method section should be easier.

If you had a program that only recorded responses, you would again reduce the possibility of researcher bias. In addition, you could have the program record behavior unobtrusively. For example, the program could record how long it took subjects to respond without subjects knowing they were being timed. Finally, because the computer is not easily bored, you could have the computer record responses for hours. For example, if you were measuring physiological responses or bar-pressing behavior over a period of hours, the computer could record the data continuously.

What can go wrong? If you are having the computer run any part of your study, you have to be concerned about two things: will subjects do what you want? and will the computer do what you want?

There are several things you can do to maximize the chances that subjects will do what you want them to do. First, you should greet them and find out if they have computer-phobia. (Computer-phobia can still be a problem, especially for those who have not been exposed to computers, such as the elderly and people from deprived backgrounds.) If participants have computer-phobia, you should do your best to allay their concerns. By all means, tell them you are available if they do not understand something. Beyond that, your efforts to get subjects to warm up to the computer could range from showing them how to press the keys to having them play a game on it.

Once you have done your best to assure subjects that the computer will not bite, the rest is up to your program. You should have made sure that your instructions are extremely detailed, clear, and repetitious. Try to get some people who know nothing about computers to be practice subjects in your study to make sure that your instructions are clear enough. Once your instructions are clear, see what happens when a subject presses the wrong button. For example, if a subject is supposed to answer "a, b, c, or d," see what happens when "4" or "e" is pressed. Ideally, the program should tell the subject that the wrong button was pressed and to please try again.

Once you have the study set up so the subject will follow instructions, make sure that the computer is doing what you want. Unfortunately, just because the computer is doing what it is supposed to in one condition, does not mean it is doing what it is supposed to in all conditions. Therefore, check each condition. In checking the conditions, run the condition and print out a listing of the program. The listing makes it easier to catch spelling errors and to compare the conditions side by side.

Once the program is working to your satisfaction, you should make at least one back-up copy (an unwritten rule of research with computers is that diskettes will go bad). Then, as an extra precaution, you should print out a listing of the final version of the program.

D

Marketing Your Research Skills in the Real World

In this course, you have learned how to conduct and evaluate research. In the process, you have refined your ability to think critically, logically, and creatively. Furthermore, you have demonstrated the ability to plan and complete projects. In short, you now possess some highly marketable skills.

ABILITY TO ASK QUESTIONS

One of the skills you have refined is the ability to ask questions. Not only have you formulated your own research questions but you have learned how to question research findings and practices.

Your mastery of the art of question asking—often called critical thinking—will be respected by researchers and nonresearchers alike. On a superficial level, this skill will help you because people will frequently judge you based on the kinds of questions you ask. From your questions, people will decide how educated, informed, and intelligent you are. The key to impressing people is often not what you know nor who you know, but what you ask.

On a deeper level (and the reason people value intelligent questioners), the ability to question is vital to success. When people make disastrous decisions, it is usually because they failed to ask the right questions. Because critical thinking is so vital to success, entrance exams to medical, law, business, and graduate schools incorporate tests of critical thinking.

ABILITY TO ASK QUESTIONS OF DATA

Although most intelligent people can ask intelligent questions, not all intelligent people can ask intelligent questions of data. To most people, data are data. But you know that not all data are created equal. That is, you know that how data are collected affect how they can be interpreted. Before accepting data at face value, you try to determine what kind of design was used and whether that design was used properly. Thus, in looking at data from an experiment, you ask how subjects were assigned, how independence was achieved, how subject and experimenter bias were reduced, etc. In looking at results from an observational design, you would question anyone who would conclude that cause-effect statements could be made. In addition, you might ask if the results might be due to observer bias. The ability to question and interpret data will become increasingly important in the future: Computers can collect and store data, but they are not experts at interpreting it (Toffler, 1990).

In addition to questioning how data were collected, you also question how the data were analyzed. Your eyes no longer glaze over when you hear terms like "interaction," and "statistically significant." In fact, you are so familiar with data that you may be able to suggest alternative ways of presenting, interpreting, or analyzing existing information. In short, you are aware of what the analyses say and what they do not say.

ABILITY TO GET ANSWERS

Although your finesse at scrutinizing, interpreting, and using existing data is very marketable, your most marketable asset may be your ability to create new data. That is, not only do you know how to ask questions, you know how to ask questions to get answers. In short, your experience in turning abstract questions into specific testable hypotheses will be very useful.

In a related way, your experience in generating operational definitions will also be useful. By operationalizing variables, you can turn unanswerable questions into answerable ones. Thus, the question "Will a diet plan be a financial success?" becomes the question "Will a diet plan with these features, marketing in this way, get X number of sales at Z price?"

You might be surprised at how rare and how valued the skill of operationalizing variables is. Even very intelligent people are mystified by individuals who can create the desired information. For example, a lawyer was defending a cartoonist in a libel suit. The other side was suing about a cartoon, claiming that everyone knew who the devious cartoon character was supposed to be. The cartoonist's lawyer was so apprehensive about the case that he hired a psychologist to help him in selecting the jury. However, even with the right jury, the lawyer was concerned: how could he defend his client against such a subjective charge? The psychologist mentioned that one way to answer such a question would be to survey people in the community and ask them who, if anybody, they thought the cartoon looked like. The lawyer's response: "You mean you could do that?" This true story shows that although you may tend to undervalue your ability to get answers, others will not.

ABILITY TO THINK LOGICALLY

In this course, you have also refined your ability to think logically. You have had to be explicit about your logic and the assumptions you are making. In writing introduction and discussion sections, you have practiced spelling out the rationale and assumptions behind your thinking.

MAKING LOGICAL ARGUMENTS SUPPORTED BY DATA

In writing introduction, results, and discussion sections, not only have you argued logically but you have also used data to support your arguments. You have used data to support the assumptions behind your arguments as well as to support your conclusions. In addition to using data to support your conclusions, you can refute arguments supported by data. For example, because you are aware of the limits of correlational data, you know that the statement "Profits have increased since Jim took over. Therefore, Jim is a good manager" is not necessarily true. In short, you are well aware of the uses and abuses of data.

ABILITY TO COMMUNICATE COMPLEX OR TECHNICAL INFORMATION

In this course, you have not only learned to think creatively, critically, and logically but you have also articulated your reasoning. You have spelled out the rationale behind your hypothesis, the procedures you used, the analyses you chose, and the conclusions you made. In addition, you have summarized the results of other studies, some of which contained complex and technical information. Your ability to coherently present complex information should be an asset, no matter what profession you enter.

ABILITY TO PLAN AND COMPLETE PROJECTS

Thus far, we have mentioned that you used the following skills to carry out your research project:

1. Manipulating data
2. Thinking logically
3. Articulating both your logic and your assumptions
4. Asking questions
5. Analyzing and interpreting data

However, these are only some of the skills you used in carrying out your research project. Planning the research project required those skills, in addition to the skills required in designing and implementing any kind of project. You had to take initiative, map out all your steps, anticipate potential flaws and problems, challenge your basic assumptions, choose from among several alternative courses of action, prepare a timeline, overcome inevitable obstacles to your progress, aggregate all the information, come to a conclusion, and compile the final report. We cannot imagine a more strenuous test of your planning and problem-solving abilities.

SELLING YOURSELF

Clearly, you have much to offer a prospective employer. To get a good job, however, you must convince an employer that you have these skills. Your initial efforts to convince an employer of your value will involve sending a resume and cover letter. To help you, we have prepared a sample resume (see box D.1).

Prospective employers will want you to be able to back up your claims about your abilities. To convince employers that you have the skills you claim, use your skills at constructing operational definitions to describe yourself in objective and quantifiable terms. For example, do not say, "I am a good student"; instead, say, "I have a 3.7." To help convince employers of your abilities, you may want to send them copies of your final research report. The report demonstrates your ability to write reports and finish projects.

Once you have convinced prospective employers of your skills, you will have to convince them that these skills will generalize to the job. That is, a prospective employer might say, "Sure, you're a good student and had a rigorous class, but how do I know you will do well at MESSON?" To successfully show the value of your skills to MESSON, you should give specific examples of how your skills would apply to the job.

Although table D.1 should give you a general idea of how research skills might apply to business, you will want your examples to be so specific and relevant that the interviewer could visualize you succeeding on the job. Of course, to generate these specific examples, you must learn as much about the job as possible before the interview. (As we have implied all along, everything boils down to having done your research.)

Despite your best efforts, some interviewers may not feel your skills will generalize to their business. Some may say, "If you were a business major, I'd hire you without reservation. But you're not." At this point, it may be tempting to give up. After all, the interviewer is judging you on the basis of a superficial criterion: face validity. Although you may be sorely tempted to quit, don't.

Instead, try to see whether you can make a case for yourself on the basis of face validity. Mention any courses or internships you have had in business.

Because face validity has a big impact in the real world, you may want to acquire experiences that will improve the face validity of your candidacy. Fortunately, because face validity is superficial, it is often easy to acquire. For example, you can improve the face validity of your candidacy by

RESUME

Ms. Ima Sharpe
100 Resource Drive
City of Industry, CA 76278
(426) 754-5533

OBJECTIVE: To be an asset to your company through the application of my skills in writing, logical thinking, organizing, research, communication, and leadership.

EDUCATION: B.A. The Wright University
                    Major: Psychology
                    Senior Thesis: Reducing errors on a motor task

WRITING SKILLS: The rigors of conducting good research have honed my competencies in research proposal and report writing.
  — I received an "A" for my research proposal.
  — My research report was handed out in class as an example of how a research report should be written.

LOGICAL THINKING SKILLS: Training in research methodology has finely tuned my inductive and deductive reasoning. These powers of critical thinking are vital for optimal problem solving in any business situation.
  — independent thinking
  — ability to recognize problems
  — ability to ask the right questions
  — ability to make the abstract concrete
  — ability to generate possible solutions
  — ability to recognize the flaws of each solution
  — ability to determine the best solution through research and analysis of relevant variables

ORGANIZATIONAL SKILLS: In order to plan, execute, interpret, and apply research, I have developed organizational skills.
  — arranged for experimental facilities and equipment
  — recruited participants (subjects)
  — supervised and conducted an experiment
  — organized The Wright University's Annual Rat Olympics

RESEARCH SKILLS: As a consequence of my course in research design, I know many research techniques.
  — how to set up timetables for studies
  — survey research
  — experimental research
  — library research
  — how to use computer packages to analyze data
  — how to interpret statistics

ORAL PRESENTATION SKILLS: To effectively speak about research, I had to make the complex sound simple, the technical sound basic. To speak convincingly about research, I had to be a good salesperson.
  — I presented an experimental report at a regional psychology conference.
  — I received an "A+" for a verbal critique of technical research in class.

LEADERSHIP:
  — President of PSI CHI
  — Vice-president of the Student Experimental Psychology Club

Reference: My research methods professor.

TABLE D.1 Similarities Between the Executive and the Researcher	
EXECUTIVE	**RESEARCHER**
Identifies problem	Identifies problem
Collects background data on problem	Collects background data on problem
Makes proposals to collect other needed information	Makes proposals to collect other needed information
Establishes timeline	Establishes timeline
Attends to detail	Attends to detail
Analyzes data	Analyzes data
Reports findings	Reports findings

1. picking up the jargon of that field;
2. subscribing to newspapers or journals in that field *(Wall Street Journal)*;
3. doing a survey for a company (even free of charge), so you can put it on your resume;
4. doing research in the area in which you want a job. (For example, one of our students wanted a job in personnel, so she did a research project on productivity and sent it to a prospective employer. She got the job.)

In addition to marketing your general problem-solving skills, you may want to market your specific research skills. These skills might be especially attractive to a small firm. Small companies may find that your ability to do research will save them from paying large fees to outside research consulting firms.

There are many ways in which a small firm might be able to use your research skills. For example, you might conduct research relating to the company's workers. In this capacity, you might design surveys to assess workers' attitudes and opinions toward the company. Alternatively, you could assess the impact of training programs and/or policy changes on productivity.

You might also do some research to get feedback from customers. This could be as simple as designing questionnaires to find out who your customers are and what they like about your company or it could be more complex. For instance, you might do research that would pretest the effectiveness of the ads your company is designing. Or, you might evaluate the effectiveness of a new advertising campaign. You may end up saving the company a lot of money by telling them where not to spend their advertising dollars.

Another avenue would be to use consumer input to develop a new product or service. For example, you might question them regarding features they desire in a product, the cost they are willing to tolerate, and where they would buy such a product. You also might do a content analysis of the competitor's successful products. That is, you might ask, "What features do these products all have in common?" Such advance planning could save a company from creating another Edsel.

If you want a job where you are constantly involved in research, there are several careers you should consider. If you enjoy the hands-on, interpersonal part of research, but do not like the writing, planning, and statistical aspects, you could become a field interviewer or a telephone interviewer. In addition, you might be able to get a job at a mental hospital as a psychological test administrator.

If you desire a job that would fully immerse you in research, you should consider market research and research assistant jobs. Market research is one of the fastest growing fields in the country. Primarily, you would conduct and analyze consumer surveys, but you might be able to do some laboratory research. Market researchers are hired not only by market research firms but also by advertising agencies and large companies.

Research assistant jobs are not as common, but they can be found. Many of these jobs focus on *evaluation research.* The purpose of evaluation research is to determine the effects of a program (job training program) or if a treatment (wellness center) is working. Thus, large hospitals and the federal government do a substantial amount of evaluation research.

Other jobs involve analyzing data the government has collected. The federal government collects data about almost anything you can imagine—from people's attitudes toward life to how much meat they buy. The government needs research assistants to help analyze the data collected from the census and from numerous other surveys.

There are also jobs working for institutions that do research for the federal government. That is, universities and large research companies (Rand Company, Battelle) which receive government money to do research often have research assistant jobs. In addition, some universities also have jobs for laboratory assistants. Usually, lab assistants maintain the university's animal laboratory.

CONCLUSION

As you know, research design requires the ability to clearly define problems, propose solutions to those problems, and implement those solutions *on time.* In performing your projects, you demonstrated initiative in problem solving, attention to detail, logical thought, and the ability to write clearly. In short, you are able to ask questions and get answers. Virtually all employers need people with your skills.

Certain employers (research firms) will immediately recognize they need your skills. Other employers, equally desperate for your skills, may not recognize they need you. You will need to convince them by using your persuasive ability and strategies we suggested earlier. In addition, you may want to improve the appearance of your application by taking courses that will improve its face validity (see table D.2). Good Luck!

TABLE D.2 Specific Jobs that Would Be Available to a Good Research Design Student and Courses that Would Help In Obtaining that Job

Job Title	Supplementary Course(s)
Businessperson	Accounting
Interviewer	Public Speaking
Laboratory Assistant	Neuropsychology w/lab
Marketing Researcher	Marketing
Newspaper Reporter	English/Journalism
Personnel Administrator	Personnel Psy.
Public Health Statistician	Biology
Public Opinion Researcher	Computer Science
Research Assistant—Company	Computer Science
Research Assistant—Government	Computer Science
Research Assistant—Hospital	Biology w/ lab
Research Assistant—Mental Health	Testing
Technical Writer	English/Journalism
Professional Psychologist	Graduate degree necessary—advanced courses in statistics and research methods increase chances of acceptance into graduate school

APPENDIX

E

Statistics and Random Numbers Tables

DIRECTIONS FOR CRITICAL VALUES OF t—USING TABLE E.1

To find the appropriate value of t, first find the row that contains the number of degrees of freedom in your study. For the simple experiment, the degrees of freedom will be two less than the number of subjects. Then, read across until you find the column corresponding to the level of significance you have chosen. To be significant, the absolute value of t you calculate must be greater than the value you found in table E.1. For example, with $df = 40$ and $p = .05$ (two-tailed test), your t-value must be greater than 2.021 if it is to be statistically significant.

DIRECTIONS FOR CRITICAL VALUES OF THE F DISTRIBUTION—USING TABLE E.3

Before using table E.3, you should have decided the level of significance for your study. If you are using the conventional level of .05, you would use the table on page 585. If using a significance level of .01, turn to page 587 of this table.

Once you have found the **page** corresponding to your **significance level,** the next step is to look up the degrees of freedom for the effect (1st df) and the error term (2d df). Thus, if you were using the $p < .05$ significance level and you had 1 df for the effect and 25 for the error term, you would look on page 585 for the column and row corresponding to 1 and 25 degrees of freedom. There, you would find the critical value of 4.24. To be statistically significant at the .05 level, the F you obtained would have to be **greater** than 4.24.

To reiterate, to be statistically significant, the F-ratio must be greater than the value you find in the table. For example, if you use the conventional $p < .05$ level of significance and you have 2 df for the effect and 30 for the error term, you would find (on the next page) the critical value of 3.32. To be statistically significant at the .05 level, the obtained F-ratio would have to exceed 3.32.

	LEVEL OF SIGNIFICANCE FOR TWO-TAILED *t*-TEST			
df	0.1	0.05	0.02	0.01
1	6.314	12.706	31.821	63.657
2	2.920	4.303	6.965	9.925
3	2.353	3.182	4.541	5.841
4	2.132	2.776	3.747	4.604
5	2.015	2.571	3.365	4.032
6	1.943	2.447	3.143	3.707
7	1.895	2.365	2.998	3.499
8	1.860	2.306	2.896	3.355
9	1.833	2.262	2.821	3.250
10	1.812	2.228	2.764	3.169
11	1.796	2.201	2.718	3.106
12	1.782	2.179	2.681	3.055
13	1.771	2.160	2.650	3.012
14	1.761	2.145	2.624	2.977
15	1.753	2.131	2.602	2.947
16	1.746	2.120	2.583	2.921
17	1.740	2.110	2.567	2.898
18	1.734	2.101	2.552	2.878
19	1.729	2.093	2.539	2.861
20	1.725	2.086	2.528	2.845
21	1.721	2.080	2.518	2.831
22	1.717	2.074	2.508	2.819
23	1.714	2.069	2.500	2.807
24	1.711	2.064	2.492	2.797
25	1.708	2.060	2.485	2.787
26	1.706	2.056	2.479	2.779
27	1.703	2.052	2.473	2.771
28	1.701	2.048	2.467	2.763
29	1.699	2.045	2.462	2.756
30	1.697	2.042	2.457	2.750
40	1.684	2.021	2.423	2.704
60	1.671	2.000	2.390	2.660
120	1.658	1.980	2.358	2.617
∞	1.645	1.960	2.326	2.576

TABLE E.2 Upper Percentage Points of the Chi Square Distribution

df \ Q	0.250	0.100	0.050	0.025	0.010	0.005	0.001
1	1.32330	2.70554	3.84146	5.02389	6.63490	7.87944	10.828
2	2.77259	4.60517	5.99147	7.37776	9.21034	10.5966	13.816
3	4.10835	6.25139	7.81473	9.34840	11.3449	12.8381	16.266
4	5.38527	7.77944	9.48773	11.1433	13.2767	14.8602	18.467
5	6.62568	9.23635	11.0705	12.8325	15.0863	16.7496	20.515
6	7.84080	10.6446	12.5916	14.4494	16.8119	18.5476	22.458
7	9.03715	12.0170	14.0671	16.0128	18.4753	20.2777	24.322
8	10.2188	13.3616	15.5073	17.5346	20.0902	21.9550	26.125
9	11.3887	14.6837	16.9190	19.0228	21.6660	23.5893	27.877
10	12.5489	15.9871	18.3070	20.4831	23.2093	25.1882	29.588
11	13.7007	17.2750	19.6751	21.9200	24.7250	26.7569	31.264
12	14.8454	18.5494	21.0261	23.3367	26.2170	28.2995	32.909
13	15.9839	19.8119	22.3621	24.7356	27.6883	29.8194	34.528
14	17.1170	21.0642	23.6848	26.1190	29.1413	31.3193	36.123
15	18.2451	22.3072	24.9958	27.4884	30.5779	32.8013	37.697
16	19.3688	23.5418	26.2962	28.8454	31.9999	34.2672	39.252
17	20.4887	24.7690	27.5871	30.1910	33.4087	35.7185	40.790
18	21.6049	25.9894	28.8693	31.5264	34.8053	37.1564	42.312
19	22.7178	27.2036	30.1435	32.8523	36.1908	38.5822	43.820
20	23.8277	28.4120	31.4104	34.1696	37.5662	39.9968	45.315
21	24.9348	29.6151	32.6705	35.4789	38.9321	41.4010	46.797
22	26.0393	30.8133	33.9244	36.7807	40.2894	42.7956	48.268
23	27.1413	32.0069	35.1725	38.0757	41.6384	44.1813	49.728
24	28.2412	33.1963	36.4151	39.3641	42.9798	45.5585	51.179
25	29.3389	34.3816	37.6525	40.6465	44.3141	46.9278	52.620
26	30.4345	35.5631	38.8852	41.9232	45.6417	48.2899	54.052
27	31.5284	36.7412	40.1133	43.1944	46.9630	49.6449	55.476
28	32.6205	37.9159	41.3372	44.4607	48.2782	50.9933	56.892
29	33.7109	39.0875	42.5569	45.7222	49.5879	52.3356	58.302
30	34.7998	40.2560	43.7729	46.9792	50.8922	53.6720	59.703
40	45.6160	51.8050	55.7585	59.3417	63.6907	66.7659	73.402
50	56.3336	63.1671	67.5048	71.4202	76.1539	79.4900	86.661
60	66.9814	74.3970	79.0819	83.2976	88.3794	91.9517	99.607
70	77.5766	85.5271	90.5312	95.0231	100.425	104.215	112.317
80	88.1303	96.5782	101.879	106.629	112.329	116.321	124.839
90	98.6499	107.565	113.145	118.136	124.116	128.299	137.208
100	109.141	118.498	124.342	129.561	135.807	140.169	149.449
z_q	+0.6745	+1.2816	+1.6449	+1.9600	+2.3263	+2.5758	+3.0902

TABLE E.3 Critical Values of F for p .10

1ST df / 2ND df	1	2	3	4	5	6	7	8	9	10	12	15	20	24	30
1	39.86	49.50	53.59	55.83	57.24	58.20	58.91	59.44	59.86	60.19	60.71	61.22	61.74	62.00	62.26
2	8.53	9.00	9.16	9.24	9.29	9.33	9.35	9.37	9.38	9.39	9.41	9.42	9.44	9.45	9.46
3	5.54	5.46	5.39	5.34	5.31	5.28	5.27	5.25	5.24	5.23	5.22	5.20	5.18	5.18	5.17
4	4.54	4.32	4.19	4.11	4.05	4.01	3.98	3.95	3.94	3.92	3.90	3.87	3.84	3.83	3.82
5	4.06	3.78	3.62	3.52	3.45	3.40	3.37	3.34	3.32	3.30	3.27	3.24	3.21	3.19	3.17
6	3.78	3.46	3.29	3.18	3.11	3.05	3.01	2.98	2.96	2.94	2.90	2.87	2.84	2.82	2.80
7	3.59	3.26	3.07	2.96	2.88	2.83	2.78	2.75	2.72	2.70	2.67	2.63	2.59	2.58	2.56
8	3.46	3.11	2.92	2.81	2.73	2.67	2.62	2.59	2.56	2.54	2.50	2.46	2.42	2.40	2.38
9	3.36	3.01	2.81	2.69	2.61	2.55	2.51	2.47	2.44	2.42	2.38	2.34	2.30	2.28	2.25
10	3.29	2.92	2.73	2.61	2.52	2.46	2.41	2.38	2.35	2.32	2.28	2.24	2.20	2.18	2.16
11	3.23	2.86	2.66	2.54	2.45	2.39	2.34	2.30	2.27	2.25	2.21	2.17	2.12	2.10	2.08
12	3.18	2.81	2.61	2.48	2.39	2.33	2.28	2.24	2.21	2.19	2.15	2.10	2.06	2.04	2.01
13	3.14	2.76	2.56	2.43	2.35	2.28	2.23	2.20	2.16	2.14	2.10	2.05	2.01	1.98	1.96
14	3.10	2.73	2.52	2.39	2.31	2.24	2.19	2.15	2.12	2.10	2.05	2.01	1.96	1.94	1.91
15	3.07	2.70	2.49	2.36	2.27	2.21	2.16	2.12	2.09	2.06	2.02	1.97	1.92	1.90	1.87
16	3.05	2.67	2.46	2.33	2.24	2.18	2.13	2.09	2.06	2.03	1.99	1.94	1.89	1.87	1.84
17	3.03	2.64	2.44	2.31	2.22	2.15	2.10	2.06	2.03	2.00	1.96	1.91	1.86	1.84	1.81
18	3.01	2.62	2.42	2.29	2.20	2.13	2.08	2.04	2.00	1.98	1.93	1.89	1.84	1.81	1.78
19	2.99	2.61	2.40	2.27	2.18	2.11	2.06	2.02	1.98	1.96	1.91	1.86	1.81	1.79	1.76
20	2.97	2.59	2.38	2.25	2.16	2.09	2.04	2.00	1.96	1.94	1.89	1.84	1.79	1.77	1.74
21	2.96	2.57	2.36	2.23	2.14	2.08	2.02	1.98	1.95	1.92	1.87	1.83	1.78	1.75	1.72
22	2.95	2.56	2.35	2.22	2.13	2.06	2.01	1.97	1.93	1.90	1.86	1.81	1.76	1.73	1.70
23	2.94	2.55	2.34	2.21	2.11	2.05	1.99	1.95	1.92	1.89	1.84	1.80	1.74	1.72	1.69
24	2.93	2.54	2.33	2.19	2.10	2.04	1.98	1.94	1.91	1.88	1.83	1.78	1.73	1.70	1.67
25	2.92	2.53	2.32	2.18	2.09	2.02	1.97	1.93	1.89	1.87	1.82	1.77	1.72	1.69	1.66
26	2.91	2.52	2.31	2.17	2.08	2.01	1.96	1.92	1.88	1.86	1.81	1.76	1.71	1.68	1.65
27	2.90	2.51	2.30	2.17	2.07	2.00	1.95	1.91	1.87	1.85	1.80	1.75	1.70	1.67	1.64
28	2.89	2.50	2.29	2.16	2.06	2.00	1.94	1.90	1.87	1.84	1.79	1.74	1.69	1.66	1.63
29	2.89	2.50	2.28	2.15	2.06	1.99	1.93	1.89	1.86	1.83	1.78	1.73	1.68	1.65	1.62
30	2.88	2.49	2.28	2.14	2.05	1.98	1.93	1.88	1.85	1.82	1.77	1.72	1.67	1.64	1.61
40	2.84	2.44	2.23	2.09	2.00	1.93	1.87	1.83	1.79	1.76	1.71	1.66	1.61	1.57	1.54
60	2.79	2.39	2.18	2.04	1.95	1.87	1.82	1.77	1.74	1.71	1.66	1.60	1.54	1.51	1.48
120	2.75	2.35	2.13	1.99	1.90	1.82	1.77	1.72	1.68	1.65	1.60	1.55	1.48	1.45	1.41
∞	2.71	2.30	2.08	1.94	1.85	1.77	1.72	1.67	1.63	1.60	1.55	1.49	1.42	1.38	1.34

TABLE E.3 Critical Values of F for p < .05

1ST df / 2ND df	1	2	3	4	5	6	7	8	9	10	12	15	20	24	30
1	161.4	199.5	215.7	224.6	230.2	234.0	236.8	238.9	240.5	241.9	243.9	245.9	248.0	249.1	250.1
2	18.51	19.00	19.16	19.25	19.30	19.33	19.35	19.37	19.38	19.40	19.41	19.43	19.45	19.45	19.46
3	10.13	9.55	9.28	9.12	9.01	8.94	8.89	8.85	8.81	8.79	8.74	8.70	8.66	8.64	8.62
4	7.71	6.94	6.59	6.39	6.26	6.16	6.09	6.04	6.00	5.96	5.91	5.86	5.80	5.77	5.75
5	6.61	5.79	5.41	5.19	5.05	4.95	4.88	4.82	4.77	4.74	4.68	4.62	4.56	4.53	4.50
6	5.99	5.14	4.76	4.53	4.39	4.28	4.21	4.15	4.10	4.06	4.00	3.94	3.87	3.84	3.81
7	5.59	4.74	4.35	4.12	3.97	3.87	3.79	3.73	3.68	3.64	3.57	3.51	3.44	3.41	3.38
8	5.32	4.46	4.07	3.84	3.69	3.58	3.50	3.44	3.39	3.35	3.28	3.22	3.15	3.12	3.08
9	5.12	4.26	3.86	3.63	3.48	3.37	3.29	3.23	3.18	3.14	3.07	3.01	2.94	2.90	2.86
10	4.96	4.10	3.71	3.48	3.33	3.22	3.14	3.07	3.02	2.98	2.91	2.85	2.77	2.74	2.70
11	4.84	3.98	3.59	3.36	3.20	3.09	3.01	2.95	2.90	2.85	2.79	2.72	2.65	2.61	2.57
12	4.75	3.89	3.49	3.26	3.11	3.00	2.91	2.85	2.80	2.75	2.69	2.62	2.54	2.51	2.47
13	4.67	3.81	3.41	3.18	3.03	2.92	2.83	2.77	2.71	2.67	2.60	2.53	2.46	2.42	2.38
14	4.60	3.74	3.34	3.11	2.96	2.85	2.76	2.70	2.65	2.60	2.53	2.46	2.39	2.35	2.31
15	4.54	3.68	3.29	3.06	2.90	2.79	2.71	2.64	2.59	2.54	2.48	2.40	2.33	2.29	2.25
16	4.49	3.63	3.24	3.01	2.85	2.74	2.66	2.59	2.54	2.49	2.42	2.35	2.28	2.24	2.19
17	4.45	3.59	3.20	2.96	2.81	2.70	2.61	2.55	2.49	2.45	2.38	2.31	2.23	2.19	2.15
18	4.41	3.55	3.16	2.93	2.77	2.66	2.58	2.51	2.46	2.41	2.34	2.27	2.19	2.15	2.11
19	4.38	3.52	3.13	2.90	2.74	2.63	2.54	2.48	2.42	2.38	2.31	2.23	2.16	2.11	2.07
20	4.35	3.49	3.10	2.87	2.71	2.60	2.51	2.45	2.39	2.35	2.28	2.20	2.12	2.08	2.04
21	4.32	3.47	3.07	2.84	2.68	2.57	2.49	2.42	2.37	2.32	2.25	2.18	2.10	2.05	2.01
22	4.30	3.44	3.05	2.82	2.66	2.55	2.46	2.40	2.34	2.30	2.23	2.15	2.07	2.03	1.98
23	4.28	3.42	3.03	2.80	2.64	2.53	2.44	2.37	2.32	2.27	2.20	2.13	2.05	2.01	1.96
24	4.26	3.40	3.01	2.78	2.62	2.51	2.42	2.36	2.30	2.25	2.18	2.11	2.03	1.98	1.94
25	4.24	3.39	2.99	2.76	2.60	2.49	2.40	2.34	2.28	2.24	2.16	2.09	2.01	1.96	1.92
26	4.23	3.37	2.98	2.74	2.59	2.47	2.39	2.32	2.27	2.22	2.15	2.07	1.99	1.95	1.90
27	4.21	3.35	2.96	2.73	2.57	2.46	2.37	2.31	2.25	2.20	2.13	2.06	1.97	1.93	1.88
28	4.20	3.34	2.95	2.71	2.56	2.45	2.36	2.29	2.24	2.19	2.12	2.04	1.96	1.91	1.87
29	4.18	3.33	2.93	2.70	2.55	2.43	2.35	2.28	2.22	2.18	2.10	2.03	1.94	1.90	1.85
30	4.17	3.32	2.92	2.69	2.53	2.42	2.33	2.27	2.21	2.16	2.09	2.01	1.93	1.89	1.84
40	4.08	3.23	2.84	2.61	2.45	2.34	2.25	2.18	2.12	2.08	2.00	1.92	1.84	1.79	1.74
60	4.00	3.15	2.76	2.53	2.37	2.25	2.17	2.10	2.04	1.99	1.92	1.84	1.75	1.70	1.65
120	3.92	3.07	2.68	2.45	2.29	2.17	2.09	2.02	1.96	1.91	1.83	1.75	1.66	1.61	1.55
∞	3.84	3.00	2.60	2.37	2.21	2.10	2.01	1.94	1.88	1.83	1.75	1.67	1.57	1.52	1.46

TABLE E.3 Critical Values of F for $p < .025$

1ST df / 2ND df	1	2	3	4	5	6	7	8	9	10	12	15	20	24	30
1	647.8	799.5	864.2	899.6	921.8	937.1	948.2	956.7	963.3	968.6	976.7	984.9	993.1	997.2	1001
2	38.51	39.00	39.17	39.25	39.30	39.33	39.36	39.37	39.39	39.40	39.41	39.43	39.45	39.46	39.46
3	17.44	16.04	15.44	15.10	14.88	14.73	14.62	14.54	14.47	14.42	14.34	14.25	14.17	14.12	14.08
4	12.22	10.65	9.98	9.60	9.36	9.20	9.07	8.98	8.90	8.84	8.75	8.66	8.56	8.51	8.46
5	10.01	8.43	7.76	7.39	7.15	6.98	6.85	6.76	6.68	6.62	6.52	6.43	6.33	6.28	6.23
6	8.81	7.26	6.60	6.23	5.99	5.82	5.70	5.60	5.52	5.46	5.37	5.27	5.17	5.12	5.07
7	8.07	6.54	5.89	5.52	5.29	5.12	4.99	4.90	4.82	4.76	4.67	4.57	4.47	4.42	4.36
8	7.57	6.06	5.42	5.05	4.82	4.65	4.53	4.43	4.36	4.30	4.20	4.10	4.00	3.95	3.89
9	7.21	5.71	5.08	4.72	4.48	4.32	4.20	4.10	4.03	3.96	3.87	3.77	3.67	3.61	3.56
10	6.94	5.46	4.83	4.47	4.24	4.07	3.95	3.85	3.78	3.72	3.62	3.52	3.42	3.37	3.31
11	6.72	5.26	4.63	4.28	4.04	3.88	3.76	3.66	3.59	3.53	3.43	3.33	3.23	3.17	3.12
12.	6.55	5.10	4.47	4.12	3.89	3.73	3.61	3.51	3.44	3.37	3.28	3.18	3.07	3.02	2.96
13	6.41	4.97	4.35	4.00	3.77	3.60	3.48	3.39	3.31	3.25	3.15	3.05	2.95	2.89	2.84
14	6.30	4.86	4.24	3.89	3.66	3.50	3.38	3.29	3.21	3.15	3.05	2.95	2.84	2.79	2.73
15	6.20	4.77	4.15	3.80	3.58	3.41	3.29	3.20	3.12	3.06	2.96	2.86	2.76	2.70	2.64
16	6.12	4.69	4.08	3.73	3.50	3.34	3.22	3.12	3.05	2.99	2.89	2.79	2.68	2.63	2.57
17	6.04	4.62	4.01	3.66	3.44	3.28	3.16	3.06	2.98	2.92	2.82	2.72	2.62	2.56	2.50
18	5.98	4.56	3.95	3.61	3.38	3.22	3.10	3.01	2.93	2.87	2.77	2.67	2.56	2.50	2.44
19	5.92	4.51	3.90	3.56	3.33	3.17	3.05	2.96	2.88	2.82	2.72	2.62	2.51	2.45	2.39
20	5.87	4.46	3.86	3.51	3.29	3.13	3.01	2.91	2.84	2.77	2.68	2.57	2.46	2.41	2.35
21	5.83	4.42	3.82	3.48	3.25	3.09	2.97	2.87	2.80	2.73	2.64	2.53	2.42	2.37	2.31
22	5.79	4.38	3.78	3.44	3.22	3.05	2.93	2.84	2.76	2.70	2.60	2.50	2.39	2.33	2.27
23	5.75	4.35	3.75	3.41	3.18	3.02	2.90	2.81	2.73	2.67	2.57	2.47	2.36	2.30	2.24
24	5.72	4.32	3.72	3.38	3.15	2.99	2.87	2.78	2.70	2.64	2.54	2.44	2.33	2.27	2.21
25	5.69	4.29	3.69	3.35	3.13	2.97	2.85	2.75	2.68	2.61	2.51	2.41	2.36	2.24	2.18
26	5.66	4.27	3.67	3.33	3.10	2.94	2.82	2.73	2.65	2.59	2.49	2.39	2.28	2.22	2.16
27	5.63	4.24	3.65	3.31	3.08	2.92	2.80	2.71	2.63	2.57	2.47	2.36	2.25	2.19	2.13
28	5.61	4.22	3.63	3.29	3.06	2.90	2.78	2.69	2.61	2.55	2.45	2.34	2.23	2.17	2.11
29	5.59	4.20	3.61	3.27	3.04	2.88	2.76	2.67	2.59	2.53	2.43	2.32	2.21	2.15	2.09
30	5.57	4.18	3.59	3.25	3.03	2.87	2.75	2.65	2.57	2.51	2.41	2.31	2.20	2.14	2.07
40	5.42	4.05	3.46	3.13	2.90	2.74	2.62	2.53	2.45	2.39	2.29	2.18	2.07	2.01	1.94
60	5.29	3.93	3.34	3.01	2.79	2.63	2.51	2.41	2.33	2.27	2.17	2.06	1.94	1.88	1.82
120	5.15	3.80	3.23	2.89	2.67	2.52	2.39	2.30	2.22	2.16	2.05	1.94	1.82	1.76	1.69
∞	5.02	3.69	3.12	2.79	2.57	2.41	2.29	2.19	2.11	2.05	1.94	1.83	1.71	1.64	1.57

TABLE E.3 Critical Values of F for p < .01

2ND df \ 1ST df	1	2	3	4	5	6	7	8	9	10	12	15	20	24	30
1	4052	4999.5	5403	5625	5764	5859	5928	5982	6022	6056	6106	6157	6209	6235	6261
2	98.50	99.00	99.17	99.25	99.30	99.33	99.36	99.37	99.39	99.40	99.42	99.43	99.45	99.46	99.47
3	34.12	30.82	29.46	28.71	28.24	27.91	27.67	27.49	27.35	27.23	27.05	26.87	26.69	26.60	26.50
4	21.20	18.00	16.69	15.98	15.52	15.21	14.98	14.80	14.66	14.55	14.37	14.20	14.02	13.93	13.84
5	16.26	13.27	12.06	11.39	10.97	10.67	10.46	10.29	10.16	10.05	9.89	9.72	9.55	9.47	9.38
6	13.75	10.92	9.78	9.15	8.75	8.47	8.26	8.10	7.98	7.87	7.72	7.56	7.40	7.31	7.23
7	12.25	9.55	8.45	7.85	7.46	7.19	6.99	6.84	6.72	6.62	6.47	6.31	6.16	6.07	5.99
8	11.26	8.65	7.59	7.01	6.63	6.37	6.18	6.03	5.91	5.81	5.67	5.52	5.36	5.28	5.20
9	10.56	8.02	6.99	6.42	6.06	5.80	5.61	5.47	5.35	5.26	5.11	4.96	4.81	4.73	4.65
10	10.04	7.56	6.55	5.99	5.64	5.39	5.20	5.06	4.94	4.85	4.71	4.56	4.41	4.33	4.25
11	9.65	7.21	6.22	5.67	5.32	5.07	4.89	4.74	4.63	4.54	4.40	4.25	4.10	4.02	3.94
12	9.33	6.93	5.95	5.41	5.06	4.82	4.64	4.50	4.39	4.30	4.16	4.01	3.86	3.78	3.70
13	9.07	6.70	5.74	5.21	4.86	4.62	4.44	4.30	4.19	4.10	3.96	3.82	3.66	3.59	3.51
14	8.86	6.51	5.56	5.04	4.69	4.46	4.28	4.14	4.03	3.94	3.80	3.66	3.51	3.43	3.35
15	8.68	6.36	5.42	4.89	4.56	4.32	4.14	4.00	3.89	3.80	3.67	3.52	3.37	3.29	3.21
16	8.53	6.23	5.29	4.77	4.44	4.20	4.03	3.89	3.78	3.69	3.55	3.41	3.26	3.18	3.10
17	8.40	6.11	5.18	4.67	4.34	4.10	3.93	3.79	3.68	3.59	3.46	3.31	3.16	3.08	3.00
18	8.29	6.01	5.09	4.58	4.25	4.01	3.84	3.71	3.60	3.51	3.37	3.23	3.08	3.00	2.92
19	8.18	5.93	5.01	4.50	4.17	3.94	3.77	3.63	3.52	3.43	3.30	3.15	3.00	2.92	2.84
20	8.10	5.85	4.94	4.43	4.10	3.87	3.70	3.56	3.46	3.37	3.23	3.09	2.94	2.86	2.78
21	8.02	5.78	4.87	4.37	4.04	3.81	3.64	3.51	3.40	3.31	3.17	3.03	2.88	2.80	2.72
22	7.95	5.72	4.82	4.31	3.99	3.76	3.59	3.45	3.35	3.26	3.12	2.98	2.83	2.75	2.67
23	7.88	5.66	4.76	4.26	3.94	3.71	3.54	3.41	3.30	3.21	3.07	2.93	2.78	2.70	2.62
24	7.82	5.61	4.72	4.22	3.90	3.67	3.50	3.36	3.26	3.17	3.03	2.89	2.74	2.66	2.58
25	7.77	5.57	4.68	4.18	3.85	3.63	3.46	3.32	3.22	3.13	2.99	2.85	2.70	2.62	2.54
26	7.72	5.53	4.64	4.14	3.82	3.59	3.42	3.29	3.18	3.09	2.96	2.81	2.66	2.58	2.50
27	7.68	5.49	4.60	4.11	3.78	3.56	3.39	3.26	3.15	3.06	2.93	2.78	2.63	2.55	2.47
28	7.64	5.45	4.57	4.07	3.75	3.53	3.36	3.23	3.12	3.03	2.90	2.75	2.60	2.52	2.44
29	7.60	5.42	4.54	4.04	3.73	3.50	3.33	3.20	3.09	3.00	2.87	2.73	2.57	2.49	2.41
30	7.56	5.39	4.51	4.02	3.70	3.47	3.30	3.17	3.07	2.98	2.84	2.70	2.55	2.47	2.39
40	7.31	5.18	4.31	3.83	3.51	3.29	3.12	2.99	2.89	2.80	2.66	2.52	2.37	2.29	2.20
60	7.08	4.98	4.13	3.65	3.34	3.12	2.95	2.82	2.72	2.63	2.50	2.35	2.20	2.12	2.03
120	6.85	4.79	3.95	3.48	3.17	2.96	2.79	2.66	2.56	2.47	2.34	2.19	2.03	1.95	1.86
∞	6.63	4.61	3.78	3.32	3.02	2.80	2.64	2.51	2.41	2.32	2.18	2.04	1.88	1.79	1.70

This table is abridged from Table 18 of the *Biometrika Tables for Statisticians* (Vol. 1, 3rd ed.) by E. S. Pearson and H. O. Hartley, (Eds.), 1970, New York: Cambridge University Press. Used with the kind permission of the Biometrika trustees.

USING TABLE E.4 TO COMPUTE TREND ANALYSES

Suppose you had the following significant effect for sugar on aggression.

	df	SS	MS	F
Sugar Main Effect	2	126.95	63.47	6.35
Error Term	21	210.00	10.00	

How would you compute a trend analysis for this data? In other words, how would you calculate an F-ratio for the linear and quadratic effects so that you could complete the following ANOVA table?

	df	SS	MS	F
Sugar Main Effect	2	126.95	63.47	6.35
Linear Component	1			
Quadratic Component	1			
Error Term	21	210.00	10.00	

Before you generate an F-ratio, you must have a sum of squares. To compute the sum of squares for a trend, you must first get the sum of the scores for each condition. Simply add up all the scores for each condition or, if you prefer, multiply each condition's average by the number of scores making up each average. Thus, if one condition's mean was 10 and there were 5 scores making up that mean, the sum for that condition would be 5 × 10 or 50.

Next, arrange these totals, starting with the total for the lowest level of independent variable and ending with the total for the highest level of the independent variable. That is, place the sum for the condition with the lowest level of the independent variable first, the sum for the condition with the next highest level of the independent variable next, and so on. In our example, you would order your sums like so:

Total Number of Violent Instances per Condition

AMOUNT OF SUGAR	TOTAL NUMBER OF VIOLENT INSTANCES
0 mg	10.0
50 mg	50.0
100 mg	12.0

Now, you are ready to consult the tables of orthogonal polynomials in table E.4. Because this example involves three conditions, you would look for the three-condition table. The table reads:

Three-Condition Case

	TREND	
	1 (Linear)	2 (Quadratic)
CONDITION 1	−1	1
CONDITION 2	0	−2
CONDITION 3	1	1
WEIGHTING FACTOR	2	6

To get the numerator for the sum of squares for the linear trend, multiply the sum for the lowest level of the independent variable by the first value in the Linear column of the table (−1), the second sum by the second value in the Linear column of the table (0), and the third sum by the third value in the Linear column of the table (+1). Next, get a sum by adding these three products together. Then, square that sum. So, for the sugar example we just described, you would do the following calculations:

$$[(-1 \times 10) + (0 \times 50) + (1 \times 12)]^2$$

or

$$(-10 + 0 + 12)^2$$

or

$$(2)^2$$

or

$$4$$

To get the denominator for the sum of squares, multiply the weighting factor for the linear trend (2) by the number of observations in each condition. Because there were eight observations in each condition, the denominator would be 16 (2×8). The sum of squares linear would be the numerator (4) divided by the denominator (16) or .25.

Once you have computed the sum of squares for the linear trend, the rest is easy. All you have to do is compute an F-ratio by dividing the mean square linear by the mean square error and then see if that result is significant.

Calculating the mean square linear involves dividing the sum of squares linear by the degrees of freedom linear. Because the degrees of freedom for any trend is always 1.00, you could divide your sum of squares (.25) by 1.00 and get .25. Or, you could simply remember that a trend's mean square is always the same as its sum of squares.

Getting the mean square error is also easy: just find the mean square error in the printout that was used to test the overall main effect. In this example, that would be 10.0.

So, to get the F-value for this linear comparison, you would divide the mean square for the comparison (.25) by the mean square error used on the overall main effect (10.0). Thus, the F would be .25/10, or .025. Because the F is below 1.00, this result is obviously not significant.

But how large would the F have had to be to be significant? That depends on how many trends you were analyzing. If you had decided to look only at the linear trend, the significant F at the .05 level would have to exceed the value in the F-table for 1 degree of freedom (the df for any trend) and 21 degrees of freedom, the df for the error term. The value is 4.32.

However, if you are going to analyze more than one trend, you must correct for the number of Fs you are going to compute. The correction is simple: you divide the significance level you want (say .05), by the number of trends you will test. In this example, you are computing two Fs. Therefore, you should use the F for .05/2 or .025. So, in this example, you would only declare a trend significant if the F for that trend exceeds the tabled value for $F(1,21)$ at the .025 level: 5.83.

Obviously, the F for the linear component $F(1,21) = .025$, falls far short of the critical value of 5.83. But what about the quadratic component? To determine whether the quadratic component is significant, you would follow the same steps as before. The only difference is that you would look at the Quadratic column of the table instead of the Linear column.

Thus, you would first multiply the treatment sums by the constants listed in the Quadratic column, add them together, and square that sum. In other words,

$$((1 \times 10) + (-2 \times 50) + (1 \times 12))^2$$

or

$$(10 + (-100) + 12)^2$$

or

$$(-78)^2$$

or

$$6084$$

Then, you would divide 6084 by 8 (the number of observations in each condition) $\times$ 6 (the weighting factor for the quadratic effect). So, SS quadratic is 6084/(8 $\times$ 6) = 6084/48 = 126.7, as is the MS quadratic (SS (126.7)/ df (1) = MS (126.7)).

To get the F, you would divide the MS quadratic by MS error. Therefore, the F would be 126.7/10 = 12.67. As before, the critical value for the comparison is the F-value for the .025 significance level with 1 and 21 degrees of freedom: 5.83. Because our F of 12.67 exceeds the critical value of 5.83, we have a statistically significant quadratic trend.

So, our complete ANOVA table, including the linear and quadratic components, would be as follows:

	df	SS	MS	F
Sugar Main Effect	2	126.95	63.47	6.35*
Linear	1	0.25	0.25	0.02
Quadratic	1	126.70	126.70	12.67*
Error Term	21	210.00	10.00	

*Significant at .05 level.

From looking at the table, you see that if you add up the degrees of freedom for all the trends involved in the main effect (1 + 1), you get the total df for that main effect (2). More importantly, note that if you add up the sum of squares for the components (126.70 + .25), you get the sum of squares for the overall effect (126.95). This fact gives you a way to check your work. Specifically, if the total of the sums of squares for all the components does not add up to the sum of squares for the overall effect, you have made a mistake.

TABLE E.4 Coefficients of Orthogonal Polynomials

	3-Condition Case Trend		4-Condition Case Trend			5-Condition Case Trend			
Condition	1 (Lin)	2 (Quad)	1 (Lin)	2 (Quad)	3 (Cubic)	1 (Lin)	2 (Quad)	3 (Cubic)	4
1	−1	1	−3	1	−1	−2	2	−1	1
2	0	−2	−1	−1	3	−1	−1	2	−4
3	1	1	1	−1	−3	0	−2	0	6
4			3	1	1	1	−1	−2	−4
5						2	2	1	1
Weighting Factor	2	6	20	4	20	10	14	10	70

	6-Condition Case Trend					7-Condition Case Trend					
Condition	1 (Lin)	2 (Quad)	3 (Cubic)	4	5	1 (Lin)	2 (Quad)	3 (Cubic)	4	5	6
1	−5	5	−5	1	−1	−3	5	−1	3	−1	1
2	−3	−1	7	−3	5	−2	0	1	−7	4	−6
3	−1	−4	4	2	−10	−1	−3	1	1	−5	15
4	1	−4	−4	2	10	0	−4	0	6	0	−20
5	3	−1	−7	−3	−5	1	−3	−1	1	5	15
6	5	5	5	1	1	2	0	−1	−7	−4	−6
7						3	5	1	3	1	1
Weighting Factor	70	84	180	28	252	28	84	6	154	84	924

	8-Condition Case Trend						9-Condition Case Trend					
Condition	1 (Lin)	2 (Quad)	3 (Cubic)	4	5	6	1 (Lin)	2 (Quad)	3 (Cubic)	4	5	6
1	−7	7	−7	7	−7	1	−4	28	−14	14	−4	4
2	−5	1	5	−13	23	−5	−3	7	7	−21	11	−17
3	−3	−3	7	−3	−17	9	−2	−8	13	−11	−4	22
4	−1	−5	3	9	−15	−5	−1	−17	9	9	−9	1
5	1	−5	−3	9	15	−5	0	−20	0	18	0	−20
6	3	−3	−7	−3	17	9	1	−17	−9	9	9	1
7	5	1	−5	−13	−23	−5	2	−8	−13	−11	4	22
8	7	7	7	7	7	1	3	7	−7	−21	−11	−17
9							4	28	14	14	4	4
Weighting Factor	168	168	264	616	2184	264	60	2772	990	2002	468	1980

(Continued)

TABLE E.4 (Continued)

10-Condition Case Trend

Condition	1 (Lin)	2 (Quad)	3 (Cubic)	4	5	6
1	-9	6	-42	18	-6	3
2	-7	2	14	-22	14	-11
3	-5	-1	35	-17	-1	10
4	-3	-3	31	3	-11	6
5	-1	-4	12	18	-6	-8
6	1	-4	-12	18	6	-8
7	3	-3	-31	3	11	6
8	5	-1	-35	-17	1	10
9	7	2	-14	-22	-14	-11
10	9	6	42	18	6	3
Weighting Factor	330	132	8580	2860	780	660

11-Condition Case Trend

Condition	1 (Lin)	2 (Quad)	3 (Cubic)	4	5	6
1	-5	15	-30	6	-3	15
2	-4	6	6	-6	6	-48
3	-3	-1	22	-6	1	29
4	-2	-6	23	-1	-4	36
5	-1	-9	14	4	-4	-12
6	0	-10	0	6	0	-40
7	1	-9	-14	4	4	-12
8	2	-6	-23	-1	4	36
9	3	-1	-22	-6	-1	29
10	4	6	-6	-6	-6	-48
11	5	15	30	6	3	15
Weighting Factor	110	858	4290	286	156	11220

12-Condition Case Trend

Condition	1 (Lin)	2 (Quad)	3 (Cubic)	4	5	6
1	-11	55	-33	33	-33	11
2	-9	25	3	-27	57	-31
3	-7	1	21	-33	21	11
4	-5	-17	25	-13	-29	25
5	-3	-29	19	12	-44	4
6	-1	-35	7	28	-20	-20
7	1	-35	-7	28	20	-20
8	3	-29	-19	12	44	4
9	5	-17	-25	-13	29	25
10	7	1	-21	-33	-21	11
11	9	25	-3	-27	-57	-31
12	11	55	33	33	33	11
Weighting Factor	572	12012	5148	8008	15912	4488

13-Condition Case Trend

Condition	1 (Lin)	2 (Quad)	3 (Cubic)	4	5	6
1	-6	22	-11	99	-22	22
2	-5	11	0	-66	33	-55
3	-4	2	6	-96	18	8
4	-3	-5	8	-54	-11	43
5	-2	-10	7	11	-26	22
6	-1	-13	4	64	-20	-20
7	0	-14	0	84	0	-40
8	1	-13	-4	64	20	-20
9	2	-10	-7	11	26	22
10	3	-5	-8	-54	11	43
11	4	2	-6	-96	-18	8
12	5	11	0	-66	-33	-55
13	6	22	11	99	22	22
Weighting Factor	182	2002	572	68068	6188	14212

TABLE E.4 Continued

	14-Condition Case Trend						15-Condition Case Trend					
Condition	**1** (Lin)	**2** (Quad)	**3** (Cubic)	**4**	**5**	**6**	**1** (Lin)	**2** (Quad)	**3** (Cubic)	**4**	**5**	**6**
1	−13	13	−143	143	−143	143	−7	91	−91	1001	−1001	143
2	−11	7	−11	−77	187	−319	−6	52	−13	−429	1144	−286
3	−9	2	66	−132	132	−11	−5	19	35	−869	979	−55
4	−7	−2	98	−92	−28	227	−4	−8	58	−704	44	176
5	−5	−5	95	−13	−139	185	−3	−29	61	−249	−751	197
6	−3	−7	67	63	−145	−25	−2	−44	49	251	−1000	50
7	−1	−8	24	108	−60	−200	−1	−53	27	621	−675	−125
8	1	−8	−24	108	60	−200	0	−56	0	756	0	−200
9	3	−7	−67	63	145	−25	1	−53	−27	621	675	−125
10	5	−5	−95	−13	139	185	2	−44	−49	251	1000	50
11	7	−2	−98	−92	28	227	3	−29	−61	−249	751	197
12	9	2	−66	−132	−132	−11	4	−8	−58	−704	−44	176
13	11	7	11	−77	−187	−319	5	19	−35	−869	−979	−55
14	13	13	143	143	143	143	6	52	13	−429	−1144	−286
15							7	91	91	1001	1001	143
Weighting Factor	910	728	97240	136136	235144	497420	280	37128	39780	6446460	1058480	426360

This table is adapted from Table VII of *Statistics* (pp. 662–664) by W. L. Hays, 1981, New York: Holt, Rinehart & Winston. Copyright © 1982 by Holt, Rinehart & Winston, Inc. Adapted by permission.

USING TABLE E.5 TO COMPUTE POST HOC TESTS

Post hoc tests, such as the Tukey test, can be used after finding a significant main effect for a multilevel factor. These tests help determine which conditions are significantly different from one another.

To see how you could use table E.5 to compute post hoc tests, suppose that an investigator uses twenty-four subjects (eight in each group) to examine the effect of color (blue, green, or yellow) on mood. As you can see from the following table, the investigator's ANOVA table reveals a significant effect of color.

SOURCE	SUM OF SQUARES	DEGREES OF FREEDOM	MEAN SQUARE	F
Color	64	2	32.0	4.0*
Error	168	**21**	**8.0**	

*Significant at .05 level.

The means for the three color conditions are

BLUE	GREEN	YELLOW
10.0	5.0	8.0

Now, the question is Which conditions differ from one another? Does yellow cause a different mood than green? Does blue cause a different mood than yellow? To find out, we need to do a post hoc test. For this example, we will do the Tukey test.

The formula for the Tukey test is

$$\frac{\text{Mean 1} - \text{Mean 2}}{\sqrt{(MSE \times 1/\text{number of observations per condition})}}$$

Because the mean square error is 8 (see original ANOVA table) and there are eight subjects in each group, the denominator in this example will always be:

$$\sqrt{(8 \times \tfrac{1}{8})}$$

or

$$\sqrt{(\tfrac{1}{8})}$$

or

$$\sqrt{1}$$

or

$$1$$

The numerator will change, depending on what means you are comparing. Thus, if you are comparing blue and green, the numerator would be $10 - 5$ or 5. So, to see whether the blue and green conditions differ significantly, you would do the following calculations.

$$\frac{\underset{\text{(blue mean) (green mean)}}{10.0 - 5.0}}{\sqrt{(8 \times \tfrac{1}{8})}} = \frac{5.0}{\sqrt{1}} = \frac{5.0}{1.0} = 5.0$$

To find out whether 5.0 is significant, go to table E.5 and look for column 3 because you have three means you are comparing. Then, go down and look at the row numbered 21 because you have 21 degrees of freedom in your error term (as you can see by looking at the original ANOVA table). The value in that table is 3.57. This is the critical value that you will use in all your comparisons. If your Tukey statistic for a pair of means is larger than this critical value, there is a significant difference between conditions. Because 5.0 is greater than 3.57, your result is significant at the .05 level.

But, do blue and yellow differ? To find out, compute the Tukey statistic

$$\frac{10.0 - 8.0}{\sqrt{(8 \times \tfrac{1}{8})}} = \frac{2.0}{\sqrt{1}} = \frac{2.0}{1.0} = 2.0$$

Because 2.0 is less than our critical value of 3.57, the difference between blue and yellow is not statistically significant at the .05 level.

Do yellow and green differ?

$$\frac{8.0 - 50.0}{\sqrt{(8 \times \frac{1}{8})}} = \frac{3.0}{\sqrt{1}} = \frac{3.0}{1.0} = 3.0$$

Because 3.0 is less than our critical value of 3.57, the difference between yellow and green is not statistically significant at the .05 level.

TABLE E.5 Critical Values for the Tukey Test for p < .05

df_{error}	αFW	NUMBER OF MEANS																			αFW	df_{error}
		2	3	4	5	6	7	8	9	10	11	12	13	14	15	16	17	18	19	20		
5	.05	3.64	4.60	5.22	5.67	6.03	6.33	6.58	6.80	6.99	7.17	7.32	7.47	7.60	7.72	7.83	7.93	8.03	8.12	8.21	.05	5
	.01	5.70	6.98	7.80	8.42	8.91	9.32	9.67	9.97	10.24	10.48	10.70	10.89	11.08	11.24	11.40	11.55	11.68	11.81	11.93	.01	
6	.05	3.46	4.34	4.90	5.30	5.63	5.90	6.12	6.32	6.49	6.65	6.79	6.92	7.03	7.14	7.24	7.34	7.43	7.51	7.59	.05	6
	.01	5.24	6.33	7.03	7.56	7.97	8.32	8.61	8.87	9.10	9.30	9.48	9.65	9.81	9.95	10.08	10.21	10.32	10.43	10.54	.01	
7	.05	3.34	4.16	4.68	5.06	5.36	5.61	5.82	6.00	6.16	6.30	6.43	6.55	6.66	6.76	6.85	6.94	7.02	7.10	7.17	.05	7
	.01	4.95	5.92	6.54	7.01	7.37	7.68	7.94	8.17	8.37	8.55	8.71	8.86	9.00	9.12	9.24	9.35	9.46	9.55	9.65	.01	
8	.05	3.26	4.04	4.53	4.89	5.17	5.40	5.60	5.77	5.92	6.05	6.18	6.29	6.39	6.48	6.57	6.65	6.73	6.80	6.87	.05	8
	.01	4.75	5.64	6.20	6.62	6.96	7.24	7.47	7.68	7.86	8.03	8.18	8.31	8.44	8.55	8.66	8.76	8.85	8.94	9.03	.01	
9	.05	3.20	3.95	4.41	4.76	5.02	5.24	5.43	5.59	5.74	5.87	5.98	6.09	6.19	6.28	6.36	6.44	6.51	6.58	6.64	.05	9
	.01	4.60	5.43	5.96	6.35	6.66	6.91	7.13	7.33	7.49	7.65	7.78	7.91	8.03	8.13	8.23	8.33	8.41	8.49	8.57	.01	
10	.05	3.15	3.88	4.33	4.65	4.91	5.12	5.30	5.46	5.60	5.72	5.83	5.93	6.03	6.11	6.19	6.27	6.34	6.40	6.47	.05	10
	.01	4.48	5.27	5.77	6.14	6.43	6.67	6.87	7.05	7.21	7.36	7.49	7.60	7.71	7.81	7.91	7.99	8.08	8.15	8.23	.01	
11	.05	3.11	3.82	4.26	4.57	4.82	5.03	5.20	5.35	5.49	5.61	5.71	5.81	5.90	5.98	6.06	6.13	6.20	6.27	6.33	.05	11
	.01	4.39	5.15	5.62	5.97	6.25	6.48	6.67	6.84	6.99	7.13	7.25	7.36	7.46	7.56	7.65	7.73	7.81	7.88	7.95	.01	
12	.05	3.08	3.77	4.20	4.51	4.75	4.95	5.12	5.27	5.39	5.51	5.61	5.71	5.80	5.88	5.95	6.02	6.09	6.15	6.21	.05	12
	.01	4.32	5.05	5.50	5.84	6.10	6.32	6.51	6.67	6.81	6.94	7.06	7.17	7.26	7.36	7.44	7.52	7.59	7.66	7.73	.01	
13	.05	3.06	3.73	4.15	4.45	4.69	4.88	5.05	5.19	5.32	5.43	5.53	5.63	5.71	5.79	5.86	5.93	5.99	6.05	6.11	.05	13
	.01	4.26	4.96	5.40	5.73	5.98	6.19	6.37	6.53	6.67	6.79	6.90	7.01	7.10	7.19	7.27	7.35	7.42	7.48	7.55	.01	
14	.05	3.03	3.70	4.11	4.41	4.64	4.83	4.99	5.13	5.25	5.36	5.46	5.55	5.64	5.71	5.79	5.85	5.91	5.97	6.03	.05	14
	.01	4.21	4.89	5.32	5.63	5.88	6.08	6.26	6.41	6.54	6.66	6.77	6.87	6.96	7.05	7.13	7.20	7.27	7.33	7.39	.01	
15	.05	3.01	3.67	4.08	4.37	4.59	4.78	4.94	5.08	5.20	5.31	5.40	5.49	5.57	5.65	5.72	5.78	5.85	5.90	5.96	.05	15
	.01	4.17	4.84	5.25	5.56	5.80	5.99	6.16	6.31	6.44	6.55	6.66	6.76	6.84	6.93	7.00	7.07	7.14	7.20	7.26	.01	

(Continued)

TABLE E.5 Continued

16	.05	3.00	3.65	4.05	4.33	4.56	4.74	4.90	5.03	5.15	5.26	5.35	5.44	5.52	5.59	5.66	5.73	5.79	5.84	5.90
	.01	4.13	4.79	5.19	5.49	5.72	5.92	6.08	6.22	6.35	6.46	6.56	6.66	6.74	8.82	6.90	6.97	7.03	7.09	7.15
17	.05	2.98	3.63	4.02	4.30	4.52	4.70	4.86	4.99	5.11	5.21	5.31	5.39	5.47	5.54	5.61	5.67	5.73	5.79	5.84
	.01	4.10	4.74	5.14	5.43	5.66	5.85	6.01	6.15	6.27	6.38	6.48	6.57	6.66	6.73	6.81	6.87	6.94	7.00	7.05
18	.05	2.97	3.61	4.00	4.28	4.49	4.67	4.82	4.96	5.07	5.17	5.27	5.35	5.43	5.50	5.57	5.63	5.69	5.74	5.79
	.01	4.07	4.70	5.09	5.38	5.60	5.79	5.94	6.08	6.20	6.31	6.41	6.50	6.58	6.65	6.73	6.79	6.85	6.91	6.97
19	.05	2.96	3.59	3.98	4.25	4.47	4.65	4.79	4.92	5.04	5.14	5.23	5.31	5.39	5.46	5.53	5.59	5.65	5.70	5.75
	.01	4.05	4.67	5.05	5.33	5.55	5.73	5.89	6.02	6.14	6.25	6.34	6.43	6.51	6.58	6.65	6.72	6.78	6.84	6.89
20	.05	2.95	3.58	3.96	4.23	4.45	4.62	4.77	4.90	5.01	5.11	5.20	5.28	5.36	5.43	5.49	5.55	5.61	5.66	5.71
	.01	4.02	4.64	5.02	5.29	5.51	5.69	5.84	5.97	6.09	6.19	6.28	6.37	6.45	6.52	6.59	6.65	6.71	6.77	6.82
24	.05	2.92	3.53	3.90	4.17	4.37	4.54	4.68	4.81	4.92	5.01	5.10	5.18	5.25	5.32	5.38	5.44	5.49	5.55	5.59
	.01	3.96	4.55	4.91	5.17	5.37	5.54	5.69	5.81	5.92	6.02	6.11	6.19	6.26	6.33	6.39	6.45	6.51	6.56	6.61
30	.05	2.89	3.49	3.85	4.10	4.30	4.46	4.60	4.72	4.82	4.92	5.00	5.08	5.15	5.21	5.27	5.33	5.38	5.43	5.47
	.01	3.89	4.45	4.80	5.05	5.24	5.40	5.54	5.65	5.76	5.85	5.93	6.01	6.08	6.14	6.20	6.26	6.31	6.36	6.41
40	.05	2.86	3.44	3.79	4.04	4.23	4.39	4.52	4.63	4.73	4.82	4.90	4.98	5.04	5.11	5.16	5.22	5.27	5.31	5.36
	.01	3.82	4.37	4.70	4.93	5.11	5.26	5.39	5.50	5.60	5.69	5.76	5.83	5.90	5.96	6.02	6.07	6.12	6.16	6.21
60	.05	2.83	3.40	3.74	3.98	4.16	4.31	4.44	4.55	4.65	4.73	4.81	4.88	4.94	5.00	5.06	5.11	5.15	5.20	5.24
	.01	3.76	4.28	4.59	4.82	4.99	5.13	5.25	5.36	5.45	5.53	5.60	5.67	5.73	5.78	5.84	5.89	5.93	5.97	6.01
120	.05	2.80	3.36	3.68	3.92	4.10	4.24	4.36	4.47	4.56	4.64	4.71	4.78	4.84	4.90	4.95	5.00	5.04	5.09	5.13
	.01	3.70	4.20	4.50	4.71	4.87	5.01	5.12	5.21	5.30	5.37	5.44	5.50	5.56	5.61	5.66	5.71	5.75	5.79	5.83
∞	.05	2.77	3.31	3.63	3.86	4.03	4.17	4.29	4.39	4.47	4.55	4.62	4.68	4.74	4.80	4.85	4.89	4.93	4.97	5.01
	.01	3.64	4.12	4.40	4.60	4.76	4.88	4.99	5.08	5.16	5.23	5.29	5.35	5.40	5.45	5.49	5.54	5.57	5.61	5.65

This table is abridged from Table 29 of the *Biometrika Tables for Statisticians* (Vol. 1 3rd ed.) by E. S. Pearson and H. O. Hartley, (Eds.), 1970, New York: Cambridge University Press. Used with the kind permission of the Biometrika Trustees.

597

TABLE E.6 Random Numbers

12	13	98	21	39	36	74	39	83	77	79	37	89	4	20	21	91	98	90
39	31	69	14	22	50	40	54	12	71	98	25	26	20	61	52	93	90	76
53	10	28	46	41	29	74	46	64	39	4	47	55	98	22	69	9	15	34
29	95	79	80	35	0	9	65	42	99	69	90	22	16	34	81	44	3	24
20	59	12	35	63	52	35	2	56	40	85	2	85	2	58	26	94	48	0
2	19	26	78	95	1	4	72	81	80	60	49	67	32	10	28	90	72	25
37	40	96	68	6	95	55	82	16	36	58	68	68	69	7	11	31	17	39
1	0	13	31	19	63	90	75	17	33	49	13	54	32	26	66	38	1	7
63	88	20	20	75	16	70	26	75	22	48	6	1	89	99	21	48	6	9
64	93	100	50	95	76	94	84	25	67	98	94	23	75	40	33	86	87	76
95	13	66	49	11	48	20	54	51	65	63	33	98	80	13	84	70	85	93
18	35	10	64	79	70	5	55	92	41	92	14	63	52	94	56	5	40	55
40	62	28	72	82	81	51	7	45	9	26	47	34	47	47	95	45	38	82
33	7	97	68	76	44	73	73	0	80	55	84	77	74	27	5	17	57	75
15	60	83	28	56	78	9	27	52	79	68	90	48	12	51	55	77	48	10
58	1	28	1	64	50	28	8	69	70	96	26	100	6	31	89	0	31	91
71	94	59	17	43	50	34	12	14	45	30	79	63	76	72	18	67	87	47
73	24	19	13	98	0	64	44	90	20	13	66	81	97	81	11	38	7	37
97	82	87	98	29	97	69	24	62	100	12	28	84	86	10	69	25	66	93
2	23	76	42	76	87	64	99	5	7	13	33	19	18	37	96	73	95	91
17	85	42	29	80	53	92	6	44	100	18	24	31	5	6	37	63	93	42
83	42	53	54	93	63	19	59	30	80	75	8	91	48	79	2	40	6	56
30	3	41	73	63	76	18	82	8	13	30	78	45	43	77	77	99	98	40
64	7	19	80	64	4	34	30	65	63	11	72	20	15	22	30	82	77	51
90	24	25	98	38	79	45	84	30	49	64	98	48	25	14	0	12	63	67
20	40	25	87	45	88	52	19	33	17	63	60	62	46	12	59	99	5	88
87	62	78	25	71	57	6	98	59	79	34	20	77	87	83	12	74	29	12
54	10	53	29	37	82	5	77	54	4	69	7	40	18	32	85	37	73	42
45	35	11	73	30	16	3	75	56	58	98	46	93	58	96	29	73	6	71
69	17	54	7	86	29	18	86	98	5	56	78	0	78	24	34	73	95	11
72	60	78	88	27	45	80	66	25	37	73	7	67	29	27	12	90	60	97
93	9	58	84	88	90	73	47	49	53	95	62	28	11	61	0	91	49	32
74	75	27	81	28	48	4	65	87	69	32	14	46	52	52	36	21	13	70
36	42	53	92	96	19	52	38	2	22	47	26	94	34	57	81	28	49	74

TABLE E.6 Continued

5	28	80	31	99	77	39	23	69	0	15	49	100	2	22	64	73	92	53
29	71	48	4	87	32	17	90	89	9	99	34	58	8	61	73	98	48	89
90	94	19	80	70	36	2	17	48	63	82	39	85	26	65	27	81	69	83
62	66	48	74	86	6	66	41	15	65	6	41	85	57	84	64	70	39	64
67	54	3	54	23	40	25	95	93	55	59	46	77	55	49	82	26	8	87
75	27	62	15	81	36	22	26	69	42	44	91	55	0	84	48	68	65	5
70	19	7	100	94	53	81	76	73	40	22	58	49	42	96	18	66	89	8
75	7	9	20	58	92	41	42	79	26	91	44	63	87	45	21	23	15	6
55	70	10	23	25	73	91	72	29	47	93	58	21	75	80	52	9	12	36
83	42	62	53	55	12	11	54	19	2	45	43	67	13	5	74	30	93	11
94	20	76	23	65	72	55	27	44	19	10	72	50	67	83	18	67	22	49
51	10	72	9	59	47	66	32	17	6	75	8	54	22	37	3	46	83	95
99	50	22	2	92	9	98	9	40	23	34	8	63	58	49	31	70	39	83
9	12	3	23	2	0	82	75	36	63	71	19	78	26	66	63	16	75	7
20	40	50	29	51	82	81	47	73	69	74	100	80	37	14	67	1	90	92
90	92	54	52	74	0	88	71	45	49	38	54	80	2	85	42	75	47	20
25	6	92	30	19	31	22	41	0	22	79	87	84	61	6	19	67	97	60
13	12	94	76	29	61	50	67	29	76	27	70	97	16	83	88	100	22	48
91	77	51	3	92	85	46	22	0	58	84	64	87	93	94	94	13	98	41
29	12	39	35	32	47	30	81	40	32	37	8	48	81	50	77	18	39	7
43	96	86	14	91	24	22	85	16	51	42	37	41	100	94	76	45	50	67
57	44	72	45	87	21	7	29	26	82	69	99	10	39	76	29	11	17	85
63	10	10	76	7	75	19	91	2	31	45	94	54	72	10	48	52	7	12
34	28	11	95	4	82	51	7	69	53	93	36	81	66	93	88	15	73	54

This table is taken from the Random numbers table in Appendix D of *Foundations of Behavioral Research*, 3rd ed. (pp. 642–643) by F. N. Kerlinger, 1986, New York: Holt, Rinehart & Winston. Copyright © 1986 by Holt, Rinehart & Winston. Reprinted by permission.

F

SAMPLE RESEARCH PAPER

Adapted from Frank, M. G. & Gilovich, T. (1988). The dark side of self- and social-perception: Black uniforms and aggression in professional sports. *Journal of Personality and Social Psychology*, 54, 74–85. Used with the kind permission of Mark Frank, Thomas Gilovich, and the American Psychological Association.

The Dark Side of Self Perception:

Black Uniforms and Aggression

Mark G. Frank and Thomas Gilovich

Cornell University

Abstract

Black is viewed as the color of evil and death in virtually all cultures. With this association in mind, we were interested in whether a cue as subtle as the color of a person's clothing might have a significant impact on the wearer's behavior. To test this possibility, we performed a laboratory experiment to determine whether wearing a black uniform can increase a person's inclination to engage in aggressive behavior. We found that subjects who wore black uniforms showed a marked increase in intended aggression relative to those wearing white uniforms. Our discussion focuses on the theoretical implications of these data for an understanding of the variable, or "situated," nature of the self.

The Dark Side of Self Perception:

Black Uniforms and Aggression

A convenient feature of the traditional American Western film was the ease of which the viewer could distinguish the good guys from the bad guys: The bad guys wore the black hats. Of course, film directors did not invent this connection between black and evil, but built upon an existing association that extends deep into our culture and language. When a terrible thing happens on a given day, we refer to it as a "black day," as when the Depression was ushered in by the infamous "Black Thursday." We can hurt ourselves by "blackening" our reputation or be hurt by others by being "blacklisted," or "blackballed," or "blackmailed" (Williams, 1964). When the Chicago White Sox deliberately lost the 1919 World Series as part of a betting scheme, they became known as the Chicago Black Sox, and to this day the "dark" chapter in American sports history is known as the Black Sox Scandal. In a similar vein, Muhammed Ali has observed that we refer to white cake as "angel food cake" and dark cake as "devil's food cake."

These anecdotes concerning people's negative associations to the color black are reinforced by the research literature on color meanings. In one representative experiment, groups of college students and seventh graders who were asked to make semantic differential rating of colors were found to associate black with evil, death, and badness (Williams & McMurty, 1970). Moreover, this association between black and evil is not strictly an American or Western phenomenon, because college students in Germany, Denmark, Hong Kong, and India (Williams, Moreland, & Underwood, 1970) and Ndembu tribesmen in Central Africa (Turner, 1967) all report that the color black connoted evil and death. Thus, Adams and Osgood (1973) concluded that black is seen, in virtually all cultures, as the color of evil and death.

The intriguing question is whether these associations influence people's behavior in important ways. For example, does wearing black clothing lead the wearer to actually act more aggressively?

This possibility is suggested by studies on anonymity and "deindividuation" which show that a person's clothing can affect the amount of aggression he or she expresses. In one study, female subjects in a "learning" experiment were asked to deliver shocks to another subject whenever she made a mistake. Under the pretense of minimizing individual identities, one half of the subjects wore nurses uniforms (a prosocial cue), and the other half wore outfits resembling Ku Klux Klan uniforms (an antisocial cue). As predicted, subjects who wore nurses uniforms delivered less shock to the "learner" than did subjects who wore the Ku Klux Klan uniforms, which demonstrates that the cues inherent in certain clothes can influence the wearer's aggressive behavior (Johnson & Downing, 1979).

Although such studies are suggestive, they involve rather contrived situations that raise troubling questions of experimental demand. Accordingly, we decided to seek parallel evidence for a link between clothing cues and aggressiveness by examining the effect of a much more subtle cue, the color of a person's uniform.

There are a couple of difficulties that confront any attempt to test whether wearing a black uniform tends to make a person more aggressive. First, any such test is fraught with the usual ethical problems involved in all research on human aggression. Second, since black is associated with violence, observers may be biased when judging the behavior of subjects wearing black. The usual solution to these twin problems is to use some version of the bogus shock paradigm (Buss, 1961). However, we chose not to use this procedure because of the difficulty in finding subjects who — given the publicity of Milgram's (1965, 1974) work — would not view the proceedings with extreme suspicion.

Our solution to these problems was to collect "behavioroid" data (cf. Carlsmith, Ellsworth, & Aronson, 1976) in the form of the subjects' intended aggressive behavior. Volunteers for an experiment on competition were led to believe that they would be vying against other subjects in several competitive events. They were also led to believe that they could exercise some control over which events they were to participate in by selecting their 5 most preferred events from a list of 12. The 12 events varied in the amount of aggressiveness they called for, allowing us to use subjects' choices as a measure of their reading to engage in aggressive action. By means of a suitable cover story, we elicited subjects' choices twice: once individually when wearing their usual clothes, and later as a team of 3 wearing black or white jerseys. We hypothesized that wearing black jerseys would induce subjects to view themselves as more mean and aggressive and thus would produce more of a "group shift" toward aggressive choices by subjects wearing black jerseys than by those wearing white (Drabman & Thomas, 1977; Jaffe, Shapir, & Yinon, 1981; Jaffe & Yinnon, 1979).

Method

Overview

Subjects participated in groups of 3 in an experiment ostensibly on the "psychology of competition." Each group was told that they would be competing against another team of 3 on a series of five games of everyone's choosing. To find out their preferences, they were asked to individually rank order 5 activities from a group of 12. After making their choices, the subjects were outfitted in either white or black uniforms in the guise of facilitating team identity. Then, while the experimenter was supposedly administering instructions to the other team, the 3 subjects were told to discuss their individual choices and to decide as a group on the rank ordering of the five activities they would like to include in the competition. This second ranking allowed us to assess whether the subjects would choose more aggressive games as a group after donning black uniforms than after putting on white uniforms. Finally, as an auxiliary measure of aggression, subjects were administered a brief version of Murray's (1943) Thematic Apperception Test (TAT) to assess their level of aggressive ideation.

Subjects

The subjects were 72 male students from Cornell University who were paid $3 for their participation. They were run in groups of 3, with the members of each group unacquainted with one another.

Procedure

As the subjects reported for the experiment they were brought together in one room and led to believe that another group of subjects was assembling in a different room. Subjects were told, that

You will be competing, as a team, on a series of five games

against another group of three subjects who are waiting in the

next room. I matched the two teams for size as you came in, so the

contests should be fair. This study is designed to mimic real-life

competition as closely as possible...[and so]...we want you to

choose the games you want to play.

Subjects were then given a list of descriptions of 12 games and were asked to indicate, individually, which games they would like to play. They were asked to choose 5 of the 12 games and to rank order those 5. After reminding the subjects not to discuss their choices with one another, the experimenter left the room, ostensibly to elicit the choices of the other team.

Upon his return, the experimenter collected the subjects' individual choices and stated that "now I would like you to make a group decision as to which games you will play, because many times people's preferences are so divergent that we need to use a group choice to serve as a tie-breaker when deciding on which games to play." The experimenter further explained that "to make the experiment more like real-world competition and to build team cohesion, I would like you to put these uniforms on over your shirts. From now on you will be referred to as the black [white] team." The subjects were then given black or white uniforms with silver duct-tape numerals (7,8, and 11) on the backs.

The experimenter once again left the room to allow the subjects to make their group choices and then returned after 5 minutes. He then explained,

> Now that I have everyone's individual and team selections, I will
> go and set up the five games that received the most votes. While I
> am doing this, I want you to complete a standard psychological
> task to get all of you in the same state of mind before we start.

Subjects were asked to write a brief story about a scene depicted in a TAT card (Card 18 BM from Murray's, 1943, original series). Subjects were given 4 minutes to write a story based on the following questions: (a) What is happening in the picture? (b) What is being thought by the characters in the picture? (c) What has led up to this picture? and (d) What will happen to the characters in the picture?

After 4 minutes the experimenter returned, collected the TAT protocols, and thoroughly debriefed the subjects. All subjects seemed surprised (and many disappointed) to learn that the experiment was over. The debriefing interview

also made it clear that none of the subjects had entertained the possibility
that the color of the uniforms might have been the focus of the experiment.

Dependent Measures

The primary measure in this experiment was the level of aggressiveness
involved in the games subjects wanted to include in the competition. A group
of 30 subjects had earlier rated a set of descriptions of 20 games in terms of
how much aggressiveness they involved. The 12 games that had received the most
consistent ratings and that represented a wide spectrum of aggressiveness were
then used as the stimulus set in this experiment. These 12 games were ranked
in terms of these aggressiveness ratings and assigned point values consistent
with their ranks, from the most aggressive (12, 11, and 10 points for "chicken
fights," "dart gun duel," and "burnout," respectively) to the least aggressive
(1, 2, and 3 points for "basket shooting," "block stacking, "and "putting
contest," respectively). Subjects were asked to choose the five games that
they wanted to include in the competition and to rank order their five choices
in terms of preference. To get an overall measure of the aggressiveness of
each subject's preferences, we multiplied the point value of his first choice
by 5, his second choice by 4, and so forth, and then added these five
products. When comparing the choices made by the subjects individually
(without uniforms), we compared the average individual choices of the 3
subjects with their group choice.

The second dependent measure in this experiment was subjects' responses
to the TAT card. Subjects' TAT stories were scored on a 5-point aggressiveness
scale (Feshbach, 1955). Stories devoid of aggression received a score of 1,
those with a little indirect aggression a score of 2, those with considerable
indirect or a little direct aggression a 3, those with direct physical
aggression a 4, and those with graphic violence a 5. These ratings were made

by two judges who were unaware of the subjects' condition. The judges' ratings were in perfect agreement on 47% of the stories and were within one point on another 48%.

Results

The mean levels of aggressiveness in subjects' individual and group choices are presented in Table 1. As expected, there was no difference in subjects' individual choices across the two groups ($\underline{MS}$ = 113.4 vs. 113.5), because they were not wearing different-colored uniforms at the time these choices were made. However, the subjects who donned black uniforms subsequently chose more aggressive games (mean change in aggressiveness = 16.8), whereas those who put on white uniforms showed no such shift (mean change = 2.4). A 2 X 2 mixed between/within ANOVA of subjects' choices yielded a significant interaction between uniform color and individual/group choice $\underline{F}(1,22) = 6.14$ $\underline{p}<.05$, indicating that the pattern of choices made by subjects in black uniforms was different from that of those wearing white. Wearing black uniforms induced subjects to seek out more aggressive activities, matched-pairs $\underline{t}(11) = 3.21$, $\underline{p}<.01$; wearing white uniforms did not, matched-pairs $\underline{t}(11) = 1.00$, $\underline{ns}$.

_____

Insert Table 1 about here

_____

The subjects who wore black uniforms also tended to express more aggressive ideation ($\underline{M}$ = 3.20) in their TAT stories than did subjects wearing white uniforms ($\underline{M}$ = 2.89), although this difference was not significant, $\underline{t}$<1.

Discussion

The results of this experiment support the hypothesis that wearing a black uniform can increase a person's inclination to engage in aggressive behavior. Subjects who wore black uniforms showed a marked increase in intended aggression relative to those wearing white uniforms.

It should be noted, however, that our demonstration involved only intended aggression. It did not involve actual aggression. It would have been interesting to have allowed our subjects to compete against one another in their chosen activities and seen whether those in black jerseys performed more aggressively. We refrained from doing so because of ethical and methodological difficulties (i.e., the difficulty of objectively measuring aggression, especially given that observers tend to be biased toward viewing people wearing black uniforms as being more aggressive). Nevertheless, the results of this experiment make the important point that in a competitive setting at least, merely donning a black uniform can increase a person's willingness to seek out opportunities for aggression. If the wearing of a black uniform can have such an effect in the laboratory, there is every reason to believe that it would have even stronger effects on the playing field (or rink), where many forms of aggression are considered acceptable behavior.

One question raised by this research concerns the generality of the effect of uniform color on aggression. It is very unlikely that donning any black uniform in any situation would make a person more inclined to act aggressively. We do not believe, for example, that the black garments worn by Catholic clergymen or Hassidic Jews don't make them any more aggressive than their secular peers. Rather, it would seem to be the case that the semantic link between the color black and evil and aggressiveness would be particularly salient in domains that already possess overtones of competition, confrontation, and physical aggression.

With this in mind, any speculation about other domains in which analogous effects might be obtained should center on those areas that also possess inherent elements of force and confrontation. The actions of uniformed police officers and prison guards may be one such area. Is it the case, in other words, that the color of the uniforms worn by such individuals influences the amount of aggressiveness they exhibit in performing their duties? This intriguing possibility could readily be tested by examining archival indicies of aggression and violence involving police officers and prison guards, such as charges of police brutality and assaults on police officers (cf. Mauro, 1984). These analyses could involve both cross-sectional comparisons of police departments (or prisons) with different-colored uniforms, as well as longitudinal comparisons within departments that have changed uniform colors. We should point out, however,that we strongly doubt whether there are any police departments or penal institutions in this country that issue black uniforms to their personnel, possibly out of implicit recognition of this article's central thesis. Nevertheless, the uniforms of police officers and prison guards do vary in color a great deal, from dark blue to light khaki. Thus, one might still expect to find an effect of uniform color on aggressiveness if the subsequent research alluded to above indicates that the uniform effect we have documented is indeed more than a simple dichotomous difference between black and nonblack uniforms.

Perhaps the most important question raised by this research concerns the exact mechanisms by which the color of a uniform might affect the behavior of the wearer. Our own explanation for this phenomenon centers upon the implicit demands on one's behavior generated by wearing a particular kind of uniform. To wear a certain uniform is to assume a particular identity, an identity that not only elicits a certain response from others but also compels a particular pattern of behavior from the wearer (Stone, 1962). Wearing an athletic uniform, for example, thrusts one into the role of athlete, and leads one to "try on" the image that such a role conveys. When the uniform is that of a football or hockey player, part of that image — and therefore part of what one "becomes" — involves toughness, aggressiveness, and "machismo." These elements are particularly salient when the color of one's uniform is black. Just as observers see those in black uniforms as tough, mean, and aggressive, so too does the person wearing that uniform (Bem, 1972). Having inferred such an identity, the person then remains true to the image by acting more aggressively in certain prescribed contexts.

More broadly construed, then, our results serve as a reminder of the flexible or "situated" nature of the self (Alexander & Knight, 1971;

Goffman, 1959; Mead, 1934; Stone, 1962). Different situations, different roles, and even different uniforms can induce us to try on different identities. Around those who are socially subdued or shy, we become a vivacious extrovert; around true socialites, we may retreat into the more reserved role of resident intellectual. In the presence of family members, we play the role of learned scholar granted us by our advanced degrees; in the company of Nobel laureates, we think of ourselves less as scientists and more as amateur musicians, devoted fathers and mothers, or fun-loving globetrotters. Some of these identities that we try to adopt do not suit us, and they are abandoned. This sustains our belief that personalities are stable and reassures us that at our core lies a "true" self. To a surprising degree, however, the identities we are led to adopt do indeed fit, and we continue to play them out in the appropriate circumstances. Perhaps the best evidence for this claim is the existence of identity conflict, such as that experienced by college students who bring their roommates home to meet their parents. This is often a disconcerting experience for many students because they cannot figure out how they should behave or "who they should be" — with their parents they are one person and with their friends they are someone else entirely.

The present investigation demonstrates how a seemingly trivial environmental variable, the color of one's uniform, can induce such a shift in a person's identity. This is not to suggest, however, that in other contexts the direction of causality might not be reversed. The black uniforms worn by gangs like the Hell's Angels, for example, are no doubt deliberately chosen precisely because they convey the desired malevolent image. Thus, as in the world portrayed in the typical

American Western, it may be that many inherently evil characters choose to wear black. However, the present investigation makes it clear that in certain contexts at least, some people become the bad guys because they wear black.

References

Adams, F. M., & Osgood, C. E. (1973). A cross-cultural study of the
    affective meanings of color. Journal of Cross-Cultural Psychology, 4,
    135-156.

Alexander, C. N., & Knight, G. (1971). Situated identities and social
    psychological experimentation. Sociometry, 34, 65-82.

Bem, D. J. (1972). Self-perception theory. In L. Berkowitz (Ed.),
    Advances in experimental social psychology (Vol.6, pp.1-62). New
    York: Academic Press.

Carlsmith, J. M., Ellsworth, P. C., & Aronson, E. (1976). Methods of
    research in social psychology. Reading, MA: Addison-Wesley.

Drabman, R. S., & Thomas, M. H. (1977). Children's imitation of
    aggressive and prosocial behavior when viewing alone and in pairs.
    Journal of Communication, 27, 199-205.

Feshbach, S. (1955). The drive-reducing function of fantasy behavior.
    Journal of Abnormal and Social Psychology, 50, 3-11.

Goffman, E. (1959). The presentation of self in everyday life. New York:
    Doubleday.

Jaffe, Y., Shapir, N., & Yinon, Y. (1981). Aggression and its
    escalation.Journal of Cross-Cultural Psychology, 12, 21-36.

Johnson, R. D. & Downing, L. L. (1979). Deindividuation and valence of
    cues: Effects of prosocial and antisocial behavior. Journal of
    Personality and Social Psychology, 37, 1532-1538.

Mauro, R. (1984). The constable's new clothes: Effects of uniforms on
    perceptions and problems of police officers. Journal of Applied
    Social Psychology, 14, 42-56.

Mead, G. H. (1934). <u>Mind, self, and society</u>. Chicago: University of

Chicago Press.

Milgram, S. (1965). Some conditions of obedience and disobedience to

authority. <u>Human Relations</u>, <u>18</u>, 57-76.

Milgram, S. (1974). <u>Obedience to authority</u>. New York: Harper.

Murray, H. A. (1943). <u>Thematic Apperception Test manual</u>. Cambridge, MA:

Harvard University Press.

Stone, G. P. (1962). Appearance and the self. In A. M. Rose (Ed.), <u>Human

behavior and social process</u> (pp. 86-118). Boston: Houghton Mifflin.

Turner, V. (1967). <u>The forest of symbols: Aspects of Ndembu ritual</u>.

Ithaca, NY: Cornell University Press.

Williams, J. E. (1964). Connotations of color names among Negroes and

Caucasians. <u>Perceptual and Motor Skills</u>, <u>18</u>, 721-731.

Williams, J. E., & McMurty, C. A. (1970). Color connotations among

Caucasian 7th graders and college students. <u>Perceptual and Motor

Skills</u>, <u>30</u>, 701-713.

Williams, J. E., Moreland, J. K., & Underwood, W. I. (1970).

Connotations of color names in the U.S., Europe, and Asia. <u>Journal of

Social Psychology</u>, <u>82</u>, 3-14.

Table 1

Mean Level of Aggressiveness Contained in Subjects' Chosen Activities,

by Condition

Uniform color	Mean individual choice (without uniforms)		Group choice (with uniforms)		Change in aggressiveness	
	M	SD	M	SD	M	SD
White	113.4	23.9	115.8	25.4	+2.4	8.5
Black	113.5	18.4	130.3	22.9	+16.8	18.1

GLOSSARY

A-B-A reversal design   A single-subject or small-*n* design in which baseline measurements are made of the target behavior (A), then an experimental treatment is given (B), and the target behavior is measured again (A).

Abstract   A short, one-page summary of a research proposal or article.

Analysis of variance (ANOVA)   A statistical test for analyzing data from experiments. Especially useful if the experiment has more than one independent variable or more than two levels of an independent variable.

Archival data   Data from existing records and public archives.

Baseline   A measure of the dependent variable as it occurs without the experimental manipulation. Used as a standard of comparison in single-subject and small-*n* designs.

Between groups variance (mean square treatment, mean square between)   A measure of the combined effects of random error and treatment. This quantity is compared to the within groups variance in ANOVA. It is the top half of the F-ratio. If the treatment has no effect, the between groups variance should be roughly the same as the within groups variance. If the treatment has an effect, the between groups variance should be larger than the within groups variance.

Blind   A strategy of making the subject or researcher unaware of what condition the subject is in.

Blocked design   Dividing experimental subjects into groups (blocks) on a subject variable (e.g., low-IQ block and high-IQ block). Then, randomly assigning members from each block to an experimental condition. Ideally, a blocked design will give you more power than a simple, between subjects design.

Carry-over   The effects of a treatment condition persist into later conditions. Often a problem with single-subject and within subjects designs because you do not know whether the subject's behavior is due to the treatment just administered or to a lingering effect of a treatment administered some time ago.

Ceiling effect   The effect of treatment(s) is underestimated because the dependent measure is not sensitive to psychological states above a certain level. The measure puts an artificially low ceiling on how high a subject may score.

Central limit theorem   If numerous large samples from the same population are taken, and you were to plot the mean for each of these samples, your plot would resemble a normal curve—even if the population from which you took those samples was not normally distributed.

Chi square (χ^2)   A statistical test you can use to determine whether two or more variables are related. Best used when you have nominal data.

Coefficient of determination   The square of the correlation coefficient; tells the degree to which knowing one variable helps to know another. Can range from 0 (knowing a subject's score on one variable tells you absolutely nothing about the subject's score on the second variable) to 1.00 (knowing a subject's score on one variable tells you exactly what the subject's score on the second variable was).

Cohort effects   The effect of belonging to a given generation (e.g., the '60s generation). Sometimes, people mistakenly assume that a difference between people of different age groups is the result of biological aging when the difference is really due to the two groups having different backgrounds because they grew up in different eras.

Compensation   When subjects in the control group try to make up for being deprived of a desired treatment. May be a problem in field research when the treatment is a training program or some other desired treatment.

Conceptual replication   An attempt to demonstrate an experimental phenomenon with an entirely new paradigm or set of measures or manipulations.

Concurrent validity   Validating a measure by giving your subject the new measure and some established measures of the construct at the same time (concurrently). You then correlate performance on the established measures with performance on the new measure. Concurrent validity is to be distinguished from predictive validity; predictive validity being seeing how well your measure predicts scores on measures that you will administer to the subject at some future time.

Confounding variables   Variables that are unintentionally manipulated. If confounding variables are present in a study, it is hard to say what caused the effect.

Construct validity   The degree to which a study measures and/or manipulates what the researcher claims it does.

Content analysis   A method used to categorize a wide range of open-ended (unrestricted) responses.

Content validity   With many measures and tests, subjects are asked a few questions from a large body of knowledge. A test has content validity if its content is a fair sample of the larger body of knowledge. Students hope that their psychology tests have content validity.

Control group   Subjects who do not receive the experimental treatment. These subjects are compared to the treatment group to determine whether the treatment had an effect.

Convenience sampling   Choosing to include people in your sample simply because they are easy (convenient) to survey.

Converging operations   A set of related studies that differ only in that they use different measures and/or manipulations of the construct.

Correlation coefficient   A number that can vary from -1.00 to $+1.00$ and indicates the kind of relationship that exists between two variables (positive or negative as indicated by the sign of the correlation coefficient) and the strength of the relationship (indicated by the extent to which the coefficient differs from 0).

Counterbalancing   Any technique used to control order effects by distributing order effects across treatment conditions.

Criterion validity   The degree to which the measure relates to other measures of the construct. Concurrent validity and predictive validity are types of criterion validity.

Cross-over (disordinal) interaction   When an independent variable has one kind of effect in the presence of one level of a second independent variable, but the opposite kind of effect in the presence of a different level of the second independent variable. Example: Getting closer to someone may increase their attraction to you if you have complimented them, but may decrease their attraction to you if you have just insulted them. Called a cross-over interaction because the lines in a graph of the interaction will cross. Called disordinal interaction because it cannot be explained by having ordinal rather than interval data.

Cross-sectional design   Trying to study the effects of age by comparing different age groups at the same point in time. For example, today, you might compare a group of five-year-olds with a group of ten-year-olds. To be distinguished from longitudinal designs where you study the same people at different times (e.g., study a group of five-year-olds today, then return five years later and study them again when they are ten).

Crosstabs   Tables of percentages used to compare different groups' responses; allows for an examination of the relationships among variables.

Crucial studies Studies that put two theories into competition.

Curvilinear A relationship between an independent and dependent variable that is graphically represented by a curved line.

Debriefing Giving subjects the details of a study at the end of their participation. Proper debriefing is one of the researcher's most serious obligations.

Deduction Applying a general rule to a specific situation.

Demand characteristics Characteristics of the study that suggest to the subject how the researcher wants the subject to behave.

Demographics Characteristics of a group, such as sex, age, social class.

Demoralization An effect of subjects knowing that they are being denied the preferred treatment. Subjects may then feel victimized and give up. A problem in field research if some subjects get training that may improve their promotability but others get no treatment at all.

Dependent groups *t*-test A statistical test used with interval or ratio data to test differences between two conditions on a single dependent variable. Differs from the between groups *t*-test or independent groups *t*-test in that it is only to be used when you are getting two scores from each subject (within groups design) or when you are using a matched pairs design.

Dependent variable The factor that the experimenter predicts is affected by the independent variable. The subject's response that the experimenter is measuring.

Diffusion of treatment When the treatment given to the treatment group is spread to the no-treatment group by treatment group subjects. For example, a professor hands out sample tests to one section of a class, but not to the other. Students who get the sample test, make copies and give them to their friends in the no-treatment class. May result in a failure to observe any difference between groups and thus falsely conclude the treatment has no effect.

Direct replication Repeating a study as exactly as possible, usually to determine whether or not the same results will be obtained.

Discriminant validity When a measure does not correlate significantly with variables from which it should differ. Example: A violence measure might have a degree of discriminant validity if it does not correlate with measures of love and desire for world peace.

Double-barreled question Several questions embedded into a single question (e.g., Are you happy and mad?).

Double-blind When neither the subject nor the person running the subject is aware of what treatment the subject has received.

Empty control group A group that does not get any kind of treatment. The group gets nothing, not even a placebo. Usually, because of subject and experimenter biases that may result from such a group, you will want to avoid using an empty control group.

Experimental group Subjects who are randomly assigned to receive the treatment.

Experimental hypothesis A prediction that the treatment will cause an effect.

Experimental realism When a study engages the subject so much that the subject is not merely playing a role (helpful subject, good person). The subject is not treating the experimental situation as a trivial, make-believe or pretend world.

Exploratory study A study investigating (exploring) a new area of research.

Ex post facto research When a researcher goes back, after the research has been completed, looking to test hypotheses that were not formulated prior to the beginning of the study. The researcher is trying to take advantage of hindsight. Often, an attempt to salvage something out of a study that did not turn out as planned.

External validity The degree to which the results of a study can be generalized to other subjects, settings, and times.

Extraneous factors Nontreatment factors.

Factorial experiment An experiment that examines two or more independent variables (factors) at a time.

Failure to follow protocol effect Contamination caused when investigators deviate from the protocol.

Fatigue effects Decreased performance on a task due to being tired or less enthusiastic as a study continues.

Field experiment An experiment performed in a nonlaboratory setting.

Fixed alternatives Items on a test or questionnaire, in which a person must choose an answer from among a few specified alternatives.

Floor effect The effect of treatment(s) is underestimated because the dependent measure artificially restricts how low scores can be.

Functional relationship The shape of a relationship.

Grand mean The mean of all the scores in a study. Often used when doing the calculations for an ANOVA.

History effect A subject's scores change between pretest and posttest because his environment has changed between pretest and posttest.

Hypothesis A testable prediction.

Hypothesis guessing When subjects alter their behavior to conform to their guess as to what the research hypothesis is. Can be a serious threat to construct validity, especially if subjects guess right.

Hypothesis testing The use of inferential statistics to determine whether the relationship found between two or more variables in a particular sample holds true in the population or whether the observed relationship is due to sampling error.

Hypothetical construct An entity that cannot be observed directly with our present technology (e.g., love, motivation, short-term memory).

Independence Factors are independent when they are not causally or correlationally linked.

Independent random assignment Randomly determining for each individual subject which condition they will be in.

Independent variable The variable being manipulated by the experimenter. Subjects are assigned to level of independent variable by independent random assignment.

Induction Creating a general rule by seeing similarities among several specific situations.

Inferential statistics Procedures for determining the reliability and generality of a particular research finding.

Informed consent If subjects agree to take part in a study after they have been told what is going to happen to them, you have their informed consent.

Instrumentation effect Apparent treatment effect being due to changes in the measuring instrument.

Interaction When you need to know how much of another variable subjects have received to say what the effect of a given variable is, you have an interaction between those two variables. If you graph the results from an experiment that has two or more independent variables, and the lines you draw between your points are not parallel, you have an interaction.

Internal consistency The degree to which each question in a scale taps the same construct.

Internal validity The degree to which a study establishes that a factor causes a difference in behavior.

Interobserver reliability An index of the degree to which different raters give the same behavior similar ratings.

Interval data Data that gives you numbers that can be meaningfully ordered along a scale (from lowest to highest) and in which equal intervals (distances) between numbers represent equal psychological distances (e.g., the difference between a rating of 3 and a rating of 2 is the same psychological distance as the difference between a rating of 5 and a rating of 4).

Interviewer bias When the interviewer influences subjects' responses by verbally or nonverbally rewarding "correct" responses.

Known groups technique Determining the validity of a measure by seeing whether groups known to differ on a characteristic differ on a measure of that characteristic (e.g., ministers should differ from atheists on a measure of religiosity).

Latency A type of dependent measure in which we measure not what the subject responds to but how long it takes to respond. Often, latency is used as a measure in reaction-time tasks.

Leading question Questions structured to lead respondents to the answer the researcher wants (e.g., "You like this book, don't you?").

Likert-type items Items that typically ask subjects whether they strongly agree, agree, are neutral, disagree, or strongly disagree with a certain statement. These items are assumed to yield interval data.

Linear A relationship between an independent and dependent variable that is graphically represented by a straight line.

Longitudinal design Trying to estimate the effects of age by testing one group of people repeatedly over time (e.g., testing them when they were five, again when they were ten, etc.).

Loose protocol effect Variations in procedure because the written procedures (the protocol) is not detailed enough. These variations in procedure may result in researcher bias.

Main effect (overall main effect) The overall or average effect of an independent variable.

Matched pairs design An experimental design in which the subjects are paired off by matching them on some variable assumed to be correlated with the dependent variable. Then, for each matched pair, one member is randomly assigned to one treatment condition, the other gets the other treatment condition. This design usually has more power than a simple, between groups experiment.

Matching Choosing your groups so that they are identical (they match) on certain characteristics.

Maturation Changes in subjects due to natural development.

Mean A measure of central tendency computed by dividing the sum of a set of scores by the number of scores in the set.

Median split The procedure of dividing subjects into two groups based on whether they are above or below the median (middle score).

Mixed designs An experimental design that contains both between subjects and within subjects manipulations of the independent variables.

Mortality (Attrition) Subjects dropping out of a study before the study is completed.

Multiple-baseline design A single-subject or small-n design in which different behaviors receive baseline periods of varying lengths prior to the introduction of the treatment variable. For example, a manager might collect baseline data on employee absenteeism, tardiness, and cleanliness. Then, the manager would reward (treatment) cleanliness while continuing to collect data on all three variables. Then, the manager would reward punctuality, etc.

Multiple operations When several different measures of the same construct are included in the same study.

Mundane realism Extent to which the research setting or task resembles real life.

Naturalistic observation A technique of observing events as they occur in their natural setting.

Negative correlation An inverse relationship between two variables (e.g., number of suicide attempts and happiness).

Nominal scale data Qualitative data; different scores do not represent different amounts of a characteristic (quantity). Instead, they represent different kinds of characteristics (qualities).

Nonequivalent control group design In quasi-experiments, a comparison group that is not determined by random assignment. Researcher hopes that this group is equivalent to the treatment group (before the treatment group received the treatment, of course), but it probably is not.

Nonreactive measures Measurements that are taken without changing the subject's behavior; also referred to as unobtrusive measures.

Null hypothesis The hypothesis that there is no relationship between two or more variables.

Null results Results that fail to dispute the null hypothesis. They fail to provide convincing evidence that the factors are related. Could mean that no relationship exists or it could mean that your design lacks the power to find the relationship.

Observer bias   Bias created by the observer seeing what the observer wants or expects to see.

Open-ended items   Questions that do not provide fixed response alternatives.

Operational definition   A publicly observable way to measure or manipulate a variable; a "recipe" for how you are going to measure or manipulate your factors.

Ordinal data   Numbers that can be meaningfully ordered from lowest to highest. With ordinal data, you know a subject with a high score has more of a characteristic than a subject with a low score. But you do not know how much more. For example, with ranked data, you know the top-ranked student has a higher score than the second-ranked student, but how much higher? You do not know if you only have ranked data. Furthermore, someone with a rank of 1 might be way ahead of the number 2-ranked scorer, but the number 2 scorer may be only slightly ahead of the number 3 scorer.

Ordinal interaction   Reflects the fact that an independent variable seems to have more of an effect under one level of a second independent variable than under another level. If you graph an ordinal interaction, the lines will not be parallel, but they will not cross. Called an ordinal interaction because the interaction, the failure of the lines to be parallel, may be an illusion. The independent variable may have the same effect under all levels of the second independent variable, but because equal psychological distances are not reflected by equal distances on your measuring scale (the difference between a 1 and a 4 is the same, in terms of amount of a construct, as is the difference between a 6 and a 7). In short, the interaction may result from having ordinal rather than interval data.

Parameter estimation   The use of inferential statistics to estimate certain characteristics of the population (parameters) from a sample of that population.

Parameters   Measurements describing populations; often inferred from statistics, which are measurements describing a sample.

Parsimonious   Explaining a broad range of phenomena with only a few principles.

Participant observation   An observation procedure in which the observer participates with those being observed.

Phi (ϕ) coefficient   A correlation coefficient to be used when both variables are measured on the nominal scale.

Placebo   A "pseudo-treatment"; allows experimenters to test the effects of expecting to get a treatment.

Positive correlation   A relationship between two variables where the two variables tend to vary together—when one increases, the other tends to increase. (E.g., height and weight: the taller one is, the more one tends to weigh; the shorter one is, the less one tends to weigh.)

Post hoc test   Usually refers to a statistical test that has been performed after an ANOVA has obtained a significant effect for a factor. Because the ANOVA only says that at least two of the levels of the independent variable differ from one another, post hoc tests are performed to find out which levels differ from one another.

Posttest   Testing subjects on the dependent measure after they have received the treatment.

Power   The probability of rejecting the null hypothesis in a statistical test when it is in fact false. The ability to find significant differences when differences truly exist.

Practice effects   The change in a score on a test (usually a gain) resulting from previous practice with the test.

Pretest   When subjects are tested on the dependent measure before they get the treatment. After getting the treatment, subjects will probably be given the dependent measure task again (the posttest).

Pretest-posttest design   Each subject is given the pretest, administered the treatment, then given the posttest.

Quasi-experiment   A study that resembles an experiment except that random assignment played no role in determining which subjects got which level of treatment. Usually have less internal validity than experiments.

Quota sampling   Making sure you get the desired numbers of (meet your quotas for) certain types of people (certain age groups, minorities, etc.). This method does not involve random sampling and usually gives you a less representative sample than random sampling would. It may, however, be an improvement over convenience sampling.

Random error   Variation in scores due to unsystematic, chance factors.

Random sampling   A sample that has been randomly selected from a population.

Ratio scale   The highest form of measurement. With ratio scale numbers, the difference between any two consecutive numbers is the same (see interval scale). But in addition to having interval scale properties, in ratio scale measurement, a zero score means the total absence of a quality. (Thus, Fahrenheit is not a ratio scale measure of temperature because 0° Fahrenheit does not mean there is no temperature. Absolute zero, 0° Kelvin, on the other hand, does mean the complete absence of temperature.) If you have ratio scale numbers, you can meaningfully form ratios between scores. If IQ scores were ratio (they are not, very few measurements in psychology are), you could say that someone with a 60 IQ was twice as smart as someone with a 30 IQ (a ratio of 2 to 1). Furthermore, you could say that someone with a 0 IQ had absolutely no intelligence whatsoever.

Regression to the mean   The tendency for scores that are extremely unusual to revert back to more normal levels on the retest.

Reliability   A general term, often referring to the degree to which a subject would get the same score if retested (test-retest reliability). More generally, reliability refers to the degree to which scores are free from random error.

Replication factor   A factor sometimes included in a factorial design to see whether an effect replicates (occurs again) if different stimulus materials are used. For example, an investigator wants to see if a new memory strategy is superior to a conventional one. Instead of having all the subjects memorize the same story, the researcher assigns different subjects to get different stories. The different stories are the replication factor in the study. The researcher hopes that the memory strategy manipulation will have the same effect regardless of what story is used. But, if story type matters (there is an interaction between memory strategy and story type), the researcher might do further research to understand why the effect was not as general as had been expected.

Researcher effect   Ideally, you hope that the results from a study would be the same no matter who was running the subjects. However, it is possible that the results may be affected by the researcher. If more than one researcher is running subjects for a given study, researcher may be included as a factor in the design to determine if different researchers get different results.

Researcher expectancy effect   When a researcher's expectations affect the results. This is a type of researcher bias.

Research realism   A study that involves the subject so that the subject is less likely to play a role during the study.

Response set   Habitual way of responding on a test that is independent of a particular test item (e.g., a subject might always check "agree" no matter what the statement is).

Restriction of range   To observe a sizeable correlation between two variables, both must be allowed to vary widely (if one variable does not vary, the variables cannot vary together). Occasionally, investigators fail to find a relationship between variables because they only study one or both variables over a highly restricted range. For example, comparing NFL offensive linemen and saying that weight has nothing to do with playing offensive line in the NFL on the basis of your finding that great offensive tackles do not weigh much more than poor offensive tackles. Problem: You only compared people who ranged in weight from 285–300.

Sampling statistics   The science of inferring the characteristics of a population from a sample.

Scatterplot   A graph made by plotting the scores of individuals on two variables (e.g., plotting each subject's height and weight). By looking at this graph, you should get an idea of what kind of relationship (positive, negative, zero) exists between the two variables.

Selection bias   Apparent treatment effects being due to comparing groups that differed even before the treatment was administered (comparing apples with oranges).

Selection by maturation interaction   The groups started out the same on the pretest, but afterwards developed at different rates or in different directions.

Self-administered questionnaire   A questionnaire filled out in the absence of an investigator.

Semistructured questionnaire   A survey constructed around a core of standard questions; however, the interviewer may expand on any question in order to explore a given response in greater depth.

Sensitivity   The degree to which a measure is capable of distinguishing between subjects having different amounts of a construct.

Sensitization   After getting several different treatments and performing the dependent variable task several times, subjects may realize (become sensitive to) what the hypothesis is.

Sequential designs   Designs that attempt to disentangle cohort, age, and history effects.

Simple main effect   Imagine a factorial experiment where you have two levels of attractiveness (ugly, pretty) and two levels of communication style (praising, insulting). If you were to look just at the difference between liking for the pretty person and liking for the ugly person in the praising condition (totally ignoring the insult condition), you would be looking at the simple main effect of attractiveness in the praising condition. To find the overall main effect for attractiveness, you would have to average this with the simple main effect of attractiveness in the insult condition.

Single-blind   To reduce either subject biases or researcher biases, you might use a single-blind experiment in which either the subject (if you are most concerned about subject bias) or the person running subjects (if you are most concerned about researcher bias) is unaware of who is receiving what level of the treatment.

Single-subject designs   Designs that require only a single subject. These designs are common in operant conditioning and psychophysics research.

Social desirability   A bias resulting from subjects giving responses that make them look good rather than giving honest responses.

Spurious   A relationship between two variables is said to be spurious if the two variables do not affect one another but are instead related because of some other variable. For example, the relationship between ice cream sales and rapes in New York is spurious, not because it does not exist (it does!) but because ice cream does not cause rape and rape does not cause ice cream sales. Beware of spuriousness whenever you look at correlational research.

Standard deviation   A measure of the extent to which individual scores deviate from the population mean.

Standard error of the difference   An index of the degree to which random sampling error may cause two sample means representing the same populations to differ.

Standard error of the mean   An index of the degree to which random sampling error may cause the sample mean to be an inaccurate estimate of the population mean.

Statistical regression   The tendency for extreme scores on some variable to be closer to the group mean when remeasured due to unreliability of measurement.

Statistical significance   When, thanks to statistics, we can be confident, beyond a reasonable doubt (usually 95% sure), that the relationship observed was not due to fluke random error but represents a real relationship.

Stratified random sampling   Making sure that

the sample is similar to the population in certain respects (e.g., certain percentage of women, etc.) and then randomly sampling from these groups (strata). Has all the advantages of random sampling with even greater accuracy.

Straw theory An oversimplified version of an existing theory. Opponents of a theory may present and attack a straw version of that theory, but claim they have attacked the theory itself.

Structured questionnaire A survey in which all respondents are asked a standard list of questions in a standard order.

Subject biases (Subject effects) Ways the subject can bias the results (guessing the hypothesis and playing along, giving the socially correct response, etc.).

Summated scores When you have several Likert-type questions that all tap the same dimension (e.g., attitude toward democracy), you could add up each subject's responses from the different questions to get an overall or summated score.

Systematic replication A study that varies from the original study only in some minor aspect.

Temporal precedence Causes come before effects. Therefore, in trying to establish causality, you must establish temporal precedence: that the causal factor was introduced before the effect occurred.

Testing effect Apparent treatment effects being due to subjects being changed by the pretest.

Theory A set of propositions from which a large number of new observations can be deduced.

Time series design A quasi-experimental design in which a series of observations are taken from a group of subjects over time before and after they receive the treatment.

Trend analysis A post hoc analysis to determine the shape of a relationship between the independent and dependent variable.

Type 1 error Rejecting the null hypothesis when it is in fact true.

Type 2 error Failure to reject the null hypothesis when it is in fact false.

Within groups variance (mean square within, mean square error, error variance) An estimate of the amount of random error in your data. The bottom half of the F-ratio.

Within subjects designs Experimental designs in which each subject is tested under more than one level of the independent variable. The order in which the subjects receive the treatments is usually determined by random assignment.

REFERENCES

ADAMS, J. (1974). *Conceptual blockbusting.* San Francisco: Freeman.

AJZEN, I., & MADDEN, T. J. (1986). Prediction of goal-directed behavior: Attitudes, intentions, and perceived behavioral control. *Journal of Experimental Social Psychology, 22,* 453–474.

ALEXANDER, C. N., LANGER, E. J., NEWMAN, R. I., CHANCLER, H. M., & DAVIES, J. L. (1989). *Journal of Personality and Social Psychology, 57,* 950–964.

ALLEN, J. L., WALKER, L. D., SCHROEDER, D. A., & JOHNSON, D. E. (1987). Attributions and attribution-behavior relations: The effect of level of cognitive development. *Journal of Personality and Social Psychology, 52,* 1099–1109.

AMERICAN PSYCHOLOGICAL ASSOCIATION. (1981). Ethical principles of psychologists. *American Psychologist, 36,* 633–638.

AMERICAN PSYCHOLOGICAL ASSOCIATION. (1983). *Publication manual of the American Psychological Association* (3rd ed.). Washington, DC: Author.

AMERICAN PSYCHOLOGICAL ASSOCIATION. (1990). Ethical principles of psychologists (amended June 2, 1989). *American Psychologist, 45,* 390–395.

ANASTASI, A. (1982). *Psychological Testing* (5th ed.). New York: Macmillan.

ANDERSON, J. R., & BOWER, G. H. (1973). *Human associative memory.* Washington, DC: V. H. Winston.

ANTILL, J. K. (1983). Sex role complementarity versus similarity in married couples. *Journal of Personality and Social Psychology, 45,* 145–155.

ARONSON, E. (1989). Analysis, synthesis, and the treasuring of the old. *Personality and Social Psychology Bulletin, 15,* 508–512.

ARONSON, E. (1990). Applying social psychology to desegregation and energy conservation. *Personality and Social Psychology Bulletin, 16,* 118–131.

ARONSON, E. & CARLSMITH, J. M. (1968). Experimentation in social psychology. In G. Lindzey & E. Aronson (Eds.), *Handbook of social psychology* (2nd ed.), 2, 1–79, Reading, MA.: Addison-Wesley.

ARONSON, E., & MILLS, J. (1959). The effect of severity of initiation on liking for a group. *Journal of Abnormal and Social Psychology, 59,* 177–181.

AYLLON, T., & AZRIN, N. H. (1965). The measurement and reinforcement of behavior of psychotics. *Journal of the Experimental Analysis of Behavior, 8,* 171–180.

AYLLON, T., & AZRIN, N. H. (1968). *The token economy: A motivational system for therapy and rehabilitation.* New York: Appleton-Century-Crofts.

BALTES, P. B. (1968). Longitudinal and cross-sectional sequences in the study of age and generation effects. *Human Development, 11,* 145–171.

BANAJI, M. R., & CROWDER, R. G. (1989). The bankruptcy of everyday memory. *American Psychologist, 44,* 1185–1193.

BARON, R. A., RUSSELL, G. W., & ARMS, R. L. (1985). Negative ions and behavior: Impact on mood, memory, and aggression among Type A and Type B persons. *Journal of Personality and Social Psychology, 48,* 746–754.

BERNIERI, F. J. (1990). Interpersonal sensitivity in teaching interactions. *Personality and Social Psychology Bulletin, 17,* 98–103.

BERSCHEID, E., DION, K., WALSTER, E., & WALSTER, G. W. (1971). Physical attractiveness and dating choice: A test of the matching hypothesis. *Journal of Experimental Social Psychology, 7,* 173–189.

BLOUGH, D. S. (1957). Effect of lysergic acid diethylamide on absolute visual threshold in the pigeon. *Science, 126,* 304–305.

BRECKLER, S. J. (1984). Empirical validation of affect, behavior, and cognition as distinct components of attitude. *Journal of Personality and Social Psychology, 47,* 1191–1205.

BREHM, S., & BREHM, J. W. (1981). *Psychological reactance: A theory of freedom and control.* New York: Academic Press.

BREWER, C. L. (1990). *Teaching research methods: Three decades of pleasure and pain.* Presentation at the 98th Annual Convention of the American Psychological Association, Boston.

BREWER, W. F. (1974). There is no convincing evidence for operant or classical conditioning in adult humans. In W. B. Weiner & D. S. Palermo (Eds.), *Cognition and the symbolic processes.* Hillsdale, N.J.: Lawrence Erlbaum.

BROAD, W. J., & WADE, N. (1982). Science's faulty fraud detectors. *Psychology Today, 16,* 50–57.

BROCK, T. C., & BALLOUN, J. L. (1967). Behavioral receptivity to dissonant information. *Journal of Personality and Social Psychology, 6,* 413–428.

BROWN, J. D. (1991). Staying fit and staying well: Physical fitness as a moderator of life stress. *Journal of Personality and Social Psychology, 60,* 555–561.

BROWN, J. D., & SMART, S. A. (1991). The self and social conduct: Linking self-representations to pro-social behavior. *Journal of Personality and Social Psychology, 60,* 368–375.

BURKE, J. (1978). *Connections.* Boston: Little, Brown.

BURKE, J. (1985). *The day the universe changed.* Boston: Little, Brown

BUROS, O. K. (ED.). (1978). *The eighth mental measurements yearbook* (Vol. I). Highland Park, NJ: Gryphon Press.

CAMPBELL, D. T., & STANLEY, J. C. (1966). *Experimental and quasi-experimental designs for research.* Chicago: Rand McNally.

CHAPMAN, L. J., & CHAPMAN, P. J. (1967). Genesis of popular but erroneous psychodiagnostic observations. *Journal of Abnormal Psychology, 72,* 193–204.

CHAIKEN, S. & EAGLY, A. H. (1976). Communication modality as a determinant of message persuasiveness and message comprehensibility. *Journal of Personality and Social Psychology, 34,* 605–614.

CHASSIN, L., PRESSON, C. C., & SHERMAN, S. J. (1990). Social psychological contributions to understanding and prevention of adolescent cigarette smoking. *Personal and Social Psychology Bulletin, 16,* 133–151.

CHLOPAN, B. E., McCAIN, M. L., CARBONELL, J. L., & HAGEN, R. L. (1985). Empathy: Review of available measures. *Journal of Personality and Social Psychology, 48,* 635–653.

CLARK, H. H. (1973). The language-as-fixed-effect fallacy: A critique of language statistics in psychological research. *Journal of Verbal Learning and Verbal Behavior, 12,* 335–359.

COHEN, J. (1976). Discussion of Wike and Church's comments. *Journal of Verbal Learning and Verbal Behavior, 15,* 261–262.

COHEN, J. (1990). Things I have learned (so far). *American Psychologist, 45,* 1304–1312.

COHEN, J. & COHEN, P. (1983). *Applied multiple regression/correlation analysis for the behavioral sciences* (2nd ed.). Hillsdale, NJ: Erlbaum.

COILE, D. C., & MILLER, N. E. (1984). How radical animal activists try to mislead humane people. *American Psychologist, 39,* 700–701.

COLEMAN, E. B. (1979). Generalization effects vs. random effects. *Journal of Verbal Learning and Verbal Behavior, 18,* 243–256.

COLLINS, A. M., & LOFTUS, E. F. (1975). A spreading-activation theory of semantic processing. *Psychological Review, 28,* 407–428.

COOK, T. D., & CAMPBELL, D. T. (1979). *Quasi-experimentation: Design and analysis for field settings.* Chicago: Rand McNally.

COREN, S. (1989). Left-handedness and accident-related injury risk. *American Journal of Public Health, 79,* 1040–1041.

COZBY, P. C. (1985). *Methods in behavioral research,* (3rd ed.). Palo Alto, CA: Mayfield.

CRANDALL, C. S. (1988). Social contagion of binge eating. *Journal of Personality and Social Psychology, 55,* 588–598.

CROWNE, D. P., & MARLOWE, D. (1960). A new scale of social desirability independent of psychopathology. *Journal of Consulting and Clinical Psychology, 24,* 349–354.

CUSTER, S. (1985). *The impact of backward masking.* Paper presented at the Thirteenth Annual Western Pennsylvania Undergraduate Psychology Conference held in Clarion, Pennsylvania.

DEVINE, P. G., & OSTROM, T. M. (1985). Cognitive mediation of inconsistency discounting. *Journal of Personality and Social Psychology, 49,* 5–21.

DIAMOND, H. (1989, September). Lights, camera . . . research! *Marketing News,* p. 11.

DILLMAN, D. A. (1978). *Mail and telephone surveys: The total design method.* New York: Wiley.

DILLON, K. (1990). Generating research ideas; or, that's salada tea. . . . *High School Psychology Teacher, 21,* 6–7.

DIPBOYE, R. L., & FLANAGAN, M. F. (1979). Research settings in industrial and organizational psychology. *American Psychologist, 34,* 141–150.

DUTTON, P. G., & ARON, A. P. (1974). Some evidence for heightened sexual attraction under conditions of high anxiety. *Journal of Personality and Social Psychology, 30,* 510–517.

EDWARDS, K. (1990). The interplay of affect and cognition in attitude formation and change. *Journal of Personality and Social Psychology, 59,* 202–216.

EDWARDS, T. (1990, July 23). Marketing grads told to take a reality check, *AMA News,* p. 9.

FECHNER, G. (1966). *Elements of psychophysics* (H. Adler, Trans.). New York: Holt. (Original work published 1860)

FESTINGER, L. (1954). Theory of social comparison processes. *Human Relations, 7,* 117–140.

FESTINGER, L. (1957). *A theory of cognitive dissonance.* Stanford, CA: Stanford University Press.

Festinger, L., & Carlsmith, J. M. (1959). Cognitive consequences of forced compliance. *Journal of Abnormal and Social Psychology, 58,* 203–210.

Festinger, L., Schachter, S., & Back, K. (1950). *Social pressures in informal groups: A study of human factors in housing.* New York: Harper & Bros.

Fiske, D. W., & Fogg, L. (1990). But the reviewers are making different criticisms of my paper! Diversity and uniqueness in reviewer comments. *American Psychologist, 45,* 591–598.

Frank, M. G. & Gilovich, T. (1988). The dark side of self- and other perception: Black uniforms and aggression in professional sports. *Journal of Personality and Social Psychology, 54,* 74–85.

Frank, R. (1984). *A half-life theory of love.* Presented at the 92nd Annual Convention of the American Psychological Association in Toronto, Canada.

Franz, C. E., McClelland, D. C., & Weinberger, J. (1991). Childhood antecedents of conventional social accomplishment in midlife adults: A 36-year prospective study. *Journal of Personality and Social Psychology, 60,* 586–595.

Frederickson, N. (1986). Toward a broader conception of human intelligence. *American Psychologist, 41,* 445–452.

Freedman, J. L., & Fraser, S. C. (1966). Compliance without pressure: The foot-in-the-door technique. *Journal of Personality and Social Psychology, 4,* 195–202.

Frey, D., & Stahlberg, D. Selection of information after receiving more or less reliable self-threatening information. *Personality and Social Psychology Bulletin, 12,* 434–441.

Frijda, N. (1988). The laws of emotion. *American Psychologist, 43,* 349–358.

Garner, D. M., & Garfinkel, P. E. (1979). The Eating Attitudes Test: An index of the symptoms of anorexia nervosa. *Psychological Medicine, 9,* 273–279.

Garvey, W., & Griffith, B. (1971). Scientific communication: Its role in the conduct of research and creation of knowledge. *American Psychologist, 26,* 349–362.

Gerard, H. B., & Mathewson, G. C. (1966). The effects of severity of initiation on liking for a group: A replication. *Journal of Experimental Social Psychology, 2,* 278–287.

Gibb, J. (1990). *The Hope Scale revisited: Further validation of a measure of individual differences in the hope motive.* Unpublished master's thesis, University of Illinois at Urbana-Champaign.

Gilbert, D. T., & Osborne, R. E. (1989). Thinking backward: Some curable and incurable consequences of cognitive busyness. *Journal of Personality and Social Psychology, 57,* 940–949.

Gilligan, C. (1982). *In a different voice: Psychological theory and women's development.* Cambridge, MA: Harvard University Press.

Gladue, B. A., & Delaney, H. J. (1990). Gender differences in perception of attractiveness of men and women in bars. *Personality and Social Psychology Bulletin, 16,* 378–391.

Glass, D. C., & Singer, J. E. (1972). *Urban stress: Experiments on noise and social stressors.* New York: Academic Press.

Glick, P., Gottesman, D., & Jolton, J. (1989). The fault is not in the stars: Susceptibility of skeptics and believers in astrology to the Barnum effect. *Personality and Social Psychology Bulletin, 15,* 559–571.

Gold, J. A., Ryckman, R. M., & Mosley, N. R. (1984). Romantic mood induction and attraction to a dissimilar other: Is love blind? *Personality and Social Psychology Bulletin, 10,* 358–368.

Goldman, B. A., & Mitchell, D. F. (1990). *Directory of Unpublished Experimental Mental Measures, 5.* Dubuque, IA: Wm. C. Brown.

Gonzalez, M. H., Pederson, J. H., Manning, D. J., & Wetter, D. W. (1990). Pardon my gaffe: Effects of sex, status, and consequence severity on accounts. *Journal of Personality and Social Psychology, 58,* 610–621.

Gould, R. L. (1978). *Transformations: Growth and change in adult life.* New York: Simon and Schuster.

Grambs, D. (1990). *Random House dictionary for writers and readers.* New York: McKay.

Greenberger, E., & Steinberg, L. (1986). *When teenagers work: The psychological and social costs of adolescent employment.* New York: Basic Books.

Greenwald, A. G. (1975). Significance, nonsignificance, and interpretation of an ESP experiment. *Journal of Experimental Social Psychology, 11,* 180–191.

Greenwald, A. G. (1976). Within-subjects designs: To use or not to use? *Psychological Bulletin, 83,* 314–320.

Greenwald, A. G., Pratkanis, A. R., Leippe, M. R., & Baumgardner, M. H. (1986). Under what conditions does theory obstruct research progress? *Psychological Review, 93,* 216–229.

Greenwald, A., Spangenberg, E., & Klinger, M. R. (1990). Which subliminal effects should we worry about? Presented at the 98th Annual Convention of the American Psychological Association, Boston.

Groves, R. M., & Kahn, R. L. (1979). *Surveys by telephone: A national comparison with personal interviews.* New York: Academic Press.

Hackman, J. R., & Oldham, G. R. (1980). *Work redesign.* Reading, MA: Addison-Wesley.

Hazan, C., & Shaver, P. R. (1987). Romantic love conceptualized as an attachment process. *Journal of Personality and Social Psychology, 52,* 511–512.

HAZAN, C., & SHAVER, P. R. (1990). Love and work: An attachment-theoretical perspective. *Journal of Personality and Social Psychology, 59,* 270–280.

HEDGES, L. (1987). How hard is hard science, how soft is soft science? *American Psychologist, 42,* 443–455.

HELSON, H. (1964). *Adaptation-level theory: An experimental and systematic approach to behavior.* New York: Harper & Row.

HERR, P. M. (1986). Consequences of priming: Judgment and behavior. *Journal of Personality and Social Psychology, 51,* 1106–1115.

HIGH-HANDED PROFESSOR'S COMMENTS CALLED HOT ERROR. (1985, August). *USA Today,* P. 2c.

HILL, C. A. (1991). Seeking emotional support: The influence of affiliative need and partner warmth. *Journal of Personality and Social Psychology, 60,* 112–121.

HILTON, J. L., & FEIN, S. (1989). The role of typical diagnosticity in stereotype-based social judgments. *Journal of Personality and Social Psychology, 57,* 201–211.

HILTON, J. L., & VON HIPPEL, W. (1990). The role of consistency in the judgment of stereotype-relevant behaviors. *Personality and Social Psychology Bulletin, 16,* 430–448.

HOLMES, D. S., & WILL, M. J. (1985). Expression of interpersonal aggression by angered and nonangered persons with Type A and Type B behavior patterns. *Journal of Personality and Social Psychology, 48,* 723–727.

HOLMES, J. G., & BOON, S. D. (1990). Developments in the field of close relationships: Creating foundations for intervention strategies. *Personality and Social Psychology Bulletin, 16,* 23–41.

HONOMICHL, J. (1990, August 6). Answering machines threaten survey research. *Marketing News,* p. 11.

ICKES, W., & BARNES, R. D. (1978). Boys and girls together and alienated: On enacting stereotyped sex roles in mixed-sex dyads. *Journal of Personality and Social Psychology, 36,* 669–683.

INJURY QUIETS RAMS. (1984, August 16). USA Today, p. 7c.

IRVING, L. M., CRENSHAW, W., SNYDER, C. R., FRANCIS, P., & GENTRY, G. (1990, May). *Hope and its correlates in a psychiatric inpatient setting.* Paper presented at the 62nd annual meeting of the Midwestern Psychological Association.

JACKSON, J. M., & WILLIAMS, K. D. (1985). Social loafing on difficult tasks: Working collectively can improve performance. *Journal of Personality and Social Psychology, 49,* 937–942.

JAMES, W. (1980). *Principles of psychology* (Vols. I and II). New York: Holt.

JANIS, I. L., & FIELD, P. B. (1959). A behavioral assessment of persuasibility: Consistency of individual differences. In C. I. Hovland & I. L. Janis (Eds.), *Personality and persuasibility* (29–54). New Haven, CT: Yale University Press.

JOHNSON, V. S. (1985). *Electrophysiological changes induced by adrostenol: A potential human pherome.* Unpublished manuscript., New Mexico State University, Las Cruces, New Mexico.

JOLLEY, J. M., MURRAY, J. D., & KELLER, P. A. (1984). *How to write psychology papers: A student's survival guide for psychology and related fields.* Sarasota, FL: Professional Resource Exchange.

KAHNEMAN, D., SLOVIC, P., & TVERSKY, A. (Eds.). (1982). *Judgment under uncertainty: Heuristics and biases.* New York: Cambridge University Press.

KENNY, D. A., & SMITH, E. R. (1980). A note on the analysis of designs in which subjects receive each stimulus only once. *Journal of Experimental Social Psychology, 16,* 497–507.

KIESLER, C. A. (1982). Public and professional myths about mental hospitalization: An empirical reassessment of policy-related beliefs. *American Psychologist, 37,* 1323–1339.

KIESLER, C. A., & SIBULKIN, A. E. (1987). *Mental hospitalization: Myths and facts about a national crisis.* Beverly Hills, CA: Sage.

KNOX, R. E., & INKSTER, J. A. (1968). Postdecision dissonance at post time. *Journal of Personality and Social Psychology, 8,* 319–323.

KOHN, A. (1988). You know what they say: Are proverbs nugget of truth or fool's gold? *Psychology Today, 22*(4), 36–41.

KROSNICK, J. A., & SCHUMAN, H. (1988). Attitude intensity, importance, and certainty and susceptibility to response effects. *Journal of Personality and Social Psychology, 54,* 940–952.

KUEHN, S. A. (1989). *Prospectus handbook for Comm 352.* Unpublished manuscript, Clarion, PA.

KUHN, T. S. (1970). *The structure of scientific revolutions* (2nd ed.). Chicago: University of Chicago Press.

LAIRD, J. D. (1984). The real role of facial response in the experience of emotion: A reply to Tourangeau and Ellsworth and others. *Journal of Personality and Social Psychology, 47,* 909–917.

LANGER, E. J., & RODIN, J. T. (1976). The effects of choice and enhanced personal responsibility for the aged: A field experiment in an institutional setting. *Journal of Personality and Social Psychology, 34,* 191–198.

LATANE, B. (1981). The psychology of social impact. *American Psychologist, 36,* 343–356.

LATANE, B., & DARLEY, J. M. (1968). Group inhibition of bystander intervention in emergencies. *Journal of Personality and Social Psychology, 10,* 215–221.

LATANE, B., & DARLEY, J. M. (1970). *The unresponsive*

bystander: Why doesn't he help? New York: Appleton-Century-Crofts.

LATANE, B., WILLIAMS, K., & HARKINS, S. (1979). Many hands make light the work: The causes and consequences of social loafing. *Journal of Personality and Social Psychology, 37,* 822–832.

LEHMAN, D. R., LEMPERT, R. O., & NISBETT, R. E. (1988). The effects of graduate training on reasoning: Formal discipline and thinking about everyday-life events. *American Psychologist, 43,* 431–442.

LEVINSON, D. (1978). *The seasons of a man's life.* New York: Ballantine.

LEVY-LEBOYER, C. (1988). Success and failure in applying psychology. *American Psychologist, 43,* 779–785.

LEWIS, D., & GREENE, J. (1982). *Thinking better.* New York: Rawson, Wade.

LINDSEY, D. (1976). Distinction, achievement, and editorial board membership. *American Psychologist, 31,* 799–804.

LOCKE, E. A., & LATHAM, G. P. (1990). Work motivation and satisfaction: Light at the end of the tunnel. *Psychological Science, 1,* 240–246.

LOFTUS, E. F. (1980). *Memories are made of this: New insights into the workings of human memory.* Reading, MA: Addison-Wesley.

MAHONEY, M. J. (1987). Scientific publication and knowledge politics. *Journal of Social Behavior and Personality, 2,* 165–176.

MARTIN, D. W. (1984). *Doing psychology experiments* (2nd ed.). San Francisco: Brooks-Cole.

MASLOW, A. H. (1970). Cited in S. Cunningham, Humanists celebrate gains, goals. *APA Monitor, 16,* 16.

McBURNEY, D. (1983). *Experimental psychology.* Belmont, CA: Wadsworth.

McDOUGALL, W. (1908). *An introduction to social psychology.* London: Methuen.

McGUIRE, W. J. (1985). Attitudes and attitude change. In G. Lindzey & E. Aronson (Eds.), *Handbook of Social Psychology,* 3rd ed. (Vol. 2, 223–346). New York: Random House.

MIKULINCER, M., FLORIAN, V., & TOLMACZ, R. (1990). Attachment styles and fear of personal death: A case study of affect regulation. *Journal of Personality and Social Psychology, 58,* 273–280.

MILGRAM, S. (1966). *Four studies using the lost letter technique.* Address given at the 85th Annual Convention of the American Psychological Association Meetings in New York. Cited in the *Handbook of Social Psychology,* (Vol. 1), Lindzey (Ed.).

MILGRAM, S. (1974). *Obedience to authority: An experimental view.* New York: Harper and Row.

MILGRAM, S., BICKMAN, L., & BERKOWITZ, L. (1969). Note on the drawing power of crowds of different sizes. *Journal of Personality and Social Psychology, 13,* 79–82.

MILLAR, M. G., & MILLAR, K. (1990). Attitude change as a function of attitude type and argument type. *Journal of Personality and Social Psychology, 59,* 217–228.

MISCHEL, W. (1974). Processes in delay of gratification. In L. Berkowitz (Ed.), *Advances in experimental social psychology* (Vol. 7, 249–292). New York: Academic Press.

MISCHEL, W. (1981). Metacognition and the rules of delay. In J. H. Flavell & L. Ross (Eds.), *Social cognitive development: Frontiers and possible futures* (240–271) New York: Cambridge University Press.

MISCHEL, W., SHODA, Y., & PEAKE, P. K. (1988). The nature of adolescent competencies predicted by preschool delay of gratification. *Journal of Personality and Social Psychology, 54,* 687–696.

MONTEPARE, J. M. & ZEBROWITZ-McARTHUR, L. (1988). Impressions of people created by age-related qualities of their gaits. *Journal of Personality and Social Psychology, 55,* 547–556.

MOOK, D. G. (1983). In defense of external invalidity. *American Psychologist, 38,* 379–387.

MOOREHOUSE, M. J. (1991). Linking material employment patterns to mother-child activities and children's school competence. *Developmental Psychology, 27,* 295–303.

MORRIS, J. D. (1986). MTV in the classroom. *Chronicle of Higher Education, 32,* 25–26.

MUEHLENHARD, C. L., & HOLLABAUGH, L. C. (1988). Do women sometimes say no when they mean yes? The prevalence and correlates of women's token resistance to sex. *Journal of Personality and Social Psychology, 54,* 872–879.

MYERS, D. G. (1990). *Social Psychology (3rd ed.).* New York: McGraw-Hill.

NEISSER, U. (1984). Ecological movement in cognitive psychology. Invited address at the 92nd Annual Convention of the American Psychological Association in Toronto, Canada.

NISBETT, R. E., & ROSS, L. (1980). Human inference: Strategies and shortcomings of social judgment. Englewood Cliffs, NJ: Prentice-Hall.

NISBETT, R. E., & WILSON, T. D. (1977). Telling more than we can know: Verbal reports on mental processes. *Psychological Review, 84,* 231–259.

O'KEEFE, M. K., NESSELHOF-KENDALL, S., & BAUM, A. (1990). Behavior and prevention of AIDS: Bases of research and intervention. *Personality and Social Psychology Bulletin, 16,* 166–180.

ORNE, M. (1962). On the social psychology of the psychological experiment: With particular reference to demand characteristics and their implications. *American Psychologist, 17,* 776–783.

PALLAK, M. S., COOK, D. A., & SULLIVAN, J. J. (1980). Commitment and energy conservation. In L. Bickman (Ed.), *Applied social psychology annual* (Vol. 1, pp. 235–254). Beverly Hills, CA: Sage.

PARDUCCI, A. (1984). Value judgments: Toward a relational theory of happiness. In J. R. Eiser (Ed.), *Attitudinal measurement* (pp. 3–21). New York: Springer-Verlag.

PENNEBAKER, J. W., DYER, M. A., CAULKINS, R. S., LITOWITZ, D. L., ACKERMAN, P. L., ANDERSON, D. B., & McGRAW, K. M. (1979). Don't the girls get prettier at closing time: A country and western application to psychology. *Personality and Social Psychology Bulletin, 5,* 122–125.

PETERS, D., & CECI, S. (1982). Peer-review practices of psychological journals: The fate of published articles, submitted again. *Behavioral and Brain Sciences, 5,* 187–195.

PFUNGST, O. (1911). *Clever Hans.* New York: Henry Holt.

PLINER, P., CHAIKEN, S., & FLETT, G. L. (1990). Gender differences in concern with body weight and physical appearance over the life span. *Personality and Social Psychology Bulletin, 16,* 263–273.

PLOMIN, R. (1990). *Nature and nurture: An introduction to human behavioral genetics.* Pacific Grove, CA: Brooks/Cole.

PRONKO, N. H. (1969). Are geniuses born or made? In *Panorama of psychology* (pp. 215–219). Belmont, CA: Brooks/Cole.

RANIERI, D. J., & ZEISS, A. M. (1984). Induction of a depressed mood: A test of opponent-process theory. *Journal of Personality and Social Psychology, 47,* 1413–1422.

RICHTER, M. L., & SEAY, M. B. (1987). ANOVA designs with subjects and stimuli as random effects: Applications to prototype effects on recognition memory. *Journal of Personality and Social Psychology, 53,* 470–480.

ROBINS, C. J. (1988). Attributions and depression: Why is the literature so inconsistent? *Journal of Personality and Social Psychology, 54,* 880–889.

ROEDIGER, H. L. (1980). The effectiveness of four mnemonics in ordering recall. *Journal of Experimental Psychology, 6,* 558–567.

ROETHLISBERGER, F. J., & DICKSON, W. J. (1939). *Management and the worker.* Cambridge, MA: Harvard University Press.

ROGERS, C. R. (1985). Cited in S. Cunningham, Humanists celebrate gains, goals. *APA Monitor, 16,* 16.

ROTTER, J. B. (1990). Internal versus external control of reinforcement: A case history of a variable. *American Psychologist, 45,* 489–493.

RUBIN, Z. (1970). Measurement of romantic love. *Journal of Personality and Social Psychology, 16,* 265–273.

SCHACHTER, S. (1959). *The psychology of affiliation.* Stanford, CA: Stanford University Press.

SCHACHTER, S. (1971). Some extraordinary facts about obese humans and rats. *American Psychologist, 26,* 129–144.

SCHACHTER, S. (1977). Studies of the interaction of psychological and pharmocological determinants of smoking: I. Nicotine regulation in heavy and light smokers. *Journal of Experimental Psychology: General, 106,* 5–12.

SCHAIE, K. W. (1977). Quasi-experimental designs in the psychology of aging. In J. E. Birren & K. W. Schaie (Eds.), *Handbook of the psychology of aging.* New York: Van Nostrand.

SCHAIE, K. W. (1988). Ageism in psychological research. *American Psychologist, 43,* 179–183.

SCHULTZ, D., & SCHULTZ, S. (1987). *A history of modern psychology* (4th ed.) New York: Academic Press.

SCHULTZ, D., & SCHULTZ, S. (1990). *Psychology and industry today: An introduction to industrial and organizational psychology* (5th ed.) New York: Macmillan.

SEMON, T. (1990, April). Beware of bedazzling number mongers. *Marketing News,* 13.

SHAFFER, D. R., ROGEL, M., & HENDRIK, C. (1975). Intervention in the library: The effect of increased responsibility on bystanders' willingness to prevent theft. *Journal of Personality and Social Psychology, 5,* 303–319.

SHEDLER, J., & BLOCK, J. (1990). Adolescent drug use and psychological health: A longitudinal inquiry. *American Psychologist, 45,* 612–637.

SHEFRIN, H. M., & STATMAN, M. (1986). How not to make money in the stock market. *Psychology Today, 20,* 52–57.

SHERMAN, L. W., & BERK, R. A. (1984). The specific deterrent effects of arrest for domestic assault. *American Sociology Review, 49,* 262–272.

SKINNER, B. F. (1956). A case history in scientific method. *American Psychologist, 11,* 221–233.

SLOVIC, P., & FISCHOFF, B. (1977). On the psychology of experimental surprises. *Journal of Experimental Psychology: Human Perception and Performance, 3,* 455–471.

SNYDER, M. (1974). The self-monitoring of expressive behavior. *Journal of Personality and Social Psychology, 30,* 526–537.

SNYDER, M., & GANGESTAD, S. (1986). On the nature of self-monitoring: Matters of assessment, matters of validity. *Journal of Personality and Social Psychology, 51,* 125–139.

SNYDER, M., & OMOTO, A. M. (1990). Basic research

in action: Volunteerism and society's response to AIDS. *Personality and Social Psychology Bulletin, 16,* 133–151.

STANOVICH, K. E. (1990). *How to think straight about psychology.* Glenview, IL: Scott, Foresman.

STEELE, C. M., & JOSEPHS, R. A. (1988). Drinking your troubles away: 2. An attention-allocation model of alcohol's effect on psychological stress. *Journal of Abnormal Psychology, 97,* 196–205.

STEELE, C. M., & JOSEPHS, R. A. (1990). Alcohol myopia: Its prized and dangerous effects. *American Psychologist, 45,* 921–933.

STEELE, C. M., & SOUTHWICK, L. (1985). Alcohol and social behavior I: The psychology of drunken excess. *Journal of Personality and Social Psychology, 48,* 18–34.

STEINBERG, L., & DORNBUSCH, S. M. (1991). Negative correlates of part-time employment during adolescence: Replication and elaboration. *Developmental Psychology, 27,* 304–313.

STONE, P. J., DUNPHY, D. C., SMITH, M. S., & OGILVIE, D. M. (1966). *The general inquirer: A computer approach to content analysis.* Cambridge, MA: The M.I.T. Press.

STRACK, F., SCHWARZ, N., & GESCHNEIDINGER, E. (1985). Happiness and reminiscing: The role of time perspective, affect, and mode of thinking. *Journal of Personality and Social Psychology, 49,* 1460–1469.

STRACK, F., MARTIN, L. L., & STEPPER, S. (1988). Inhibiting and facilitating conditions of the human smile: A nonobtrusive test of the facial feedback hypothesis. *Journal of Personality and Social Psychology, 54,* 768–777.

SWETS, J. A., & BJORK, R. A. (1990). Enhancing human performance: An evaluation of "new age" techniques considered by the U.S. Army. *Psychological Science, 1,* 85–96.

SYKES, C. J. (1989). *ProfScam.* New York: St. Martin.

TEIGEN, K. H. (1986). Old truths or fresh insights? A study of students' evaluations of proverbs. *British Journal of Social Psychology, 25,* 43–50.

TOFFLER, A. (1990). *Power shift.* New York: Bantam.

TOLMAN, E. C. (1932). *Purposive behavior in animals and men.* New York: Century.

TOLMAN, E. C., & HONZIK, C. H. (1930). Introduction and removal of reward and maze performance in rats. *University of California Publications in Psychology, 4,* 257–275.

TVERSKY, B. (1973). Encoding processes in recognition and recall. *Cognitive Psychology, 5,* 275–287.

WARD, W. C., & JENKINS, H. M. (1965). The display of information and the judgment of contingency. *Canadian Journal of Psychology, 19,* 231–241.

WEBB, E. J., CAMPBELL, D. T., SCHWARTZ, R. D., & SEECHRIST, L. (1981). *Unobtrusive measures: Nonreactive research in the social sciences.* Chicago: Rand McNally.

WEDELL, D. H., PARDUCCI, A., & GEISELMAN, R. E. (1987). A formal analysis of ratings of physical attractiveness: Successive contrast and simultaneous assimilation. *Journal of Experimental Social Psychology, 23,* 230–249.

WEDELL, D. H. PARDUCCI, A., & LANE, M. (1990). Reducing the dependence of clinical judgment on the immediate context: Effects of number of categories and types of anchors. *Journal of Personality and Social Psychology, 58,* 319–329.

WICKENS, T. D., & KEPPEL, G. (1983). On the choice of design and of test statistic in the analysis of experiments with sampled materials. *Journal of Verbal Learning and Verbal Behavior, 22,* 296–309.

WIKE, E. L., & CHURCH, J. D. (1976). Comments on Clark's "The language-as-fixed-effect fallacy." *Journal of Verbal Learning and Verbal Behavior, 15,* 249–255.

WILLIAMS, K. B., & WILLIAMS, K. D. (1983). Social inhibition and asking for help: The effects of number, strength, and immediacy. *Journal of Personality and Social Psychology, 44,* 67–77.

WILLIAMS, R. L., & LONG, J. D. (1983). *Toward a self-managed lifestyle* (3rd ed.). Boston: Houghton-Mifflin.

WILSON, T. D., & LINVILLE, P. W. (1985). Improving the performance of freshmen with attributional techniques. *Journal of Personality and Social Psychology, 49,* 287–293.

WILSON, T. D., & SCHOOLER, J. W. (1991). Thinking too much: Introspection can reduce the quality of preferences and decisions. *Journal of Personality and Social Psychology, 60,* 181–192.

WOHLFORD, P. (1970). Initiation of cigarette smoking: Is it related to parental smoking behavior? *Journal of Consulting and Clinical Psychology, 34,* 148–151.

WURMAN, R. S. (1990). *Information anxiety: What to do when information doesn't tell you what you need to know.* New York: Bantam.

SELECTED READINGS

AMERICAN PSYCHOLOGICAL ASSOCIATION. (1981). Guidelines for the use of animals in school-science behavior projects. *American Psychologist, 36*, 686.

AMERICAN PSYCHOLOGICAL ASSOCIATION. (1982). *Ethical principles in the conduct of research with human behavior.* Washington, DC: Author.

ARONSON, E., & CARLSMITH, J. M. (1968). Experimentation in social psychology. In G. Lindzey & E. Aronson (Eds.), *Handbook of social psychology* (2nd ed.) (pp. 1–79). Reading, MA: Addison-Wesley.

ARONSON, E., & LINDER, D. (1965). Gain and loss of esteem as determinants of interpersonal attractiveness. *Journal of Experimental Social Psychology, 1*, 156–171.

BALAY, J., & SHEVRIN, H. (1988). The subliminal psychodynamic activation method: A critical review. *American Psychologist, 43*, 161–174.

BALTES, P. B., REESE, H. W., & NESSELROADE, J. R. (1977). *Life-span developmental psychology: Introduction to reseach methods.* Monterey, CA: Brooks and Cole.

BANDURA, A. (1977). *Social learning theory.* Englewood Cliffs, NJ: Prentice-Hall.

BANDURA, A. (1986). *Social foundations of thought and action: A social cognitive theory.* Englewood Cliffs, NJ: Prentice-Hall.

BANDURA, A. (1989). Human agency in social cognitive theory. *American Psychologist, 44*, 1175–1184.

BARBER, T. X. (1976). *Pitfalls in human research: Ten pivotal points.* New York: Pergamon.

BARBER, T. X., & SILVER, M. J. (1968). Fact, fiction, and experimenter bias effect. *Psychological Bulletin, 70*, 1–29.

BARON, R. A. (1987). Effects of negative ions on interpersonal attraction: Evidence for intensification. *Journal of Personality and Social Psychology, 52*, 547–553.

BARON, R. M., & KENNY, D. A. (1986). The moderator-mediator distinction in social psychological research: Conceptual, strategic, and statistical considerations. *Journal of Personality and Social Psychology, 51*, 1173–1182.

BAUM, A., & NESSELHOF, S. E. A. (1988). Psychological research and the prevention, etiology, and treatment of AIDS. *American Psychologists, 43*, 900–906.

BEM, D. J. (1967). Self-perception: An alternative interpretation of cognitive dissonance phenomena. *Psychological Review, 74*, 183–200.

BEM, S. L. (1974). The measurement of psychological androgyny. *Journal of Consulting and Clinical Psychology, 42*, 155–162.

BERKOWITZ, L., & DONNERSTEIN, E. (1982). External validity is more than skin deep. *American Psychologist, 37*, 245–257.

BERSHEID, E. (1985). Interpersonal attraction. In G. Lindzey & E. Aronson (Eds.), *The Handbook of Social Psychology.* New York: Random House.

BLOUGH, D. S. (1961). Animal psychophysics. *Scientific American, 205*, 113–122.

BORGIDA, E., & DeBONO, K. G. (1989). Social hypothesis testing and the role of expertise. *Personality and Social Psychology Bulletin, 15*, 212–221.

BORNSTEIN, R. F., KALE, A. R., & CORNELL, K. R. (1990). Boredom as a limiting condition on the mere exposure effect. *Journal of Personality and Social Psychology, 58*, 791–800.

BOUSFIELD, W. A. (1953). The occurrence of clustering in the recall of randomly arranged associates. *Journal of General Psychology, 49*, 229–240.

BRADY, J. V. (1958). Ulcers in "executive" monkeys. *Scientific American, 199*, 95–100.

BRIGHAM, T. A. (1989). On the importance of recognizing the difference between experiments and correlational studies. *American Psychologist, 44*, 1077–1078.

BURNKRANDT, R. E., & UNNAVA, H. R. (1989). Self-referencing: A strategy for increasing processing of message content. *Personality and Social Psychology Bulletin, 15*, 559–571.

BUSS, D. M. (1985). Human mate selection. *American Scientist, 73*, 47–51.

BYRNE, D. (1971). *The attraction paradigm.* New York: Academic Press.

CAMPBELL, D. T., & FISKE, D. W. (1959). Convergent and discriminant validation by the multitrait-multimethod matrix. *Psychological Bulletin*, 56, 81–105.

CAMPBELL, J. P., DAFT, R. L., & HULIN, C. L. (1982). *What to study*: *Generating and developing research questions*. Beverly Hills, CA: Sage.

CARLI, L. L. (1989). Gender differences in interaction style and influence. *Journal of Personality and Social Psychology*, 56, 656–567.

CARVER, C. S. (1989). How should multifaceted personality constructs be tested? Issues illustrated by self-monitoring, attributional style, and hardiness. *Journal of Personality and Social Psychology*, 56, 577–585.

CHWALISZ, K., DIENER, E., & GALLAGHER, D. (1988). Autonomic arousal feedback and emotional experience: Evidence from the spinal cord injured. *Journal of Personality and Social Psychology*, 54, 820–828.

COHEN, A. S., ROSEN, R. C., & GOLDSTEIN, L. (1985). EEG hemispheric asymmetry during sexual arousal: Psychophysiological patterns in responsive, unresponsive, and dysfunctional men. *Journal of Abnormal Psychology*, 94, 580–590.

COHEN, J. (1977). *Statistical power analysis for the behavioral sciences* (rev. ed.). New York: Academic Press.

CORCORAN, K., & FISCHER, J. (1987). *Measures for clinical practice*: A sourcebook. New York: The Free Press.

CRONBACH, L. J., & MEEHL, P. (1955). Construct validity in psychological tests. *Psychological Bulletin*, 52, 281–302.

DIAMOND, H. (1989). Lights, camera . . . research! *Marketing News*, September, 11.

DICKMAN, S. J. (1990). Functional and dysfunctional impulsivity: Personality and cognitive correlates. *Journal of Personality and Social Psychology*, 58, 95–102.

DOMJAN, M. (1987). Animal learning comes of age. *American Psychologist*, 42, 556–564.

ERICCSON, A., & SIMON, H. A. (1980). Verbal reports as data. *Psychological Review*, 87, 215–251.

ERON, L. D. (1982). Parent-child interaction, television violence, and aggression in children. *American Psychologist*, 37, 197–211.

EYSENCK, H. J., & EYSENCK, M. (1983). *Mindwatching*. Garden City, NY: Anchor Press/Doubleday.

FAZIO, R. H. (1990). On the value of basic research: An overview. *Personality and Social Psychology Bulletin*, 16, 5–8.

FEENEY, D. M. (1987). Human rights and animal welfare. *American Psychologist*, 42, 593–599.

FEENEY, J. A., & NOLLER, P. (1990). Attachment styles as a predictor of adult romantic relationships. *Journal of Personality and Social Psychology*, 58, 281–291.

FIELDS, H. L., & LEVINE, J. D. (1984). Placebo analgesia: A role for endorphins. *Trends in neuroscience*, 7, 271–273.

FISHBEIN, M., & AJZEN, I. (1975). *Belief, attitude, intention and behavior: An introduction to theory and research*. Reading, MA: Addison-Wesley.

FRANK, M. G., & GILOVICH, T. (1988). The dark side of self- and other perception: Black uniforms and aggression in professional sports. *Journal of Personality and Social Psychology*, 54, 74–85.

GARNER, W. R., HAKE, H., & ERIKSEN, C. W. (1956). Operationism and the concept of perception. *Psychological Review*, 63, 149–159.

GELLER, E. S. (1983). Rewarding safety belt usage at an industrial setting: Tests of treatment generality and response maintenance. *Journal of Applied Behavior Analysis*, 16, 189–202.

GESCHEIDER, G. A. (1976). *Psychophysics: Method and theory*. Hillsdale, NJ: Erlbaum.

GILBERT, D. T. (1991). How mental systems believe. *American Psychologist*, 46, 107–119.

GLASER, R. (1990). The reemergence of learning theory within instructional research. *American Psychologist*, 45, 29–39.

GOLDMAN, B. A., & MITCHELL, D. F. (1990). *Directory of Unpublished Experimental Mental Measures*, 5 Dubuque, IA: Wm. C. Brown.

GOLMAN, M., PULCHER, D., & MENDEZ, T. (1983). Appeals for help, prosocial behavior, and psychological reactance. *The Journal of Psychology*, 113, 265–269.

GONZALEZ, M. H., PEDERSON, J. H., MANNING, D. J., & WETTER, D. W. (1990). Pardon my gaffe: Effects of sex, status, and consequence severity on accounts. *Journal of Personality and Social Psychology*, 58, 610–621.

GRAZIANO, W. G., RAHE, D. F., & FELDESMAN, A. B. (1985). Extraversion, social cognition, and the salience of aversiveness in social encounters. *Journal of Personality and Social Psychology*, 49, 971–980.

GREENWALD, A., SPANGENBERG, E., & KLINGER, M. R. (1990). *Which subliminal effects should we worry about?* Presented at the 98th Annual Convention of the American Psychological Association, Boston.

GUTHRIE, E. R. (1952). *The psychology of learning*. New York: Harper.

HALL, C. S. (1954). *A primer of Freudian psychology*. Cleveland: World Publishing.

HAMMOND, K. R. (1948). Measuring attitudes by error-choice: An indirect method. *Journal of Abnormal and Social Psychology*, 43, 38–48.

HARCUM, E. R. (1989). The highly inappropriate calibrations of statistical significance. *American Psychologist*, 44, 964.

HARKINS, S. G., LATANE, B., & WILLIAMS, K. (1980). Social loafing: Allocating effort or taking it easy? *Journal of Experimental Social Psychology*, 16, 457–465.

HARLOW, H. F. (1958). The nature of love. *American Psychologist*, 13, 673–685.

HAYS, W. L. (1981). *Statistics* (3rd ed.). New York: Holt, Rinehart, & Winston.

HENDRICK, C., & HENDRICK, S. S. (1988). Lovers wear rose colored glasses. *Journal of Social and Personal Relationships, 5,* 161–183.

HEREK, G. M. (1989). Hate crimes against lesbians and gay men: Issues for research and policy. *American Psychologist, 44,* 948–955.

HERRNSTEIN, R. J. (1962). Placebo effect in rats. *Science, 138,* 677–678.

HERRNSTEIN, R. J. (1990). Rational choice theory: Necessary, but not sufficient. *American Psychologist, 45,* 356–368.

HESS, E. H., & POLT, J. M. (1960). Pupil size as related to interest value of visual stimuli. *Science, 132,* 349–350.

HESSINGER, D. J., ELFFERS, H., & WEIGEL, R. H. (1988). Exploring the limits of self-report and reasoned action: An investigation of the psychology of tax evasion behavior. *Journal of Personality and Social Psychology, 54,* 405–413.

HIGH-HANDED PROFESSOR'S COMMENTS CALLED HOT ERROR. (1985). *USA Today,* August, P. 2c.

HUCK, S. W., & SANDLER, H. M. (1979). *Rival hypotheses: Alternative interpretations of data based conclusions.* New York: Harper and Row.

HULL, C. L. (1952). *A behavior system.* New Haven: Yale University Press.

JAMES, W. (1950). *Principles of psychology.* New York: Dover.

KELLEY, H. H. (1971). *Attribution in social interaction.* Morristown, NJ: General Learning Press.

KENNY, D. A. (1979). *Correlation and causality.* New York: John Wiley & Sons.

KERLINGER, F. N. (1986). *Foundations of behavioral research* (4th ed.). New York: Holt, Rinehart, & Winston.

KIMBLE, G. A. (1990). A search for principles in principles of psychology. *Psychological Science, 1,* 151–155.

KOHLBERG, L. (1981). *The meaning and measurement of moral development.* Worcester, MA: Clark University Press.

KOHLER, W. (1925). *The mentality of apes.* New York: Harcourt.

KROSNICK, J. A., & ALWIN, D. F. (1989). Aging and susceptibility to attitude change. *Journal of Personality and Social Psychology, 57,* 416–425.

KUEHN, S. A. (1989). *Prospectus handbook for Comm 352.* Unpublished manuscript. Clarion, PA.

LANGER, E. J. (1983). *The psychology of control.* Beverly Hills, CA: Sage.

LATANE, B., & NIDA, S. A. (1981). Ten years of research on group size and helping. *Psychological Bulletin, 89,* 307–324.

LATANE, B., NIDA, S. A., & WILSON, D. W. (1981). The effects of group size on helping behavior. In J. P. Rushton & Y. R. M. Sorrentino (Eds.), *Altruism and helping behavior: Social, personality, and developmental perspectives.* Hillsdale, NJ: Erlbaum.

LEMON, N. (1973). *Attitudes and their measurement.* New York: Wiley.

LEWIN, K. (1951). *Field theory in social science.* New York: Harper.

LIGHT, R. J., & PILLEMER, D. P. (1984). *Summing up: The science of reviewing research.* Cambridge, MA: Harvard University Press.

LINZ, D. G., DONNERSTEIN, E., & PENROD, S. (1988). Effects of long-term exposure to violent and sexually degrading depictions of women. *Journal of Personality and Social Psychology, 55,* 758–768.

LOCKE, E. A., & LATHAM, G. P. (1984). *Goal-setting: A motivational technique that works.* Englewood Cliffs, NJ: Prentice-Hall.

LYKKEN, D. T. (1979). The detection of deception. *Psychological Bulletin, 86,* 47–53.

LYKKEN, D. T. (1981). *A tremor in the blood: Uses and abuses of the lie detector.* New York: McGraw-Hill.

MARTIN, C. L. (1987). A ratio measure of sex stereotyping. *Journal of Personality and Social Psychology, 52,* 489–499.

MAYZNER, M. S., & DOLAN, T. R. (EDS.). (1978). *Mini-computers in sensory and information-processing research.* Hillsdale, NJ: Erlbaum.

MCCANN, I. L., & HOLMES, D. S. (1984). Influence of aerobic exercise on depression. *Journal of Personality and Social Psychology, 46,* 1142–1147.

MCCLOSKEY, M., & ZARAGOZA, M. (1985). Misleading postevent information and memory for events: Arguments and evidence against memory impairment hypotheses. *Journal of Experimental Psychology: General, 117,* 171–181.

MCGILLICUDDY, N. B., WELTON, G. L., & PRUITT, D. G. (1987). Third-party intervention: A field experiment comparing three different models. *Journal of Personality and Social Psychology, 53,* 104–112.

MILLER, G. A. (1969). Psychology as a means of promoting human welfare. *American Psychologist, 24,* 1063–1075.

MILLER, N. E. (1985). The value of behavioral research on animals. *American Psychologist, 40,* 423–440.

MILLSTEIN, S. G. (1989). Adolescent health: Challenges for behavioral scientists. *American Psychologist, 44,* 837–842.

MORI, D., CHAIKEN, S., & PLINER, P. (1987). "Eating lightly" and the self-presentation of femininity. *Journal of Personality and Social Psychology, 52,* 693–702.

MYERS, J. L. (1979). *Fundamentals of experimental design* (3rd ed.). Boston: Allyn and Bacon.

Myerscough, R., & Taylor, S. (1985). The effects of marijuana on human physical aggression. *Journal of Personality and Social Psychology, 49*, 1541–1546.

Ozer, D. J. (1987). Personality, intelligence, and spatial visualization: Correlates of mental rotations test performance. *Journal of Personality and Social Psychology, 53*, 129–134.

Padilla, E. R., & O'Grady, K. E. (1987). Sexuality among Mexican Americans: A case of sexual stereotyping. *Journal of Personality and Social Psychology, 52*, 5–10.

Parsons, H. M. (1974). What happened at Hawthorne? *Science, 183*, 922–932.

Phillips, D. P. (1985). Natural experiments on the effects of mass media violence on fatal aggression: Strengths and weaknesses of a new approach. In L. Berkowitz (Ed.), *Advances in experimental social psychology, 19*. Orlando, Fl: Academic Press.

Piaget, J., & Inhelder, B. (1969). *The psychology of the child*. London: Routledge & Kegan Paul.

Pratkanis, A. R., Greenwald, A. G., Leippe, M. R., & Baumgardner, M. H. (1988). In search of reliable persuasion effects: The sleeper effect is dead. Long live the sleeper effect. *Journal of Personality and Social Psychology, 54*, 203–218.

Rescorla, R. A. (1988). Pavlovian conditioning: It's not what you think it is. *American Psychologist, 43*, 151–160.

Rinn, W. E. (1984). The neuropsychology of facial expression: A review of the neurological and psychological mechanisms for producing facial expressions. *Psychological Bulletin, 95*, 52–77.

Robinson, P., & Shaver, P. R. (1973). *Measures of social psychological attitudes*. Ann Arbor, MI: Institute for Social Research.

Rodin, J., & Ickovics, J. R. (1990). Women's health: Review and research agenda as we approach the 21st century. *American Psychologist, 45*, 1018–1034.

Rodriguez, M. L., Mischel, W., & Shoda, Y. (1989). Cognitive person variables in the delay of gratification of older children at risk. *Journal of Personality and Social Psychology, 57*, 358–366.

Rosenthal, R., & Rosnow, R. (1969). *Artifact in behavioral research*. New York: Academic Press.

Russo, N. F. (1990). Overview: Forging research priorities for women's health. *American Psychologist, 45*, 368–373.

Scarr, S. (1989). Race and gender as psychological variables: Social and ethical issues. *American Psychologist, 43*, 56–59.

Schachter, S., & Singer, J. (1962). Cognitive, social, and physiological determinants of emotional state. *Psychological Review, 69*, 379–399.

Schachter, S. (1971). Some extraordinary facts about obese humans and rats. *American Psychologist, 26*, 129–144.

Seligman, M. E. P. (1975). *Helplessness: On depression, development, and death*. San Francisco: Freeman.

Sherman, S. J., Hamilton, D. L., & Roskos-Ewoldsen, P. R. (1989). Attenuation of illusory correlation. *Personality and Social Psychology Bulletin, 15*, 559–571.

Siegel, J. M. (1990). Stressful life events and use of physician services among the elderly: The moderating role of pet ownership. *Journal of Personality and Social Psychology, 58*, 1081–1086.

Skinner, B. F. (1938). *The behavior of organisms: An experimental analysis*. New York: Appleton-Century-Crofts.

Smith, R. E. (1989). Effects of coping skills training on generalized self-efficacy and locus of control. *Journal of Personality and Social Psychology, 56*, 228–233.

Smith, R. E., Smoll, F. L., & Ptacek, J. T. (1990). Conjunctive moderator variables in vulnerability and resiliency research: Life stress, social support, and coping skills, and adolescent sport injuries. *Journal of Personality and Social Psychology, 58*, 360–369.

Snyder, C. R., Harris, C., Anderson, J. R., Holleran, S. A., Irving, L. M., Sigmon, S., Yoshinobu, L., Gigg, J., Langelle, C., & Harney, P. (1991). The will and the ways: Development and validation of an individual-differences measure of hope. *Journal of Personality and Social Psychology, 60*, 570–585.

Snyder, M., & Gangestad, S. (1986). On the nature of self-monitoring: Matters of assessment, matters of validity. *Journal of Personality and Social Psychology, 51*, 125–139.

Solomon, R. L. (1980). The opponent-process theory of acquired motivation: The costs of pleasure and the benefits of pain. *American Psychologist, 35*, 691–712.

Sternberg, R. J., & Grajek, S. (1984). The nature of love. *Journal of Personality and Social Psychology, 47*, 312–329.

Stevens, S. S. (1946). On the theory of scales of measurement. *Science, 103*, 677–680.

Stevens, S. S. (1957). On the psychophysical law. *Psychological Review, 64*, 153–181.

Sudman, S., & Bradburn, N. M. (1982). *Asking Questions: A practical guide to questionnaire design*. San Francisco: Jossey-Bass.

Taylor, S. E. (1990). Health psychology: The science and the field. *American Psychologist, 45*, 40–50.

Taylor, S. E., Buunk, B. P., & Aspinwall, L. G. (1990). *Personality and Social Psychology Bulletin, 16*, 74–89.

Thayer, R. E. (1987). Energy, tiredness, and tension

effects of a sugar snack versus moderate exercise. *Journal of Personality and Social Psychology, 52,* 119–125.

TOULIATOS, J., PERLMUTTER, B. F., STRAUS, M. A. (EDS.). (1990). *Handbook of Family Measurement Techniques.* Newbury Park, CA: Sage.

TULVING, E., & PEARLSTONE, Z. (1966). Availability versus accessibility of information in memory for words. *Journal of Verbal Learning and Verbal Behavior, 5,* 381–391.

TVERSKY, A. (1985). Quoted by K. McKean, Decisions, decisions. *Discover,* 22–31.

TVERSKY, A., & KAHNEMAN, D. (1971). Belief in the law of small numbers. *Psychological Bulletin, 76,* 105–110.

VARELA, J. A. (1977). Social technology. *American Psychologist, 32,* 914–923.

VELEBER, D. M., & TEMPLER, D. I. (1984). Effects of caffeine on anxiety and depression. *Journal of Abnormal Psychology, 93,* 120–122.

WASON, P. (1960). On the failure to eliminate hypotheses in a conceptual task. *Quarterly Journal of Experimental Psychology, 12,* 129–140.

WEDELL, D. H., & PARDUCCI, A. (1988). The category effect in social judgment: Experimental ratings of happiness. *Journal of Personality and Social Psychology, 55,* 341–356.

WELLS, G. L., & LUUS, C. A. E. (1990). Police lineups as experiments: Social methodology as a framework for properly conducted lineups. *Personality and Social Psychology Bulletin, 16,* 106–117.

WINER, B. J. (1971). *Statistical principles in experimental design.* (2nd ed.). New York: McGraw-Hill.

WOHLWILL, J. F. (1970). Methodology and research strategy in the study of developmental change. In L. R. Goulet & P. B. Baltes (Eds.), *Life-span developmental psychology: Research and theory.* New York: Academic Press.

WOOLFOLK, M. E., CASTELLAN, W., & BROOKS, C. I. (1983). Pepsi versus Coke: Labels, not tastes, prevail. *Psychological Reports, 52,* 185–186.

YERKES, R. M., & DODSON, J. D. (1908). The relation of strength of stimulus to rapidity of habit formation. *Journal of Comparative Neurology and Psychology, 18,* 459–482.

ZAJONC, R. B. (1965). Social facilitation. *Science, 149,* 269–274.

ZAJONC, R. B. (1968). The attitudinal effects of mere exposure. *Journal of Personality and Social Psychology, 9,* 1–27.

ZAJONC, R. B., & SALES, S. M. (1966). Social facilitation of dominant and subordinant responses. *Journal of Experimental Social Psychology, 2,* 160–168.

ZIMBARDO, P. G. (1975). Transforming experimental research into advocacy for social change. In M. Deutsch & H. A. Hornstein (Eds.), *Applying social psychology: Implications for research, practice, and training.* Hillsdale, NJ: Erlbaum.

ZUCKERMAN, M., BERNIERI, G., KOESTNER, R., & ROSENTHAL, R. (1989). To predict some of the people some of the time: In search of moderators. *Journal of Personality and Social Psychology, 57,* 279–293.

ZUCKERMAN, M., KLORMAN, R., LARRANCE, D. T., & SPIEGEL, N. H. (1981). Facial, autonomic, and subjective components of emotion: The facial feedback hypothesis versus the externalizer-internalizer distinction. *Journal of Personality and Social Psychology, 41,* 929–944.

Index